Instrumental Music in an Age of Sociability

Sociability may be a key term of reference for eighteenth-century studies as a whole, but it has not yet developed an especially strong profile in music scholarship. Many of the associations that it brings do not fit comfortably with a later imperative of individual expression. W. Dean Sutcliffe invites us to face up to the challenge of re-evaluating the communicative rationales that lie behind later eighteenth-century instrumental style. Taking a behavioural perspective, he divides sociability into 'technical' and 'affective' realms, involving close attention both to particular recurring musical patterns and to some of the style's most salient expressive attributes. The book addresses a broad span of the instrumental production of the era, with Haydn as the pivotal figure. Close readings of a variety of works are embedded in an encompassing consideration of the reception of this music.

W. DEAN SUTCLIFFE is Professor in the School of Music at the University of Auckland, and co-editor of *Eighteenth-Century Music*, published by Cambridge University Press. His research interests focus on the eighteenth century, and publications have covered composers such as Domenico Scarlatti, Scarlatti's Spanish contemporary Sebastián de Albero, Boccherini, Mozart, Manuel Blasco de Nebra and above all Haydn. His most recent large-scale publication is an edition of the three string quartets Op. 42 by Adalbert Gyrowetz (2017). He was awarded the Dent Medal for 2009 by the Royal Musical Association.

Instrumental Music in an Age of Sociability

Haydn, Mozart and Friends

W. DEAN SUTCLIFFE
University of Auckland

CAMBRIDGE
UNIVERSITY PRESS

University Printing House, Cambridge CB2 8BS, United Kingdom

One Liberty Plaza, 20th Floor, New York, NY 10006, USA

477 Williamstown Road, Port Melbourne, VIC 3207, Australia

314–321, 3rd Floor, Plot 3, Splendor Forum, Jasola District Centre, New Delhi – 110025, India

79 Anson Road, #06–04/06, Singapore 079906

Cambridge University Press is part of the University of Cambridge.

It furthers the University's mission by disseminating knowledge in the pursuit of education, learning and research at the highest international levels of excellence.

www.cambridge.org
Information on this title: www.cambridge.org/9781107013810
DOI: 10.1017/9781139012126

© W. Dean Sutcliffe 2020

This publication is in copyright. Subject to statutory exception and to the provisions of relevant collective licensing agreements, no reproduction of any part may take place without the written permission of Cambridge University Press.

First published 2020

Printed in the United Kingdom by TJ International Ltd. Padstow Cornwall

A catalogue record for this publication is available from the British Library.

ISBN 978-1-107-01381-0 Hardback

Cambridge University Press has no responsibility for the persistence or accuracy of URLs for external or third-party internet websites referred to in this publication and does not guarantee that any content on such websites is, or will remain, accurate or appropriate.

Contents

List of Music Examples   [*page* vii]
Preface   [xi]

1 The Sociable Muse   [1]
   Introduction   [1]
   Modern Reception   [24]
   The Listener   [42]

2 Reciprocity   [55]
   The Gracious Riposte   [55]
   The Order of Things   [89]
   Agency and Motive   [120]
   The Language Model and 'Conversation'   [140]
   Thematic Interaction   [162]
   Contrast as Incongruity   [199]
   Topics   [230]
   Variety   [245]

3 Formula   [267]
   Convention   [267]
   Renewal   [276]
   The Simplifying Cadence and the Soft Ending   [313]
   Reduction   [339]
   Attention and Boredom   [346]
   Versatility   [371]
   Formal Function   [384]
   Middle Function: What Are Development Sections Doing?   [407]

4 Tone   [428]
   Sociable Feeling   [428]
   Sociable Surface   [453]
   The Minor Mode   [503]

5 Final Focus [515]
   The Pastoral [515]
   The Tempo di Menuetto Finale [531]

References [559]
Index [586]

Music Examples

1.1	Haydn, Quartet in E flat major Op. 33 No. 2/iv, bars 136–172	[*page* 29]
2.1	Pleyel, Quartet in E flat major Op. 1 No. 2/i, bars 1–11[3]	[58]
2.2	Türk, Sonata No. 4 in C major/i, from *Sechs leichte Klaviersonaten, Erster Teil*, bars 1–12	[60]
2.3	Beethoven, Sonata in C minor Op. 10 No. 1/i, bars 1–16	[61]
2.4	Abel, Keyboard Concerto in B flat major, Op. 11 No. 2/ii, bars 1–8	[64]
2.5a	Clementi, Violin Sonata in E flat major Op. 15 No. 1/i, bars 1–8	[73]
2.5b	Clementi, Violin Sonata in E flat major Op. 15 No. 1/i, bars 28–37[1]	[73]
2.6	Haydn, Sonata in E minor H34/ii, bars 12–20	[75]
2.7	Boccherini, Quartet in C major Op. 32 No. 4/i, bars 19–31	[80]
2.8a	Stamitz, Symphony in E flat major Op. 4 No. 6/i, bars 1–8	[83]
2.8b	Stamitz, Symphony in E flat major Op. 4 No. 6/i, bars 61–86	[84]
2.9	C. P. E. Bach, Rondo in E major Wq57/1, bars 1–8	[86]
2.10	J. C. Bach, Sonata in G major Op. 5 No. 3/i, bars 1–6	[86]
2.11	Mozart, Quintet in D major, K593/ii, bars 1–4[2]	[88]
2.12	J. C. Bach, Symphony in G minor, Op. 6 No. 6/i, bars 25–41	[93]
2.13	Haydn, Symphony No. 67 in F major/ii, bars 41–48	[96]
2.14	Wanhal, Flute Quartet in C major Op. 7 No. 6/i, bars 31–42	[98]
2.15	Mozart, Violin Sonata in B flat major K454/iii, bars 1–8[2]	[101]
2.16	Mozart, Variations for Piano Duet in G major, K501, bars 1–18	[104]
2.17	Haydn, Quartet in C major Op. 64 No. 1/iv, bars 1–62	[127]
2.18a	Mozart, Violin Sonata in G major K301/i, bars 1–18	[134]
2.18b	Mozart, Violin Sonata in G major K301/i, bars 25–33	[136]
2.18c	Mozart, Violin Sonata in G major K301/i, bars 80–84[3]	[136]
2.18d	Mozart, Violin Sonata in G major K301/i, bars 84[4]–92	[137]

2.18e   Mozart, Violin Sonata in G major K301/i, bars 113–122   [138]
2.18f   Mozart, Violin Sonata in G major K301/i, bars 134–144   [139]
2.18g   Mozart, Violin Sonata in G major K301/i, bars 190–194   [139]
2.19   Haydn, Quartet in B minor Op. 33 No. 1/i, bars 1–8   [151]
2.20a   Dittersdorf, Quartet in G major, K193/ii, bars 1–8   [153]
2.20b   Dittersdorf, Quartet in G major, K193/ii, bars 16–26   [153]
2.21   Hoffmeister, Quartet in F major Op. 14 No. 1/i, bars 1–10^1 [155]
2.22   Hoffmeister, Quartet in B flat major Op. 14 No. 2/ii, bars 20–31   [156]
2.23   Hoffmeister, Quartet in D minor Op. 14 No. 3/iv, bars 138–149   [157]
2.24   Boccherini, Quartet in D major Op. 32 No. 3/i, bars 1–8   [160]
2.25   Jadin, Quartet in F minor, Op. 1 No. 3/iii, bars 1–36^2 (cello part only)   [162]
2.26   Haydn, Sonata in E minor H34/i   [169]
2.27   C. P. E. Bach, Rondo in E flat major, Wq61/1, bars 1–47   [178]
2.28   Clementi, Sonata in G major Op. 37 No. 2/i, bars 1–54^3 [184]
2.29   Dittersdorf, Quartet in C major, K194/ii   [209]
2.30   Mozart, Quartet in D major K499/i, bars 1–23^1 [243]
3.1   Haydn, Sonata in D major H33/i, bars 37–58   [283]
3.2a   Haydn, Quartet in E flat major Op. 50 No. 3/iii, bars 1–12^2 [285]
3.2b   Haydn, Quartet in E flat major Op. 50 No. 3/iii, bars 43–57^2 [285]
3.3a   Haydn, Symphony No. 97 in C major/i, bars 1–18   [288]
3.3b   Haydn, Symphony No. 97 in C major/i, bars 96–103^2 [292]
3.4   Romberg, Quartet in E flat major Op. 1 No. 1/i, bars 1–18   [293]
3.5a   Gyrowetz, Quartet in B flat major Op. 44 No. 2/i, bars 16–21^1 [298]
3.5b   Gyrowetz, Quartet in B flat major Op. 44 No. 2/i, bars 42–46^3 [298]
3.5c   Gyrowetz, Quartet in B flat major Op. 44 No. 2/i, bars 83–86   [299]
3.5d   Gyrowetz, Quartet in B flat major Op. 44 No. 2/i, bars 262–266   [299]
3.6   Haydn, Quartet in G major Op. 54 No. 1/iv, bars 185–193   [301]
3.7   Pleyel, Quartet in G major Op. 1 No. 5/ii, bars 102–126   [306]
3.8   Beethoven, Sonata in F minor Op. 2 No. 1/iii, bars 1–28^2 [307]

3.9   Brunetti, Quartet in B flat major L192/i, bars 54–61   [310]
3.10   Haydn, Quartet in C major Op. 33 No. 3/i, bars 1–15   [311]
3.11a Dussek, Sonata in D major Op. 31 No. 2/i, bars 8^2–31^1 [313]
3.11b Dussek, Sonata in D major Op. 31 No. 2/i, bars 110–135   [314]
3.12   Dittersdorf, Quartet in D major, K191/i, bars 33–43   [316]
3.13   Pleyel, Quartet in A major Op. 1 No. 3/i, bars 75–83   [317]
3.14a Kraus, Violin Sonata in C major VB160/ii, bars 57–60   [318]
3.14b Kraus, Violin Sonata in C major VB160/ii, bars 1–2   [318]
3.15   Haydn, Quartet in B flat major Op. 50 No. 1/iv, bars 57–66   [319]
3.16   Mozart, Sonata in F major K332/iii, bars 218–245   [320]
3.17   Kozeluch, Quartet in E flat major Op. 32 No. 1/i, bars 37–60   [323]
3.18   Gyrowetz, Quartet in A flat major Op. 44 No. 3/ii, bars 43–57   [327]
3.19   Beethoven, Sonata in E flat major Op. 31 No. 3/i, bars 1–25^1 [331]
3.20   Mozart, Quartet in D major K499/i, bars 251–266   [334]
3.21   Krommer, Oboe Quartet in F major, P IX:22/iii, bars 194–211   [335]
3.22   Clementi, Violin Sonata in E flat major Op. 15 No. 1/iii, bars 187–199   [338]
3.23   Mozart, Violin Sonata in E flat major K302/iii, bars 162–175   [344]
3.24   Haydn, Quartet in B flat major Op. 50 No. 1/i, bars 1–6   [362]
3.25   Haydn, Quartet in C major Op. 33 No. 3/i, bars 156–167   [363]
3.26   Dittersdorf, Quartet in G major, K193/ii, bars 37–48   [364]
3.27   Dittersdorf, Quartet in E flat major, K195/ii, bars 45–60   [366]
3.28a Beethoven, Bagatelle in C major Op. 33 No. 2, bars 1–16   [369]
3.28b Beethoven, Bagatelle in C major Op. 33 No. 2, bars 118–138   [369]
3.29a Clementi, Sonata in G major Op. 40 No. 1/i, bars 1–8   [378]
3.29b Clementi, Sonata in G major Op. 40 No. 1/i, bars 24–30^2 [378]
3.29c Clementi, Sonata in G major Op. 40 No. 1/i, bars 34–40   [378]
3.30a Haydn, Symphony No. 58 in F major/iv, bars 1–12   [382]
3.30b Haydn, Symphony No. 58 in F major/iv, bars 60–71   [382]
3.30c Haydn, Symphony No. 58 in F major/iv, bars 105–117   [383]
3.31a Kraus, Symphony in C major VB139/ii, bars 1–10   [391]
3.31b Kraus, Symphony in C major VB139/ii, bars 64–82   [392]
3.32   Shield, String Trio No. 2 in D major/i, bars 10–19   [396]

3.33	C. P. E. Bach, Rondo in C minor, Wq59/4, bars 103–109	[399]
3.34a	Dittersdorf, Quartet in G major, K193/i, bars 167–178	[400]
3.34b	Dittersdorf, Quartet in G major, K193/i, bars 198–204	[400]
3.35a	Kraus, Quartet in B flat major, Op. 1 No. 2/i, bars 1–13	[416]
3.35b	Kraus, Quartet in B flat major, Op. 1 No. 2/i, bars 72–87[1]	[417]
3.36	Haydn, Symphony No. 93 in D major/i, bars 108–163	[418]
3.37	Pleyel, Quartet in C major Op. 1 No. 1/i, bars 108–125	[424]
4.1	C. P. E. Bach, Rondo in E major Wq 57/1, bars 89–94	[476]
4.2	Gyrowetz, Quartet in A flat major Op. 44 No. 3/ii, bars 74–82	[480]
4.3	Gyrowetz, Quartet in B flat major Op. 44 No. 2/ii, bars 95–103	[480]
4.4a	Kraus, Rondo in F major, VB191, bars 1–20	[482]
4.4b	Kraus, Rondo in F major, VB191, bars 37–54	[482]
4.4c	Kraus, Rondo in F major, VB191, bars 118–128	[483]
4.4d	Kraus, Rondo in F major, VB191, bars 173–191	[483]
4.5	Haydn, Quartet in B flat major Op. 55 No. 3/iii, bars 32^3–42^2	[502]
4.6	Kozeluch, Piano Trio in E minor Op. 28 No. 3/i, bars 1–28 (piano part only)	[507]
5.1	Haydn, Symphony No. 50 in C major/iii, bars 56^3–102	[527]
5.2	Kozeluch, Piano Trio in B flat major Op. 41 No. 1/ii, bars 124–141	[532]
5.3a	Haydn, Piano Trio in F major H17/ii, bars 1–11	[536]
5.3b	Haydn, Piano Trio in F major H17/ii, bars 33–43	[537]
5.4	Schobert, Sonata in E flat major Op. 6 No. 1/iii, bars 1–29	[543]
5.5	Clementi, Sonata for Piano Duet in E flat major Op. 3 No. 2/ii, bars 1–30	[548]
5.6a	Haydn, Piano Trio in F major H6/ii, bars 1–32^2	[552]
5.6b	Haydn, Piano Trio in F major H6/ii, bars 135^3–148	[556]

Preface

This study aims both to define and to defend a strain of Western art music that achieved particular prominence in the latter part of the eighteenth century. I have encapsulated it under the rubric of sociability, a widely understood shorthand for certain developments that characterized the eighteenth-century Enlightenment, but not a term that has often featured more than incidentally in music scholarship. I aim to show how a sociable ethos informs not only the general affective character of this repertory, but also the precise ways in which music could be shaped by composers and received by listeners.

Why should this sociable strain need defending? If it often prompted reactions ranging from incomprehension to indifference to hostility from the listeners and critics of the time, it has, equally ironically, continued to do so up to the present day. This may seem a far-fetched claim when some of the most illustrious composing names in the canon were operating at this time. Yet a great deal of the literature has implied that the accessible character of galant musical language was an obstacle to true creative expression: that the 'real music' was somehow to be found behind or beyond the everyday pleasantries that formed the communicative surface. As will soon become clear in Chapter 1, I believe that an imperative of 'expression' controls such discourse, and we might ask – not just of this repertory, incidentally – just what we mean by expression, and just how it relates to the listening experience. We might want, for example, to ponder the thoughts of Elizabeth Hellmuth Margulis when she writes, in *On Repeat: How Music Plays the Mind* (New York: Oxford University Press, 2014):

> I would submit that interest is an important part of our emotional response to music, and that repetition facilitates the interest response. To my knowledge, the notion of interest as an affective response to music has not been deeply explored. Much has been made of emotional responses to music that entail sadness or happiness or some such feeling, yet often my own involvement with a piece, although deeply engaged, consists not of such feeling-states, but rather of a kind of committed and sustained interest. (18)

If this is not exactly the line of thinking I will be emphasizing – though in Chapter 3 I do specifically consider interest's evil twin, boredom –

Margulis's cognitive approach offers another point of departure when we consider what makes for 'interesting' music. In addition, her perspective is clearly not confined to the eighteenth century, and I would like to note here what I will go on to say at greater length in what follows: that my focus on sociability should not imply that such a perspective has no relevance for other (Western) musical idioms. It may indeed prove to be a particularly rewarding means of reorientation for later eighteenth-century music, but there is a counterbalancing danger of reification – that my study will simply end up reinforcing prevailing views about the 'complacency' and 'lightness' of the style.

However, I don't want to start rehearsing all the arguments that are about to be launched. Any reader will surely end up agreeing that these are expounded at sufficient length in what follows – and besides, a preface should not be a way of making good any flaws in the substance of what succeeds it. I should signal here, though, that I confine my attentions almost entirely to instrumental music, both for reasons intrinsic to the topic and also on logistical grounds. The amount of musical material on which I could draw for this study was already just about limitless, and I have tried to avoid concentrating on any particular genre. I have also, it will be apparent, not confined myself to the usual handful of composers who normally figure in accounts of the era. I have been given a very generous allowance of music examples, but there are many movements I discuss where no score has been provided. In all such cases I have tried to describe them in such a way that the accounts will still make sense in the absence of visual evidence.

A few other logistical matters should be mentioned. I have aimed to give the dates for all works mentioned in the book, which are dates of composition where securely known or, if not, dates of publication. Where I use the simple terms 'quartet' and 'sonata', these refer to the string quartet and solo keyboard sonata unless otherwise qualified. And I should clarify a larger-scale matter that might cause confusion. The term 'galant' functions as a value-neutral description of the musical style that prevailed for most of the eighteenth century, up to the last decades, where most of my interest has been concentrated. The dread word 'Classical' appears only in (scare) quotes.

This book has been a long time in the making. I have given many conference papers and other presentations relating to my subject from 2005 to the present, and I draw on a number of these throughout the book. In addition, at various times I draw on previously published material, acknowledged in all cases through footnotes at the relevant point of the text. This material derives from the journals *Eighteenth-Century Music*, *Journal of Musicological Research*, *Journal of the Royal Musical Association*, *Music & Letters* and *Notes: Quarterly Journal of the Music Library Association*, and from the books *Haydn and His Contemporaries II: Selected Papers from the Fifth Biennial Conference of the Society for Eighteenth-Century Music at the College of Charleston in Charleston, SC, 13–15 April 2012*, ed. Kathryn Libin (Ann Arbor: Steglein, 2015); *Instrumental Music in Late Eighteenth-Century Spain*, ed. Miguel Ángel Marín and Màrius Bernardó (Kassel: Reichenberger, 2014); *SECM in Austin 2016: Topics in Eighteenth-Century Music II*, ed. Janet K. Page (Ann Arbor: Steglein, 2019); *The Cambridge Companion to the String Quartet*, ed. Robin Stowell (Cambridge: Cambridge University Press, 2003); *The Cambridge Haydn Encyclopedia*, ed. Caryl Clark and Sarah Day-O'Connell (Cambridge: Cambridge University Press, 2019); and *The Oxford Handbook of Topic Theory*, ed. Danuta Mirka (New York: Oxford University Press, 2014). I am grateful to all the publishers and presses who allowed me to reuse and/or adapt my thoughts. I should like to thank the University of Auckland and, in the earlier days of the project, the University of Cambridge for support towards attendance at conferences and other events. Many thanks are also due to those bodies that granted me subventions to cover some extra publication costs: the University of Auckland, once more, the Society for Music Theory and the Margarita M. Hanson Endowment of the American Musicological Society, funded in part by the National Endowment for the Humanities and the Andrew W. Mellon Foundation. I am also grateful to all those who have responded positively to both publications and presentations: no author can have too much encouragement. I did not inflict the following chapters on anyone, since by the time they were in a fit and final state, it really was time to go public, after such a long gestation. I would also like to thank Kathryn Puffett and Gordon J. Callon for setting the music examples, Victoria Cooper, Eilidh Burrett, Lisa Sinclair and Kate Brett of Cambridge University Press for all their help, and my copy-editor Barbara Wilson. Finally, thanks and much love to my partner, Geoff, and to my late parents, Patricia and Bill, who started it all off, and were the most encouraging of all.

1 | The Sociable Muse

Introduction

> *When something seems 'the most obvious thing in the world' it means that any attempt to understand the world has been given up.*
>
> Bertolt Brecht[1]

While sociability has long been a key term of reference for eighteenth-century studies as a whole, it has not developed an especially strong profile in music scholarship.[2] Allusions to a sociable art are scattered freely in musicological literature, certainly with regard to the instrumental music of the later eighteenth century, the subject of this book, yet this cultural strain has not been examined as directly and explicitly as it has been in other fields. Scholarly approaches sometimes seem to take their discursive or critical cues from the perceived character of the music being examined: sobriety for the North German Baroque, a headier brew for the romantic generation, and so on. If so, then the mantra for studies of the later eighteenth century might be good taste, meaning that certain fundamental precepts may be taken as read, or perhaps touched on only lightly and in passing: to do more would be to give the game away. In other words, the friendly face that our repertory typically presents is 'the most obvious thing

---

[1] Bertolt Brecht, 'Vergnügungstheater oder Lehrtheater?' (Theatre for Pleasure or Theatre for Instruction?), from 'Über eine nichtaristotelische Dramatik', in *Bertolt Brecht: Schriften zum Theater*, seven volumes (Frankfurt am Main: Suhrkamp, 1963), volume 3: *1933–1947*, 55; *Brecht on Theatre: The Development of an Aesthetic*, ed. and trans. John Willett (London: Methuen, 1964), 71. This established translation is quite a free rendering of the original, 'Bei allem "Selbstverständlichen" wird auf das Verstehen einfach verzichtet.'

[2] Parts of this opening section are based on various passages found in my articles 'Before the Joke: Texture and Sociability in the Largo of Haydn's Op. 33 No. 2', *Journal of Musicological Research* 28/2–3 (2009), 92–118, www.tandfonline.com/loi/gmur20, and in particular 'The Shapes of Sociability in the Instrumental Music of the Later Eighteenth Century', *Journal of the Royal Musical Association* 138/1 (2013), 1–45, copyright ©The Royal Musical Association, reprinted by permission of Taylor & Francis Ltd, www.tandfonline.com, on behalf of The Royal Musical Association.

in the world', so why should one labour the point any more than did the musicians of that time? Matthew Riley has characterized what could be seen as a related tendency, a tradition of what he calls 'polite criticism' in regard to this music, 'in which the writer poses as a gentleman-connoisseur and assumes a similar pose from his readers'.[3] What might seem to contradict such a thesis is a long-standing theoretical attachment to the nuts and bolts of the musical language of the time, recently revivified in a formidable series of studies by William E. Caplin, Robert O. Gjerdingen, and James Hepokoski and Warren Darcy.[4] Yet for all of the more or less systematic approaches they offer, they also suggest a permissive ethos: an appeal to individual circumstance and free choice amongst formal or schematic alternatives – in other words, taste. Here too there has been a certain reticence to engage too heavily with the social implications of what all acknowledge to be an especially listener-directed art.[5]

Indeed, it is the very directness of address to a listener that constitutes one of the great novelties of this instrumental repertory. In order for this to come about, an especially clear system of communication must have been established, and our one relies strongly on familiar signs, whether these be topics or formulas or schemata.[6] From our perspective, systematic approaches such as those mentioned above are very much to the point: sociability too necessitates constant attention to form. While such form

---

[3] Matthew Riley writes: 'In the twentieth century, the study of "classical style" in Anglophone scholarship seems to have become a haven for the otherwise embattled genre of polite criticism, in which the writer poses as a gentleman-connoisseur and assumes a similar pose from his readers. Its echoes are recognizable in the prose styles of Tovey, Rosen, Joseph Kerman, and perhaps even Cone.' Riley, 'Sonata Principles' (review of Hepokoski and Darcy, *Elements of Sonata Theory*), *Music & Letters* 89/4 (2008), 596.

[4] William E. Caplin, *Classical Form: A Theory of Formal Functions for the Instrumental Music of Haydn, Mozart, and Beethoven* (New York: Oxford University Press, 1998); Robert O. Gjerdingen, *Music in the Galant Style* (New York: Oxford University Press, 2007); James Hepokoski and Warren Darcy, *Elements of Sonata Theory: Norms, Types, and Deformations in the Late-Eighteenth-Century Sonata* (New York: Oxford University Press, 2006).

[5] As will subsequently become clear, various scholars have indeed touched on these social concerns. Wye Jamison Allanbrook was one individual who did make sociable qualities a fundamental point of orientation for her work, as encapsulated in her posthumous *The Secular Commedia: Comic Mimesis in Late Eighteenth-Century Instrumental Music*, ed. Mary Ann Smart and Richard Taruskin (Berkeley: University of California Press, 2014). James R. Currie's 'Waiting for the Viennese Classics', *The Musical Quarterly* 90/1 (2007), 123–166, places particular emphasis on the ethics of a style that conducts a dialogue with the listener, based on recognition – and often distortion – of conventions, and will be discussed in Chapter 3.

[6] It is not, of course, as if any preceding and following musical styles are exactly lacking in familiar signs that can be recognized by a listener. What may enhance the sensation of familiarity in later eighteenth-century instrumental music is the way in which such features are packaged. This will be a major concern throughout my study, and will be explored further in Chapter 2.

may not literally be of the music-theoretical type, it does imply the need to read the signs, to negotiate one's way through what may be largely a series of familiar gambits.

Of course, one could hardly claim that social interaction itself was a novelty to the eighteenth century. What does seem to be new, though, is the very conception of the social as an encompassing category: Daniel Gordon, in his *Citizens without Sovereignty: Equality and Sociability in French Thought, 1670–1789*, writes of 'the invention of the social as a distinctive field of human experience',[7] and this goes beyond all those concrete manifestations like the coffee-house and the salon. It entails a belief that keeping company is the natural human state and that interaction with others generates what we would call collective wisdom, a better take on things as they are than anything an individual alone can achieve. In French the very term 'sociabilité' was coined early in the eighteenth century.[8] Also being added to the lexicon around this time, or at least acquiring new resonance, are the cognate term 'society' and the related notion of 'the public'. In their newer senses both terms try to comprehend a sort of sum total of all human activities and views. 'Society' is no longer just a specific collection of people gathered in one place, but something more permanent and larger-scale, and 'public' no longer refers solely to the exercise of state authority.[9] Both come to refer above all to a discursive culture that involves the expression of opinion. This need not mean that agreement or even consensus is reached, that everyone speaks with one voice, or indeed that conformity is achieved. But it does imply that the interaction happens through the free association of individuals, beyond the direct control of such entities as church, state or monarchy. It is the very fact of communication – the process rather than the result – that is pivotal.[10] 'Society' and 'the public' have since become such naturalized

---

[7] Daniel Gordon, *Citizens without Sovereignty: Equality and Sociability in French Thought, 1670–1789* (Princeton: Princeton University Press, 1994), 5.

[8] Gordon, *Citizens without Sovereignty*, 6.

[9] The latter point is clarified in James van Horn Melton, *The Rise of the Public in Enlightenment Europe* (Cambridge: Cambridge University Press, 2001), 1: while the older sense of the term 'public' still exists in such phrases as 'public building' or 'public property', the newer meanings 'were unrelated to the exercise of state authority. They referred rather to publics whose members were private individuals rendering judgement on what they read, observed, or otherwise experienced.'

[10] Compare T. C. W. Blanning, *The Culture of Power and the Power of Culture: Old Regime Europe 1660–1789* (Oxford: Oxford University Press, 2002), 8–9: 'What matters about [the public sphere] is not what it contains in terms of ideas or feelings or even its social composition, but the fact that those contents are actively communicated. It is the effort of communication which creates the "public".

concepts that it is hard to think one's way back into a time when they were only just gaining these new implications. Gordon notes of 'society' that it has become 'indispensable' to any historiographical 'discussion of collective life',[11] and indeed it is only through the existence of such a frame of reference, for better or worse, that this present study can take place at all.

While claims for the intrinsically social nature of human beings may once have had the force of novelty, they soon became so common that many writers acknowledged the fact. Joseph Addison, for instance, stated in 1711 that 'Man is said to be a Sociable Animal', while Henry Fielding began his 1743 *Essay on Conversation* by noting that 'Man is generally represented as an Animal formed for and delighting in Society'.[12] The very framing of such statements in the passive voice ('is said', 'is represented') itself appeals to a wider authority than the individual writer. A variant was to regard sociability as a birthright. Thus the *Dictionnaire de Trévoux* of 1704 stated that 'Man is born to be *sociable* to such an extent that this quality is just as much attached to his essence as reason is',[13] while in an issue of *The Lounger* of 1785 Henry Mackenzie (it is thought) wrote, 'Men were born to live in society, and from society only can happiness be derived'.[14] Caroline Pichler, whose father's Viennese salon was attended by composers such as Haydn in the 1780s and who in turn became a celebrated cultural arbiter as well as writer, could still reiterate the point in an essay of 1819: 'Der Mensch ist zur Geselligkeit gebohren' (man is born to society).[15] This could also be expressed in reverse, offering a negative image of those who wanted to renounce their human inheritance. The Third Earl of Shaftesbury – like Addison, regarded as something of a founding father of eighteenth-century sociable culture – opined that 'whoever is unsociable, and voluntarily shuns Society, or Commerce with

---

[11] Gordon, *Citizens without Sovereignty*, 7. Blanning, *Culture of Power*, 2, writes: 'By exchanging information, ideas, and criticism, these individuals created a cultural actor – the public – which has dominated European culture ever since.' For a discussion of the development of the terms 'social' and 'société' in France see Keith Michael Baker, 'Enlightenment and the Institution of Society: Notes for a Conceptual History', in *Main Trends in Cultural History: Ten Essays*, ed. Willem Melching and Wyger Velema (Amsterdam: Rodopi, 1994), 95–120.

[12] Joseph Addison, *The Spectator* (10 March 1711), 48, and Henry Fielding, 'An Essay on Conversation', in *Miscellanies*, volume 1 (London: A. Millar, 1743), 117.

[13] *Dictionnaire universel françois et latin [Dictionnaire de Trévoux]* (Paris: Estienne Ganeau, 1704), 'Sociable', cited in translation in Gordon, *Citizens without Sovereignty*, 52.

[14] Hortensius [Henry MacKenzie], *The Lounger* 9 (2 April 1785), 75.

[15] Caroline Pichler, 'Überblick meines Lebens' (1819), in *Prosaische Aufsätze*, two volumes (Vienna: Anton Pichler, 1822), volume 2, 189. All translations are mine unless otherwise indicated.

the World, must of necessity be morose and ill-natur'd'.[16] A specifically musical application of this sentiment comes from Gaspar de Molina y Saldívar, Marquis of Ureña, who in his *Reflexiones sobre la arquitectura, ornato, y musica del templo* of 1785 wrote: 'One must nourish oneself with ideas, since men are contrivers, not creators. To renounce imitation is a great mistake: among a thousand gifted musicians there will scarcely be one who can develop without hearing others perform and imitating them. Anyone who imagines that he can find within himself the museum that will make him wise is just deceiving himself.'[17] Through the metaphor of a museum, a repository of knowledge made publicly available, the marquis strongly affirms our principle of collective wisdom, even as he makes clear that contrary views did exist.

Indeed, sociability does not deny the existence of private thoughts and feelings; rather, it implies respect for the thoughts and feelings of others in a group situation. Rather than being a monolithically collective phenomenon, it arises from the cooperation of individual sensibilities. In other words, sociability is not impersonal, it is interpersonal. It involves such concepts and qualities as reciprocity, politeness, decorum, exchange, friendliness, pleasantness, comfort, ease, goodwill, graciousness, wit and humour. But since it entails an emphasis on human deportment rather than direct self-expression, it departs from the expressive aesthetics to which we are still so loyal, with their connotations of personal integrity and individual self-sufficiency. This means that watchwords of sociable interaction like politeness, comfort and moderation of utterance don't seem like promising vehicles for memorable aesthetic experience. Indeed, resistance to such qualities has been stronger and more sustained in the musical sphere than elsewhere, and one does not have to dig far into the reception history of later eighteenth-century music to recognize the signs. The controlling image is of creativity and individuality blighted by convention, so that only exceptional talents were able to produce music that can still engage our interest today.

The operative term in this equation, and the real sticking-point when we consider the reception of the style, is expression. We need to consider,

---

[16] Anthony Ashley Cooper Third Earl of Shaftesbury, *Characteristicks of Men, Manners, Opinions, Times*, three volumes (London: John Darby, 1714), volume 2, 137.

[17] Gaspar de Molina y Saldívar, Marqués de Ureña, *Reflexiones sobre la arquitectura, ornato, y musica del templo* (Madrid: Joachin Ibarra, 1785), 388, cited in translation in Teresa Cascudo, 'Iberian Symphonism, 1779–1809: Some Observations', in *Music in Spain during the Eighteenth Century*, ed. Malcolm Boyd and Juan José Carreras (Cambridge: Cambridge University Press, 1998), 156.

though, whether expression as commonly understood is not so much a universal truth as a widely held assumption. While many forms of artistic activity have been understood to involve making productive capital out of personal feeling, this has been nowhere more consistently asserted than in the case of music. Whether in the academic or the wider public imagination, for many the very raison d'être of music resides in the way it connects directly with emotion, as variously expressed and experienced by composer, performer and listener.[18] Music's relatively weak referential capacities have no doubt encouraged the sense that it all 'comes from inside', most plainly in the case of wordless instrumental forms. However, the belief that personal emotion – more broadly, subjectivity – is being expressed is itself socially conditioned. As Sianne Ngai puts it on a larger scale, 'far from being merely private or idiosyncratic phenomena ... feelings are as fundamentally "social" as the institutions and collective practices that have been the more traditional objects of historicist criticism'.[19] Feelings, in other words, have to be learnt based on the practices of a particular culture. Within that framework, the notion of expression is built on the culturally specific idea of a 'centred subjectivity', the sense that each of us contains a stable core of identity and character that is not shared by any other individual.[20] Even if we were to accept the link between music and emotion as a given, there remains the question of just how that might operate. As Celia Applegate wonders, is music 'a sphere of emotional education or compensation or expression or action, or some combination of all these?'.[21]

In fact, when it comes to music, expression tends to be understood in a specific way. While in theory available to all emotional modalities, including those mentioned above under the banner of sociability, expression most commonly connotes introspection, measured speeds and melancholy affects:

---

[18] In conjunction with this, it is worth noting that 'music and the emotions' has become a hot topic in recent scholarship, though not necessarily taking the same line as I aim to develop here. A representative recent contribution is the Special Issue on Music and Emotion of *Music Analysis* 29/1-2-3 (2010), ed. Michael Spitzer. A sample of the wider, longer-standing interest in the subject is Ute Frevert and others, *Emotional Lexicons: Continuity and Change in the Vocabulary of Feeling 1700-2000* (Oxford: Oxford University Press, 2014).

[19] Sianne Ngai, *Ugly Feelings* (Cambridge, MA: Harvard University Press, 2005), 25.

[20] This is addressed on a musical plane by Susan McClary throughout *Conventional Wisdom: The Content of Musical Form* (Berkeley: University of California Press, 2000), for instance when she writes of Alessandro Scarlatti's character Griselda 'displaying the centered subjectivity – the belief in the unshakability of that inner core – that is still one of our favorite myths, poststructuralism notwithstanding' (79).

[21] Celia Applegate, 'Introduction: Music among the Historians', *German History* 30/3 (2012), 345.

slow and sad, in other words.²² In sum, while it commonly connotes a focus on inner feelings, free from social constraint, 'expression' may in fact be regarded as the master convention of them all. It is something that has been learnt and internalized. But since this study will be emphasizing the positive and productive aspects of (artistic) convention, and the socialization of feeling, it would be inconsistent to regard this in a negative light. We simply need to note the existence of this convention, and its continuing hold over us.

It would be easy to ally the idea that music expresses personal emotion with developments that occur chiefly in the earlier nineteenth century, with romanticism, and to declare expressive aesthetics anachronistic to our concerns. Yet expression was in fact a very familiar watchword in treatises and other writings on music throughout the eighteenth century. Indeed, expression, together with 'taste', are probably the most commonly encountered terms of reference in such discussions. Johann Georg Sulzer, for example, in his *Allgemeine Theorie der Schönen Künste* of 1771–1774, asserted that 'Expression is the soul of music. Without it, music is but an entertaining diversion.'²³ Further to the point, composers were increasingly discussed as though they had distinct personas, their music interpreted as an expression of their personality. In the case of Haydn, for instance, many of his more unaccountable and odd musical moments came to be explained with reference to his reputation as a 'humorist'.²⁴

Nevertheless, this may not be quite the same thing as saying that Haydn 'expresses himself' in music. What is implied is less that listeners are given an insight into the inner life of the composer, than that they recognize that

---

[22] A revealing instance of this may be found in the article 'Emotions in Music' by Jenefer Robinson and Robert S. Hatten, *Music Theory Spectrum* 34/2 (2012), 71–106. They offer a rich theoretical account of just what it might mean to say that 'music has an especially intimate connection with the emotions' (71), but then choose pieces for closer study that fit the customarily narrow understanding of 'expression'. First they analyse J. S. Bach's Prelude in E flat minor from Book 1 of the *Well-Tempered Clavier*, which is quite definitively slow and sad, and then in an account of the (also) slow movement of Brahms's Piano Quartet in C minor, Op. 60, they emphasize its 'yearning' character, which is surely one of the definitive expressive conventions of 'romantic' music.

[23] Johann Georg Sulzer, *Allgemeine Theorie der Schönen Künste*, four volumes (Leipzig: M. G. Weidmann und Reich, 1771–1774), volume 1, 271, cited in translation in *Aesthetics and the Art of Musical Composition in the German Enlightenment: Selected Writings of Johann Georg Sulzer and Heinrich Christoph Koch*, ed. and trans. Nancy Kovaleff Baker and Thomas Christensen (Cambridge: Cambridge University Press, 1995), 51.

[24] Reception of Haydn in terms of his perceived personality has been treated at length, with a visual and an iconographical focus, in Thomas Tolley's *Painting the Cannon's Roar: Music, the Visual Arts and the Rise of an Attentive Public in the Age of Haydn, c.1750 to c.1810* (Aldershot: Ashgate, 2001). See in particular chapter 5, 'Musical Icons and the Cult of Haydn', 162–206.

he has a distinctive manner – in other words, a way of behaving.[25] And behaviour means how we appear to the outside world. Personality, therefore, becomes apparent in interaction rather than being understood as an essence, as 'how one really is', which was a private matter and hence not readily knowable. And so if sociability is to be lined up alongside an imperative of 'expression', it implies an expression of feeling that is directed outwards, that is concerned with how one's own nature and one's own views interact with those of others. To put it differently: no matter how strong one's personal feelings or convictions are, one can be sure that they are unlikely to be felt in the same way by one's fellows. As this might suggest, the modern sense of expression as issuing from an individual – rather than involving the codified affects or 'passions' of an earlier time[26] – has in fact already emerged, and complicates any attempt to place expressive aesthetics outside our purview.

Another way to try to capture this is to suggest that in later eighteenth-century instrumental music the emphasis lies in communication rather than expression, in the now-customary sense of revealing 'pure', internal feelings. The brand of discourse is one of constant qualification, of always conceding another point of view or way of feeling; it is relativistic rather than revelatory. Indeed, sociability may be understood as involving a strongly performative orientation, which means being less concerned to tell a single truth, as it were, than to investigate the nature of utterance. This type of performativity approximates that found in J. L. Austin's theory of speech acts, which 'reverses the priority held by language as truth and correspondence over language as action and creation'.[27] This is a musical style that rarely declaims, that does not seem to want to persuade in any straightforward way, but is instead more self-conscious about its mission in the world. Often the main information conveyed to a listener seems to be less a determinate affect, or even series of affects, than something akin to what we might call 'discourse', or 'structure', or indeed 'language as action' – an invitation to contemplate the agency of all parties in the construction of a work of music.

---

[25] Wye Jamison Allanbrook puts this in terms of a more specific sort of outward sign, physical movement as embodied in dance steps, and more broadly rhythms and the metres within which they are held, in *Rhythmic Gesture in Mozart: 'Le nozze di Figaro' and 'Don Giovanni'* (Chicago: University of Chicago Press, 1983). For example, 'rhythm ... is a primary agent in the projecting of human postures and thereby of human character. ... a character in the motion of action would reveal himself more naturally than could any number of explanatory soliloquies' (8–9).

[26] On the replacement of the passions by 'sentiment' see Georgia Cowart, 'Sense and Sensibility in Eighteenth-Century Musical Thought', *Acta musicologica* 56/2 (1984), 251–266.

[27] Benjamin Lee, *Talking Heads: Language, Metalanguage, and the Semiotics of Subjectivity* (Durham, NC: Duke University Press, 1997), 23.

This comes about because of a self-consciousness that is evident in such aspects as the constant changeability of rhythm and texture or the playing with musical formulas and their implications. And the way in which the listener is more or less directly addressed by such phenomena may generate self-consciousness at the receiving end too, a sense of 'guilt by association' when a musical work takes odd turns, as happens frequently enough. The listeners who are implied by such stylistic traits need to be alert, to keep their wits about them, to exercise judgment – all sociable attributes – rather than simply immerse themselves in the musical flow. If – as suggested earlier – the style of music under examination can imprint itself on the style of scholarly discourse associated with it, then such self-awareness may explain the characteristically allusive, decentred way in which later eighteenth-century music has often been discussed, relatively bashful about making grand claims or engaging head on with aesthetic properties and implications.

If constructs like 'discourse' and 'communication' may help to loosen the hold of 'expression' (though certainly not replace it) in addressing the instrumental music of the later eighteenth century, another point of orientation might be 'behaviour'. Certainly, as already implied, sociable music provides some equivalent for the mental processes of qualification and inhibition that we undergo in order to interact with others, which are then manifested in musical action. Behaviour has the advantage over discourse that it is less narrowly linguistic in its implications, enabling us to invoke analogies not just of verbal language but also of body language, such as gesture, and of course interpersonal conduct is generally marked by a mixture of the two.[28] Behaviour also encompasses the notion of manners, which allows us to start to account for such perceived musical attributes in this repertory as politeness and pleasantness. Once more, such qualities may seem to us today to be inimical to the proper purpose of art, certainly by the standards of our current expressive model, in which inhibition plays no part. But manners – how one acts – could not always be separated so readily from what was inside – how one feels. As Wye J. Allanbrook has commented: 'Comportment was for the eighteenth century ... no thin veneer of society manners, but an expression of character and the key to

---

[28] For a gloss on this from a sociological standpoint see Tia DeNora, *Music in Everyday Life* (Cambridge: Cambridge University Press, 2000), 17: 'Music may influence how people compose their bodies, how they conduct themselves, how they experience the passage of time, how they feel ... about themselves, about others, and about situations. In this respect music may imply and, in some cases, elicit associated modes of conduct.'

a man's worth.'[29] In fact, as we shall see in due course, there was always anxiety that good manners were indeed a 'thin veneer', but this contended with the ideal articulated by Allanbrook, that manners were a holistic expression of the human being and thus something more akin to ethics, a complete system of behaviour. This broader understanding of manners, explicitly linked to the art of music, is apparent in John Brown's 1763 *Dissertation on the Rise, Union, and Power . . . of Poetry and Music*. In a section in which Brown contemplates the stages that will be gone through by 'savages' should the 'use of letters' (literacy) come among them, he suggests that

> The Genius of their *Music* would *vary* along with their *Manners*: For Manners being the leading and most essential Quality of Man; All his other Tastes and Accomplishments naturally correspond with *These*; and accommodate themselves to his Manners, as to their chief and original Cause. / As a Change of Manners must influence their Music, so, by a reciprocal Action, a Change in their Music must influence Manners.[30]

Clearly 'manners' here are to be considered as more than outward signs, and it is striking in Brown's closing proposal that music functions symbiotically with them: music does not just reflect but actively influences human conduct. Positing a relationship between the two was not exactly a new idea, of course, as was apparent when Thomas Twining, in a comment to his 1789 translation of Aristotle's *Poetics*, affirmed that 'music alone possesses this property of resemblance to human manners'.[31] But the behavioural model can also be situated within a development that is more peculiar to the eighteenth century: simply put, the intense interest in how people get on with each other. This is one aspect of Gordon's 'invention of the social as a distinctive field of human experience', and it led to the rise of what we might call the human sciences over the course of the century.[32]

My characterization of a self-conscious brand of musical behaviour may well seem remote from some widely held perceptions of later eighteenth-century instrumental style: where are the qualities such as ease, elegance and

---

[29] Allanbrook, *Rhythmic Gesture in Mozart*, 69–70.

[30] John Brown, *A Dissertation on the Rise, Union, and Power, the Progressions, Separations, and Corruptions, of Poetry and Music* (London: L. Davis and C. Reymers, 1763), 45.

[31] Thomas Twining, *Recreations and Studies of a Country Clergyman of the Eighteenth Century, Being Selections from the Correspondence of the Rev. Thomas Twining, M. A.* (London: John Murray, 1882), 54, cited in David P. Schroeder, *Haydn and the Enlightenment: The Late Symphonies and Their Audience* (Oxford: Clarendon, 1990), 116.

[32] See Nicholas Cronk, Introduction to Denis Diderot, *Rameau's Nephew and First Satire*, trans. Margaret Mauldon, with Introduction and notes by Nicholas Cronk (Oxford: Oxford University Press, 2006), vii–xxv.

naturalness that have so often been ascribed to it, and to which I have already alluded above? One answer is to note that the 'natural' – another favoured term of the time – already presupposes a degree of self-consciousness. True naturalness is unaware of itself, and does not need to posit itself explicitly as a category. Secondly, the self-consciousness is a global attribute rather than necessarily one that intrudes at every moment. It is evident in the way in which material is organized, and includes the changeability and play with formulas referred to earlier. This leads to the important point that musical sociability must be treated partly as a technical matter. The area of phrase rhythm illustrates this. The ways in which composers manipulate its parameters – whether through clearly demarcated phrase units, through strongly signalled approaches to a cadence or through differentiations between the formal functions of beginning, middle and end[33] – exemplify an artistic imperative of intelligibility, of making musical utterance accessible to a wide range of listeners.

A further regulating principle is reciprocity. Reciprocity must lie at the heart of any form of sociable conduct, and our repertory makes this structurally vivid in all sorts of ways. One way is the marked preference for binary constructions, where phrases are arranged in matching or complementary pairs. But this can be felt and heard on smaller and larger scales, too. A single phrase unit may contain all sorts of checks and balances of contour, dynamics, rhythm, articulation and the like, while whole sections and movements can be shaped so as to feature quite explicit 'dialogues' of contours. This call-and-response method can be understood as inherently social, implying the interaction and mutual adjustment of different ideas or styles or affects. Later generations have been more inclined to hear in such attributes a desire for balance pure and simple, something more architectonic and 'classical' and less to do with the controlling of utterance. Of course the historical engagement with form, on all its levels of operation, is quite understandable in the case of a type of music that seems very conscious of how it organizes itself: as already noted, this encourages contemplation of its formal behaviour as an autonomous category. And the changeability we have highlighted derives from an imperative of keeping one's listeners – those with whom one interacts musically – engaged at all times, not allowing them to drift off into reverie (or perhaps into a state of boredom).

---

[33] On formal functions see the chapter 'Introversive Semiosis: The Beginning–Middle–End Paradigm' in Kofi Agawu, *Playing with Signs: A Semiotic Interpretation of Classic Music* (Princeton: Princeton University Press, 1991), 51–79.

Such features mean that sociable and communicative urges seem to be built into the very utterance of the music, independent of affect, as it were. Sociability, in other words, can exist from the point of view of musical technique alone even when the tone does not seem especially friendly or obliging. Thus the music at issue need not convey only what we might define as sociable emotions or affects. A useful shorthand would be to distinguish between affective sociability, encompassing our feelings of good fellowship, ease, warmth, friendliness, relaxation, good humour and the like, and technical sociability, which encompasses all the communicative principles and devices that can be applied in order to court a listener.

These are not, it should be clear, mutually exclusive categories. Indeed, the strains of technical sociability mentioned above, which involve the ways in which utterance is organized, suggest that musical syntax is not to be regarded as some sort of neutral frame upon which we hang meaning. Several studies by Susan McClary concerning seventeenth- and eighteenth-century music have attempted to move beyond such an assumption, guided by the 'claim [that] musical syntax cannot be understood apart from the effects it was designed to produce at various moments in history'. This means 'assum[ing] that musicians produce the kind of music that appeals to them and those for whom they write and perform. It is the job of historians to reconstruct the contexts within which those preferences prevailed and made sense.'[34] In his work on eighteenth-century musical schemata Gjerdingen has been guided by a similar belief, that there is a mutual relationship between 'pure' syntax and a particular culture within which it is embedded and heard: musical pattern functions as a 'medium of exchange'.[35] Listeners are primed by the replication of patterns to recognize and make sense of them, and composers can only continue to employ these patterns as long as listeners assent to receive them.

To say as much may seem self-evident, and such an equation would surely also apply well beyond the period with which we are concerned.[36] But what helps bring this alive for the later eighteenth century is the sense that sociable style goes out of its way to encourage listener competence and

---

[34] Susan McClary, *Desire and Pleasure in Seventeenth-Century Music* (Berkeley: University of California Press, 2012), 6 and 8. See also McClary, *Conventional Wisdom*.

[35] Robert O. Gjerdingen, 'Courtly Behaviors', *Music Perception: An Interdisciplinary Journal* 13/3 (1996), 367.

[36] As Leonard B. Meyer remarks, 'explaining replication is an important concern of music history': 'Nature, Nurture, and Convention: The Cadential Six-Four Progression', in *Convention in Eighteenth- and Nineteenth-Century Music: Essays in Honor of Leonard G. Ratner*, ed. Wye J. Allanbrook, Janet M. Levy and William P. Mahrt (Stuyvesant: Pendragon, 1992), 475.

comprehension, and that it is historically fairly exceptional in the extent to which it does this. In fact, this very accessibility has created a problem. These attributes have helped to make some of this repertory an entrenched and fundamental part of various forms of music teaching, whether practical or theoretical, as well as of the performing canon, lasting up to the present day. Such familiarity may mean that we are particularly liable to overlook the original historical charge that the musical syntax could have carried. Less familiar repertories of European art music are, in some senses, easier to grasp in this respect precisely because they feel more remote from our common experience. But if this familiarity can be ascribed partly to subsequent historical circumstance, it plainly also seems to have been a particular artistic aspiration of the time. It can be grasped not just in compositional tendencies and the listening practices that they encouraged but also in, for example, contemporary music-theoretical writings, which – it is widely agreed – focus on immediately perceptible structures. These writings are apparently much less concerned with larger-scale matters like musical form, which for many present-day scholars is in fact an anachronistic category, one whose time had not yet come. Certainly, Gjerdingen's schema theory sets itself squarely against any such notion, arguing instead that the characteristic syntax of the time is concatenationist: in other words, both composing and listening are much more concerned with immediate continuation, with the way in which one thing follows another.[37]

While reserving judgment on such a reading of the music of this time, I would like to stress the importance of pattern as a construct, understood mostly on quite a small scale, together with the idea that patterns in themselves can convey cultural implications and so be subject to critical interpretation. Such patterns will not always be susceptible of tight definition. While they will often involve characteristic shapings of the parameters of pitch, rhythm, dynamics, texture and the like, they may sometimes be better understood as behavioural-expressive trajectories. Concentrating on various forms of pattern offers us the chance to consider what music specifically brought to the culture of its day. What, in other

---

[37] The term concatenationism in relation to music was first applied by Jerrold Levinson in *Music in the Moment* (Ithaca: Cornell University Press, 1997). Gjerdingen, *Music in the Galant Style*, writes that 'Rather than failing to understand form, and being unable to articulate its "deeper" secrets, galant composers and writers about music understood it very well. They understood the practical abilities of listeners to follow schemes of repetition, digression, or return, to attend to the rise or fall of melodic or bass progressions, and they understood that the real art of composition lay in guiding their patron's and audience's moment-to-moment experiences.' (424)

words, did music bring that could not be replicated in any other domain of human experience?[38]

One contemporary answer would have been that music offered a universal language, precisely because it was non-verbal, and to a large extent this held even in vocal genres, when texts were involved.[39] That music was routinely described as a language in the eighteenth century attests to an emphasis on comprehensibility and to a communicative orientation, and also simply to the human scale of the operation – transcendental explanations of music's powers were out of favour.[40] All of these aspects – language, universality, comprehensibility – come together in Haydn's famous pronouncement 'meine Sprache verstehet man durch die ganze Welt' (my language is understood throughout the world). Armin Raab has suggested that these words may represent an invention by one of the composer's biographers, Albert Christoph Dies, rather than anything that Haydn himself ever spoke,[41] but even if that was the case, it would not invalidate the sentiment. It would still encapsulate a cultural truth of the time.

---

[38] Compare Applegate, 'Music among the Historians', 331–332: 'historians have often chosen to find music's meaning in history as a reflection (or confirmation or expression) of something else ... But even that history shares with musical formalism a tendency ... to make music passive in society, reflecting the world out of which it emerged, not acting in it.' Leo Treitler specifically addresses patterns when asking whether 'music's internal patterns and structure can also be understood to reflect its wider historicity. At issue is ... whether the historical understanding of music is totally dependent on extramusical matters, or whether historical understanding of *music* is possible and, if so, what it entails. Then musical works would themselves be interpreted as items of history'; they would not simply be 'inert records of the conditions of their creation; it would be important to see them as having been active participants in the dynamics of those conditions'. Treitler, 'The Historiography of Music: Issues of Past and Present', in *Rethinking Music*, ed. Nicholas Cook and Mark Everist (Oxford: Oxford University Press, 1999), 366.

[39] Paul Cobley remarks that the ability of music in the eighteenth century to make a '"universalist" or "internationalist" contribution to the public sphere' depended on its 'status as a nonverbal communication'. Cobley, 'Communication and Verisimilitude in the Eighteenth Century', in *Communication in Eighteenth-Century Music*, ed. Danuta Mirka and Kofi Agawu (Cambridge: Cambridge University Press, 2008), 23. In 'Tartini and the Tongue of Saint Anthony', *Journal of the American Musicological Society* 67/2 (2014), 429–486, Pierpaolo Polzonetti examines the 'utopian goal of equating instrumental music with language in order to overcome idiomatic boundaries' (430), meaning the different languages that people spoke.

[40] Julian Rushton sums up the 'Encyclopaediste position' thus: 'science and art are the products of human endeavour and their goal is the better understanding not of transcendental matters but of the world and of ourselves': *Classical Music: A Concise History from Gluck to Beethoven* (London: Thames and Hudson, 1986), 116–117.

[41] Armin Raab, 'Ein Porträt des Künstlers als alter Mann: Joseph Haydn und seine Biographen', *Haydn-Studien* 10/3-4 (2013), 378. Haydn apparently spoke these words to Mozart shortly before his first departure for London.

While we may grant that music was widely understood in eighteenth-century Europe to be universal in its application and effects, I would not wish to claim absolute powers for my particular field in its historical context. Sociability, as suggested at the outset, could hardly be a phenomenon peculiar to the eighteenth century, even if it seems to have been fully conceptualized only from about that point.[42] Nor should its application to music be made in any way exclusive to that century.[43] Of all the arts, music may readily be thought the most intrinsically social and sociable. It will always carry social traces, may always be regarded as modelling forms of interaction. And all music-making represents a form of social behaviour – even playing a solo piece for oneself alone. Christopher Small has made such interaction between sounds and participants the core of his theory of 'musicking',[44] which clearly has a much wider application than solely to our period, while Edward Cone had earlier given this idea a more purely acoustic twist: 'We do not . . . inhabit the depicted space of a painting . . . We do not occupy the actual space of a statue. We do not live inside the minds of characters. But music creates an environment that all share, for it surrounds and permeates all equally; it unifies characters, agents, and auditors in a single world of sound.'[45] My thesis is simply that such social attunement is more pronounced in the era of Haydn than at other times in the history of Western music, and had more profound consequences for the ways composers wrote music and listeners listened to it.

---

[42] Compare the thoughts of Patricia Meyer Spacks: 'One can never prove that a new feeling has entered the world. . . . If new feelings arguably never manifest themselves, new concepts unequivocally do.' Spacks, *Boredom: The Literary History of a State of Mind* (Chicago: University of Chicago Press, 1995), 28.

[43] For instance, in his 'On the *Scherzando* Nocturne', concentrating on instances of the genre in Chopin, Jeffrey Kallberg describes 'how contemporary witnesses depicted a genre that supported structures of sociable communication'. In *Variations on the Canon: Essays on Music from Bach to Boulez in Honor of Charles Rosen on His Eightieth Birthday*, ed. Robert Curry, David Gable and Robert L. Marshall (Rochester, NY: University of Rochester Press, 2008), 176.

[44] 'When we perform, we bring into existence, for the duration of the performance, a set of relationships, between the sounds and between the participants, that model ideal relationships as we imagine them to be and allow us to learn about them by experiencing them.' Christopher Small, *Musicking: The Meanings of Performing and Listening* (Hanover, NH: Wesleyan University Press, 1998), 218.

[45] Edward T. Cone, *The Composer's Voice* (Berkeley: University of California Press, 1974), 155. Compare also Elizabeth Hellmuth Margulis in *On Repeat: How Music Plays the Mind* (New York: Oxford University Press, 2014), 74: 'Since music comes from other people . . . and is often experienced in a social setting, with other people jointly moving to the beat or listening together, this sense of being played from outside can feel intensely bonding and communal, and serve to construct a sense of shared subjectivity.'

Further, purely within the field of eighteenth-century music, I do not wish to imply that sociability needs to form some sort of all-encompassing category for interpretation, displacing other rubrics or emphases. Rather, it should be understood as an interpretative or thematic strand that can coexist with others, as one might hope given its ethos of fruitful interaction.[46] Coexistence would also be a fair way to characterize its reception at the time, since what I am defining as musical sociability was certainly a contested matter. After all, our eighteenth-century 'society' itself is, as I have said, no unified block speaking with one voice but something that arises through interpersonal interaction, involving many different perspectives and points of view, all hoping to have the last word.

While 'sociable' and its cognates were on the lips of so many,[47] one will struggle to find many specifically musical discussions of the concept in the eighteenth century. In that respect, though, it shares much with other rubrics subsequently proposed as central to later eighteenth-century music, such as 'classical' or 'topic' or 'rhetoric'. This is partly a function of a relatively light weight of the sort of literature we would want to find to support them, with many writings on music taking on a more speculative, theoretical or pedagogical character, and composers yet to assume the oracular role that demanded they leave copious traces of their creative process and views. Of course, to return to the question of music's specific contribution to a social history, if something is truly being said through music alone, we cannot expect to find this mirrored precisely in prose (though even using the verb 'say' tends to skew the matter, implying that music's message can be equated with a verbal construct). In fact some of the strongest confirmations – and most vivid evocations – of a sociable musical manner come from hostile parties, from those who did contest the matter. In 1784 William Jones referred to the division of music lovers 'into

---

[46] Examples of other recent approaches that aim to tease out particular thematic strands of later eighteenth-century musical culture, primarily with respect to its instrumental repertory, include Anselm Gerhard, *London und der Klassizismus in der Musik: Die Idee der 'absoluten Musik' und Muzio Clementis Klavierwerke* (Stuttgart: Metzler, 2002); Roger Moseley, *Keys to Play: Music as a Ludic Medium from Apollo to Nintendo* (Oakland: University of California Press, 2016); Annette Richards, *The Free Fantasia and the Musical Picturesque* (Cambridge: Cambridge University Press, 2001); and Annette Richards, 'Haydn's *London* Trios and the Rhetoric of the Grotesque', in *Haydn and the Performance of Rhetoric*, ed. Tom Beghin and Sander M. Goldberg (Chicago: University of Chicago Press, 2007), 251–280.

[47] See, for example, Antoine Lilti, *The World of the Salons: Sociability and Worldliness in Eighteenth-Century Paris*, trans. Lydia G. Cochrane (New York: Oxford University Press, 2015), 29: 'The lexical field of sociability was ... a field of experimentation where the political concept of "society", so important in Enlightenment thought, led to a number of neologisms (*socialité, sociabilité, socialisme*).'

parties for the old and the new Music, in which there is undoubtedly a great diversity of Style and an attention to different effects':

> As for *Haydn* and *Boccherini*, who merit a first place among the Moderns for *invention*, they are sometimes so desultory and unaccountable in their way of treating a Subject, that they may be reckoned among the wild warblers of the wood: And they seem to differ from some pieces of *Handel*, as the Talk and the Laughter of the Tea-table (where, perhaps, neither Wit nor Invention are wanting) differs from the Oratory of the Bar and the Pulpit.[48]

This usefully equates the music of two leading modern composers with a lively, but clearly trivial, social situation. Jones's reference to their 'desultory and unaccountable . . . way of treating a Subject' suggests that he heard an informal, unpredictable flow of thoughts, and also, crucially, a difference in agency from the music of his older school. This agency now resides in multiple points of view, in many people, as it were ('the Talk and the Laughter of the Tea-table'), rather than being delivered in authoritative fashion from the centralized figure of the composer.

Heinrich Christoph Koch, by contrast, seems simply to be offering advice to the budding composer on how to express sentiment rather than critical commentary on the contemporary musical scene. His advice, however, is also being written against trends that he dislikes:

> The feelings may follow one another only as they do according to the nature of our soul. The composer may not leave any gaps, and he may not jump randomly from one feeling to the other . . .[49]

The prohibition against 'jump[ing] randomly from one feeling to the other' is in fact a covert reference to what Koch – like other writers from his milieu – saw as the noisy, chattering, inconsequential music of the Italian school. Koch in effect prescribes a kind of 'method' technique for composers, involving sustained immersion in an expressive role – and we know that his composing hero, C. P. E. Bach, recommended the same to a performer. (Charles Burney has left a memorable account of hearing

---

[48] William Jones, *A Treatise on the Art of Music; in which the Elements of Harmony and Air are practically considered, and illustrated by an hundred and fifty examples in notes[,] Many of them taken from the best Authors: The whole being intended as a Course of Lectures, preparatory to the practice of Thorough-Bass and Musical Composition* (Colchester: W. Keymer, 1784), iii and 49–50.

[49] Heinrich Christoph Koch, *Versuch einer Anleitung zur Komposition*, three volumes, volume 2 (Leipzig: Adam Friedrich Boehme, 1787), part 1, 22, cited in translation in *Aesthetics and the Art of Musical Composition in the German Enlightenment*, ed. and trans. Baker and Christensen, 147.

Bach perform by means of such total immersion.[50]) Further, like Jones, Koch objects to an instrumental style that is multi-centred or discursively informal. Just as Jones refers to the treatment of a musical 'Subject', in the singular, so Koch makes clear elsewhere in his writings that any musical movement should offer only one principal theme and one accompanying sentiment.[51]

Such critiques testify, if negatively, to the existence of an instrumental style that cannot readily be understood to embody a single consciousness, but the idea of a sociable style of music was certainly not problematic for all. In his *Essay on Musical Expression* of 1752 Charles Avison stated that 'it is the peculiar Quality of Music to raise the *Sociable and happy Passions*, and to *subdue* the *contrary ones*'.[52] In his *Theory of Moral Sentiments*, first published in 1759, Adam Smith more or less agreed with this, but made the distinction on a more technical basis:

When music imitates the modulations of grief and joy, it either actually inspires us with those passions, or at least puts us in the mood which disposes us to conceive them. But when it imitates the notes of anger, it inspires us with fear. Joy, grief, love, admiration, devotion, are all of them passions which are naturally musical. Their natural tones are all soft, clear, and melodious; and they naturally express themselves in periods which are distinguished by regular pauses, and which upon that account are easily adapted to the regular returns of the correspondent airs of a tune. The voice of anger, on the contrary, and of all the passions which are akin to

---

[50] 'After dinner, [Bach] played, with little intermission, till near eleven o'clock at night. During this time he grew so animated and *possessed*, that he not only played, but looked like one inspired. His eyes were fixed, his under lip fell, and drops of effervescence distilled from his countenance.' Charles Burney, *The Present State of Music in Germany, the Netherlands, and United Provinces*, two volumes (London: T. Becket, J. Robson and G. Robinson, 1773), volume 2, 269.

[51] On the relevance of Koch's views to the Viennese style of the later eighteenth century see Felix Diergarten, '"Auch Homere schlafen bisweilen": Heinrich Christoph Kochs Polemik gegen Joseph Haydn', *Haydn-Studien* 10/1 (2010), 78–92. An earlier English version appeared as '"At Times Even Homer Nods Off": Heinrich Christoph Koch's Polemic against Joseph Haydn', trans. Michael Schubert, *Music Theory Online* 14/1 (2008) www.mtosmt.org (10 February 2012). Diergarten argues that both aesthetically and technically Koch's views have very limited application to compositional practice of the time, especially that of a Haydn. See also Michael Spitzer's review of Anselm Gerhard's *London und der Klassizismus in der Musik* in *Eighteenth-Century Music* 3/2 (2006), 331: 'Gerhard is motivated by the scandal at the heart of the Viennese classical style – namely, the apparent absence of a Viennese intellectual context. . . . The most influential aesthetic writings flowed instead from north Germany, from the Berlin philosophical circle of Moses Mendelssohn and C. P. E. Bach (about which Gerhard has edited a collection of essays), and the Sulzer circle of Schulz, Kirnberger and Koch. None of these fits the style of Haydn or Mozart particularly well'.

[52] *Charles Avison's 'Essay on Musical Expression', with Related Writings by William Hayes and Charles Avison*, ed. Pierre Dubois (Aldershot: Ashgate, 2004), 6.

it, is harsh and discordant. Its periods too are all irregular, sometimes very long, and sometimes very short, and distinguished by no regular pauses. It is with difficulty, therefore, that music can imitate any of those passions; and the music which does imitate them is not the most agreeable. A whole entertainment may consist, without any impropriety, of the imitation of the social and agreeable passions.[53]

In contemplating which feelings the art of music was best able to evoke, Smith notes that feelings like anger and hatred do not fit well with what he sees as music's naturally periodic syntax, unlike those which 'express themselves in periods which are distinguished by regular pauses, and which upon that account are easily adapted to the regular returns of the correspondent airs of a tune'. This, of course, suggests that Smith primarily has vocal models in mind. Because of this differentiated suitability for periodic expression, a 'whole [musical] entertainment' may well comprise 'the imitation of the social and agreeable passions'.

But even with such endorsements of our central theme, one should not assume that sociability was straightforwardly translated into either social or artistic practice during this time. It was at least as much an ideal as a feature of lived experience. While Fielding's *Essay on Conversation* may describe man as 'an Animal formed for and delighting in Society', it is clear from his discussion of 'numberless Offences given too frequently' in company that truly sociable conduct was as much aspiration as reality.[54] In his conduct manual *Über den Umgang mit Menschen* Adolph Freiherr von Knigge, whose voice could easily have been added to the chorus earlier on when he wrote of 'man, who by nature is designed to be a social being', also remarked on the rarity of 'a congenial harmony of thinking and of sentiments ... in our social circles'.[55] However, music could be something of a case apart in such a context. For instance, when trying to define 'l'esprit

---

[53] Adam Smith, *The Theory of Moral Sentiments* (first edition, London: A. Millar, 1759), ed. D. D. Raphael and A. L. Macfie (Oxford: Clarendon, 1976), 37.

[54] Fielding, 'An Essay on Conversation', 129.

[55] Adolph Freiherr von Knigge, *Über den Umgang mit Menschen*, two volumes (first edition, Hanover: Schmidt, 1788), trans. P. Will as *Practical Philosophy of Social Life, or The Art of Conversing with Men*, two volumes (London: T. Cadell junior and W. Davies, 1799), volume 2, 308 and 286. Here and on two subsequent occasions I have not been able to match translation and original. The Reverend P. Will, Minister of the Reformed German Congregation in the Savoy, not only reordered the contents of Knigge's two volumes, but also included some material not immediately derived from them: 'as the original is entirely modified after the local wants, customs, and situation of Germany ... I was obliged almost entirely to new-mould it, in order to render it more congenial to the soil into which I intended transplanting it' (Preface, xii). Nevertheless, almost all the passages I subsequently cite may readily be matched in the two versions.

de conversation', Germaine de Staël suggested that conversation was akin to playing an instrument ('c'est un instrument dont on aime à jouer') and continued:

> Le genre de bien-être que fait éprouver une conversation animée, ne consiste pas précisément dans le sujet de cette conversation; les idées ni les connaissances qu'on peut y développer n'en sont pas le principal intérêt; c'est une certaine manière d'agir les uns sur les autres, de se faire plaisir réciproquement.[56]

The type of well-being that a lively conversation makes us feel does not derive exactly from the subject of that conversation; the principal interest does not lie in the ideas and knowledge that can be developed; rather, it is a certain manner of interacting with others, of giving reciprocal pleasure.

The initial reference to music was no accident: the genius of conversation lies not in its subject, but effectively in its patterns and the pleasures they can bring. Since music does not convey 'ideas' or 'knowledge' of the literal sort, it can be viewed as the perfect embodiment of what de Staël was attempting to convey through the comparison with conversation. What counts are the rhythms of exchange, the very fact of exchange, the processes of modification and mutual interaction that unfold. It is also revealing that the writer reached for the analogy of a musical instrument: the 'abstract' nature of exchange in music can be most readily grasped in the absence of a controlling text.

And music altogether had a further advantage. Sociable conduct was open to the charge that it involved 'mere form', that it was a token of insincerity, motivated only by a wish to get on in the world. Further, it could mean alienation from one's own true nature. Jean-Jacques Rousseau expressed this in extreme form: 'The savage lives within himself; the sociable man, always outside of himself, knows how to live only in the opinion of others; and it is, so to speak, from their judgment alone that he draws the sentiment of his own existence.'[57] Musical sociability, though, was less likely to generate wary reactions. First there was the widespread understanding of music as a 'language of feeling',[58] expressed 'naturally'

---

[56] Madame de Staël, *De l'Allemagne* (first edition, 1810/1813) (Paris: Didot, 1868), 54.

[57] Jean-Jacques Rousseau, *Discours sur l'origine et les fondemens de l'inégalité parmi les hommes* (first edition, Amsterdam: Marc-Michel Rey, 1755), in *J.-J. Rousseau: oeuvres complètes*, ed. Bernard Gagnebin and Marcel Raymond, five volumes (Paris: Gallimard, 1959–1995), volume 3 (1991), 393, cited in translation by Elena Russo, 'The Self, Real and Imaginary: Social Sentiment in Marivaux and Hume', *Yale French Studies* 92 (1997), 130.

[58] Carl Dahlhaus, for instance, notes that the maxim of music as a language of feeling was 'repeated endlessly in the eighteenth century'. Further, music was described as being 'gefühlsbildend': through musically expressed feelings, sympathy could be created between

rather than artificially and so almost by definition above suspicion. Then there was the fact that music's lack of clear referentiality meant that it was at least one degree removed from those points of contention or difference that might inhibit any real-life social conduct. Thirdly, the very act of musical performance, while of course an artifice in its own way, patently required full commitment and cooperation, and hence sincerity of intention, on the part of each player. In such senses music was able to suggest something closer to an ideal sphere of sociability.

The motley crew of historical witnesses that I have called upon to testify so far, without strong definition of geographical or temporal boundaries, indicates the synchronic nature of the approach I will be taking to the subject. This is no systematic history that will focus on origins, development or destination, nor an attempt to offer a complete lexicon of sociable musical gestures from the time, even if that were possible. Instead, the aim is to approach and define a 'structure of feeling',[59] a musical ethos. The field of enquiry is instrumental music, but without any particular generic limitation. Certainly, this ethos is not to be tied to the 'intimacy' of a genre such as the string quartet, since a solo sonata, concerto or symphony are equally liable to contain the sorts of sociable pattern I will describe. In 1789 Charles Burney noted with approval the 'great progress that has been made in instrumental Music, since the decease of Pergolesi' in 1736,[60] and while we might now not wish to endorse such a teleological judgment, there is no doubt that the eighteenth century saw instrumental composition increase markedly in both prominence and relative quantity. A virtual mass market for publication of such works arose in due course, which in itself required composers to think carefully about how they would address a more or less anonymous 'public' of potential consumers. Rudolf Rasch has noted how in the eighteenth century, composers 'started keeping

---

human beings. Dahlhaus, *Geschichte der Musik*, seven volumes (Laaber: Laaber, 2010), volume 5: *Die Musik des 18. Jahrhunderts* (reprint of *Neues Handbuch der Musikwissenschaft*, ed. Dahlhaus and Hermann Danuser, thirteen volumes (Laaber: Laaber, 1980–1991), volume 5 (1985)), 9.

[59] The term derives from Raymond Williams, in *Marxism and Literature* (Oxford: Oxford University Press, 1977). In the light of the discussion of the term by Mitchum Huehls in 'Structures of Feeling: Or, How to Do Things (or Not) with Books', *Contemporary Literature* 51/2 (2010), 419–428, sociability would not entirely qualify as a 'structure of feeling' of its time, since it had been articulated too fully and openly: 'structures of feeling actually precede articulation' (420). *Musical* sociability, though, given the lack of literature that directly addressed such a notion at the time, might just about qualify for admission.

[60] Charles Burney, *A General History of Music from the Earliest Ages to the Present Period* (first edition, London: author, 1776–1789), *Volume the Second*, with critical and historical notes by Frank Mercer (New York: Dover, 1957), 924.

systematic records of their compositions, something rarely, if ever, done before'.[61] This must above all have been the case precisely because of the proliferation of works that not only lacked accompanying texts, but in general lacked readily identifiable titles. Because this was a young market, a constant turnover of new products seemed to be required; this was not necessarily the case with vocal genres, with works such as Pergolesi's *Stabat mater* or Piccinni's opera *La buona figliuola* remaining in the public performing repertory on a long-term basis.[62]

While this study is not to be aligned with any particular genre of instrumental music, it will take its bearings from the work of one composer, Joseph Haydn. There are good historical reasons for this: Haydn was indubitably a market leader both critically and commercially, and on a broader scale one of the major artistic figures of the entire eighteenth century. But this focus has had to overcome major strategic reservations on my part. First, I believe that a sociable orientation was widely displayed in various hues by many of his composing contemporaries; it is far from peculiar to Haydn, though he unquestionably did much to shape it. Second, there is a danger that such an emphasis simply colludes with established aspects of the Haydn image – funny and friendly – that have often been thought to represent limitations. After all, such epithets are, as explored earlier, not necessarily terms of endearment when it comes to assessing the Western musical canon. They represent limitations from the point of view of a reception history that has often used such perceived attributes to circumscribe the extent of his artistic achievement. But they are also limiting from the point of view of his advocates who have felt compelled to push back against them, and often in the process confirmed that great art has to present itself more 'seriously'. This is linked to a third reservation, that this study could readily be understood as yet another attempted rescue act. The basic opening gambit of much Haydn scholarship of recent generations, after all, is an acknowledgment of a particularly narrow and relatively uncomprehending reception history. In fact, I would not wish to deny the perception of such qualities in Haydn's music. Even if we accept

---

[61] Rudolf Rasch, 'Luigi Boccherini and the Music Publishing Trade', in *Boccherini Studies 1*, ed. Christian Speck (Bologna: Ut Orpheus, 2007), 67.

[62] In *Music in the Eighteenth Century* (New York: Norton, 2013), 95, John Rice notes that Piccinni's *La buona figliuola* (Rome, 1760) received 112 performances at the King's Theatre in London alone between 1767 and 1810. A similar case would be that of Duni's opera *Les deux chasseurs et la laitière* (Paris, 1763), the performing history of which is traced by Julia Doe in 'Two Hunters, a Milkmaid and the French "Revolutionary" Canon', *Eighteenth-Century Music* 15/2 (2018), 177–205. During the 1790s alone, Doe shows, it was performed at least 355 times (178).

the terms of reference at face value, being funny and being friendly were in fact highly novel impressions to produce in the minds of listeners and performers. Of course they do not represent the full story, but in the first instance this study indeed aims to take them seriously, to show that there was an ethical backbone to them, and to show that they were widely reinforced elsewhere.

Joseph Martin Kraus, for one, was not amused or filled with warm fuzzy feeling when he visited Haydn at Eszterháza in October 1783, as he related to his parents in a letter:

> In Haydn I have met quite a decent soul, save for one point – [and] that is money. He could not comprehend that I had not equipped myself with a selection of scores for my travel in order to present them to people as opportunity arose. I answered quite drily that I was not cut out to be a Jewish merchant; *Enough! Sterkel* wrote to him and requested from him several arias for his sister and offered him an equivalent number of arias from his Neapolitan opera. Haydn shook his head, for there were no jingling coins. This is the most marvelous thing about the majority of artists. The closer one illuminates them, the more they lose the halos that the Herr amateurs, critics, etc., etc., have painted around them like saints.[63]

Whatever else it suggests, Kraus's letter tells us that hagiographical attitudes towards creative artists, and Haydn in particular, already existed, well before the point where Haydn achieved patent celebrity status on his two visits to London in the 1790s. Of course, his impressions must be kept distinct from the compositional persona suggested by Haydn's musical works. Regardless of the sort of reality that Kraus encountered that day, Haydn the creative persona seems to have offered something that was hard to resist. This persona had exceptionally finely tuned social antennae, including a highly developed sense of irony, that made him an especially welcome companion for many listeners. Nevertheless, it is interesting to contemplate whether the sort of fine social attunement that can be found in the music was matched by the actual historical person. There is in fact plenty of evidence that Haydn's real-life social skills were also of a high order, from his many interventions on behalf of himself and other musicians at Eszterháza to his demeanour at the Salomon concerts in London, where it was reported that Haydn 'conducts himself ... in the most modest

---

[63] Kraus, letter to his parents from Eszterháza, 18 October 1783; Bertil H. van Boer, *The Musical Life of Joseph Martin Kraus: Letters of an Eighteenth-Century Swedish Composer* (Bloomington: Indiana University Press, 2014), 169.

manner'.[64] But such evidence of diplomatic capacities is scarcely earth-shattering next to the impact made by the music, through which Haydn achieved such supreme success.

Such success was hardly immediate and comprehensive, any more than that of the sociable style that the composer did much to establish. And, indeed, the fact that this sociable style has not exactly been embraced as such by subsequent scholarship shows that its success was only ever provisional. In a discussion of public listening practices in the eighteenth century William Weber cites Peter Gay's accounts of raucous audience behaviour and his accompanying remark that 'Philosophers provided alibis for the shallow, sociable view of what music should mean.' Weber takes him to task with the rejoinder 'But what is so "shallow" about music being "sociable"?'.[65] This is a useful point from which to depart.

Modern Reception

As it turns out, perceptions of shallowness are deeply rooted. That we have yet to come fully to terms with the sociable musical art of Haydn and his contemporaries, in the scholarly as well as the popular imagination, may be grasped when we consider the relatively poor representation of much of this repertory in the academic and concert canons.[66] In the area of instrumental music, aside from Haydn, Mozart, and to an extent C. P. E. Bach, and for all the recent growth of interest in figures such as Boccherini and Clementi, the landscape is still sparsely populated; it is difficult to think of another era where advocacy is so narrowly concentrated, even as recordings and editions have opened up so much new territory. It remains a common assumption that composers were hamstrung by the conventions

---

[64] 'Ueber den jetzigen Zustand und die Moden der Musik in England', *Journal des Luxus und der Moden* 9 (1794), 342–343, cited in translation in Emily I. Dolan, *The Orchestral Revolution: Haydn and the Technologies of Timbre* (Cambridge: Cambridge University Press, 2013), 134. One might also cite biographer Albert Christoph Dies's account of how during his London visits the composer would often invite 'the most important players' of Salomon's orchestra to dinner, 'so that they appeared gladly for private rehearsals in his home'. He then 'praised them and interwove reprimand, when it was necessary, with praise in the subtlest fashion', which 'won him the affection of all musicians with whom he came into contact'. Dies, *Biographische Nachrichten von Joseph Haydn* (Vienna: Camesinaische Buchhandlung, 1810), in *Haydn: Two Contemporary Portraits*, ed. and trans. Vernon Gotwals (Madison: University of Wisconsin Press, 1968), 124. However, this information presumably derives from Haydn himself, so should carry less weight when it comes to assessing the composer's perceived social skills.

[65] William Weber, 'Did People Listen in the 18th Century?', *Early Music* 25/4 (1997), 680.

[66] This sentence and the next few sentences are based on my 'Before the Joke', 93.

of the musical language, in other words that the language itself was inherently uninteresting, and so artistically interesting results – music that can still engage us today – could only be achieved by denying the pressures of this language or at least problematizing it. I have already associated that lack of a broader engagement with several factors. The style is perceived to be at odds with an expressive imperative that is music's true mission, and its products therefore need some 'added value' to be worth continued consideration. A second factor might seem to contradict the first: the fact that 'Classicism' represents a core repertory, one that has been indispensable for pedagogical purposes, whether theoretical or practical. This has created high levels of familiarity, but within certain set frames of reference, limited to a tiny cohort of composers and to preferred perspectives such as 'form', 'balance' and 'elegance'. Not that such notions have no foundation, but they have helped to create a feeling of inertia around the larger image of later eighteenth-century instrumental music.

In addition, such extensive pedagogical use has tended to make this repertory a kind of norm or neutral ground against which we measure other idioms, and so we have trouble grasping what could be called the cultural specificity of the style. Yet if we are to take a bird's-eye view of Western art music, I would argue that so-called classical music is precisely not normal or exemplary – it is, rather, anomalous. The larger-scale consistencies of texture and rhythm that mark the styles on either side – baroque and romantic – are replaced by conspicuously short units, their brevity only thrown into sharper relief by a characteristic changeability of musical material from one unit to the next. It is such restless contrasts – like a kind of attention-deficit disorder writ large – that topic theory attempts to account for. And such a syntax also promotes an exploitation of incongruity that leads to another anomalous feature: the style's widespread adoption of comic accents and procedures.[67]

The sway of traditional approaches over the longer term might explain why two highly enriching theoretical entities, topic and schema, have only been 'discovered' or at least codified relatively recently.[68] Since they have

---

[67] This paragraph is based on a passage in my chapter 'The Simplifying Cadence: Concession and Deflation in Later Eighteenth-Century Musical Style', in *Haydn and His Contemporaries II: Selected Papers from the Fifth Biennial Conference of the Society for Eighteenth-Century Music at the College of Charleston in Charleston, SC, 13–15 April 2012*, ed. Kathryn Libin (Ann Arbor: Steglein, 2015), 165.

[68] Topic theory was initially outlined by Leonard Ratner in *Classic Music: Expression, Form, and Style* (New York: Schirmer, 1980); see in particular chapter 2, 'Topics', 9–29. Gjerdingen's schema theory, as comprehensively outlined in *Music in the Galant Style*, has more recent precedents, such as Leonard B. Meyer in 'Exploiting Limits: Creation, Archetypes, and Style

been shown to constitute fundamental aspects of later eighteenth-century musical discourse, it is astonishing that what now appears so obvious had not been noted as such earlier: routine frames of reference, it would seem, meant that we couldn't see what was staring us in the face. Together with an equally surprising revival of formal approaches – nothing could have better represented the tired face of 'Classical' music than a preoccupation with form, and especially the story of sonata form – one might well claim that, theoretically at least, inertia has been well and truly overcome. Yet what has changed less amidst the welter of new approaches is the narrowness of repertory adduced in support, which continues to focus on our tiny cohort; one might even suspect a pretext to find new ways of talking about the same old music. And the wider problem of image remains unresolved. This is in spite of numerous studies in the field that have moved well beyond the routine and suggested new approaches to take – and to be fair, the new theoretical angles have all contributed in this respect, too, by offering fresh perspectives on creative and listening practices of the time.

A fundamental part of the image problem concerns the perceived lack of moral integrity and ethical weight to this musical style. It is insufficiently 'serious'. There is a particular problem with this term in the field of art criticism.[69] It has two meanings: while it refers to a manner that is direct and earnest, and hence avoids humour, it also refers to artistic intent, and so readily becomes a loaded term of value judgment. Thus we talk about serious as opposed to trivial or popular, of serious art as against light art. While the word can function as a relatively neutral way of distinguishing between genres, whether in opera or in literature, the difficulty is that the two meanings are readily conflated – and it can be hard to argue the claims of an art that is not perceived as 'serious'.

Wye Allanbrook – whose work on the image problem is of particular relevance to the current study – has dealt with just this difficulty concerning the music of our period, with reference to the reception history of Mozart. It often seems to have been felt necessary to hold Mozart above the fray, to rescue him from the damaging associations of the lightness that

---

Change', *Daedalus* 109/2 (1980), 177–205, as well as in Gjerdingen's own earlier work such as 'Courtly Behaviors' and *A Classic Turn of Phrase: Music and the Psychology of Convention* (Philadelphia: University of Pennsylvania Press, 1988); and the fact that he can point to the historical precedent of a theorist like Joseph Riepel, as well as a wealth of contemporary partimento practice, means that 'rediscovery' might be a more apt term than 'discovery'.

[69] The rest of this paragraph and the following paragraph are based on my 'Before the Joke', 95–96.

surrounded him. Taking Mozart seriously, Allanbrook suggests, has meant taking him tragically – the concept of 'the Gloomy Mozart'. And it has often meant emphasizing his alleged 'subversive' nature, at the expense of the sunnier side that was supposedly forced on the composer by his historical circumstances. Such a critical agenda has often been determined by a wish to undermine the 'sentimental adoration' that has been another strain in responses to the composer. However, if such adoration is marked by a certain naivety, 'is it not equally naive and uncritical', Allanbrook asks, 'to exalt the dark and the troubled'?[70] Such uncritical vaunting of the sombre and the turbulent reflects, she believes, a shift in outlook that occurred in the transition to the nineteenth century. Eighteenth-century philosophers stressed 'not the fall of man but the possibility of redemption ... essentially a comic notion'.[71] This formed part of the Enlightenment faith in universal reason and human perfectibility. The 'tragic outlook' we have acquired from the Romantics, says Allanbrook, 'leads us to admire the loss of this faith as a sign of personal growth'.[72] In other words, we grow up out of our immature optimistic state; musically, we leave behind the state of innocence that later eighteenth-century style represents. There is an ingrained assumption that profundity and melancholia go hand in hand; we have already noted how 'expression' tends to be firmly wedded to an affect of melancholy introspection. However, prevailing attitudes in the eighteenth century stood against such pessimism. This had a correlative in terms of social behaviour, what Weber describes as 'a sense of propriety that abhorred speaking in excessively serious terms'.[73] This did not mean, of course, that either socially or musically one was lacking in serious intent, simply that a consistently earnest tone was unlikely to win many friends for one's point of view.

Yet it often seems as though most musical commentators have not absorbed what Allanbrook had to say. Or at least such thinking has struggled to be heard over the voice of critical tradition. The prevalence of comic accents in our instrumental style, even beyond a prevalent tone of energetic optimism, has undoubtedly been a major obstacle. This was certainly a matter of comment at the time, often already in the negative,

---

[70] Wye J. Allanbrook, 'Mozart's Tunes and the Comedy of Closure', in *On Mozart*, ed. James M. Morris (Cambridge: Cambridge University Press, in association with the Woodrow Wilson Center Press, 1994), 170.
[71] Allanbrook, 'Mozart's Tunes', 171.
[72] Allanbrook, 'Mozart's Tunes', 172. For a further, more sustained argument from Allanbrook on such matters see *Secular Commedia*.
[73] Weber, 'Did People Listen?', 683.

and unsurprisingly so. Comedy had not been a customary way to conduct one's compositional business, and it would not be afterwards. Our music has a seemingly inexhaustible appetite for comic incident, spinning off into the realms of wit and irony, and it needs to be stressed again how exceptional this is, historically speaking. There is no other Western musical style that has a fraction of this capacity for tickling a listener's funny bone.[74] Otherwise, it is largely 'serious' business all the way. In an article revealingly entitled 'Must Classical Music Be Entirely Serious?', where 'Classical' primarily takes on its narrower application to the later eighteenth century, Alfred Brendel writes, 'Nobody seems to doubt that music can "sigh", metaphorically speaking, but I have read denials that music can laugh.... To some people ... laughter is vulgar, seriousness a sign of maturity, and everything that is hilarious a desecration of loftier states of mind.'[75] To spell out the entrenched critical equation against which Allanbrook and Brendel are arguing: because the manner of this music is often light and comic rather than heavy and serious, then the artistic intent must likewise not be serious.

All this is not to suggest a widespread sense-of-humour failure on the part of critics, let alone listeners. It is rather a question of priorities: a feeling that humour is all very well, but that it must ultimately cede the stage to weightier matters. A classic case to consider would be the famously funny finale of Haydn's String Quartet in E flat major Op. 33 No. 2 (1781). It is impossible not to be caught in the act of listening at the end of this work (see Example 1.1). We are compelled to keep on listening, just in case there is any more music to come. It is strange enough when from bar 152 the four phrase units that make up the movement's theme are performed separately, with silences in between – having been preceded by a portentous Adagio that seems to have absolutely nothing to do with the movement at hand – but then, after a very long silence, we hear the first of these four units again, from bar 170. So, we will imagine, we are to hear yet another elongated performance of the theme. But as the following silence continues – not notated in the score but an essential part of the music – we

---

[74] This sentence is also borrowed from Sutcliffe, 'Simplifying Cadence', 165.

[75] Alfred Brendel, 'Must Classical Music Be Entirely Serious?: 1 The Sublime in Reverse', in *Alfred Brendel on Music: Collected Essays* (London: Robson, 2001), 108. Andras Schiff testifies to the problem: 'I had the pleasure and privilege of conducting Haydn's Symphony No[.] 80 in D minor in Salzburg recently. It's an astonishing work, full of surprises, and almost completely unknown. ... The last movement – the Presto – is a tour de force of rhythmic ambiguities ... It's ingenious, and extremely funny. But in Salzburg no one laughed. No one even smiled.' Schiff, 'Did You Hear the One about ... ', *The Guardian* (29 May 2009) www.theguardian.com (20 November 2017).

Example 1.1 Haydn, Quartet in E flat major Op. 33 No. 2/iv, bars 136–172

must assume that what we have heard countless times through the movement as a beginning, as marking the return of the theme, is in fact to be understood as an ending. And it is the listener alone who must perform this perceptual U-turn – the composer has provided all that he is going to provide. Haydn has effectively absented himself, with a parting message to the listener, 'Over to you; *you* work it out'. He forces the listener to interact with the music, to take an active role in making sense of the sounding data. It is a collaborative aesthetic.

This movement has given the whole string quartet the nickname 'The Joke', which seems reasonable enough. But that should not obscure the fact that this is a revolutionary movement. It encapsulates a new approach to the listener – indeed, a new consciousness that there is a listener out there to be wooed.[76] And it does this by focussing on a basic fact of musical life – that all good pieces must come to an end – so fundamental that no one can fail to engage with it. But because listener response is now elevated to such a prime position, we need not agree even on the basic fact of the music coming to an end. I have outlined one likely response, that we must – even if reluctantly, or with bemusement – acknowledge that the piece has finished. On the other hand, we know full well that it hasn't really done so – it has finished with the first of the four units that made up the theme. The sound may have stopped, but the music hasn't. The finale therefore in a sense stretches out into infinity: it will never be properly completed.

Not surprisingly, this movement has been much written about, yet it does not exactly occupy the exalted position I have claimed for it in music history. A recent account by Byron Almén is a case in point. He offers a compelling step-by-step account of the increasing fragmentation of the final page, which means that 'the structure of the piece must be reinterpreted again and again',[77] and he also notices something about the earlier part of the movement that is often overlooked: the relative 'homogeneity' of the B and C sections of this rondo form, consisting as they largely do of 'static pedal point passages and straightforward sequential activity'.[78] The modern rondo form was premised on variety, and these two episodes fail to deliver it; instead, at least in retrospect, they help to create a sense of relentless, even mechanical motion, for all the popular accents of the musical material. From this point of view the ending provides a form of escape – not in terms of material, of course (with the exception of the strange Adagio), but rather in terms of how it is delivered, in halting uncertainty.

---

[76] The last few phrases derive from Sutcliffe, 'Before the Joke', 92.
[77] Byron Almén, *A Theory of Musical Narrative* (Bloomington: Indiana University Press, 2008), 85.
[78] Almén, *A Theory of Musical Narrative*, 171.

Almén describes the movement as an instance of an ironic narrative archetype that 'portrays the defeat of an initial hierarchy by transgressive elements'.[79] These elements come to the fore at the end of the movement as the previous balance between 'naïve' and 'skeptical mode[s] of listening' is tipped in favour of the latter:[80] with this he alludes to the tension between the self-evidently popular flavour of the music, its straightforward accessibility, and hearing it instead as having parodistic elements (surely that tune comes back just too often?). Yet ultimately Almén finds the defeat of the hierarchy to be rather gentle; he feels compelled to conclude that the 'humorous inclusiveness' of Haydn's strategies has 'worked against the corrosive influence of the formal manipulations'. In the end we are left with 'a playful, rather than a serious, challenge to the prevailing hierarchy'.[81] Once again, therefore, we stumble over the word 'serious'. Contemplating similar Haydnesque strategies elsewhere, Scott Burnham reaches a similar verdict: that the composer is 'playful without being iconoclastic, witty without being subversive'.[82]

These formulations can hardly provoke full dissent: there is indeed something inclusive about such strategies, there is indeed a playful irony in that stylistic and formal norms may be at once undermined and upheld. But there is clearly a 'but'. Full scholarly endorsement is being withheld. What is waiting in the wings is the concept of 'commitment', and the modernist ideology of 'subversive' art, what Nicholas Mathew encapsulates as 'the belief, common to much Modernist thought, that resistance is the only authentic aesthetic and political stance'.[83] It is no coincidence that Mathew passes these remarks when considering the reception of Beethoven, who is the unspoken point of comparison with such verdicts. Of course the tone of Haydn's movement is playful, friendly, and so forth, and there is no overtly cataclysmic *Durchbruch*, no renting of stylistic garments. But the 'seriousness' of what Haydn has done could not be greater. This is a eureka moment in the history of Western art music – revolutionary in the way in which it alters the balance of power between composer and listener, in which it acknowledges the existence of a listener whose participation is essential to the meaning of the music.

In any case, one must ask, if Haydn had chosen to be 'iconoclastic', what would that sound like? How would that have been different from his

---

[79] Almén, *A Theory of Musical Narrative*, 169.   [80] Almén, *A Theory of Musical Narrative*, 173.
[81] Almén, *A Theory of Musical Narrative*, 174.
[82] Scott Burnham, 'Haydn and Humor', in *The Cambridge Companion to Haydn*, ed. Caryl Clark (Cambridge: Cambridge University Press, 2005), 72.
[83] Nicholas Mathew, *Political Beethoven* (Cambridge: Cambridge University Press, 2013), 6.

strategy of complete contradiction – a piece that is complete on the page but incomplete off the page, a piece that fails to finish yet must finish in the mind of the listener, to whom all agency is ultimately given? And if there was a more iconoclastic way of denying the most fundamental fact about a piece of music – that it will finish – what difference would that have made, historically, and what difference would that make to us now? For an answer to the latter, it is difficult to get beyond what Allanbrook might have said of such a case – simply that, because of the hold of the 'tragic' perspective, it makes us feel better.[84]

One should also not assume that the events of this movement can do nothing but generate mirth – logically enough, given the interpretative agency now being handed over to the listener. Tom Service suggests a different kind of reaction:

Haydn's jokes can be funny, for sure, but they can also be existential observations of musical time.

At the end of his quartet Op 33 No 2, the joke seems, on the face of it, self-consciously humorous. Haydn gives the audience a whole series of false endings, weird pauses and wrong places to clap, concluding the movement with the same phrase it started with. But I don't think it's laugh-out-loud funny. This finale can be a strange and disturbing experience; you become disoriented and confused, and when it finally does end it's through no musical logic other than that it has stopped.

It's not just that Haydn pulls the rug from under you: for a second the certainties and continuities of classical music are suspended. Is this comedy? If it is, it's pretty serious in its implications, and its sophistication. Few other composers, before or since, have managed such moving playfulness.[85]

This reminds us of a point that should seem obvious, except that it seems to escape the grasp of much music criticism. Comedy need not be one-dimensional; it may not only be 'serious in its implications', but may also be entwined with other affective states.

Yet it is understandable that this is not always kept in mind. Comedy, in all its shades, can have what Jean Paul in the case of Haydn called an 'annihilating' quality;[86] it may displace all the other affective qualities with

---

[84] I am echoing Allanbrook's remark that 'It is a curious quirk of the psychology of our fallen nature that when we hear that a reading of a text or art work enshrines that fallen nature, we feel better.' Allanbrook, 'Mozart's Tunes', 171.

[85] Tom Service, 'Haydn Composed Existential Comedy', *The Guardian* (29 May 2009) www.theguardian.com (4 October 2017).

[86] Mark Evan Bonds notes how, in the second edition of his *Vorschule der Ästhetik* (1813), 'Jean Paul compares the "annihilating humor" of Sterne's prose with Haydn's music': 'Haydn, Laurence Sterne, and the Origins of Musical Irony', *Journal of the American Musicological Society* 44/1 (1991), 63.

which it is mixed. It creates a distancing effect, undermines the possibility of emotional identification or emotional transport; from this point of view, the somewhat reserved reception of later eighteenth-century musical comedy makes sense. It is unlikely to inspire purple prose. Hence the rhetorical gambit of 'it really is serious' that both Tom Service and I have had to deploy above.

It might have been to counter charges that what Haydn offered in such circumstances was ultimately 'not enough' that Charles Rosen wrote that 'Haydn was the most playful of composers, but his frivolity and his whimsicality never consisted of empty structural variants',[87] but at times that has just about seemed to be the critical consensus. It has evidently been difficult to sense any weight, any Big Ideas, the sort of thing that attracts academic mandarins, including those philosopher-musicians who visit the field of music. They have had remarkably little to say about Haydn, which is especially remarkable given his weight as a cultural figure in the later eighteenth and early nineteenth centuries.[88] In this situation, of course, it is not so much Haydn in particular as his period in general that fails to inspire, and Haydn acts primarily as a figurehead. Ways have been found – among which are those detailed by Allanbrook above – to rescue Mozart from these associations.

These associations move beyond humour as such to a conception of lightness in general – and this affects the reception of the whole field of galant instrumental style. In the case of Haydn, his so-called *Sturm und Drang* period of the later 1760s and early 1770s has been used as a stick with which to beat the surrounding output for its apparent lack of 'commitment'. Thanks to the *Sturm und Drang*, wrote Karl Geiringer in 1963, the composer 'acquired the courage to break away from the fashionable grace and shallow gaiety [of the galant] and strove truthfully to express what he felt. In this way his idiom gained immeasurably in profundity and power'.[89] This might now raise some smiles, but it only expresses baldly a belief that retains some currency. Later biographer Ludwig Finscher writes of the 'danger' present in the symphonies of 1774–1780 of Haydn's 'slipping into a general playful elegance', of giving in to 'mere

---

[87] Charles Rosen, *The Classical Style: Haydn, Mozart, Beethoven* (London: Faber, 1971), 129.
[88] One evident exception would be Alain Badiou and his 'Haydn event', as discussed in Naomi Waltham-Smith, *Music and Belonging between Revolution and Restoration* (New York: Oxford University Press, 2017), chapter 2, 'Haydn's Revolution', 40–79.
[89] Karl Geiringer, 'Joseph Haydn, Protagonist of the Enlightenment', in *Joseph Haydn and the Eighteenth Century: Collected Essays of Karl Geiringer*, ed. Robert N. Freeman (Warren, MI: Harmonie Park Press, 2002), 56. The original article appeared in *Studies on Voltaire and the Eighteenth Century* 25 (1963), 683–690.

play' and 'cutting a fine figure in society [gesellschaftliche ... Repräsentanz]'; in this period 'Haydn seems not to have had the power or the will, perhaps also not the opportunity, to write serious, substantial [vollwertige] ... instrumental music.'[90] Historian Tim Blanning suggests that the *Sturm und Drang* symphonies could take the form that they did because they were written for Haydn's princely patron Nikolaus Esterházy II: 'One must wonder whether [Haydn] could have created the extraordinarily original symphonies of his so-called *Sturm und Drang* period ... if he had been writing for London or Paris and not for the discerning and tolerant Prince Nicholas Esterházy. I cannot be alone in preferring the stark emotional vitality of these earlier works to the more polished Paris and London symphonies.'[91] This preference is perfectly defensible, of course, but one suspects that a point is being made above and beyond personal taste.

Such suspicions of 'polish', 'shallow gaiety' and 'mere play' continue to surface outside the academy too. In my local newspaper *The New Zealand Herald* a few years ago one could read of a piano recital at which the performer made the decision to replace the Haydn sonata planned to open the programme with Chopin's nocturne Op. 9 No. 3 in order to 'create a better atmosphere' for the following works by Schubert and Chopin, both, according to her, 'works of great sorrow'. The headline for the review read 'Pianist's decision to replace Haydn Sonata keeps emotions real',[92] which says it all. One sure index for a lack of 'emotional reality' is the predominance of the major mode, as we may find in this *New York Times* review:

The program consisted entirely of Mozart sonatas for piano and violin. While there may be bodies of the composer's work from which any given handful will automatically form a varied and compelling program, these sonatas are not among

---

[90] Ludwig Finscher, *Studien zur Geschichte des Streichquartetts. Die Entstehung des klassischen Streichquartetts: Von den Vorformen zur Grundlegung durch Joseph Haydn* (Kassel: Bärenreiter, 1974), 242. Such a view is considered and countered in James Webster, 'Haydn's Symphonies between *Sturm und Drang* and "Classical Style": Art and Entertainment', in *Haydn Studies*, ed. W. Dean Sutcliffe (Cambridge: Cambridge University Press, 1998), 218–245.

[91] Tim Blanning, *The Triumph of Music: The Rise of Composers, Musicians and Their Art* (Cambridge, MA: Belknap Press of Harvard University Press, 2012), 27–28. Note how Michael Spitzer has turned around these common elements of Haydn reception in his 'Haydn's Reversals: Style Change, Gesture and the Implication-Realization Model', in *Haydn Studies*, ed. Sutcliffe, 217: 'The *Sturm und Drang* is poised; the *galant* is stormy. That is Haydn's most dramatic reversal.' The larger point is the relative continuity of compositional procedure between idioms or styles that are often framed as virtual opposites.

[92] William Dart, review of piano recital given by Ingrid Filter, *The New Zealand Herald* (10 September 2013), A36.

them. In this case Mr. Neikrug and Mr. Zukerman selected four three-movement works, all in major keys: the Sonatas in D (K. 306), E flat (K. 380), A (K. 526) and F (K. 547). In fact, only one of the 12 movements was in the minor mode, the peculiar Andante con Moto of K. 380, with touching sighs prominent in its main theme.

Nor, with the possible exception of the K. 526 Andante, was any real profundity to be found. For that, and for a healthy inoculation of the minor, listeners had to attend the preconcert recital, at which Andreas Haefliger, a young Swiss pianist, played the great C-minor Fantasia (K. 475) and Sonata (K. 457).[93]

As Allanbrook has pointed out, this is to put things the wrong way around: 'In the musical language that Mozart inherited from his Baroque predecessors, the prevalence of major keys' was a 'striking new trope'.[94]

Nevertheless, these common contemporary critical sentiments cannot simply be attributed to conventions of thought that have been foisted upon us by the nineteenth century. The notion that the lightness of later eighteenth-century style was enforced by commercial pressure, with composers having to defer to 'public taste', was certainly alive at the time. C. P. E. Bach, for one, is on record with words to this effect, meaning that it has been possible to cast him as a heroic resister of his age. He made much of being 'restrained' when he had to write for particular people or the public rather than for himself; he was pessimistic about the capacity of the general public to appreciate his more 'personal' and 'difficult' music.[95] A strange kind of myopia arises when such views are uncritically replicated in the present. Just as happens with the collocation of 'light' and 'serious', writers stumble over the notion of a music written to satisfy public taste or to entertain, as if this were somehow an impediment to good art or a historical anomaly. But doesn't all the 'great' music we listen to today fulfil these criteria? If it didn't do so at the time, by definition it does so now.

This has been a particular problem for Mozart scholarship, since no composer's output could be currently more popular than his. Ways have to be found to place him above 'public taste', both then and now, as well as above the supposed stylistic mediocrity of his time (it is no accident that

---

[93] James R. Oestreich, 'Mostly Mozart: Neikrug and Zukerman Play Four Piano-Violin Sonatas', review of concert in series Mostly Mozart, *New York Times* (12 August 1990), *The New York Times Archives* 001053.

[94] Allanbrook, 'Mozart's Tunes', 175.

[95] For example, there is Bach's advice in a letter of 31 August 1784 to the young composer Johann Christoph Kühnau, 'In things that are to be printed, and therefore are for everyone, be less artistic and give more sugar.' *The Letters of C. P. E. Bach*, ed. and trans. Stephen L. Clark (Oxford: Clarendon, 1997), 213.

the term *Kleinmeister* has attached itself specifically to our period[96]). We have already touched on one solution, that redemptive strain of Mozart criticism that includes Allanbrook's 'gloom' but also encompasses narratives of difficulty, alienation and 'subjectivity'.[97] Thomas Irvine tells a nice tale about this in connection with the finale of the Quintet in D major, K593 (1790). The long anacrusis figure that opens the movement exists in two versions, one chromatic (in the autograph) and the other describing a diatonic 'zigzag' pattern (in the first edition and all contemporary performing material). Irvine notes the belief of most textual critics that the 'difficult' chromatic version must be the original, since 'chromaticism is the talisman of "true" Mozart'. For such critics, 'an entire critical perspective – [that of] the difficult/incongruous/alienated composer – would collapse if the "zig-zag" were to be linked convincingly with Mozart'.[98]

Another critical strain may not deny the sociable virtues of Mozart's music but nevertheless makes everything ineffable, beyond ordinary reach; even an apparently routine turn of events may become transfigured in the composer's hands, with the preferred term of reference being a pure, absolute, inexplicable 'beauty'.[99] This is a way of acknowledging that the composer in fact uses the patterns and forms of his day with few signs of rebellious intent. The prose often strains for superlatives, and the tone of

---

[96] In a discussion of this term and its connotations, Wolfgang Hirschmann writes of 'the common *feuilleton* view of eighteenth-century music history' that 'is obviously still dominated by a concept of heroes' tales'. Hirschmann, 'Editorial', *Eighteenth-Century Music* 11/2 (2014), 167.

[97] Classic instances of more recent times would include Joseph Kerman, 'Mozart's Concertos and Their Audience', in *On Mozart*, ed. Morris, 151–168, and Susan McClary, 'A Musical Dialectic from the Enlightenment: Mozart Piano Concerto in G Major, K. 453, Movement 2', *Cultural Critique* 4 (1986), 129–169. Both, making use of the obvious textural set-up of the concerto genre, deploy the trope of a composer alienated from his (paying) audience.

[98] Thomas Irvine, '"Das Launigste Thema": On the Politics of Editing and Performing the Finale of K. 593', *Mozart-Jahrbuch* (2003–2004), 20.

[99] For recent examples see Roman Ivanovitch, 'Mozart's Art of Retransition', *Music Analysis* 30/1 (2011), 1–36, and Scott Burnham, *Mozart's Grace* (Princeton: Princeton University Press, 2013). To be clear, both these works contain remarkable insights, and, rather than simply reproducing the trope, the authors try to analyse just what factors produce the impression of 'absolute beauty' that so many listeners, after all, seem to have felt. I applaud any efforts to see beyond an image of 'mere formula' in the musical language of this time, to show how the actual handling of the everyday is what counts, and that this is where we find an individual creative imprint; the problem is the assumption that such special handling is a mark of Mozart's creativity alone. James Webster makes the point that in the case of Mozart 'genuinely canonical status was not achieved until the second half of the 20th century ... ; it was only after World War II that Mozart emerged from Beethoven's shadow [and became] a figure who engendered ... ineffable feelings of sublimity and awe'. Webster, 'The Century of Handel and Haydn', in *The Century of Bach and Mozart: Perspectives on Historiography, Composition, Theory, and Performance*, ed. Sean Gallagher and Thomas Forrest Kelly (Cambridge, MA: Harvard University Press, 2008), 311.

such criticism may suggest a love affair; Eric Blom in fact finished his biography of Mozart with an open 'declaration of love'.[100] It is not, of course, a question of the rightness of loving a composer's music – that would, after all, be a plausible starting-point for any engagement with the art – but rather a question of why such rhetoric hardly exists outside these confines. The notion that Mozart's music is uniquely resistant to ordinary explanation becomes an article of faith, and may well have some experiential basis, but in respect of what musical output does 'beauty' become easy to capture?

Just as a love affair renders the lover entirely indifferent to other charms, so it is difficult otherwise to explain how both Karol Berger and Stephen Rumph, for example, could have advanced recent large-scale explications of eighteenth-century musical culture with such a firm focus on Mozart alone. Berger's charting of the development of a progressive sense of musical time over the eighteenth century, culminating in 'Mozart's Arrow', should hardly be able to do without Haydn's continual questioning of accepted sequences of temporal events, among many other attributes (nor, indeed, to move back further in time, the multi-temporal perspectives offered by Domenico Scarlatti[101]). Our earlier encounter with the finale of Op. 33 No. 2 alone, that 'existential observation ... of musical time', makes that clear. Nevertheless, Haydn is conspicuous by his near-complete absence from Berger's book.[102] Rumph's study of musical semiotics also finds a new kind of dynamism in later eighteenth-century music, one that abandons the 'underlying premises of persuasive rhetoric',[103] and is less concerned to promote fixed ideas than to explore the processes of cognition. Such a thesis is highly sympathetic to the strands I am exploring in the

---

[100] Eric Blom, *Mozart*, The Master Musicians (London: Dent, 1962; first published 1935), 300.

[101] See my 'Temporality in Domenico Scarlatti', in *Domenico Scarlatti Adventures: Essays to Commemorate the 250th Anniversary of His Death*, ed. Massimiliano Sala and W. Dean Sutcliffe (Bologna: Ut Orpheus, 2008), 369–399.

[102] Karol Berger, *Bach's Cycle, Mozart's Arrow: An Essay on the Origins of Musical Modernity* (Berkeley: University of California Press, 2007). Compare Berger's thesis with, for example, the 'hypothesis' of Nicole Schwindt-Gross, in *Drama und Diskurs: Zur Beziehung zwischen Satztechnik und motivischem Prozeß am Beispiel der durchbrochenen Arbeit in den Streichquartetten Mozarts und Haydns* (Laaber: Laaber, 1989), that 'Haydn's musical thought was oriented towards the idea of discourse and Mozart's towards a model of drama' (10), elsewhere characterized as respective orientations towards time and space. Subsequently she suggests, by way of amplification, that while 'Mozart's motivic modifications are always at base variants' ('Mozarts motivische Modifikationen sind im Kern immer variativen, Varianten bildenden Charakters'), Haydn's motivic variants are 'not reversible and cannot be swapped around' ('nicht umkehrbar ist und in seiner Binnenstruktur keine Umstellung zuließe') (177).

[103] Stephen Rumph, *Mozart and Enlightenment Semiotics* (Berkeley: University of California Press, 2012), 21.

current study. However, to make Mozart the principal protagonist of this change is unconvincing. Haydn, for instance, is sidelined on the dubious grounds that in his so-called monothematic sonata-form movements 'the traditional model of rhetorical *elaboratio* lives on'.[104]

However, the fallback position for Mozart's exceptionalism is biographical. In spite of a scholarly consensus that the composer's professional difficulties and public indifference to his music in the later part of his career have been greatly exaggerated,[105] the 'Tragic Mozart' has by no means ceased to exist. Nor has the 'Political Mozart', in spite of studies such as William Weber's 'Myth of Mozart, the Revolutionary', which describes that image as a 'red herring'.[106] The special status of minor-key works as a site of alienation remains alive, and in a recent study Rupert Ridgewell has tested the claims of one of them, the Piano Quartet in G minor, K478 (1785). A story that derives from the 1828 biography of the composer by Georg Nikolaus von Nissen has it that Franz Anton Hoffmeister had commissioned three such quartets from Mozart, but unfavourable public reaction to the G minor work caused him to cancel the agreement. As Ridgewell points out, this story has fed into notions of Mozart's music being misunderstood during his lifetime, that it was 'judged unsuitable for wider commercial distribution', and that the feeling was mutual, with the composer in turn being 'indifferent to the need to "write for the market"'.[107] Having carefully examined all the circumstances, which include the fact that at least four further publishers brought out editions of K478 within two years of its original appearance, Ridgewell concludes that 'almost every aspect of the publication of Mozart's piano quartets has been misinterpreted'; the 'remarkably resilient' Nissen anecdote 'emerges as a product of a romantic ideology that deemed autonomous music to be superior to music created to meet the demands of commerce and popular taste'.[108]

---

[104] Rumph, *Mozart and Enlightenment Semiotics*, 43. To be fair, Rumph also associates *elaboratio* with the so-called *thematische Arbeit* (thematic work) of 'the high Viennese style' in general.

[105] For a concise account of this and other relevant matters see William Stafford, 'The Evolution of Mozartian Biography', in *The Cambridge Companion to Mozart*, ed. Simon P. Keefe (Cambridge: Cambridge University Press, 2003), 200–211.

[106] William Weber, 'The Myth of Mozart, the Revolutionary', *The Musical Quarterly* 78/1 (1994), 45. Note that 'red herring' also applies to the author of the original play, Beaumarchais ('The idea of Beaumarchais and Mozart as protorevolutionaries is a red herring').

[107] Rupert Ridgewell, 'Biographical Myth and the Publication of Mozart's Piano Quartets', *Journal of the Royal Musical Association* 135/1 (2010), 41.

[108] Ridgewell, 'Biographical Myth and the Publication of Mozart's Piano Quartets', 48 and 105.

Ridgewell's acknowledgment of 'resilience' hints at the difficulties involved in this sort of revisionist enterprise. The prospects are that the technical and/or affective difficulty, and therefore 'seriousness', of Mozart's output will continue to be a fulcrum for many interpretations, for all the counterevidence, whether musical or circumstantial. It is too good a story to give up, both in its own right and as a more or less oblique comment on the state of the art in later eighteenth-century Europe.

It has also proved an attractive option as a form of compensatory history, making amends for the perceived lack of consistent public success for Mozart during his lifetime. This may be described as the heart of the hurt, the long-running trauma that has scarred the collective approach to musical 'classicism'.[109] Something or somebody must be to blame, and 'public taste' has been one convenient object of scorn. The target may take more particular forms; in several recent studies, for example, Pleyel, by any measure a much-loved and commercially successful composer, has been used as a whipping boy.[110]

But, of course, the more obvious counterpole is Haydn. Haydn's success during his lifetime is also beyond doubt; as noted earlier, it was no triumphal march, though the many negative reviews, the frequent 'difficulty' of the music and the professional frustrations have often been conveniently overlooked. The interesting aspect is that the popularity often becomes a 'problem' that must be solved, the success something that must be 'explained', generally meaning that the excellence of the music cannot be the root cause (whereas with Mozart the excellence is often treated as having been an impediment to contemporary comprehension). Elaine Sisman has coined the nicely objectifying term 'success narrative' to mark the gap between the common conception of a triumphal march and the fact that Haydn often thought himself misunderstood, was often 'defensive' about his work.[111]

A common thread in addressing the 'problem' of the composer's success gives the impression that Haydn, of all composers of his time, was somehow uniquely interested in reaching and pleasing his audience; a particular point of emphasis has been what Haydn did differently in his London

---

[109] The latter phrase derives from near the opening of my review of Melanie Lowe, *Pleasure and Meaning in the Classical Symphony*, *Music & Letters* 89/4 (2008), 628.

[110] See Mark Evan Bonds, 'Replacing Haydn: Mozart's "Pleyel" Quartets', *Music & Letters* 88/2 (2007), 201–225, and Melanie Lowe, 'Amateur Topical Competencies', in *The Oxford Handbook of Topic Theory*, ed. Danuta Mirka (New York: Oxford University Press, 2014), 601–628.

[111] Elaine Sisman, 'Haydn's Career and the Idea of the Multiple Audience', in *The Cambridge Companion to Haydn*, ed. Clark, 6.

works to accommodate his changed professional circumstances and a new musical environment. For example, in a study that focusses on topical interplay in Haydn's later symphonies, Melanie Lowe suggests that 'The secret to Haydn's accessibility and public success, particularly in England, was to provide some listeners [with] a musical corroboration of Europe's stratified society while offering others a momentary, if imaginary, musical escape from this inescapable premise.'[112] Yet it is hard to believe that any composer of the time whose work mixed materials associated with different social levels could not be understood to have promoted a similar agenda. The subtext here is a familiar one: that Haydn made it big by deferring to the status quo. Less subtextual is Lawrence Kramer, who once wrote that *The Creation* 'forms a celebration of rigid social hierarchy', given that it was 'underwritten by a consortium of aristocrats' and 'composed by a man whose enormous success was inextricable from his unprotesting subordination'.[113] In an often penetrating and largely sympathetic treatment of the composer in his *Oxford History of Western Music*, Richard Taruskin nevertheless feels obliged to remind us of these moral limitations: 'his art [is] one that seems uncommonly given to complimenting the discernment of its listeners'; 'while Haydn is often applauded for his peasant origins (even by himself in retrospect when talking to fawning biographers), it is evident that his artistic sympathies and loyalties were entirely aristocratic'.[114] Christopher Small works from a similar premise, but makes the moral equation a gendered one. In contrast to Mozart's 'subtle . . . perception of the feminine', 'the feminine seems hardly to exist' in Haydn, whose works 'exist in an ideal of masculine order of Enlightenment rationality and possess a curiously sexless quality'.[115] Small bases his claim principally on Haydn's 'monothematic' sonata-form movements, the same feature that leads Rumph astray: the lack of a contrasting second subject would appear to have been deliberately contrived by the composer so as to keep women from the door.

The fact that Small makes his pronouncement on a highly anachronistic formal basis (sonata form had not yet been formulated as such, and it had yet to attract essentializing gendered explanations) is less relevant here

[112] Melanie Lowe, *Pleasure and Meaning in the Classical Symphony* (Bloomington: Indiana University Press, 2007), 134.
[113] Lawrence Kramer, *Classical Music and Postmodern Knowledge* (Berkeley: University of California Press, 1995), 93. To be fair, the writer's later accounts of Haydn have shown considerably greater sensitivity.
[114] Richard Taruskin, *The Oxford History of Western Music*, volume 2: *Music in the Seventeenth and Eighteenth Centuries* (New York: Oxford University Press, 2005), 540–541 and 550.
[115] Small, *Musicking*, 176–177.

than the fact that he reaffirms this most conventional of critical subtexts about Haydn and the status quo. It is remarkable that the name of Haydn can release such reserves of aggression – although, once again, the composer's role is at least partly symbolic, standing as he often does for the wider moral failure of galant music. Often enough, in fact, the tone is milder than that, and takes the form of damning with faint praise rather than outright attack; this is particularly the case when so-called *Kleinmeister* are being discussed. In either case, this attitude might be thought to derive from the nineteenth century. Yet a significant body of recent work suggests that it was not quite like that: that the supposed fall of Haydn's reputation over that time was primarily at the hands of critics, while his music continued to be loved by listeners.[116] This suggests a nice symmetry with the case of Mozart's reception during his lifetime: just as the image of neglect and/or incomprehension of his music is becoming less and less tenable, so the same is emerging with respect to Haydn's posthumous fate. Even so, when we consider the broader treatment of Haydn, we may find once more that the old story is too good to give up. And these old stories continue to intrude even at a high critical level – which is the level at which most of the work I have cited in this section operates.

The notion that Haydn was somehow uniquely accommodating of his audience can be easily pushed over. We might note, for instance, as Julian Rushton does, that Mozart wrote his Symphony in D major K297 (1778) for Paris in three movements, 'in accordance with local expectations'; Haydn, on the other hand, ignored this local preference and stuck with his customary four-movement design when he wrote his six symphonies for Paris (Nos 82–87, 1785–1786).[117] Shortly thereafter, Haydn conceived the idea of dedicating his Op. 50 string quartets (1787) to the cello-playing King Friedrich Wilhelm II of Prussia, but no particular favours are granted to that instrument;[118] when Mozart subsequently dedicated the three quartets K575, 589 and 590 to the King in 1790, he literally aimed to please,

---

[116] See James Garratt, 'Haydn and Posterity: The Long Nineteenth Century', in *The Cambridge Companion to Haydn*, ed. Clark, 226–238; Jess Tyre, 'Reviving the Classic, Inventing Memory: Haydn's Reception in Fin-de-Siècle France, *HAYDN* 2/1 (2012) www.rit.edu/haydn (1 December 2014); and Bryan Proksch, *Reviving Haydn: New Appreciations in the Twentieth Century* (Rochester, NY: University of Rochester Press, 2015).

[117] Rushton, *Classical Music*, 110.

[118] Precisely how the composition and dedication of Op. 50 interwove is not entirely clear; see my account in *Haydn: String Quartets, Op. 50* (Cambridge: Cambridge University Press, 1992), 30–32. It is likely that at least the first two works were written before the prospect of dedicating the set to the King of Prussia had arisen. Thus a common explanation for the opening of Op. 50 No. 1 in B flat major with a series of repeated B♭s for cello alone – that it was a joke at the expense of the cello-playing king – may have no basis in fact.

since the cello attains great melodic prominence and enforces a more concertante texture altogether. The point of this is not, of course, merely to turn the tables, nor indeed to reinforce the idea that *not* writing to please confers moral superiority on the composer concerned; it is simply to suggest how selective the reading of musical and historical evidence must be in order to maintain the 'old stories'.

We have got into the very familiar, not to say tedious, territory of playing Haydn and Mozart off against each other – a Tale of Two Composers – even if solely in terms of their respective traditions of reception. Given the imbalance in the scholarly literature, though, the confinement to our 'tiny cohort' of figures, it would have been difficult to do it any other way. Yet it has been enough to establish the difficulties that attend our conception of the instrumental music of the period. The aim is not to downplay any amount of fine work that has been devoted to the repertory, but rather to suggest the power of certain assumptions that retain their grip – assumptions that are all about occupying a moral high ground above the image of a 'shallow sociability'. When else, after all, in Western music history has a whole style been so often understood negatively, as a problem in need of a solution?

The Listener

One danger in the account given above is that, in squaring off against certain constants in the reception of later eighteenth-century style, I am perpetuating the notion of an identikit type of music – that it is all the same. Surely the picture was more varied than that? Indeed it was, but in attempting to get at the heart of a problem, I am concentrating on where I believe the point of greatest resistance lies. This is a cluster of associations that can be more positively understood under the rubric of sociability. It is not to imply that lightness, humour, grace and the like are all that the style offers – it would be reasonable to assume that musicians of the time thought they were covering more affective bases than that – but instead to note that such perceived attributes are what most need further thought.

One widely held assumption may be more happily reproduced: the listener-friendliness of this music. In fact, an emphasis on the listener is a relatively recent development. It has arisen logically out of the fields of topic and schema theory, for instance, but these have formed just part of a wider programme: to demystify the repertory, to move it away from the dreaded clutches of 'absolute music' and to reimagine it on a more human scale. Topic and schema give priority to a bar-by-bar engagement with patterns, with familiar configurations of musical material, in an attempt to break the hold of the traditional 'absolute' assumption that listeners 'listen for form' on a larger scale. Earlier I reserved judgment on this, and in light of the finale of Haydn's Op. 33 No. 2, the reservation should make some sense. This movement – which we have already marked out as a symbol of a new orientation towards the listener – patently asks that listener to range back beyond the immediate context and consider what the last two-bar phrase unit has meant over the course of the whole finale. It has functioned not just as the beginning of the movement altogether, but as a return to the beginning, both within the three-part structure that constitutes the first section of the movement (its 'A' section) and, on a larger scale, the return to that complete sequence of sounds (the repeated refrain within an ABACA rondo). Hence the double signification of the end – that we are expecting more to follow to complete another version of the familiar tune and that, when this doesn't happen, we must come to terms with the palindromic absurdity of the conclusion. To have to think along such lines more or less equates to 'form' on the large scale, as a way of trying to grasp the shape of the complete listening experience.

In favour of the concatenationist, bar-by-bar, perspective is that smaller-scale musical units were precisely the novelty of the eighteenth century, arising in symbiosis with our new more listener-friendly orientation. Phrases are now prone to be made up of our short, well-defined parts, clearly signalled to the listener by gaps, which may extend into something we can perceive as a silence or a pause. They are easy to grasp and easy to remember. But such units build into longer stretches of sound that may also be signalled with a new clarity, so that larger-scale form, too, becomes something to reckon with. What helps to reconcile the two perspectives is the principle of articulation – that sections of varying sizes are marked for perception as such. Paul Griffiths encapsulates the novelty of the outcome, not coincidentally in connection with Haydn's Op. 33: 'The idea that music could be "followed", understood as a course of sound events without any metaphorical interpretation, was quite new, and it was the main social reason that the late eighteenth century developed a musical style of such lucidity'.[119]

We can take this further by returning to the language model. As we have seen, a dominant way of understanding music as the eighteenth century progressed was to describe it as a language. To do this suggests, first, that

---

[119] Paul Griffiths, *The String Quartet: A History* (London: Thames and Hudson, 1983), 42.

music is also an agent of communication between people; both media, after all, communicate through sound (and also take a silent written form). Second, there is an expectation of intelligibility, that there is mutual understanding between the users of the language. Third, and especially important for current purposes, language is made up of discrete units that build up into larger utterances: words build into sentences, notes into longer units such as phrases. The importance of the comparison between music and language is hard for us to grasp, since it is such a familiar idea nowadays, but it carried a sharper edge at the time. There had been and would be other ways to understand the nature of music – as celestial sounds (the 'music of the spheres' of earlier times), as a primal force, as something that washes over us – but for the eighteenth century music was, above all, linguistic. In other words, it was a worldly, man-made phenomenon. Johann Joachim Quantz wrote in his famous flute treatise of 1752 that 'music is nothing but an artificial language through which we seek to acquaint the listener with our *musical* ideas'.[120]

We can place this new sense of music as language within a broader development, of a culture in which art music became conspicuously accessible. One aspect of that accessibility was the clear articulation of sound into digestible units: 'punctuation' was the favoured term of the time, evidently reflecting a linguistic ontology.[121] Another is evident in the fact that at no other time was high-art music so popular in its accents as it became in the later eighteenth century – often embracing music that could have been heard on the streets or in the fields. Simplicity and naturalness were buzzwords. The highest compliment one could pay to a piece of music was to call it 'natural', and there was often a connection drawn between sincerity and simplicity of expression.[122] Simplicity could be thought the highest form of eloquence; overt complication was suspect.

---

[120] Johann Joachim Quantz, *Versuch einer Anweisung die Flöte traversiere zu spielen* (Berlin: Johann Friedrich Voß, 1752), 102; *On Playing the Flute*: A Complete Translation with an Introduction and Notes by Edward R. Reilly (London: Faber, 1966), 120.

[121] For an instance of the many recent treatments of 'punctuation' in connection with historical music theory see Stefan Eckert, '"[...] wherein good Taste, Order and Thoroughness rule": Hearing Riepel's Op. 1 Violin Concertos through Riepel's Theories', *Ad Parnassum* 3/5 (2005), 23–44. Eckert notes that such accounts of the time presuppose an 'audience's ability to comprehend the unfolding of [musical] syntax' (44).

[122] Note the pronouncement of Ruth Katz and Carl Dahlhaus: 'that simplicity guarantees the "genuineness" of an emotion was the central thesis of the aesthetics of the Enlightenment'. Katz and Dahlhaus, *Contemplating Music: Source Readings in the Aesthetics of Music*, volume 2: *Import* (Stuyvesant: Pendragon, 1989), 114. We return to this 'thesis' later in the book, especially in Chapter 4.

This meant avoiding what was perceived as the 'laborious', 'Gothic' writing of earlier generations. Immediately after the reference above to 'musical ideas', Quantz writes, 'If we execute those ideas in an obscure or bizarre manner which is incomprehensible to the listener and arouses no feeling, of what use are our perpetual efforts to be thought learned?'.[123] The practical upshot of such an anti-academic orientation was a focus on melody, simply accompanied. The idea was that this corresponded more realistically to what an average listener could take in at any one point in time – as opposed to the endless multiplication of lines in the texture of strict counterpoint. Witness the criticisms of Johann Adolph Scheibe: 'a composer usually sinks into the bombastic manner when he gives all parts the same amount to do and when they constantly squabble with one another'.[124] The terms of Scheibe's disapproval are significant. The very word 'bombastic' implies a language model: it more or less refers to a manner of speaking (down) to other people.[125] And more broadly, it refers to behaviour, a way of conducting oneself in relation to those others.

It would, of course, be a big exaggeration to suggest that intricate textures disappeared from art music over the eighteenth century, or indeed that 'complexity' was avoided – after all, there are other ways to be complex aside from the textural – but it is certainly the case that more accessible homophonic textures became common practice. These could work in tandem with our short, well-defined units of musical utterance. The very brevity of individual musical units takes us back to the language model, but in particular it's a language model that tends to the more informal end of the spectrum. To put it in terms that were greatly favoured by the eighteenth century, it is a model based on the typical rhythms of conversation. Conversations, after all, tend to consist of quite short exchanges, since if the individual contributions grow too long, the raison d'être of informal interaction will naturally be lost.

If there was a concern for comprehensibility, as the words of Quantz suggest, this would readily lead to a realization that music might mean

---

[123] Quantz, *Versuch einer Anweisung die Flöte traversiere zu spielen*, 102; *On Playing the Flute*, trans. Reilly, 120.
[124] Johann Adolph Scheibe, *Der critische Musikus* (Leipzig: Breitkopf, 1745), 132, cited in translation in Warren Kirkendale, *Fugue and Fugato in Rococo and Classical Chamber Music*, trans. Margaret Bent and Warren Kirkendale, revised and expanded second edition (Durham, NC: Duke University Press, 1979), 23.
[125] The translation of Scheibe's 'schwülstig' as 'bombastic' has been challenged in Beverly Jerold, 'The Bach-Scheibe Controversy: New Documentation', *Bach: Journal of the Riemenschneider Bach Institute* 42/1 (2011), 15, in which the author claims that Scheibe's usage carries rather the meaning of 'unintelligible to the ear'.

different things to different people – that not all listeners were the same. This, too, became an established part of the discourse, and was often linked with the desirability of variety, another key term of cultural exchange. C. P. E. Bach, for all his apparent diffidence in private on the matter, wrote in his *Versuch über die wahre Art das Klavier zu spielen*, 'Since nature has so wisely endowed music with such diversity that it can be enjoyed by everyone, the musician, too, has the duty, insofar as he is able, to satisfy all kinds of listeners.'[126] The key exhibit in the matter has often been Mozart's famous letter to his father about his concertos K413–415 (1782–1783), which were 'a happy medium between what is too easy and too difficult' and contained passages 'from which the connoisseurs alone can derive satisfaction; but these passages are written in such a way that the less learned cannot fail to be pleased, though without knowing why'.[127] Of course, this was also a means of reassuring publishers, just as Mozart was arguably reassuring his father: in a letter to publisher Robert Birchall in 1817, Leopold Kozeluch was still able to employ such a gambit, writing that some sonatas of his were 'not difficult', but nevertheless 'melodious and brilliant'.[128] This reminds us that there was no clear line between ethical and marketing motivations: on the one hand, a desire to communicate, rather than obfuscate, as Quantz might have put it, and, on the other hand, the self-evident need to earn one's living by selling one's product as widely as possible. Burney gave a characteristically wry twist to the theme: 'With respect to excellence of Style and Composition, it may perhaps be said that to practised ears the most pleasing Music is such as has the merit of novelty, added to refinement, and ingenious contrivance; and to the ignorant, such as is most familiar and common.'[129]

Burney's epigram is necessarily rather deterministic; taste, he would have known, was a little more elusive than that. In addition, it was informed by

---

[126] Carl Philipp Emanuel Bach, *Versuch über die wahre Art das Klavier zu spielen*, part 1 (Berlin: Christian Friedrich Henning, 1753), 123; translated in *Music and Culture in Eighteenth-Century Europe: A Source Book*, ed. Enrico Fubini, trans. Wolfgang Freis, Lisa Gasbarrone and Michael Louis Leone, trans. ed. Bonnie J. Blackburn (Chicago: University of Chicago Press, 1994), 295.

[127] Mozart, letter to Leopold Mozart, 28 December 1782; *The Letters of Mozart and His Family*, ed. and trans. Emily Anderson, third edition, revised by Stanley Sadie and Fiona Smart (London: Palgrave Macmillan, 1985), 833. Simon P. Keefe notes that there is a 'risk of overinterpreting' this letter, since such pronouncements were common at the time: 'The Concertos in Aesthetic and Stylistic Context', in *The Cambridge Companion to Mozart*, ed. Keefe, 78.

[128] Kozeluch, letter to Robert Birchall, 22 November 1817, cited in translation in Christopher Hogwood, 'The Keyboard Sonatas of Leopold Kozeluch', *Early Music* 40/4 (2012), 625.

[129] Charles Burney, *A General History of Music from the Earliest Ages to the Present Period* (first edition, London: author, 1776–1789), *Volume the First*, with critical and historical notes by Frank Mercer (New York: Dover, 1957), 22.

a dualism that it still carries today. Taste is a function of personal choice, but it also carries a collective, comparative import. In that sense, it shares much with the sociability for which it was a key term of reference. There is the awareness of oneself and one's own preferences, and then there is the awareness of others and their views. Taste could be a tyrant – coercive at a collective level and meaningless in isolation (tastes don't mean much if they can't be expressed to and discussed with other people). The ideal was more consensual, a mediation between the two extremes. Lest that seem like a euphemism for the tyranny of the majority, we should bear in mind the new sense of 'society' and 'public' outlined at the outset, and the liberating notion that a work could be 'validated not simply by its conformity to pre-established rules but also by its public reception'.[130] And because it was not foreordained, that reception could shift, giving dissenting voices an incentive to reiterate their views.

In any case, we should not leave the impression that our music simply waited passively for approbation or otherwise. It could lead by example, set the parameters within which a response could be made, for instance by embodying the virtues of variety, clarity, naturalness and the like; it could, in other words, imply a certain kind of listener, suggest a particular kind of subject-position.[131] It could encourage certain values and preferences, but could not determine them. While this may be a principle that applies to musical repertories of all kinds, one could argue that the sense of mutual conditioning is particularly strong in the case of later eighteenth-century music. This music invites the listener inside, as it were, though its accessibility, through familiar materials that have specific shapes (schemata), stylistic associations (topics) or kinds of placement (formal functions), but it also leaves much up to the judgment of that listener – what we are to make of the relationships between materials presented side by side, what we are to make of unfamiliar or unconventional elements, what we are to make of the whole (the finale of Haydn's Op. 33 No. 2 again). Friedrich Blume encapsulated this ethos: 'one of the fundamental tenets of the Classic style [was] to make a composition easily accessible to the listener

---

[130] James van Horn Melton, 'School, Stage, Salon: Musical Cultures in Haydn's Vienna', in *Haydn and the Performance of Rhetoric*, ed. Beghin and Goldberg, 89; this is how the author characterizes the arguments of Joseph Addison and Jean-Baptiste Dubos.

[131] On subject-position in relation to music see Eric F. Clarke, 'Subject-Position and the Specification of Invariants in Music by Frank Zappa and P. J. Harvey', *Music Analysis* 18/3 (1999), 347–374. See also Lawrence Kramer, 'The Mysteries of Animation: History, Analysis and Musical Subjectivity', *Music Analysis* 20/2 (2001): 'the basic work of culture is to construct subject positions, contingent frames of reference within which certain forms of action, desire, speech and understanding become possible' (156).

for his co-operation in its fulfillment'. To this he opposed the 'sovereign' character that was 'increasingly pressed upon' romantic music, 'compelling the listener to passive surrender'.[132] This is amusingly at odds with the liberation narrative that is usually assumed, and which underpins the suspicions of sociability that we have observed in operation in the previous sections of this chapter. Ruth Katz, for instance, who certainly does understand the notion of the later eighteenth-century listener being expected to 'follow the "sense" of a composition' as it unfolded, nevertheless believes that with the arrival of the nineteenth century 'a dynamic mode of listening replaced the more static way of perceiving that primarily rested on the implementation of "logical" procedures, on those learned cognitive schemata shared by composer and listener'.[133]

But accessibility and comprehensibility could produce their own demands; certain kinds of simplicity do not rule out certain kinds of complexity. Some historical sympathy is required in order to make this case, since one is up against the 'easy listening' that is today's wider image of the style. Blume suggests that the listener has to play a part rather than simply 'surrendering' to the music, and most recent accounts have stressed that active listening is required.[134] The premium that the style places on humour sums this up very well. Humour both demands and rewards attention, and often prompts an active (physical) response from an audience; yet it is not always so easy to get the joke. One might speak of a sliding scale of humour fading into wit fading into irony, whereby each successive term demands greater prior knowledge and greater concentration, though the level of responsiveness will not be as neat and tidy as that. The tone of our music is often hard to read: in other words, whether we are to take a particular piece of material or an expressive typology 'seriously'. Related to such uncertainties of response, and often enough productive of them,

---

[132] Friedrich Blume, *Classic and Romantic Music: A Comprehensive Survey*, trans. M. D. Herder Norton (New York: Norton, 1970; based on entries from *Die Musik in Geschichte und Gegenwart*, 1958), 34 and 16. For a more recent perspective along similar lines see Currie, 'Waiting for the Viennese Classics', who notes how the dialogic basis for the style 'works against the notion of authoritative control' (137).

[133] Ruth Katz, *A Language of Its Own: Sense and Meaning in the Making of Western Art Music* (Chicago: University of Chicago Press, 2009), 102 and 180.

[134] One instance from beyond the field of instrumental music might be cited: in 'Pergolesi's *Stabat Mater* and the Politics of Feminine Virtue', *The Musical Quarterly* 87/3 (2004), Richard Will stresses how the composer gives listeners 'an active role, allowing them to sympathize with feeling rather than tremble before sublimity' (609). This is, of course, not quite the same thing as the sort of engagement I was arguing for in the case of the finale of Haydn's Op. 33 No. 2; it is more a question of sympathetic participation rather than the sort of drawing-in of the listener that invites critical judgment.

are the very frequent silences and pauses that mark the style. Gretchen Wheelock draws attention to the 'freely extended pause' as a way of reminding us that it is not just players who interact within a piece; listeners are also involved in the 'conversation', and the pause implies a 'particularly focused moment of listening'.[135] But even if one thinks of breaks, pauses, silences and general oddities of timing purely from an executive point of view, it is clear that they require players to listen to each other much more attentively than ever before; the continuo no longer forms the centre of gravity that allows for an untroubled unfolding of contents. Performers must listen in hard so as to coordinate, and this virtually enforces one of the fundamental proprieties of sociable conduct, the need to think about the responses of others. Silence is indeed loaded from this point of view.

Even a basic term of reference like variety, so often thematized as a way of attracting different kinds of listener, could in practice prove confusing rather than stimulating. For instance, the dramatist Lessing wrote in 1769 of a new style of music that 'leaves us in uncertainty and confusion'; the 'disorderly feelings' produced by quick changes from one affect to another were 'more fatiguing than agreeable'.[136] Burney lamented the fact that while treatises were being produced in abundance, none were written 'to instruct ignorant lovers of Music how to listen, or to judge for themselves'.[137] This acknowledges not only that listening was not always an easy occupation, but also that the listener ought to be actively involved.

There were plenty of others who testified to the sorts of difficulties experienced by Lessing, and Burney had an answer to the most famous of them – the 'Sonate, que me veux-tu?' (Sonata, what do you want of me?) uttered by the Frenchman Bernard le Bovier de Fontenelle:[138] 'If a lover and judge of music had asked the same question as Fontenelle, the sonata should answer "I would have you listen with attention and delight to the ingenuity of the composition . . . as well as to the charms of refined tones, lengthened and polished into passion."'[139] The notion of the sonata

---

[135] Gretchen A. Wheelock, 'The "Rhetorical Pause" and Metaphors of Conversation in Haydn's Quartets', in *Haydn & das Streichquartett*, ed. Georg Feder and Walter Reicher (Tutzing: Schneider, 2003), 73.

[136] Gotthold Ephraim Lessing, *Hamburgische Dramaturgie, Erster Teil* (Hamburg and Bremen: J. H. Cramer, 1769), 212, cited in translation in Allanbrook, *Secular Commedia*, 24.

[137] Burney, *General History of Music, Volume the Second*, 7–8.

[138] Beverly Jerold suggests that the usual translation, of which I have offered one version, may miss the mark, and that the phrase abridges a common idiom that should translate to 'Sonata, what do you mean to me?': 'Fontenelle's Famous Question and Performance Standards of the Day', *College Music Symposium* 43 (2003), 150.

[139] Burney, *General History of Music, Volume the Second*, 11.

speaking back signals not only a linguistic orientation (instrumental music has its own 'voice') but also an interactive model of musical communication (question and answer between listener and composition). More relevant to the current purpose, the sonata asks for 'attention' from its auditors. Even if the request is politely phrased, it still mandates a level of engagement that goes beyond our later image of easy listening. There was another way of framing this: in his *Idee sull'indole del piacere* of 1774 Pietro Verri asserted that 'music leaves more to the imagination of the listener' than the other arts. The diversity of reactions that music could produce were less prevalent when it came to judging either painting or poetry, since in those cases the receiver is 'almost entirely passive'. 'With music, however, the listener has to go above himself [l'ascoltatore deve coagire sopra se stesso].'[140] Once more, therefore, the ideal listener will need to take an active role.

There were different contemporary ways of tackling the problem of 'difficulty'. The *Wiener Zeitung* in February 1791 announced the publication of Haydn's Op. 64 quartets in this manner: 'There have in the past been many complaints about the extraordinary difficulties of execution in Haydn's works. Haydn has avoided this in these six quartets ... in that he has combined art, dalliance and taste with the easiest execution, in such a way that the *Künstler* as well as the mere *Liebhaber* will be completely satisfied.'[141] This is of course a sales pitch, though it implies that the composer has a moral obligation to meet the needs of all kinds of listener, to be approachable as well as artful (echoing the sorts of sentiments we saw in Mozart's letter on the concertos K413–415). On the other hand, Burney (again) wrote that Haydn's compositions 'are in general so new to the player and hearer that they are equally unable, at first, to keep pace with his inspiration. The first exclamation of an embarrassed performer and a bewildered hearer is, that the Music is very *odd*, or very *comical*; but the queerness and comicality cease when, by frequent repetition, the performer and hearer are at their ease.'[142] In this instance the moral obligation falls rather onto the consumer, who will find that persistence has its rewards.[143]

---

[140] Pietro Verri, *Idee sull'indole del piacere* (Milan: Giuseppe Galeazzi, 1774), 63–64. It is not entirely clear from context whether Verri is thinking specifically of instrumental music or rather of music as a whole, though the only specific generic reference he makes is to 'the melody of a fine concerto'.

[141] *Wiener Zeitung* (23 February 1791), 463, cited in Horst Walter, 'Zum Wiener Streichquartett der Jahre 1780 bis 1800', *Haydn-Studien* 7/3–4 (1998), 306.

[142] Burney, *General History of Music, Volume the Second*, 959–960.

[143] Compare Simon McVeigh's summation in *Concert Life in London from Mozart to Haydn* (Cambridge: Cambridge University Press, 1993) that Haydn's symphonies 'played a crucial role' in the development of notions of 'cultural responsibility': 'It was recognised at an early

Other kinds of complexity – or at the very least, a greatly enriched sense of contemporary composing and listening possibilities – have emerged through the engagement with theoretical writings from the time. Danuta Mirka, for example, basing her work on the writings of Koch and Joseph Riepel (1709–1782), has uncovered a dizzying range of rhythmical-metrical manipulations in the string chamber music of Haydn in particular. To learn to perceive at least some of these features would certainly get us beyond an assumed 'easy listening': it 'turns today's listener from a passive consumer into an active partner of the eighteenth-century composer in a game played with the compositional rules of the time'. She is careful not to claim that present-day listeners can thereby acquire a genuine 'period ear', but at least 'we can try to reconstruct the "historical listener" of the eighteenth century' as a step in that direction.[144]

Similar considerations arise in the case of schema theory. The writings of Riepel in fact also form one of the bases for recognition of galant schemata, given that he provided names for several patterns that have been taken up by Gjerdingen.[145] (The home territory for the practice, though, was in the first instance Neapolitan, and it was a primarily oral tradition rather than one that left substantial verbal traces.) Schematic analysis gives a particularity and tangibility to what might otherwise have been blankly received as routine turns of phrase; an ability to hear schemata brings not just the pleasure of recognition, but also the pleasure of hearing how exactly they are realized. It is perhaps their relative compactness – a model of the short, sharp, readily perceptible musical utterance – that has fostered a belief that we too can enjoy the benefits. Vasili Byros suggests that schemata, which 'configure a situated psychology of hearing', can provide access to historical modes of listening even today.[146] This line of thought can be traced back to the work of Leonard Meyer, who, in the words of Michael Spitzer, taught us 'that listeners' stylistic competence (including their internalisation of schemata as mental models) inextricably

---

date that [Haydn's symphonies] required some application on the part of the listener ... This trend closely matched a current of improvement and instruction throughout the entertainment industry.' (64)

[144] Danuta Mirka, *Metric Manipulations in Haydn and Mozart: Chamber Music for Strings, 1787–1791* (New York: Oxford University Press, 2009), xii. As the title of the book makes clear, Mirka concentrates on a particular selection of Haydn's quartets, and Mozart also plays a part in the study, albeit a relatively minor one.

[145] Joseph Riepel, *Anfangsgründe zur musikalischen Setzkunst*, five volumes (1752–1768).

[146] Vasili Byros, 'Meyer's Anvil: Revisiting the Schema Concept', *Music Analysis* 31/3 (2012), 327. See also his 'Towards an "Archaeology" of Hearing: Schemata and Eighteenth-Century Consciousness', *Musica Humana* 1/2 (2009), 235–306.

blends cognition with historical consciousness'.[147] This more optimistic note might be reinforced in the case of schemata by noting their avowedly practical dimension: schemata were (and again now are) taught and internalized physically through keyboard playing. This reminds us, more broadly speaking, that the roles of player and listener overlap. Players are always also listeners, of course, but they are likely to have particularly high levels of embodied knowledge. Nor should we forget the very significant role that arrangements played in the later eighteenth century, meaning that a wide range of players could get their hands on a particular piece of music; thus hearing was more frequently mediated through playing than is the case today.[148]

In detailing some of the perceived complexities and difficulties of later eighteenth-century instrumental style, one needs to be careful not to reaffirm the very equation that created the problems of reception in the first place: 'the more demanding, the better'. The importance of accessibility as a first principle remains paramount – and it is still the greatest impediment to latter-day comprehension of the style, ironically enough. In critical and compositional terms, the more or less automatically positive valuation of complexity retains a hold through to contemporary Western art music, yet it can hardly have escaped notice that levels of listener engagement do not match that. One has to be careful, after all, not to equate surface complexity, or complexity on the page, with complexity of perception. Without some framework of expectation, the listening experience can readily become rather one-dimensional. On the other hand, our later eighteenth-century style gives an impression of familiarity that can draw the listener in, even if the total package turns out to be not so transparent. The finale of Haydn's Op. 33 No. 2, for instance, could hardly do more to make us feel at home, with its simple rhyming refrain, yet at the end, as we have seen, it spins off into all kinds of cognitive complexity. This movement, admittedly at an extreme end, points to an apparent paradox in the style's orientation towards the listener: that it may be both welcoming and demanding at the same time. Yet, in terms of sociable properties, no

---

[147] Michael Spitzer, 'Guest Editorial: The Emotion Issue', *Music Analysis* 29/1–3 (2010), 5.
[148] Wiebke Thormählen notes the views of Baron van Swieten, that arbiter of taste in later eighteenth-century Vienna, that only active engagement with works via such means as arrangements would yield the full benefits: 'the inner sensation of taste is best inspired by the recipient's socializing with and through the work'. Thormählen, 'Playing with Art: Musical Arrangements as Educational Tools in van Swieten's Vienna', *The Journal of Musicology* 27/3 (2010), 373.

contradiction need be felt: both comfort and alertness are required for successful social transactions.

We can also refer this duality to the emergence of the compositional persona: as suggested early on, attributing musical characteristics to the perceived personal qualities of the composer was a way of controlling the listening experience, and of course this is now firmly embedded in our reception of much musical art, as indeed is the notion of 'expression' that arose at a similar time. Haydn's persona could be read as anything from 'mad, bad and dangerous to know' (which is the rough sense of Christian Friedrich Daniel Schubart's phrase '*Haiden*, den verwegenen Launischen'[149]) to something akin to a tease (Ignaz Arnold wrote that the composer 'teases us in every way until we grow tired of trying to guess what will come next' ('uns von allen Seiten zu *necken*, bis wir müde, zu errathen, was kommen wird'[150])). This development may owe something to the growth in publishing of instrumental music, from the point of view of both producer and consumer. The very anonymity of the process may have brought an extra degree of self-consciousness to the discourse, since the composer had to imagine a response in people who were for the most part not personally known, and the same would apply in reverse on the part of the purchasers, who might start to recognize a personal brand. That contemporaries could hear plenty of differences between the characteristic manners of different figures, when we are more likely to hear an 'identikit' approach, is evidenced from many quarters. For example, a 1787 review of some sonatas by Johann Ludwig Willing (1755–1805) commented, 'Admittedly, these sonatas do not have Haydn's humour, or Vanhall's liveliness, or [C. P. E.] Bach's seriousness, or Kozeluch or Clementi's passion'.[151] Schubart's reference to Haydn above formed part of a similar list in the preface to his third volume of *Musicalische Rhapsodien* (1786), which included reference to '*Kozeluch*, den Prächtigen' (the splendid (or grand) Kozeluch) and '*Mozart*, den Schimmernden'[152] (possibly untranslatable, though to describe Mozart as 'shimmering' or 'glimmering' might just be a new term within a bulging lexicon).

---

[149] Christian Friedrich Daniel Schubart, *Musicalische Rhapsodien*, volume 3 (Stuttgart: Buchdrukerei der Herzoglichen Hohen Carlsschule, 1786), Preface ('Klavierrezepte'), [3].
[150] Ignaz Arnold, *Joseph Haydn: Eine kurze Biographie und ästhetische Darstellung seiner Werke* (Erfurt: Müller, 1810), 82.
[151] *Neue Leipziger gelehrte Zeitungen* 3/2 (26 April 1787), 49, cited in translation in Hogwood, 'Keyboard Sonatas of Leopold Kozeluch', 630.
[152] Schubart, *Musicalische Rhapsodien*, Preface ('Klavierrezepte'), [3].

In the case of Haydn, while the common emphasis on humour, misdirection and even just sheer lunacy[153] might seem to more recent eyes to confine him to the harmless end of the artistic spectrum, such 'personal' attributes were not understood in that way at the time. Rather, they testify to his power over listeners, who are encouraged to follow the train of thought and may then find themselves upended. The air of good-humoured familiarity, though, can be so strong that it overrides all other impressions. Certainly, this has been a feature of subsequent critical reception. After all, even some modern-day musicologists can with a straight face still associate Haydn with rule-making, leaving the rule-breaking for the likes of Mozart and C. P. E. Bach, which shows that the familiar manner can even now dupe a sophisticated listener into imagining that there is 'nothing to see here'.[154] We have also observed that Haydn (though he is far from alone in this) leaves much up to the judgment of the listener, and that of course includes many of the more subtle infringements of discourse that can often pass unheard. Thus we return to the duality of sociable consciousness. Haydn exercises a position of authority over the listener yet at the same time gives the impression of being accommodating, 'arguing' for a lessening of composer authority, most obviously so when the musical discourse seems in some way to go wrong. This means that the listener must help to make good the error, must exercise powers of discrimination. Thus we encounter a sociable musical persona who is at once undogmatic and manipulative.

---

[153] Note in connection with this term the thoughts of Marshall Brown: 'Much discussed in connection with Haydn is the contemporary characterization of the composer as "launisch". But scholars who relate *Laune* either to British "wit" or Romantic "irony" are looking too far afield. Both translations are too intellectual for the moody unpredictability targeted by *Laune*, whose etymological associations lie with lunacy.' Marshall Brown, 'Editorial', *Eighteenth-Century Music* 5/1 (2008), 5–6.

[154] For example, in a discussion of how difficult it can be to 'sell' eighteenth-century music to music undergraduates – something with which it is easy to sympathize – Susan McClary writes: 'With the exception of the works of Bach, Mozart and Beethoven, all of whom are perceived – rightly or wrongly – to push the conventional envelope and thus to call for a brand of analysis that rewards transgression, the eighteenth-century repertory seems to students to lack substance. Note that I am including in this latter category Handel (an astonishing composer of melodies, which current music theory undervalues) and Haydn (the forger of many of the genres students have learned to regard as always already available); both these composers are very dear to me, and yet they are very hard sells so long as we are saddled with criteria that favour deviation. The one relatively unfamiliar rabbit I can pull out of my hat during that school term is C. P. E. Bach, whose music never fails to amaze.' While McClary is rightly leery of 'transgression' as a marker of worth, she nevertheless gives no sense that Haydn (and indeed Handel) might also be shown to 'deviate' from time to time in their compositions. McClary, 'Editorial', *Eighteenth-Century Music* 6/1 (2009), 3.

2 | Reciprocity

The Gracious Riposte

In the first chapter I suggested that sociability might be understood partly as a technical category – in other words, as relating to levels of musical syntax independent of affect. A stormy movement in the minor mode may contain few tokens of friendship towards the listener, but it may still be organized in a manner that we can understand as interactive, as involving relationships between different ideas and gestures. A key concept in this regard is reciprocity. Reciprocal thinking saturates later eighteenth-century instrumental style. We might grasp it by invoking various turns of phrase – *give and take, back and forth, question and answer, statement and response*, and the like – but these need not imply that two elements alone are in play over the course of a section or a movement. Rather, at any one point a number of binary relationships can be in operation, between phrase units, dynamic levels, textural types, registers, styles and so forth. These may interlock for a particular gesture – for instance, high register and soft dynamics may contrast with low and loud – but then go their separate ways immediately thereafter. The typically rapid turnover of material can then encourage the listener to hear these differences not as discrete features, as simple juxtapositions, but instead as being in some sort of responsive relationship to each other. And while at any one point we might hear a kind of oscillation on the level of the individual parameter – hence such explanatory concepts as give and take – when one then factors in the behaviour of other parameters the overall effect is more akin to a network of interactive gestures.

One could hardly claim that this reciprocity has not received due recognition in the literature, yet, as noted earlier, it has often been accounted simply a 'Classical' virtue, in the name of such artistic ideals as 'balance' and 'perfection'. This is particularly the case when it comes to one of the more intensively examined manifestations of the principle, periodic phrase syntax. As reinforced through a weighty pedagogical tradition, the arrangement of phrase units that are interdependent in terms of both their materials and their proportions is often portrayed as a primarily architectonic matter. The types of symmetry that result feed into an image of balance that excites no one, part of the wider image of a 'Classical' style that is satisfied with small returns. But reciprocity should not be understood in such a static fashion. We should try to recover a sense of the dynamism it could convey, as a property of the changeable style that marked the musical modernity of the time; as Julian Rushton reminds us, 'What academics later classified ... as models of balanced structure ... were novel for the composers who used them'.[1] In the eyes of hostile critics, this was not so much 'balanced' or 'perfect' as unprincipled, illogical, conveying no firm substance or consistent point of view, and while such objections may seem to have subsided as the changeable style turned into something like a lingua franca, countercurrents of hostility remained throughout the century.

Of course one thing that anchored what Charles Burney described in 1789 as the 'favourite desultory style of the present times'[2] was precisely periodic phrase syntax, the recursive arrangement of units of material that could yield a more transparent sense of musical structure than anything previously known. But one could also approach this from the opposite direction: clear-cut, short-order contrasts strengthen the force of the unprecedentedly accessible syntax. Such contrasts helped to provide sharp perceptual edges, encouraging a kind of 'structural hearing', though current wisdom is that such structure is primarily a matter of immediate concatenations – of how one short passage leads to the next short passage rather than the kind of global overview that 'structure' has normally tended to suggest.[3] In any case, such an idiom could only have prevailed given a sufficiently large number of musical agents – listeners, performers, critics, composers – who were prepared to accept this new mode of musical behaviour. This is, indeed, implicit in the notion of style – that, as Robert O. Gjerdingen has it, 'a musical style and its listeners mutually organize each other'.[4]

Aside from the pedagogical resonances that have accrued to reciprocal syntax, another obstacle to a fresh appreciation is simply how natural it appears to us. This goes beyond its domestication by means of classroom

---

[1] Rushton, *Classical Music*, 10. [2] Burney, *General History of Music, Volume the Second*, 449.
[3] The phrase 'structural hearing' alludes to the title of Felix Salzer's *Structural Hearing: Tonal Coherence in Music* (New York: Dover, 1962), which adopts the Schenkerian voice-leading perspective against which 'concatenationist' approaches have rebelled.
[4] Gjerdingen, 'Courtly Behaviors', 381.

example. A system of checks and balances must surely be a fundamental for any kind of composition – contours must be managed, levels of tension and energy controlled – and we can readily conceptualize this as a process of constant negotiation between different musical elements. Even just on the level of phrase structure, periodicity is hardly the exclusive property of the later eighteenth century. So why might one want to associate reciprocal utterance with this period in particular? The answer may lie in the way the product is packaged, the combination of brief units of utterance, periodic symmetrical syntax and clearly defined syntactical function forcing its way into the listener's consciousness, becoming an obvious attribute of the music's communicative regime. The reciprocity has a salience that is not readily matched elsewhere. Any music student will associate four-bar phrases with the music of this period rather than the following 'romantic' age, even though, as William Rothstein has pointed out, the four-bar phrase in fact becomes more entrenched in the nineteenth century, and phrase rhythms in general become squarer and less supple. This is what he dubs the 'Great Nineteenth-Century Rhythm Problem'.[5] Yet it is indicative that this property of romantic style has not registered in the same way.

It may be that the rate at which material alternates is what makes the difference. Certainly by the terms of most Western compositional styles, this property – the marked avoidance of long stretches of the same thing – is exceptional. It is anything but 'natural' by their standards. One of the most readily grasped embodiments of quick reciprocal action is what I have called the gracious riposte.[6] Typically, this means that an assertive musical gesture will be succeeded by a gentler one, where the latter has a concessive, mollifying force. Example 2.1, the opening of Pleyel's Quartet in E flat major Op. 1 No. 2 (1782–1783), demonstrates the pattern.

The opening couple of bars present a typical attention-grabbing gesture, whose dotted rhythms might trace their lineage to the French overture. The *fortissimo* dynamic marking, rising contour, staccato articulation and unison scoring all suggest forceful utterance. But rather than continue in the same vein, as would certainly have happened in the case of the French overture, this gesture is immediately countered in every way imaginable. The tutti presentation gives way to a solo violin, the loud dynamic is replaced by *piano*, and a mainly rising contour gives way to a falling one. Table 2.1 attempts to sum up these and other differences between the two

---

[5] William Rothstein, *Phrase Rhythm in Tonal Music* (New York: Schirmer, 1989), 184.
[6] So dubbed in Sutcliffe, 'The Shapes of Sociability', 6, from which most of the following paragraphs are taken ('The Shapes of Sociability', 6–9).

Example 2.1 Pleyel, Quartet in E flat major Op. 1 No. 2/i, bars 1–11[3]

musical gestures. Note that the gracious riposte also features a number of appoggiaturas (or sometimes restruck suspensions), which are a classic component of this style of answer. The most prominent of these, the ab^1–g^1 in first half of bar 5, encapsulates the opposition between the strong plain marking of the downbeats in the first three bars and the smoother handling of metrical accentuation that follows.

Such a network of relationships can clearly be thought to show reciprocal behaviour in action and hence embody sociability in a technical sense.

Table 2.1 Assertive and concessive gestures in Pleyel, Quartet in E flat major Op. 1 No. 2/i, bars 1–7

bars 1–3^2	bars 3^3–7^1
loud	soft
rising	falling
staccato	legato
unison	homophonic
downbeat-oriented	anacrusic
tutti	solo
dotted rhythmic values	even rhythmic values
monorhythmic	differentiated rhythm

A strong statement is counterbalanced by something that is socially smoother, that is more ingratiating. This need not imply that there is anything 'wrong' with the initial gesture in itself. However, if the music were to continue for too much longer in the same vein, it might become insufferable from a social point of view, given its categorical character. We need not construct a narrative reading in which one element must triumph over the other; as suggested in Chapter 1, the style of discourse is rather one of constant qualification. Indeed, it is precisely a sociable orientation that tolerates differences or disagreements and allows them to be constructively sustained.

That it is not really a question of a riposte that triumphs over the first utterance is apparent in the continuation from bar 7, after the softening phrase unit has come to an end. The melodic conduct in the first violin now mediates between the two impulses on a small scale, in its mix of falling legato pairs with rising staccato scales, which are now rendered in plain quaver rhythms. Only in the termination of the trills does the dotted rhythm live on. The way in which the viola line counterpoints that of the first violin, in each bar moving in the opposite direction, further suggests the attempt to negotiate an equilibrium, though as a whole this material remains in the domain of the gracious.

Pleyel's realization of the gracious riposte is representative of its class. In fact, the only unusual aspect to this example of reciprocal exchange is that normally the second part has stronger linear continuity than the first: in this case, the initial assertive material also moves largely by step, though the larger shape traced by successive downbeats is a rising triad. More typical in this respect is the opening of Daniel Gottlob Türk's Sonata No. 4 in C

Example 2.2 Türk, Sonata No. 4 in C major/i, from *Sechs leichte Klaviersonaten, Erster Teil*, bars 1–12

major from a collection of 'easy keyboard sonatas' published in 1783. Here the initial strong gesture is countered by a softer, higher melodic fragment that features just two skips amidst the predominant steps (Example 2.2). A further difference lies in the scale of the operation: the assertive and lyrical materials are shorter and alternate several times. Thus bars 3–4 replicate the exchange of the first two bars, with upward transposition of the right-hand part, and each alternation constitutes a unit within the larger structure. Together the two two-bar units form the presentation part of a musical sentence, meaning that on that larger scale the opposing sentiments are in fact working together to create continuity. This exemplifies the symbiosis of sharp contrast and periodic definition referred to earlier – the gestural contrast gives each part of the presentation a memorable character and aids perception of structure, while on the other hand the confinement of the gestures within a composite periodic unit controls the utterance.

The crisp contrasts of assertive and lyrical heard at the start of Türk's movement seem to highlight one of the pairings suggested in Table 2.1 – that of tutti versus solo. Indeed, many of the more immediately recognizable instances of the gracious riposte in forms such as the solo sonata or string quartet call to mind a symphonic idiom, in particular an Italianate

Example 2.3 Beethoven, Sonata in C minor Op. 10 No. 1/i, bars 1–16

overture idiom, which mingled with what we nowadays tend to think of as a separate genre – the symphonic first movement. Thus the collective force of a full ensemble is countered by a smaller grouping; the few modify the many. But these associations were readily absorbed into other instrumental media, becoming entirely idiomatic there. The opening movement of another solo sonata, Beethoven's Sonata in C minor Op. 10 No. 1 (1798; Example 2.3), begins similarly to Türk's. An initial loud tonic chord refracts into a jagged arpeggiated ascent, the composite gesture being countered by the briefest of ripostes, a harmonized falling-sigh figure. This riposte is effectively interrupted by a return of the assertive material before the sigh figure is then heard again, and the double pairing of gestures turns out once more to be the presentation phase of a sentence structure. Whereas the continuation part of Türk's sentence was dominated by the 'tutti' material, in Beethoven's case it is the lyrical motive that now expands, describing from bar 9 a series of stepwise descents that counter the rocketing arpeggios. In fact, each descending arc is initiated by a rising triad, thus co-opting an aspect of the assertive material for more lyrical ends. This rapprochement is taken further in the movement's second theme from bar 56, where the same arpeggiated rise (retaining a trace of the initial dotted rhythm) is followed by a falling step, but now without any contrast of dynamics or other separation of the two gestures. Instead, the two form a natural-sounding melodic contour.

The existence of the two-part gesture that I call the gracious riposte has been acknowledged often enough in the literature. But recognition of the pattern has mainly been confined to opening statements, and its larger behavioural implications have not regularly been explored. The very fact that there is no generally agreed name for the phenomenon might be indicative; like many aspects of this repertoire, it may be so familiar that we simply take it for granted. Modern commentators often describe it by invoking opposed expressive stances, as indeed I have myself done. Thus we have such adjectival pairs as 'bold' and 'timid', 'aggressive' and 'pleading', 'stern' and 'tender', and 'assertive' and 'receptive'. These refer to music by Tartini, Vivaldi, Haydn and Mozart respectively,[7] the former two references suggesting that the procedure was not native to the later eighteenth century. Yet, as argued earlier, the clearer syntactical packaging at that time does mean that the alternation of gestures is liable to be experienced more vividly. In fact, some writers imply that the technique is specifically Mozart's. These include Leonard Ratner, who notes how the composer's Sonata in C minor, K457 (1784), begins by 'alternat[ing] bold tutti figures with legato song-like figures in pathetic style' before suggesting that this 'became a model for a similar opening statement in the Jupiter Symphony written four years later'.[8] Of course, viewing later eighteenth-century music through a Mozartean lens – in this case suggesting that the composer was borrowing from himself rather than simply realizing anew a common gestural type – has been a recurring impediment to a better balanced appreciation of our repertory.

While Charles Rosen provides a wider perspective with his discussion of the category of the theme with 'built-in contrast' that 'represents opposing

---

[7] Daniel Heartz, *Music in European Capitals: The Galant Style, 1720–1780* (New York: Norton, 2003), 224 (Tartini's Violin Concerto in D major D39 'begins with an idea that has both "bold" and "timid" components ... within the same theme'); Michael Talbot and Janice B. Stockigt, 'Two More New Vivaldi Finds in Dresden', *Eighteenth-Century Music* 3/1 (2006), 53 ('Characteristic, too, is the pleading *piano* phrase that responds to the aggressive unison opening ... ; Vivaldi was a pioneer in the creation of an opposition between a (so-called) masculine antecedent and a feminine consequent.'); Webster, 'Haydn's Symphonies between *Sturm und Drang* and "Classical Style"', 240 (the slow introduction to Haydn's Symphony No. 71 'contrasts topics of stern majesty and tenderness or pleading'); and Eric F. Clarke, *Ways of Listening: An Ecological Approach to the Perception of Musical Meaning* (New York: Oxford University Press, 2005), 86 (at the opening of the development section of Mozart's quintet K515 'the cello and violin parts specify very different kinds of motion (one assertive and energetic, the other receptive and accommodating)').

[8] Leonard Ratner, 'Topical Content in Mozart's Keyboard Sonatas', *Early Music* 19/4 (1991), 616. When he implies the Mozart-specificity of the technique Ratner keeps distinguished company. See also Robert S. Hatten, who compares the use of 'dialectical oppositions' in just these two works in *Interpreting Musical Gestures, Topics, and Tropes: Mozart, Beethoven, Schubert* (Bloomington: Indiana University Press, 2004), 135, while Daniel Heartz notes how Mozart's violin sonata K454, together with the slow introductions to the composer's 'Linz' Symphony in C major (K425) and Quintet for Piano and Winds in E flat major (K452), 'alternate loud, forceful chords with soft, pleading melodies, mostly falling by step': *Mozart, Haydn and Early Beethoven, 1781–1802* (New York: Norton, 2009), 56–57.

sentiments',[9] which he believes comes to the fore in the late eighteenth century, most of his examples also derive from Mozart. The opening of the 'Jupiter' Symphony (K551; 1788) – a clear example of big being answered by small – features once more, though Rosen's emphasis lies on the way in which the counterstatement from bar 24 liquidates the contrast between the two initial gestures, a loud tutti call to attention (bars 1–2^1) and a soft lyrical response that features three separate appoggiatura-resolution pairs (bars 2^4–4^3). In the counterstatement the 'opposition' between the two elements 'has disappeared, united by the flute obbligato'[10] that covers the original gap between them. Not noted by Rosen, but strengthening his reading, is the fact that this counterstatement is given at a uniform *piano* level. When one then takes account of the fact that the movement's initial eight bars of *forte-piano* alternations are followed by a full fifteen bars of swaggering tutti, an unrelieved procession of grand gestures, it becomes apparent that our assertive–concessive pairing is also operating on a larger scale. The timbrally mediated soft counterstatement, incorporating both the original *tirata* and the lyrical rejoinder, acts as a second-order gracious riposte to the entire first section (bars 1–23).[11]

Something akin to our gracious-riposte formula is invoked by James Hepoksoski and Warren Darcy's description of the 'strong-launch option' for the first theme of a sonata-form movement, which may feature 'an initial *forte* basic idea . . . riddled with back-and-forth interpolated *piano* responses – hesitant, gentler, contrasting, or questioning replies, as in J. C. Bach, much of Mozart, and so on'.[12] But perhaps the nearest theoretical approximation to our category is to be found in Gjerdingen's account of galant phraseology, which has a propensity to offer 'paired gestures simulating . . . on-the-one-hand-on-the-other-hand forms of rhetoric'. Within that regime, 'one preferred riposte acted to balance an assertive, ascending

---

[9] Charles Rosen, *Music and Sentiment* (New Haven: Yale University Press, 2010), 50.
[10] Rosen, *Music and Sentiment*, 52.
[11] In a review of *Music and Sentiment*, Michael Spitzer suggests that the labelling of emotions in Rosen's account of the passage is less to the point than 'the symbolic sociability of Mozart's question-response dialogues', in which the 'complementary sentiments of Mozart's subphrases . . . echo and cleave to each other like those of feeling subjects' – in other words, that any supposed opposition between the gestures is less important than the larger sociable process of which they form distinct parts. Spitzer, review of Charles Rosen, *Music and Sentiment*, *Music & Letters* 93/2 (2012), 223. Carl Dahlhaus offers a further perspective on the complementary nature of the symphony's opening gestures when noting the reciprocal relationships between harmony, 'governed by an xyyx shape', and motive, governed 'by an xyxy shape'. Further, the two ideas are 'governed by the same basic dotted rhythm'. Dahlhaus, *Die Musik des 18. Jahrhunderts*, 47.
[12] Hepokoski and Darcy, *Elements of Sonata Theory*, 66.

Example 2.4 Abel, Keyboard Concerto in B flat major, Op. 11 No. 2/ii, bars 1–8

opening gambit with a concessive, descending pattern'.[13] The most typical of these descending patterns is what Gjerdingen, reviving a term invented by Joseph Riepel, has labelled the 'Prinner Riposte'. Occupying the second half of a phrase, the Prinner operates on the basis of paired tenths between outer voices that fall by a fourth: $\hat{6}$–$\hat{5}$–$\hat{4}$–$\hat{3}$ in the upper voice together with $\hat{4}$–$\hat{3}$–$\hat{2}$–$\hat{1}$ in the bass.[14] Example 2.4, from the final movement of Abel's keyboard concerto Op. 11 No. 2 (1774), shows an instance of the schema beginning in bar 5, in this case extending down to a half cadence on $\hat{2}$ over the dominant.[15] Given its falling stepwise contour and its answering function within the larger phrase unit, this shares much with the category I am pursuing: a Prinner riposte is likely also to be a gracious one. Gjerdingen's characterization of the device is a little different, though. He relates the larger pattern to an imagined world of courtly conversation in which the second half represents an 'elegant' reply, 'a certain flair at just the right moment'.[16] This may indeed be the effect, but such a characterization is too narrow to cover even the few samples we have considered above. By the same token, my 'gracious' should hardly be regarded as a binding attribute, merely an approximation of the characteristic affect. The main analogy

---

[13] Gjerdingen, 'Courtly Behaviors', 368.
[14] See the discussion, for example, in Gjerdingen, 'Courtly Behaviors', and then the fuller description in Gjerdingen, *Music in the Galant Style*, especially chapter 3, 45–60, where the term used has been shortened to 'Prinner'.
[15] Compare this with the sole example of such an extension given by Gjerdingen in *Music in the Galant Style*, from a solfeggio by Giovanni Aprile, in his Example 3.16, page 54.
[16] Gjerdingen, *Music in the Galant Style*, 45.

should be discursive rather than emotive: the core of the technique is simply the fact of riposte, of one gesture 'answering' or contradicting or completing another. This brings us back to the notion of technical sociability, whereby reciprocity is more fundamental than any affective sequence that we try to define verbally. The most expressively specific thing about the individual elements is how they contrast with others; their 'relational content' is easier to define than any intrinsic character they possess.[17]

If the gracious riposte has been an irregular subject of attention in more recent literature, the same would certainly apply to the musical writings of the eighteenth century. Recognition tends to be more implicit than overt, and, as has also been the case in our times, it tends to involve the attribution of contrasting expressive characteristics.[18] Türk himself in fact wrote that 'if a passage of gentle sensitivity [von sanfter Empfindung] follows a fiery and brisk thought, then both periods must ... be more carefully separated than would be necessary if they were of the same character',[19] which not only recognizes the sort of affective sequence we saw realized in his own sonata movement but also testifies to the encapsulation of the individual affects within discrete phrase units. In a 1779 issue of his *Betrachtungen der Mannheimer Tonschule* Georg Joseph Vogler referred to symphonies having two main themes, the first strong and giving material for thematic development, the second gentle, mediating the heated din and offering the listener a pleasing change of pace: 'In den [S]infonien befinden sich meistentheils zwei Hauptsätze. Erstens ein starker, der zur Ausführung den Stof giebt. Zweitens ein sanfter, der die hizigen Getöse vermittelt und das Gehör in einer angenehmen Abwechslung erhält.'[20]

---

[17] Gregory Karl outlines this (structuralist) position thus: 'the semantic and expressive qualities we can reasonably attribute to passages of absolute music in isolation ... are necessarily unspecific. ... elements only vaguely defined as to their intrinsic expressive qualities and semantic potential may yet be defined with considerable precision in relational terms with respect to other elements'. Karl, 'Structuralism and Musical Plot', *Music Theory Spectrum* 19/1 (1997), 18–19.

[18] Elaine Sisman notes that instead of identifying topics, as we modern analysts would like them to have done, writers on music of the time tended to focus on contrasts of character: they 'do no more than discuss the contrasting "character" of different parts of a piece ("strong" and "gentle", "singing" and "roaring")'. Sisman, 'Genre, Gesture, and Meaning in Mozart's "Prague" Symphony', in *Mozart Studies 2*, ed. Cliff Eisen (Oxford: Clarendon, 1997), 50.

[19] Daniel Gottlob Türk, *Klavierschule, oder Anweisung zum Klavierspielen für Lehrer und Lernende* (Leipzig: Schwickert and Halle: Hemmerde und Schwetschke, 1789), 342, cited in translation in Stephanie D. Vial, *The Art of Musical Phrasing in the Eighteenth Century: Punctuating the Classical 'Period'* (Rochester, NY: University of Rochester Press, 2008), 167.

[20] Georg Joseph Vogler, *Betrachtungen der Mannheimer Tonschule* 2/1 (1779), 62, cited in Jane Stevens, 'Georg Joseph Vogler and the "Second Theme" in Sonata Form: Some 18th-Century

The context of the discussion and the examples Vogler gives to support his claim suggest that he is referring not to the two themes of a sonata-form first movement, as we might assume, but in fact to the opening material alone, making this a notably direct contemporary acknowledgment of our category. Of one particular example he remarks: 'Der zweite Period würde mit seinen sanften Pinselzügen lang nicht jenen Eindruck machen, wenn das rasche nicht vorhergegangen wäre'[21] (The second phrase, with its gentle brush-strokes, would make nothing like this impression if the lively one hadn't preceded it). As Türk does, Vogler characterizes the second unit as being gentle or soft ('sanft'), and it is notable that he understands it as helping to sharpen listener perception, to bring a piece of material to life simply through clear contrast. Ultimately, he seems to place greater weight on the more 'technical sociable' terms of syntactical clarity and mutual definition than on the 'affective sociable' terms of withdrawing from assertive behaviour. One can also find negative testimony to the riposte technique: Johann Georg Sulzer warned that the composer 'must be especially careful when composing longer themes that consist of several smaller segments [*Einschnitten*] to observe the closest cohesion so that the main theme possesses real unity and is not just a pairing of two different ideas'.[22] This suggests that Sulzer has heard themes with internal contrast, quite probably along our lines of assertive/conciliatory, and thinks they are improper.

Further contemporary recognition is apparent in Burney's comment on Johann Christian Bach:

Bach seems to have been the first composer who obeyed the law of *contrast*, as a *principle*. Before his time, contrast there frequently was, in the works of others; but it seems to have been accidental. Bach in his symphonies and other instrumental

---

Perceptions of Musical Contrast', *The Journal of Musicology* 2/3 (1983), 280, note 9. Stevens argues that Vogler refers to internal contrast within a theme rather than to the familiar first theme/second theme division of later sonata-form terminology.

[21] Vogler, *Betrachtungen der Mannheimer Tonschule* 1/5–6 (1778), 148, cited in Stevens, 'Vogler and the "Second Theme" in Sonata Form', 284, note 24.

[22] Sulzer, *Allgemeine Theorie der Schönen Künste*, volume 2, 489, cited in translation in *Aesthetics and the Art of Musical Composition in the German Enlightenment*, ed. and trans. Baker and Christensen, 102. Regarding authorship, it is known that Sulzer sought the help of both Johann Philipp Kirnberger and Johann Abraham Peter Schulz on more technical musical matters. Christensen comments that 'it is not possible to disentangle with certainty the respective contributions' of all, and cites the entry from which the current extract is taken, 'Hauptsatz' (Main Theme), as an example, since it plainly mixes aesthetic and technical considerations: Introduction, *Aesthetics and the Art of Musical Composition in the German Enlightenment*, 14, note 23.

pieces, as well as his songs, seldom failed, after a rapid and noisy passage to introduce one that was slow and soothing.[23]

The succession of 'rapid and noisy' and 'slow and soothing', in that order, certainly approaches the idea of the gracious riposte. Significantly, there is no suggestion of a hierarchy between these two types of material, but simply an assertion that contrast is deliberate and part of an aesthetic programme.[24] The 'noisy' and 'soothing' are interdependent; they mutually define each other. That they can work together rather than simply representing a flat contrast is apparent in a 1787 review of a violin sonata by Johann Ludwig Willing that contained an Allegro 'where liveliness and charm offer their hands to each other' ('wo Munterkeit und Annhemlichkeit sich beyde die Hände bieten').[25] This is a nice way of describing the reciprocal play of different sensibilities, imagined as actual gesture.

That Burney describes the fact of contrast as a 'law' suggests that contrast forms a fundamental in the system, and that it could be taken as read at that time. But his description also starts to move us towards the wider view of the gracious-riposte pattern that I believe is necessary: Burney also implies that this contrast could operate on a larger scale, and was not necessarily confined to opening positions. Ratner in fact has provided a modern confirmation of this, moving beyond a preoccupation with Mozart when he states that 'the contrast between the brilliant-vigorous and the gentle-cantabile ... permeates classic rhetoric on every scale of magnitude'. He makes an intriguing suggestion about the origins of such contrast, that it was 'probably a continuation of the tutti-solo relationship of baroque music'.[26] If accepted, this would remind us once more that gracious-riposte technique was not new in the later eighteenth century, though it surely was reimagined and intensified – in other words, what Burney termed 'accidental contrast' in music prior to J. C. Bach becomes a calculated point of principle in his modern musical style. Further, Ratner's 'tutti-solo' relationship will not necessarily involve a contrast of materials, and, similarly, the Prinner need not be marked by a dynamic or textural change from the

---

[23] Burney, *General History of Music, Volume the Second*, 866.
[24] The last few sentences and several from the start of the following paragraph derive from Sutcliffe, 'The Shapes of Sociability', 11–12.
[25] Anonymous, *Neue Leipziger gelehrte Zeitungen* 3/2 49 (26 April 1787), cited in Mary Sue Morrow, *German Music Criticism in the Late Eighteenth Century: Aesthetic Issues in Instrumental Music* (Cambridge: Cambridge University Press, 1997), 124 (translation) and 218 (German original).
[26] Ratner, *Classic Music*, 219.

preceding unit; the extract from Abel shown in Example 2.4 features no such differentiation.

Ratner does not frame his definition of contrast in our terms, as a form of social action. One aspect of the riposte, however, has been consistently understood by writers in just this way: the appoggiatura, associated with a softening of utterance. Türk once more is a useful contemporary witness, in recommending to the performer that material that needs to be played in a 'defiant and sharply accented manner' should not be ornamented by appoggiaturas, 'because through them the melody would receive a certain smoothness which, in such cases, would not be desirable'.[27] Heinrich Christoph Koch associated appoggiaturas with 'the pleasing passions' ('die angenehmen Leidenschaften'), and in fact included them in a collocation of attributes that comes close to our definition of the gracious riposte: these pleasing passions produce 'notes that are more gently legato than staccato and generally also more conjunct than disjunct, with fewer sharp accents in the whole, but with a stronger and more swelling stress on the appoggiaturas'.[28] That appoggiaturas could supply an affective charge in their own right can be confirmed, once more, by hostile reaction: a 1769 review of a sonata movement by Georg Simon Löhlein (1725–1781) characterized its chromatic appoggiaturas as merely 'fashionable prettiness' ('bloß eine Modeschönheit')[29]. This also suggests that an abundance of them was a marked feature of the modern musical manner.

Among more recent (and positively minded) writers, Robert S. Hatten tries to define the social character of the falling stepwise two-note slur that is found so often in our repertory; appoggiaturas will naturally form an important part of this category. While this short slur may represent a plaintive sigh, more often this figure becomes the 'musical analogue to ... ritualized social gestures' such as bows and nods. When appearing in its characteristic location of 'the weak-beat galant cadence[, it] captures the ... character of all gracious social gesturing in the eighteenth century, male and female alike'.[30] Hatten's final phrase reinforces his disavowal of the familiar term 'feminine cadence' for this musical event. Matthew Head might agree when he describes the musical aesthetics of the later eighteenth century

---

[27] Türk, *Klavierschule*, 206n, cited in translation in Vial, *The Art of Musical Phrasing*, 187.
[28] Heinrich Christoph Koch, *Musikalisches Lexikon* (Frankfurt am Main: August Hermann der Jüngere, 1802), 'Leidenschaft, Affect', 898, cited in translation in Allanbrook, *Secular Commedia*, 68. Allanbrook translates 'die angenehmen Leidenschaften' as 'tender passions'; I prefer the apparently milder 'pleasing'.
[29] Anonymous, *Unterhaltungen* 7/5 (May 1769), cited in Morrow, *German Music Criticism*, 53 (translation) and 182 (German original).
[30] Hatten, *Interpreting Musical Gestures*, 140.

altogether as aspiring towards an 'androgynous balance of antithetical elements',[31] of which our gracious-riposte pattern would represent a particular embodiment. Nevertheless, it is undeniable that characterizations of the gracious element may well invoke perceived feminine virtues – or indeed vices, as 'fashionable prettiness' aimed to do. Femininity forms one of a set of associations that cluster around our riposte: appoggiatura-stepwise-galant-gracious-tender-smooth, a mixture of character traits, specific musical phenomena and stylistic imprints. This mixture might also correspond to Johann Adolph Scheibe's definition of the 'middle style' as 'ingenious, pleasing and fluent' ('sinnreich, angenehm und fließend'), as opposed to a 'high style' that 'must be stately and emphatic' ('prächtig und nachdrücklich').[32] This suggests hearing our pairing of assertive and gracious as high being answered by middle, a function of class rather than gender politics, but this is just one possibility: the assertive gesture may also be heard as rough and the gracious as a civilizing move, and therefore 'higher' up the scale of social virtues.

This brings us back to the priority we should give to a 'technical' reading of the pattern as a whole. While it is the gracious unit that carries the sociable character as such, it is in the interaction as a whole that the sociable process lies. The softening words only assume their full meaning in relation to material that is less so. To imagine a whole style comprised of gentle, conciliatory utterance would be to deprive the discourse of tension, to make it idyllic rather than properly social.[33] We also need to grasp that the 'pleasing' itself need not mean 'bland', as the image of a 'Classical' moderation of extremes can readily suggest. Elisabeth Le Guin, for example, notes the sensation of pleasure or 'gratification' that may arise for a performer when realizing a gesture of withdrawal. In the first movement of a Boccherini cello sonata in E flat major a passage that features a series of descending lines after a 'precarious starting point' in the treble clef shows 'retreat and subsiding manifest[ing themselves] as desirable'.[34] This feeling of gratification may of course be experienced by listeners as well.

That the process of interaction ultimately counts for more than a set sequence of social-musical events is apparent in the fact that our pattern may be reversed. Stephen Rumph notes an instance of this in the first

---

[31] Matthew Head, *Sovereign Feminine: Music and Gender in Eighteenth-Century Germany* (Berkeley: University of California Press, 2013), 17.
[32] Scheibe, *Der critische Musikus*, 128 and 126.
[33] The last three sentences derive from Sutcliffe, 'Simplifying Cadence', 167.
[34] Elisabeth Le Guin, *Boccherini's Body: An Essay in Carnal Musicology* (Berkeley: University of California Press, 2006), 18 and 19.

movement of Mozart's Piano Concerto in B flat major K450 (1784), which opens with 'the lyrical motive tak[ing] the lead' in oboes and bassoons, followed by a 'triadic fanfare' in first violins which by rights ought to have been heard first.[35] While there is no doubt about the basic reversal of presentation, various factors mute the sense of contrast. The exchange takes place at a uniform *piano* level, and the beginning and end of the first violins' answering figure represent less a fanfare than a continuation of the wind instruments' material. Matters seem to be more straightforward in the opening bars of Haydn's Quartet in B flat major Op. 55 No. 3 (1788): four bars of *piano* material are followed by four bars of contrasting material played *forte*. In many other respects, though, the sequence of events matches the norm. Bars 1–4 are in unison, and therefore a kind of call to attention, and while each bar features a slurred stepwise pair of notes, each of these is connected by leap; then bars 5–8 are harmonized, more melodic in character and more predominantly stepwise. On the other hand, with its strange contours and uncertain tonal sense (it begins on B♭ and finishes on an E♮), the opening unison sounds more mysterious than assertive – it is hardly a firm enunciation. From that point of view, when the lyrical consequent bursts in *forte*, restoring a sense of diatonic order, it does indeed carry the greater authority.[36] In mixing and matching expressive signals in such a manner, Haydn manages to have it both ways at once.

Some sort of gestural reversal is particularly likely in symphonic style, though this begins to take us away from the smaller-scale, more readily recognizable operation of the riposte pattern towards a broader management of character contrast. Within first movements, a slow introduction makes an unassuming start to the quicker material particularly likely, as we hear in the case of Mozart's 'Linz' Symphony, K425 (1783). The theme of this Allegro spiritoso sets out quietly; it is in our terms entirely gracious. It turns out, though, to be a ten-bar antecedent to a loud tutti consequent, so that now the gracious is answered by the assertive in an 'assertive riposte'.[37]

---

[35] Rumph, *Mozart and Enlightenment Semiotics*, 127.

[36] Note Charles Rosen's account of this movement in *The Classical Style*, 130–131. He makes much of the conjunction of the E♮ that finishes the first unit and the first violin's E♭ that opens the second, an awkward transition that somewhat weakens my claim that bars 5–8 restore diatonic order. An obvious point of comparison with Haydn's strange opening – which heralds a thoroughly angular and cryptic movement – is the opening of Mozart's Quartet in E flat major K428 (1783), which forms part of the set that the composer dedicated to Haydn. It is therefore possible that, just a few years later, Haydn decided to take up the challenge of Mozart's equally odd *exordium*.

[37] Hepokoski and Darcy, *Elements of Sonata Theory*, 66, refer to this as the 'weak-launch option' for a primary theme, and note that it is 'especially attractive after a slow introduction'. However, they note that this option 'invites a [transition] of the *forte* affirmation or restatement type',

In this case the immediate contrast is purely one of dynamics, not of material, which remains the same. However, the theme soon takes on a different cast: the understated IV–I progression that ended the first four-bar phrase of the Allegro (bar 23) is transformed at bars 33–36 into a series of repeated IV–I alternations that radiate majesty – certainly in this instance an example of high style.[38] But this larger scale of reversal is hardly confined to symphonies. The first movement of Gaetano Brunetti's Quartet in A major L191 (1792) opens most unusually without a theme; instead, we hear *pianissimo* tonic chords in the lower three instruments, one per downbeat. Melodic material emerges only in bar 5, and, while it has a clear lyrical impulse, it does not organize itself into anything that could be called a 'theme'. The ensuing music seems to linger in pastoral fashion rather than suggest a sense of direction. The opening material is then repeated from bar 17, but with the harmony soon swerving into the submediant, F sharp minor; this only increases the sense of stasis, pleasant though that may be. However, the passage is quickly inflected by *rinf.* markings, and eventually by means of a *crescendo* we reach a brilliant transition. This represents a negative image of the usual assertive–gracious dynamic. In this case, especially given that this is an opening movement, there is too much gentleness, and indeed the gentle material doesn't seem to know how to behave in its unaccustomed opening slot; thus an injection of assertive energy is needed to generate a sense of momentum.

One larger-scale manifestation of the gracious riposte will come as a surprise to no one: its use as a secondary theme. Something of this sort is enshrined in sonata-form lore, and was being stipulated as early as 1796 when Francesco Galeazzi wrote that a theme that falls in the middle of the first section (what he called 'Il Passo Caratteristico, o Passo di mezzo') 'must be gentle, expressive and tender in almost all kinds of compositions' ('dolce, espressivo e tenero quasi in ogni genere di composizione').[39]

---

which would not apply to the current case, since Mozart's 'assertive riposte' is clearly an altered/expanded consequent phrase rather than a transition. It leads to a firm cadence in the tonic before the transition gets underway.

[38] Richard Will is one writer who recognizes not just the gracious riposte as I have formulated it here, but also the possibility of reversing the equation. Of Haydn's Symphony No. 71 he notes that, after the slow introduction, its Allegro 'suggests a similar encounter [to the assertive–gracious opening of Haydn's Symphony No. 82] but in reverse', with 'a languid, descending arpeggio' being 'answered by a loud, unison voice'. Will, 'When God Met the Sinner, and Other Dramatic Confrontations in Eighteenth-Century Instrumental Music', *Music & Letters* 78/4 (1997), 194.

[39] Francesco Galeazzi, *Elementi teorico-pratici di musica*, two volumes, volume 2 (Rome: Puccinelli, 1796), part 4, section 2, paragraph 30. For further discussion see Siegfried Schmalzriedt, 'Charakter und Drama: Zur historischen Analyse von Haydnschen und

However, we should not assume, as sonata lore has it, that this gentler theme is in dialogue specifically with the opening material. It may be responding not so much to the first-theme area but to what has come immediately before it – the typically vigorous, often rough gestures of a transition section, often enough given in an unrelieved *forte* dynamic.[40] This seems to be the case, to name just one example, in the first movement of J. C. Bach's Sonata in D major Op. 5 No. 2 (1766), and when the new theme arrives in bar 19, the composer quickly signals the change of tone not just through a reduction to *piano*, but also by means of a Lombard rhythm, with its connotations of playful elegance.[41]

On the other hand, in the first movement of Clementi's violin sonata Op. 15 No. 1 (1786) the second theme is plainly in dialogue with the first (Example 2.5a and b). It in fact opens in bar 30 with the same material that we heard at the outset, but transforms it in almost every way. The original motto, heard twice in bars 1–4 at a decisive *forte* dynamic, is now played *pianissimo*, and the original rising staccato crotchet dyads are inverted so as to fall by step (compare bars 2 and 31). The bass, which originally played more or less in rhythmic unison with the motto, now features repeated-note crotchets; at *pp* these clearly aid the softening of utterance. Thus, while the reuse of the opening material from bar 30 is significant in that it acts as a formal marker for the listener, the changes are even more so – they enact on a large scale our pairing of assertive and conciliatory gestures. More commonly, of course, this is done by means of straightforward thematic contrast. There is a further level of mollification, in that the two-bar motto is not then repeated, as happened at the opening. Instead, bars 32–33 offer a separate level of reciprocity as the violin now answers the piano with a lyrical figure that features a very prominent appoggiatura in its second bar, reached by downward leap of a sixth. The

---

Beethovenschen Sonatensätzen', *Archiv für Musikwissenschaft* 42/1 (1985), 37–66, and Bathia Churgin, 'Francesco Galeazzi's Description (1796) of Sonata Form', *Journal of the American Musicological Society* 21/2 (1968), 181–199.

[40] This seems to be the conclusion reached by Mark Richards when trying to answer the question of why second themes so often begin at a soft dynamic level. Following up on Hepokoski and Darcy's term 'energy gain', in which a loud dynamic is maintained all through a transition, Richards suggests that a *piano* beginning to the following section provides a striking contrast. Richards, 'Sonata Form and the Problem of Second-Theme Beginnings', *Music Analysis* 32/1 (2013), 11.

[41] Quantz hears a 'cheeky' quality in such rhythms: 'Das Freche wird mit Noten, wo hinter der zweyten oder dritten ein Punct steht... vorgestellt'. Quantz, *Versuch einer Anweisung die Flöte traversiere zu spielen*, 116, cited in Josef Gmeiner, *Menuett und Scherzo: Ein Beitrag zur Entwicklungsgeschichte und Soziologie des Tanzsatzes in der Wiener Klassik* (Tutzing: Schneider, 1979), 67.

Example 2.5a Clementi, Violin Sonata in E flat major Op. 15 No. 1/i, bars 1–8

Example 2.5b Clementi, Violin Sonata in E flat major Op. 15 No. 1/i, bars 28–37[1]

whole four-bar unit is then reiterated in a reciprocal harmonization at bars 34–37 so as to offer a larger-scale sense of lyrical composure. In fact Clementi subsequently repeats the entire eight-bar passage later in the exposition, from bar 62, where it now acts as a closing theme after the decisive cadence in the dominant; and, as had also happened earlier, it offsets the busier, predominantly *forte* figurative writing that has been heard in the interim.

This postcadential placement of a larger-scale gracious riposte is by no means unusual, though in fact the riposte technique may occur at any juncture. And while the most readily identifiable forms tend to be symmetrical, with the two gestures being of comparable dimensions, this need not be so, as the preceding Clementi example has shown – the eight-bar gracious ripostes are quite compact in comparison with the assertive passages that they temper. The initial eight-bar sentence of Beethoven's Sonata in F minor Op. 2 No. 1 (1795) offers another instance, on a smaller scale: after six bars that feature rising staccato arpeggios and a broader ascent built around accelerating use of the main rhythmic motive, the falling stepwise legato reply occupies just the final two bars of the phrase. When the second theme arrives, from bar 20, we hear a more sustained form of riposte: keeping the same basic rhythm as heard during the first two-bar unit, and the same arpeggiated basis, the riposte inverts the rising contour of the initial theme and substitutes legato for detached articulation.

If the gracious riposte need not be confined within a single thematic or form-functional area, and may operate on a broader canvas, one should also note that it is not confined to fast outer movements, as our examples thus far might suggest. The scherzo movement from Peter Hänsel's Quartet in D major Op. 5 No. 3 (1797) is spiky and syncopated throughout aside from a single six-bar phrase that begins the second section, from the last beat of bar 30. This suddenly switches to a smoother legato manner, featuring longer note values and a fuller texture. As gracious ripostes are liable to be, the material here is relatively plain, less 'characteristic' than what it moderates, but it still has a powerful effect in context: amidst eighty-odd bars when the players seem to be fighting against the metre, this is the one moment of regularity and lyrical repose, strengthened by a move to the subdominant, G major. As if to allow it a greater chance to speak, the composer then bases his Trio on the material and character of this single cantabile phrase, and this thus forms a longer-range riposte to the scherzo section as a whole.

A striking slow-movement example comes from the Adagio of Haydn's Sonata in E minor H34 (1784; Example 2.6). The build-up towards the

Example 2.6 Haydn, Sonata in E minor H34/ii, bars 12–20

close of the first section features a tarrying on the supertonic in bar 15 (an instance of the Indugio schema[42]), followed by a full bar first of V6/4 then of V5/3, the melody working its way towards a bar-long cadential trill at 17, at which point the left hand suddenly plunges down to a low A octave. This all adds up to a surprisingly grand approach towards a cadence, seemingly out of scale with the intimate, intricate lyrical writing with which the movement began. What follows the arrival on the local tonic at bar 18^1 can once more be referred to the principle of the gracious riposte. Most of the melodic lines to this point have tended to drive upwards, whereas now we hear a huge arc of downward movement, a lengthy descending scale in demisemiquavers followed by a slower line that continues to trace an overall downward trajectory, especially marked in a leap down from d^1 to e at bar 19^3. And we hear the signature use of accented dissonances on the downbeats of bars 18 and 19, though neither is technically an appoggiatura (the a♯ at 18 is an accented chromatic passing note and the c♯ at 19 a restruck suspension). The melody then finishes on d, way lower than we could have imagined given the generally high tessitura of the earlier melodic lines. The bass similarly descends to previously unsuspected depths. These bars patently represent a withdrawal after the lengthy cadential build-up that we have just heard. The 'bold' is answered by

---

[42] For a definition see Gjerdingen, *Music in the Galant Style*, chapter 20, 273–283.

something much gentler, but, unlike our previous example by Hänsel, one would be hard pushed to find the riposte less characterful than the material it counteracts. In fact, the wide downward arc, expansive enough in its own right, makes for a decidedly poignant conclusion. This reminds us once more that the gracious riposte may be best understood as a habitual gesture connoting withdrawal that need not have any particular affect attached to it.

For all that, several composers of the time did try to thematize such a contrast by invoking 'moral characters'.[43] In the case of Dittersdorf's symphony *Il combattimento delle passioni umani* (c1771) this takes place between the first two of its seven movements, with *Il Superbo* (Pride) being succeeded by *Il Humile* (Humility).[44] *Il Superbo* is in the grand key of D major. Played tutti almost throughout, it offers a panoply of ceremonial features: open intervals, fanfare-like flourishes, dotted rhythms, and also 'Hallelujah'-like motives of the sort we noted in the first movement of Mozart's 'Linz' Symphony. Some of these gestures may derive from the French overture, and certainly encourage our earlier association of the assertive component with high style. The succeeding movement, *Il Humile*, is in D minor, for strings only, to be performed *sempre piano*. The parts move mostly by step, creating a fundamental contrast of gesture that finds an obvious parallel in real human behaviour: large musical intervals connote confident, big gestures, while small intervals suggest a more contained and careful comportment.

A similar programme is at play in Francisco Javier Moreno's single-movement sinfonia 'a grand'orchestra titolata le due opposti caratteri Superbia ed Umiltà', written in the early 1800s for performance between the acts of operas and plays at the Madrid theatre Los Caños del Peral.[45] In this case, though, the 'opposed characters' are contained within a single movement, and they interact throughout. The Introduzione, marked Maestoso, begins with a typical call to attention – unison, *forte*, built

---

[43] For some background on this concept see Richard Will, *The Characteristic Symphony in the Age of Haydn and Beethoven* (Cambridge: Cambridge University Press, 2002), 4ff. The concept may fit the Dittersdorf symphony particularly well given that each movement of his work is ostensibly devoted to portraying one moral or character type; on page 137 Will points out that this may well have gained the approval of German critics who were disturbed by the admixture of affects they heard within single movements.

[44] Richard Will, *Characteristic Symphony*, 257, gives the title of this movement as 'L'Umile', but the edition I have consulted, ed. Allan Badley (Wellington: Artaria, 1995), based on the Kremsmünster source, has 'Il Humile'.

[45] Jacqueline A. Shadko, Introduction to *The Symphony in Madrid: Seven Symphonies*, ed. Shadko (New York: Garland, 1981), xiii.

around the tonic triad and with prominent dotted rhythms. In bars 3–4 comes the 'humble' reply – *piano*, with even quaver rhythms, a more lyrical flavour, and a chromatic accented passing note-cum-appoggiatura that softens the outline. These two gestural types alternate fairly quickly, and the 'proud' adds to its repertoire some flashing arpeggio figures. After thirty bars, this gives way to an Allegro in 3/4, and it is the 'humble' that now begins proceedings while the 'proud' has the interrupting role. This is another example of that common symphonic procedure that we noted above in the case of Mozart's 'Linz' Symphony. The 'humble' material earns its name by virtue of its phrase syntax, which is always regular and uncomplicated, its texture, which is generally quite thin, and a predominantly soft dynamic level. Moreno continues to alternate the two types at short intervals throughout the movement, without noticeable development in the rhythms of the exchange. This might suggest that while they are opposed, the proud and humble are also interdependent – they work in tandem to create a broader continuity.

A much better-known movement, the Andante con moto of Beethoven's Piano Concerto No. 4 in G major, Op. 58 (1805–1806), operates on a similar basis. Unison strings, playing *forte* and *sempre staccato* in persistently dotted rhythms, are answered by the soloist offering steady chorale-like harmony, playing *una corda* and *molto cantabile*, and tracing a long melodic line that descends by an octave (from e^2 in bar 7 to e^1 in bar 13). Unlike in Moreno's movement, though, the rate of exchange between the two 'characters' varies: initially the exchange involves complete phrases, but it soon accelerates, and not too long after that the unison strings start to fade away dynamically, eventually falling silent before the lyrical eloquence of the piano. Only near the very end (bars 64–66) do we hear a faint echo of the initial dotted-rhythmic bravado, ghosted out in the bass line of the string section at *pianissimo*. While this famous movement has often been imagined as a confrontation between two protagonists, and indeed thought to have had a programmatic basis,[46] its fundamental gestural contrast is no

---

[46] See Owen Jander, 'Beethoven's "Orpheus in Hades": The *Andante con moto* of the Fourth Piano Concerto', *19th-Century Music* 8/3 (1985), 195–212. Discussing a passage in the development section of Mozart's piano concerto K449, Simon P. Keefe suggests that 'the specific alternation of loud unisons and contrasting material (often a melody accompanied homophonically) might have been recognized as a sign of confrontation by Mozart's Viennese audiences', citing various works by Gluck and Dittersdorf that feature such alternations. Keefe, '"An Entirely Special Manner": Mozart's Piano Concerto No. 14 in E Flat, K. 449, and the Stylistic Implications of Confrontation', *Music & Letters* 82/4 (2001), 570. One of the Gluck works cited by Keefe, *Orfeo ed Euridice*, forms the centrepiece of Jander's programmatic interpretation of the Beethoven movement.

novelty; what it does do is dramatize the pairing of assertive and gracious elements on the scale of a whole movement. While Moreno's movement-length interplay does not offer this kind of dramatic arc, it does become more flexible towards the end. From bar 366, for instance, we hear a comparatively long utterance from one side: Pride initiates a form of Mannheim crescendo, which lasts for a full ten bars. This is then countered by a very soft mock-comic rejoinder, whereby the humble clearly undercuts the pretensions of the proud.

Undercutting pretension reminds us that our gracious manoeuvre can always embody what Richard Taruskin calls 'contrast as irony' in later eighteenth-century instrumental style.[47] If one understands the contrasting materials as interactive, as 'talking to' or commenting on one another, then the gentle or gracious can be heard as implicitly admonishing the grand or proud or assertive. The effect may be overtly comic, as it is in Moreno's movement, though irony is a more encompassing category for understanding the gracious withdrawal – the hedging of strong affirmative utterance by a subsequent gesture that suggests it to have been trying too hard or assuming too much.

This is a particularly characteristic effect in retransitions, where the effectiveness of the riposte is often inversely proportional to its duration: a few well-chosen words, as it were, undercut the bluster. A retransition section in the finale of Pleyel's Quartet in C major Op. 1 No. 1 (1782–1783), from bar 78, gives us a grand orchestral-style *crescendo* over eight bars, the cello playing a drum bass while the upper three instruments play rapid syncopated chords in the service of a rising arpeggio. The end of the passage brings three *forte* hammerblows that are a common closing formula, in this case telling the listener that the retransition has achieved its harmonic goal and the rondo theme may now reappear. Overlapping with the last of these hammerblows is a brief falling chromatic fragment in the first violin, softening to *piano*, taking us from a climactic g^2 via $f\sharp^2$ and $f\natural^2$ to the e^2 with which the rondo theme will resume. Much of the ironic effect derives from the brevity of the gesture. Just two bars and three notes are needed to send us smoothly back to the rondo theme; just the lightest of touches is needed to deflate the previous grandeur, which in retrospect is made to sound like so much huffing and puffing. There is a similar sense of deflation in the final movement of the octet version of Mozart's Serenade in E flat major, K375 (1782). After an effortful retransitional passage built on a

---

[47] Taruskin, *The Oxford History of Western Music: Music in the Seventeenth and Eighteenth Centuries*, 439.

rising chromatic line in the bassoons, who along with oboes and horns play in persistent *sforzando* syncopations, and a circling figure in the clarinets marked *forte*, the eight instruments come together in bar 160 on a chord suddenly marked *piano*. The tension from this build-up is then dispersed by staccato scale fragments played in contrary motion, just four notes on each instrument, that sound like a collective throwaway remark. Once again in a retransition a mere handful of notes does the trick; replacing many more effortful notes, they lighten the tone and imply that what went before need not have protested so much.[48]

The elements of a gracious riposte can also undercut previous bravado on a larger scale than in these two retransitions. In the first-movement exposition of Boccherini's Quartet in C major Op. 32 No. 4/G204 (1780) a cello melody that began in bar 15 takes off into the stratosphere from bar 22, outlining a rising G-major-seventh arpeggio, and soon reaches grotesque registral heights – presumably the main reason why the movement carries the designation 'Allegro bizzarro' (Example 2.7). This display seems to silence its colleagues, who have dropped out by the end of bar 24. The cello pauses to admire the view on its high F, repeating three parts of its dominant-seventh harmony *a piacere*. Clearly the soloist has overstepped generic limits (this is more like concerto behaviour), and there is another error of discourse, too, since the arpeggio figure outlines the wrong harmony for this point in the movement; it moves us back towards the tonic key of C major when the harmonic territory should be that of the dominant, G major.

Not surprisingly, a stunned silence follows, with the composer instructing the players to wait a long time (*aspettar molto*); there could be no clearer musical embodiment of mutual embarrassment. Then the whole ensemble re-emerges *pianissimo* at a low tessitura from bar 26, moving exclusively in cautious steps: all these elements represent the opposite of what we have just heard. The dynamic level gradually grows towards a boisterous, folksy, *fortissimo* closing theme that kicks in mid-way through bar 29, as confidence is restored. Great social comedy is made of a virtuoso impulse, and the best touch of all is that the re-emergence is done via a

---

[48] In the sextet version of this passage (1781), one misses the oboe parts that were added by Mozart a year later. It is the oboes that play a rising version of the scale fragment in bar 162, while the clarinets play the line in falling parallel tenths with the bassoons. Thus the sextet version, minus that rising oboe line, does not feature contrary motion between outer voices, and some of the insouciant effect of this gesture of withdrawal is lost. One should note too that the dynamic markings are rather different in the sextet version, but without affecting the sense I find in the passage.

Example 2.7 Boccherini, Quartet in C major Op. 32 No. 4/i, bars 19–31

collectively modest, melody-less texture, thus tactfully avoiding the musical element that has occasioned the impropriety. If there is no melody, there is no overt leadership, and no leadership means no chance for anyone to go over the top.[49]

Pride also leads to something of a fall in the final movement of Dittersdorf's Quartet in E flat major, K195 (1789). From bar 60 we witness a huge episode in which the three lower instruments, each double-stopped, hold a C minor chord *fortissimo* for nearly forty bars without a break while

---

[49] As Elisabeth le Guin notes, the composer 'shows signs of being aware of the philosophical stakes' in regard to virtuoso display: 'In certain sonatas, he distances and ironizes the performer in specific regard to his virtuosity'. Le Guin, *Boccherini's Body*, 6.

Example 2.7 (continued)

the first violin performs a gypsy lamentation. This material is brazen not just in style but in its length and unrelieved intensity. What follows is a bar (98) of total silence. Thereafter all four players resume *pianissimo* in a low register, in a uniform texture, with the harmonic rhythm starting to move again after its near-complete extinction. This is reminiscent of what happened after the cello histrionics in Boccherini's movement: a low, soft, relatively undifferentiated texture, melody-less, as though the best way for the group to start functioning normally again is to concentrate on the basics. Thus we move from melody with a six-part drone to more or less pure harmony – one of those occasions when harmony lives up to its frequently evoked billing as a symbol of social cohesion. In both these examples we can hear the principles of the gracious riposte writ large – something bold, indeed exotically different, is countered by something 'smaller', more considerate, more socially minded.

On the basis of the range of examples covered thus far, we could suggest that the gracious riposte constitutes an affective schema. It features a cluster of likely attributes for each of the two parts no one of which has to be present on any particular occasion.[50] Dynamics, pitch trend, texture,

---

[50] As Robert Gjerdingen notes, 'individual exemplars of a schema may not contain all the features that define the schema': *Music in the Galant Style*, 13.

intervallic construction, even the sequence of the two events can be altered from the mental template without the schema ceasing to operate. We have seen that it need not occur just in opening position, need not involve straightforwardly paired phrase units, and that it can operate on different timescales. In other words, there are many apparent exceptions to the line-up of contrasting parameters presented in Table 2.1. In our Boccherini and Dittersdorf examples above, it is not so much a case of tutti or at least full texture followed by solo, but instead a soft collective riposte to a 'loud' individual display; in Mozart's Serenade K375 the riposte features staccato articulation rather than the more usual legato; in Clementi's Op. 15 violin sonata the reply reconfigures the same material rather than offering a clear change of utterance. In addition, it bears repeating that my preferred descriptive term 'gracious' is an approximation to the typical character of the answering unit, a likely rather than a mandatory affect. There may not even be any clear-cut dynamic contrast, as was the case in Beethoven's Op. 2 No. 1 – there the initial assertion is marked *piano* and then builds to a *fortissimo*, at which level the lyrical element begins its reply before fading away, and in fact when the theme returns to mark the recapitulation, it begins *forte*, and then the entire riposte is marked to be played *fortissimo*. The character of the whole theme, encouraged by a dramatic retransition, is transformed, most obviously so when a number of originally offbeat chords are resituated on downbeats to create a more decisive, not to say angry effect. This just about suggests that we hear a large-scale reversal of the usual affective sequence: here the relatively nuanced mode of presentation heard at the outset is replaced by an all-out aggressive one.

Indeed, sometimes dynamics alone are enough to invoke the properties of our putative schema. The contrast often takes a particularly elemental form in the symphonies of Johann Stamitz, as in the first movement of his Symphony in E flat major Op. 4 No. 6, part of a set published by Huberty in Paris in 1758. This shows that contrasting dynamics need not be associated with contrasting material. The opening eight bars, for instance, present a single triadic impulse, and could easily be played at one dynamic level, but instead two bars of *piano* are followed by two bars of *forte*, an alternation that is then repeated (Example 2.8a). (Of a comparable example in another Stamitz symphony Carl Dahlhaus writes of 'a wealth of contrast in the smallest space [Kontrastreichtum auf engstem Raum]', everything taking place 'within the field of one harmony, the tonic'.[51]) The *piano* passages feature a slur between first and second beats of the bar, and the *forte*

---

[51] Carl Dahlhaus, *Die Musik des 18. Jahrhunderts*, 204.

Example 2.8a Stamitz, Symphony in E flat major Op. 4 No. 6/i, bars 1–8

passages are completely staccato and played in a tutti unison, which does of course correspond to elements of the assertive–gracious pairing. Later on, bars 61ff, which are *fortissimo* in the strings, with a fanfare-like upper voice, tremolos and a repeated quick rising-octave scale in the bass, are repeated in a *pianissimo* variant from bar 69 (Example 2.8b). This might be understood simply as echo dynamics, hardly a novel practice for the 1750s, but in fact the material is rethought. The quaver and semiquaver tremolos become gentler repeated crotchets in the bass and sustained pedals in the horns. The oboes repeat their melody but replace the fanfare-style repeated-note tattoo with sustained dotted crotchets. While there is no contrast of material as such, there is nevertheless a strong contrast of execution, of musical behaviour. Further, this softer version then receives a long extension from bar 77 that continues the more lyrical flavour, and this includes our classic softening device of appoggiaturas (restruck suspensions). A keyboard equivalent of this example can be found at the start of C. P. E. Bach's Rondo in E major from the third book of pieces written *Für Kenner und Liebhaber* (Wq57/1; 1779). Here bars 5–8 are a somewhat varied repetition of the theme presented in bars 1–4, and the individual two-bar phrases are turned into assertive–gracious pairings, at 5–6 and then 7–8, simply through contrasts of texture and dynamics (Example 2.9).

Example 2.8b Stamitz, Symphony in E flat major Op. 4 No. 6/i, bars 61–86

The continual alternations between loud and soft dynamic levels in a movement such as Stamitz's also serve other purposes that we have already alluded to. Since they are generally allied with phrases or phrase units, they sharpen the sense of periodicity, and thus help to create a very clear sense of

Example 2.8b (continued)

hypermetrical organization. This in turn fosters the dynamism and drive that is so characteristic of this Italianate symphonic idiom, the sense that the listener is taking a ride in a fast machine. There is thus a symbiotic

Example 2.9 C. P. E. Bach, Rondo in E major Wq57/1, bars 1–8

Example 2.10 J. C. Bach, Sonata in G major Op. 5 No. 3/i, bars 1–6

relationship between contrast of character and syntactical definition. The constant jolts of dynamic level – whether allied to contrasting material or the same material performed in a different way – act as prompts for the listener's attention, as part of what one might call a sensationalist aesthetic. Many of the dynamic alternations in Stamitz seem to exist at this level of pure sensation – which can mean that they feel counterintuitive, to the player as well as to the listener.

One hears something similar in many works by Abel, J. C. Bach and the earlier Mozart. Bach's Sonata in G major Op. 5 No. 3 (1766), for instance, opens with a two-bar phrase unit that could readily sustain performance at one dynamic level (Example 2.10). Above a constant Alberti bass, a falling stepwise fragment is answered by a rising octave scale and a long appoggiatura, which sounds like a unified 'basic idea'.[52] However, Bach

---

[52] For definition and discussion of the term 'basic idea' see Caplin, *Classical Form*, 37. For Caplin, the basic idea forms the 'fundamental building block' for our repertory: 'the classical work

subdivides the phrase unit into *forte* and *piano*, a pattern that is replicated in the answering unit, and so out of nothing makes us hear a strong gesture that is pacified by what follows. According to our schematic rules of thumb, the dynamic alternation should if anything operate in reverse, since here it is the rising contour that softens the utterance. Such dynamic markings are likely to get under the skin of the modern-day player, but there is little reason to think that they were ever heard or felt as natural. Instead, they actively grab the attention, by causing a perceptual jolt. And this back-and-forth relationship will not be mechanically applied – what continually brings it alive in the case of the Stamitz symphonies, for example, is the unpredictability of the operation. Alternations take many different forms, and occur on different scales. Often enough, in fact, the dynamic alternations in Stamitz's symphonies do ally themselves with different types of material, and so do exemplify the classic type of gracious riposte. This type was to prove more enduring.

A more dramatic kind of pure dynamic interplay tended to replace the sort we often find in Stamitz: the contradiction of a dynamic build-up by means of a *subito piano*. Stamitz himself in fact offers an example in the Trio of his Symphony in F major Op. 4 No. 1 (1758). At the start of its second section we hear four bars of standing on the dominant, with successive dynamic markings of *piano, cresc., forte* and *fortissimo*. This would naturally be expected to lead to a forceful following downbeat as the harmony resolves back to a 5/3 over C, but instead the dynamic level is suddenly reduced to *piano*. Another concise example may be found at the start of the Adagio of Mozart's string quintet K593 (1790; Example 2.11). The first four bars suggest an assertive–gracious pairing even though few of the elements of a normal assertive gesture are present. Indeed, bars 1–2 are clearly lyrical in style, and intervallic movement is predominantly by step. They also begin softly, but a *crescendo* hairpin quickly follows. After the elaboration of tonic harmony by means of a Quiescenza schema – which involves a voice-leading pattern of $\hat{8}$–$\flat\hat{7}$–$\hat{6}$–$\sharp\hat{7}$–$\hat{8}$[53] – there is every reason to expect not only that there will be a change of harmony at the start of the third bar, but that this will be played at the loud dynamic level to which the *crescendo* is leading us. Instead, the pre-dominant chord that begins bar 3 is marked *piano*, an abrupt change of dynamic level. The falling motion in the first violin's melody and chain of

---

initially groups together several motives into a single gesture, a larger idea lasting two real measures'.

[53] For further information and examples see Gjerdingen, *Music in the Galant Style*, chapter 13, 181–195.

Example 2.11 Mozart, Quintet in D major, K593/ii, bars 1–4²

restruck suspensions create a series of sighs that very readily fit the notion of a gracious riposte. In addition, the full texture of bars 1–2 is lightened by the use of quavers and rests in all the parts in bar 3. Thus there is an unmistakable feeling that high (and growing) intensity has taken a concessive turn; it has been softened.

An inherited sense that 'classical' music must be smooth at all costs determines that many such moments in Mozart and elsewhere are underplayed. One might suggest, for instance, that the arrival back on I5/3 at the end of the Quiescenza in bar 2^3 is a natural point at which to relax the dynamic level, even though the composer's notation hardly seems to allow this possibility (the hairpins extend to the third beat of the bar). But I would argue that a *subito piano* at bar 3^1 is entirely appropriate not just in view of our riposte pattern but more broadly in view of a style that operates by means of so many hard edges. There is, however, one difference in this realization of the schema. There is no separation of the elements; in all our previous examples there has been some kind of break, whether between phrase units or indeed between larger-scale sections, sometimes spaced well apart. Given a *subito piano* reading, the first element abuts on the second, or, rather, one replaces the other at an expected moment of fulfilment. But what remains is the fundamental sense of pulling back from categorical expression. From a behavioural perspective, inhibition is put to positive use.

Such behaviour is magnified in the output of Beethoven, with whom the 'crescendo to nothing' becomes a real creative fingerprint: a build-up of weight and power followed by a sudden withdrawal to *piano*. Once more, the effect can be physically quite disturbing and can feel counterintuitive to both player and listener. The slow movements of his sonatas Op. 10 No. 3 (the famous Largo in D minor; 1798) and Op. 28 (the so-called Pastoral; 1801), for example, are rich in *subito piano* effects. The sense of latent disruptive power that inheres in his assertive material may well be more vivid in Beethoven than in the music of his predecessors, yet the trademark 'crescendo to nothing', the choking-back to a more overt level of control, is premised on the same sort of discursive self-consciousness.

The Order of Things

As already noted, there is a high degree of consensus on the modus operandi of later eighteenth-century musical syntax, on how this music composes itself, so to speak. Binary principles are paramount. This binarism has two aspects: symmetry (two things match) and contrast (two things differ). Because the immediate scale of the operation is quite small, and therefore readily perceptible, we can imagine that the two units (gestures, motives, phrases, whatever they may be) 'notice' each other, that they communicate. And so when sameness meets difference under these terms, we can understand the resulting process as a reciprocal one. Characteristic formulations of this phenomenon include Karol Berger's 'ideal of bipartite, symmetrical balance, in which the second half answers the first' or Michael Spitzer's 'essential principles of complementary balance',[54] and both authors note that this binary dynamic operates on various levels of structure. This means in fact a kind of bifocal perspective – one eye on the immediate view, and one eye on the larger shaping of utterance, as cells and motives build into phrase units, which build successively into phrases, periods, functional groupings, sections and whole movements – the definition of each aided by an unprecedented cultivation of silence. This need not amount to something we would actively perceive as silence, but does involve a constant recourse to short breaks in the musical flow. The *horror vacui* we might associate with baroque style turns into something like its opposite, an aversion to infinitely proliferating utterance.

---

[54] Berger, *Bach's Cycle, Mozart's Arrow*, 187, and Michael Spitzer, 'Haydn's *Creation* as Late Style: Parataxis, Pastoral, and the Retreat from Humanism', *Journal of Musicological Research* 28/2–3 (2009), 239.

Not always explicitly theorized is that this binarism is not just a vehicle for content: it is content itself, meaningful in its own right. Binary syntax is not just intrinsic – in other words, a purely formal feature within the domain of music – it is also extrinsic – it points to, and can be most readily grasped in connection with, other domains of human experience. For Rumph this is the 'choreographic symmetries of the body', as encapsulated in dance.[55] For David Lidov, on the other hand, it is linguistic; he describes phrase structure as becoming a 'topic' in the later eighteenth century. In other words, interest accrues to the structure of utterance per se, not simply to its particular realization: it's not what you say, it's how you say it.[56] This represents, once more, what I am calling the technical side of sociability, and in this case the idea that the structure or pattern communicates independently of any affect suggested by the musical materials. And because the 'packaging' is so clear-cut in our repertory, the syntactical message is foregrounded; other brands of musical syntax, after all, may also have something to say in their own right, but may not call attention to the fact in quite such strong terms.[57]

It is surely the prominence of such packaging that has led to an assumption that is particularly prevalent with regard to our repertory: that expression comes from the disruption of patterns. In other words, binary symmetry and reciprocity are intrinsically neutral, not to say unexciting, properties, and need to be interrupted in some way in order for expression to 'break through'. This common working assumption can hardly be denied flat out. Pattern disruption can certainly sharpen perception, though within limits: if too prevalent, it would flatten listeners' expectations and so cause them to lose any stake in the listening experience. And the gracious riposte is after all a kind of disruption – a swift change of

---

[55] Rumph, *Mozart and Enlightenment Semiotics*, 36.
[56] David Lidov, *Is Language a Music? Writings on Musical Form and Signification* (Bloomington: Indiana University Press, 2005), 119. He encapsulates his argument by invoking Ferdinand de Saussure's binary pairing: 'this attraction to *langue*, language-like phrase structure, contrasts with earlier and later generations' fascination for *parole*, reflected by interest in rhetoric and … resonance with the kinesthesia of personal utterance'. This is perhaps too categorical, but still a useful shorthand for distinguishing what makes our period so different.
[57] Scott Burnham put this eloquently in the context of the 'analysis wars' of the 1990s when he wrote: 'Yet it is difficult to deny that musical syntax *is* to a large degree musical significance. This is not the same as insinuating that music is entirely self-referential and culturally isolated. It is rather to say that music's potential for signification is largely bound up with the space between a tacit, internalized sense of general style … and the claims of an individual work. Prior to speculation about extramusical meanings, we as listeners put into play any number of (often subliminal) assumptions about musical syntax without which interpretive claims could not be made, assumptions which allow us to read a piece's "body language".' Burnham, 'The Criticism of Analysis and the Analysis of Criticism', *19th-Century Music* 16/1 (1992), 72.

expressive stance, a contradictory gesture. This then returns us to the dialectic previously explored between changeable materials and periodic phrase syntax – that they can both contradict and reinforce each other. And there is a further dialectic, one that emerges with particular force in our repertory: disruption of a pattern or of a norm may call it into question, but also reaffirms it. Even where that norm is not ultimately upheld in context, it still forms a point of departure for assessment of the disruption. Yet the more fundamental point at this juncture is that the brand of binary organization found in this music does not need 'added value' in order to communicate. Some level of significance derives from the very fact of matching (symmetry) and the very process of exchange between more or less symmetrical units (reciprocity).

While such attributes could be understood grammatically – Koch, for instance, referred to 'subject-predicate' relationships[58] – a common strategy in eighteenth-century critical writings was to humanize them. A favoured term of reference was dialogue, meaning an interchange between musical materials or 'characters'. As one strand in his intensive treatment of the subject, for instance, Anton Reicha noted how dialogue could be created by means of 'the difference between instruments and the difference in their timbres; in the difference in the value of notes; in the different chords; in the *forte* and the *piano*; in the choice of keys; in high and low notes; in the succession of unison and harmony; in the different sections of which the orchestra is composed'.[59] And this was hardly just a critical gambit; it was also a commercial one, as endless title-pages for instrumental works promised an up-to-date *dialogué* style.

We can see this modernity being written into the discourse in the first movement of J. C. Bach's Symphony in G minor, Op. 6 No. 6 (published in Amsterdam in 1770). The opening of the movement is very typical of the minor-key idiom one hears in other symphonies from the 1760s and

---

[58] For one treatment of Koch's subject-predicate distinction, noting the typical antithesis present between the first two units, see Walther Dürr, 'Music as an Analogue of Speech: Musical Syntax in the Writings of Heinrich Christoph Koch and in the Works of Schubert', in *Eighteenth-Century Music in Theory and Practice: Essays in Honor of Alfred Mann*, ed. Mary Ann Parker (Stuyvesant: Pendragon, 1994), 227–240. Dürr notes how this arrangement eventually breaks down: 'the relationship of subject and predicate [undergoes] a change', as 'antithetical patterns now no longer yield fulfillment', but 'take the listener farther afield' (239–240).

[59] Anton Reicha, *Art du compositeur dramatique, ou cours complet de composition vocale* (Paris: Richault, 1833), 43, cited in translation in Simon P. Keefe, *Mozart's Piano Concertos: Dramatic Dialogue in the Age of Enlightenment* (Woodbridge: Boydell, 2001), 33. While a book from 1833 may seem to be of dubious relevance to our period, Keefe notes that the listing of dialogue techniques presented here builds on concepts of dialogue already advanced in the *Traité de mélodie* of 1814 (Paris: J. L. Scherff).

1770s.[60] Plentiful repeated notes, stabbing accents and abrupt alternations of dynamic level create an *agitato* affect, partly because of the lack of eloquent melodic leadership; instead, texture and rhythm seem to drive the process. However, this affect changes immediately once the music jumps to the mediant major from the end of bar 25 (Example 2.12). What is most interesting from our point of view about the more cantabile material that follows is the way in which it modulates stylistically. It starts off with the baroque idiom of a walking bass in crotchets, above which the second violin plays a rising figure that is then imitated by the first violin a step above. This material promises to turn into one of those Corelli-style suspension chains in which the two melodic instruments reach over each other in turn to create a composite rising scale. But after a few bars, and just a single suspension in the second violin in bar 28, the material melts away; the phrase unit is already over by the downbeat of 29. Then violin 1 plays a bar of staccato quavers unaccompanied. These quavers are patently a link or filler; they signal a modern paratactic style that operates by means of short intelligible units of discourse – quite the opposite of the continuity and fullness promised by the walking-bass idiom. The parallel phrase that follows moves slightly further away from an evocation of the idiom in that violin 2, which now answers violin 1, plays its C a seventh below the B♭ rather than a step above. This voicing weakens the suspension-chain model, and a further stylistic failure is the fact that the harmony in the following bar 32 does not shift as expected – harmonic prolongation replaces the anticipated harmonic change.

In the following phrase, after another bar of linking staccato quavers – a playful half-inversion of the equivalent in bar 29 – the walking-bass shape is isolated and repeated by the oboes in parallel sixths. (Compare the falling legato D–C–B♭ heard from the second to fourth beats of bar 26 in the bass with what the oboes play in bar 34.) In other words, the material is turned into a modern motive. After a complementary repetition in the next bar, this is then answered by the violins at bar 36 in parallel-moving arpeggios. They play the same rhythm as the oboes, but the rhythm is now delivered in detached quavers with quaver rests in between. Several basic reciprocal equations operate: the oboes' falling-step shape is answered by rising leaps in the violins, and legato is answered by staccato. Within those operations, the violins answer their own rising triads with falling ones (bar 37) to create

---

[60] For a comprehensive study of this symphonic type, though restricted to the Viennese orbit, see Matthew Riley, *The Viennese Minor-Key Symphony in the Age of Haydn and Mozart* (New York: Oxford University Press, 2014).

Example 2.12 J. C. Bach, Symphony in G minor, Op. 6 No. 6/i, bars 25–41

an internally 'dialogued' contour. Note in addition how the full strings-plus-horn punctuation of the downbeats of 34 and 35 is met by sustained oboes and a lighter viola–bass downbeat at 36 and 37.

All these forms of answering represent contemporary dialogue technique as opposed to the older-style imitation at close range with which the section started. And these types of reciprocal action can readily be grasped on several larger scales. There is the very contrast between the baroque-style passage from the end of bar 25 (suggesting a trio sonata) and the material that ensues, the first suggesting dignified consistency of means and the second the sort of 'favourite desultory style of the present times' that Burney was to celebrate. Zooming further back, though, and in spite of those differences, we can see that by comparison with what went before in the movement, the whole passage from bar 25^4 is marked by relatively even rhythmic values and a predominance of conjunct movement. Thus as a whole it acts as a gracious calming of the previous bluster, just as Burney suggested was characteristic of this composer, and creates a larger-scale social balance. We can also see how binary principles – at their most abstract, 'this thing' versus 'that thing' – can operate at different levels, yet in a way that is more or less separate from binary phrase structure as such, which is where the principles have received their most ready recognition.

The flexibility of binary or 'dialogue' thinking is another feature to consider, leaning on its reciprocal rather than its symmetrical aspects. To revisit the first-movement exposition of Mozart's 'Linz' Symphony, K425: after the gracious–assertive reversal noted earlier, we encounter a typically robustious transition section that is surprisingly undercut by various means, leading to a soft, lightly scored cadence in the dominant at bar 71. Closure is achieved by means of understatement, an ironic glance at the typical 'bullying tactics' of a full orchestra. The short gap that follows – a medial caesura – tells us to prepare for confirmation of the new key. Instead there is an unexpected jump into E minor, together with a loud tutti texture, and the vigorous, driving language of the transition reasserts itself. A triadic melodic line that builds on a two-minim motive from the transition (compare bars 44 and then 62–65 with 72–73) is heard over busy continuous quavers in the bass that also revive the transitional style. This rude interruption is immediately countered by the wind band alone, playing *piano*, twisting the same material into C major; the triadic fanfare turns into a lyrical fragment, and the busy quavers disappear. E minor is then further banished with a bantering reply from the violins as a close in G major is achieved. These two brief ripostes make light of the previous heavy gesture.

The whole multi-part phrase is then repeated, but with terms reversed. Instead of the *forte* two-part counterpoint of fanfare and busy bass, the E minor phrase unit is played *piano* and legato and with a melody-and-accompaniment texture, led by a tune in oboe and bassoon (bars 79–83). Now the triad is partially filled in by smooth steps. Following this, the *piano* wind-band material is restyled as a *forte* tutti, and the busy bass quavers return to reinforce the point. The subsequent bantering material is varied and continues the more assertive rendition. What this all demonstrates is that our reciprocity, which once more clearly operates on several distinct levels in this instance, is driven less by (static) character contrast than by a protean principle of interaction. Any piece of material can take on any guise, it seems, according to circumstances. This binarism can be compared with the dynamic of social interaction, which comes from a consciousness of oneself on one hand and others on the other hand, and what one does in order to bridge the gap. How are we the same? How are we different? In what ways do we differ? In what ways do we agree? It's a matter of constant fine adjustments, in which similarities suddenly produce differences and contrasts can just as suddenly be bridged or dissolved.

Such compulsive concentration on the process of exchange is evident in one creative habit that seems to have escaped critical attention as such. This is a repeated alternation of short phrase units that takes place after the decisive structural cadence at the end of a major section, thus in a codetta or coda (if in sonata form, after what is now known after Hepokoski and Darcy as the essential expositional (or structural) closure[61]). The more common form entails a contrast between an initial fragment played *piano* and a correcting *forte* figure, suggesting a kind of bashfulness about the need for assertive closure. For example, at bars 32–36 of the first movement of the Quartet in D major Op. 1 No. 3 (*c*1765) by Gaetano Latilla (1711–1788) a three-note figure played twice softly by the two violins is met by a loud chordal response, I–IV–V–I, from all the players. The soft fragments seem to suggest some further (individual) things might remain to be said, and the loud chords are like a corporate reply in the negative. This form of postcadential interplay always features at least two rotations of the contrasting pairs, but often there are more: four, for example, at bars 142–150 of the first movement of Boccherini's Quintet in C major Op. 10 No. 4/G268 (1771). There are also four rotations at bars 43–48 of the Adagio of Haydn's Symphony No. 67 (*c*1778), but the dynamic pattern is reversed – at least initially (Example 2.13). A sharp rat-a-tat on oboes, bassoon and

---

[61] See Hepokoski and Darcy, *Elements of Sonata Theory*, 120–124.

Example 2.13 Haydn, Symphony No. 67 in F major/ii, bars 41–48

horns, three loud repeated notes, is followed by a soft falling scale on the violins, but after the next wind figure, the answer comes from the whole string section, rising instead of falling, and played *forte*. This means that there is internal dialogue between the two string fragments; they answer each other as well as answering the military-sounding wind figure. A repetition of the whole from bar 45 brings us up to eight alternating units in succession, following which, in bar 47, the strings concede the point. They now play the same forceful figure as the winds, if still in alternation, but with the rate of interchange doubled so as to create a stretto effect.[62]

This common device clearly bears comparison with the interplay of assertive and gracious elements as explored in the previous section, but the compressed time-scale and repeated alternations, together with a fixed postcadential function, make it distinct enough. Further, the two contrasting types of material don't always fit readily under those affective categories. At bars 36–44 of the first movement of Mozart's Violin Sonata in F major K376 (1781) the dynamic level is uniformly soft, and the alternating one-bar units are not strongly distinguished rhythmically. An unaccompanied rising third in the piano, decorated by a turn, is answered by an accompanied cadential formula; following that, the initial figure returns, slightly extended, before being answered by a different accompanied cadential formula. The complete package is then reiterated with violin taking the melody, making once again for eight alternating units in total. Rather than there being any strong affective opposition between the two elements, it is as if we are hearing a kind of bartering between them. The main distinction is that the odd-numbered units, with their rising contours, suggest further energy remains to be expended before closure can arrive, while the even-numbered ones want rather to settle on a point of rest. The effect is teasingly indecisive, necessitating a separate *forte* postcadential unit (44–47) that offers a straightforward confirmation of closure.

In the opening movement of Wanhal's Flute (or Oboe) Quartet in C major, Op. 7 No. 6 (1771), there is again no clear-cut contrast of dynamic levels or character when this device appears near the end of the exposition (Example 2.14). In this case a one-bar unit, consisting of a rising scale played in unison with a downward octave displacement on the final note, is answered by a harmonized phrase that lasts for two bars and falls by step from an initial high point down to a cadential close marked by a trill (bars 31^2–34^1). Both figures are marked for *forte* execution. A sense of question and answer arises not just from the swift alternation of gestures, but also from the basic intonation contour of the whole, as rise is succeeded by fall. Indeed, the marked displacement of a falling seventh that we hear at the end of the first unit creates a more specific kind of interrogative mood. This is because the note arrived on at the end of that unit, an F♯, the local leading

---

[62] In fact, the strings have already been echoing the winds' rhythm at the start of each of their contributions, but now it is ironed out into the same repeated-note form.

Example 2.14 Wanhal, Flute Quartet in C major Op. 7 No. 6/i, bars 31–42

note, demands completion. This demand is met when the following unit ends at 34^1 on a tonic G, also played in unison, meaning that we hear an answer to that dangling leading note not just in terms of pitch but also in terms of scoring.

The sense of interplay between the two units seems set to apply on a larger scale when the passage begins its obligatory repetition at bar 34^2, since the first unit is now played *piano*. We would then expect the continuation to remain at that level as part of that larger-scale 'game of pairs'. Instead it goes off course first harmonically – by briefly tonicizing V of V, through what in retrospect turns out to be a parenthetical addition at 35^3–36^1 – and then also dynamically – by switching back to *forte*. This harmonic 'mistake', so close to what we imagine is the end of the first half of the movement, seems to prompt the return to *forte*, as if the extra dynamic energy is needed to correct the harmonic and phrase-structural error and get us back on course. In fact, that is no sooner done than the phrase shrinks back to *piano* from bar 38 to give us an understated, matter-of-fact close to what has become an extended answering unit. Thus purely from the point of view of dynamics, this fourth part of the postcadential passage (starting at bar 36^3) first of all allies itself with the first and second units before subsequently matching the third unit after all, meaning there are two twists in this tale: departure from the expected *piano*, then a swerve away from the unexpected *forte* and back to the original larger plan.[63] As in Mozart's K376 above, there is a sense of teasing, of a juggling of gestures, as if the players are uncertain about how to mark the impending closure. And as in that movement, these manoeuvres lead to a further, much firmer *forte* conclusion. The rhetorical point of our device would seem to be breaking up the headlong charge towards an end through fragmentation, a process of repeated small-scale interchange which suggests that unanimity has not quite yet been achieved. As such it exemplifies the dialectic noted earlier between contradiction and reinforcement of a norm. The expectation of strong unanimous closure is put in doubt by these rapid oscillations, which will include elements of dynamic and textural instability, yet at the same time they ultimately serve to strengthen the close when it finally arrives. And, as it turns out, this type of delaying tactic is found commonly enough that it can be thought of as a norm in its own right.

Readers may well have noted how many words it has taken me to evoke these seemingly simple sequences of events. It has at least been worth it in order to suggest how readily basic principles of binary reciprocity can spin off into a more complex interplay of similarity and difference. The musical sense of such a device can in fact be comprehended in an instant, and it might be more apt to imagine not the verbal parallel of 'dialogue' but a more purely gestural equivalent – a kind of musical pantomime, something akin to the *lazzi* of the *commedia dell'arte*.

The kind of short-order binary balancing-act that we hear in the repeated alternations of this postcadential pattern is, as noted, not that

---

[63] It should be noted that the 1771 Huberty parts show some differences in the dynamic markings applied to this fourth unit, both at this point and then when the material returns transposed near the end of the movement. But on balance the plan of unexpected *forte* followed by the now unexpected return to *piano* seems in little doubt.

different in principle from what we hear in various forms of the gracious riposte, but it does differ in scale. The examples cited also reveal that the interplay between gestures need not involve any marked opposition. At times the primary driver seems to be simply contour – the ways in which rising and falling pitch configurations alone can be heard to relate to each other. These configurations then ally themselves with various other parameters to create more comprehensive forms of reciprocal play. While such reciprocity of contour is of course to be found everywhere and on various scales, it often takes a particularly concentrated form in movements of moderate tempo. One might almost speak of a typology, involving themes in cantabile style, with patently symmetrical phrase structures, and generally without clear internal contrasts of affect. It is as if the tempo character (most commonly involving an Andante designation) encourages the cultivation of this manner, which is especially associated with an opening function. It also overlaps with what Wye Allanbrook dubbed the 'sensitive style'. This is not to be confused with the German *empfindsamer Stil*, since the sensitive style controls its utterance more carefully; there is a patent concern for the fine print of melodic conduct, for polished diction. At the same time the very sensitivity to detail can imply an expressive register that is not so remote from *Empfindsamkeit*: Allanbrook wrote of an affect that was 'at once intense and demure'.[64]

It is no accident that Allanbrook devised her label as a means of trying to capture a Mozartean trait, since the composer evidently delights in forms of interplay in which fine adjustments count for a lot. Take, for example, the opening theme of the finale of his Violin Sonata in B flat major K454 (1784), an Allegretto (Example 2.15). Its first four bars basically describe a falling movement, from an apex of $b\flat^2$ by step all the way down to f^1, while the next four bars ascend from a $b\flat^1$ up to a d^3 before resting on a medial f^2. This is a clear-cut, readily apprehensible 'dialogue' of contours within a melodic line. But the most marked shape within the first four bars is in fact a rising one – a chromatic passing note marked *sfp*, heard twice in descending sequence at bars 2^3–3^1. The second phrase answers this feature by means of two prominent dissonances of its own, restruck suspensions that are heard on the downbeats of bars 5 and 6. However, these figures also rise by step, just as the chromatic passing notes did in the first phrase, and this similarity cuts across the basic idea that the second phrase is inverting

---

[64] Wye J. Allanbrook, 'Two Threads through the Labyrinth: Topic and Process in the First Movements of K. 332 and K. 333', in *Convention in Eighteenth- and Nineteenth-Century Music*, ed. Allanbrook, Levy and Mahrt, 145.

Example 2.15 Mozart, Violin Sonata in B flat major K454/iii, bars 1–8[2]

the contour of the first. On the other hand, the restruck suspensions of 5 and 6 also have a sort of resolving function relative to the two earlier figures: they are diatonic rather than chromatic. Further, these two dissonance–resolution pairs are arranged into a rising sequence, as opposed to the descending sequence of the first phrase. Thus, purely in terms of contour, there is a complex network of similarity and difference across the two phrases, involving various kinds of repetition, resolution and inversion. This is musical behaviour where nuances count. In traditional terms, it could well be described as a kind of 'classical balance', but, once again, that lends an inappropriately static aspect to the process. Our term reciprocity offers a better guide: it implies a dynamic interplay between different elements, each with its own agency, as it were. Elements of agreement are offset by elements of difference; symmetry is offset by asymmetry. And such properties do not exist in a timeless 'classical' realm, as if the whole style was set up to be a model to us all, but represent an unprecedented self-consciousness about the act of communication.

Mozart was hardly alone in his exacting cultivation of contour within this particular expressive typology. The earlier Clementi in particular left many memorable examples, as in the Andante espressivo from his piano duet Op. 12 (1784) or the Larghetto con moto from his piano duet of Op. 6 (1780–1781), which show the same eloquence of asymmetrical detail within a framework of lyrical regularity. An instructive example by Haydn can be found in the Andante second movement of his String

Quartet in F sharp minor, Op. 50 No. 4 (1787). The first section, in A major and rounded-binary form, features all the checks and balances of its kind. For example, falling legato steps in the first two-bar unit are answered by rising staccato steps in the second. In the second half of this section a rising sequence, at bars 8–10, is answered by a falling sequence, at 12–14, with sustained high register in between, and following that a version of the initial falling contour is used to lower the register still further. The overall shape represents an arch of tension, peaking in the middle and subsiding thereafter, which can also be felt in most of the individual two-part units that make up the whole.

This movement is in double-variation form, but the succeeding section, in A minor, doesn't really have a 'theme' to vary. Not only does it lack a melodic profile, but it seems to go out of its way to avoid the syntactical clarity of the A major section. Instead of the interplay of concise two-bar units, the definition of which was sharpened by those contrasts of contour, we seem to hear two continuous eight-bar phrases. There is imitation between the parts throughout, which obviously provides a type of reciprocity, yet the lack of internal caesuras and consistently full textures mean that the players seem to be suffocating under the weight of sound; there is no place at which they can breathe. And the second part of this section (bars 29–36) features no rounding at all: in terms of thematic organization it is through-composed. Altogether this section provides a sort of negative image of the reciprocal charm of the previous A major music. Thus modern good musical manners are played off against something that is much less polished in its conduct, that lacks any sense of 'dialogue' between its materials.

These sensitive musical manners would seem to represent another feature of later eighteenth-century instrumental style that has been taken as read, more commonly acknowledged in passing rather than contemplated in detail. Yet the larger field of which these manners form a part – phrase syntax, form altogether – could hardly have received more loving and sustained attention, and so it would seem that these manners have not proved especially congenial to later generations of scholars. This undoubtedly reflects the problem previously noted that 'balance', and indeed the constant modification of utterance that this entails, is not an enticing property within an 'expressive' regime. That said, the use of what Gjerdingen calls 'complementary contours'[65] need not always lead to a result that sounds perfectly poised. Friedrich Blume noted that the '"closed" character' created by so many complementary relationships within the 'Classic theme' was not inevitable: while this was normally the

---

[65] Gjerdingen, *A Classic Turn of Phrase*, 148.

case in Mozart, many of Haydn's themes remain 'open' and 'leave the feeling that continued development is needed'.[66] Nevertheless, the Andante typology that I am focussing on normally takes great pains to appear self-contained.

One particularly poised example of this typology, to return to Mozart, may be found in his Variations in G major for Piano Duet, K501 (1786). This is an unusual independent variation set that uses the composer's own theme rather than a pre-existing one. A carefully contoured style of melodic conduct is apparent from the start of this theme (Example 2.16), which once more carries an Andante marking. The first eight bars form (roughly, given that 3–4 are such a free variant of 1–2) a sentence. The first two-bar unit basically arcs upwards in the melody against relatively static lower voices, with two types of ascent, the relatively unmarked rising tonic triad from d^2 to d^3 that encompasses the whole unit, and the more marked, 'yearning' interval of a rising sixth from $f\sharp^2$ to d^3 at the end. The second two-bar unit then executes a complementary descent, and finishes on the same note with which the melody started, d^2. The descent is more intricate, with its introduction of dotted rhythms, more varied and detailed articulation (slurred figures, staccato markings plus a turn, as opposed to the near-complete legato of the first unit) and greater use of stepwise intervals. While this could hardly count as an assertive–gracious pairing, we do at least hear something that is relatively expansive being answered by something that is gesturally 'small(er)', though all within a restrained soft dynamic. The greater attention to detail at bars 3–4 is characteristic of the small and lyrical side.

Bar 5 then brings greater intensity, with a whole bar of repeated notes in all parts plus the change of harmonic colour provided by the flattening of the leading note; this balances the tonicization of V that occurred in the previous two bars. Bar 5 stands out harmonically (slowest harmonic rhythm so far), melodically (static – a kind of neutral ground between the previous rise and fall), texturally (unison of parts), rhythmically (plain quavers) and in terms of articulation ('portamento' staccato). In retrospect we will understand that this bar (which turns out to act as an applied dominant to the following subdominant harmony) acts as the apex of an arch of intensity over the course of the eight-bar phrase. As writers such as Rosen have pointed out, such proportions – whereby a peak is reached between half and three quarters of the way through the structure – can be felt at various levels of a complete movement.[67] A characteristic feature is

---

[66] Blume, *Classic and Romantic Music*, 50.
[67] See, for example, Rosen's discussion of how Haydn expands the second theme in the first movement of his Piano Trio in G minor H18 (1794), which shows the composer's 'consciousness of [the] relation of large-scale form to phrase'. The variation is expanded into a miniature sonata form,

Example 2.16 Mozart, Variations for Piano Duet in G major, K501, bars 1–18

that the lessening of intensity sets in well before the end of the whole unit – part of a 'rounding' quality that might suggest a concern to exhibit grace and control of deportment. It means we do not 'fall onto' the cadence; it is

> revealing that form to be 'an immense melody, an expanded classical phrase, articulated, with its harmonic climax three-quarters of the way through and a symmetrical resolution that rounds it off in careful balance with the opening'. Rosen, *The Classical Style*, 83 and 87.

choreographed well in advance. Bar 6 takes us back to a more normal course of events for this theme, and tension is released with the arrival of the cadence. The melodic figure used to articulate this cadence rhymes with the one that closed the first four bars of music (at bars 3^2–4^1). Note the finicky elegance of detail that surrounds the cadential arrival: a trill in the secondo part heard at the same time as the turn figure in the primo, then a bass figure in dotted rhythm to fill in the gap before the next melodic anacrusis.

The momentum towards the cadence is increased by the fact that the third two-bar unit has no clear-cut point of ending, as did the first two, which both featured a significant hiatus. The pivotal note in this respect is the final g^2 quaver of bar 6: it could be heard as belonging to the preceding melodic unit (the repeated g^2s thus being weakly sequential with the repeated $f\natural^2$s in the second half of bar 5 in the primo melody) or as an anacrusis into the fourth two-bar unit. Note, though, that the secondo's bass line through bars 6 and 7 is entirely connected by a slur, and so there are grounds for hearing the second four bars of the whole phrase as a single unit (which would fit with the classic 2 + 2 + 4 construction of a sentence). Therefore, while this four-bar unit reaches a point of resolution, and features a melodic rhyme with the end of the first four bars, it also has more momentum. This is our classic reciprocal equation: elements of agreement are offset by elements of difference. There is no way to capture this quality, too often taken as read, except by the sort of patient, literal account I am providing; sweeping prose won't do it.

The level of intensity rises immediately after the double bar with an abrupt move to E minor, and imitation of the opening motive in the primo part by the secondo a bar later. This imitation soon deviates so that the harmony swerves from a tonicized vi to a tonicized IV, meaning that the rate of activity continues to accelerate. Further heightening features follow: in bar 11 the primo's melodic line ascends to by far its highest sustained register, and either side of the arrival on D at bar 12^1 the secondo has an internal imitation of a short C♯–D figure. After arrival on D, which is quickly reinterpreted as a standing on the dominant, the sense of textural activity remains high, but note the predominance of falling pitch contours that counterbalance the previous melodic rise (especially the falling sevenths in the top voice). Also at bars 13–14 the device of imitation continues – the primo's left-hand line across the bar at 12–13, involving a suspension, is answered by the secondo's right-hand line across the bar at 13–14 – yet this sounds less 'competitive' than the imitation heard at 9–10. The imitative process is partially disguised through a textural thickening that involves a sort of complementary counterpoint between the players; first at 12–13 the secondo's middle voice plays the same figure as the primo right hand but with partially inverted contour (mirroring), and then in the next bar the primo's left hand does something similar in relationship to the imitating secondo top line. Thus the process of imitation is blurred through the rhythmic unanimity of voices in the different players' parts. This means that the level of tension is falling, at least texturally; harmonically, we are still hovering on the dominant.

This dominant preparation leads to a return of the opening two bars of the theme, but now the secondo imitates the primo's melodic gambit one bar later. This is just what we heard at bars 9–10; it gives an internal balance within the second section (symmetry), but on the other hand it creates a more active version of bars 1–2 (asymmetry, progression). The final two-bar unit (bars 16^2–18^1) combines later events from the first section, the melodic repeated notes of bar 5 merging into an exact echo of the close of that section (7–8), in all voices, which rhyme tells us we are back at that earlier, and lower, level of intensity. We can understand this as an interaction between the forces of symmetrical organization (space) and forward momentum (time). Such a perspective also obtains in the fact that when the opening returns, we might expect a version of the complete first eight-bar section to follow, but this expectation is denied when cadential activity arrives, seemingly prematurely, in the third bar of the phrase. In retrospect, therefore, the opening material that returns at bars 14^2–16^1 is not so much a fresh beginning – from the top, so to speak – as the beginning of the end. Its formal function is transformed from one of opening up to one of closing down. The sense of symmetry we would have felt on hearing a rhyme with the opening shape is undercut (though certainly not destroyed) in favour of dynamic reinterpretation, through a compression of expected events.

My account of the way in which this theme unfolds has attempted to bring to life the dynamic nature of its reciprocal interaction, the sense that every detail sparkles with significance. Dynamism need not, of course, translate into affect, entailing driving tempo or forthright utterance, and in this case the music creates an impression of charm and ease. At the same time, paradoxically, it appears highly self-conscious in its exacting concern for diction, for the finest grains of sound. The management of contours alone, based on a play of simple differences such as up versus down, is eloquent.

But how much faith should be invested in this claim – that the careful management of contours is in its own right a trademark of our style and, further, can be understood under a rubric of sociable interaction? Rising and falling are, after all, the two basic motions that music can accomplish. From a purely melodic point of view, any tune has in various ways to balance rise and fall, leap and step, in order to remain (theoretically or actually) singable and memorable; some sort of 'balance' must be created. The rise normally precedes the fall, creating an arch of tension, and the fall is more likely to involve increasing recourse to stepwise movement as a marker of impending closure. This can be affirmed with reference to quite varied theoretical perspectives. William E. Caplin, for instance, contrasts the 'characteristic' material that typically 'opens up' a melody or theme with the less characteristic, cadential material that 'conveys the sense of "closing down" a melodic process', and this has implications for the types of interval found, as larger give way to smaller. Steve Larson's three categories of gravity, magnetism and inertia can take us a long way in accounting for the behaviour of any (tonal) melody. Leonard B. Meyer notes how secondary parameters (all the elements of music apart from pitch and duration) provide 'natural signs of closure' that include 'lowering of dynamic level, slowing of tempo, ... simplification of texture [and] descending pitch contours'.[68] And even a nodding acquaintance with Schenkerian voice-leading analysis will make one aware that descending linear progressions tend to cluster towards the ends of phrases and sections, at various structural levels, and how the rate at which they fall tends to increase towards the close. More broadly, as acknowledged earlier, any and all composition can be expected to involve a handling of different parameters through a series of checks and balances. All such perspectives threaten a cold shower for my arguments about the stylistic specificity of particular identified techniques. Once more, though, the difference in sociable music may lie in the way that the handling of contours, in this case, is tightly wrapped up with other factors such as dynamic level, type of articulation and, above all, phrase structure, which means that these 'natural' processes become events in their own right. They do not need to be teased out of the wider flow; they are there up front for our comprehension.

To this point we have mainly explored the reciprocal aspects of eighteenth-century binarism, but there is a more purely formal, and symmetrical, side to the equation. This means periodicity in its own right, where the focus lies less on the words, as it were, than on how they are punctuated. While not all

---

[68] Caplin, *Classical Form*, 43; Steve Larson, *Musical Forces: Motion, Metaphor, and Meaning in Music* (Bloomington: Indiana University Press, 2012), chapter 4, 82–109; and Leonard B. Meyer, *Style and Music: Theory, History, and Ideology* (Chicago: University of Chicago Press, 1989), 16 (italics removed from 'natural') and 15.

writers on music of the time directly addressed semantics – for instance, the challenges posed by rapid changes of affect – it seems that they all concerned themselves with grammar. The two could be combined, as Charles Henri Blainville did in 1767 when, as Stephanie D. Vial relates, he wrote that 'all melody must be . . . "conversed" (*dialogué*) through the use of full stops and commas, which impart a sense of completion, repose, and suspension'.[69] This suggests that musical punctuation – achieved through all those breaks in the sound that set up a periodic style, and through a hierarchy of various cadential events[70] – was not just a grammatical feature but in fact also already reciprocal. A highly punctuated brand of syntax promotes a social ethos in the way that it constantly leaves gaps for new or at least separate utterances. But a greater number of writers emphasized the virtues of punctuation in its own right, for the clarity and comprehensibility it offered from a listener's point of view. This in itself, of course, represents a social rationale, based on consideration for listeners who need to make sense of the sounds that they hear. Punctuation applied regularly on a larger scale gives rise to the periodic style. Jacqueline Waeber has traced the history of the catch-cry 'unité de mélodie' associated with Rousseau and finds that it became more and more associated with giving priority to periodicity, culminating in the *querelle des Gluckistes et des Piccinnistes* of the later 1770s. The first figure to link 'unité de mélodie' with periodic construction, she notes, was Chastellux, who wrote in 1765: 'In order to make the sentence of the melody periodic, a certain unity must be maintained, a proportion in the parts that compose it, a roundness in the melody that holds the attention and sustains it to the end.'[71] Thus what held a melody together – what gave it 'unity' – was not so much the materials it used as their arrangement, the 'proportion in the parts' that translates into periodic phrase syntax. And when those parts match in various ways, the listener's ability to grasp the whole becomes all the greater. A simple analogy is with rhyming verse, easier to remember than prose because of sounds that match in a regular rhythm.

[69] Charles Henri Blainville, *Histoire générale, critique et philologique de la musique* (Paris: Pissot, 1767), 27; Vial, *The Art of Musical Phrasing*, 79.
[70] As an example of the hierarchy of musical punctuation, Robert O. Gjerdingen cites Galeazzi offering a sequence of four cadential types of increasing strength by analogy with marks of verbal punctuation. Gjerdingen, *Music in the Galant Style*, 156.
[71] François-Jean de Chastellux, *Essai sur l'union de la poésie et de la musique* (Paris: Merlin, 1765), 18, cited in translation in Jacqueline Waeber, 'Jean-Jacques Rousseau's "Unité de Mélodie"', *Journal of the American Musicological Society* 62/1 (2009), 93. Compare the thoughts of Jean-François Marmontel (*Essai sur les révolutions de la musique en France* (Liège: Bassompierre, 1777), 451) on Leonardo Vinci, who 'traced the circle of periodic song . . . in a pure, elegant and sustained design', thus revealing 'the great mystery of melody', cited in translation in Heartz, *Music in European Capitals*, 102.

This clarity of internal structure has continued to impress itself upon listeners to the present day, both for better and for worse. One negative consequence is apparent in Ratner's remark of the later eighteenth century that 'Since most of this music had to be composed quickly, for immediate use, composers relied on familiar and universally accepted formulas for its organization and handling of detail.'[72] This can hardly be denied, especially since we are in the middle of exploring the more or less 'universally accepted formula' of periodic phrase construction, and the notion that a relatively international musical lingua franca had developed across the eighteenth century is what allows the very thesis of this book to be advanced in the first place. But it raises the question of what happened when composers had to write quickly in other eras. Surely they too must have had recourse to familiar patterns – and this may well have happened even when they were not pressed for time. What must make the difference with this widely held perception – an image of composition-by-numbers that has done later eighteenth-century style no favours – is precisely the clarity of periodic phrase syntax, which allows the formulas to be perceived more vividly. This rather drives home the point of an aesthetic of ready intelligibility. We continue to get the message – even if it has lost much of its original freshness.

If Chastellux implies that periodic melody has to be consciously made, another strain of criticism held it up as natural. An exchange in Diderot's *Le neveu de Rameau* (Rameau's Nephew) on the subject 'What is a melody?' turns to the music of 'our young composers' like Egidio Duni (1708–1775), whereupon the character of 'Him' suggests that declamation, understood as a kind of intrinsic human eloquence, is the model. Indeed, 'The more powerful and true the declamation ... the more the song mirroring it will break it into separate phrases; then the truer the song, and the more beautiful. And that's what our young musicians have understood so well.' Thus the dividing of melody into 'separate phrases' is not only stylistically progressive, being contrasted here with the possibly 'dull' older ways of the likes of Lully, Campra and Rameau, but is also framed as being truer to natural human utterance.[73] The naturalness could also be tied not so much to the breaking-up of utterance through declamatory punctuation, but to the symmetry that

---

[72] Ratner, *Classic Music*, xiv.
[73] Diderot, *Rameau's Nephew*, trans. Mauldon, 63–64. It is not known precisely when Diderot wrote *Le neveu de Rameau*.

was likely to result on a larger scale – the preference for even-numbered phrase units. For Riepel in 1752, durations of four, eight, sixteen or thirty-two bars were 'implanted in our natures, to the extent that it is hard to hear any other arrangement with pleasure'.[74] For Koch in 1793, four-bar phrases represented 'the most pleasing melodic sections for our sensibilities',[75] which retains the idea that symmetry brings pleasure, but with 'sensibilities' starts to suggest that this was something that needed to be cultivated. In *Der musikalische Dilettant* of 1773, Johann Friedrich Daube also wanted to have it both ways:

> Of what does symmetry in architecture consist? Of the beautiful proportions of the various dimensions of the component parts from which the building is constructed. This proportional division is pleasing. Even the uninformed peasant will praise it, although he does not know by what means this beauty is produced. . . . Beautiful symmetry is found today in painting, sculpture, dancing, poetry, literature, etc., in which it always brings forth beauty and edification. It is this which we recognize in music, too, and of which very little was known by our forefathers, many of whom believed that one must give his thoughts free rein and let the idea itself conclude the piece.[76]

Thus while musical symmetry can be grasped even by the uneducated – because it is, once again, intrinsically 'pleasing' – at the same time, somewhat inconsistently, there is a historical dimension to it. As we also saw in Diderot's dialogue, this brand of syntax is seen as a decidedly modern feature. Daube's notion of earlier generations giving '[their] thoughts free rein' sounds like what we would now characterize as *Fortspinnung*, the much more continuous syntactical style associated with baroque music. Significantly, Daube's phrase also carries strong behavioural implications: he makes *Fortspinnung* sound anti-social, a way of proceeding that ignores the needs of the listener for clarity of utterance. The phrase 'let[ting] the idea itself conclude the piece' may indicate a disregard for musical

---

[74] Riepel, *Anfangsgründe zur musicalischen Setzkunst*, volume 1: *De Rhythmopoeia oder von der Tactordnung* (Regensburg: Emerich Felix Bader, 1752), 23. Citing Riepel's remark, Georg Feder notes how often Haydn deviates from such an arrangement with his use of three-, five- and six-bar phrases, to say nothing of his manipulation of metre on a larger scale. Feder, *Haydns Streichquartette: Ein musikalischer Werkführer* (Munich: Beck, 1998), 25.

[75] Koch, *Versuch einer Anleitung zur Komposition*, three volumes, volume 3 (Leipzig: Adam Friedrich Böhme, 1793), 53, cited in translation in Danuta Mirka, 'Punctuation and Sense in Late-Eighteenth-Century Music', *Journal of Music Theory* 54/2 (2010), 247.

[76] Johann Friedrich Daube, *Der musikalische Dilettant* (Vienna: Johann Thomas edlen von Trattnern, 1773), 81; *The Musical Dilettante: A Treatise on Composition by J. F. Daube*, trans. and ed. Susan Snook-Luther (Cambridge: Cambridge University Press, 1992), 98.

punctuation – for the need to finish with a full stop, as it were, rather than simply pursuing 'the idea' to the bitter end.

Daube's architectural metaphor also makes clear that symmetrical proportions could exist at various levels of the whole structure. The imperative that these should be audible is answered in some seemingly unlikely contexts in the music of the time. The cancrizans minuet offers a nice example. It is built on unimpeachably symmetrical binary principles – that from the half-way point in the movement all the music so far heard will be played backwards, creating a perfect mirror image. However, this could by no means be described as a 'natural' course of events, and, being more of a learned conceit, should be very difficult to grasp aurally. But in such movements from their symphonies both Haydn (Symphony No. 47 in G major of 1772) and Kraus (Symphony in C sharp minor, VB140, of 1782) go out of their way to help listeners, using marked contrasts of texture, timbre and dynamics, that will, with any luck, also sound conspicuous enough when the music goes into reverse gear.[77] There are no dynamic contrasts marked in the 'Trio al roverscio' from the Quartet in G major Op. 29 No. 2 (1800) by Adalbert Gyrowetz, and little rhythmic differentiation within the material that will be made to run backward, but the composer makes strategic use of short silences to the same end.

A more dynamic conception of musical periodicity than Daube's is offered by Adam Smith, who wrote in 1795 that 'In the contemplation of that immense variety of agreeable and melodious sounds, arranged and digested, both in their coincidence and in their succession, into so complete and regular a system, the mind in reality enjoys not only a very great sensual, but a very high intellectual, pleasure, not unlike that which it derives from contemplation of a great system in any other science'.[78] While Smith is describing the virtues of modern instrumental music

---

[77] In 'More than a Copy: Joseph Haydn's *Menuet al roverso* in Context', HAYDN 3/2 (2013) www.rit.edu/haydn (1 July 2014), Balázs Mikusi examines precedents for Haydn's *roverso* movement. Confirming that such a technical procedure carried older associations, Mikusi cites the words of Türk, who included a *minuetto riverso* in his *Klavierschule* of 1789: 'Nowadays one wastes less time and effort on such tricks than formerly' (22). Of Haydn's movement Mikusi also notes that the composer must have wanted it to be 'perceptible to all attentive listeners' (14). Perhaps because of his concentration on the pre-history of Haydn's movement, Mikusi does not note the existence of Kraus's example, and to this one could add the final movement of the Kraus String Quartet in G minor, Op. 1 No. 3 (VB183; 1784). Here both outer sections form a perfect cancrizans, separated by a trio, but with no obvious dynamic or other anomalies that would help the listener. But the generic context of the string quartet may account for the less helpful compositional approach.

[78] Adam Smith, *Essays on Philosophical Subjects* (London: T. Cadell junior and W. Davies, 1795), 172.

altogether, what is striking for our purposes is the repetition of the word 'system'. That it is 'complete and regular' suggests that Smith hears an art that moves like a great machine, with individual working parts that function in perfect synchrony with the 'logic' of the whole. But, as we saw in Chapter 1, Smith had also noted that periodicity constrains utterance. For him, it naturally favours 'the sociable and agreeable passions', since feelings such as anger are harder to reconcile within a system of periodic phrase syntax. But for Christian Friedrich Daniel Schubart, in his *Ideen zu einer Ästhetik der Tonkunst* of 1784–1785, what was constrained was not so much anger as all higher feelings, because of the devastating 'taste for the comic' that had swept all before it. Looking forward to the future of music, he urged that 'our best effort must go towards limiting this taste as much as possible and making a place anew for the serious, heroic and tragic, for pathos and the elevated'. What would be especially important would be 'to seek out a new rhythm in which the ever-present caesuras will not make our music monotonous'. By avoiding such caesuras – the constant punctuating gaps of the periodic style – music will get 'led back to its former dignity and sublimity'.[79]

If for Schubart periodic rhythms delivered monotony and triviality, most musical evidence from the time suggests that it was rather the lack of periodicity that was open to question. Certainly, this was likely to count as a special effect if pursued for any length of time. Many of the most extreme examples have an avowed programmatic basis, involving disorder of various kinds. Storms and battles were likely occasions for a breakdown of the 'great system'. A battle is indicated for the final movement of Dittersdorf's *Les Quatre Ages du Monde* (The Four Ages of the World), one of his series of *Symphonies on Ovid's Metamorphoses* (premiered in 1786). This finale depicts the Iron Age, the end of a downward spiral of civilization that is reached after the paradise of the Golden Age depicted at the outset. Richard Will notes that the final movements of all these works after Ovid's tales involve a 'dissolution of musical order',[80] but the Iron Age does this spectacularly. Once past its initial phases, the movement produces a torrent of sequential figuration that offers regularity in the immediate sense, but there is no larger-scale patterning that would offer functional

---

[79] Christian Friedrich Daniel Schubart, *Ideen zu einer Ästhetik der Tonkunst*, ed. (by his son) Ludwig Schubart (Stuttgart: J. Scheible, 1839; first edition, Vienna: Degen, 1806), 280; Ted Alan DuBois, 'Christian Friedrich Daniel Schubart's *Ideen zu einer Ästhetik der Tonkunst*: An Annotated Translation' (PhD dissertation, University of Southern California, 1983), 327–328 (translation slightly adapted).

[80] Will, *Characteristic Symphony*, 29.

clarity, telling the listener how one pattern relates to the next. A lack of melodic definition and cadential articulation means there is no proper sense of phrase, so that the entire passage ends up feeling like a transition with no end. The lack of complementarity or reciprocity between the various gestures that we hear, the lack of 'consideration' of the materials for other possible types of utterance, suggests the anti-social wickedness of the Age: the syntactical ethos seems to be 'every man for himself'.

Eventually the tumult, which has lasted over sixty bars, dies away, to be succeeded by an Allegretto that restores recognizable musical conduct. We hear the reciprocal symmetry of an antecedent–consequent phrase construction, reminiscent of the opening Golden Age, which inhabits a paradise of periodicity. And indeed, after the unbridled assertiveness of what has gone before, we might understand the Allegretto section as a large-scale version of our gracious riposte. If so, the restoration of order and social consciousness that it symbolizes has a dark irony. Dittersdorf describes the section as portraying the cries of triumph of the victors and sorrow of the vanquished, but even without that prompt, it is evident that nothing can ever be the same again. After what we have witnessed, the 'natural order' of periodicity has been exposed as contingent. Haydn's depiction of the earthquake at the end of *The Seven Last Words* (1787) is comparably apocalyptic in its abandonment of syntactical norms. Once more it tells us that periodicity entails more than immediate and hence 'symmetrical' repetitions of material, since there are plenty of those here. It is the superstructure of utterance that falls apart. In the *Representation of Chaos* that opens Haydn's *Creation*, written in 1796, the opposite seems to apply. We hear almost no immediate repetitions of material, yet for all sense of confusion and mystery, four-bar units are in control almost throughout – in the absence of cadential articulation, they cannot properly be described as four-bar phrases. This creates an undertow of regularity, a symmetry of large-scale rhythm, that provides some base for recognition of the many chaotic irregularities.

The lesson that modern binary syntax involves a negotiation between forces of symmetry and reciprocity is also taught in many more modest contexts. At this point we are concerned only with occasions where 'system failure' is apparent across a complete unit, not the more immediate interplay of what Caplin calls 'tight-knit' and 'loose' styles of organization,[81] nor the sort of relative breakdown that may occur in say a development section. One self-contained example of such failure is heard in Dittersdorf's

---

[81] See Caplin, *Classical Form*, 17, for initial comment on this distinction.

symphony *Il combattimento delle passioni umani*, immediately following the two movements that we considered earlier (*Il Superbo* and *Il Humile*). This is a minuet dubbed *Il Matto* (Madness, Eccentricity). Amidst some patently odd features – hemiolas, prominent tritones, an awkward descending sequence – the most significant feature for our purposes is the over-insistence on a few rhythmic motives. The music appears to be closed in on itself, unable to consider alternative shapes or ideas. Also notable is that all but a few bars of the minuet are played in unison, meaning that texturally as well as thematically variety is excluded. This portrayal of an unbalanced one-track mind is paired with a trio called *Il Amante*. Much more varied in its seductive moves, this makes the point effectively by contrast: love, at least ideally, is the most reciprocal of states of feeling.

Various forms of exotic evocation may also be understood in opposition to the syntactical norm, often reinforcing the point made above that a highly sectional phrase structure alone does not fully equip a movement in the modern musical world. Over-repetition – too much symmetry, in effect – often characterizes the *alla turca* style, for instance,[82] and the same holds as the exotic shades into the rustic. The discursive style is relatively inflexible, lacking not just 'pleasing variety' but also the suppleness of phrase rhythm that allows for expansions of content. Such sections or movements tend to finish without ceremony, with 'the idea itself', as Daube might have said. Yet we need not imagine that listeners were laughing up their sleeves, since there was clearly a market demand for such styles. And at a global level such idioms offered variety of utterance, an encompassing desideratum. The mania for Scottish folklore in England in the late eighteenth century produced some nice examples, such as Dussek's Op. 31 set of piano trios from 1795 (which also in fact advertised the use of 'German Airs' within its pages, making for a refreshing change of exotic locale). The slow movement of Op. 31 No. 3, based on the Scotch air 'Auld Robin Gray', follows the captivating eight-bar theme with a minore section based on the head-motive of the air. Not so much a contrast as an intensification of the gentle melancholy of the theme, it also contains a phrase extension as an expected four bars are turned into six before the cadence arrives. Then the opening eight bars return exactly, to be followed by a varied version of the same as the surface rhythm speeds up to sextuplets. At the end of this variation the movement simply stops, without even an extra chord or two to signal the close of the

---

[82] For a recent examination of Turkish style, and indeed the Hungarian style with which it was largely interchangeable, see Catherine Mayes, 'Turkish and Hungarian-Gypsy Styles', in *The Oxford Handbook of Topic Theory*, ed. Mirka, 214–237.

movement. This apparent simplicity is in fact something of a special effect, all the more marked given the greater flexibility evident in the central minore section.

It is a similar story in the second movement of Pleyel's piano trio Ben448 (1794), part of a batch of eighteen trios the composer wrote for George Thompson that use Scotch airs. The tune of this 'Rondo Ecossois' in A minor is syntactically 'lame', unexpectedly sitting down at cadence points, and its initial unison presentation by the three players emphasizes the material's lack of tractability. Nor, once more, can there be any coda at the end – the tune simply stops, unable to extend itself. The episodes heard in between identical recurrences of the theme offer the more customary syntactical flexibility, for instance through short-range dialogue between violin and piano, though the composer then takes great care to dissolve such eloquence in readiness for the return of the unpolished Scotch air.[83]

But unpolished does not mean unattractive, and one can imagine the relish with which players across Europe would have tackled such a movement. And, as we shall see in later chapters, it is unrealistic to posit any sort of a firm aesthetic gap between such untutored pastoralism and a more flexible reciprocal style given how strongly galant music aspires to the openness and accessibility of popular idioms. In any case, the tables can be turned, as they seem to be in the six Pastorelas by Manuel Blasco de Nebra (written some time before the composer's death in 1784). Each of these works consists of an Adagio followed by a movement that is itself named Pastorela and concludes with a Minuet. The middle movements, without tempo markings but clearly meant to be played fast, all offer the same rhythmically quirky idiom marked by unexpected accents on the second and fifth quavers of the 6/8 bar, but just as striking is their extreme paratactic syntax. While particular shapes do recur from phrase to phrase, in general there is a conspicuous lack of art in the way individual phrases succeed one another. We tend to hear an untidy profusion of ideas. While this is a common feature of pastoral music in general – one would not expect artful transitions in a style that is meant to evoke rustic music-making – the composer takes it to an extreme.[84]

---

[83] This material derives from my review of the recording *Ignaz Pleyel: Piano Trios*, played by Trio 1790 (cpo 777 544-2, 2011), in *Eighteenth-Century Music* 9/2 (2012), 284–285.

[84] The last few sentences derive from my article 'Poet of the Galant: The Keyboard Works of Manuel Blasco de Nebra', in *Instrumental Music in Late Eighteenth-Century Spain*, ed. Miguel Ángel Marín and Màrius Bernardó (Kassel: Reichenberger, 2014), 320. Following this, at 320–321, I offer an inventory of the shared features of these six strikingly original pastorela movements.

The minuets that follow these explosions of rhythmic exuberance, varied though they are, all represent a regaining of stylistic equilibrium. This is apparent in the much more polished nature of their diction, with phrases arranged in reciprocal pairings and rhythms more settled after the 'disorder' of the pastorelas. Yet these minuets are typically very brief, and three of them (in Pastorelas Nos 2, 3 and 6) never leave their tonic key. Allied with this is a reserved tone, as if disciplined by the 'civilized' nature of the dance form.[85] After the messy generosity of the pastorelas, the minuets leave a somewhat inscrutable impression; they suggest the inhibiting side of civilized discourse. Blasco de Nebra's juxtaposition of syntactical types in these works exposes the ambivalence that can often be sensed in attitudes to the modern syntactical style, with its clustered conceptual bases of symmetry, periodicity and reciprocity. Modern musical syntax is unmarked and natural, 'implanted in our natures', as Riepel had it, but it is also a sign of civilization, a man-made accomplishment. The same tension exists with regard to the sociable impulses that I argue this syntax specifically embodies – they are at once a natural part of being human but also something that must be cultivated.

An opposed to the overly sectional, paratactic types discussed above, exceptional effects can also arise from extreme syntactical continuity. At the level of a complete structure this can only really be found in slow movements, and the sense of otherness tends to be temporally rather than geographically based. Often this is achieved via some version of ground-bass or passacaglia technique, as in the slow movements from Haydn's Sonata in E major H31 (1776) and Piano Trio in E major H28 (1797), both set in the tonic minor. In the sonata movement the ground bass is not always present, but the continuous quaver rhythms it embodies always are, while the equivalent pattern in the Trio movement is relentlessly maintained until just before the end.[86] The Andante of Mozart's Violin Sonata in A major, K526 (1787), offers a bass pattern that should be subordinate but often dominates because the melody only arrives in very short bursts, and where the pattern is not literally present, the sense of continuous motion is maintained. Mozart's bass line has a less antique flavour than those of Haydn. What it shares with them, though, especially with the piano-trio movement, is a spooky, even gothic, feeling brought about by the stylistic sense that so much unrelieved even rhythmic

---

[85] The last few sentences are also based on extracts from my 'Poet of the Galant', 322 and 324.
[86] Charles Rosen gives an especially inspired account of this movement in *The Classical Style*, 360.

motion is unnatural. At the same time, an overlay of periodicity – of the music's dividing into distinct phrases – is never in doubt. The Adagio of Clementi's Sonata in G major Op. 37 No. 2 (1798) utilizes a virtual ostinato in dotted rhythm throughout, and gives the game away through its subtitle: 'In the solemn style'. Several breathtaking moments when the seamless rhythmic motion is arrested, and silence breaks out, seem to acknowledge what from a late eighteenth-century perspective is an unnatural way for music to proceed.

Another way of stepping outside the bounds of syntactical norms arises with the genre of fantasia, even if this is largely confined to solo keyboard performance. From our current perspective, its typically unpredictable profusion of material is not a distinguishing feature, since this was a charge often levelled at music that did not aspire to give the impression of being improvised. What is more germane, once more, is the unruly superstructure. As an avowedly personal genre, the fantasia can resist, or at least play with, the collective values that reciprocity and periodicity imply. This need not entail only 'unruly' affects. Clementi's Capriccio in F major, Op. 34 (1795), opens with a typical mixture of passionate and brilliant gestures, but is then derailed courtesy of material that makes its first appearance from bar 87. Marked by a change to 3/4 time and the direction Moderato, and featuring consistent dotted rhythms, it has an amiable character, but it stumbles over itself, returning again and again to its opening gesture. The improviser is lost for a sense of direction, it would appear, and so we hear a sort of desultory playing-around with not very much at all, and this lasts for nearly one hundred moderately paced bars. The material may present a friendly face, but it goes on too long and is therefore lacking in consideration – a sociable vice. Saying things at length is not what one does. Appropriately enough given the genre, the material lacks the usual 'composed' presentation typical of sociable style.

The fantasia spirit runs through much of the output of C. P. E. Bach, beyond the fact that he published so many specimens of the genre and wrote so prolifically about its requirements.[87] This is apparent in a consistent unruliness of syntax: in the composer's tendency to avoid straightforward periodic construction and his preference for various kinds of harmonic interruption and deflection. This affects full cadences above all; even when present, which of course they must be often enough, there is

---

[87] Carl Philipp Emanuel Bach, *Versuch über die wahre Art das Klavier zu spielen*, part 2 (Berlin: Georg Ludewig Winter, 1762), 'Von der freyen Fantasie', 325–341; C. P. E. Bach, *Essay on the True Art of Playing Keyboard Instruments*, ed. and trans. William J. Mitchell (New York: Norton, 1949), 'The Free Fantasia', 430–445.

often some quirk of shaping or some unusual means of arrival that weakens their effect. Curiously, this does not extend to half cadences, which tend to take a very similar form through much of Bach's output.[88] It is in fact not so much the specific form and articulation of the cadence that is problematized as the approach to it, demonstrating what Annette Richards calls the composer's 'almost obsessive resistance to closure'.[89] For example, the first movement of the Sonata in F major from the second collection of keyboard works *für Kenner und Liebhaber* (Wq56/4; 1780) opens with four bars that sound like a typical antecedent phrase, but the consequent is nothing like what we would expect, and six bars later the music reaches an authentic cadence in A minor. Thus symmetry is upset both thematically and in terms of duration, and harmonically we arrive at an unexpected destination. Nevertheless, the actual form taken by this cadence is the most prototypical available at the time: the Cudworth Cadence, which offers an octave descent in the melody to a more or less set rhythm, heard against a set succession of bass degrees.[90] The whole ten bars are then repeated in 'varied reprise' manner, which creates symmetry at a higher level, no matter how disruptive the internal contents of the passage happen to be.

Such higher symmetry in fact plays an essential role. The Sonata in E minor from book 6 of *Kenner und Liebhaber* (Wq61/5; 1785) has a first movement that is at an extreme of impulsiveness. Practically every bar brings a contradiction of any expected continuation, with disjunct handling of texture, register, dynamics, harmony and theme. What holds it together is the fact that most phrases are two or four bars long. The phrases thus 'breathe' regularly on a large scale – which means periodicity. This demonstrates how such large-scale regularity can allow any amount of impulsive, 'improvisatory' changeability within its bounds. If this returns us to our earlier dialectic between changeable materials and periodic phrase syntax, it must be said that Bach's approach often puts extreme pressure on the stability of that equation. However, we must resist the notion that periodicity constrains composition, that it inhibits creativity – that hallowed strain of the reception of later eighteenth-century instrumental style. Even in the relatively exceptional cases we have been considering above, it is not a matter of either/or: the particular type of periodicity that developed in the

---

[88] The last few sentences derive from my review of ten volumes from *Carl Philip Emanuel Bach: The Complete Works* in *Notes: Quarterly Journal of the Music Library Association* 65/3 (2009), 845.

[89] Richards, *Free Fantasia and the Musical Picturesque*, 55.

[90] The Cudworth Cadence was so dubbed by Robert Gjerdingen in honour of Charles Cudworth, who was the first to discuss the pattern in print; see *Music in the Galant Style*, 146–149.

eighteenth century was a basic ground for utterance, for comprehension, and all composers had to work with it, alongside it, against it, in fact often shifted fluidly between these poles.

A nice example of such fluidity, on a larger structural scale, may be found in the first movement of the Sonata in G major from *Kenner und Liebhaber* book 4 (Wq58/2; 1781). Marked Grazioso, with its diction embodying the 'sensitive style', it opens with a four-bar phrase finishing on the dominant. When the second phrase begins in the same way, we may project that a musical period will unfold, involving both symmetry (roughly rhyming antecedent and consequent phrases) and complementarity (the second phrase will offer a different, stronger cadence in response to the initial half cadence). However, this consequent phrase is only just underway when it veers off towards the dominant. While the music initially follows the outlines of the equivalent antecedent material, it is nothing like a match, and soon were are hearing an echo-repeat of a new one-bar unit, which destroys the prospects of a matching four-bar phrase. Once more the composer shows that he is, as Richard Kramer has it, 'impatient with the idea of a conventional continuity'.[91] The phrase eventually does close, in D major, but can barely be heard as a normal modulating consequent. It ends up being six bars long, and the last two consist of a loud brilliant descending scale of D major in a new rhythm of triplet semiquavers, which hardly fits affectively in this 'sensitive' environment. It sounds instead like an impulsive disruption. Then we hear a varied repetition of the whole ten bars, creating a compensatory larger-scale symmetry: a similar plan to that found in the Sonata in F major Wq56/4 above. In the current case this means that by the time we reach bar 20, we have heard four phrases all of which start on I and finish on or in V. A new four-bar phrase that resumes the sensitive style moves us back to being on V, rather than in V. It acts as a retransition to the return of the opening four-bar phrase, which initially exactly matches what we heard at the beginning, but is then lightly varied so as to finish on I. While at first this return seems to function as a reprise, the way it continues to a close on the tonic makes it assume a different structural identity: a delayed consequent that finishes 'properly' in I. After a varied repetition of the retransitional phrase, we hear from bar 32^3 a decorated version of our first phrase, at first exactly matching the form it took from the end of bar 10. But then it too finishes on I, and that, in fact, is the end of the movement. Thus the two aberrant modulating consequent phrases from earlier on are replaced – and answered – by two that close on

---

[91] Richard Kramer, *Unfinished Music* (New York: Oxford University Press, 2008), 240.

the tonic, and these two later versions also answer each other in a symmetrical relationship. From our current syntactical perspective, therefore, the plot of the whole movement is about reaching a proper consequent phrase, in a problematizing of the principle of reciprocity between phrases.

Agency and Motive

Many of the noteworthy developments in music scholarship of the past generation or so might be said to pivot on questions of agency. The term itself might not always have been invoked, but the sense behind it has animated much rethinking of scholarly obligations. Such notions as composer authority and musical autonomy have been comprehensively challenged, as has a perceived preference for investigating production rather than consumption: both summon up the spectre of that now infamous phrase 'the music itself'. A kind of compensatory history has rushed to the aid of performers and listeners, stressing their agency in the musical equation via such terms of reference as 'voice', 'body' and 'musicking',[92] and on a broader scale the simple word 'context' has become a mantra to ward off our spectre of work autonomy and the associated notion of the 'purely musical'. What has allegedly been unmasked is a flow-chart of agency that moves in just the one direction – whereby the scholar-analyst simply brings out what is immanent in the work, which is entirely in the gift of the composer, and performers in turn simply bring out this content, to be faithfully recorded by the listener, who is always highly literate, stylistically aware and attentive.

Yet, even if one accepts this diagnosis of an earlier state of affairs, one might argue that the problem of autonomy and the one-way traffic it implies have not so much been solved as deflected. While we may have been looking elsewhere, the sense of some kind of intrinsic musical agency has not gone away. Eric F. Clarke suggests that listening typically involves a mixture of agential impressions, among which is precisely a kind of autonomy:

The autonomous character of music is *not* entirely illusory, but it is also only one aspect of what I experience in music ... At times music does have the power ... to draw a listener into a virtual reality consisting of objects and events that are experienced simultaneously as motifs, rhythmic groups, and cadences, as well as spaces, actions, places, and agents. And at other times it remains firmly anchored in

---

[92] This term entered the lexicon with the appearance of Small, *Musicking*.

the everyday world through the real actions, objects, ideologies, words, and social functions with which it is entwined.[93]

Clarke evokes a state of immersion within an intrinsically musical world – a world of pure sound, as it were – that contends with elements that pull us away from such a state, which might include sitting in a concert hall or becoming conscious of the physical production of sound. The sense of action that issues from a musical experience can thus be both virtual – not readily translatable outside the music world in which it is understood – and real. It is surely this virtual, immersive state, which I imagine most of us have experienced, that encourages the sense that there is something we can reify as 'the music' and attempt to account for in our writings.

My focus here lies in one aspect of music's pulling power, which seems to draw us into that virtual reality – the musical motive. It is of course a dependent aspect, but then, as Clarke makes clear, there are no stand-alone elements to our experience of music. After all, even the agency of performers is not absolute in the Western classical tradition; since they take their cue from notated scripts, they are also dependent parts of the complete equation. And of course the composer is hardly absolute either, relying on the agency of performers in order for music to exist more than conceptually. As for music scholars, when we think and write about music, we are also listeners – and indeed also performers of a kind when we attempt to bring to life an individual piece or movement or work. Seth Monahan's recent dissecting of agential implications in music-analytical writing makes this explicit by granting the analyst a separate sphere of agency: his four basic categories of agent, in ascending order of weight, are (1) individuated elements, (2) the work persona, (3) the fictional composer and (4) the analyst.[94] Indeed, the analyst is Monahan's controlling category, and this owes something to the disciplinary developments of recent times: without them it would have been harder to construe the analyst's role in such a proactive fashion.

But even if we all concede that understandings of musical agency involve a messy mixture of protagonists – the performer, the listener, the scholar, music's virtual world and, finally, let us not forget, the composer – it is unlikely that the mixture is not inflected by historical and cultural circumstances. As Monahan notes, writings to this point, including arguably the pioneering work of Edward T. Cone, have been based on canonical

---

[93] Clarke, *Ways of Listening*, 187.
[94] Seth Monahan, 'Action and Agency Revisited', *Journal of Music Theory* 57/2 (2013), 321–371.

nineteenth-century repertory,[95] which means bringing certain assumptions to bear that seem to be a comfortable fit for that music. Thus the level of agency within a work that Monahan dubs the 'work persona', an experiencing – often suffering – subject whose presence is understood within the music. This can readily be equated with a kind of encompassing subjectivity, which often translates into the direct expression of emotional states, and this can just as readily be transferred outwards, involving an appeal to the circumstances of the real-life composer. There might now be a consensus that such assumptions are only awkwardly applicable to the musical outputs of the eighteenth century – though there is no shortage of prior example, if one considers traditions of treating the music of say C. P. E. Bach or Mozart as a more or less rebellious expression of personal subjectivity.

If this represents one challenge when considering agency in eighteenth-century music, another arises with the concepts under which we gather together such impressions – 'narrative', for instance, or 'drama' (an important precursor to Monahan's examination of agency, by Fred Everett Maus, is entitled 'Music as Drama'[96]). But, one might ask, why narrative; why drama? Language per se might be a better fit. After all, language models are widely acknowledged to have been a formative influence on both the composition and the critical conception of eighteenth-century music: we have seen earlier the influence of such models on contemporary notions of what music was doing, or ought to be doing, evident in the emphasis on various levels of punctuation, for instance. A broader concept than language would be, simply, discourse, suggested as a point of orientation in Chapter 1, and defined there as an invitation to contemplate the agency of all parties in the construction of a work of music.

Michael Spitzer's metaphor theory offers a useful means of refining our sense of how musical agency was both understood and enacted historically. He writes, 'The illusion that music can embody human qualities is irreducible from our musical experience', but we 'have plenty of latitude in *how* to hear its human aspects'.[97] That latitude he defines in terms of preferred modes of musical understanding from three successive stylistic periods of the common-practice era. His governing metaphors are representation, language and embodiment, mapped onto music of the baroque era, the later eighteenth century and the nineteenth century respectively. An

---

[95] Monahan, 'Action and Agency Revisited', 323n.
[96] Fred Everett Maus, 'Music as Drama', *Music Theory Spectrum* 10/1 (1988), 56–73.
[97] Michael Spitzer, *Metaphor and Musical Thought* (Chicago: University of Chicago Press, 2004), 12.

alternative collocation would be, again in chronological order, music as painting, music as language and, for the nineteenth century, simply music as life. Therefore to engage a preferred metaphorical mode for music in the nineteenth century, he states, 'is to compare music to a person, rather than a picture (baroque) or a language (classical)'.[98] This offers a way to historicize current understandings of musical agency: they remain rooted in romantic aesthetics.

So what, then, of the linguistic metaphor; if we accept the point, what does music as language imply for the works of the later eighteenth century? We might answer that, from the point of view of the time, language is a shared phenomenon, premised on an expectation that utterance will be intelligible, as opposed to the perhaps less articulate states implied by the nineteenth-century model. Expression is certainly a valid term of reference, but – as explored earlier – it is not so much libidinal as behavioural in orientation, meaning that, while one has one's own feelings and points of view, one also considers those of others. This can bring in its wake a certain self-consciousness about the act of communication, reaffirming the notion that discourse might be a more appropriate term than drama within which to organize our impressions of musical sound.

This self-consciousness even allows Rumph to speak of an 'erosion of voice' in later eighteenth-century music. In his account, the balanced regular phrase rhythms of the style encourage a mixture of elements, a 'combinatorial play', that undermines an earlier rhetorical tradition.[99] This certainly makes sense if we consider the topical plurality that is such a striking development of the time, whereby dance rhythms, horn calls, learned counterpoint and the like mingle in unpredictable combinations. Musical topics can hardly be identified with the utterance of any single work persona. Rather they seem to represent a plurality of 'outside voices' making their way into the work. From the many negative contemporary reactions to such a style we can gather that hearing music as the expression of an individual temperament was not anachronistic: for the enemies of the 'mixed style', it offended against just this assumption. What they heard was a clatter of conflicting gestures that, as Sulzer claimed, 'does not engage the heart' ('ein artiges und unterhaltendes, aber das Herz nicht beschäftigendes Geschwätz'[100]). In other words, agency had become de-centred and uncertain, something we have seen in the words of William Jones, who

---

[98] Spitzer, *Metaphor and Musical* Thought, 278.
[99] Rumph, *Mozart and Enlightenment Semiotics*, 37.
[100] Sulzer, *Allgemeine Theorie der Schönen Künste*, volume 3, 431.

contrasted Handel at his pulpit with Haydn and Boccherini at the tea-table. Yet this need not equate to a weakening of the 'composer's voice'. While any sense of a feeling work persona may indeed be questionable, at the level of Monahan's 'fictional composer' – the creative agency that is in control of the notated product – that voice may in fact be strengthened. Any patent manipulation of musical events – such as Haydn's endless games with the formal function of material, as when beginnings and endings are mixed up – strongly implies the agency of a composer. Similarly, Rumph's 'combinatorial play' both strengthens the sense of an omniscient composer – who decides what materials to deploy at what particular time – yet also weakens it, since the composer as it were abdicates creative responsibility, by inviting all and sundry to the musical party. Multiple materials with multiple points of view interact, while the composer 'stands aside' in 'philosophical' manner. This creative ambivalence also extends, as Danuta Mirka has often demonstrated, to the composer's assuming the role of an incompetent ('artful imitation of bungling'[101]), unable to manage the materials that crowd on into the musical picture.

A similar ambiguity arises when we come to consider the ontology and agency of the musical motive. The individualization of motive represents another striking development in the music of the later eighteenth century. While motives are certainly recognizable as such earlier than this time, they are less 'characteristic', partly because they are embedded in a more continuous brand of musical syntax (so-called *Fortspinnung*), and partly because they tend to be rhythmically more homogeneous. There is the sense that they form what Rita Benton calls 'part of the general motion of the piece, not an entirely independent or contrasting segment of it'.[102] In the later eighteenth century, though, aided by the growing taste for periodic phrase structures, motives can 'stand out from the crowd' and become agents of a new, listener-oriented sense of musical process. As a result of their brevity, their rhythmic memorability and their relative isolation within a wider web of sound, they can start to be thought of as distinct 'ideas'.[103] They may function as the 'hook' does in popular music, drawing the listener in, standing in for the whole, giving the listener something to

---

[101] Mirka, *Metric Manipulations in Haydn and Mozart*, 301.
[102] Rita Benton, 'Form in the Sonatas of Domenico Scarlatti', *The Music Review* 13/4 (1952), 267.
[103] And the larger entity of the theme also starts to be equated with 'idea'; see Mark Evan Bonds, *Wordless Rhetoric: Musical Form and the Metaphor of the Oration* (Cambridge, MA: Harvard University Press, 1991), 164, who notes that 'The perception of *Thema* as *Gedanke* reflects the growing belief in an inherent, self-referential meaning within musical works that have no text', which reminds us of a level of agency that has been the focus of much musicological attention in the past generation.

latch on to. In other words, motives aid the process of entrainment; as we sing them or hum them, they seem to be absorbed into our nervous system. But their individuality extends beyond their local make-up to the ways in which they behave on a larger scale; they may change markedly over the course of a movement, either in their form or in their placement relative to other materials, a phenomenon that is already vividly embodied in a repertory such as the Domenico Scarlatti sonatas.[104] Such unpredictability may foreground the agency of the composer, whose persona can intrude in a way that is historically quite novel. But it can also do something quite different, and possibly contradictory: create the impression that the material concerned has taken on a life of its own.

We can consider this with reference to the 'philosophical' stance mentioned earlier. Lidov writes that 'Among Haydn's bequests to Beethoven [was] the method of giving a philosophical tone to music', which involves what he calls 'objectification' and 'distancing'.[105] The 'philosophical' method[106] means that 'musical forms and figures are subject to play': 'To *play* with the theme is to set it partly free, free from one sound, one context, one definite arrangement'.[107] This may indeed be understood as a kind of abstraction, but it also highlights qualities of versatility and adaptability, which are sociable virtues too: being able to see other points of view. Lidov's perspective also reinforces the duality of our 'motivic agency'. Objectification heightens the agency of the fictional composer, but it does so as that fictional composer patently 'sets free' his materials, as represented by the most prominent and memorable ones – those we could describe as motivic. The motive is 'free to roam' in the same way that the composer in a mixed and periodic style is 'free to roam' over all sorts of possibilities.

While this kind of motivic independence can most readily be imagined when a movement features strongly contrasting materials, so diffusing any sense of a controlling authorial voice, I will concentrate on cases where one motive or gesture dominates. In the finale of Haydn's Quartet in C major Op. 64 No. 1 (1790; Example 2.17) a simple but rhythmically vital motive projects an energy that seems to carry all before it. This movement would

---

[104] For an exploration of this see W. Dean Sutcliffe, *The Keyboard Sonatas of Domenico Scarlatti and Eighteenth-Century Musical Style* (Cambridge: Cambridge University Press, 2003), 325–334.

[105] Lidov, *Is Language a Music?*, 56.

[106] On the historical roots of this 'philosophical' strain see Leon Botstein, 'The Consequences of Presumed Innocence: The Nineteenth-Century Reception of Joseph Haydn', in *Haydn Studies*, ed. Sutcliffe, 1–34.

[107] Lidov, *Is Language a Music?*, 57.

seem to confirm what Rosen asserts, that in Haydn we have the sensation that 'the material can be made to release its charged force so that the music no longer unfolds, as in the Baroque, but is literally impelled from within'.[108] The energetic charge is provided by a classic motive – concise, concentrated, immediately apprehensible by the listener. It is plainly a motive that motivates, yet when one tries to define just what this motive is, a confusion of agential levels becomes apparent. At the start of Example 2.17 I have labelled it *x*, suggesting that it consists of just two notes, an upbeat followed by a downbeat, both on the same pitch, played by three of the four instruments. We can see that this motive is immediately repeated, but at this point things become less straightforward. Violin 2 and viola now edge upwards by step, suggesting a nervous energy that culminates when the next upbeat is subject to rhythmic diminution. It is this, I would suggest, that is the greatest hook of all. The initial short isolated two-note units, stuttering in buffa fashion, are followed by a semiquaver tattoo that gives the most decided character to the whole phrase unit (marked *x'*). It seems to demand a release of tension that follows in the plain quaver rhythms of bar 2, marked *y*, plus the fact that all three instruments descend. In light of these events, and in light of the forms we will subsequently hear, it is indeed hard to define just what constitutes the motive. In one sense it is motive *x* as individually labelled – irreducible, primal, upbeat leads to downbeat, end of story – but in another sense, particularly given the magnetizing aural power of the semiquaver tattoo, and the way in which the repetitions build up to it, the whole two-bar unit is where the agency lies. This I have labelled *M* (for the larger-scale motive). If we take the more monadic option, we are opting for a gesture so simple it barely sounds like it has been composed. But when it seems to generate its own continuation, and then its own elaboration, the sense of independent agency becomes vivid: this is exactly what Rosen characterizes as being 'impelled from within'. Motive *x* even leaves its mark on the contrasting material that follows in bars 3–4, a smooth cantabile rejoinder (and a form of gracious riposte), since a repeated-note upbeat-downbeat succession sets this in train on the pickup into bar 3.

Because trying to determine the precise definition of motive *x* proves elusive, this undermines my agency as an analyst. The controlling power seems to be with the motive, as it were, for ever dancing playfully out of reach. Haydn often presents extreme cases of this sort of ambiguity, leaving us flailing at thin air. Hepokoski and Darcy try to capture this sensation

---

[108] Rosen, *The Classical Style*, 120.

Example 2.17 Haydn, Quartet in C major Op. 64 No. 1/iv, bars 1–62

Example 2.17 (continued)

Example 2.17 (continued)

(albeit with regard to the composer's recapitulatory practices) by invoking the eighteenth-century concept of 'vitalism, according to which individual living particles are understood to grow spontaneously and continuously'. Haydn, they write, 'may be suggesting ... that the task of the composer [when] facing such self-willed vitalistic (musical) particles is to trim and shape their innate tendency toward unstoppable growth and self-mutation'.[109] This suggests not just that the analyst may not be able to keep up, but that the composer himself cannot control his invention. A glance at the annotated Example 2.17 will suggest something of the invasive power of the motive, or in fact the larger motive-complex. Even the main contrasting material of the movement, the strings of continuous semiquavers (y'), can also be interpreted as an outflow from x. See bars 8–9, when they are first launched, courtesy of x', which here moves by step. These semiquavers are themselves a rhythmic diminution of the even note values and stepwise movement first encountered in bar 2, marked y. Once more in bar 9 they could be read as a wave of energy being released after the coiled-spring repetitions of motive x, and are therefore dependent on that motive to bring them into being.

Subsequently x and y are joined even more closely. From the upbeat to bar 15, for example, the original chain of x figures returns in violin 1 as violin 2 and viola simultaneously take up y'. The continuation at 16–17 seems be new, but in fact is an augmentation of the descending shape from bar 2, both melodically (falling stepwise fourth) and in terms of texture (the parallel 6/3 chords). Thus we can understand the whole three-bar unit as a further version of M, now expanding its range texturally, temporally and rhythmically. Further, one of the means of stretching out y is x itself, with repeated-note upbeat–downbeat pairs initiating each note of the descending line.

Part of the way in which x proliferates through the movement is that it can shrug off its original accentual pattern. Witness the stretto effect in bars 18–21, when x expands its duration so that in one part or other we hear repeated notes on every quaver of the bar, presenting a real *imbroglio* of possibilities. The shifting of accentual weight becomes clearer not too long afterwards, when the original short-form x is played by violin 2 and viola at 27–28 with the accented note now coming first, not second. There is a third permutation possible, and this arrives in the first-violin part in bars 33 then 35: here the weight falls on neither of the notes, which now have an

---

[109] Hepokoski and Darcy, *Elements of Sonata Theory*, 233.

afterbeat function. This is plainer in bar 35, where the two repeated notes are preceded by a rest on the downbeat.

Matters of accentual weight within a motive also come to the fore in the finale of Beethoven's Sonata in D major Op. 10 No. 3 (1798). A three-note shape is presented twice in isolation at the start, surrounded by gaps, just as in the Haydn, though here extended so as to sound like true silences. But in this case a different sort of *imbroglio* unfolds: the notation throughout the movement tells the player that the accent consistently falls on the second of the three notes, yet this is easier seen than heard. Especially on the many occasions when the motive returns in isolated form, the accent seems naturally to fall on the first, rather than the second, note; this is supported by the legato slur that encompasses the whole motive (which itself according to convention of the time implies an initial accent) and the fact that the greatest textural weight falls at the start (thinning out with each subsequent note). Thus trying to make the sound match the notation is likely to prove difficult, if not frustrating. Even if succeeding to the player's aural satisfaction, there is every chance, given the way the odds are stacked, that the listener will perceive a first-note accent anyway. Much of the accentual ambiguity – the awkward collision of texture, articulation and notation – therefore has to be internalized by the pianist, as a sort of constant irritant. Once again the motivic agent has the upper hand, as it were; it can't be pinned down to a stable identity.

The proliferation of forms of x in Haydn's movement, growing indifferent to metrical placement, seemingly occurring wherever they like, becomes even stronger after the double bar. Various forms of imitation take the accentual versatility further, combined with both extensions and contractions of the original form of the motive. Note, for example, the juxtaposition of two forms of M two quavers apart from bar 56, or how from bar 49 in the first violin even the metre can be sacrificed to the all-consuming nature of the material: this is a metrical modulation into groupings of three, into 9/8.

While an earlier scholarly perspective might have emphasized the thematic unity that this movement seems to embody, surely what counts for more are the endlessly different inflections, the versatility, the recombinations that all promote the idea of a musical gesture with a vivid sense of its own agency, drawing on its own internal resources. In this respect the motive functions like a kind of selfish gene: while we like to imagine that what we call the music is a complete functioning system that encompasses features like a motive, in reality the music is simply a vehicle for the motive, which is what vividly impresses itself upon the player and listener. It's what we remember; the rest of the supposed music falls away from our memory. But there is, of course, a fundamental difference from true genetic replication: with such highly individualized motives, their life is confined to a particular delimited stretch of musical time – normally a single movement. They are not the same thing as a schema or a cadential formula, which does indeed hop from work to work, as it were (and compare the 'memetic paradigm' formulated by Steven Jan[110]). With that realization we may adopt the wider perspective, noting the agency of the composer in effecting such manipulations, for all the distancing 'philosophical' strains that may attend the attitude to musical materials. This dichotomy is nicely captured in Gretchen Wheelock's statement that 'in displaying his materials as capable of ever-changing shapes and uses, Haydn animates his subjects as seemingly autonomous'.[111]

On occasions, in fact, that autonomy is explicitly written in. In the rondo finale of Haydn's Flute Trio in G major, H15 (1790), the garrulous main motive is twice used extensively as a means of retransition back to the A sections. Repeated in isolation and surrounded by rests, it anticipates its own reappearance in the context of the full theme. Such a technique is often to be found in a rondo, but the forms it takes here are particularly intrusive. This is especially the case the second time around (from bar 117), when a marked breakdown occurs – the tempo becomes 'sempre più largo', and mystifying chromatic alterations are introduced. This retransition thus becomes anything but an efficient preparation for return; instead, it is reduced to immobility and uncertainty. The collective needs of the music, as it were, are ignored as the motive 'selfishly' decides to explore some different possibilities of delivery, out of time and out of place. More considerately situated is a similar process in the finale of Beethoven's Symphony No. 1 (1801), in which a germ of an idea holds up proceedings while it shapes itself into a form with which it is happy. After an initial loud tutti unison G in Adagio tempo, the first violin offers a rising figure that is elongated and given different rhythmic inflections with each playing. Each time the interval covered is one note more, until after an uncertain pause it reaches a rapid rising octave that will be the head motive for the movement. Once more we gain the sense that a motive may simply want to do its own thing.

---

[110] Steven Jan, 'The Evolution of a "Memeplex" in Late Mozart: Replicated Structures in Pamina's "Ach, ich fühl's"', *Journal of the Royal Musical Association* 128/1 (2003), 30–70.

[111] Gretchen A. Wheelock, *Haydn's Ingenious Jesting with Art: Contexts of Musical Wit and Humor* (New York: Schirmer, 1992), 132.

If I have suggested that the analyst may not be able to keep up with Wheelock's 'ever-changing shapes and uses', and that composer and performer too may struggle for control, we should spare a thought for the listener who experiences similar sensations. On account of their brevity and intrinsic rhythmic basis, motives are by definition memorable and should therefore be easy to follow as they recur, certainly in conjunction with the perceptual ordering provided by periodic phrase syntax. However, given the intricacy of the motivic behaviour in a movement like the finale of Op. 64 No. 1 and the speed of events, both conceptual and actual (Presto), that can hardly be taken as read. Another characteristic example would be the minuet from Haydn's String Quartet in D major Op. 50 No. 6 (1787), which trades in units so short that they are really more submotivic particles or rhythmic cells rather than full motives, and these units interact unpredictably and with great rapidity. While we know that such movements were often found to be hard to follow, we should not assume that this epigrammatic style was in fact an impediment to appreciation. Indeed, Haydn may have had particular success because his methods of presentation are typically very concise and 'argumentative', immediately generating consequences and necessitating reinterpretation. The composer's enormous acclaim in Paris – the acknowledged home of the conversational arts – may have been related to this trait. Thus being in fact less obviously sociable in his discourse, knottier, in many respects more eccentric, may have made Haydn especially companionable – just as we enjoy interacting with those people who say outrageous or striking things, as long as they can find ways of justifying them or integrating them into the discourse. In addition, the quickness with which basic terms or ideas are recast and reformulated suggests something of the exhilaration of verbal repartee – except that, because of the weak referentiality of the musical 'words' or 'phrases', it is the construction itself that draws the attention. And so not being able quite to keep up with all the adventures of a motive need not preclude enjoyment; as expressed by Germaine de Staël in Chapter 1, it may be the very rhythms of exchange that count for most.

The motive whose behaviour I want to trace in the first movement of Mozart's Violin Sonata in G major K301 (1778) does not assume the same generative role that we found in Haydn's Op. 64 No. 1. Its agency derives less from any sort of omnipresence – since it does not dominate the movement statistically – than from its distinctive make-up. We first hear it in bars 8–12 (see Example 2.18a), where it immediately stands out because of its quasi-interrupting role. It follows a soft smooth eight-bar theme for violin with piano accompaniment. After this straightforward

Example 2.18a Mozart, Violin Sonata in G major K301/i, bars 1–18

homophony, our passage is *forte* and played in (near-)unison between the two instruments. It also stands out because of its rhythm – first as an abrupt two-note shape over the barline, which is then filled in by quavers and so made a four-note shape, which is then further filled in by semiquavers, making seven notes in total, and this form is then repeated. But in fact this fourth and final version is perceptually faster than the third one, since its C♯ and D both form part of a larger-scale rising fifth from G up to D that occupies bars 9–12 (as marked on Example 2.18a); this creates a feeling of acceleration from start to finish. This arresting material may seem out of place after such a gentle start to the movement, but one might argue that it is needed since the theme lacks a sufficiently dynamic balance within its confines: after a big leap up of an octave in bar 2, everything else falls. This is an obvious gap-fill (note the falling fourth at 2–4, and then a falling sixth at 6–8), but for an opening theme in particular one would expect greater complexity of contour and interval type. The rising sequential construction of 8–12, together with the rhythmic acceleration, help to counteract the shape of the theme, in a reversal of the usual assertive–gracious schema. (Mozart uses similar material, also constructed as a rising sequence, after the first subject of the first movement of his Sonata in G major K283, written four years earlier than the violin sonata.)

What Mozart's motive has in common with Haydn's is that it is multi-part: both are made up of an initial two-note unit that then replicates itself immediately, meaning that both can also be understood as composite complete entities. Thus yet again there is ambiguity about just what the core gesture is: is it the simple, irreducible two-note unit or rather the larger gestalt? Certainly once more we can hear a motive that generates its own continuation, that is able to move under its own steam. The visceral impact of the motive in context makes it possible to hear it as an autonomous musical action. At the same time, the agency of the fictional composer is clearly involved. Mozart wants to give a dual presentation of the theme, in line with the etiquette for duo sonatas, and a second presentation does follow from the end of bar 12, with violin and piano right hand swapping melodic and accompanying roles. But, given the gentle nature of the theme, it would be weak to proceed immediately to that second version, and so the composer provides some material that balances the theme by various kinds of inversion.

The formal function of bars 8–12, however, is not entirely clear. It might initially sound postcadential, though it then works its way from tonic to dominant, so suggesting a transitional role. When we next hear our material, following a close on the tonic in bar 28 (see Example 2.18b), it quickly becomes obvious that it does now act as a transition. Various changes of form back up this change (or clarification) of meaning. The unison texture is replaced by dialogue, with violin imitating piano; a descending sequence replaces a rising one; and the dynamic level is now *subito piano* rather than *subito forte*. Finally, the treatment of material differs: the initial two-note shape is omitted, and instead the middle two parts of the original passage are presented twice as part of the descending sequence. This helps to soften the more purely forward-driving character of the original version. Along the same lines, the passage is not preceded by silence, nor is it followed by it – instead it segues straight into further transitional material. Thus the motive clearly integrates itself into its surroundings. The original rhythmic form of the motive-complex returns after a cadence in the dominant at bar 80 (Example 2.18c), together with a unison delivery by violin and piano. However, it is now counterpointed by *Trommelbass* repeated Ds and a harmonization that first flattens then

Example 2.18b Mozart, Violin Sonata in G major K301/i, bars 25–33

Example 2.18c Mozart, Violin Sonata in G major K301/i, bars 80–84³

restores the leading note (a Quiescenza schema), which together strongly articulate a postcadential function. The dynamic level now begins *piano* and crescendos to *forte*, which seems to mediate between the two earlier appearances: thus to start with here, the motive is an integrated part of its surroundings, but by the end it once more sounds assertive.

Immediately thereafter, at the start of the second section, a fourth version is heard (Example 2.18d). While our motive thus far has had various middle and ending roles, there is no doubt about its formal function now: it opens proceedings. Yet the precise way in which it does so makes it sound more assertive than ever, as if continuing on from where the third version in Example 2.18c had left off. The whole passage is played *forte* again and is in simple unison without any other material being

Example 2.18d Mozart, Violin Sonata in G major K301/i, bars 84⁴–92

present, for the first time since Version 1. The reversal of formal function might seem to be symbolized by the inversion of contour, with each individual motive form now falling rather than rising. Further, the falling is intervallically expanded, taking place by leaps of a third rather than by step. Thus instead of the larger-scale linear progression of a rising sixth that we have just heard in Version 3 (F♯ rising up to D), we now hear a large-scale descending arpeggio moving (as per the circled notes on Example 2.18d) from D to B to G♯ and then to E. This outlines a dissonant seventh chord, which also means that the motive-complex is now left harmonically open. Therefore, in spite of Version 4 occupying a supposedly more settled formal function than Version 1, the net effect is once again somewhat disruptive.

This version is immediately succeeded by another, fifth one from bar 88, but this time the material fulfils a middle or transitional function, standing on V of the supertonic A minor, and at a *piano* level. Thus the material now generates its own abrupt dynamic contrast of *forte* and *piano* between successive versions. And we return to dialogue between the two players, as we heard on the second appearance. However, on that basis one expects that violin will follow and echo piano, yet when it enters at bar 89 the violin jumps in with the second unit (the four quavers) half a bar ahead of time, and in fact it is suddenly the piano that is following. In addition, the echoing is no longer at pitch, as it was in Version 2, but in sequence. An alternative interpretation would suggest not so much dialogue as conflict,

Example 2.18e Mozart, Violin Sonata in G major K301/i, bars 113–122

in particular conflicting downbeats between the two performers. As marked on Example 2.18d, the violin's downbeats seem to be falling on the third beat of each bar.

Version 6 (see Example 2.18e) leaves behind such ambiguities and uncertainties as it reverts to a loud unison presentation and to the original rising contour, so is the closest version to the original. However, what it takes from Version 4 – with which it forms a frame for the development section – is the use of an interval of a third between units. These thirds now rise to outline a large-scale V7 of G, D–F♯–A–C, meaning once more a harmonically open end to the whole passage. The function is now clearly one of retransition – a new feature. This version ushers in the reprise, and it is notable that this time the two reciprocal playings of the eight-bar theme are not separated by the original interruption. This has effectively displaced itself to a new, earlier position, and while it is again assertive in character, it is not disruptive. Version 7 (Example 2.18f) is an initially untransposed match for Version 2 (Example 2.18b), but the model is significantly altered. Every two-part statement–imitation pair is now heard at a different dynamic level, with alternations of loud and soft. Further, there is expansion of material at the end, something that must happen since this is one of those recapitulatory transitions that needs to end up going nowhere harmonically (we are in the tonic already and will be remaining there). At the

Example 2.18f Mozart, Violin Sonata in G major K301/i, bars 134–144

Example 2.18g Mozart, Violin Sonata in G major K301/i, bars 190–194

point of expansion, in bar 141, imitation at pitch is replaced by each instrument outlining successively lower notes of a descending line, in the service of a falling linear progression of a sixth. In addition, the regular alternation of quaver and semiquaver versions of the motive gives way to a free exchange between the two, while the alternating loud–soft pattern is maintained, creating conflict between parameters.

In terms of pitch structure, our eighth and final version (Example 2.18g) more or less transposes the form we heard at the end of the exposition. However, there is no unison, nor any kind of imitation – and so, for the first time, only one instrument (the piano) participates in the presentation of the motive. The violin plays various forms of G almost throughout, matching those played by the piano left hand, so that the material is framed by pedals at both top and bottom of the texture. And at the end a single extra note, harmonized by a tonic chord, is added on the second beat of the bar, which surely offsets the strong arrival on a downbeat that has always characterized the motive. If this arguably represents a kind of blurring, the rescoring may do so too, as a kind of textural liquidation.

While localized in import compared to that found in Haydn's Op. 64 No. 1, the motive (or motive-complex) in K301 shares its dynamism, as well as its sense of spontaneity. It also shows flexibility of thought, with implications for an ideal of social interaction in which one must always be alive to the different temperaments and circumstances of others. What starts off as disruptive and functionally ambiguous ends up fulfilling all sorts of roles and is clearly integrated in various ways thereafter: the motive ends up in the 'trusted' position of closing each half of the movement. It is almost like a point of honour for no two appearances of the idea to be the same. (Table 2.2 encapsulates the adventures undergone by the motive or motive-complex.) This bespeaks a sort of 'thematic psychology'[112] whereby a true motivating motive never stands still – it is always looking to do something different, not 'obedient' to the dictates of composer, listener or analyst. As noted earlier, this versatility arises in tandem with the increasing individualization of motives over the course of the eighteenth century. A greater degree of uniformity in appearance of the motive would lessen any perception of such virtual agency. If one hears thematic material as carrying such agency, the underlying social model could be either discursive (seeing an idea from different angles) or more simply behavioural (fulfilling different roles according to circumstances).

The Language Model and 'Conversation'

The centrality of the language model to both production and reception of later eighteenth-century music is, as we have seen, hardly in doubt. Musicians of the time virtually line up to bear historical witness to the

---

[112] I borrow this term from my *Keyboard Sonatas of Domenico Scarlatti*, 328.

Table 2.2 Different appearances of a motive in Mozart, Violin Sonata in G major K301/i

Version	Texture	Dynamics	Larger Shape	Formal Function	Other Features
1	unison	forte	rising sequence, rising fifth	postcadential?; transitional?	rhythmic 'acceleration'
2	imitation	piano	falling sequence, falling third	transitional	initial two-note version not present
3	unison melodic lines, harmonized over bass pedal	piano increases to forte	rising sequence, rising 6-prg.	closing (postcadential)	realized as part of Quiescenza schema
4	unison	forte	falling sequence, falling arpeggio of a seventh	opening	individual motive forms reversed; they now fall
5	imitation	piano	falling sequence, falling fourth	transitional	unclear which instrument leads and which follows, conflicting downbeats between instruments
6	unison	forte	rising sequence, rising arpeggio of a seventh	retransitional	displaced equivalent of Version 1, which does not return as expected eight bars into the reprise
7	imitation	forte and piano alternate	falling sequence, falling 3-prg., then falling 6-prg.	transitional	expanded equivalent of Version 2; alternating motive forms give way to free exchange
8	no unison or imitation; piano only plays motive forms while violin plays mostly repeated Gs	piano increases to forte	rising sequence, rising 6-prg.	closing (postcadential)	equivalent to Version 3, with Quiescenza schema, but extra note added at the end, on second beat of the bar

notion that music is a language, and to those already cited we might add, by way of reinforcement, Vincenzo Manfredini. In a revised version of his *Regole harmoniche*, from 1797, he noted how a cadence can be used to conclude not just a complete composition but also an individual musical phrase or period, 'it being the case that music, like verbal discourse, has its phrases, its periods, its punctuation marks of every sort, its digressions, etc.'.[113] Note that Manfredini's invocation of the language model also entails a clear sense of hierarchy, of what we might call grammatical or structural levels, similar to what Daube praised in modern musical symmetry, its 'beautiful proportions of various dimensions of component parts from which the building is constructed'. And the rise of historically informed performance has only reinforced the model: as Tom Beghin and Sander M. Goldberg assert, 'Eighteenth-century music, as the study of period instruments and the manuals for playing them has taught, could be thought to behave much like language in its need for punctuation, accent, articulation, and phrasing to determine content.'[114] Even without detailed historical knowledge, most performers will know of the special care needed to 'point' this music; constant alertness is required.

Nevertheless, language represents another area where it can be hard to see the wood for the trees, since attributes often specifically associated with our era can readily be held to be of more global application. The management of melodic contour as detailed earlier or the use of periodic phrase structure, for example, can scarcely be confined to the later eighteenth century (nor, indeed, can the embodied social aspects of music-making that form the larger thesis of this book). But the music–language equation operates much more broadly than these. Brian Hyer notes how 'language exists within music as sediment in the form of phrase and cadence, rhythm and meter, and so forth. Music is languaged matter, so much so that if one were to factor out language it is hard to imagine what would remain behind, or how one would recognize it as music.'[115] What is at issue is not whether music is in fact a language, but that we can hardly apprise it without recourse to concepts that are also linguistic ones. Nor is this conundrum specific to music, since any communicative behaviour can be

---

[113] Vincenzo Manfredini, *Regole armoniche, o sieno precetti ragionati per apprender la musica*, second edition (Venice: Adolfo Cesare, 1797), 41, cited in translation in Gjerdingen, *Music in the Galant Style*, 155.

[114] Tom Beghin and Sander M. Goldberg, 'Coda', in *Haydn and the Performance of Rhetoric*, ed. Beghin and Goldberg, 327.

[115] Brian Hyer, review of Rose Rosengard Subotnik, *Deconstructive Variations: Music and Reason in Western Society* and Lawrence Kramer, *Classical Music and Postmodern Knowledge*, *Journal of the American Musicological Society* 51/2 (1998), 420.

conceived of as a language with a vocabulary ('body language', the 'language' of a painter). At this level, the power of metaphor to direct our thinking becomes apparent. Justin London is careful to note that the particular metaphor 'MUSIC IS LANGUAGE' is no kind of absolute; rather, there is a significant 'linguistic overlap' that does not dissolve music's 'aesthetic and cognitive independence',[116] the ways in which it may function aside from or beyond the reach of the powers of language.

However, one must not be too relativistic about this metaphorical pairing. Especially if we focus on spoken language, music patently shares with this a basis in sound (though both may also exist in silent notated forms on the page). A visual or gestural dimension may then augment what the sound says. And music too may be broken down into distinct, closed units, uses intonation to express both mood and structure, and so forth. Over and above this is the growing evidence from neuroscience that the two domains overlap, that they are processed in very similar ways.[117]

So where does this leave our music-is-language model in the later eighteenth century? It was not exactly a new idea at the time, but the intensity and frequency with which the comparison was evoked has some novelty about it. There is a deconstructive, analytical bent to many written accounts – the sense that music is a machine with many moving parts – that finds an echo in compositional practice, whereby motives, phrase units, whole phrases and so on up the chain are clearly articulated as such. Most vividly in the case of Haydn, but certainly not in his output alone, there is an interest in 'how things work', in the operation of individual grammatical elements. (It is significant that Hyer's thoughts on the language model in general are exemplified by means of a speech–act analysis precisely of a movement from our period, and one by Haydn, the famous finale of the quartet Op. 33 No. 2.) But any more specific applicability of the language model goes beyond such technical concordances to encompass a broader communicative ethos. This involves values such as intelligibility and familiarity, and more broadly the sense of explicit human

---

[116] Justin London, 'Musical and Linguistic Speech Acts', *The Journal of Aesthetics and Art Criticism* 54/1 (1996), 62. For another take on the music–language equation ('music and discourse') see Carol L. Krumhansl, 'A Perceptual Analysis of Mozart's Piano Sonata K. 282: Segmentation, Tension, and Musical Ideas', *Music Perception* 13/3 (1996), 401–432.

[117] See Ian Cross, 'Music, Speech and Meaning in Interaction', in *Music, Analysis, Experience: New Perspectives in Musical Semiotics*, ed. Costantino Maeder and Mark Reybrouck (Leuven: Leuven University Press, 2015), 24: 'the idea that music and language – in the form of speech – are overlapping communicative domains is backed by an increasing amount of evidence from the cognitive sciences and neuroscience, as well as by ethnographic cases'.

agency: music is less a divine gift or reflection than something that is patently made, something that is uttered.

If such considerations help to rescue the language model for our purposes, we still have to ask: what kind of language? That it is in the first instance spoken language should be clear, but we might further specify that informal speech is the preferred perspective. This means, as we have seen, that 'dialogue' is often invoked as an explanatory term, and at least as common is the idea of conversation. The informality can be grasped with reference to an element that has not thus far been emphasized: variety of surface rhythm. If periodicity and symmetry could allow a general changeability or 'irregularity' of material and gesture, as previously explored, they could, perhaps more fundamentally, allow small-scale rhythm to operate in many different gradations. Thus at a local level patterns of grouping and stress are conspicuously flexible. 'Speech' is delivered less in a measured way than with the constant changes of pacing that characterize lively, informal utterance. Such rhythmic admixture is most brazen in earlier galant music, for instance in the practice of 'breaking into triplets' in the middle of a phrase previously ruled by binary groupings; we can see a trace of this in bar 4 of Example 2.18a, with the sudden triplet flourish in the violin.

Because of this kind of informality, and the broader mixing of musical messages, the place of rhetoric in this language model is uncertain; Rumph's 'erosion of voice' was noted earlier, to which we might add Wheelock's question about how compatible rhetoric is with the 'play' that is a fundamental in the instrumental music of the time – 'one implying a strategy of controlling the listener, the other an invitation to participate in an open-ended … game'.[118] The 'persuasive speech' of the rhetorical tradition is hard to reconcile with the more de-centred sense of agency that characterizes this brand of instrumental music, with what we might call its anti-authoritarian ethos.

The frequent recourse to terms like dialogue and conversation at the time – and ever since – helps to express the interactive side of this ethos. Conversation may even have achieved wider currency than dialogue,

---

[118] Wheelock, *Haydn's Ingenious Jesting with Art*, 201. An earlier questioning of the applicability of rhetoric may be found in Denes Bartha, 'On Beethoven's Thematic Structure', *The Musical Quarterly* 56/4 (1970), 759–778. Bartha coins the term Quaternary Stanza Structure to describe a sentence-like thematic structure found in Haydn and Beethoven that shows the roots of their style not so much in prose rhetoric as in popular song and dance. Among the virtues of Quaternary Stanza Structure is that it can 'relieve our great classic heritage of music from the anachronistic burden of sterile late-Baroque rhetoric' (778).

perhaps because it implies a more diffuse, more informal type of social interaction. It too could appear on title-pages, as in Boccherini's *Sei conversazioni a tre per due violini e violoncello*, Op. 7/G125–130, of 1770, or John Marsh's 'A Conversation Sinfonie, for two orchestras' of 1778, which divided its two groups into high and low. If nothing else, this shows that 'conversation' was highly marketable, just as the addition of 'dialogué' to a title-page promised something that ought to be coveted by the modern musical consumer. If conversation was soon to become attached to one particular genre, the string quartet, that was not the original state of affairs, and indeed this particular linguistic analogy had been around for a long time.[119] Once more, the basic difference from such prior usage lies simply in the frequency and intensity of reference. It was certainly given a push by the prestige of 'conversation' altogether in eighteenth-century life, associated most strongly with a French salon environment but readily translated into other media. Hence the dominance of the letter as a literary form,[120] both in its own right and in the context of the epistolary novel; a letter expects a reply, which in turn expects a reply, creating a potentially endless chain of reciprocal actions. A nice example closer to home is the structure of Riepel's treatise *Anfangsgründe zur musicalischen Setzkunst*, which is couched as a dialogue between teacher and student. Even without any such structure, interactivity could be presumed, as when Baron Freiherr von Knigge stated outright that 'The writing of books ... in our times' is 'nothing else than a literal conversation between an author and the reading public [schriftliche Unterredung mit der Lesewelt]'.[121] Knigge makes sure to stress the modernity of such a linguistic relationship.

---

[119] See Finscher, *Studien zur Geschichte des Streichquartetts*, concluding section, 'Die Theorie des Streichquartetts', 279–301, 285 in particular.

[120] See Dena Goodman, *The Republic of Letters: A Cultural History of the French Enlightenment* (Ithaca: Cornell University Press, 1994), 137: 'only through the translation of salon values into writing and then into print could enlightenment be spread. The key ... is the letter, the dominant form of writing in the eighteenth century. ... The epistolary genre became the dominant medium for creating an active and interactive reading public.' We might also note the use of the genre within moral weeklies, which, as James van Horn Melton notes, 'were innovative in their inclusion of real or fictitious letters to the editor. This technique fostered the impression of a direct dialogue between editor and public'. Melton, 'School, Stage, Salon', 90.

[121] Knigge, *Über den Umgang mit Menschen*, volume 2, 308; *Practical Philosophy of Social Life*, trans. Will, volume 2, 270. Note that translator Will's 'literal' is not an exact translation of 'schriftliche', which means 'written'. Along comparable visual lines, note the iconographical evidence examined in Nancy November, 'Theatre Piece and *Cabinetstück*: Nineteenth-Century Visual Ideologies of the String Quartet', *Music in Art* 29/1–2 (2004), 135–150: listeners were typically represented as being in 'conversational' contact with the performers

In fact, the basic connection we are considering could be turned around: music could be the metaphor for conversation. As we saw from Germaine de Staël in Chapter 1, conversation was akin to playing a musical instrument, all the better for being a kind of ideal social exchange unencumbered by specific worded ideas. Adam Smith drew on a separate, long-standing metaphor of MUSIC IS HARMONY when noting that 'The great pleasure of conversation and society ... arises from a certain correspondence of sentiments and opinions, from a certain harmony of minds, which like so many musical instruments coincide and keep time with one another.'[122]

However, we must remain aware that linguistic analogies such as conversation and dialogue are susceptible to other rationales – they could be as much a justification as an explanation for the modern instrumental manner that could, after all, cause such a commotion. For Richard Will, this amounts to 'a framework for listening that would encourage audiences to think differently from the many in the eighteenth century who complained that instrumental music was just so much meaningless noise'.[123] Nevertheless, the factors outlined above make much about this framework intrinsically persuasive: the interactive ethos, variety on a small scale, the informal linguistic register. The concise dimensions of musical units, clearly defined and variously shaped so that they seem to respond to each other, readily yield an impression of 'different things being said' in short order; the gaps, pauses or even silences between utterances are a further element of 'realism'; and the pronounced mixture of rhythms and gestures supports the conversational ideal of the time of variety of subject matter. There is also the matter of 'speed of thought', as evoked for the finale of Haydn's quartet Op. 64 No. 1 (Example 2.17), whereby a listener need not be able to keep up with the motivic arguments in order to grasp the quick-witted behaviour that is on display. Informality is found in both what is said – utterances are often ordinary, maybe even formulaic – and how it is said, the tone of address. While the art of conversation was well entrenched before the eighteenth century, what does emerge in this time, as Peter Burke points out, is a greater 'stress on informality'.[124]

---

prior to the nineteenth century, during which time painters began rather to emphasize 'introspective, private listening' (135).

[122] Smith, *Theory of Moral Sentiments*, 337.

[123] Will, 'When God Met the Sinner', 183–184. See also Simon P. Keefe: 'Eager to demonstrate the aesthetic value of instrumental works, writers frequently focused linguistic analogies around the concept of dialogue'. Keefe, *Mozart's Piano Concertos*, 1.

[124] Peter Burke, *The Art of Conversation* (Ithaca: Cornell University Press, 1993), 112.

Beyond that, though, there are the ethical implications of the model, based on the ideally consensual nature of conversation. Such a conversation does more than produce 'musical' sympathy between human beings, it also constitutes what Henry Fielding described as 'the only accurate Guide to Knowledge'.[125] Conversation, in other words, should not proceed from a basis of ideas that are known in advance, and which it is the point of the practice to prove – which would be the rhetorical model – but instead generates knowledge through a collaborative effort, arriving ideally at a kind of collective wisdom. It has a dynamic rather than didactic orientation, since any conclusions that may be reached cannot be foreseen. In any case, as I have already stressed, the larger point is interaction itself, process rather than product. It is an emphasis on process that allowed Charles Avison in 1766 to imagine that even a keyboard improvisation could embody this conversational ideal:

> This unpremeditated Display of the musical Talent, when excited in the Performer by the Perfection of his Instrument, may be considered as an interlocutary Discourse among Friends – when Time – Place – and other Occasions concur, – the Intercourse of sensible People, conversing on Subjects interesting and agreeable, seldom fails to inspire a Variety of Thoughts, and lead to Observations, thus put in Practice, if I may so term it, which otherwise might have lain dormant in the Mind.[126]

One would not imagine that solo performance, let alone an improvised solo performance, would naturally stir thoughts of conversational interaction. Yet what transpires on the sociable occasion that Avison envisages is a 'Variety of Thoughts' leading to unpredictable, indeed previously unsuspected, insights. The individual's own feelings and thoughts are not kept pure and celebrated in solitude, but are brought out, encouraged and realized precisely through interaction with others. From a purely musical perspective, the improvisation itself, and the inherent 'Talent' of the improvising individual, are also both realized to best effect in congenial company.

The apparently unlikely context of Avison's paean to sociability exposes a fundamental weakness in the conversational model as it is most frequently applied. Barbara Hanning, for example, defines the *style dialogué* as 'a musical texture in which each of the instruments of a chamber music

---

[125] Fielding, 'An Essay on Conversation', 119.
[126] Avison, *Essay on Musical Expression*, ed. Dubois, 185.

ensemble at some time or other is assigned to play the melody'.[127] Thus musical conversation – and more broadly the idea of interplay – is straightforwardly associated with texture, to the relative exclusion of the sorts of factors considered above. Within that textural template, conversation is generally held to take place through melodic activity, and melody is equated with voice, which in turn is equated with 'speaking'. One of the greatest difficulties with this lies in the logical implication that all other material, broadly the 'accompaniment', should be equated with listening. Yet even the purest kind of accompanimental figuration, say a repeated note or a series of close-position broken chords, still represents a kind of utterance, a form of musical 'speech'. Further, given the basis of galant style in accessible homophonic textures, the statistical reality is that the sorts of melodic exchanges held to embody conversation are going to be relatively uncommon, except when melodic leadership is rotated more or less systematically. Such a procedure then risks losing the sense of spontaneity that is vital to social interplay.[128]

Other difficulties arise in the firm linking of conversation to chamber music (in its modern sense), and indeed to the string quartet in particular. These links may be hard to break given the weight of reception history, but it is simply untenable to hear all other instrumental genres of the time as 'less conversational', even if we confine ourselves to the narrow melody-based understanding given above. In addition, we should note that, according to the traditional understanding, exchange is held to take place not so much between voices as such, as between different instruments and players. This would therefore rule out Avison's improviser, and indeed any and all solo performance. To be fair, these are by no means recent restrictions of perspective; the notion that conversation arises from melodic exchange between different players was very much the rule at the time too. Thus Reicha, for example, wrote in 1814 that 'to dialogue the melody is to distribute the phrases and the members, the ideas, and the periods between two or more voices or instruments'.[129]

---

[127] Barbara Hanning, 'Conversation and Musical Style in the Late Eighteenth-Century Parisian Salon', *Eighteenth-Century Studies* 22/4 (1989), 512. Much of the rest of this paragraph draws on Sutcliffe, 'The Shapes of Sociability', 13–14.

[128] A recent sustained contemplation of these difficulties may be found in Edward Klorman's *Mozart's Music of Friends: Social Interplay in the Chamber Works* (Cambridge: Cambridge University Press, 2016), resulting in the author's coinage of 'multiple agency'; this offers a much more comprehensive and conceptually stronger means of understanding the interaction between performers and parts. As he notes, 'Several of Sutcliffe's objections to equating string quartets with conversation are resolved by substituting multiple agency for conversation' (123).

[129] Reicha, *Traité de mélodie*, 89, cited in Keefe, *Mozart's Piano Concertos*, 24, and Keefe quotes many other figures of the time to similar effect.

Outside of such textural matters, further reservations can be put forward. One is that a musical conversation – regardless of the instrumental medium in which it is found – is not spontaneous, since the players, of course, know their lines in advance. This suggests that a theatrical analogy might better serve the purpose: 'a staging . . . of carefully rehearsed dialogues', as Wheelock describes it. But Wheelock also offers us a way around this difficulty by noting that conversation itself required 'study and practice'.[130] If the very existence of so many conversation manuals at the time rather undermines the catch-cry of informality, the same would apply to those supposedly spontaneous arts of ornamentation and improvisation, which were also not short of 'how-to' guides in the eighteenth century. In all cases, it would seem, the impromptu required careful advance preparation; the 'unplanned' needed planning.

Another widely proclaimed attribute of salon conversation was its politeness. André Morellet's listing of things to avoid in this sphere, as noted by Hanning, included 'being inattentive, interrupting someone else or speaking simultaneously, showing off, being pedantic or egotistical [and] dominating the conversation'.[131] Morellet noted that participants often fell into these traps; but then, along with so many other treatise writers, his aim may have been not so much to reflect as to improve current practice. And, indeed, the same 'faults' might be found in many musical 'conversations' of the time, but with a difference: these faults do not detract from the sense of interaction, but rather make it more vivid. I suggested earlier that Haydn's especially 'argumentative' style may have contributed to the particular resonance his music found with his audiences. Similarly, one could cite countless instances of more or less subtle rudeness in his works, such as the openings of his quartets Op. 50 No. 5 (1787), in which the viola and cello are not listening and then enter with a complete (harmonic) non sequitur, and Op. 54 No. 3 (1788), in which the first violin repeatedly undermines the second violin and viola's train of thought.[132] The bad manners are all the more delicious for being held within the 'polite' framework of periodic phrase structures, as if nothing were amiss. But we should not forget the events of Boccherini's Op. 32 No. 4 (Example 2.7), in which the cello goes right off topic and so occasions a kind of collective embarrassment, marked by a very long silence directed by the

---

[130] Wheelock, 'Rhetorical Pause', 70 and 69.
[131] André Morellet, 'De la conversation', in *Éloges de Mme Geoffrin, contemporaine de Madame du Deffand, par MM. Morellet, Thomas et D'Alembert*, ed. Morellet (Paris: Nicolle, 1812), 169–170; Hanning, 'Conversation and Musical Style', 515.
[132] On Op. 50 No. 5 see Sutcliffe, *Haydn: String Quartets, Op. 50*, 94–95, and on Op. 54 No. 3 see Rosen, *The Classical Style*, 141–142.

composer (*aspettar molto*). Allanbrook has a different, though related, reason for misgivings about what she calls the 'civilized metaphors' of conversation and dialogue. For her they suggest the wrong aesthetic register, since they detract from the bigger historical point: an unruly mixture of styles and points of view that should not be tamed by 'imagin[ing] a conversation between recognizably consistent participants'.[133] This is a salutary reminder of what can be missed when metaphor of conversation, as so often happens, is applied too literally.

However, there is more to say about that more literal, textural end of the matter. The need for every player to have a social stake in proceedings, undoubtedly a desideratum of the time, is not readily compatible with the predominance of accessible homophonic textures. As pointed out earlier, rotating melodic lines among the participants, while not unknown, could never have become the preferred solution. What is in fact more common is for a composer to inflect the predominant homophony by complicating any clear distinction between melodic and accompanying lines. This is often accomplished by the simplest possible means, for example by using repeated notes in various parts of the texture so that each part is involved in 'discussing' the same thing.[134] While the exchange of melodic material can undoubtedly convey a strong sense of reciprocal behaviour, it is far from the only possibility under the rubric of sociable music-making.[135]

A wonderful example of how the use of repeated notes can complicate matters of textural agency may be found in the opening movement of Haydn's Quartet in B minor Op. 33 No. 1 (1781; Example 2.19). In a fine account of the logical problems inherent in the metaphor of conversation – albeit applied only to the string quartet – Hans-Joachim Bracht asserts that the individual voices in this movement speak not just one after another, but at the same time ('Es zeigt sich jedoch, daß die Einzelstimmen nicht nur nacheinander, sondern auch gleichzeitig als sprechende Individuen hervortreten können'). Consistent with that, he notes that the repeated-note figure heard in the second violin in bar 1 is important material rather than simply being subordinate, but in describing it as an 'accompanying figure'

---

[133] Allanbrook, *Secular Commedia*, 117.

[134] Charles Rosen puts it thus: that the challenge for composers 'was to retain the late-century hierarchy of melodic voice and accompanying parts while giving the accompaniment motivic significance', and 'the most fruitful solution was to learn how to make themes out of formulas of conventional accompaniment'. He describes this as 'Haydn's discovery'. Rosen, *Sonata Forms*, revised edition (New York: Norton, 1988), 181. He subsequently notes that the 'simplest way to transform accompaniment into melody ... was to make a theme out of repeated notes' (182). See also the material cited from *The Classical Style* below.

[135] The last few sentences are taken from Sutcliffe, 'The Shapes of Sociability', 14.

Example 2.19 Haydn, Quartet in B minor Op. 33 No. 1/i, bars 1–8

('Begleitfigur') Bracht shows he has not quite grasped how the composer softens the boundaries between melody and accompaniment. The second violin's figure must initially be heard as an imitation of the first violin's 'melody', which starts with the same weak–strong repeated-note cell, before the listener can subsequently start to categorize it as subordinate, and it is from this ambiguity that much of the discursive brilliance of the Allegro moderato unfolds.[136] Rosen has certainly picked up on such ambiguity, writing about Haydn's 'invention of classical counterpoint' in this movement, which he finds later in the opening phrase. While the cello begins bar 3 in clear melodic charge, at some point, imperceptibly, the first violin takes over, so that by the end of bar 4 it now has the tune: 'All that one knows is that the violin starts measure 3 as accompaniment and ends measure 4 as melody.'[137] Taking this as his cue, Rosen writes expansively

---

[136] Hans-Joachim Bracht, 'Überlegungen zum Quartett-"Gespräch"', *Archiv für Musikwissenschaft* 51/3 (1994), 172 and 173. Much of this passage also derives from Sutcliffe, 'The Shapes of Sociability', 14n.

[137] Rosen, *The Classical Style*, 117.

about the 'revolution in style' that this kind of textural thinking represents.[138] Curiously, though, he fails to note the ambiguity already present in the first two bars, or that the predominant repeated-note cell is the fulcrum for the revolutionary disposition of the entire four-bar passage.[139] And the same cell patently generates a new kind of textural uncertainty in the following two-bar unit (5–6). This famous movement has attracted much commentary, yet it tends to focus almost entirely on the harmonic ambiguity that is felt at the start, with no reference to the textural ambiguity that is its companion.[140]

A similarly fluid textural conception features in the Menuetto from Dittersdorf's Quartet in G major, K193 (1789; Example 2.20a). The three upper instruments play repeated parts of a root-position G major triad and are thus texturally indistinguishable; in bar 2 they play repeated components of a V6 chord in the same rhythm, but there is a first hint of textural differentiation as the first violin decorates its downbeat note with a trill. Even though the first violin alone continues to play the same note as it did in the first bar, one may start to assume that this most static of the three parts is in fact carrying the melody, and an expansive flourish in the third bar confirms the fact. At the same time, second violin and viola continue their stepwise descent with the repeated-note shape as part of the Romanesca pattern on which the first four bars are based. Thus, as it turns out, we have a melody made in the image of the accompaniment, or vice versa, a blurring of the distinction between leading and supporting roles. The two repeated notes played by the cello in bar 8 take this further: they are clearly a bass filler at the end of the phrase but also in this particular context just as 'melodic' as anything we heard in the first bar of the movement.

Later in the Menuetto, from bar 16 (Example 2.20b), the top three instruments blend perfectly once again, just as we heard in bar 1. This time, though, they move in descending waves of parallel 6/3 chords, a *fauxbourdon* effect. This is countered by a lengthy cello solo that replaces

---

[138] Rosen, *The Classical Style*, 116.

[139] One drawback of Rosen's reading is that he has used a corrupt older edition of this movement as the basis for his analysis. This features an initial a♮^{1} above the f♯^{1} in the second-violin part that should not be present; no doubt introduced at some point to clarify precisely the harmonic ambiguity, it simply blunts the cunning of Haydn's conception. The new edition of *The Classical Style* that appeared in 1997 (London: Faber) did not remedy this problem.

[140] Markus Bandur, for example, offers a fine close reading of harmonic ambiguity in the movement, but never mentions the textural conceit regarding repeated notes and their dual thematic/accompanimental identity. Bandur, 'Plot und Rekurs – "eine gantz neue besondere Art"?', in *Haydns Streichquartette: Eine moderne Gattung*, Musik-Konzepte 116, ed. Heinz-Klaus Metzger and Rainer Riehn (Munich: edition text + kritik, 2002), 62–84.

Example 2.20a Dittersdorf, Quartet in G major, K193/ii, bars 1–8

Example 2.20b Dittersdorf, Quartet in G major, K193/ii, bars 16–26

the entirely stepwise progress of the upper voices with a very wide-ranging arpeggio – up over two octaves of a dominant-seventh harmony and then back down again. While we may pick up that the cello line is acting as a retransition, since solo textures often do this,[141] there is surely a mismatch between form and function: the expansiveness of the cello's gesture seems

---

[141] See Janet M. Levy, 'Texture as a Sign in Classic and Early Romantic Music', *Journal of the American Musicological Society* 35/3 (1982), 498–499.

overdone, as if it is making up for its absence from the previous passage. In the last full bar of this solo (24), on the second beat, the two violins enter with repeated notes that sound like a discreet accompaniment to the cello's line, and they continue with the same figure into the following bar (25). But this bar soon reveals itself as a return to the opening material, and so those same repeated notes now take on a thematic profile once more. This enforces a major change in aural perspective, building on the ambiguous textural relations that we witnessed at the start. The finest touch of all is that the viola does not join in until the second beat of bar 25 (compare bar 1, where it was present from the start). This means that it in fact imitates the two violins' figures at a distance of one bar. That the preceding three notes in the two violins could form a point for imitation implies that they form a stable unit in their own right, and are therefore already in a sense 'back in charge' rather than simply being supportive. This little imbroglio of possibilities means that it is hard to perceive that decisive alignment of parameters that normally signals the return of an opening theme in the tonic key. Instead, the return is diffused through time, and, as Rosen remarks of Haydn's Op. 33 No. 1, there is a barely perceptible shift between melodic and accompanying roles. And a repeated-note figure, which should be incidental, merely a typical supporting element in the homophonic galant apparatus, ends up being a focal point.

There are plenty of other ways in which the conversational model's notion of accompaniment as 'listening' can be complicated. To remain with the string quartet for now, so as to show how little the genre needs to depend on the traditional textural assumptions, we might take several brief examples from one opus, Franz Anton Hoffmeister's Op. 14, published in 1791. The first movement of Op. 14 No. 1 in F major (Example 2.21) opens with violin 2 and viola playing a short fanfare-like figure; initially, this sounds like a plausible *Hauptstimme*, though it soon settles on repeated quaver Fs. Then violin 1 and cello enter with something more obviously melodic, phrased across the strong beats and involving mostly semitonal movement. This line draws the ear, but then every other bar the first pair break up their even repeated quavers with the dactylic rhythm they first played at the start of bar 2. This rhythmic kink draws the ear irresistibly back towards this strand of the texture, creating a very fine balance between the claims of melodic fluency and rhythmic insistence. (We could in addition understand the texture as a simultaneous presentation of assertive and gracious elements, the military drum rhythms being fused with the more delicate lyrical gestures.) Not surprisingly, Hoffmeister does not leave his teasing textural conception at that. The ambivalence about textural

Example 2.21 Hoffmeister, Quartet in F major Op. 14 No. 1/i, bars 1–10[1]

priorities is in fact spread over the whole Allegro, since the 'accompanying' repeated-note figure is heard frequently throughout in various contexts and turns out to be the most characteristic, magnetic element of the movement.

In the second movement of Hoffmeister's Op. 14 No. 2 in B flat major (Romance: Adagio), the first section comes to a close with a cadence at bar 26 (Example 2.22). While harmonic closure is achieved, and the lower three instruments then prolong the E flat major harmony, an expected postcadential event, an unexpected rise in dynamic level to *fortissimo* makes the material sound less like a continuation than an interruption. In the following bar, violin 2 continues its figure but abruptly drops its dynamic level to *piano* to usher in a cantilena in the first violin; then the two lower instruments start to play simple supportive lines. The change of dynamic level alone transforms the lower parts into the sort of murmuring accompaniment that typically supports a lyrical line (this one marked *dolce*). This dramatic effect, repeated twice later in the movement, at bars 31 and 64, highlights the agency of the accompanying parts: they start assertively but then consent to reduce their stridency in order to support a colleague. Their accompanimental submissiveness, in other words, is actively chosen rather than being imposed from without.

Example 2.22 Hoffmeister, Quartet in B flat major Op. 14 No. 2/ii, bars 20–31

What strengthens this impression is the individual imprint of the parts. In the interrupting *fortissimo* of bar 26, each part has its own shape and rhythm, and this in fact continues more subtly once the dynamic reduction takes place: second violin with its murmuring semiquavers, cello marking the main beats in typical bass-like fashion, and viola singing a long note in the middle of each phrase unit. Hans Keller devised the term 'homophonic polyphony' to cover those many passages in the Haydn quartets where the textural sense cannot readily be captured by either of these two supposedly opposed terms.[142] While in fact there are a great many textures that could

---

[142] Hans Keller, *The Great Haydn Quartets: Their Interpretation* (London: Dent, 1986), 6.

Example 2.23 Hoffmeister, Quartet in D minor Op. 14 No. 3/iv, bars 138–149

fit under this umbrella, and in many genres, this may indeed be a type of texture that is most resourcefully cultivated in string chamber music. But it is hardly specific to Haydn: in Hoffmeister's movement we hear what is plainly a melody-and-accompaniment texture, but inflected by the different types of support that the melody receives, so that from the point of view of agency we hear a combination of individual utterance and agreement. Boccherini in particular is a master of this kind of textural stratification, the individual supporting parts often refracting into a series of separate ostinatos, distinct not just rhythmically but often also in terms of articulation and even dynamic level.

Our final example from Hoffmeister's Op. 14 set comes from the last movement of No. 3 in D minor. In the postcadential material that ends the first section (bars 36ff), a softly played viola figure alternates three times with *fortissimo* chords for the full ensemble; the viola's chromatic neighbour notes around its A, in particular its B♭, suggest a minor colouration that has not been extinguished in spite of the finale's moving into the tonic major, D. Hence this is a little more than simply a contrast of dynamics and texture: the viola hints at a certain independence of (harmonic) spirit.

From bar 138 (Example 2.23) this passage returns, again in three rotations, but this time the viola transposes its figure down by a third on each occasion and so enforces a collective modulating sequence from D via B minor down to the subdominant key of G. Thus it now takes an active role in promulgating its desire for harmonic difference. After the third *fortissimo* tutti has concluded the viola is once more heard by itself (bar 144), but now playing a very different kind of material: a simple repeated broken-triad figure, starting at an assumed loud dynamic before being marked *mancando*. This lasts for three complete bars without contradiction, but especially as the dynamic level softens, there is only one way to interpret it: as an accompaniment. This kind of 'accompaniment to nothing' is common enough; it normally promises that cantabile material will follow, and this duly arrives from bar 147 while the accompanying part continues with its pattern. But the circumstances here are out of the ordinary. The viola has not only taken the initiative harmonically prior to this, but has then taken the initiative once more in setting up a new texture, melody-accompaniment, and topic, a simple comic-rustic style. (The two violins' playing of the subsequent tune in octaves is a classic sign of a lower linguistic register.) It just happens to do the latter by 'volunteering' to play the most subordinate part, and the *mancando* marking seems to suggest the player's change of heart, from directing the discourse to setting up a situation for others to shine.

All this then means, of course, that when the rustic material unfolds from bar 147, it would be absurd to equate what the viola is doing there with 'listening', given the way in which we arrive at this broken-chord accompanying figure. Yet the conversational model as customarily applied cannot account for such circumstances, focussed as it is on melodic or thematic material and notions of textural 'equality'. Even when contemplated in isolation, aside from this particular context, such a broken-chord figure still 'speaks', still plays a role in the total utterance. Melody, after all, can scarcely unfold without a more regular ground against which it can be heard, and so that supporting material must carry agency in providing that ground, if nothing else. In one respect, though, equating regular, repeated accompanimental figuration with listening does make sense: those very attributes mean that such material lacks the sort of intonation contour that would encourage us to identify it with speech. But the larger point stands: 'speaking' agency is diffused throughout a texture and, further, the rapid rate at which textures typically change in the instrumental music of the time helps to maintain a dynamic social sense.

The ways in which Hoffmeister diffuses the sense of textural agency in his Op. 14 offer just a sample of what is possible. The basic compositional problem – how to balance the claims of accessible homophonic utterance and social inclusiveness – was an abiding preoccupation. A different solution is offered at the start of Boccherini's String Quintet in F major Op. 28 No. 1/G307 (1779). The first four bars present mainly staccato lines played in unison by all five performers. This would seem to be a thematic statement, though the *pianissimo* dynamic and uniformity of material might make the listener doubt this. From the end of bar 8 the staccato lines are repeated by the two cellos, but now in support of a melody played by the first violin – and so what had seemed to be a theme is revealed to be an accompaniment. If this sounds familiar, it is because Haydn took up the same conceit in the famous opening of his 'Lark' Quartet, Op. 64 No. 5 (1790).[143] But whereas the material that the first violin plays from bar 8 of Haydn's work is undubitably the tune, Boccherini does not decisively solve the textural puzzle. At the start of both development and recapitulation different lines are added to the staccato material, first a repeated melodic figure on first cello and then a brief suspension chain played by the two violins. But on none of these three occasions does it feel as if a decisive theme has been launched.

A different problem of agency is apparent in the use of unison texture. In spite of their obvious unanimity, unisons tend to be intrinsically unstable and ambiguous as to their social implications. While they can of course represent agreement, they can equally unsettle a sense of discursive equilibrium.[144] We have seen how unison proclamation can often be overturned in the gracious-riposte formula, whereby reciprocal harmony replaces unilateral monophony. And especially when a full unison – of pitch as well as rhythm – is given softly, the effect can be uncanny or uncertain. As an opening device, a soft unison may seem to be a contradiction in terms, but it is often employed. In a sense it draws even greater attention to the material that is being collectively delivered. The quartet first movements of Kozeluch's Op. 32 No. 3 (1790) and Gyrowetz's Op. 44 No. 2 (1804) are characteristic examples, and at the openings of Mozart's K428 (1783) and Haydn's Op. 55 No. 3 (1788) this goes with twisting, harmonically ambiguous lines, to which one might add the start of

---

[143] If Haydn may not have come across Boccherini's textural conceit, he is more likely to have known Pleyel's set of Op. 1 string quartets (1782–1783), since they were dedicated to him. In the first movement of Op. 1 No. 5 in G major a very tuneful second subject, from bar 28, begins in a way that is remarkably akin to the famous opening material of 'The Lark'.

[144] For excellent discussions of unison textures along such lines see Levy, 'Texture as a Sign', 507–530, and Mary Hunter, 'Unisons in Haydn's String Quartets', *HAYDN* 4/1 (2014) www.rit.edu/haydn (2 July 2014), who concludes that 'it is the multivalence and ambiguity of unison, rather than its apparent embodiment of unanimity and agreement, that makes it so fascinating' (36).

Example 2.24 Boccherini, Quartet in D major Op. 32 No. 3/i, bars 1–8

Mozart's Piano Concerto in C minor, K491. The social ambiguity of unison delivery is cleverly dealt with by Boccherini at the outset of his String Quartet in D major Op. 32 No. 3/G203 (1780; Example 2.24). This is a rhythmically and texturally differentiated unison pronouncement of a leaping Romanesca pattern, again at a soft dynamic. The first violin is squarely sequential, while the other parts enter off the beat. There is a basic form of imitation between cello and viola, while the second violin, without the octave leap of its lower counterparts, imitates the first. Agreement comes in many shades of opinion, it would seem.

However, if unisons represent a social 'problem', it is a local one. Because individual textural conformations are rarely sustained at length in our changeable style, unisons will be surrounded by other types of texture, with which they will interact. In this larger sense they are intrinsically 'conversational'; they expect a response, a different way of organizing sound. However, if unison textures are sustained at any length, this comfortable expectation may start to weaken. We saw an instance of this in the 'mad' minuet (*Il Matto*) from Dittersdorf's symphony *Il combattimento delle passioni umani*, delivered almost entirely in unison as part of its embodiment of unbalanced behaviour.

A similar case could be made for the first movement of Mozart's Violin Sonata in E minor, K304 (1778), which opens in a distinctly uneasy atmosphere, which the soft unison texture does much to create; by no means can it be taken to represent a desirable state of agreement between the two parties. Further, the unison then crosses boundaries of gesture and material. The first eight bars constitute a harmonically rounded phrase, after which point one might expect the players to go their separate ways, yet the unison continues for another four bars, in a *forte* passage made up of contrasting material – shorter staccato units after the long melodic trajectory of the first eight bars. Both the opening theme and the unison texture undergo a series of adventures over the course of the movement, but aside from the exposition repeat, they never return in combination. Subsequent treatments of the theme, including a canonic presentation and the piano's dissonant accompaniment of the violin at the point of reprise, maintain the tension, and it is worthy of note that the most 'resolved' textural presentation, of melody plus subordinate oscillating accompaniment, is heard last of all, in the coda, from bar 192^4. (In the version of the theme heard at bars 13–20, the piano plays repeated units characteristic of accompanimental function, yet these maintain a fairly independent profile.) By making this a kind of ultimate solution to the opening textural problem Mozart, like Hoffmeister, shows the sense of active agency that can inhere in a simple homophonic texture.

The minuet from Boccherini's Quintet in D minor Op. 25 No. 1/G295 (1778) likewise opens with a complete phrase in soft unison. This is not just an unnatural presentation for a minuet, so is the twisting aperiodic rhythm, which makes it hard to get one's bearings. There is a gothic flavour to it which is heightened when this material is played in canon in the following phrase. But the gothic flavour seems more literal in the second movement of Hyacinthe Jadin's Quartet Op. 1 No. 3 in F minor of 1795 (this was one of many sets of debut string quartets dedicated to Haydn[145]). This too is a minuet, at least in name, and takes its *pianissimo* unison texture to spectacular lengths (Example 2.25). The entire minuet is delivered in this way, and multiple ties across the bar-line together with a complete lack of rests mean that a listener has little chance of grasping either metre or grouping. Yet there is a periodic impulse at work, if heavily disguised. The wave-like contours of the line are in fact organized into a modulating period up to the

---

[145] For a listing and discussion of all these sets of quartets see Horst Walter, 'Haydn gewidmete Streichquartette', in *Joseph Haydn: Tradition und Rezeption. Bericht über die Jahrestagung der Gesellschaft für Musikforschung, Köln 1982*, ed. Georg Feder, Heinrich Hüschen and Ulrich Tank (Regensburg: Bosse, 1985), 17–53.

Example 2.25 Jadin, Quartet in F minor, Op. 1 No. 3/iii, bars 1–36[2] (cello part only)

double bar, and there is a return to the opening shape in the second half, albeit early and with a different continuation. If one was to try and pin down where this material could have come from, what stylistic associations it evokes – in other words, what musical topic is at play – plainchant might be a reasonable guess. The Trio, moving into the tonic major, offsets this mysterious apparition of a minuet by offering an interlude of modern lyrical homophony.

Thematic Interaction

One of the ways of broadening our guiding idea of reciprocity beyond the familiar conversational model – where the agents of exchange are individual instrumental parts, in the case of chamber music delivered by individual performers – is to consider how musical materials themselves might interact. Conversation, after all, tends to be invoked as an explanatory category only when the exchange is quite literal, generally involving imitation or alternation of a set piece of musical material. Statistically this is not in fact that common, and could hardly account in full for the impression of reciprocal action that is so strong in our repertory. That this reciprocity need not be literally embodied in the relationships among individual parts should already be apparent in the category of the gracious riposte. Understanding that interaction can arise between different thematic entities as well as between constituent parts of a texture offers us a wider canvas on which to recognize fundamental patterns of social exchange, and this is encouraged by the individualizing nature of periodic syntax, in which thematic units can readily assume a distinct, memorable profile: they become characters or social entities in their own right.[146] We have already seen how musical motives can act in this capacity.

Trying to understand a musical discourse in such terms is hardly novel in itself. One only need consider the notorious theoretical prescription that hears a contrast between 'masculine' first and 'feminine' second subjects in the exposition of a sonata-form structure. But it is far less common to imagine such interplay in explicitly social terms, or to suggest that it can itself form a kind of musical 'conversation' or dialogue. In addition, it is our period that initiated such possibilities of interpretation, with its unprecedented admission of strong discontinuities of material into the frame of an individual movement. Thus they had the force of novelty; our perception of them is inevitably worn down by several subsequent centuries of art music in which such contrasts are no longer remarkable as such. That these might be understood as a form of more or less intimate social interplay owes much to the typically rapid rhythm of thematic exchange, made possible in turn by the duration of the units. Short and sharp, they can readily be grasped by an attentive listener. And this characteristic rhythm of exchange helps to keep the behavioural sense informal, and hence 'social'. It is less common for the individualized materials to encompass a whole theme or 'subject', which would create the kind of epic sweep we would associate with the nineteenth-century handling of thematic contrast, and which that century's invention of 'sonata form' encapsulates in its broad-brush prescription of contrast between first- and second-subject areas. Yet while the units at play are often very concise in our earlier brand of thematic interaction, this interaction may also be sustained on a large scale.

This type of interplay is recognized in Janet M. Levy's account of the second movement of Haydn's quartet Op. 77 No. 2 (1799), in which she describes how differing materials seem in fact not to get on with each other: 'Several different sets of patterns or "gestural characters" behave rigidly, absent-mindedly, as if without regard to the behavior of the others.'[147] This lack of mutual listening might seem anything but sociable, yet the larger point is that Levy conceives the musical materials in social terms, as sounds that behave relative to one another. In the eighteenth century, as we have seen, such interplay was often assimilated to verbal models such as

---

[146] This sentence derives from Sutcliffe, 'Before the Joke', 107.
[147] Janet M. Levy, '"Something Mechanical Encrusted on the Living": A Source of Musical Wit and Humor', in *Convention in Eighteenth- and Nineteenth-Century Music*, ed. Allanbrook, Levy and Mahrt, 233.

conversation, and has certainly been since as well, and it could also be understood under the rubric of character, often leaning on some sort of theatrical model.[148] The *sinfonía de argumento*, for example, was conceived on the basis of opposing character types – as we saw with the Moreno symphonic movement that set Pride and Humility against each other – lending 'the illusion of a theatrical representation', in the words of Teresa Cascudo.[149]

Yet the kinds of thematic interaction that we often find are much finer-grained than these models allow for. The musical materials may lack the fixity of definition that the term 'character' would suggest, since their behaviour may be almost endlessly fluid and flexible. And the tone of the interaction may not resemble anything we would associate with sociability. Such would certainly seem to be the case in the initial Presto of Haydn's Sonata in E minor H34 (1784; Example 2.26), a movement that hardly leaves a friendly impression. Here our two typical opposed tendencies, bold and gracious, are not so much presented in successive units as interlinked on a smaller scale. The opening bars give us rhythmically complementary ostinatos in the two hands, and these will go on to dominate the movement. The bolder gesture, x, is the left hand's four-note tonic arpeggio – rising, all skips and no steps, staccato, rhythmically decisive, downbeat-oriented. The softer gesture, y, follows immediately in the right hand, a three-note figure that is mostly falling, stepwise, legato and anacrusic. However, its softness can only be a question of 'gestural character', since the whole exchange takes place at a dynamic level of *piano*. While I have immediately proposed a kind of interchange with my reference to two ostinatos and two gestures, it would be possible to hear the material as comprising one larger-scale impulse, especially at a Presto tempo that is unusually quick for an opening movement. And indeed there are other thematic and textural ambiguities. If we do hear two contrasting units in this opening, which one takes the lead – which one attracts the ear more? Initially it would seem that the right hand's material is subordinate to that of the left hand. Starting on the fifth quaver of the bar, it fills in the gaps until the next left-hand reiteration,

---

[148] On 'character' see Matthew Pritchard, '"The Moral Background of the Work of Art": "Character" in German Musical Aesthetics, 1780–1850', *Eighteenth-Century Music* 9/1 (2012), 63–80. For the more theatrical perspective on the concept see Allanbrook, *Secular Commedia*, among her many writings on the matter.

[149] Cascudo, 'Iberian Symphonism', 153. One chamber-music equivalent of this symphonic genre that comes readily to mind is C. P. E. Bach's trio sonata *Sanguineus und Melancholicus* of 1749 (Wq161/1), which is discussed along with other such 'confrontational' works of the time in Will, 'When God Met the Sinner'.

which with its downbeat beginning forms a stronger focal point for listener attention. Figure *x* might also take priority simply because it is heard first, and so what the right hand then plays can be heard to respond to it.[150]

Yet while the left hand's figure may feel dominant, more 'characteristic', it is also initially static for the first three bars while the right hand shows greater flexibility by moving upwards more or less in sequence. From this point of view the left hand represents a typically fixed 'accompaniment', even if its initial solo presentation and immediate reiteration might mark it out as being motivic. The right hand's more flexible behaviour and use of closer intervals suggest that it functions as a melodic and therefore leading part. That sense of flexibility in response is typical of gracious ripostes, of which the current right-hand material represents a very compressed form. Such ripostes are often in fact less immediately memorable than the gestures they 'tame'.

At the fourth time of asking, the left hand starts to adjust its behaviour. It now moves sequentially upwards too, but more strikingly it plays the first three notes of its rising arpeggio legato. The right hand does not finish its motive after the first quaver of bar 4, but holds its dyad for three further quaver pulses, so that the hands, having more or less alternated, now play together in earnest for the first time. The left hand then does something similar, so instead of its fourth note lasting a quaver, it is held for the rest of the bar. The right hand begins its next iteration on schedule on the fifth quaver, but instead of falling by step it drops by thirds each time, yielding the contour e^2–c^2–a^1–$f\sharp^1$ over the course of bars 4–5^1. Its former steps are completely replaced by leaps, and in that respect it is now behaving like *x*. One might even hear it as a quasi-inversion of the left hand's rising-arpeggio shape. It is clear that the two elements are now borrowing from one another.

The left hand keeps its basic rhythm once more in bar 5, but with a crucial difference – the C on the downbeat is tied over from the previous bar, which destroys the energetic downbeat nature of the gesture. Since it

---

[150] Another uncertainty about the opening of the movement is its very character as a thematic unit. As noted by Roni Y. Granot and Nori Jacoby, 'there is little in the way of rhetorical cues that define this theme as an opening one': 'Musically Puzzling II: Sensitivity to Overall Structure in a Haydn E-Minor Sonata', *Musicae Scientiae* 16/1 (2011), 75. The authors' experiment involved splitting Haydn's movement into an '8-segment puzzle task', playing the segments out of sequence to four groups of participants and asking them to reconstruct the likely original order. Just 20.7% of participants decided that bars 1–8 (the first segment) needed to be placed first, prompting the authors' explanation noted above. In other words, not only does Haydn's movement sound affectively unfriendly, it may be cognitively unfriendly too.

once more holds the last note of its rhythmic motive, as the right hand has also done, we suddenly find that the left hand is playing the same basic rhythm as the right: two anacrusic quavers followed by a longer note that falls on the beat. In other words, the left hand is imitating the right hand rhythmically. And because of the right hand's move to falling thirds instead of falling steps, and the left hand's subsequent continuance of its rising-triad contour in this bar, there is now a clear dialogue of intervallic shapes: the left hand answers the right hand in inversion. This is a remarkably rapid change from the first bar, when the two hands seemed to offer opposing (if complementary) shapes. The materials show a gregarious, socializing tendency, shedding their sharper edges and coming to seem like two sides of the same coin.

After these moments of parity, it is arguably the right hand that then dominates to the end of the phrase. Its next reiteration of y in bars 5–6 continues the downward trend of before, though it now reverts to falling steps. The left hand in bar 6 keeps its rhythmic model of the previous bar but tightens its edges so as to play a discrete three-quaver figure, which is exactly the form in which y began. The fact that the left hand has now adopted the articulation of y as well (two-note slur plus a final unattached note) represents another role reversal. A third reversal of activity becomes evident when we note that it is now y alone that is heard on the downbeat of this bar. In addition, y is now elongated beyond a three-note gesture.

Meanwhile the contour of x has changed too – the second and third notes are a step apart, A♯ rising to B. This pitch succession is immediately echoed by the right hand one octave above, on the fifth and sixth quavers of bar 6, which is the first instance of one hand directly matching the other. When bars 7 and 8 repeat the same materials, the resulting threefold reiteration takes us back to how x started in bars 1–3. The difference now is that y also literally repeats itself three times, and it has clearly assumed the leadership: note that the right hand in fact plays continuously from the end of bar 3 to the end of the phrase. Just how one subdivides this continuous activity becomes ambiguous. The right hand's A♯–B pairs heard at the end of bar 6 and then of bar 7 could either be heard as the beginnings of their respective units – so continuing the pattern whereby each version of y begins with the fifth quaver of the bar – or else there is a change of grouping at this point, and these two-note pairs form the fifth and sixth quaver beats of units that begin on the downbeat of each bar. If the latter possibility is preferred, it means that y has assumed yet another of the initial characteristics of x. For all these possibilities, note that there is one constant throughout the whole phrase: x basically rises and y basically falls.

In sum, through the first phrase of this sonata we hear a complex series of mutual adjustments between two sonic personalities. They are caught somewhere between cooperation and competition, with the sense of textural hierarchy uncertain and open to change. These adjustments happen swiftly, suggesting the sort of instantaneous interaction that might be understood as verbal ('conversation'), but could also be grasped under the broader categories of social behaviour or human gesture. In relation to similar textural ambiguities in the first movement of Haydn's quartet Op. 33 No. 1, we earlier noted Rosen's assertion of a 'revolution in style', whereby melodic and subordinate roles could almost imperceptibly be exchanged. The current case shows that this revolutionary conception of texture does not require multiple performers to come into being. Only one performer is required to execute this sonata, though of course Haydn has found a substitute in the two hands wielded by the keyboard player.

After a pause the music begins again with what sounds like it will be a parallel phrase. But now the two hands maintain their original rhythmic shapes for longer, for five consecutive bars, reinforcing their ostinato character. This time, it appears, the hands are less prepared to listen to each other. This means that a certain social-textural tension starts to build, even if from the harmonic point of view the hands are cooperating in shifting towards the mediant. In bar 14 x suddenly erupts into the first *forte* of the movement, the G major arpeggio reinforced by octave doubling, to create a clearly aggressive gesture. In response the right hand plays a burst of semiquavers, also *forte*. This material retains the falling steps and anacrusic nature of y, but, as if unsettled by the outburst from x, loses any obvious melodic properties. Just two bars later, though, x presents itself very differently. It is not just legato after the previous detached form but a written-in legato, with each note of the rising arpeggio being held on so as to build up to a four-part chord. This provides an unexpected textural richness after the spare sonorities heard to this point. The chordal presentation suggests an accompanimental role, and y is quick to seize on this opportunity. While the right hand seems as though it will simply repeat its material of bars 14^4–16^1 one octave higher, each one-bar unit is now elongated by a restruck suspension, resolving by step onto the third quaver of the bar. This change immediately suggests a more melodic profile, so that bars 16–18 give us the first straightforward melody-and-accompaniment texture of the movement.

To describe this passage simply as a variation on the immediately preceding bars 14–15 would not really do justice to the sense of musical process. It may well entail a varied replaying of the same material an octave higher, but it also shows the two types of material reacting quickly to changing circumstances, as if they are independent agents. Gesture x

counters its sudden aggression with a much more conciliatory form of behaviour, and gesture *y* is able to transform its outburst of semiquavers into something with a lyrical twist. Thus the interplay takes place not just between the two types of material, but also internally, within each one in its own right. And it takes place, once more, at a tempo that is not just literally quick but also perceptually quick. This illustrates László Somfai's observation that Haydn's music is dense not so much vertically as horizontally;[151] in other words, it changes rapidly through time.

This is soon apparent once more as bar 19 brings yet another gambit, with a rhythmic acceleration into continuous semiquavers. The hands take turns to play them in the service of material that feints towards some of the properties of *x* and *y*. The predominance of stepwise movement takes its cue from *y*, and more specifically the form that *y* has taken in the immediately preceding bars, but rhythmically there are echoes of *x*. This is apparent not just on the small scale (most obviously if one compares the left-hand rhythm of bars 19–20 with that of bars 1–3) but also on the larger scale: bars 19–21 and then bars 22–24 both represent three-bar units built up from the same reiterated rhythms, which was just how *x* originally presented itself in the first three bars of the movement. This passage culminates in bars 27–29 in a brilliant flourish in which the hands operate in unison, the first time that they have come together in this way.

After a further pause we hear a second theme that is completely different in effect. It is a lyrical effusion in continuous quaver rhythms (until we approach the cadence point). Initially it is created through a sort of stretto treatment of *y* in its original guise: three-note falling figures, mostly falling by step, the third note occurring on a strong beat. While each individual form falls, each successive one starts higher to yield an overall rising trajectory. This is just what happened at the start of the movement, and so bars 30–31 simply compress that action. From bar 32 the specific motivic traces of *y* are largely dissolved, and what is retained is just the basic stepwise behaviour, now taking its place within a new texture of free three-part counterpoint. The more fluid melodic activity evident in this

---

[151] Somfai writes that 'Because of the fast speed of events, Haydn quartets are not vertically "dense" (like, for example, the synchronous contrapuntal or rhythmical complexities of Beethoven or Brahms), but rather horizontally "dense" in their rapid rhythmic and motivic successions, in the refined network of motives which refer to one another'; this creates a style that 'is so much more fluent, so much more condensed and restless that it is closer, practically speaking, to ... 20th[-]century chamber music, than to the Viennese classical and romantic generations following him'. László Somfai, notes to recording of Haydn, *String Quartets, Op. 33 Nos 1–6* by the Tátrai Quartet, trans. Charles F. Carlson (Hungaroton: HCD 11887 88 2, 1979), 6–7.

Example 2.26 Haydn, Sonata in E minor H34/i

phrase suggests a large-scale riposte to the type of phrase syntax that has dominated the movement to this point – that the lyrical impulse associated with *y* has come into its own at the expense of the reiterative energy of *x*. Yet for all this fluidity, the phrase is surrounded by silence: preceded by a pause in bar 29, it is followed by a further pause in bar 35. These pauses 'frame' the melodic flow, suggesting perhaps that *y* has a more hesitant character, consistent with its anacrusic nature, as opposed to the firm downbeat-oriented reiterations of *x*. In any case, after the break at bar 35 the whole phrase is repeated (with an internal expansion), creating a further block of lyricism, and this time the cadence is elided with a brief postcadential confirmation from bar 42. This resumes the toccata-like style of bars 19ff. 'Hidden' within the right hand's compound-melodic structure is the rhythm of *y*, going from fifth quaver of one bar to the downbeat of the

Example 2.26 (continued)

next. It also moves by step, but now upwards rather than downwards, which means that the right hand is inverting its characteristic contour from the start of the movement: compare the reiterated g^2–a^2–b^2 shapes that conclude on the first beats of bars 43, 44 and 45 with, for example, the b^1–a^1–g^1 succession heard at bars 2^5–3^1. This is followed by a final three-note comment at bar 45 that once more recalls *y*.

Figure *x*, which had disappeared in the latter part of the exposition, immediately returns at the start of the second section as both hands resume their original roles – chains of *x* in the left hand interspersed with chains of *y* in the right hand. Yet another pause arrives in bar 50, without any interaction having occurred between the two types of material, or indeed any harmonic progress having been made (the music remains poised on V

Example 2.26 (continued)

of A minor). Thereafter *x* does just what it did at bar 14, creating a shock by entering *forte* and doubled at the octave, though this time the chord it outlines (C major) is unprepared. Bars 51–54 in fact transpose bars 14–17, meaning that once again *x* has no sooner imposed itself than it melts into a softer accompanimental rendering of its rising arpeggio. As before, the right hand takes up the implied invitation to behave more melodically. But this time, instead of an almost immediate switch into a more toccata-like style, the lyrical effect is sustained and more fully realized. While forms of *x* pile up to create accompanimental chords, the right hand's semiquaver

Example 2.26 (continued)

units start to become unpredictable in their exact contour and in their relationship to each other. Each of these units leads to either a suspension or an appoggiatura, which together with unstable harmony dramatically intensifies the discourse. These factors together with the sheer length of the passage heighten the effect of a 'lyrical breakthrough'.[152] But while the

[152] 'Lyrical breakthrough' is a term I have used in relation to similar events in the sonatas of Domenico Scarlatti, whereby a previously thwarted lyrical impulse is finally – but normally quite briefly – allowed to blossom. See Sutcliffe, *Keyboard Sonatas of Domenico Scarlatti*, 358–367, for a definition and discussion.

Example 2.26 (continued)

conjunct melodic movement associated with *y* may seem to dominate affectively, the rhythm of *x* is nevertheless heard the whole way through. In fact both hands continue to play rhythmic ostinatos, for all the unpredictability of pitch structure.

Eventually in bar 64 this material leads, as it did in the exposition, to something more toccata-like, but the proportions continue to be quite different. Just as the lyrical material has expanded well beyond its original bounds, so the toccata has shrunk. After three and a half bars it is effectively overridden, via a phrase overlap, by what sounds like new material. While the left hand at bar 67^4 takes over the perpetual semiquaver motion, the right hand plays a melodic line in relatively slower note values than anything heard to this point. Together they create the first straightforward melody-and-accompaniment texture of the movement. The use of many falling stepwise intervals in the right hand naturally aligns the material with *y*, but more to the point is that the material begins firmly on a beat rather than being anacrusic, and this stress pattern is continued by the trochaic crotchet-quaver rhythms that ensue. What this means, of course, is that the right hand, and by association *y*, is assuming a feature firmly associated with *x* and the player's left hand.

Just as the phrase arrives at its cadence at the start of bar 71, another overlap occurs, and the melodic line is unexpectedly extended into a rising B minor arpeggio. This is nothing less than figure *x*, being played for the first time in the right hand. For all the changes in profile of our two thematic characters, to this point they have been fairly firmly associated with one of the keyboard player's two hands. The right hand's takeover of *x* has, though, been nicely anticipated by its move to downbeat-oriented phrase units from bar 67^4, as just described. What unfolds from bar 71 is textural inversion on a large scale: if the right hand has assumed responsibility for *x*, the left hand is left with no choice, as it were, but to fill in the gaps by means of *y*. The right hand goes on to reiterate *x* no fewer than eight times over bars 71–78, while the left hand has the simplest form of *y*, a falling three-note figure in parallel thirds. The left hand organizes that figure into a long sequence that falls also by thirds, moving relentlessly down until we reach D♯ and F♯, on which there is a further pause while the right hand arrives at a high b^2. This is an extraordinarily far-flung sonority, an inevitable result of the left hand's moving further and further away from the right hand while the latter stays in the same register.

While to this stage we have heard many adjustments of contour on the part of the two hands as they react to each other's thoughts, as it were, the inversion of texture that we hear from bar 71 represents reciprocity on a larger scale. This passage responds to – is in dialogue with – the normal presentation of *x* and *y* in left and right hands respectively over the rest of the movement. And the tables have also been turned with regard to thematic behaviour. Figure *y* has here become mechanically repetitive, moving implacably down in perfect sequence, and so losing much of its more differentiated melodic character. Figure *x*, on the other hand, while retaining its characteristic rhythm, shows more flexibility in its intervallic construction: with each successive reiteration from bar 72 it changes one pitch of its rising arpeggio. But this is only a relative freedom. More than ever at this point, one might hear the hands as comprising less two separate ideas than a single super-ostinato, carried through for a duration that starts to feel alien to a style based on periodic organization of its elements. The 'lyrical breakthrough' passage earlier in this section was in fact similarly mechanical in its rhythms, but that was masked by the intensity and unpredictability of its harmonic and melodic behaviour.

It is not surprising in light of this driving reiteration of the movement's two main elements that Haydn radically compresses events almost as soon as the recapitulation has begun. After just two bars of literal return, in bar 81 *x* takes its accompanimental form, holding each note of its rising arpeggio so as to form a chord, and *y* starts to blossom melodically, with its falling semiquavers leading to a suspension. While seemingly rushing us on to the equivalent of the exposition's bar 16, the precise shapes assumed by each hand actually evoke the extended lyrical passage from the development. This compression – or rather, juxtaposition – of earlier events clearly avoids redundancy, not to say anti-climax, after the heightened treatments of the *x*–*y* complex heard in the middle section. But this also means that the recapitulation has within six bars reached a stage where there will be no further overt confrontations of *x* and *y*. The second theme returns reworked in the tonic minor from bar 95, again cut off on either side by pauses at the first time of asking. On its second playing, the theme is extended still further than it was in the exposition, and a falling chain of suspensions now occupies a full four bars at 103–106. This becomes a kind of learned equivalent of the big lyrical blossoming in the development section, which featured similar chains of dissonance–resolution pairs.

If the recapitulation proper was compressed, this is compensated for by a big extension of the original four-bar codetta into a nineteen-bar coda. The codetta's material is heard three times, but each time that it reaches its third bar it is cut short. The first version, starting in bar 109, is cut off in bar 111 by a dramatic intervention on the part of *y*. There is no rhythmic trace of *y* in the two dotted crotchets that the right hand plays, but the falling step has been well established as a behavioural trait of that gesture, and the longer note values, together with the left hand's Alberti-style accompanimental shape, clearly signal lyricism. The second melodic note, F♮, deflects the harmony towards a tonicized submediant, C major. The communicative sense on the part of *y*, which interrupts both the reiterated figuration and the process of tonic confirmation, is something like 'no, hold, on – I have more to say'. The C major version of the closing figuration that this ushers in is in turn cut short at bar 114 by a falling sequence. If the previous interruption represented the lyrical impulse, this interrupting material is the opposite of that. In fact it builds on the falling parallel tenths used by y in its earlier brief manifestation (bars 111–112^1 using the pairs e^1–g^2, $d\natural^1$–$f\natural^2$ and c^1–e^2), but extends the pattern over four bars into a hard-driven toccata idiom. This material builds up a head of steam that propels us into a third playing of the codetta material, now back in E minor. For a third time this material is cut short of its original three-bar duration, but on this occasion what ensues represents a seamless continuation, increasing the momentum still further. From bar 120 we hear a two-bar cadential pattern involving a bass-line cycle of scale degrees 8–6–4–5 (the so-called *cadenza lunga*[153]). This pattern and its immediate repetition – which is just what occurs here at bars 122–123 – is a trademark device used to signal a grand close, associated especially with big operatic numbers such as act finales. That is the exact sense in which it appears here, promising an exciting and brilliant finish.

Most unexpectedly, however, the cadence at bar 124 overlaps with a return to the opening material of the movement. We hear the first three bars once more, meaning that x repeats itself three times in a row and is answered each time by the more flexible y that fills in the metrical gaps. (And y shows further flexibility in that its second iteration, at bars 125^5–126^1, takes a different form compared to the beginning; it is now a near-sequential repetition of the first playing of the figure, with its diminished fourth between notes 1 and 2.) The return to the first few bars – back to the beginning, as it were – suggests circularity, a sense that 'we haven't got anywhere', and this seems to be confirmed by what happens in the fourth bar of the unit, and the final bar of the movement. After the third version of y, now higher in register than expected, closes on the downbeat of 127, we hear three high bare octaves, presumably best played softly. That this is a three-quaver unit beginning on the second quaver of a beat suggests motive y, but it has now lost all its contour. No longer does it move by step or trace a melodic shape against the insistent repetitions of x; it is simply a static repeated note. This makes for a remarkably anticlimactic, even bleak ending. The movement effectively peters out, though with much tension remaining in the air: the build-up of figuration through the coda virtually demands a tension-releasing chord or series of chords to conclude the discourse, but these do not eventuate.

---

[153] The term derives from Nicola Sala and is adopted and explained in Gjerdingen, *Music in the Galant Style*, 169–170.

Yet this lack of resolution is in a way consistent with the prevailing tone of the movement, which, as suggested at the outset, is hardly friendly: David Wyn Jones calls the Presto 'unsmiling' and 'precise'.[154] The way in which the movement closes in on itself at the end prompts this brief account by Monika Möllering:

The [first] movement seems to come from nowhere and, after hastening past, it disappears again into nowhere; the relatively long coda quotes the beginning before it dies out in three empty octaves. Hardly anything takes on a firm shape; a few bars of polyphony in the subsidiary theme and a forlorn little B minor melody in the development do not contradict that impression, they strengthen it.[155]

But for all the cryptic quality of the Presto, one must stress that the basic working method is a sociable one, underpinned by the interaction of motivic 'characters', as I have shown in some detail. We might encapsulate this interaction as pitting propulsion (x) against lyricism (y), meaning that much of the coda, with its insistent repetitions and strong downbeat emphases, belongs to x, as if in response to the large-scale expression of y in the preceding section (bars 95–109). Whether we finish with an uneasy compromise between the two tendencies rather than a true meeting of minds is therefore beside the point for present purposes. What counts is the idea of some sort of mutual adjustment, of the capacity of materials to 'notice' other types. The lyrical breakthrough in the middle of the movement is perhaps the most striking large-scale example. This is where y declares itself most fully, but it is underpinned throughout by the rhythm of x, which has adjusted its behaviour so as to function as a legato chordal accompaniment, and the passage as a whole is built on the basis of quite 'mechanical' repetition, which is primarily a property of x.

While Haydn's may seem an exceptional movement, in terms of the type of thematic behaviour that I have isolated, it in fact has plenty of companions. Two other movements for solo keyboard can be cited to make the point, and to confirm that such interaction does not require multiple performers to come into being. C. P. E. Bach's Rondo in E flat major, Wq61/1, from the sixth collection of the *Kenner und Liebhaber* series (1785–1786; Example 2.27), is headed Andantino, an indication that already suggests the likely manner of the opening material. And indeed,

---

[154] H. C. Robbins Landon and David Wyn Jones, *Haydn: His Life and Music* (London: Thames and Hudson, 1988), 206.

[155] Monika Möllering, trans. Eugene Hartzell, notes to recording of Haydn keyboard music by Alfred Brendel (Philips 412 228-4, 1985), cited in W. Dean Sutcliffe, 'Haydn's Musical Personality', *The Musical Times* 130/1756 (June 1989), 344.

Example 2.27 C. P. E. Bach, Rondo in E flat major, Wq61/1, bars 1–47

this material conforms to expectation, being written in tuneful, graceful 'middle style'. The first phrase, a sentence construction built on a rising bass, comes to an end on V in bar 8, and we might predict that this will be answered by a second sentence ending on I, to form a period on a larger scale. This indeed also happens, but in other respects the consequent phrase is realized in such unlikely fashion that one might hardly notice. As soon as the antecedent phrase has ended, the bass thunders out a repeated B♭ in *fortissimo* octaves, a flat contradiction of the gentle manner we have heard to this point. The right hand then answers with a soft lyrical figure from the opening, and the whole process is then repeated in bars 10–12. Thus it sounds as if the original material alternates with the rude interruption.

In fact, though, the left hand is doing nothing more than play the first two notes of the original tune, a repeated B♭ over the bar line; the shock derives from the fact that it performs them at an unexpected register and dynamic level. And then the right hand picks up where the left has left off, as its upper line follows on from that B♭ with a g^2 which then moves down by step to f^2, $e♭^2$ and finally d^2. And so the whole phrase unit at bars 8^4–10^3 simply reiterates the melodic line that we heard at the start, but this is now presented in hocket-like fashion, being split between the hands. Thus what was a unified flow of sound has become interactive, being turned into a classic assertive–gracious pairing: loud and gesturally abrupt is answered by soft and measured. Note the difference from the type of interaction we saw in Haydn's sonata movement. There two kinds of gesture could immediately be understood as being in dialogue, whereas Bach draws a potential for contrast – indeed, conflict – from material that seemed to contain no such thing. It is a striking *trompe l'oreille* effect, and it takes some effort (and luck) even to notice just how close the respective phrase units are. Bach seems to be playing off different aspects of the music against one another. In terms of melodic pitch structure, the two units are identical – a perfect match, one might say – whereas in terms of register and dynamics their realization is wildly different. These differences extend to texture: note how the gracious riposte heard from the second quaver of bar 9 is made even more gracious and mellifluous by the doubling of the tune a sixth below, and then in bar 10 by the addition of a rising two-note figure in the tenor register that moves in contrary motion to the falling right-hand line. These two changes increase the sense of considered, reciprocal behaviour within this unit, so counterbalancing the impulsive repeated note.

The following two bars continue to track the original phrase: the left hand repeats its loud octaves on B♭, while the right hand then continues with the equivalent third and fourth bars of the tune. Properly speaking, the left hand should in fact move to A♭ to replicate the course of the original line; by not doing so, and instead insisting on the B♭, it in fact helps to alter the harmonic sense of this part of the phrase, which now sounds like a prolongation of the dominant. But a more drastic harmonic change follows from the last quaver of bar 12 as the left-hand *fortissimo* octaves return and this time do move down a step to A♭, and they are then reiterated through the whole of bar 13. There is no equivalent for this in the original phrase. Thus the left hand's gesture can no longer be understood as an eccentric realization of what was already present in the original phrase; the low octaves now become disruptive in every sense. Further, the right hand joins in with these repeated A♭s an octave above. This destroys the notion of a dialogue between the hands and registers that had been developing since the start of the phrase. The repeated notes are followed by an especially dramatic shift in register to a high dominant-ninth chord at bar 14^1, which suddenly dissolves into a routine-sounding cadence on the tonic.

Then we begin again from the beginning, and the following sixteen bars will turn out to be a modified version of what we have just heard, forming the second half of a double period. If the preceding consequent phrase 'analysed' a bifurcation inherent in the original material, splitting it into stubborn repeated notes versus mobile steps, then from the upbeat to bar 17 the original melodic material is 'dialogued' in a different, more civilized way. It is realized in two right-hand voices, while the left hand plays a more hesitant version of its original pulsing crotchets. The repeated-note figure, back at a dynamic level of *piano*, is now heard at the top of the texture rather than the bottom, and its second note is sustained throughout the rest of the two-bar phrase unit. This entirely removes the disruptive aspect that it had taken on in the previous phrase. The melodic continuation from the initial repeated note occurs in a separate voice, underneath the pedal; it maintains the rhythm of the original tune, though not its pitch contour. In the continuation part of the sentence structure, at bar 22, the pedal note flowers into a variant of the original sixth bar, joined a sixth below by the other voice, reinforcing the harmonious sense of the whole phrase.

The disruptive consequent phrase does then return, but with textural reversal. The *fortissimo* octaves are now in the right hand, and it is the left hand that provides the gracious riposte with soft legato lines. While the first of the left hand's units at bars 25–26 falls, matching the contour of the melody in bars 1 and 9, the second unit at 27–28 balances this by moving upwards, so that once more an extra level of gracious reciprocal behaviour is added to counter the rude loud repeated notes. Yet on a larger scale the *fortissimo* octaves themselves now take part in a form of reciprocal patterning: the very reversal of the roles of the hands compared with the earlier consequent phrase (bars 9–16) provides a balancing gesture. This considerably tames their effect, since on this larger scale they are no longer just a shock but match a previous event. They are at once disruptive and symmetrical.

As in the earlier consequent phrase, at the third time of asking the *fortissimo* octaves generate a more sustained disruption. After the right hand has played the repeated-note figure on high E♭ octaves, there is a registral correction in bar 29, as the right hand starts to play in a middle register while the left hand reverts to low octaves. The hands move by step in contrary motion within a harmonic progression that takes us from the tonic to the subdominant in bar 31. Bars 29–30 express their aggression even more dramatically than any of the earlier figures in octaves, both because of their textural weight (chords in up to five parts) and because this disruption lasts for longer (an extra bar compared with 12^4–13). In addition, each chord is repeated in a weak-strong placement before moving to the next one in the progression – in other words, each chord is expressed in the terms of the original *fortissimo* repeated-note motive. At the same time, because the progression involves stepwise voice leading, this represents a cross-fertilization between our two types of basic musical gesture: steps and repeated notes. As in the Presto of Haydn's Sonata in E minor, two types of material constantly shift in relation to each other, sometimes seeming to form part of a larger whole, and at others being plainly opposed, and, as we have just seen, they may also approach each other in terms of actual shaping.[156]

What seems to encourage such thematic behaviour is that property we studied earlier in this chapter: the organization of musical units according to binary principles. This involves double presentations at various levels, in the current case three: the two two-bar units that begin the eight-bar sentence, then the two eight-bar sentences that make up the sixteen-bar parallel period, then the varied repetition of that structure to make up a double period of thirty-two bars. While such shaping has an

---

[156] Note, as a further instance of this, that the lyrical material in fact contains another repeated-note figure, as heard at the start over the bar lines between bars 1–2 and 3–4. This could have the same explosive potential as the initial repeated-note figure that subsequently isolates itself from the second phrase onwards, but this particular repeated note takes the form of a restruck suspension, meaning that it always resolves down a step and so represents a softening move.

obviously symmetrical aspect, it also encourages complementarity. Thus the phrase that begins on the upbeat to bar 17, for example, represents the start of the double period and so can be understood as a variant on bars 1–8, but on the other hand it is also to be heard in the light of the immediately preceding eight-bar phrase, and stands as a correction to that, reassembling the various musical ingredients in more cooperative guise.

Not that such operations are confined to period structures, either in general or in the case of this rondo: no sooner has the double period concluded in bar 32 than the basic materials appear in a new configuration. Now the repeated-note motive is repeated softly each bar in an alto voice, while two other voices either side play the lyrical continuation in mellifluous sixths. Moments later, yet another transformation of the basic materials arrives. From the end of bar 36 the repeated notes are heard in stepwise chains, as occurred in the chordal eruption of bars 29–31, but now there are slurs between each stepwise interval of the rising sequence. This provides a closer marriage between steps and repeated notes. Meanwhile, the repeated-note figure is now heard at the end of each two-bar incise, in the bass, at bars 38 and 40, and has moved onto the second beat of the bar rather than the first – a metrically gentler placement.

However, this second conciliatory treatment of the thematic materials is based on a rising sequence, which suddenly seems to spin out of control and produces a strong climax on a V4/2 chord from bar 44. At the same time the isolated form of the repeated-note motive reappears, but now it is played by both hands in rhythmic imitation. This means that for the first time the motive is in dialogue with itself. As this process unfolds, the hands move further and further apart; their eventual wide separation picks up on the association of the motive on its first 'real' appearance in bars 8^2–9^1 with registral incongruity. After the thematic integration and prevailing middle register found in the earlier part of the phrase, this means that the motive once more assumes a disruptive role, and this is emphasized by the dissonant V4/2 harmony and the growth to a *fortissimo* dynamic level. On the other hand, the imitation between the hands here suggests reciprocity, so that from a behavioural point of view one can read this passage in different ways. In sum, this music shows an almost inexhaustible level of flexibility and responsiveness in the ways that its materials interact. Yet this is based on very simple, fundamental musical properties – note repetition versus stepwise continuation, static versus fluent, loud versus soft – and the short duration of the elements in play means they are readily accessible to perception. Thematic interplay there is, but it does not take the form of contrast between entire phrases or themes: it takes place at a more intimate level.[157]

A third instance of close thematic interaction is the first movement of Clementi's Sonata in G major Op. 37 No. 2 (1798; Example 2.28). In textural terms it begins much like Bach's rondo, with a right-hand melody supported by a repeated-note accompaniment in the left hand, a 'natural' hierarchy. This accompaniment, though, operates at quicker speed than the melody (y) and never moves from its repeated pitch of G; it is thus what was known at the time as a drum bass, a definitive sign of contemporary style, though it is a feature more commonly encountered in writing for strings than for keyboard. But the drum bass arrives via a small initial kink, an anacrusic slurred pair that rises a semitone from scale degrees 7 to 8 (F♯ to G). This seems a peripheral detail. However, the continuation phrase from bar 5 abandons any trace of the broad cantabile manner of y and immediately offers us the small 'kink' from the start, joined to two further note repetitions. This four-note unit was precisely what we heard at the outset, before the entry of the melodic line drew attention elsewhere. Now, though, this shape is played in thirds in the melodic register and then repeated in rhythmic sequence as the left hand joins in, playing it in contrary motion to the right hand. This procedure isolates the shape, turning into a recognizable entity – motive x. A *forzando* marking on the final beat of bar 5 emphasizes the disruption to the metrical sense occasioned by a chain of motivic forms that begin on second and fourth beats of the bar; it may sound as if the bar-lines have shifted. Thus what was peripheral, seemingly accompanimental, becomes the centre of attention, and the dramatic change of perspective is emphasized by the disruptive rhythm. In bar 8 the left hand presents what seems like an obvious bass-line filler to take us to the start of the next phrase, moving chromatically in quavers from a D back up to the tonic note G. But at 8^4-9^1 this merges imperceptibly into the same bass figure we heard at the start, so that once more what had seemed to be a routine bit of musical behaviour turns out to be of more specific relevance to the piece at hand. The familiar is made fresh by means of this motivic-syntactical pun.

---

[157] Another instance of this kind of interplay, in the first movement of C. P. E. Bach's Sonata in A major from the first collection *für Kenner und Liebhaber* (1779), Wq55/4, is discussed by Charles Rosen in *Sonata Forms*. Rosen demonstrates how the opening theme 'is essentially the combination of two tiny motifs' (181), though he does not suggest quite the kind of dynamic interaction that I am currently trying to define.

Example 2.28 Clementi, Sonata in G major Op. 37 No. 2/i, bars 1–54[3]

When *x* rises to prominence at the equivalent point of the restatement, from bar 13, it expands dramatically. From bar 15 chains of the motive are played over four octaves in the two hands and marked *fortissimo*. Liberally marked with *forzandi*, *x* grows even more insistent up to the medial caesura. From bar 17 it replaces its third and fourth notes with a single longer note, which gives the motive a stronger melodic identity. After the break *y* re-enters, now on the dominant. But it does so alone,

Example 2.28 (continued)

without any anticipatory drum bass, and then the left hand decides to try *y* for size, ushering in a lengthy passage of sinuous two-part counterpoint that leaves no room for *x* to recur. To this point the interaction between the two types of writing is taking place on a broader scale than in our Bach and Haydn examples, as first one then the other aims to expand its territory. Yet it is animated by similar types of fundamental contrast: disjunct against conjunct, staccato against legato, even melodic focus against rhythmic focus.

After the sustained spell in the company of *y*, the expected cadence at the start of bar 33 is abruptly overwritten by the arrival of brilliant figuration, amidst which a form of *x* quickly makes itself felt. Soon the dynamic is *fortissimo* as the music begins to wind up towards a strong close. But while this time the point of cadential arrival, at the start of bar 42, is unimpeded, the approach to the cadence is not what we expect. Instead of a loud final flourish in the preceding bars, the opening materials return, once more in tandem, but with significant changes. As Haydn and Bach had done in their movements, Clementi takes advantage of the built-in stereo capacities of the medium – one keyboard, one player, but two hands. From bar 39^4 the texture is turned upside down, with *x* followed by the drum-bass repetitions on top, in the right hand, and *y* on the bottom, in the left hand. This encapsulates the way in which the seemingly insignificant *x* has risen in importance since the start at the expense of what sounded like the movement's signature material, *y*. Melodic continuity is still provided by *y*, but it now acts as a bass voice; with a few adjustments of contour it provides the harmonic foundation for the approaching cadence. There is a further reversal in this phrase, relating to formal function: what had been opening material now acts as continuation towards a close. And the dynamic level, suddenly reduced to *piano* after the *fortissimo* build-up, emphasizes the wit of the reversals that have taken place.

After the understated cadence at the start of bar 42, a closing theme is heard in which *y* reasserts itself as a carrier of lyrical breadth. It returns to the right hand and is roughly inverted in contour, so creating two kinds of interplay with the form just heard at bars 40–41. Motive *x* does make several appearances within this theme, but only in the form of repeated notes, in other words without the initial slurred step. Hence its role is once more subordinate. Meanwhile, the left hand's figuration also features a form of *x*, with a D being reiterated on the second quaver of every beat from bar 42 all the way through to the start of bar 52. This means that the drum-bass repetitions associated with *x* have in fact returned, and on a larger scale than ever. But on the first quaver of each beat in the left hand we hear a shadow version of *y* in a tenor range that effectively breaks up the percussive, insistent aspect of *x*'s repeated notes. Thus in this latest reconfiguration of material *y* has expanded texturally and melodically while *x*, though still present in various forms, takes on more supportive roles. But then at bars 52–54 *x* plainly reasserts itself, *forte*, as a chain of original four-quaver versions outlines a falling D major arpeggio. What the endlessly dynamic process of Clementi's exposition section shows us is that textures can be contested by their constituent elements; they are subject to constant negotiation.

The versatility of behaviour does not flag through the rest of the movement. We could take, for example, the two subsequent passages that refer to bars 39^4–42^1, where the hands explicitly reversed their roles. In the first of these, from bar 94, x splits into two right-hand voices that form a lengthy 2–3 suspension chain underneath which y enters in the left hand, forming a circle-of-fifths sequence that starts to guide us back towards the tonic. In the earlier such textural reversal, the hands combined to express a new closing function, but now that changes yet again, as the formal function becomes retransitional, or middle. The second of these passages arrives when we reach the equivalent point in the recapitulation, at the end of bar 127. Here the textural reversal is reversed: it is the left hand once more that plays x, melting into the drum bass, and the right hand plays y. Further, y now takes its opening guise – to be more specific, it replays its consequent-phrase version of the tune from bar 9, with the same melodic variants. This is therefore a second reversal, in that we are expecting to hear a phrase that moves us towards a cadence, but instead hear material that was associated with presentational function. A third level of reversal is apparent in the fact that the bass plays not a local tonic pedal on G, but a dominant one on D. This means that the syntactical implications of the two hands are in conflict: the right hand suggests opening while the left hand suggests continuation.[158]

One cannot but be struck by the technical adroitness of this type of music-making, which strong elements of functional definition and periodic syntax help to make possible. It creates a sense of cleverness, an abiding part of the tone of our musical style, as if the composer is a master manipulator or raconteur. But the plaudits need not exactly rest with the figure of the composer, though this style of writing certainly encourages listeners to engage with a creator who leads them on. The constant changes of perspective on the materials of the movement also encourage us, once more, to conceive of the interacting musical elements as independent agents.[159]

---

[158] When y returns, in its second-subject guise, at bar 109, this would seem to exemplify Hepokoski and Darcy's Type 2 sonata form, whereby the recapitulation begins with the second subject (see *Elements of Sonata Theory*, chapter 17, 353–387). However, if we track backwards, we find that the retransition that began at bar 96 offers a close rhythmic replica first of bars 1–8 – though with a rhythmic augmentation of the rising chromatic fourth in the bass that had linked the first sentence to the second – followed by a cut to a more plainly recalled bars 17–20 at 105–108. Thus from a rotational perspective Clementi is simply continuing with the earlier sequence of events when the second subject returns at bar 109.

[159] My article 'Before the Joke' offers a lengthy analysis along these lines of the slow movement of Haydn's quartet Op. 33 No. 2, with a distinct emphasis on thematic – rather than just textural – interaction.

Such interactions need not lead to a clear point of resolution. This was already clear in the case of Haydn's E minor movement, and in the Clementi the climax to the dialogue arrives in the passage just described, in which the two hands and two motives are at greatest odds, wanting to 'do their own thing'. In a way the main 'moral', as already suggested in other contexts, as with Germaine de Staël's words on conversation, is interaction itself: the moment-by-moment process of adjustment, turn-taking and 'listening' that the various materials seem to enact.

While, as I have stressed, these thematic characters tend to express themselves concisely, they may also operate on a larger scale. The first movement of Haydn's Symphony No. 43 in E flat major, written around 1771, is marked by strong thematic contrast, though this cannot be aligned with any sonata-form template: rather, we are presented with two basic types of musical behaviour, one lyrical and the other much more kinetic. The opening passage is punctuated by loud tutti tonic chords (bars 1, 5 and 9) that suggest the kind of momentum proper to an opening movement, but everything else contradicts that. We hear *piano* singing-style material that meanders along for twenty-six bars without suggesting a strong sense of direction. While bar 8 closes on the tonic, it does so weakly, and in what follows – an implied continuation phrase of a sentence structure – the music keeps landing on first-inversion tonic chords, and the melodic lines loop back on themselves rather than suggesting forward movement.[160] In bar 26 this material is effectively interrupted by loud figuration played in octaves by the two violins, which quickly generates a strong perfect cadence in the tonic, from which point it feels like the movement is finally underway in earnest. Henceforth the movement alternates between frequently ferocious propulsive figuration, marked by even quaver and semiquaver rhythms and often organized sequentially, and the lyrical lines, which move mostly in even crotchets. The particular point of this conjunction is that the singing style is musing and 'inefficient' – it lacks control of harmonic movement and of phrase structure, so absorbed does it appear to be in its cantabile world. The figuration then comes to the rescue by restoring a sense of forward momentum.

While the contrast generally involves alternating blocks of the two types of behaviour, there are also points where the materials interact on an intimate scale, and so demonstrate a greater suppleness of utterance.

---

[160] It is quite understandable that Charles Rosen took this opening passage to be an instance of lack of compositional control, serving his thesis that the increased expressive power of Haydn's music of the later 1760s and earlier 1770s was bought at the expense of musical coherence and technical security; see *The Classical Style*, 149–150.

From bar 60, for instance, the opening theme returns to mark the arrival on the dominant, but it is now underpinned by a repeated-note quaver bass that ensures continuity of rhythm and pulse, and this helps to drive it towards a strong perfect cadence at the end of the phrase. And the lyrical material is now compressed into a shorter sentence structure that is completed without delay. The two types of gesture are in fact mutually dependent, since, while it is clear that the lyricism needs the help of the figuration in order to achieve a coherent shape, the figuration needs the lyricism too: given that its energy gets channelled into a number of different forms over the course of the movement, it lacks the thematic profile to govern the Allegro in its own right. And in fact initiating function is always given to the lyrical material; quite naturally, given its propensity for small-scale reiteration and sequence, the figuration can only fulfil continuation or closing functions.

In the second half of the movement, these roles will be sorely needed, since the lyrical material brings about a series of structural accidents that threaten to derail the movement. A very early return of the opening theme in the tonic (bar 113)[161] is countered by a further stretch of forceful figuration, but then in short order we are treated to returns of the singing theme in A flat major (bar 152), then F minor (157), and finally back in the tonic of E flat major (162), these events being awkwardly spaced five bars apart, and linked by tentative-sounding chromatic scales. The loud tutti thumps that mark the beginning of each phrase only accentuate the awkwardness. After the tonic return at bar 162 the lyrical material spins itself out at greater length than ever before, pleasantly enough, but heightening the feeling around this point that the movement is losing its sense of direction. Eventually our figuration comes to the rescue by injecting a further wave of reiterative energy, from bar 197, but because we have been made to wait longer than expected for its arrival, it carries a renewed sense of agency. In its various manifestations the figuration drives us through to the end of the movement.

The broader brand of thematic interaction that is apparent in this movement may be especially idiomatic in a genre like the symphony, since the contrasting musical agents can be allied to especially vivid contrasts of textural mass and volume. The final movement of Haydn's Symphony No. 50 in C major (1773) offers a comparable instance. It

---

[161] Whether such a return can rightly be described as a 'false recapitulation' or 'false reprise' remains contentious. One foundational contribution to the debate is Peter A. Hoyt, 'The "False Recapitulation" and the Conventions of Sonata Form' (PhD dissertation, University of Pennsylvania, 1999).

opens with an eight-bar tune, played *pianissimo* by the strings, whose catchy popular style and simple parallel-period construction are just what we could expect to hear at the start of a finale. But the generic expectation operates on a larger scale too: the listener of the time would have been primed to hear an immediate repetition of the tune, typical of the squarer phrase syntax of a concluding movement, and this would then be followed by a loud tutti section. However, such a series of anticipated events is quickly complicated by a *forte* unison passage in the strings, four bars long plus an initial anacrusis, that interjects before any repetition of the theme can get underway (bars 8^4–12^2). The opening then returns *piano*, though in the violins alone, and so our gratification has merely been delayed, it appears. But after four bars of this, the *forte* unison material begins again – and so the interruption now occurs within the period rather than after it. This means it is no symmetrical match for the previous one; its changed timing, 'too soon', means it retains its surprising force. And because on both occasions it seems not to acknowledge the demands of periodic symmetry that the opening has set up, this material gives the impression of operating 'outside the system', as if it is an independent agent.

This impression is strengthened by the ways in which the surprising gesture continues to surprise. Having come in 'too soon' at the second time of asking, the interruption then turns out to be 'too short', since it now lasts for just two bars (plus anacrusis). Thus it is halved in duration. The two violins then from bar 19 play a four-bar complement to the four-bar antecedent that has just been interrupted, and as we approach the end of the phrase, it would seem that, once more, gratification has simply been delayed, and we are now back on track. The phrase completes itself perfectly well harmonically, closing with a cadence on the tonic, and melodically, moving $\hat{7}$–$\hat{1}$ in the upper voice, but in terms of dynamics and timbral mass it is all change. At the point of the conclusive V-I progression, the dynamic level suddenly jumps to *forte* once more, and the whole orchestra enters. Thus we have a resolution and an interruption simultaneously. The material that enters at this point is new thematically, but the *forte* marking allied to the anacrusis clearly point to the previous loud interruptions. That once again the *forte* gesture does not tally with the expected divisions of the phrase syntax strengthens the impression that it is acting as a kind of free agent. At the same time, we have now reached the tutti section that the soft opening would have promised to deliver. Therefore on a broad scale the anticipated sequence of events after that tune is delivered softly at the outset does come to pass. From this point of view the loud unison gesture could be conceived as a musical character that is unable to wait its turn in the unfolding of the movement: on three separate occasions it pre-empts the proper exposition of the opening tune.

If on this larger scale expectation is satisfied, the rest of the movement continues to display an unpredictable association between the two thematic characters, which to a great extent can be understood as involving a simple contrast of *piano* and *forte* execution. The soft side generally repeats the opening tune, beginning squarely on the downbeat, while the loud side is less thematically focussed, and is associated with 'impatient' anacrusis beginnings. The latter continues to show its agency by interrupting, or overruling, the catchy tune in ever-varied ways, and in fact it sometimes appropriates the tune's opening phrase for its own purposes. The agency of the tune itself is of a different kind. With its innocent demeanour comes a seeming obliviousness to its surroundings; over the course of the movement it continually begins again 'from the top', in a succession of different keys, as if perpetually unaware of the fate that will befall it when it is cut short. Allied with the elemental pairing of soft and loud dynamic levels are contrasts between melodic and figurative writing, and between strings-only and tutti scoring.

These equations are reminiscent of those that operated in the first movement of Haydn's Symphony No. 43, with its dialogue between wandering lyricism and highly charged figuration. In both cases the louder material takes no consistent form, but it has been implicit in the accounts above that this does not disqualify it from being perceived as a focussed agent in the conduct of the movement. In other words, as proposed earlier, the 'thematic' in our 'thematic interaction' needs to be understood broadly. While it may often be allied with 'motivic', as in our earlier case studies of Haydn, Bach and Clementi keyboard works, and so entail a clearly defined rhythmic-melodic identity, it may often be better understood simply as 'characteristic'. However, as already noted, that term also has its limitations, given the range and adaptability that our musical materials display. In many instances, the contrasts either take off from or turn into an interplay of types of execution. This may involve a simple contrast of dynamic levels, as in our two symphonic movements, or of types of articulation, such as legato and staccato. Other kinds of elemental, readily perceived, difference may come into play, such as between steps and repeated notes in Bach's Rondo, and often enough, as noted at the very start of this chapter, such binary relationships are (unpredictably) paired with other ones to create a network of differentiated musical behaviours. The contrasts of mass and timbre evident in the Haydn symphonic movements were to be retained in his later output, and, if anything, made more dramatic. Emily Dolan notes how many movements in the London symphonies (Nos 93–104) 'unfold as a working-through of opposing sonorities or textures', with the use of 'sonic extremes' being especially characteristic of their slow movements.[162]

While in a symphonic context such interaction would naturally be expected to conclude with the whole ensemble playing together, and therefore most likely with the louder side of the dynamic equation, this need not be so. In the finale of Brunetti's Symphony No. 9 in D major (date unknown) it is in fact soft material that has the final say, the movement closing with a *pianissimo assai* arpeggio for strings alone. The first and final refrain sections of this five-part rondo contrast a thinly scored theme, played *pianissimo*, with robustious tutti fanfares, played *fortissimo*, while in the first episode, in D minor, *forte* unisons are met by *piano* versions of the opening motive. The tutti fanfares are absent from the middle version of the refrain, meaning that the opening theme is able softly to run its course without any dynamic competition. The tables are then turned in the second episode, however, which is played *fortissimo* throughout in an agitated B minor.

While this all suggests an alternation of blocks of sound allied with some familiar binaries – loud versus soft, the many versus the few – there are in fact two points in the movement where we hear a reconciliation. The first arrives at the end of the opening refrain, from the upbeat to bar 33, when the initial eight-bar period returns. The theme, now heard in bass and woodwinds, is transformed into a *fortissimo* tutti, combined with traits of the fanfare, with its characteristic military rhythm returning in the timpani. This is like a marriage of the two previously opposed characters: the material is predominantly that of the opening, though intermixed with elements of the fanfare, while the full scoring and dynamic level clearly derive from the latter.

At the equivalent point in the final refrain, from the upbeat to bar 181, the basic idea is the same, but differently inflected. The tune is heard in the bass and woodwinds for just two bars instead of the original four, with the third and fourth bars now being given over purely to fanfare style, and this plan is repeated in the four-bar consequent phrase. If this restores some sense of alternation between the two characters, an ethos of reconciliation still seems to hold. Then we hear four bars of pure fanfare material, which in fact takes a similar form to what we heard on its first appearance in bars 9–12. This suggests not so much that the fanfare suddenly prevails as that it assumes its

---

[162] Dolan, *Orchestral Revolution*, 120.

'natural' role of providing an affirmative conclusion, especially since this is a final movement. We only need a few bars of extension and the movement will have finished (it would be too abrupt if it finished on the downbeat of bar 192). But what ensues is no such thing; instead, the rising D major arpeggio heard at the top of the fanfare texture is echoed by the string section in unison, and at the dynamic level of *pianissimo assai*. Each note of the arpeggio lasts a full minim, played under a single slur in the four-bar phrase for maximally smooth effect. And there the movement stops.

In a sense this conclusion – four bars of loud followed by four bars of soft – strikes a perfect balance between the opposing elements. On the other hand, it is hugely counterintuitive, and breaks a generic norm, especially for the finale of an instrumental work, and even more so in the case of a symphony, which brings together relatively large forces. The soft gesture overwrites the expected conclusion – which would entail a series of chords played forcefully by all in the ensemble – that the previous fanfare material has so strongly set up. Yet it does so simply by copying one element associated with the fanfare, a rising tonic arpeggio. This could certainly be understood as a further form of rapprochement, but in context – because we were expecting something else, at a different dynamic level – imitation proves to be the sincerest form of disruption. Added to this is the fact that the imitation involves replicating a rising contour, suggesting a kind of interrogative intonation that is an unnatural way to finish. This finale provides a further example of how pivotal parameters like dynamics and texture can be to an interactive discourse.

On the basis of the movements covered thus far, it remains an open question whether the long-range interactions we have traced need to reach some sort of diplomatic entente. It was suggested earlier that the process of interaction may itself be regarded as the main 'moral': in other words, this process is impelled by an ethos that is more social-behavioural than narrative or dramatic, and so no final resolution need be anticipated. The possibility that this aspect of a movement may be left open would seem to jar with an overwhelming emphasis in the relevant literature on the resolution of constituent elements. Much of this no doubt is underpinned by the image of the later eighteenth century as the era of 'form', of 'balance', of tonal harmony at its cleanest, where movements drive towards an explicit close in a central key, with harmonic resolution achieved after clearly delineated movements into other tonal areas.[163] This reflects a

---

[163] In 'Haydn's "Irregularities": Ambiguous Openings in the B-Minor String Quartets, Op. 33/1 and Op. 64/2' Mathieu Langlois challenges assumptions that resolution must be achieved in this repertory, especially when it comes to ambiguities; in *Topics in Eighteenth-Century Music I: Selected Papers from the Fourth Biennial Conference of the Society for Eighteenth-Century*

traditional emphasis on the supremacy of pitch structure within our experience of this music, and on a large historical scale it would be hard to deny the force of such equations, as Susan McClary for one has made clear.[164] However, many commentators have argued for resolution precisely in terms of the musical materials themselves. For Allanbrook, an explicit resolution of contrasting elements inheres in the fundamentally comic mission of later eighteenth-century style; for Leon Botstein, the style places a premium 'on the symbolic achievement of resolution within the musical experience', which 'meant the reconciling of the disparate and conflicting elements of an emotional experience, as mirrored by contrasts in the music'.[165] And certainly in our Brunetti finale reconciliation does takes place, even if it is in some ways undone by those quizzical final four bars. The two guiding impulses of the movement are separated once more after they had seemingly been united for a celebratory close, and arguably we finish with a juxtaposition rather than with a proper resolution of the 'conflicting elements'.

The larger point, though, is that the prospect of reconciliation is clearly evoked, and one can readily find other movements in which that prospect comes to pass. In the first movement of his Symphony in E flat major Murray A28 (1786) Antonio Rosetti puts a learned spin on the process. The Largo introduction opens in two-part counterpoint, with a rising triadic shape written against a repeated-note figure that is treated in imitation to form a rising suspension chain in best Corelli style. These ideas immediately come back when the Allegro assai starts, but inverted, so that the triadic figure is now heard in the top line and the repeated notes occur lower in the texture. Both thematic elements – effectively contrapuntal 'tags' – retain their separate identities as they are used in the rest of the movement, even when they are variously combined during a learned development section. Right near the end, though, something quite unexpected takes place. After a series of closing gestures that rhyme with the end of the exposition, and so lead us to imagine that the end is nigh, the two elements are suddenly fused into one melodic line, played by flute and

---

Music at St. Francis College in Brooklyn, NY, 8–11 April 2010, ed. Margaret R. Butler and Janet K. Page (Ann Arbor: Steglein, 2014), 103–130.

[164] This forms a focal point of McClary's *Conventional Wisdom*.

[165] See, for instance, Allanbrook, 'Mozart's Tunes', 179 ('the sense of a just end – of a close that completes a dynamically balanced process – was important as it had not been in music before and has not been since'); Botstein, 'The Consequences of Presumed Innocence', 28–29. Note also Stephen Rumph's remark, when discussing 'neutralization', that in 'the music of Mozart's generation ... so many processes involve overcoming binary oppositions': *Mozart and Enlightenment Semiotics*, 100.

oboes, and echoed approvingly by horns. The rising triadic figure is followed immediately by the repeated notes, to create a union of the two separate thematic 'characters'. This is a distinctly modern form of coming-together compared with the previous conjunction of the two elements. Such explicit reconciliation is not within the terms of the older technique of invertible counterpoint that Rosetti has drawn on to this point. The older contrapuntal procedure certainly involves its own brand of thematic interaction, but it would not naturally produce this kind of unexpected agreement, where two become one. Rosetti seems to acknowledge the stylistic impropriety, as it were, of such a move by placing it outside the proper formal frame of the movement, so that it feels like a sort of amusing afterthought. But from our current perspective it is not peripheral. This moment of reconciliation attests to the dynamic way in which musical materials can now interact, as what was a simultaneous relationship becomes a successive one, and what was contrapuntal becomes melodic.

If the late melodic consensus of the two figures in the Rosetti movement was unexpected, the materials were at least in a sense always together. This is not the case in the first movement of Clementi's Piano Duo in B flat major, Op. 12 (1784). Here the two musical ideas inhabit different spaces in a way they could not readily do in an older style; in fact, they coincide with the two subject groups of a sonata-form movement, which means they are presented separately at widely spaced points of the discourse. The first idea (first subject) is marked by a strongly rhythmic head-motive consisting of repeated notes followed by a falling semiquaver scale fragment, whereas the softer second subject opens in bar 23 with finickety elegance: it alternates neighbour-note figuration with a fragment of melody, so creating a small-scale internal dialogue. This second subject is given a dual presentation, creating a larger scale of dialogue and indeed a kind of reciprocity that is second nature to the duo medium. Before the second keyboard player takes over the material, an 'empty bar' (34) is filled by the first player with a recollection of the head-motive from the first subject. It retains the same rhythm and initial repeated notes, but for the falling scalic contour it substitutes a turn shape that fits with the second subject's emphasis on neighbour notes ('around-ness' instead of 'to-ness'). This then recurs every two bars as a complementary comment to the second subject.

This relatively inconspicuous commingling of the two elements is taken much further during the development section. After a silence of almost two bars (68–69), the first subject begins *pp* in the hands of the first keyboard in E flat major. Then, one bar later, seemingly out of nowhere, the second keyboard begins the second subject! Not only that, but these iterations are sustained: the first five bars of the first subject are given verbatim by one player at the same time as the other perfectly renders the first four bars of the second subject. It sounds little short of a miracle that these two separate, and affectively distinct, pieces of material can be so neatly spliced together: they can be heard simultaneously in their full form without any need for adjustment. In other words, they can retain their complete sonic identity while at the same time being reconciled with each other. The hushed dynamic level only increases the sense that something special is unfolding. As the passage continues, we are given an aural reminder of the earlier interaction, when the second subject was repeated in the first section. Here too the first keyboard interjects versions of the first subject's head-motive while the second keyboard is engaged in performing the second subject. The difference now, of course, is that the first keyboard is also performing the first theme in its entirety. This difference seems to point to what has changed: what in the exposition had seemed to be a simple bit of musical glue, providing continuity between the short phrase units of a typically galant theme, turns out to hint at a much larger-scale compatibility of the two musical subjects. The basic (social) message: things that seem to be separate and different turn out to be compatible. And, unlike all our previous cases, no flexible 'interaction' is required: the compatibility of the two thematic agents turns out to be inbuilt.

The first movement of Michael Haydn's Symphony in D major ST287 (before 1781) offers another case where two elements that were not in overt dialogue turn out to be compatible. Whereas in the Clementi duo the fusion occurred in the middle of the movement, in this case it takes place at the end. The coda starts with the movement's opening triadic motive, previously played by oboes and horns, being transferred to unison strings (bars 171–174). As they repeat the motive, the dynamic level rises from *piano* to *fortissimo*, and this climaxes in a most unexpected return of the striking two-note gesture that opened the movement's second theme: a loud unison falling sixth, the first note of which lasts a whole bar and so interrupts the rhythmic flow (compare bars 26–27 and 175–176). The figure's subsequent appearance at the start of the theme's consequent phrase had an even more striking effect as it crashed in ahead of time, by means of a phrase overlap, effectively undercutting the previous phrase; this reinforces its peremptory character. Thus in the movement's coda two elements that were previously entirely separate in their occurrence are now conjoined, and an unexpected similarity is revealed: the falling-sixth shape that opened the second subject is cognate with the triadic horn-call motive that opened the first subject. In fact, the falling sixth did not fit especially well with the material that followed it in its original surroundings, which was more conjunct and lyrical; the wide falling interval sounded more like a formal marker ('here begins the second thematic group') than part of an integrated statement. Now, though, it seems to find a more congenial home, amidst the disjunct intervals of the opening theme.

A further change of circumstance as this loud falling sixth recurs is that it is now no longer heard as a beginning of a larger unit, but occurs at a later point of the phrase. And this appearance of the two-note shape is immediately followed by a further version that dissolves some of its previous attributes. First, this subsequent version is marked *pianissimo* in all parts, meaning that a shape that had always been performed forcefully is now given a complementary soft answer, countering not just the previous dynamic level but also its 'social loudness' in the original context. Secondly, the strings answer the original falling sixth with a falling fifth, on $\hat{5}$–$\hat{1}$, which means a resolution to more stable scale degrees. Third, the previous unison presentation of the figure now yields to homophony, as the oboes and horns harmonize this falling fifth to create a gentle but firm V–I cadence. Thus the figure that started life as a brusque beginning has transformed itself into a stable close. After this turn of events, as a final touch, the first subject comes back in its original scoring, with oboes and horns playing the triadic motive, and another beginning becomes an ending.[166]

In this Michael Haydn movement and the Clementi before it, the reconciliation of thematic materials was all the more surprising since they had originally been presented as part of separate groups. The materials were in dialogue only in a broad formal sense, with contrast being implicit in the sonata-form structure rather than explicit, as was the case with the more immediate cut and thrust found in some of our earlier examples. The Clementi duo involves a quite unexpected 'simultaneous transmission' of ideas whose variety seemed to be self-evident, an unmarked aspect of later eighteenth-century musical language. In other words, there was no particular reason to anticipate an encounter between the two ideas. In the case of the Michael Haydn symphony, it is only once the two elements are conjoined that we may realize that a certain problem of compatibility has been addressed – namely, the tension in the second subject between a brash motto and the gentler material that succeeds it. Over and above this, what is striking about both moments of reconciliation, and indeed that found in

---

[166] This is reminiscent of what brother Joseph does at the end of the first movement of his 'Hornsignal' Symphony in D major, No. 31 (1765).

the earlier Rosetti movement, is how brief they are. While each moment is made formally prominent – whether through placement near the end so as to act as a peroration (Rosetti, Haydn) or by means of a preceding silence (Clementi) – none is insisted on at length. Rather, they all have the flavour of the epigram about them, wittily finding common ground between things that seemed to be unrelated to each other. The lack of insistence upon the process forms part of the social style of this music, just indeed as wit represents a flash of recognition rather than a sustained exploration. In this respect too such thematic practice differs from the nineteenth-century examples that still represent our normal point of orientation; the interaction between musical elements need not be framed according to the favoured terms of reference for that repertory, involving some heroic or epic narrative whereby one element finishes in triumph or two elements experience a sustained climactic unification, and need not involve anything that we would now recognize as a 'breakthrough'.

Not that such moments of concord need always come as a complete revelation: in the opening Allegro of Kraus's Symphony in F major VB128 (c1775–1776), the two elements at play are within earshot of each other from the start. The first theme begins with a bar of assertive unisons involving a written-out trill that decorates a single repeated note (*a*) followed by two bars of gracious material (*b*), rising legato steps leading to a softening appoggiatura-like ending. The whole is then repeated, but with the gracious part now descending by step. This creates a perfect balance with regard to contour, but since each constituent phrase is three bars long, the phrase rhythm is clearly less comfortable. When this material comes again at the end of the movement, the appoggiatura in the third bar receives a sequential answer in a fourth bar, and then the stepwise ascent that had preceded the appoggiatura is subjected to rhythmic diminution to lead to a new cadential close. Thus the original grouping of three-bar antecedent followed by three-bar consequent is replaced by a broader, continuous six-bar phrase, but this is followed by a series of postcadential extensions, the second of which repeats the opening bar, our unison trill motive. This motive now acts as a close rather than an opening, and within the same large phrase.

This close can be seen as both a completion and a correction of the initial theme. The two distinct elements that it contained, assertive and gracious, are more fully integrated within a longer statement, and with a chiastic balance of *abba*. The start of the development section had split the complementary parts of the theme, first of all taking the lyrical component further and then from bar 82 concentrating on the assertive trill. Then at the point of recapitulation (bar 96) the initial unison trill motive was not followed by its gracious complement. This was replaced by a series of rising arpeggios in violin 1 with syncopated rhythms heard beneath, which clearly cannot count as a gracious riposte. Therefore after the exposition Kraus has deliberately kept the two gestures apart, in order for the final integration to register more strongly. Here it is not so much a case of two elements being reconciled to each other, since they already coexisted at the start, but of being reconciled to the need for a different mode of presentation. This turn of events is still likely to generate a sense of surprise on the part of the listener – in common with our previous cases, it still sounds like a rabbit has been pulled out of the hat – but the realignment of contrasting materials takes place on a different level.

One should note that the more or less explicit kinds of thematic reconciliation outlined in the last few case studies are relatively rare; it is the principle of interaction altogether that prevails, without any clear point of resolution or revelation needing to be reached. We must also distinguish between contrast as a self-evident phenomenon that will exist in almost any stream of sound, variety as a normal state of affairs within our repertory, and the more focussed interactions that I have been aiming to describe in this section. It would appear that these interactions always take place between two basic tendencies. Must these always be binary operations? While at any one point this generally seems to be the case, perhaps reflecting the limits of listener perception, each term of the binary pair, as I have stressed, typically carries a number of associations which can all operate separately. Thus we are likely to end up with a larger field than just the two original entities, amounting to a constellation of separate binary relationships. These may involve volume, articulation, texture, tessitura, interval size, pitch trend, rhythm and the like, each of which is a potentially independent agent in the musical movement.

Contrast as Incongruity

But what if variety, however it seems to be organized, fails to convey any sense of give and take? When does it become simple incongruity? Certainly for those eighteenth-century critics who were uneasy with the modern plurality of style and gesture, the threshold for a perception of incongruity was rather low. In the cases detailed above, I was able to argue that various materials 'notice' each other – and therefore that they can be felt to interact. As already suggested, this need not mean that any sort of resolution or reconciliation is achieved, since the name of the game is the very process of interaction. On a number of occasions, though, the implicit 'tolerance' that underpins galant variety is put to the test, when materials simply seem to be incompatible and remain stubbornly so throughout. The contrast seems to be two-dimensional, or 'flat', with no obvious softening of edges between the different kinds of gesture.

The distinction between 'pleasing variety' and flat contrast is, naturally, not easy to discern or maintain, any more than it would be in the wider realm of social behaviour of which music forms a part. Might we just say, adopting that perspective, that such differing materials 'agree to disagree'? When David Hume wrote that 'Opposite sentiments, even without any decision, afford an agreeable amusement', this might seem to give a blessing to our presumptive category, but one imagines that some level of rapprochement was envisaged none the less. The same might go for Morellet's 'spirit of contradiction', which gives rise to verbal interchanges that 'consist almost entirely in doubting, modifying, or combating what another advances'.[167] This only remains viable with at least some element of acknowledgment of the other point of view; otherwise the threshold for civilized sociable behaviour is not reached. But even 'contradiction' may not capture the impression one gains in the case of such opposed musical elements, since they often don't seem even to acknowledge each other. It can appear rather that they simply occupy different realms or planes of existence.

One need not wait until the later eighteenth century for such issues to arise. They already do so in the case of Domenico Scarlatti, who may be accounted the first composer who routinely brings strongly contrasting materials together within the frame of a single instrumental movement.[168] While these materials often do appear to listen to each other, at other times we find harsh interruptions, not to say ruptures in the musical fabric. These can give the impression that a new piece of music has begun, as in the Sonata in D major K236, in which the second half starts with a complete change of gear into a rushing toccata idiom, or the Sonata in B flat major K202, where at the same point material in the style of a quick Italian

---

[167] David Hume, *Dialogues concerning Natural Religion*, second edition (London, 1779), 8; André Morellet, 'De l'esprit de contradiction', in *Éloges de Mme Geoffrin*, ed. Morellet, 231, cited in translation in Daniel Gordon, *Citizens without Sovereignty*, 207.

[168] See Sutcliffe, 'Topics in Chamber Music', in *The Oxford Handbook of Topic Theory*, ed. Mirka, 122: 'Scarlatti offers us perhaps the first recognizably topically volatile repertory'; and also Sutcliffe, *Keyboard Sonatas of Domenico Scarlatti*, especially chapter 3, 'Heteroglossia', 78–144.

pastorale interrupts and proceeds to dominate the rest of the sonata.[169] What results, via the use of what Wilfred Mellers calls 'permutation and contradiction', is a form of 'open-ended' listening experience.[170]

It is certainly the case that there are gradations to such a phenomenon, as interaction shades into straight contrast which in turn shades into incongruity or incompatibility. Seemingly unaccountable contrasts may occur within a single movement, but we can only finally judge them as such once a movement is over. We have noted in the case of a movement like the Allegro of Haydn's Symphony No. 43 that materials or parameters that seem strongly opposed may eventually seem to adjust their behaviour, but then there are cases like the first movement of Haydn's Quartet in B flat major Op. 76 No. 4 ('Sunrise'; 1797). George Edwards describes this as consisting of 'contrasting monologues' in which the 'hushed rapture' of the famous opening 'alternates with loud passages of rather generic passage work and cadential material'; and there is 'almost no mediation between these extremes except when the development begins to prepare the recapitulation'. The 'monologues' then return in the reprise, 'to be resolved, if at all, in later movements'.[171] For Edwards such ambiguity concerning resolution is of a piece with Haydn's wider equivocation about the fact of musical ending. From the symphonic sphere, we might note the slow movement of Haydn's Symphony No. 88 in G major (1787), one of those movements that trades in the 'sonic extremes' noted by Dolan. This Largo is often singled out for the beauty of its main theme, most commonly carried by solo oboe and solo cello playing one octave apart, a strikingly original timbre, yet this material is also interrupted – increasingly so as the movement progresses – by *fortissimo* and *forzando* repeated chords. These are played by the full orchestra, with trumpets and drums making their presence felt; not only was the participation of these instruments in a slow movement a novelty at this time, but their impact is all the stronger given

---

[169] See Sutcliffe, *Keyboard Sonatas of Domenico Scarlatti*, 134–136, for commentary on these two works.

[170] Wilfred Mellers, *The Masks of Orpheus* (Manchester: Manchester University Press, 1987), 85 and 86.

[171] George Edwards, 'The Nonsense of an Ending: Closure in Haydn's String Quartets', *The Musical Quarterly* 75/3 (1991), 241. For a possible counterexample, see the interpretation of the first movement of Haydn's quartet Op. 71 No. 1 by Wilhelm Seidel, which similarly trades in a contrast between melody and figuration, but whose governing principle involves the 'modification of two antithetical ideas'. Wilhelm Seidel, 'Haydns Streichquartett in B-Dur Op. 71 Nr. 1 (Hob. III: 69): Analytische Bemerkungen aus der Sicht Heinrich Christoph Kochs', in *Joseph Haydn: Tradition und Rezeption*, ed. Feder, Hüschen and Tank, 3–13.

that they had played no role in the first movement.[172] The intensity of this material is amplified by the fact that while winds and timpani play in straight crotchets, the strings divide each beat into eight aggressively repeated demisemiquavers. The collective impression is of an undifferentiated brute force that is entirely at odds not just with the melodic eloquence but also with the highly refined orchestration that we have been hearing up to this point. While the loud tutti material later acquires some sense of melodic and harmonic direction, just what constructive role it plays is never clarified. The juxtaposition of the two basic gestures – long-breathed melody and obsessively accented chords – is never 'explained'.

While in this Largo and the first movement of Op. 76 No. 4 the contrasts may seem to be unaccountable, we do at least encounter both types of material several times over the course of the movement, and so there is at least a sense of alternation between them. At other times, a single moment or gesture seems to be so much at odds with the rest of the music that one also wants to account for it under this rubric. Of course one could simply speak of a surprise, but characteristic of such cases is the placement of the gesture late on in the piece, so that there is little time for the surprise to resonate, for the listener to consider what to make of it before the movement concludes. One instance comes in the slow movement of J. C. Bach's Symphony in E flat major Op. 9 No. 2 (1773). This is an Andante con sordini in C minor in which muted first violins carry the melody while the lower strings play pizzicato. The movement weaves a gently melancholy spell in serenade style until the final two bars, after the opening eight-bar period has been recapitulated. The mutes come off the first violins, the lower strings play arco, oboes and horns rejoin the texture, and everyone plays *fortissimo*. The material is more or less a decorated version of the previous two, cadential bars, but the changes of scoring, timbre and dynamics combine to create a real dramatic jolt right at the end of the movement. The changes in these parameters are enough to overturn the melancholic serenade; they frame it as something contingent. And we should note that these final two bars stand outside the double-bar lines that stipulate a repeated performance of the second half of this rounded-binary-form Andante. Thus the listener will hear two endings that are congruent with the style of the movement before the final passage throws everything into doubt.

---

[172] See A. Peter Brown, *The Symphonic Repertoire*, volume 2: *The First Golden Age of the Viennese Symphony: Haydn, Mozart, Beethoven, and Schubert* (Bloomington: Indiana University Press, 2002), 227.

A similar impression may be left by a better-known middle movement, the Andante from Beethoven's Sonata in G major Op. 14 No. 2 (1799). The theme of what is an unmarked series of variations marries chorale texture with march rhythm, but the predominant staccato articulation of the chords, which are also separated by rests, works against the dignified associations of those topics, creating an air of comic disparity. Subsequent sections alternate detached and legato treatments of the theme before a further staccato version begins at bar 85. Quite quickly, though, this breaks down into fragments, the dynamics decrease from *piano* to *pianissimo* and the register starts to vacillate between high and low. In addition, the gap between each chord, previously a crotchet, is doubled to half a bar (88–89). This rhythmic augmentation together with the other changes signal liquidation – that the movement is running out of steam and is drawing to a close. It does so punctually with a single tonic chord on the downbeat of bar 90, but this is realized as a thickly scored, widely spread *fortissimo* bang, which nobody can have heard coming after the carefully engineered fade-out. Charles Rosen describes this as 'a joke in Haydn's style',[173] which is certainly plausible given the general mood of the movement. Yet one need not hear (or attempt to play) it in this way. It could be understood more as a crude or angry or grand obliteration of everything that has gone before. But ascribing an imagined character to this final moment may not be of the first importance; any character one chooses simply rationalizes the more basic fact of flat, unmediated contrast, one that occurs right at the end of the movement and so allows the listener little time to assimilate it.

The contrasts in the Beethoven and J. C. Bach movements involve single, 'dissonant' gestures that contradict or overturn the previous musical flow, and their late placement means that they can hardly be heard to interact with earlier material. But, as noted above, sometimes this type of contrast sounds entirely unpurposive; it suggests not so much contradiction as simply a different plane of musical existence. Boccherini is one of the kings of this kind of abrupt swerve: in the second movement of the Quintet in D major Op. 10 No. 6/G270 (1771), for example, the middle section brings a phrase that sounds like a complete non sequitur (bars 60–61). It employs the Romanesca schema, with the characteristic bass line and a succession of

---

[173] Charles Rosen, *Beethoven's Piano Sonatas: A Short Companion* (New Haven: Yale University Press, 2002), 147. In his similarly named *A Companion to Beethoven's Pianoforte Sonatas (Bar-to-Bar Analysis)* (London: Associated Board of the Royal Schools of Music, 1931), 79, Donald Francis Tovey nicely describes the final few bars as an 'ostentatiously perfunctory cadence dispersed over different octaves'.

scale degrees 1–5–1–5 in the upper voice.[174] While using the dotted rhythms that are already well integrated within this Allegro maestoso movement, the phrase still seems to arrive out of the blue, emphasized by harmonic and dynamic incongruity: *fortissimo* G major after the previous phrase ends on V of E minor, and a subsequent version in B flat major after a preceding D major chord (bars 66–67). The material sounds like a quotation from a different piece of music; further, it sounds what Matthew Riley would call 'untimely' in style,[175] like a baroque remnant. This sudden sharp contrast seems neither to have nor to need any specific rationale – it simply forms part of a world of restless difference.

More characteristic than these last few examples, though, is where the type of unaccountable contrast I am investigating takes more of a block form. Several sectional formal types positively encourage such a tendency, such as rondo and ternary, the latter most commonly heard in the middle movements of an instrumental cycle. It might seem all too convenient to enlist such formal types under the current category: after all, one expects the episodes in rondo forms, the middle sections of ternary-form slow movements or the trios to minuets to provide clearly contrasting material. However, that would be to overlook how these contrasts typically became much sharper during our period, compared to an earlier type of rondo that was more nearly monothematic and trios that did not necessarily differ strongly in style from their companion minuets. The sharp contrasts may have become conventionalized, but that does not mean that the convention meant nothing. Thus the typical trio would invoke a lower style than the preceding minuet, often pastoral, sometimes taking a conspicuously rustic route, and the contrast between the two sections was generally unmediated: in other words, the different materials and topics succeed each other in block form, without any apparent interaction.

That said, some ternary forms make the contrast more striking than others. The third movement of Haydn's Symphony No. 58 in F major (c1767–1768) is a 'Menuet alla zoppa', but this is not the *alla zoppa* (limping) manner that involves two parallel lines that move out of phase with each other.[176] Instead we have a perversion of dotted style, and hence of a stately minuet. The nearly constant crotchets of the bass line embody

---

[174] For a concise introduction to the Romanesca see Gjerdingen, *Music in the Galant Style*, chapter 2, 25–43.

[175] See Riley, *Viennese Minor-Key Symphony*, 5. Riley's phrase will be amplified later in this chapter.

[176] This idiom, characteristic of earlier Haydn, tends to be found in the trios of minuet movements, for instance in the Piano Trio in E major H34 and the Sonata in A major H12.

the sort of steady flow one would expect from a normal example of the genre, but the dotted rhythms of the upper voice are anything but steady: generally the tune limps towards a longer note on the weak second beat of the bar, but sometimes the longer note is on the downbeat, and once (bars 9^3–10^1) it falls on the third beat. In spite of this wildly un-minuet-like behaviour, the music is organized in regular four-bar phrase units. The following Trio also features a perfectly regular phrase rhythm, four four-bar units, but the expressive difference from the Minuet is enormous. It turns to the minor mode and never departs from it, the solemn tone augmented by the scoring for closely packed strings in a low register. After the wild irregularities of the minuet, the rhythmic values are mostly straight crotchets; the dynamic is *piano* after the implied *forte* of the minuet.

What is the listener to make of such a change in style and tone? The difference is electrifying. A grotesque minuet is succeeded by something entirely 'serious', hushed, perhaps rather eerie, the almost exactly matching rhythms of each phrase unit almost like a rebuke to the frivolous 'limping' dance that has gone before. Also remarkable is that while the Trio ends with an F major chord, this cannot be heard as a tonic or indeed a *tierce de Picardie*. Rather, we finish on V of iv, the dominant of B flat minor, a device that is quite often found at the close of minor-mode movements.[177] This carries a distinctly archaic tinge, far removed from any expectation of pastoral contrast for a trio section. It would, on the other hand, be possible to hear this Trio as exotic rather than archaic; A. Peter Brown suggests 'eastern European folk music' as an inspiration.[178] Ultimately fixing on a stylistic or topical origin for this material – as with the earlier discussion of 'character' in the case of Beethoven's Op. 14 No. 2 – seems less to the point than acknowledging the basic hard-edged conflict between the sections, and we must remember that after the fundamental change of orientation in the Trio the limping Minuet will return verbatim to reinforce the puzzle. In

---

[177] The device, for reasons I cannot explain, is particularly common in association with the endings to G minor movements. Examples may be found in Haydn's quartet Op. 20 No. 3 (the endings to both minuet and trio sections of the second movement, and also the finale) and his *Salve regina* in G minor, and in Beethoven's cello sonata Op. 5 No. 2 (first movement) and his Bagatelle in G minor, Op. 119 No. 1.

[178] Brown, *First Golden Age of the Viennese Symphony*, 117. H. C. Robbins Landon hears 'slightly sinister Gypsies' at work: *Haydn: Chronicle and Works*, volume 2: *Haydn at Eszterháza, 1766–1790* (London: Thames and Hudson, 1978), 290. Commenting on this, Mark Ferraguto notes that such a suggestion is 'conjectural', and suggests that the basic 'otherness' of the Trio relative to the Minuet is more important. I agree with this. Ferraguto, 'Haydn as "Minimalist": Rethinking Exoticism in the Trios of the 1760s and 1770s', *Studia musicologica* 51/1–2 (2010), 71.

his commentary on this movement, as part of a study of Haydn's 'minimalist' trios, Mark Ferraguto reaches a comparable conclusion about the relationship between the two sections: 'If pressed, one might find motivic connections linking the unusual trio back to the minuet; however, one senses that the movement's intended effect is less to promote such inquiries than to startle, even bewilder, the listener through its astonishing juxtapositions.'[179]

Such juxtapositions can be if anything more striking in a 'free' ternary form, in a movement-type where ternary is just one possible shape the music could take as it unfolds; the minuet and trio, after all, rarely allows for any other form than a straight ABA. Slow movements are the most likely location. The Andante of Haydn's late Piano Trio in C major H27 (1797) is set in A major, a bold third-relationship typical of the composer's later harmonic practice, and one that seems to elevate the calm lyrical style of the music. The middle section overturns this composure, entering abruptly at the very point one is awaiting the completion of a cadence in the tonic A major. Switching to A minor, though not staying there for long, it displays obsessive-compulsive rhythmic behaviour, the cello and piano heavily accentuating each strong beat, while the violin keeps up an unending stream of close-position broken chords. There is a brief lull, in which music draws breath, as it were, before the obsessive accentuation resumes, together with a sequence of grace notes (bars 48–49) that imparts a distinctly sardonic touch to proceedings. Rosen hears in this middle section 'a dramatic power that is close to brutality',[180] yet, however one frames it, the mood vanishes as abruptly as it came, and we are back to the sweet lyricism of the opening material, 'as if nothing had happened'. It is only once we reach the end of the movement, of course, when no sign of the earlier tempest has reappeared, that we can grasp the material as a central section that is not only self-contained formally but also, it would seem, emotionally. Once more, no 'explanation' is forthcoming, though certainly one could argue that the events of the middle section heighten our appreciation of the initial material when it returns. The juxtaposition of lyricism and explosive gesture clearly has something in common with the Largo of Haydn's Symphony No. 88, but in this instance the 'interruption' is sustained, and comes but once. There are many such cases in later Haydn in particular; another would be the slow movement of the string quartet Op. 54 No. 3 (1788), where the central section offers a wild 'gypsy' style in which the first violin plays fantastic arabesques over a vamping accompaniment.

[179] Ferraguto, 'Haydn as "Minimalist"', 71.   [180] Rosen, *The Classical Style*, 358.

While this kind of block contrast within a ternary (or indeed rondo) form is commonly aligned with the individual sections of the complete structure, the contrast can also be an internal one, within an individual section. The Trio to the Minuet of Haydn's Symphony No. 93 in D major (1791) abruptly juxtaposes timbres and dynamics: *forte* winds and timpani versus *piano* strings. The loud material is a call to attention in military style, played all on one note, D, and just about the last thing one would expect to hear in a trio section. The more pliant, lyrical material played by the string section could certainly be described as a gracious riposte, but that might only be the point of behavioural origin. In spite of some integration of timbres at the point of reprise, the sense of stark juxtaposition between opposed gestures remains; there is no answer to the conundrum.

This also applies harmonically. The strings twist the repeated Ds of the alarum into different harmonic contexts – first of all B minor, then G major, and then at the point of the reprise, when the fanfare Ds should lead to a confirmation of D major, once more towards G major. While the section finishes in D major, the trio as a whole might more properly be described as having a central pitch, D, rather than truly being 'in a key'. This is thus another uncertainty that is never really resolved. Peter Brown plausibly imagines that listeners would have been 'baffled' by the alternation of 'aggressive fanfares and the more introspective writing for the strings'. By way of explanation he invokes a 'juxtaposition of the sublime and the beautiful', further suggesting that the 'apparent contradictions' point to Haydn's role as father of musical romanticism.[181] Yet this kind of conflict, not mitigated by any evident programmatic or narrative thrust, does not quite seem amenable to such comfortable contextualization. There is, as suggested earlier, a 'flatness' to the procedure that seems specifically characteristic of the later eighteenth century.

A more radical example, which cuts across all the divisions of an ABA form, can be found in the second movement of Dittersdorf's String Quartet No. 4 in C major, K194 (1789; Example 2.29). While the A section is headed Menuetto, there can be few examples of the kind that are more remote from any sort of dance step. Instead of that, the players perform horn calls, at a brisk Allegro assai tempo, cycling again and again through the same three dyads. Immediately after the double bar the cello holds pedal notes on the fifth G and D, which continues the openness of sonority. For four bars this is all we hear, but when the other instruments then enter, it is clear that the topical ground has shifted. The harmony has shifted too, jumping

---

[181] Brown, *First Golden Age of the Viennese Symphony*, 255.

into the dominant key without ceremony. The first violin plays an identical two-bar shape four times in a row, a dominant-major-ninth arpeggio alternating with a G major reply, these alternations backed up by second violin and viola above the cello's drone. What we seem to be hearing is a rustic dance played by a peasant band. While a present-day listener might hear no strong break of style after the double bar, it is by no means evident that these two types of material are compatible. Certainly both represent outdoor topics, and both are exuberantly energetic, but horn calls evoke hunting, a distinctly aristocratic activity, while the subsequent material pulls the listener well downmarket.

After a retransition executed by first violin alone at bars 24–30, the horn-call material is greatly extended upon its return, building up a real head of steam. Yet there is no strongly affirmative close to cap this off. This would hardly be possible given the harmonic behaviour that in fact unites the two types of material. In neither case does the harmonic vocabulary extend beyond alternating tonic and dominant; there isn't so much as a single pre-dominant chord heard throughout, and without such a harmonic function no proper cadential preparation, or strong cadential arrival, can eventuate.[182] Since there is no deviation whatever from the purest form of horn call, the close of the 'Menuetto' remains weak, and literally weak too, since the final sonority we hear is a tonic 6/3 chord. The music simply stops rather than properly finishing. Another feature that unites the two topical fields is the near-complete lack of normal periodic construction. Everything is built up on the basis of short repeated units, which certainly creates symmetry, but the modern periodicity of the time, as we have seen, depends on reciprocal relationships between these units. This music, on the other hand, simply accumulates by repetition. Such technical characteristics issue from what one might call the brazenly pictorial stance of the minuet as a whole.

For all these elements that horn call and rustic dance have in common, the extent to which they cohere as a topical succession remains an open question. There is little chance, however, of hearing the slightest continuity between the final horn call of the Menuetto and the start of the Alternativo section that follows. The Alternativo (a term that Dittersdorf consistently uses in his string quartets in place of 'Trio') moves directly into A minor and a very different texture: instead of the open spaces of the minuet, we hear close-position chords. Much more striking, though is the style of the

---

[182] The need for a pre-dominant harmony as part of the approach to a genuine cadence in this style is a point made particularly clearly in William E. Caplin, 'The Classical Cadence: Conceptions and Misconceptions', *Journal of the American Musicological Society* 57/1 (2004), 51–117.

Example 2.29 Dittersdorf, Quartet in C major, K194/ii

material. Riley's 'untimely' would be too gentle a description for what we hear, which is distinctly archaic, with its hemiola in bars 53–54 and the use of the Phrygian cadence to end the phrase. Here, indeed, we have our first predominant harmony of the movement, the D minor 6/3 chord at bar 54^2, but

Example 2.29 (continued)

the way it leads to the E major dominant chord in the following bar means that it does not behave according to modern diatonic manners. While Phrygian cadences can be readily found in baroque music, most characteristically as part of a linking strategy between movements, the total context here rules out hearing this phrase as an echo of baroque practice. What we

Example 2.29 (continued)

hear is some sort of echo of a more distant musical past, and the very archaism implies that the imagined performance space has moved indoors after the outdoor orientation of the minuet.

Yet just as remarkable as this utter change of stylistic perspective is how short-lived the material is. It consists of a four-bar unit that is marked for

Example 2.29 (continued)

repetition, which at an Allegro assai tempo means that almost immediately, before we can assimilate the sounds we have just heard, it has disappeared. What replaces it is surely just as unexpected – our rustic dance material returns verbatim, transposed into the dominant major (E major). Such sharing of material between minuet and trio is most uncommon, still less a literal reappearance of minuet material *en bloc*. The fact that it is the rustic dance that returns strengthens the sense that it operates as a Lord of Misrule; it breaks into the antique style that opens the Alternativo with its own less decorous, lower-life, strains. Once more the rustic dance is followed by a passage for first violin alone, which borrows from the equivalent passage in the Menuetto rather than recalling it exactly; compare the broken-thirds figuration at bars 28–30 with what we hear from the upbeat to bar 68. This time, however, it does not exactly fulfil the transitional role that it did in the earlier section. Instead, it comes to an abrupt halt at bar 76, followed by a silence, so that it has in the end done nothing more than circle (brilliantly) around the established E major harmony. This seems to embody the untutored exuberance of the rustic fiddler.

After this silence the archaic material returns, but now in extended form, just as happened to the horn calls when they returned in the Menuetto. Our original four-bar unit is repeated in decorated form and is then answered by two further four-bar phrases in similar style. Yet again, any sort of orthodox modern cadence is denied, and in its place we hear a distinctly modal-sounding succession of A major to E major triads to conclude the section. At this greater length the 'swing' of the hemiola rhythms is even more striking than it was before, and one starts to wonder whether Dittersdorf is in fact invoking a Renaissance dance form – as if the composer had by some means come across music from the era of Thomas Morley and couldn't resist trying his hand at a replica. (Some of the gift for mimicry that Dittersdorf claimed to have in real life seems also to have been one of his compositional proclivities.[183])

A further jolt naturally awaits when the players return from this stylistic sphere to their horn calls and we hear the complete 'minuet' once more – but they are not finished. After the minuet has run its course, our rustic dance returns yet again in a specifically named coda. It too is an exact match for the original version, but now transposed into the tonic C major. As this material concludes, the first violin performs a series of glissandos that reach ever higher while the three lower strings hold a tonic drone. These glissandos are based on the first violin's transitional material from the minuet (compare the rhythm and pitch contours of bars 24–28 and

---

[183] In his autobiography Dittersdorf writes that he 'possessed the not very edifying gift of mimicking the oddities and weaknesses of other people': *The Autobiography of Karl von Dittersdorf, Dictated to His Son*, trans. A. D. Coleridge (London: Richard Bentley and Son, 1896), 29.

104–108), but with a different formal function. Now they are used to effect closure, but yet again this does not happen through conventional harmonic-cadential means. Instead, the long-held final tonic chord (nearly seven bars long) and the first violin's figuration effectively produce a fade-out, an unorthodox but picturesque conceit.

In a sense the fade-out is consistent with the technical behaviour of this movement – lacking any sort of full modern harmonic and syntactical vocabulary, it is unable to turn structural corners, and hence more or less jumps from one block of material to another. This is most obvious in the case of the rustic dance, which on each occasion simply enters unbidden, without ceremony. What are we to make of such abrupt, seemingly unaccountable contrasts, and indeed of the movement as a whole? There is no doubting the immediate appeal of the individual blocks of material, yet the complete conglomeration can hardly be said to provide easy listening. Yet while there is no mediation or reconciliation 'in' the music, a process of mediation is implied, one might argue, by the very incompatibility of the materials contained within this single span of sound. They demand some sort of completion, and that lies with the agency of the listener. A challenge is being thrown out to that listener to make sense of the extreme contrasts, to fill in the gaps. Once more, therefore, we encounter a paradox of sociable instrumental style: it invites the listener in through its accessibility (here through a vivid embodiment of (mostly) popular topics) yet also demands active engagement.

The listener is put to work once more in the finale of this quartet, a series of variations at Andante tempo and in 2/4 time. Just as we seem to be approaching the final cadence of the movement, the tempo changes to Allegro and the rustic dance material in 3/4 appears yet again. It takes exactly the form it took when acting as coda to the Minuet and Trio, complete with violin glissandos and final fade-out. It is, arguably, even more out of place when returning here than it ever was in the previous movement. Not only is its reappearance an extremely unlikely event so late in the piece, but it jars very strongly with the galant lyrical conduct of the finale. The full heading for the movement, Andante e con gusto, almost makes as if to ensure that standards of stylistic decency are reaffirmed after the events of the minuet and trio, though when subsequent variations start to involve heavily chromatic decorations, the suggestion of parody is not too far distant. At the same time as it disrupts anew, the rustic dance of course acts to unify our experience of the quartet as a whole – yet it hardly makes immediate sense of that experience.

If the listener might once more be challenged to make sense of this further incongruity, to take an active approach in completion of the whole work, another perspective might refer us back to the master category of tolerance that, as alluded to earlier, underpins the variety of galant style. This would mean simply to accept the contrasts in 'philosophical' fashion: to put it differently, no particular action is required; enjoy the motley parade. But that may be easier said than experienced. In November 1832 writer Franz Grillparzer recorded in his diary a concert in Vienna in which works by Handel and Boccherini were played alongside a Dittersdorf quartet. The Dittersdorf work (which may or may not have been K194) was 'now and then all too racy and contrived [mitunter gar zu pikant und daher gesucht]'.[184] This represents a perfectly understandable nineteenth-century reaction to the seemingly unprincipled, 'plot-less' succession of incommensurable materials that we hear in Dittersdorf's quartet (and indeed most of the other works in the composer's set of six quartets offer similar incongruities). But there must have been plenty of contemporaries of Dittersdorf's too who wondered what to make of what they were hearing.

In fact the finale of K194 opens up a further category within our field of unaccountable contrast. The preceding minuet and trio may indeed present obstacles to ready comprehension, but the materials are at least held together by a consistent tempo throughout. When changes of tempo and/or metre occur within the frame of an individual movement, as they do in the finale of K194, the potential incompatibility of contrasting materials becomes more blatant. Slow movement and finale are the two most likely locations for this phenomenon; it seems to be almost unknown in first movements, perhaps because of the 'overture' typology that they typically display, which means contrasts press in quickly, almost disallowing the possibility of a seismic stylistic shock. This is to leave aside the possible presence of a slow introduction, which was common enough a device to mean that any contrast between it and the ensuing Allegro could hardly disconcert. On the other hand, with slow movements at least the generic expectation would be for a more even flow of material, for a more reflective, purely lyrical brand of expression[185] – and so this would be the last place where one would expect any sort of harsh temporal contrast.

---

[184] Cited in Hubert Unverricht, 'Carl Ditters von Dittersdorf als Quartettkomponist: Ein Konkurrent Haydns, Mozarts und Pleyels?', *Haydn-Studien* 7/3–4 (1998), 325.

[185] See my article 'Expressive Ambivalence in Haydn's Symphonic Slow Movements of the 1770s', *The Journal of Musicology* 27/1 (2010), 84: 'The relative slowing of tempo and pulse seems to have brought certain associations that have remained quite stable through to the present day. The broad expectation is that such a movement will provide such qualities as warmth, lyricism, and gravity, that it will tend to suggest reflection rather than action. There is plenty of evidence that this expectation was shared by the listeners of Haydn's day.'

A case in point is the second movement of Paul Wranitzky's Sextet No. 4 in C major for flute, oboe, violin, two violas and cello (1795).[186] An Adagio set in the subdominant F major and in 3/4 time, it exemplifies the hymn-like style of slow movement that was also being cultivated by figures such as Clementi, Haydn and Beethoven. This entails homogeneity of texture and rhythm, the use of relatively long note values and a distinct absence of ornamentation, together creating the sense of a noble simplicity of utterance. The music eases its way towards a firm cadence in the dominant at bar 43, which is followed by a brief transition, and suddenly, in bar 46, we are in A flat major. But more arresting than that is that the style changes utterly – the time signature is now 2/4, the tempo is Allegro non troppo, and flute and oboe drop out, leaving just the four string players. The texture becomes straightforwardly homophonic, with a lightly accompanied melodic line that moves mostly in semiquavers, unlike the predominant crotchets and quavers of the Adagio. Short repeated units, the odd syncopation and some dithering trill figures (bars 54–57) all contribute to what is plainly a very different mood, though the dynamic remains *piano*. How can such material relate to what has gone before? It would certainly be possible to understand it as a form of comic relief. After the solemn emotion represented by the Adagio, it draws us back from such sustained intensity, lightening the tone. On the other hand, many other slow movements of the time find ways of fulfilling this imperative without effectively breaking the generic code; Wranitzky's players sound like they have simply started a different piece of music.

After this section closes in A flat major we hear a *forte* unison tattoo on and around the note C that lasts for eight bars (70–77). This leads to a prolongation of a single diminished-seventh chord for no fewer than twelve bars (78–89): flute, oboe and violin unceasingly repeat the same constituent notes while the lower strings deliver the harmony as ominous-sounding descending arpeggios. In light of what we have just heard, it is hard to take this *ombra*-style passage seriously: it sounds like unmotivated bluster. While the previous material in A flat major may have been a disorientating contrast, there was nothing especially crass about it. At least the current section, by turning us towards an implied F minor, does then allow the opening material to return in F major. It thus acts as a

---

[186] Nancy November notes that the six sextets published in 1795 may be arrangements from earlier symphonies; for a fuller explanation see November, Introduction to *Paul Wranitzky, Six Sextets for Flute, Oboe, Violin, Two Violas, and Cello*, ed. November (Middleton, WI: A-R Editions, 2012), viii.

transition – but it is a very intrusive one, as incongruous in its way as the sudden speeding-up to Allegro was in the first place.

After a brief silence, we return to the elevated world of the Adagio. To be more precise, we hear a rerun of the first part of that section (bars 1–23), which finished with a perfect cadence in the tonic. There the music simply stops. The shortening of a returning A section is certainly not uncommon, but in this case it is cut to half its original length. In addition, such an elevated style of utterance would normally at this time entail some sort of 'ennobling' coda, achieved perhaps through some sort of harmonic enrichment or at the least an extension of closing material. But there is no such extension here, which makes the close of the movement sound somewhat abrupt, if not premature. It is as if the Adagio is entirely self-sufficient, deaf to the intervening events of the movement. In a formal sense this might also hold: the Adagio resumes at the point where it has been cut off, after the cadence in the dominant of bar 43 that might lead the listener to expect a thematic return as part of a small ternary form. It is as if the middle section and transition were simply an interpolation that can now be discarded from memory ('as if nothing has happened'). Yet if we move out beyond the point of view of the Adagio, as it were, the movement as a whole seems to consist of a series of non sequiturs.

Such enigmatic qualities are shared by other slow movements that break ranks in similar fashion. The third movement of Gyrowetz's Notturno for piano trio, Op. 31 (1800), witnesses a Larghetto in A major and 6/8 being interrupted by an Allegretto in 2/4 and the same key before the Larghetto returns in much reduced form; in this case the middle part is so extensive as to suggest that the Larghetto sections simply form a frame. From Wranitzky as well there is the second movement of his String Quartet in E minor, Op. 23 No. 2 (1793), which has a similar juxtaposition of affects. A solemn hymn-like Adagio in C major, played *con sordini,* is followed by a rather flippant Allegretto, once again in the lighter metre of 2/4, before the Adagio returns. On this occasion, though, the first section finishes with a cadence in the tonic key, and then the Allegretto section remains firmly in the tonic, raising the possibility that they might be heard simply as separate movements. It is only the return of the Adagio (bar 60) that definitively overrules such a perception. Unlike the literal reprise of the first twenty-three bars in the sextet movement, here the Adagio behaves more freely. It begins with the equivalent of the fifth bar of the opening section, suggesting that the material has re-emerged in mid-stream, and soon blossoms lyrically, suggesting more a continuation than a recapitulation of the earlier material.

An even less literal return can be found in the third movement of Andreas Romberg's Quartet in E flat major Op. 1 No. 1 (1799). A highly wrought Andante sostenuto is replaced from the upbeat to bar 47 by an Allegro, but without any change of metre, which remains 2/4. When the original Andante tempo resumes (107), it lasts for just three bars, and then the movement, most disconcertingly, is over. Further, there is no return of the initial material; instead, we hear a version of the three bars that closed out the sixteen-bar theme (14–16), which were then repeated in more elaborate form at bars 30–32. To recapitulate only a final cadential flourish is a cryptic procedure. Given that listeners recognize the beginning of a thematic unit more readily than its ending,[187] this passage may not even register as a return, and its relative brevity will not help matters. Further, Romberg takes care to provide motivic continuity between the end of the Allegro and the resumption of the Andante, and so all a listener may be able to determine is that the music has slowed down before coming to an abrupt halt.

Just how the Allegro section relates affectively to the preceding Andante is also obscure. As it enters, the Allegro certainly lightens the mood, with distinct popular accents, and its almost exclusive concentration on a single repeated-note motive could hardly differ more from the long-breathed lines of the Andante. On the other hand, it features a series of chromatic complications that undermine the initially straightforward diatonic language and are in fact quite compatible with the harmonic intensity of the Andante. And from a rhythmic point of view the Allegro may not be such a shock: there is an acceleration of note values in the Andante from the opening, from a base rate of quavers in bars 1–16 to semiquavers from bar 17 through to cascading demisemiquavers from bar 35. This culminates in a brilliant flourish in bar 45, where the two violins and viola execute a sequence of falling parallel 6/3 chords in demisemiquaver values. The subsequent change of tempo to Allegro might therefore be heard as a plausible next step. Further, the Allegro is based in the tonic key, and since the movement has already suggested a kind of variation shape, with the opening material being resumed and decorated from bars 17 and 40,

---

[187] This would seem to follow straightforwardly, for example, from the distinction Caplin makes between the 'characteristic' material that typically begins a phrase or larger unit and the more 'conventional' material that leads to its cadence: see *Classical Form*, 11. On the other hand, Leonard B. Meyer, in attempting to distinguish between eighteenth- and nineteenth-century syntactical and aesthetic principles, writes, 'though the beginnings and ends of Classic melodies are remembered more or less equally well, with Romantic melodies the beginnings are usually much better remembered than the ends'. Meyer, *Style and Music*, 231–232.

the underlying model could be that type of variation form that leads to a quicker final section. The difficulty with that, though, is the lack of any obvious connection of the Allegro material to the Andante. This would lead to a different formal conclusion – an unusual 'open' binary form, AB, with a final very brief glance at A in order to close the movement.

Not that such 'broken' slow movements are confined to the very end of the century. The slow movement of Michael Haydn's Symphony in B flat major ST62 (1763), which carries the unexplained title 'La Confidenza', is an Andante in E flat major, but it twice moves briefly to Allegretto and different material in a much lighter, more comic style. In the fifth movement of brother Joseph's Symphony No. 60 (1774), 'Il Distratto', we hear an Adagio that has all the signs of a broad cantilena, with sextuplet second-violin accompaniment and pizzicato lower strings supporting the song of the first violin. One does not expect it to be interrupted by a loud fanfare for full orchestra, as happens from bar 29, even though the aria quickly re-establishes itself thereafter. Just as disconcerting is what happens at the end of the movement: what sounds like postcadential closing material at bars 71–74, with regular alternations of tonic and dominant, is repeated, but at Allegro tempo, and the movement comes to an abrupt end. The impression is of the affecting soulful Adagio being impatiently dismissed.

As is well known, Haydn's Symphony No. 60 derives from incidental music the composer wrote for Jean-François Regnard's play *Le distrait*, and this raises the question of whether our mixed-tempo slow movements – and more broadly our category of abrupt sectional contrasts – could have some specific theatrical inspiration behind them (as opposed to the broader 'theatrical' orientation that is often read into the galant style's mixture of musical elements). One might call to mind a much earlier exemplar, the aria 'A Serpina penserete' from Pergolesi's epochal intermezzo *La serva padrona*. This starts Larghetto as serving-maid Serpina pretends to be leaving her master Uberto, but is punctuated by Allegro asides in which the character turns to the audience to celebrate the seeming success of her ruse. Allanbrook describes the juxtaposition of two very different brands of music as 'subversive', continuing: 'Against the conventional modern assumption that the serious is the locus of truth telling, this "aria" frames a serious gesture as theatrical, a false face, a caricature, the comic topos exposing its pretense. The mixed mode of comedy undermines the elevated style, making it difficult to take the serious seriously.'[188] Something similar might be concluded from our sample of movements in

---

[188] Allanbrook, *Secular Commedia*, 19–22.

which an 'elevated style' is undermined, though, as we have seen, matters are generally more complicated than that, and there are no words and no obvious 'plots' by means of which to grasp the ruptures of style. That such ruptures could remain especially objectionable in a 'serious' slow movement is evident from a 1785 review of a such a case in a concerto by Kozeluch: 'For most of the piece it is earnest, touching, heartrending, and then, when it should be fully developed, the entire stream of the earlier torrent of emotions is hemmed in by four measures that would fit into a merry Allegretto better. This strengthens the reviewer's opinion that every piece would be better if it adopted a definite character, or at least not a contradictory one'.[189]

One final example of such 'contradictory character' comes from (Joseph) Haydn's Symphony No. 79 in F major (1783–1784). The second movement, while headed Adagio cantabile, represents a pleasing rather than exalted vein of lyric expression. It is almost excessively comprehensible in its phrase syntax, starting with an eight-bar phrase three of whose sub-phrases last for about a bar and a half – in other words, there is plenty of air in between each unit, so that one can grasp the construction. The larger-scale organization is clear too: an eight-bar theme immediately given a decorated repetition (bars 1–16), an eight-bar continuation and close based on similar material, which is then also repeated with variations (17–32), then a further decorated form of the first eight bars (33–40) followed by a further decorated form of the continuation-close material (41–48). This is immediately followed at bars 49–56 by yet another decorated form of the phrase we have just heard, by which point the accessible clarity of structure and procedure is in fact becoming distinctly blurred. The music seems to be going around in circles, with the sense of formal process (or lack of it) starting to suggest a spoof of the 'complaisant' expressive typology. In one technical sense this is beyond doubt. The music has not left the tonic key of B flat major for a second, and even passages of standing on the dominant involve no tonicization. This is a grammatical impossibility for a movement that has been going on this long. Restfulness has turned into inaction, for all the charm of the material.

At bar 57 another variant of earlier material begins, and then finally in bars 59–60 F major is tonicized, albeit weakly via the harmonic progression vii°6-I of V. This progression normally sets up a return to the tonic key, which is indeed what happens, but this is at the cost of abandoning the

---

[189] 'R.', *Magazin der Musik* 2/1 (7 March 1785), cited in Morrow, *German Music Criticism*, 141 (translation) and 229 (German original).

Adagio. In its place, entirely new material enters, at a new tempo (Un poco allegro) and switching from triple to duple time. This 'comments on' the lyrical charm by replacing it with something more robustious, but it does not solve the harmonic problem: it is barely any more able to leave the tonic key than the Adagio was, and is just about as transparent in phrase syntax and repetitive thematically. One important difference from our previous case studies is that here the contrasting material prevails until the end; there is not even the ghost of a return to the opening tempo or material, as there was even in Romberg's slow movement. Thus we are left with a strongly bifurcated AB structure, make of it what one will.

Yet there is one small-scale, but aurally powerful, hint of the Adagio material. In the seventh bar (67) of the Allegro we hear the same pungent half-diminished vii°4/3 chord that we heard in the seventh bar of the Adagio, scored identically, using the same actual pitches in each of the string parts, and on both occasions a *forzando* reinforces the harmonic colour. Given all the varied repetitions of that phrase in the Adagio, this means we have heard that sonority quite a few times before the arrival of the Allegro, and in fact at the very same point of the alternating eight-bar phrase, the continuation and close (first of all in bar 23), we hear a similar pre-cadential harmony. It is based on the same outer-voice structure, E♭ in the bass and G in the treble, and is also heightened by a *forzando* marking. This resemblance suggests that the Allegro might be a parody in substance as well as spirit of the pleasantries that were passed in the first part of the movement. That this is a marked gesture and a marked sonority is apparent in how the movement ends – at bar 101 it stumbles over this much-repeated move, the phrase stops dead, and after a silence there is a decorated version of the same chord, followed by another silence. Then the harmony is 'corrected' to V4/2 (which only entails replacing a G with an F), which leads to a series of *fortissimo* closing chords.

One way of trying to come to terms with Haydn's movement, and indeed with many of our previous examples, is to understand the quicker material as representing a finale typology, both expressively and syntactically. None of the interrupting fast sections suggest that they could have strayed in from an opening Allegro: the lighter time signatures, more straightforward types of phrase structure and foot-tapping rhythms are all generic markers of a final movement. Since finale tempos are typically fleeter than those of first movements, and their character more exuberant, this helps to create a particularly stark clash in the movements under review: slow and serious versus fast and frivolous. Yet there are clear limits to this equation, not least because in the case of Haydn's Symphony No. 79, for example, the Adagiocum-Allegro is only the second movement of the work; there is still a minuet and trio in prospect before we even reach an actual finale. It would be hard to dupe any sort of seasoned listener into accepting that the final movement has actually begun.

Matters may be different when the slow movement forms the penultimate part of the whole work. This is the case in Boccherini's String Quintet in F minor Op. 42 No. 1/G348 (1789), in which the third-placed Adagio cantabile barely gets beyond the repeated first section of what seems likely to unfold as a sonata-form movement. The composer finishes this section with a series of firm repeated chords, a trademark closing formula and one that promises a rhyming repetition later on. After the double bar this formula is immediately echoed but becomes disruptive, and so just the opposite of what it previously was, a simple and widely comprehensible marker of closure. It is heard in four consecutive bars, each time set to a different diminished-seventh chord, creating a dramatic break from the sweet lyricism of the preceding section. Thereafter the music clouds over into F minor at *pianissimo* level, and this leads immediately to the final rondo.

While this amounts to another slow movement with an unexpected, and seemingly inexplicable, disruption, one difference here is that the slow movement undermines itself in the first instance: it unravels from within, using its own materials. Secondly, it also represents a far commoner category: the incomplete slow movement that proceeds directly to a finale. The current example just happens to accelerate the process, the slow movement 'failing' when all the signs suggest that it has not yet reached its half-way point. But what this has in common with our original category is a joining-together of blocks of material that contrast in tempo, affect and, almost always, metre – and technically such slow movements remain incomplete, as they fail to finish in their tonic, thus forming together with the ensuing finale a larger-scale version of an 'open' AB structure. In this case there is certainly historical precedent, with many slower movements of the baroque era abutting directly onto a following faster movement, but rarely with the sense of dramatic juxtaposition that can attend the process in the later eighteenth century.

If, as suggested above, our category of interrupted slow movement might represent a collision of two fundamentally different kinds of musical behaviour – that appropriate to a contemplative inner movement and that appropriate to a finale – the equation should be able to operate in reverse. And indeed, final movements can be invaded by what sounds like slow-movement material. However, one could not readily claim the same shock value for this procedure. It is, for a start, considerably more common than the reverse; this may be mainly because a finale is typically less tight-knit in its organization than say a fast first movement, and so clear breaks and contrasts form part of a listener's horizon of expectations. After all, rondo, which became so greatly favoured as a final-movement form, is premised on clear-cut sectional contrasts. And one might suggest that the typically extrovert expressive stance of finales makes it easier for listeners to take any abrupt changes in their stride; such changes could even be understood as intrinsic to the 'showing off' that often comes to the fore in the final movement of an instrumental work. Slow movements, though, as noted earlier, carry expressive connotations that were (and are) relatively fixed. This is also a matter of temporal character: to state the obvious, events unfold more slowly, more spaciously, inducing a particular kind of listener entrainment. To have the 'spell' broken, especially by material that seems irrelevant and possibly irreverent, can be an unsettling experience.

Yet mixed-tempo finales can provide their own hard edges. This is certainly the case if that finale begins in a slow tempo, which is what happens in the third movement of Pleyel's String Quartet in E flat major Op. 1 No. 2 (1782–1783). We hear a harmonically closed sixteen-bar unit, Adagio ma non troppo, suggesting a theme for subsequent variation. Whatever the larger shape might turn out to be, this is plainly the start of a slow movement (it could not represent any sort of slow introduction, which is occasionally present at the start of a finale). Yet, instead of bar 17 delivering the start of a first variation, it brings an extreme switch of speed, to Presto, and music that is seemingly unrelated to that of the Adagio, though still in the tonic. While the Presto material initially organizes itself into a sixteen-bar unit with internal repeats, suggesting it is offering an alternative proposition to the Adagio, this is not quite the case. This material is not so much expository as celebratory: it contains the sorts of gestures one would expect to hear towards the end of a movement, winding up the momentum towards a brilliant close. The Presto has barely moved beyond its repeated sixteen-bar confines when it gets stuck harmonically: for six bars (40–45) it remains on V4/2 of the tonic key.

The Adagio then resumes. If the manner in which the Presto runs aground is comedic behaviour – as though the material were suddenly overcome with a sense of embarrassment at being in the wrong place at the wrong time – a more understated comic charge attaches to the return of the slower music. The all-but identical reappearance of the Adagio (one glancing change in in bar 50 aside) is quite incongruous in context. The straight repetition suggests the slow material is oblivious to what has just transpired; as we have noted before in earlier cases, it returns 'as if nothing had happened'. This is a musical embodiment of dramatic irony – the character knows nothing, the audience knows better.

Indeed, with our Olympian listeners' perspective, we can probably predict that we have not heard the last of the Presto. But this time the Presto enters four bars earlier than before (in bar 58); in other words, we only hear twelve bars of Adagio material. Thus the surprise surprises anew – it is now an interruption of the expected not just in terms of tempo and character, but also in terms of phrase syntax. This is technical as well as more general behavioural bad manners. This time the Presto has no crisis of confidence and continues on its way to the end of the movement. However, it still provides only material of a closing character. Indicative of this is the presentation, almost immediately, of two successive Grand Cadence formulas[190] (starting in bars 69 and 79). These formulas, as their name suggests, should always signal some sort of final achievement of the cadential goal. And in fact they do; after the second version has concluded in the tonic at bar 85, all the subsequent material is postcadential, and there are fifty bars of it, a gross disproportion in the context of the movement. In other words, the Presto prevails at the second time of asking as the proper material to constitute a finale, but celebrates prematurely, almost immediately reaching the harmonic-structural goal of a final firm cadence in the tonic. From the perspective of the movement as a whole, the only proper opening function is provided by the Adagio, and the only proper closing function is provided by the Presto. Thus these utterly opposed musical gestures turn out to be formally interdependent.

It is nice to imagine that Haydn, remembering his pupil's Op. 1, took up the challenge of such a formal conceit when he wrote the final movement of his String Quartet in C major Op. 54 No. 2 (1788), which alternates material bearing the same tempo indications Adagio and Presto. This movement ends up being more unsettling than its possible model, and we will return to it when considering the parent issue of formal function in Chapter 3.

---

[190] The term derives from Gjerdingen, *Music in the Galant Style*, 152, but my usage of it reflects the adaptations made by Floyd Grave in 'Freakish Variations on a "Grand Cadence" Prototype in Haydn's String Quartets', *Journal of Musicological Research* 28/2–3 (2009), 119–145. The Grand Cadence typically involves a rise to a high note, either by scale or by arpeggio, followed by an abrupt drop to a low note, which is then connected, via some form of rising figuration, to a trill that normally occupies a register somewhere in between the two extremes already delineated. This trill, often accompanied by repeated-quaver figuration, then leads to the moment of cadence. It is almost always brilliant in style and typically marks a major cadence point. We return to this formula in Chapter 3.

A more common phenomenon in mixed-tempo final movements is for the slower tempo to appear once the finale proper seems to have established itself. At the start of the last movement of Mozart's Piano Concerto in C major K415 (1782–1783) the soloist gives the cue by announcing the 6/8 Allegro theme, and then leaves the orchestra to give its exposition of the thematic material. The orchestra in turn sets up the reappearance of the soloist, who obliges in bar 49 by commencing an elaborate elegiac Adagio in C minor and 2/4 time – not quite the ticket for a concerto finale. From bar 61 we hear a standing on the dominant that ought to signal a return of the opening Adagio material. But instead the soloist – having got that mood out of the system, as it were – now returns to the opening Allegro theme, and normal finale service seems to be resumed. Much later in the movement, when the faster motion and material seem to have gained unstoppable momentum, the Adagio comes back (from bar 216) in decorated form. That completed, the soloist once more signals a return to finale etiquette by playing through the Allegro theme, but immediately thereafter the movement starts to wind down – rather than wind up to a brilliant finish. Against a continual stream of written-out trills for soloist and/or strings, we hear one of Allanbrook's 'tunes' that 'sprouts from the top', her coinage for the popular-sounding new materials that Mozart sometimes introduces in his coda sections.[191] The dynamic level is an unvarying *piano*, reducing to *pianissimo* for the last few bars. To this extent we might imagine a form of interaction between the seemingly incompatible materials that have placed themselves side by side: the Allegro material 'notices' the pathos-ridden stance of the Adagio and decides it might be tactful to finish in less triumphalist style.

If the alternations of fast and slow in K415 and the two previous movements at least allow listeners an opportunity to 'compare and contrast', a single incursion of slow material may not prove so helpful. In the final movement of Rosetti's Flute Concerto in F major, Murray C21 (before 1778), this incursion arrives very late in the piece – after three statements of the refrain, when we can expect the movement to be drawing to a close. Sterling E. Murray comments: 'the light-hearted flow of the piece is brusquely interrupted by a change of meter and tempo. The inserted 3/4 Adagio that follows show no obvious link with the rest of the movement, and its presence is perplexing. Although only sixteen measures in length, this dramatic aside is sufficient to confound the movement's prevalent mood. With no emotional resolution, the movement rushes to its

---

[191] Allanbrook, 'Mozart's Tunes', 177.

conclusion in one final statement of the refrain.'[192] While, as already suggested, any expectation of 'emotional resolution' may be anachronistic, Murray's reaction testifies to how alienating and inexplicable such incursions can be; they cannot just be comfortably ascribed to an Enlightenment celebration of variety or difference. Similarly placed is an Adagio that appears towards the end of the finale in Rosetti's Oboe Concerto in D major, Murray C33 (1778). Also marked 'Tempo di Menueto [sic]', this section does not differ dramatically in character from what we have heard previously in this Allegretto rondo, but there is still the puzzle of how it fits into the whole. This is all the more so since the Adagio gives the impression of starting in the middle; within eight bars it has reached what sounds like a plausible conclusion to a quite separate movement, via use of a *cadenza lunga* pattern in the bass. In Haydn's Symphony No. 45 in F sharp minor ('Farewell'; 1772), famously, the unexpected reduction of speed is not reversed, and an Adagio permanently succeeds the previous Presto; eventually, as we know, there is not just a slowing of tempo, but also a thinning to vanishing-point of the assembled orchestral forces. At least in this case we can take our bearings from a known programmatic impetus behind the composition of the symphony; we are not entirely left to our own devices when trying to make sense of events.

On some occasions the slower material we encounter in a mixed-tempo finale does not seem to derive from a slow movement. This is already the case in the finale of Rosetti's Oboe Concerto C33. There the slow incursion plainly invokes, in spite of the Adagio tempo, a different final-movement typology: the tempo di menuetto. The leisurely triple time and distinct affect – tenderness mixed with grace – suggest a different way of closing a multi-movement instrumental work, one that was starting to recede into the past, as we will explore further in Chapter 5. Two Mozart keyboard concertos in E flat major suggest the same mixture of finale types, though on both occasions the minuet-like material (in A flat major) forms a self-contained central section. In K271 (1777) this section is in fact headed 'Menuetto. Cantabile', making clear the composer's sense of this contrasting material, and while in K482 (1785) it is simply headed 'Andantino cantabile', the elegant gait of a minuet is unmistakable. But other typologies may contend too. In Mozart's Violin Sonata in D major K306 (1778) the final movement alternates between Allegretto and Allegro sections, and between their respective 2/4 and 6/8 metres. It sounds like a dialogue

---

[192] Sterling E. Murray, *The Career of an Eighteenth-Century Kapellmeister: The Life and Music of Antonio Rosetti* (Rochester, NY: University of Rochester Press, 2014), 246.

between two styles of finale: the relatively gentle, low-key type represented by the Allegretto (comparable in fact to the tempo di menuetto finale) and the quicker, louder, more virtuoso style of the Allegro. The Allegretto appears three times over the course of the movement, on each occasion virtually identical in form, whereas the Allegro is dynamic and changeable; on its second iteration it boils over into an enormous cadenza for both instruments that lasts for nearly fifty bars. As we have seen in some previous instances, the way in which the original slower material of the movement resumes unchanged after a brusque interruption suggests a kind of innocence or ignorance of what has transpired in the interim.

An alternative way of accounting for mixed-tempo finales that slow up in the middle is to invoke historical precedent. This has been the case for the final movement of Haydn's Symphony No. 67 in F major (c1778). A vigorous Allegro di molto section in cut time reaches a firm cadence on the dominant – the end of an exposition in a sonata-form structure, one presumes – but an expected continuation is denied. Instead, this material is promptly succeeded by a most affecting Adagio e cantabile in 3/8. This consists of a lengthy sectional rounded-binary movement back in the tonic key of F, mostly played by a solo string trio of two violins and cello, with the full orchestra joining in for the return of the initial theme. This is followed by a section in B flat major led by a wind trio of two oboes and bassoon, which continues the expansive lyrical style – there is all the time in the world for this music to unfold, it would seem, and any finale imperative to wind up to a bracing close seems very remote. Immediately this further section has concluded, a loud interruption from the full orchestra disrupts the idyll, but the lyrical material attempts to continue after this and two further *fortissimo* pronouncements. These recall the head-motive of the Allegro, and eventually the lyricism shapes itself into a transitional role. The Allegro di molto then recapitulates itself in full, creating a clear large-scale ternary form. For Rosen such a sequence of events shows the imprint of the da-capo aria – he dubs such a form 'the sonata with central trio'[193] – while for Hepokoski and Darcy it exemplifies the mid-century tradition of the 'da capo overture'.[194] One familiar example of the latter would be the overture to Mozart's *Die Entführung aus dem Serail* (1782), in which an Andante in C minor is sandwiched between two Presto sections in C major.

---

[193] Rosen, *Sonata Forms*, 163.
[194] Hepokoski and Darcy, *Elements of Sonata Theory*, 221 (note that the authors take this term from Jan LaRue).

Such generic precedents can hardly be thrown out of court, of course, but they may well underplay the strangeness of the listening experience, whether for prospective eighteenth-century or for present-day listeners. In the case of Symphony No. 67 the Adagio e cantabile is much more than a simple interpolation: it sounds like it has arrived from a different musical universe, especially, as noted above, in the 'timeless' way in which it unfolds its lyrical riches. And indeed its sheer length – some seventy-four bars at Adagio tempo out of the movement's total count of 209 bars – means that it dominates in terms of duration. By comparison, the Andante 'trio' in Mozart's *Entführung* is relatively short, and the composer goes on to integrate it into the larger whole by returning to a major-mode version of the material to open the first act of the opera (Belmonte's aria 'Hier soll ich dich denn sehen, Konstanze!'). A passage near the very end of Haydn's finale, well after the Allegro di molto has resumed, seems calculated to exacerbate the sense of unaccountable difference between the movement's two expressive worlds. From bar 199 a three-note closing fragment is passed between various woodwind pairs to the accompaniment of a continuous written-out trill in the first violins. The falling intonation of the repeated material together with the continuous trill are uncannily similar to the concluding gestures in the finale of Mozart's concerto K415, but instead of the gentle subsiding of momentum apparent there, Haydn's passage sounds teasing, even bizarre. The closing gesture (bars 208–209) is two *fortissimo* tutti chords, supporting an upper-voice progression from $\hat{2}$ to $\hat{3}$, a succession of scale degrees that is surprisingly open for the end of a final movement.[195] These events leave a decided sting in the tail, perhaps suggesting a dismissal of the elevated discourse of the Adagio.

The finale of Symphony No. 67 is an apt example with which to conclude our account of 'contrast as incongruity' since it is so difficult to come to terms with. The differences of tempo, metre and affect, and the formal sense of the whole, are far from transparent; they cannot be readily absorbed or readily comprehended. Indicative of the status of such movements is that where their coherence is not actively questioned – as Murray bracingly does for the finale of the Rosetti flute concerto – they have tended

---

[195] Stephen Fisher suggests that this movement in fact began life literally as an overture, and further that it would originally have ended quietly, lacking the last two bars. Stephen Carey Fisher, 'Haydn's Overtures and Their Adaptations as Concert Orchestral Works' (PhD dissertation, University of Pennsylvania, 1985), 183–184 and 352–353. The idea that an original version would have concluded with the dying-away via the continuous trill figures is an attractive one; certainly, many overtures did indeed finish with such a fade-out. On the other hand, the fast material of this movement simply doesn't sound like a possible opener; it has the slightly looser-knit thematic and phrase-structural organization that typifies a finale compared with a first movement.

to draw a critical blank. The contrasts may be reported quite neutrally, as if there is 'nothing to see here'. Yet such movements may be particularly valuable in allowing us to get closer to the mindset of those later eighteenth-century listeners and critics who could not deal with the 'modern style' – who simply heard a sequence of unmediated meaningless contrasts. As has already been stressed, the sheer variability of this idiom is hard for us to appreciate now; it has become domesticated under the rubric of 'classical style'. But in the case of these movements, where contrasts are presented on a larger canvas, and in unpredictable ways, those contrasts may seem to be more elemental, even cruder, and it is easier to understand how our positively framed 'variety' could instead be perceived as a less friendly 'instability' or 'inconsistency'.

Logically, if these juxtapositions of formal and affective blocks within a movement can cause bemusement, this must also be possible when moving from one self-sufficient movement to another. However, just as the bar must be set high for maintaining that differences of material sound less like a natural variety and more like flat incongruity, so must it be set even higher for inter-movement relationships. One can sense this difficulty in connection with Elaine Sisman's 'opus concept', whereby groups of published instrumental works can be understood to communicate both with their listeners and with each other through a process of 'tertiary rhetoric': the works, and their various individual movements, relate to each other by way of elaboration, refutation, corroboration, ironic commentary and the like.[196] But similarity and difference are slippery concepts in this regard: when is meaningful (or indeed meaningless) difference in fact just self-evident variety? This question has haunted my consideration of intra-movement incongruity, especially since 'variety', however defined or understood, was such an aesthetic desideratum for our period.

Lawrence Kramer is a rare writer who has dealt squarely with our phenomenon of apparently irreconcilable difference, but has done so precisely at the level of inter-movement relationships. After the Largo cantabile of Haydn's String Quartet in D major Op. 76 No. 5 (1797), set in the remote mediant major and for Kramer an early example of a deeply contemplative style of slow movement, 'the ensuing minuet is so sturdy and earthy that it seems . . . false',[197] and in fact he believes that the quartet

---

[196] Elaine Sisman, 'Six of One: The Opus Concept in the Eighteenth Century', in *The Century of Bach and Mozart*, ed. Gallagher and Kelly, 89.
[197] Lawrence Kramer, 'The Devoted Ear: Music as Contemplation', in *Musical Meaning and Human Values*, ed. Keith Chapin and Lawrence Kramer (New York: Fordham University Press, 2009), 62.

altogether deliberately fails to add up to a satisfactory whole. Kramer compares the role of Haydn's Largo cantabile within the complete work with what we hear in Beethoven's Rasumovsky quartets, Op. 59 (1806), where the slow movements 'all seem to respond to something in the movement preceding them rather than to step unforeseeably into an alternat[ive] expressive universe', as Haydn's seems to do.[198] An 'alternative expressive universe' is just what one might hear in many of the case studies presented earlier. Kramer sums up his case by suggesting that, in comparison with Beethoven, 'Haydn shows more confidence in simple difference, which might be glossed as a confidence in forgetting, a willingness to take the present moment as sufficient unto itself.' In other words, incompatibility may be allowed to stand – nothing needs to be 'done about it'. Kramer traces this tolerance of 'simple difference' to Haydn's being part of 'a culture of feeling where emotions more often coexist than interact'.[199] This might seem an unlikely conclusion to draw given the plurality of material and topic that underpins later eighteenth-century style, since those topics suggest associations not just of place but also of various states of feeling. It might also seem unlikely given the processes that were outlined in our previous section on thematic interaction. However, at a more abstract level, and in light of the examples considered in the current section, the notion of coexistence – not necessarily peaceful, and instead possibly unsatisfactory or downright disconcerting – is entirely plausible.

Topics

'Topic theory', first formulated by Leonard Ratner,[200] seeks to account for the kinds of contrast that we have been contemplating above: in particular, the possibility that an individual movement may now incorporate disparate materials, leading to abrupt changes of style.[201] Such materials typically derive from some original functional context in which their defining musical elements are heard – a social dance, a ceremonial fanfare or music for worship, for example – and are then lifted out of that context. Thus a keyboard instrument can play a horn call or a string quartet can evoke sacred polyphony. This sense of music being imported from elsewhere is the most characteristic aspect of topical discourse. It implies a world with

---

[198] Kramer, 'The Devoted Ear', 63.   [199] Kramer, 'The Devoted Ear', 65.
[200] Ratner, *Classic Music*, chapter 2, 'Topics', 9–29.
[201] The first part of this section is based on the start of my chapter 'Topics in Chamber Music', 118–121.

newly enlarged musical horizons, suggests that music can be found everywhere in a society and readily transferred from one place to another; it also tends to overturn hierarchies that may exist when types of music are confined to their original functional contexts. High, middle and low styles may now rub shoulders. As noted above, this is often understood as part of a thoroughgoing theatrical orientation, as if the different topics can be heard as characters interacting on a stage; more broadly, it can be understood as – to put this into a contemporary vernacular – a celebration of difference. The larger discourse within which these styles are held is socially heterogeneous, tolerant of different ways of existing in the (musical) world. And because the styles are supposed to be readily recognizable, derived from shared knowledge, that larger discourse seems to express a welcoming, sociable ethos.

However, given that the field of topical analysis is now well enough established, its proponents have generally shown little curiosity about the origins of topical mixture. While Ratner writes that 'music in the early 18th century developed a thesaurus of *characteristic figures*',[202] the examples and writings cited in support derive almost entirely from the late part of the century. More recently, the work of Raymond Monelle showed plenty of curiosity, though this was directed more towards establishing a cultural history of individual topics or topical fields, namely the hunt, military and pastoral.[203] He did not address the historical emergence of a topically mixed style as such nor the conditions whereby that seems to have become a norm. There is a general consensus that topical mixture emerges from the world of opera, in particular opera buffa, but this has been more assumed than widely demonstrated.[204]

If the field of enquiry has been rather restricted chronologically, this also seems to apply geographically. Both are evident in the fact that the scholarly literature has concentrated on a particular, traditional repertory, Viennese classicism, and indeed on a single composer, Mozart. In fact, one might argue that topic theory, as a means of accounting for developments in the art music of the later eighteenth century, has been made in the image of Mozart; in other words, what may be a peculiarly suitable way of accounting for some of his compositional procedures has been taken to represent a more widespread practice to which the theory may not entirely

---

[202] Ratner, *Classic Music*, 9.
[203] Raymond Monelle, *The Musical Topic: Hunt, Military and Pastoral* (Bloomington: Indiana University Press, 2006).
[204] For an examination of this see Mary Hunter, 'Topics and Opera Buffa', in *The Oxford Handbook of Topic Theory*, ed. Mirka, 61–89.

apply. One might even argue that it came about from a desire to elevate Mozart in the face of prevailing Beethoven-inspired assumptions about what constitutes the core of classicism's technique and spirit (above all organicism). Such essentializing may be especially apparent when one considers the 'hard end' of the theory, whereby the speed of topical interplay becomes a defining feature. Thus the quick-fire juggling of seemingly disparate material is held up as a stylistic norm, and Mozart is then proclaimed, in the words of Ratner, to be 'the greatest master at mixing and coordinating topics, often in the shortest space'.[205]

However, one might question whether this is even a fair characterization of Mozartean procedures. Many topical exegeses deal with sonata-form first movements of multi-movement instrumental works, which do tend to be highly varied in their types of musical material. Certain showpieces, such as the first movement of Mozart's Sonata in F major K332 (1783), are undoubtedly remarkable in their rapid changes of texture and topical stance, but may not be that typical of the composer. Other movement types like slow movements, variations, rondo finales, and minuets and trios, which would not seem readily to allow such mercurial shifts of expression, have also been neglected. Indeed, it may be that what I have referred to on occasion as an overture typology is the most direct source for a style of quick topical mixture, which would explain why it is much more characteristic of instrumental first movements than subsequent ones.

If we expand our terrain geographically, the status of topical play as it has been defined is also uncertain. Rather than a European universal, it is closely bound to Italianate composers and compositional traditions – though admittedly that can encompass much of the continent. In particular, connection with the world of opera does seem to have been a stimulus. C. P. E. Bach, who never engaged with that world compositionally, is an instructive figure in this regard. His music does not seem to have become part of the canon for topical explication – understandably so, since there is but intermittent evidence that he sought to mix and match material in the quasi-theatrical way that is suggested by the literature.

On the other hand, no creative output could be more marked by quick changes, and a distinct taste for discontinuity, which often amounts to the impulsive pulling-apart of individual phrase units. If we wish to reconcile such features with the notion of topical mutability, we may need to revise our terms of reference. There is little doubt about the increasing cultivation over the course of the eighteenth century of a manner that offers contrast

---

[205] Ratner, *Classic Music*, 27.

and interaction between types of musical material, within the span of a single movement – but whether topic is the best controlling term for such a syntactical aesthetic is open to debate. More fundamental, perhaps, is simple changeability of discourse, made possible by the rise of periodic phrase structures – which encourage such 'short-term' thinking – and underpinned by an attitude of scepticism or relativism about the nature of musical utterance. A relativistic attitude derives from the fact that individual expressive tokens – whether we call these topics or gestures or textures – are potentially worlds unto themselves and may often have 'filled the screen' in some original functional or generic context. However, when they are conjoined with other material within a single musical unit, they lose any absolute claims, becoming merely another possible means of musical expression. Within such a style, topics may be symptomatic rather than foundational,[206] the larger development being a sort of creative abdication of discursive authority; a musical utterance marked by variety of stance and gesture no longer seems to compel a particular response or enforce a single 'message'. Thus greater weight is now placed on the listener, who is invited to make sense of such plurality.

One way of asserting the foundational status of topics has been to widen the terms of engagement, as Ratner attempted to do: in addition to various well-known musical styles, 'we can include specific figures – appoggiaturas, tiratas, arpeggios, suspensions, turns, repeated notes etc. – in the theatrical climate generated by the constant presence of topical content. These short figures take on topical character as postures, as gestures that carry affective value. They enter the discourse as subjects that surround the more sharply delineated topics.'[207] Given that such figures can indeed carry particular kinds of affective and gestural character, it seems plausible to suggest that they might not be so different in that respect from topics proper. Allanbrook also considered just how far 'topicality' extends in this repertory: 'All topical identities are relational. "Legato" and "lyrical" are topoi by virtue of being juxtaposed to and hence differentiated from passages that are staccato, or that clearly mimic orchestral rather than vocal idioms. The mercurial gestural shifts of the style delimit one another in a variegated web across the surface, and the absence of a fortunate name for a particular gesture does not mean that it is not differentiated from its neighbor in the

---

[206] As Elaine Sisman notes in a discussion of Mozart's 'Prague' Symphony, K504: 'Were frequent surface contrasts in texture, rhythm, and melody perceived as rapidly changing topics or as more general gestures producing an aesthetically desirable variety?'. Sisman, 'Genre, Gesture, and Meaning', 28.

[207] Ratner, 'Topical Content in Mozart's Keyboard Sonatas', 616.

topical thread of the piece.'[208] Unlike Ratner, who differentiates phenomena such as repeated notes or arpeggios from topics by dubbing them 'figures', Allanbrook states that different types of articulation (legato, staccato), for example, also assume a topical identity.

This might seem to be backed up by Charles Avison, for instance, who in 1752 equated legato and staccato playing on the violin ('the *Sostenute* and *Staccato*') with a 'Change of Styles'.[209] The notion that such contrasting materials are defined relative to each other is hardly controversial,[210] yet the larger assumption made by both writers exposes a tension in the conception of the field. On the one hand, topics are understood as conventional gestures or figures of any kind, including the phenomena proposed by Ratner and Allanbrook (an appoggiatura, legato articulation and so forth). On the other hand, topics are understood as larger-scale phenomena, as characteristic combinations of such figures, recognizable more or less as styles that are lifted from some original functional context and placed elsewhere. Certainly, the latter is the prevalent working assumption for most scholars in the field. One might argue that the more inclusive definition, implying a brand of musical discourse that is always topically saturated, reduces the explanatory power of 'topic theory'. It becomes just another 'theory of everything', an 'organic' or holistic world of its own, and there is no ready means to differentiate topical phenomena from other strands that go towards making up such music. From a more style-historical point of view, other periods also produced musical works that are full of such 'figures'; why should they not therefore carry the same theatrical and gestural weight in those circumstances? If they do, then how is topical analysis in any way addressing the particularities of later eighteenth-century style and its social premises?

One thing that is clear, though, regardless of how quickly we think it should take place and for all the tension between permissive and more restrictive understandings of the term: topical mixture challenges the listener. The middle movement of Dittersdorf's String Quartet K194 (Example 2.29), with its multiple juxtapositions of horn call, rustic dance and strange archaic

---

[208] Allanbrook, *Secular Commedia*, 123. This passage derives from Allanbrook's earlier 'Theorizing the Comic Surface', in *Music in the Mirror: Reflections on the History of Music Theory and Literature for the Twenty-First Century*, ed. Andreas Giger and Thomas Mathiesen (Lincoln: University of Nebraska Press, 2002), 214, where she also wrote '*Topoi* articulate each other's differences in same way as modern linguists understand phonic units as delimiting each other: by juxtaposition and opposition, by rubbing shoulders'.

[209] Avison, *Essay on Musical Expression*, ed. Dubois, 52.

[210] In a recent survey of the literature on topics Nicholas MacKay remarks, 'Semioticians know that meaning resides not in the signs themselves but in the relation among signs.' MacKay, 'On Topics Today', *Zeitschrift der Gesellschaft für Musiktheorie* 4/1–2 (2007), 167.

material, offered an extreme form of such a challenge. Such brazen variety acts as a goad, virtually enforcing an attempt to pin down an identity for each of the distinct materials that we are hearing, so that we can make more focussed sense of our listening experience. From this point of view, the development of an intellectual superstructure such as topic theory might seem to have been inevitable – though, as with other perspectives we now bring to the repertory, there is limited contemporaneous support for the fine print of the theory. Whether we need, and in fact will always be able, to pin down our aural impressions exactly, by means of a precise topical label, is another question. Exercising the imagination of the listener may be a more fundamental outcome; this is similar to what was suggested above with the category of thematic interaction, whereby the main point may be interaction itself, rather than the need to settle on a decisive plot or story. This much might be suggested by the words of Koch: in the galant style 'music aims to please individual persons or a whole group of them through the expression of a capricious sequence of gay, tender, sad, or sublime feelings, or to present such tone pictures as allow the imagination free play with the ideas created'.[211] The notion of allowing the listener free play might suggest that, while the fixing of topical labels can hit the nail on the head, as I hope it has done in some of my earlier readings, it can also miss the point. After all, many listeners (both then and now) may be unable to assign an exact stylistic identity to a piece of material yet can still participate 'authentically' in the process, by being alive to difference and stimulated to respond to it: curiosity is its own reward.[212] From that point of view the possibly indeterminate identity of any particular gesture within a regime of topical mixture need not matter; more important is the attitude it embraces of openness to the diversity of the (musical) world.[213]

---

[211] Koch, *Musikalisches Lexikon*, entry 'Styl, Schreibart', 1454, cited in translation in Wheelock, *Haydn's Ingenious Jesting with Art*, 39.

[212] An interesting modern perspective on this comes from the field of music cognition, in Carol L. Krumhansl, 'Topic in Music: An Empirical Study of Memorability, Openness, and Emotion in Mozart's String Quintet in C Major and Beethoven's String Quartet in A Minor', *Music Perception* 16/1 (1998), 119–134. Having based the study on Kofi Agawu's identification of topics in those two works in his book *Playing with Signs*, the author concludes that Agawu's 'parsing of the music into topics' was reflected in the experiences of 'all listeners, even . . . those with little training and experience with classical music. That the topics influenced the judgments suggests that their distinctive characteristics (such as tempo, rhythm, melodic figures) established them as psychological entities. . . . The results call into question the assumption made in the music literature that extensive stylistic familiarity is prerequisite to the appreciation of topics.' (132–133)

[213] Note in this respect the view of Robert P. Morgan, in response to Wye J. Allanbrook's injunction for analysts to focus more upon surface than on 'hidden unities': 'she too must reach beyond the "given" surface to embrace generalising analytical categories. In her case this means "topics", which are – even if they are historically sanctioned – conceptual abstractions

Koch's remark that the chamber style is meant to please 'individual persons or a whole group of them' supports the idea that topical plurality is rooted in an ideal of accessibility, and by offering the two alternative constituencies he suggests that not everyone is certain to be pleased in the same way at the same time; characterizing a sequence of changeable events as 'capricious' helps to signal this. At the same time Koch usefully exposes a further tension in how such mixture might be understood. There is the worldly side, the mirror held up to humanity, whereby topics represent a common coinage that everyone can recognize, but there is also the level of individual response, which will not be so uniform.

A similar duality is apparent in Türk's 1783 publication of twelve easy keyboard sonatas that we encountered earlier. In his Preface the composer hopes that his efforts 'will meet the expectations of most of the subscribers, since, given how tastes vary, it is hardly possible to satisfy all' ('Möchte doch diese Arbeit wenigstens der Erwartung des größern Theils entsprechen; da es, bei dem verschiedenen Geschmack, doch wohl nicht möglich ist, Alle zu befriedigen!').[214] While this is obviously indebted to the gambit of the prefatory disclaimer, Türk shows himself strongly conscious of different parties who will be pleased with different musical materials. The twelve works in fact could hardly do more to cater to such differences; there is a clear plan to introduce the player to various idioms, to various formal and expressive types, so that there will be 'something for everyone'. At the same time, by encompassing such variety, the set presents a certain encyclopedic perspective, a worldly summation of possibilities. This might reinforce Ratner's view that topical mixture embodies an eighteenth-century 'trend toward codification, toward the ordering of materials and processes'.[215] To codify, however, is to put individual agency aside in favour of a god's-eye view. And to revert to our previous concern, if everything is tidily topical, if everything is already 'known', there is less room for individual imagination and response. The tension between these two approaches to topical signification need not be seen negatively, though; after all, the same applies to 'taste', which can be a matter of individual agency, as Türk depicts it above, but is also a collective phenomenon.

(and are arguably much further from the work's actual surface than say a Schenkerian reduction). ... Allanbrook too ends up subsuming individual events under generalising features, which is precisely what analysis must do.' Morgan, 'The Concept of Unity and Musical Analysis', *Music Analysis* 22/1–2 (2003), 45, note 6.

[214] Daniel Gottlob Türk, Preface to *Sechs leichte Klaviersonaten, Erster Teil* (Leipzig and Halle: Breitkopf, 1783), unpaginated (first page).

[215] Ratner, 'Topical Content in Mozart's Keyboard Sonatas', 615.

Koch also seems to appeal to individual response in describing a mixture of materials as a succession of moods – 'a capricious sequence of gay, tender, sad, or sublime feelings' – rather than styles, as topic theory would have it. Of course the two are hardly mutually exclusive, since many topics brings particular affects with them (a grand fanfare, a rustic drone), even if these are not binding;[216] and as we have noted earlier, 'character' was at the time a common means of trying to come to terms with a musical manner that offered such clear-cut contrasts. In sum, there are a number of uncertainties concerning the application and definition of musical topics. Should we understand them as being in the first instance affective or stylistic categories? If they are by definition public, shared phenomena, is listener response foreordained or may it appropriately be more personal? Finally, as we touched on in an earlier section, what sense of agency can arise from such stylistic mixture: are musical topics a series of 'outside voices' that make themselves heard, or may they also be understood as the expression of an individual temperament, a single 'voice' that experiences different moods and adopts different accents?

On the first of these counts, affect versus style, one would not want to dispense with the stylistically more precise terminology offered by topic theory, since it helps to suggest other kinds of differentiation between materials. Koch's 'tone pictures' can become more vivid when we consider how topics can evoke different spaces and places. For instance, to return to the fifth-movement Adagio of Haydn's Symphony No. 60, 'Il Distratto', we witness an aria-like cantilena being interrupted by a fanfare, and so we are transported from the theatre to some ceremonial occasion, possibly held out of doors. In the middle of the same symphony's second movement, from the upbeat to bar 64, we hear a brief passage that sounds quite incongruous. Against a bass that moves in continuous even quavers, the violins play an elaborate line with many dotted rhythms, furnished with *forzando* trills on eight consecutive downbeats. While picking up on the incongruity of this material in the context of a lyrical Andante will already provide food for the imagination, this will be sharpened if one can work out

---

[216] Robert L. Martin, 'Musical "Topics" and Expression in Music', *The Journal of Aesthetics and Art Criticism* 53/4 (1995), lists the 'expressive connotations' that arise from various types of topics, citing Allanbrook that these derive from 'the circumstances in which they are habitually employed' (418). However, Martin finds that such connotations do not always hold, and for him the real value of a topical view 'is to give to the work a feeling of being connected to other experiences of life ... This accounts for something very important in the experience of many listeners – the feeling that even "abstract" music has very close connections to the fullness of life's experiences.' (420). This conclusion firmly supports the 'worldly' orientation towards topical signals.

that these features amount to a particular style. This style in fact belongs to the past; it is baroque pastiche, with the lower line representing a 'walking bass' and the violins performing in the 'dotted style'.[217] This gives us our classic definition of topic – material taken out of some original context and thrust into a movement, in this case a singing Andante, where its features are no longer self-evident. The passage signs off at bars 73–74 with a quick unison descending scale that sounds like a Vivaldian flourish. In the case of this movement the change of style suggests that we are travelling not so much in space as in time.

One locale that a topical perspective has taught us to appreciate more thoroughly is the dance floor, and it is hardly possible to overstate the importance of dancing as a social activity during our period. The importance of dance, though, goes beyond topical explication. It is, after all, an inherently socializing and collective activity; its indissoluble association with music, and its embodiment through gesture rather than word, means that it in many ways provides a more powerful model than verbal ones such as dialogue or conversation when one tries to evoke the ethos of sociable instrumental music. On the other hand, when it comes to identifying particular dance types, uncertainties of definition can readily arise. It often feels as though topical identities are asserted in the literature rather than argued through. Must every fast finale in 6/8 derive from the gigue, for instance; must every fast finale in 2/4 represent a contredanse; must every passage in a moderate 3/4 time be in minuet style?[218] A certain interpretative promiscuity would of course be quite consistent with the level of individual response that I have argued for above – the notion that topics' prompting of the imagination is more fundamental than settling on an agreed point of origin for a particular piece of musical material. On the other hand, many claims regarding topical identity do imply rather the god's-eye view, an act of codification that leaves no particular room for dispute.

---

[217] For an examination of this stylistic field (which has not really achieved the status of a topic) see David Fuller, 'The "Dotted Style" in Bach, Handel, and Scarlatti', in *Bach, Handel, Scarlatti: Tercentenary Essays*, ed. Peter Williams (Cambridge: Cambridge University Press, 1985), 99–117.

[218] Note in this respect Michael Talbot's remark that while many instrumental finales of the eighteenth century have dance-like properties, 'recognition of a generalized relationship to the dance needs ... to be coupled with a much more rigorous definition of individual dances. One should never call a movement a "gigue" because a modern semiotician has assigned this word as a handy label to a given "topic".' He then notes that 'many Classical finales ... are on any analysis totally devoid of dance connotations'. Michael Talbot, *The Finale in Western Instrumental Music* (Oxford: Oxford University Press, 2001), 57.

There is, however, one topical area which implies just such a laying-down of the law. It has often gone by the name of 'learned style', though it has been increasingly recognized how blunt an instrument that name can be.[219] While most topics derive from some original functional context where they 'filled the screen', before being mixed up with others, learned style may stand somewhat apart. If we understand it to imply the practice of strict counterpoint, it precisely does not allow any wavering from its sole mission, the development of a central subject or subjects. In his definition of what he called 'the *strict* style, which is also called the *bound* style or the fugal style', Koch noted its 'strict adherence to the main subject', as well as the absence of the 'ornamentation and breaking-up of the melody into small fragments' that were reliable markers of the modern. For Koch, everything else was called, significantly, the 'free style'.[220] Therefore the learned is a topic that leaves no room for contrast, and certainly not the often abrupt contrasts we encounter in the mixed style; its world is self-contained and self-sufficient, not one that allows for difference of that kind. However, on the vast majority of occasions when the strict style makes its presence felt in instrumental music, it is precisely part of a mixed menu. James Currie notes the dissonance this creates with the ethos of the style: 'Since learned style's identity is founded on its authority, stylistic interaction will often produce a lessening of its characteristic effect'.[221] Such authority derives from its associations with learning, genre (sacred) and location (church), and, simply, from its age – the weight of tradition.

Not that this always needs to translate into what Koch called the 'serious character' which made the strict style 'best suited for church music':[222] plenty of fugues from older times, for example, convey lighter affects than that. And indeed, in the later eighteenth century contrapuntal procedures often take an explicitly comic turn; the finales of Beethoven's piano sonata Op. 10 No. 2 (1798) and Haydn's Symphony No. 66 (c1778) are representative instances. However, these start to move us away from anything that

---

[219] For an excellent account of the problems of definition that pertain to 'learned style' see Keith Chapin's chapter 'Learned Style and Learned Styles' in *The Oxford Handbook of Topic Theory*, ed. Mirka, 301–329.

[220] Koch, *Musikalisches Lexikon*, entry 'Styl, Schreibart', 1451–1452, cited in translation in Ratner, *Classic Music*, 23.

[221] James R. Currie, *Music and the Politics of Negation* (Bloomington: Indiana University Press, 2012), 22. Compare Stephen Rumph's discussion of this matter in *Mozart and Enlightenment Semiotics*, 153, where he remarks that the learned style 'provided an escape from the whole system of representation in which topics operate'.

[222] Koch, *Musikalisches Lexikon*, entry 'Styl, Schreibart', 1452, cited in translation in Ratner, *Classic Music*, 23.

could be called strict or learned style; various forms of imitation surface sporadically throughout, but never dominate. In his treatise of 1773 Daube noted a distinction between such imitation and 'the fugal style or canonic procedure'.[223] Arguably in such cases we are also moving away from that sense of conceptual separation that allows us to speak of a topic at all. On the other hand, in the finale of Dittersdorf's String Quartet in A major, K196 (1789), a quite extensive fugato section is heard twice as part of an episode within the rondo form and is clearly contrasted with other types of writing. Thus it counts both as a topic and as 'learned' or 'strict'. The demeanour is entirely 'serious', and any comic charge derives from its juxtaposition with other materials. The most obvious incongruity derives from the way in which the fugato is prepared, from bar 33, by means of a texture that makes the quartet sound like a rustic band, complete with cello drone and repeated two-bar fragments in the upper instruments. (The idiom is very similar to that we encountered in the second movement of the composer's K194, discussed above.) Then, out of nowhere, the rustic sonority gives way to a single line in the first violin, which almost immediately can be grasped as the subject of a fugal exposition. The folk fiddler, it would seem, has suddenly morphed into the polyphonic pedant. Another unusual aspect, as Warren Kirkendale has pointed out, lies in the very positioning of the fugato, in the middle of the movement, plus the fact that it takes up a theme not previously heard.[224] Together with the unusual preparation, these factors cut against an expectation that learned discourse will announce itself at the outset and reign uncontested throughout. In such a case, its 'authority' is certainly lessened.

If many later eighteenth-century contrapuntal textures can hardly be straightforwardly linked with learned style, there is, on the other hand, a category of materials that sound old but need not involve any strong polyphonic apparatus. Matthew Riley's useful coinage 'untimely rhetoric' covers any material that has an aura of age, that refers to 'pre-galant idioms'. These can indeed include types of strict counterpoint but can also encompass such phenomena as 'species[-]counterpoint textures, ritornello gestures, Corellian trio-sonata textures [and] fast-moving basslines'.[225] We have already encountered a number of movements that evince further 'untimely' features: the all-unison minuet in F minor from Jadin's Op. 1 No. 3 that suggested plainchant, the passacaglia bass of Haydn's Piano Trio in E major H28, and indeed that strangely archaic material that surfaces in the Alternativo of Dittersdorf's

[223] Daube, *The Musical Dilettante*, ed. and trans. Snook-Luther, 111.
[224] Kirkendale, *Fugue and Fugato*, 85.   [225] Riley, *Viennese Minor-Key Symphony*, 5.

K194. In many cases such materials can sound uncanny, if not gothic, in context. These need not be understood negatively, of course, given the 'tolerance' that underpins topical mixture, but that is a possibility. The third movement of Dittersdorf's *Four Ages of the World* represents the Brazen Age, the penultimate stage on the downward spiral that culminates in the chaotic 'Iron Age' finale that we looked at earlier. It is a minuet in A minor that represents 'le despotisme', while the trio paints 'the groans of those who find themselves [its] victims'.[226] The minuet presents many wide leaps and dotted rhythms, together with much unison writing. These features could all point to a martial mode; in any case, they do anything but suggest a graceful minuet. When the opening material returns in the second section, it is manipulated into a classic 'untimely' feature, a rising suspension chain after the manner of Corelli that is heard in the oboes and bassoons. In conjunction with the prevailing dotted rhythms, the lack of any contrasting material and the fact that the first section cadences unusually in the dominant minor,[227] this pushes us in the direction of a different topical field. We might loosely call this baroque dotted style; the eighteenth-century category of high style might also serve. Ratner remarks that the high style 'was a heritage from the earlier 18th century, when one of the main objects of this style was to celebrate authority'.[228] In the current case, though, 'celebrate' would not be the operative word; authority here is plainly authoritarian, and the old style is meant to inspire some sort of terror in the auditors.

My mixed impressions of the topical identity of the minuet's material may represent an exemplary case of listener freedom – an invitation extended and accepted on the basis of prior listening experience and stylistic 'competence', with no one conclusion necessarily having to be drawn.[229] On the other hand, such ambivalence might seem to undermine the claims of topic theory that the stylistic sources of material were widely understood and intersubjectively valid. However, in some such cases at least one can understand that topical traits overlap, on the basis of simple

---

[226] Cited in translation in Will, *Characteristic Symphony*, 60.
[227] John Rice describes this as an archaic feature in 'New Light on Dittersdorf's Ovid Symphonies', *Studi musicali* 29/2 (2000), 464, cited in Will, *Characteristic Symphony*, 60n.
[228] Ratner, *Classic Music*, 365.
[229] Note that Richard Will hears a different combination of elements in this material, which seems to exclude the 'untimely'. For him the 'ominous' character of the minuet is created not just by the setting of the movement in the relative minor (the work is in C major), but by 'the unison scoring, suggestive of a voice issuing commands, and a jagged melody composed in equal parts of the dotted rhythms of military fanfares and the wide leaps associated in contemporary vocal music with high-flown emotion'. Will, *Characteristic Symphony*, 60.

figures that they have in common.[230] In this instance the two topical fields share a dotted rhythm that imparts an aura of authority. In fact we might conceive of a merger between the military and 'untimely' dotted styles, an instance of what Hatten has described as 'topical troping'.[231]

A more elusive instance of this arises at the start of Mozart's String Quartet in D major K499 (1786; Example 2.30). If one were to announce in advance that the players will begin by performing a tonic arpeggio in unison in quickish duple time, a listener could readily imagine the sort of opening that is in store – it will be loud, confident and probably redolent of a fanfare. Yet what we hear is none of these things. A fanfare topic is certainly not extinguished, but what we hear is *piano*, rather than *forte*, and, rather than rising, it falls. Further, the slurred pairings of triadic notes group upbeat with downbeat to create anacrusic groupings that almost sound like a series of sighs. As the theme unfolds, some larger-scale ambiguities of grouping become apparent. The real metre may in fact be 4/2 rather than the advertised cut time, and the hypermetrical structure is not clear (in other words, which downbeats are stronger than others). Fanfares are normally decisive in such respects, with clearly marked strong beats and square phrase rhythms. Altogether, rather than hearing a confident announcement, we hear something that is low-key, almost diffident; it has a concessive rather than an affirmative character.

It would not make sense to twist a topic in this way unless a reciprocal syntactical dynamic was in place. What seems to be happening is that a typically strong, unambiguous opening and a graceful rejoinder are being superimposed; we hear the latter more plainly, but given its position in the discourse it is inflected by or heard against the former. The opening of K499, in other words, could not arise without a sense of the mutually conditioning influences of what I have been calling assertive and gracious tendencies. Nor could it have arisen without a fairly focussed sense of what we now call 'topic', together with the relativistic attitude towards musical expression that I have suggested underpins it: if 'topic' suggests that musical materials are no longer absolutes, merely possibilities in a wider field, that is what allows our composer to produce a seeming contradiction in terms, a gentle fanfare. However, it is not just the opening two-bar unit

---

[230] Stephen Rumph explores the idea that various fundamental figures (*figurae*) can underpin multiple topics in his chapter 'Topical Figurae: The Double Articulation of Topics' in *The Oxford Handbook of Topic Theory*, ed. Mirka, 493–513.

[231] See Hatten, *Interpreting Musical Gestures* and 'The Troping of Topics in Mozart's Instrumental Works', in *The Oxford Handbook of Topic Theory*, ed. Mirka, 514–536.

Example 2.30 Mozart, Quartet in D major K499/i, bars 1–23[1]

which might be heard in relation to that topic: the two-bar unit that follows, still in unison, has other characteristics of ceremonial opening material. After the first two-bar unit's paired groupings of triadic notes, the second starts with a dotted rhythm and continues with repeated notes, both very much part of the fanfare style. These features also start to suggest the march, nominally a separate topic but clearly compatible with fanfare as part of the same topical field or 'mode'.[232]

Another unusual aspect to the handling of the topic comes with the continuation. Normally a fanfare would be clear-cut syntactically, with a definite ending point. In this case the second two-bar figure is extended through several further repetitions while violin 1 rises by leap at the start of each new phrase unit. While both might in theory be compatible with fanfare activity, other factors work against that: the gradual refraction of the unison texture into more strongly individuated parts, and the presence of pedal notes in the cello (almost suggesting a musette). Through such means the fanfare/march topic does not so much end as gradually drain away. By the time the whole phrase comes to an end, the instruments are moving almost exclusively by step, as opposed to the disjunct triadic intervals with which they started, and the cadence point in bar 12 is decorated by appoggiaturas (restruck suspensions) in the upper three parts – a classic softening device.

In fact, this is far from the end of the story. In what follows Mozart continues to combine an assertive or 'open' topic with a conciliatory realization. The two halves of the fanfare material are played simultaneously, or put in dialogue with each other, by the two violins, which might represent another kind of topical distancing, but then this phrase is repeated exactly by the viola-cello duo down an octave (bars 12^4–16^3 then 16^4–20^1). Such antiphonal repetition of material is an idiomatic element of fanfare style. This is taken further when the final bar of the phrase is repeated in decorated form first by the higher pair (violins 1 and 2) and then by the lower pair of viola and cello (bars 20^2–22^1). The rate of antiphonal exchange has greatly quickened, and the suggestion of a fanfare (or indeed a horn call) is unmistakeable. Further fragmentation follows, when the second half of that one-bar unit is isolated and repeated antiphonally in turn, the topical identity becoming absolutely plain. But the dynamic level remains soft throughout, so we still retain a sense of merged types of utterance, 'light' and 'heavy', gracious and assertive.

Such equivocal topical treatment represents a fairly extreme end of the merging of styles. In a greater number of cases, there is a more explicit process of reconciliation between materials that are initially presented as separate spheres of activity. The basic topical plot of the finale of Mozart's

---

[232] Hatten uses the term 'mode' to describe such larger collocations of supposedly separate topics; his term 'heroic mode', which includes 'triumphant marches [and] fanfares', could suitably be applied to the opening material of this quartet. Hatten, 'The Troping of Topics', 523.

quintet K593 contrasts rustic and learned, and in the recapitulation the composer shows how they are compatible by combining them. The slow movement of Haydn's Symphony No. 96 in D major (1791) is animated by a similar contrast, though it is a higher, Arcadian form of pastoral that bumps up against a middle section that exemplifies the attributes of 'ancient music' for its English audience.[233] The rapprochement takes place in an unexpected cadenza that features two solo violins, solo winds and pizzicato ripieno strings. While the pastoral remains in charge, not least because of the picturesque scoring, there are many elements that recall the central fugato material. Such interpenetration of opposites need not be heard to happen, of course. A 'philosophical' coexistence may be the likely outcome, as explored earlier in this chapter. Certainly when the topical contrasts take place at the level of whole sections or movements, as in a minuet and trio, that is often the more plausible reading. But even there the sequence of events may not be certain. Brunetti, for example, tends to eschew the minuet as the third movement in his symphonies, replacing it by other dance forms, though often no dance is named. What he does do consistently, though, is to give the outer sections to a 'Quintetto' of wind soloists while the trio is played principally by the string section. If this virtually reverses the expected timbral focus for such a movement, so does the topical succession, since frequently the outer sections, strictly symmetrical in phrase syntax, carry a pastoral flavour of the outdoors while the trios offer 'untimely' gestures from the scholar's study.

Variety

For all the possible merging of topics considered above, on many occasions there is little sense of common ground. Instead a succession of topics can seem like so much 'raw data' that is thrown at the listener, encouraging identification and interpretation but not guaranteeing that any synthesis will emerge. Even to understand topics under an umbrella term such as 'theatrical' is arguably to domesticate them, turning each topical strand into a distinct 'character' – someone or something that has a recognizable, relatively stable identity – when in fact, as we have seen above, establishing

---

[233] A. Peter Brown suggests that 'the eighteenth-century London musical sophisticate' would probably have heard the central section as 'typical of the ancient style': *First Golden Age of the Viennese Symphony*, 248.

an identity can be a matter of individual response, nor is the separation between such personages by any means always clear-cut.

This sense of uncompromising parataxis, of simple juxtaposition, takes us back to the point suggested earlier: that changeability, over and above 'topic', is the more fundamental point of reference for later eighteenth-century instrumental style. This can mean abrupt, seemingly unaccountable swerves. The first movement of Gyrowetz's Quartet Op. 44 No. 2 in B flat major (1804) begins smoothly enough before collectively played material in dotted rhythm arrives out of the blue in bar 12. We can readily categorize this figure as march-like, though that might be to miss some of the point. Apart from being unrelated to anything that has gone before, the figure is heard in the middle of an expected eight-bar phrase, not a natural place for all four players suddenly to try a different gambit. This misplacement is all the more vivid given the functional implications of the specific topic: marches would normally declare themselves at the outset of a section. One would also expect a confident execution, whereas this passage is to be played *piano*. The march then vanishes after four bars; it has been a temporary distraction, it would appear. A different kind of unaccountable change marks the first movement of Boccherini's Piano Quintet in C major, Op. 57 No. 6/G418 (1799), in which the flow of material is continually interrupted by a two-note cell, often treated in dialogue between the five players. This seems to represent a kind of distraction, as if the players are unable to concentrate on the matter at hand. If the instrumental style of this time displays an openness to anything and everything from the musical world – which topic theory after all acknowledges through its very existence and its almost exclusive application to this repertory – then it is reasonable to imagine that this may produce a distracted condition. It is as if the impressions of the musical world crowd in on the musical agents, leading to over-stimulation.

We must of remind ourselves, though, that such parataxis of material exists in counterpoint with a strongly hypotactic phrase syntax, a sense of interlocking grammatical levels that the language model of the time helped to capture. Periodic organization brings regularity – and it typically involves forms of medium- and larger-scale repetition. Yet on the smaller scale, exact repetition is very frequently avoided. This is especially so with thematic presentations, as we have seen in the case of the 'sensitive style'. The Presto finale of Mozart's 'Linz' Symphony, K425, opens with a four-bar unit based on the intervallic shape of a fourth up then a third down, the latter filled in by step, and this unit is followed by three successive variants at bars 5–16. If this suggests a high degree of symmetry, the actual sounding result is anything but; various forms of elaboration give each of the four-bar units its own distinct identity. It is almost like a point of honour for the symmetry to be underplayed in favour of resourceful difference. Even outside presentational contexts, such a principle might obtain. In Riepel's treatise *Anfangsgründe zur musicalischen Setzkunst* the teacher warns the student against writing a literally symmetrical Monte (two-part ascending sequence): 'two identical statements one after the other sound bad'.[234] The second version should in some way be different. Of course there is any amount of sequential writing from the time in which units are indeed exactly transposed, and it also depends on the scale of the operation and the character of the material, but the force of the warning stands. This is also a question of editorial and performance practice. Differing versions of parallel passages in the source(s) for a piece have often troubled later editors or performers, or both, resulting in an overwhelming tendency to tidy up the differences. Relatively less common, but arguably more appropriate in many individual instances, is to accept the differences and try to make positive capital out of them. One performer-scholar who aims to do so is Robert Levin, who argues that 'variety of characterization' is a more fundamental value than 'consistency' for the style.[235]

Consideration of such an issue should remind us that a preference for variety encompasses more than thematic, motivic or topical concerns. It can exist also, for instance, with regard to dynamics, as with those unpredictable alternations of *forte* and *piano* in Stamitz that seem to exist at the level of pure sensation. In the area of articulation, one might note the rarity of long unchanged stretches of the same style in later eighteenth-century instrumental music; instead, various types of touch and sound production constantly intermingle. The same also applies to rhythm in its more immediate sense – as opposed to the larger-scale hypermetrical regularities

---

[234] Riepel, *Anfangsgründe zur musicalischen Setzkunst*, volume 2: *Grundregeln der Tonordnung* (Frankfurt and Leipzig: Christian Ulrich Wagner, 1755), 45, cited in translation in Gjerdingen, *Music in the Galant Style*, 106.

[235] Robert D. Levin, 'Performance Practice in the Music of Mozart', in *The Cambridge Companion to Mozart*, ed. Keefe, 232 (italics removed from 'variety'). Levin prefaces his 'variety versus consistency' equation by stating that 'there is every reason to challenge the general aesthetic tendency of modern editions to standardize readings according to parallel passages'. James Webster notes that the very term 'inconsistency' tends to load the dice when one considers varying markings within a source; hence he prefers to use 'the more neutral concept of *variability*'. Webster, 'The Triumph of Variability: Haydn's Articulation Markings in the Autograph of Sonata No. 49 in E Flat', in *Haydn, Mozart, & Beethoven: Studies in the Music of the Classical Period. Essays in Honour of Alan Tyson*, ed. Sieghard Brandenburg (Oxford: Clarendon, 1998), 58.

generated by periodic organization. As we saw earlier, this is especially pronounced in the earlier galant, whether that means C. P. E. Bach or Galuppi, whereby the basic rhythmic denomination may vary from bar to bar, even beat to beat. On a broader scale, long passages that are dominated by one rhythmic value are also exceptional, and may be a special effect. This does not apply when regular rhythms can be understood as forming an accompaniment, since the melody they support will contain the necessary variegation to meet the stylistic requirement.

That literal repetition could be a matter of comment is apparent in Burney's strictures on Tartini, who 'certainly repeats his passages, and adheres to his original *motivo*, or theme, too much' for what Burney nicely encapsulated, as we saw earlier, as 'the favourite desultory style of the present times'.[236] On a much larger scale, there is the case of the two movements in Haydn's 'Auenbrugger' sonatas published in 1780 that are based on the same incipit: the opening movement of the Sonata in G major H39 and the middle movement of the Sonata in C sharp minor, H36. However this resemblance came about,[237] Haydn asked for an 'Avertissement' to be placed after the title-page specifically noting that there were 'two single movements in which the same subject occurs through several bars'. The composer wrote in his letter to publishers Artaria, 'For of course I could have chosen a hundred other ideas instead of this one; but so that the whole *opus* will not be exposed to blame on account of this one intentional detail (which the critics and especially my enemies might interpret wrongly), I think that this *avertissement* or something like it must be appended, otherwise the sale might be hindered thereby.'[238] Of course it was more than commercial damage that Haydn was concerned about; there was the damage to his reputation that might arise if he was said to be repeating himself rather than offering something different.

There are several Dittersdorf symphonies in which 'the favourite desultory style' is more or less programmatically promoted. The *Sinfonia nazionale nel gusto di cinque nazioni* (1767) offers musical portraits of the German, Italian, English, French and Turkish in successive movements

---

[236] Burney, *General History of Music, Volume the Second*, 449.

[237] For a full recent discussion of all the circumstances of this affair, and its many varied interpretations, see Tom Beghin, *The Virtual Haydn: Paradox of a Twenty-First-Century Keyboardist* (Chicago: University of Chicago Press, 2015), 169–179.

[238] Haydn, letter to Artaria, 25 February 1780; *Joseph Haydn: Gesammelte Briefe und Aufzeichnungen*, ed. H. C. Robbins Landon and Dénes Bartha (Budapest: Corvina, 1965), 90–91, cited in translation in Landon, *Haydn at Eszterháza*, 431.

before bringing them all together in a finale. The very form in which they are combined is significant – rondo, which in its modern incarnation was precisely premised on variety of material. There were earlier types of the form that were also based on alternation between theme and episode, but those episodes did not necessarily form a strong contrast – as so often with the French *rondeau*, where the couplets would continue the business of the refrain.[239] In the later eighteenth century, though, clear-cut differences became the norm, and in the current case they carry an extra charge: the episodes revisit the various national styles to which we have already been exposed in previous movements. Thus what had been presented as separate phenomena are now 'tolerantly' gathered together into a single larger statement. The prototypical modern form of the rondo precisely builds difference into its structure, and in the case of this particular movement provides a form of reconciliation. Still more significant is that Dittersdorf has arguably shown the limitations of the individual styles in the preceding movements; all feature elements of parody. These limitations are then overcome when those styles mix and mingle in the finale; as we saw when considering the model of conversation, a sort of collective wisdom arises from the interaction of different types or views, transcending the limited perspectives of the individual participants.

That said, it is worth noting that the good-humoured rondo theme that helps to unite the various styles is marked 'Tedesco'. This might seem to represent double-dipping, with the first movement having already offered the German perspective; we might also recognize a familiar tale of musical universality being equated with *Deutschtum*. However, as Allan Badley has pointed out, these two German portraits may not be the same thing at all: the Germans depicted in the first movement 'appear to be a little old-fashioned, probably North-Germans and more than likely, given the date of the work (c. 1766), hostile to the avant-garde style of the Viennese. In the *Finale,* however, the Germans – now almost certainly Southern Germans and Austrians – are clothed in modern dress (with oboes and horns) and speaking the new musical *lingua franca* of Europe with great fluency.'[240] By this measure there is a different Germanophone mentality organizing

---

[239] See Joel Galand, 'Form, Genre, and Style in the Eighteenth-Century Rondo', *Music Theory Spectrum* 17/1 (1995), 27–52. Galand notes that the development of a rondo with clearly contrasting episodes was not universal, with the 'monothematic' rondo continuing to have some currency in north Germany: 'descriptions of the rondo by North Germans such as Reichardt, Forkel, and Cramer do not call for contrast; these critics uphold as models the monothematic rondos of C. P. E. Bach' (37).

[240] Allan Badley, notes to *Dittersdorf: Sinfonias*, Failoni Orchestra, conducted by Uwe Grodd (Naxos 8.553975, 1998), 5–6.

affairs in the finale, one that is not only open to variety but also more prone to humour and the popular touch.

The same applies in the finale of Dittersdorf's symphony *Il combattimento delle passioni umani*. We have already touched on some of the characters depicted by earlier movements: the 'proud' opening movement with its submissive successor *Il Humile*, and the 'madness' of its minuet countered by the more socially attuned *Il Amante*. The final two movements offer another contrasting pair – the penultimate depiction of melancholy, *Il Malinconico*, leads to the finale's depiction of lively high spirits, *Il Vivace*. Importantly, as with the final rondo of the *Sinfonia nazionale*, this is the first movement of the work to feature clear internal contrasts, to offer an intimate dialogue between different textures and materials – and therefore the first to operate fully in the most up-to-date style. Not only are vivacity and cheerfulness being cast as the normal modern state of mind, but the movement shows how this mood naturally generates contrast. In fact, some of this contrast involves recourse to the minor mode in several episodes, suggesting how a lively modern mindset can absorb unhappy setbacks and still come out smiling, as it were.

It needs to be stressed that it is the finales of these symphonies that show modern variety in its truest colours. Variety between movements, while marked enough in these cases, and advertised by means of titles, is nothing new.[241] But the fact that strong differences nevertheless exist between the individual movements exposes the slippery nature of the principal term of reference. What exactly did 'variety', this mantra of the time, mean? The difficulty for us is that variety now seems like bland coinage; as we noted earlier of 'balance', it does not exactly set critical pulses racing. As in the case of that concept, as well as others such as 'music as language', we have to try to recover some sort of fresh imprint. This is not to say that our 'variety' had some original sharply defined sense which has since got lost. It was a contested term in the sense that it could clearly mean different things to different people. Nobody was going to disagree with the principle of variety: that artworks needed some form of light and shade, some kind of internal differentiation of texture or treatment or metre or similar, in order

---

[241] For example, in his account of the origins of the Italian solo keyboard sonata, Gregory Barnett emphasizes the importance of varied expressive and stylistic typologies as the multi-movement form took hold. The four movements of the third of Lodovico Giustini's twelve sonatas Op. 1 (1732), for instance, offer successively 'folksy, erudite, lyrical, and energized moods'. Such works, of course, already represent a trend that one might characterize as galant. Gregory Barnett, 'The Early Italian Keyboard Sonata: Origins, Influences, and Disseminations', in *The Early Keyboard Sonata in Italy and Beyond*, ed. Rohan Stewart-MacDonald (Turnhout: Brepols, 2016), 38.

to make them worthy of respect. Yet while its particular manifestation in changeable modern instrumental style was to its proponents a stimulating embodiment of that principle, for opponents it was less variety that was on offer than sheer inconsistency. For those opposed or simply confused, 'raw data' was all they perceived, with the composer ducking the responsibility of bringing order to an arrangement of sounds. Another way of saying this: it was a matter of taste.

Taste was, of course, another mantra of the times, and, like variety, it could take on different inflections. Its most modern sense implied individual preference, the ability to choose, and it therefore presupposed a variety of things from which to choose. Those preferences might then be compared with those of others, making taste an instrument of social negotiation, something that was both personal and comparative. But that process could result in commonly agreed preferences, which might then mute the taste of the individual. A further relevant link in our chain of Enlightenment buzzwords is cosmopolitan. The stylistic orientation of galant music has often been thus described: for Daniel Heartz, for instance, the galant 'was little swayed by nationalism. It was, above all, cosmopolitan.'[242] This too can imply an acknowledgment of diversity, a worldly tolerance of difference. But, like taste, it may also acquire a more collective shading. As Roy Porter explains, a cosmopolitan attitude was underpinned by the belief that 'there was a single uniform human nature, all people being endowed with fundamentally the same attributes and desires';[243] particularities of custom, dress, spoken language and the like were decorative rather than fundamental. While this need not be seen as oppressive, since there is a benevolent side to this belief,[244] in musical practice a certain conformity did arise: cosmopolitan really meant Italian.

---

[242] Heartz, *Music in European Capitals*, xxii. For a case study of such cosmopolitanism in musical action see David Hennebelle, 'Nobles, musique et musiciens à Paris à la fin de l'Ancien Régime: les transformations d'un patronage séculaire (1760–1780)', *Revue de musicologie* 87/2 (2001), 395–418. The focus is on the patronage of Louis Duc de Noailles (1713–1793).

[243] Roy Porter, *The Enlightenment*, second edition (Basingstoke: Palgrave, 2001), 47.

[244] I allude here to the many negative critiques of what the Enlightenment stood for and accomplished, if anything heightened under a current prevailing regime whereby the particular, local and contingent are preferred terms of reference, against which Terry Eagleton, for instance, writes his defence of the concept of 'shared humanity: 'It is difficult for us to recapture the imaginative excitement that must have burst upon the world with the concept of universality. What could have sounded more scandalous to a profoundly particularist culture, one in which what you were was bound up with your region, function, social rank, than the extraordinary notion that everyone was entitled to individual respect quite independently of these things? . . . It was one of the greatest emancipatory ideas of world history, one that postmodernism has come so much to take for granted that it can apparently only identify it by its blind spots. Everyone's freedom mattered in theory, and "in theory" was a

That might be one reason to treat any musical application of the term with caution, but then the same might apply to 'taste' and 'variety'. Mary Helen McMurran notes that while *cosmopolite* and equivalents became used more frequently in the last quarter of the eighteenth century, to acknowledge one's allegiance to 'the great community that comprehends all mankind',[245] it hardly settled on an agreed definition. But this was no impediment; in fact, the lack of clear definition of what cosmopolitan entailed 'was an enabling condition for its discursive energy'.[246] Of course instrumental music, because of its 'universal' communicative capacities, had a better than even chance of deserving the epithet, for all its Italianate accents. The same productive fuzziness would obtain in the case of 'taste' and 'variety' – words of the moment that could be invoked in defence of various shades of opinion, words that could cover sins as well as express virtues.

As we have seen, one of the arenas in which variety was consistently called for was the salon. Conversation, verbal interaction with others, 'requires we should be in possession of various materials to keep it alive', as Knigge wrote.[247] But variety might not only be consciously sought during the conversational encounter, it could be a treated as a prerequisite. Thus the success of the Parisian salon of Madame Geoffrin (1699–1777) was said to be due not only to her moderating abilities when disagreements flared, but also to the fact that she would assemble a variety of temperaments and social stations: 'the reunion of all ranks, like that of all types of minds, prevented any one tone from dominating'.[248] This could just about pass as a global description of the aspirations of the mixed style as 'hosted' by composers of the time. But other forms of verbal variety could be considered. Reading practices seem to have changed over the eighteenth century in tandem with an exponential increase in the publication of journals, newspapers and weeklies. As James van Horn Melton describes it, alongside the older 'intensive' practices arose a new type of 'extensive' reading that consumed a wider range of material, more quickly.[249] The

sizeable improvement on its not mattering at all.' Eagleton, *The Illusions of Postmodernism* (Oxford: Blackwell, 1996), 112–113.

[245] Archibald Campbell, *An Enquiry into the Original of Moral Virtue* (Edinburgh, 1733), 62, cited in Mary Helen McMurran, 'The New Cosmopolitanism and the Eighteenth Century', *Eighteenth-Century Studies* 47/1 (2013), 30.

[246] McMurran, 'The New Cosmopolitanism', 32.

[247] Knigge, *Über den Umgang mit Menschen; Practical Philosophy of Social Life*, trans. Will, volume 2, 298.

[248] Antoine-Léonard Thomas, 'À la mémoire de Madame Geoffrin', in *Éloges de Mme Geoffrin*, ed. Morellet, 89, cited in translation in Goodman, *Republic of Letters*, 101.

[249] Melton, *Rise of the Public*, 91.

editors of the Stuttgart *Real-Zeitung* captured this in 1765 when stating that 'most inhabitants of our blessed territory have no particular inclination to read good and useful books... So we believed the easiest way to stimulate a taste for reading would be to publish a weekly that would cover diverse topics, alluring the reader through the variety of material'.[250] Once more a musical parallel readily suggests itself: music in the mixed style can be understood as a form of journalism, 'reporting' in short doses on what is happening 'out there' in the world.

Yet again, though, this raises the question of agency that we considered in specific relation to topics. Variety may be understood as a worldly property, a reflection of what is 'out there' – a matter of representation – but it can also be understood as an embodiment of personal experience – a matter of feeling, involving changing reactions to outer stimuli and, simply, changing moods within the individual. The latter perspective leaves aside the objectifying aspect of 'topic' and instead derives its sense from the trope of music as a language of feeling. In Diderot's *Le neveu de Rameau* the character 'Him' mimes the part of a harpsichordist playing Alberti or Galuppi: 'His features revealed the play of successive emotions: tenderness, fury, pleasure, pain. You could tell when he was playing *piano*, when *forte*.'[251] While hardly a straightforward endorsement, given that what is being described is a mute performance, this passage nevertheless testifies to a notion that galant music embodied a succession of feelings experienced by the individual. That same notion could be turned around and used as a means of attack. In 1746 Noël-Antoine Pluche wrote:

> In instrumental music [the composer] increased the various styles that are displayed..., and juxtaposed fast and slow passages, great noise [le grand fracas] and silence, then a long line of crackling sounds, jolts, and sudden bursts of fire.
>
> ... But we never think well of a mind that passes from sadness to great bursts of laughter, and from banter to seriousness, to tenderness, to anger, and to rage without having any cause to laugh or to become angry. Now, sonatas and many other types of music – are they anything but what we have just described?[252]

Here the understanding of variety as issuing from a single 'mind' is precisely what brings about accusations of incoherence and instability. While the fleeting feelings that are portrayed in Diderot's passage do not seem to be negatively charged in their own right, they do issue from a

---

[250] Cited in translation in Melton, *Rise of the Public*, 93 (italics removed from the final phrase).
[251] Diderot, *Rameau's Nephew*, trans. Mauldon, 22.
[252] Noël-Antoine Pluche, *Le spectacle de la nature*, seven volumes, volume 7 (Paris: chez la veuve Estienne, 1746), 115–116, cited in translation in *Music and Culture*, ed. Fubini, 83.

character who is unstable, if entertainingly so, and thus Diderot at least flirts with the negative line taken by Pluche. There might also be an element of codification in the portrayal of feeling, a sense that we are dealing with (known) affects or passions rather than (unpredictable) personal sentiment.[253] Any ambiguity is largely removed if the feelings are thought to reflect those of the composing agent, which had certainly become more common by the end of the century. In 1797 Boccherini was being described as 'the sentimentalist par excellence ... who is turn by turn somber, tender, heart-rending, graceful, and yet very gay, all by fits and starts'.[254] In this case the variety is plainly understood as an internal phenomenon, as representing the succession of feelings in one individual. 'Character' is another of our fundamental but slippery terms of reference that we might revisit at this point, since it was a further means of trying to deal with the ambiguities of agency generated by the changeable modern instrumental style. It too could be applied against that style – as in the critical demands that a piece of music should embody one recognizable, stable character – as well as in favour of it, and it too could be understood as a question of representation or one of individual temperament, a complex bundle of feelings held within a single experiencing subject.[255]

Another term that could be used either to undermine or to uphold modern musical variety was 'natural'. It too derived great discursive energy from its slipperiness of definition. One proponent, Daube, compares 'the art(fulness) of the old music with the grace and natural beauty of the modern variety [die Kunst der alten Musik mit der Anmuth und natürlichen Schönheit der itzigen]', thus finding the free modern style

---

[253] On the distinction between passion and sentiment, and the history of how one is supplanted by the other, see Cowart, 'Sense and Sensibility'.

[254] Anonymous reviewer ('P') of Grétry, *Mémoires, ou essais sur la musique*, *Journal des savans* (1797), 171, cited in translation in Heartz, *Music in European Capitals*, 995.

[255] In his discussion of Christian Gottfried Körner's 1795 essay 'On the Representation of Character in Music' Matthew Pritchard argues that, for Körner, character could only be inferred by the listening subject: 'the creation of character was not the sole responsibility of the composer, but invited, and indeed required, the participation of the listener and his or her imagination. It was this *freedom* in the imaginative creation of character', on the part of both composer and listener, 'that for Körner, as for Kant and Schiller, was of the greatest aesthetic worth.' Pritchard, 'The Moral Background of the Work of Art', 71. The last sentence here makes clear that Pritchard sees this as a romantic, idealist project, whereas I would argue that a stress on the agency and responsibility of the listener is already fully in place before the very late eighteenth century – even if that may not be reflected in the literature of earlier decades. See also Craig Comen, 'Hoffmann's Musical Modernity and the Pursuit of Sentimental Unity', *Eighteenth-Century Music* 15/1 (2018), whose summation of the matter is: 'To say that a musical work had a character was to claim that the work cohered in spite of its fragmented appearance.' (23)

more 'natural' than that of the 'ancients',[256] but through his comparison of an instrumental discourse with the operations of the human mind Pluche clearly feels otherwise: any mind that passes through a series of unrelated moods is not of a normal kind. But Burney wrote that 'a liberal and enlightened musician, and hearer of music, receives pleasure from various styles and effects', implying that we are naturally disposed towards variety – at least those listeners who are sympathetic to the modern manner, as 'liberal and enlightened' might suggest.[257] And if an inclination towards variety in all things was not natural, it needed to be cultivated. This is apparent in that idealized figure of the time, the man of letters, who would show a variety of interests, would be able to discourse on a variety of subjects, rather than having a narrow interest in a few.[258] One can see this translated into musical terms by C. P. E. Bach in his autobiography: 'Since I have never liked excessive uniformity in composition and taste, ... and since I have always been of the opinion that one may make use of good elements wherever they may be found ... it is presumably precisely these considerations ... that explain the variety noticed in my work.'[259]

The charge from opponents that the new style lacked control did not have to be framed in terms of affect. It could be made on a more formal level, on the hallowed basis of unity, a unity that had to be materially apparent. But this demand was in fact often justified by invoking affect, as Sulzer did when stating that 'the main phrase' of a movement should be 'repeated with these connecting ideas in various harmonies and keys and with little melodic variations appropriate to the main expression until the listener's spirit is sufficiently taken by the sentiment and has, as it were,

---

[256] Daube, *Der musikalische Dilettant*, 332 (my translation). To clarify, Daube is at this point proposing that the virtues of older and newer manners are combined, rather than simply glorifying modern music.

[257] Charles Burney, review of William Jackson, *Observations on the Present State of Music*, in London, *Monthly Review* (October 1791), 198. The complete review is cited in Landon, *Haydn: Chronicle and Works*, volume 3: *Haydn in England, 1791–1795* (London: Thames and Hudson, 1976), 100–104.

[258] See the characterization given by Antoine Lilti: 'The man of letters was distinguished by his lack of specialization, by his capacity for excelling in different literary genres, by his mastery of codes of behavior elaborated by the urban aristocracy, and by a disinterest in things financial. ... For Voltaire, the man of letters could "proceed from the thorns of mathematics to the flowers of poetry, and judge equally well a book of metaphysics and a work of drama".' Lilti, *World of the Salons*, 109.

[259] Carl Philipp Emanuel Bach, autobiography, in *Carl Burney's der Musik Doktors Tagebuch seiner musikalischen Reisen*, volume 3: *Durch Böhmen, Sachsen, Brandenburg, Hamburg und Holland* (Hamburg: Bode, 1773), 208, cited in translation in Christopher Hogwood, Introduction to *'Kenner und Liebhaber' Collections I*, Carl Philip Emanuel Bach: The Complete Works, series 1, volume 4.1, ed. Hogwood (Los Altos: Packard Humanities Institute, 2009), xv.

sensed it from all sides'.²⁶⁰ Without such a thematic and affective focus (which clearly does admit variety on its own terms) there would be nothing for the listener to hold on to. There would be 'nothing for the heart', a common frame of reference in the criticism of modern variety. A Koch polemic against an unnamed symphony (which Felix Diergarten believes to be one by Haydn, and probably the conspicuously varied Symphony No. 60) proceeded: 'composers have tried to introduce characteristic pieces whose characteristic aspect is not feeling but play for the mind [*Spielwerk für den Verstand*] . . . Instead of using art to work on the heart, they try to occupy the minds of the listeners with wit'.²⁶¹ Here variety has precisely left the realms of sentiment and has become a kind of mental gymnastics.

However, one should not imagine that unity was a criterion that was abandoned by the moderns in debates about the nature of modern instrumental style – that their vaunted 'variety' was as unprincipled as the ancients could make it sound. In her reflections on this issue Judith L. Schwartz contrasts an 'older, single-theme notion of unity' with a 'newer conception subsuming striking thematic contrast', whereby 'complementarity of contrasting ideas' becomes 'a binding force'.²⁶² This newer conception encompasses the principles of reciprocity and periodicity that have formed the focus for the whole of this chapter; they can be taken to offer 'unity' of a different kind, one that arises out of an acknowledgment of difference. There was also a tribal dimension to the debate. Schwartz encapsulates it thus: 'Those who found pleasure in distinctive thematic contrasts were typically pro-Italian', while 'those who upheld narrower standards of thematic unity tended to be staunch supporters of their local musical traditions, whether German, French, or English (meaning for the most part Handelian or Corellian).'²⁶³ This is nicely put given that much of the focus for scholarship on the later eighteenth century has been on (North) German critics of the newer ways. It also reinforces our equation that the varied modern 'cosmopolitan' style was in fact fundamentally

---

²⁶⁰ Sulzer, *Allgemeine Theorie der Schönen Künste*, volume 1, 522, cited in translation in Matthew Riley, *Musical Listening in the German Enlightenment: Attention, Wonder and Astonishment* (Aldershot: Ashgate, 2004), 9.
²⁶¹ Koch, *Versuch einer Anleitung zur Komposition*, volume 2, 40, cited in Felix Diergarten, 'At Times Even Homer Nods Off' www.mtosmt.org (10 February 2012). Diergarten gives the translation from *Aesthetics and the Art of Musical Composition in the German Enlightenment*, ed. Baker and Christensen, 155, but I have here used my own.
²⁶² Judith L. Schwartz, 'Conceptions of Musical Unity in the 18th Century', *The Journal of Musicology* 18/1 (2001), 57.
²⁶³ Schwartz, 'Conceptions of Musical Unity', 59.

Italian, either by association or because of the weight of the Italian musical diaspora across the continent during the eighteenth century.

That cosmopolitan – and more broadly 'modern variety' – meant Italian may be seen from a weight of negative testimony from that time. Its negativity is in fact useful from our point of view, since it helps to provide a sharp perceptual edge to variety, to rescue it from the aura of blandness that often settles over favoured terms of reference for later eighteenth-century instrumental style. Against this testimony we must weigh the success of modern variety with paying customers (including of course patrons and noble employers): if it wasn't working, it wouldn't have continued to be offered. This helps to explain the defensiveness of much of the more disparaging discourse.

Complaints, however, did not have to refer specifically to Italians or Italianism. Pluche's description of an instrumental work jerking implausibly between different states of mind does not do so. Joseph Fowke, a diamond merchant living in Calcutta, and a card-carrying member of the 'ancients', focussed specifically on the figure of Haydn, who was certainly as good an individual target as any. In a letter of 1785 he wrote of the 'nonsensical compositions of that Prince of Coxcombs – Haydn', whose success clearly showed that 'fashion governs the world in music as it does in dress'.[264] Haydn's music, personified as a composer who was all show and no substance, is nonsense in the same way that 'sonatas' in general were nonsense to Pluche. One other aspect of Pluche's complaint might be returned to at this point, his description of composers 'juxtapos[ing] fast and slow passages, great noise and silence, then a long line of crackling sounds, jolts, and sudden bursts of fire'. This is a rather poetic way of making a very characteristic complaint from the time – that modern music was noisy. Joseph Fowke's reference to Haydn as 'Prince of Coxcombs' in fact provides a visual equivalent to this: the composer was, as it were, loudly dressed.

When 'noise' became a term of reference, the Italians were usually to be found in the near vicinity. In *Le neveu de Rameau* the character of 'Him', referring to the *querelle des bouffons* of the earlier 1750s, notes that for the defenders of French ways the *bouffons* were offering 'trashy fairground music'.[265] This associates Italian music with the cheap and nasty, and undoubtedly noisy. For Johann Christoph Gottsched in 1754, Italian

---

[264] Ian Woodfield, 'Haydn Symphonies in Calcutta' (Correspondence), *Music & Letters* 75/1 (1994), 142.

[265] Diderot, *Rameau's Nephew*, trans. Mauldon, 65.

instrumental works represented 'a mere jangle [ein blosses Geklingel]',[266] while in 1774 Johann Abraham Peter Schulz criticized 'the Italians and their imitators' for producing 'a great noise of notes following randomly one after another [ein Geräusch von willkührlich auf einander folgenden Tönen]'.[267] One such imitator was Ferdinand Fischer, who was criticized in a review of 1766 for producing 'Symphonies that are full of the Impotent, the Unmelodic, the Vulgar, the Farcical and the Chopped-up, plus the feverish attacks of alternating *Piano* and *Forte* that you find in the latest Italian fashion composers'.[268] These testaments to meaningless noise all reinforce the worldly side of modern variety, the sense of something that was directed outwards in order to catch the ears of the masses. And for such critics, because nothing remained in the heart from this mere outward show, variety became noisy monotony. The complaints surely also go beyond the literal; they testify to the cognitive 'noise' that would have been experienced when confronted with a music that presented too much to take in too quickly.

However, similar terms of reference could turn up in surprising places. Haydn, who suffered severely enough at the hands of North German critics on this score (recall Koch's criticisms above),[269] recounted in his old age to biographer Georg August Griesinger that he attempted when composing 'to develop and sustain [an idea] in keeping with the rules of the art'. However, that 'is what so many younger composers lack: they string one little idea after another; they break off when they have scarcely begun'. This meant that 'nothing remains in the heart'.[270] Given his immense celebrity at the time when the composer made these reported remarks to Griesinger,

---

[266] Johann Christoph Gottsched, *Auszug aus des Herrn Batteux schönen Künsten aus dem einzigen Grundsätze der Nachahmung hergeleitet* (Leipzig: Breitkopf, 1754), 201, cited in translation in Bellamy Hosler, *Changing Aesthetic Views of Instrumental Music in 18th-Century Germany* (Ann Arbor: UMI, 1981), 3.

[267] [Johann Abraham Peter Schulz,] 'Sonate', in Sulzer, *Allgemeine Theorie der Schönen Künste*, volume 2, 1095.

[268] Anonymous, *Allgemeine deutsche Bibliothek* 2/1 (1766), cited in Morrow, *German Music Criticism*, 51 (translation) and 181 (German original).

[269] In his 'Becoming Original: Haydn and the Cult of Genius', *The Musical Quarterly* 87/2 (2004), 335, Thomas Bauman wonders who 'the shadowy "nobody"' was to whom Haydn was referring in his conversation with Griesinger when he said 'there was nobody in my vicinity to confuse and annoy me in my course'. For Bauman, 'the image of a distant, irritating, captious "nobody"' must refer to 'the tribe of North German music critics whose aesthetic conservatism exercised itself with schoolmasterly rigor on the new musical rhetoric of Haydn and other Viennese composers'.

[270] Georg August Griesinger, *Biographische Notizen über Joseph Haydn* (Leipzig: Breitkopf & Härtel, 1810), 114, cited in translation in James Webster, 'Haydn's Sensibility', *Studia musicologica* 51/1–2 (2010), 19.

Haydn may well have felt in a position to turn upon other composers the criticisms that had once been levelled at himself – and to be fair, his ability to 'draw such rich and varied developments' from one idea, as a reviewer in the *Mercure de France* put it,[271] had become something of a creative trademark.

But if we are inclined to let Haydn off the hook here, it might be harder to do so in the case of Dittersdorf. In his autobiography the composer tells us of a conversation with Joseph II about the music of Mozart, who has 'such an amazing wealth of ideas; I could almost wish he were not so lavish in using them. He leaves his hearer out of breath; for hardly has he grasped one beautiful thought, when another of greater fascination dispels the first, and this goes on throughout, so that in the end it is impossible to retain any one of these beautiful melodies.'[272] Unsurprisingly, this passage has been quoted to death, since it helps to sustain an important aspect of the Mozart mythology – that he was too good for the listeners of his time – but it is a bit rich for Dittersdorf of all figures to find this fault in the music of another composer, given how 'mixed' his own manner is. We have touched several times already on the brazen style of contrast favoured by Dittersdorf, which caused Johann Karl Friedrich Triest, in his overview of eighteenth-century German music, to place the composer in the category of thematic spendthrifts: 'he wrote too much' and 'succumbed too easily to the general tendency to write mixed compositions [gab auch er dem allgemeinen Hange zu gemischten Kompositionen zu sehr nach]'.[273] Further evidence that the operating principle was 'do what I say, not what I do' is that Dittersdorf felt able to satirize the Italian manner in the second movement of his *Sinfonia nazionale nel gusto di cinque nazioni*, which is crude and 'noisy'.[274] Dittersdorf's characterization of a highly paratactic style – one thing after another, so that nothing really remains – clearly recalls Haydn's

---

[271] Anonymous, 'Spectacles: Concert Spirituel', *Mercure de France* (12 April 1788), 77, cited in translation in Bernard Harrison, *Haydn: The 'Paris' Symphonies* (Cambridge: Cambridge University Press, 1998), 22.

[272] Dittersdorf, *Autobiography of Karl von Dittersdorf*, trans. Coleridge, 251–252.

[273] Johann Karl Friedrich Triest, 'Bemerkungen über die Ausbildung der Tonkunst in Deutschland im achtzehnten Jahrhundert, *Allgemeine musikalische Zeitung* 3 (25 February 1801), column 378; 'Remarks on the Development of the Art of Music in Germany in the Eighteenth Century', in *Haydn and His World* (Princeton: Princeton University Press, 1997), ed. Elaine Sisman, trans. Susan Gillespie, 362.

[274] Elsewhere in his autobiography Dittersdorf recounts a visit to Parma, during which he heard *Catone in Utica* by J. C. Bach. He notes that while some of the airs were beautiful, 'the main body of the work was written very sketchily, after the Italian style'. Dittersdorf must therefore have been thinking of himself as a 'good German' composer in this regard. Dittersdorf, *Autobiography of Karl von Dittersdorf*, trans. Coleridge, 125.

complaint, and taps into a familiar source of pejorative imagery about modern musical style. What may be positively viewed as (my) pleasing variety becomes negatively viewed as (your) uncontrolled proliferation.

One of the most eloquent hostile witnesses to contemporary musical developments was Schubart. As we have seen, he hoped that music would in the future be able to recover its 'former dignity and sublimity', having been led astray by the 'taste for the comic' and the accompanying tedium of 'the ever-present caesuras'. It was 'the ever more destructive search for smallness among the moderns [die immer mehr einreißende Kleinheitssucht der Neueren]' that had 'all but eliminated the taste for such gigantic pieces' as the 'original genius' J. S. Bach had written.[275] One symptom of this 'smallness' was undoubtedly the quick passing from one musical event to the next, so injurious to the dignity of the art. Of particular note is how Schubart holds C. P. E. Bach aloof from his critique. While there was some truth to accusations of 'capricious taste [and] frequent oddities' against this 'extraordinary genius', and while in response 'one notices in his newest pieces some concession to the spirit of the times', the composer 'never descend[s] to the reigning spirit of pettiness [*Kleinheit*]'.[276] This echoes many similar treatments of C. P. E. Bach from northern Germany. Sulzer, for instance, lauded the 'character and expression' with which 'our Hamburg Bach' managed to infuse his sonatas, so unlike the 'cacophony of arbitrarily connected tones' that he heard in 'today's Italian sonatas'.[277] In all such cases it is a puzzle how to reconcile such critical views with the patent eccentricities and mood swings of the compositional output; as we noted above, while Bach has barely featured at all in the literature on musical topics, no music of the later eighteenth century is more changeable, moment by moment, than his. It seems hard to look beyond pure parochialism as an explanation.

One leitmotif that marks Schubart's discussion of individual composers is composing for oneself, with integrity, as opposed to debasing oneself for the sake of wider public taste. Schobert, for example, who had 'set the fashion in France', had to 'compose ... much for students of a moderate capacity'. Yet 'Whatever he composed for himself was always written in the

---

[275] Schubart, *Ideen zu einer Ästhetik der Tonkunst*, 108; DuBois, 'Schubart's *Ideen zu einer Ästhetik einer Tonkunst*: Annotated Translation', 151.

[276] Schubart, *Ideen zu einer Ästhetik der Tonkunst*, 185–186; DuBois, 'Schubart's *Ideen zu einer Ästhetik einer Tonkunst*: Annotated Translation', 232–233.

[277] Sulzer, *Allgemeine Theorie der Schönen Künste*, volume 4, 425, cited in translation in *Aesthetics and the Art of Musical Composition in the German Enlightenment*, ed. and trans. Baker and Christensen, 104.

best style and repeatedly gave evidence of traces of a fiery soul.'[278] On the other hand, Dittersdorf, whose acumen for comic opera is noted, 'has a completely individual manner which degenerates only too often into burlesque and vulgar comedy [Niedrigkomische]. One often has to burst out laughing loudly in the midst of a stream of sentiments because he blends into his pictures such checkered passages.'[279] Once more mixed musical manners occasion disapproval, though presumably the laughter brings at least temporary pleasure. Still more compromised artistically was J. C. Bach, who was all too happy to 'submit himself to the trivial spirit of the masses'.[280] According to Schubart, 'His brother in Hamburg [C. P. E. Bach] often wrote to him "Don't turn into a child!" But he always replied "I have to babble so that the children can understand me."' ('Sein Bruder in Hamburg schrieb ihm öfters "Werde kein Kind!" Er aber antwortete immer "Ich muß stammeln, damit mich die Kinder verstehen."')[281] Schubart had no doubt about the London Bach's vast talents, but summed up his ultimate artistic failure thus: 'His adoption of the fashionable taste, his often too great complaisance, his pleasing condescension to the people's taste, his trifling which so ill suited his great mind, facility in his composition despite his natural inclination to severity – all these things originated from his all too great love for the female sex. He was the darling of English women.'[282] This startling passage shows that the negative press could have its gendered as well as national component; it brings in yet another item to our collocation of disapproving terms for the modern varied and pleasing style, which might run something like Italian-superficial-fashionable-easy-feminine-noisy-chatty, and we could readily add more.[283]

Schubart's approach to the music of his time is considerably more nuanced than the excerpts I have offered above might seem to suggest. But his particular value in the current context is that he offers a whole cluster of ideas – his appeal to qualities like the 'serious, heroic and tragic', a

---

[278] Schubart, *Ideen zu einer Ästhetik der Tonkunst*, 236–237; DuBois, 'Schubart's *Ideen zu einer Ästhetik einer Tonkunst*: Annotated Translation', 284–285.

[279] Schubart, *Ideen zu einer Ästhetik der Tonkunst*, 239–240; DuBois, 'Schubart's *Ideen zu einer Ästhetik einer Tonkunst*: Annotated Translation', 288.

[280] Schubart, *Ideen zu einer Ästhetik der Tonkunst*, 208; DuBois, 'Schubart's *Ideen zu einer Ästhetik einer Tonkunst*: Annotated Translation', 255.

[281] Schubart, *Ideen zu einer Ästhetik der Tonkunst*, 209 (my translation).

[282] Schubart, *Ideen zu einer Ästhetik der Tonkunst*, 210–211; DuBois, 'Schubart's *Ideen zu einer Ästhetik einer Tonkunst*: Annotated Translation', 257.

[283] For one examination of such an equation in this cultural context see Matthew Head, '"Like Beauty Spots on the Face of a Man": Gender in 18th-Century North-German Discourse on Genre', *The Journal of Musicology* 13/2 (1995), 143–167.

deep suspicion of the listening public and their predominantly trivial tastes, and the notion that the best musical art is done solely for the composer's own satisfaction – that will soon become a more dominant discourse, and one that has hardly lost its force through to the present day. Much of his rhetoric, and that of his fellow nay-sayers, feels defensive, and indeed they may be said to have lost the battle, at least in their own lifetimes. Yet they also assuredly won the war.

It is also important to dwell on such views as a reminder that what I am characterizing as musical sociability was a contested phenomenon. It was not universally acclaimed, even if it had indeed become the 'cosmopolitan' default modern style of instrumental music; and where it did exist, it came in many shades of conception and execution. C. P. E. Bach himself is a model example. To take him at his word alone, he may indeed have distinguished between writing for himself, when one could 'allow [one's] diligence full rein', and writing 'things that are to be printed, and therefore are for everyone', where one had to 'be less artistic and give more sugar'.[284] Yet we have also seen him endorse that mantra of his times: a search for continual variety, that spice of contemporary musical life. And certainly much of his musical output provides plenty of that 'raw data' that would keep the listener constantly stimulated – or, alternatively, confused.

One means of trying to control the contemporary reception history of galant style has been to pitch the north against the south. Schwartz does this relatively indirectly in her characterization of two camps on the matter of musical unity, and we noted her inclusion of French, English and German critics among the representatives of the north. For Dahlhaus the north is a more exclusively German one, but he also offers a broader religious explanation for hostilities: 'Viennese Classicism was part of a southern Catholic tradition', as opposed to the musical aesthetics of 'Protestant North Germany'.[285] This has also received a broader confirmation in Holly Watkins's association of the critical rhetoric of 'depth' with Pietist culture in particular, which 'represented an intensification of Lutheran inwardness'.[286] However, such equations were not unknown at the time. In Burney's diplomatic parlance, it was a matter of climate:

---

[284] C. P. E. Bach, letter to Johann Christoph Kühnau, 31 August 1784, cited in translation in Jonatan Bar-Yoshafat, '*Kenner und Liebhaber*: Yet Another Look', *International Review of the Aesthetics and Sociology of Music* 44/1 (2013), 28 (translation modified from that in *Letters of C. P. E. Bach*, ed. and trans. Clark, 213).

[285] Dahlhaus, *Die Musik des 18. Jahrhunderts*, 339.

[286] Holly Watkins, 'From the Mine to the Shrine: The Critical Origins of Musical Depth', *19th-Century Music* 27/3 (2004), 182.

'Climate seems to operate so much on Music ... that what is admired in one country is detested in another. In cold climates *labour* is necessary to circulation; in hot, *ease* is the grand desideratum. The principle is carried to such excess in Italy, that whatever gives the hearer of Music the least trouble to disentangle, is Gothic, pedantic, and *scelerata*.'[287] This reminds us that the negative press could certainly also run the other way, against the earnestly laboured and learned. But the larger point is that the north–south equation is only a useful shorthand. Burney himself, to name but one northern advocate of the modern manner, was hardly the progeny of a southern Catholic culture. We have already noted Dittersdorf's satirical treatment of Italian style in his *Sinfonia nazionale nel gusto di cinque nazioni*. And while Mozart and Haydn may both confessionally and musically fall more or less into the southern camp, that did not equate to any sort of solidarity. Haydn was very quick to dismiss any influence from the Milanese Sammartini on his early quartets, calling him a 'Schmierer' (hack writer),[288] while acknowledging C. P. E. Bach as an inspiration. Then there is Mozart's famous racist rant against Clementi, who, 'like all Italians', was a '*ciarlatano*'.[289]

And against all this, an even larger point needs to be made. There is simply a lack of weight of words on what musicians thought they were writing or playing and what listeners thought they were hearing – at least in comparison with the far greater critical mass that makes writing about music of the nineteenth century and later a much more comfortable occupation. And once more this is not just a product of later perception. Burney himself had noted that 'musical criticism has been so little cultivated in our country, that its first elements are hardly known', and the only exception he knew of was Avison's *Essay on Musical Expression*. Burney was specifically excluding treatises on composition and performance; what he meant, as we saw in Chapter 1, was works that could 'instruct ignorant lovers of Music how to listen, or to judge for themselves'.[290] Burney later noted that across Europe as a whole, only Germany provided an

---

[287] Burney, *General History of Music, Volume the Second*, 931. Elsewhere Burney rather confirms the confessional equation of Dahlhaus when he writes 'there seems an unwillingness in the inhabitants of the protestant states of Germany to allow due praise, even to the musical works and opinions of the Catholics. And, on the contrary, the Catholics appear equally unwilling to listen to the musical strains of the Protestants.' *General History of Music, Volume the Second*, 950.

[288] Griesinger, *Biographische Notizen*, 15, cited in translation in Elaine Sisman, 'Haydn, Shakespeare, and the Rules of Originality', in *Haydn and His World*, ed. Sisman, 4.

[289] Mozart, letter to Leopold Mozart, 7 June 1783; *Letters of Mozart*, ed. and trans. Anderson, 850.

[290] Burney, *General History of Music, Volume the Second*, 7–8.

exception,[291] and that is, of course, precisely where the most concentrated opposition to modern variety was articulated.

But even there a different overview might be taken. Writing in 1801, Triest noted that 'During [the] general expansion of the amateur engagement with music [toward the end of the past century], the *theory* and the *literature* of music did not entirely fail to progress, even if they have had slight influence, *until now*, on the *course* of music itself.'[292] Considering this scholarly difficulty in more recent times, William Weber states plainly 'We just do not know what musicians thought analytically about the music they heard and read.' He continues: 'Books of musical rules usually represented the most conservative side of musical taste; the intellectually most vital side of that field remained a spoken tradition among the musically educated.'[293] A nice concrete example of that might be the visit to Eszterháza in October 1785 of the Venezualan military leader and revolutionary Francisco de Miranda (1750–1816), who reported that he spent much of his two days there talking music with Haydn, including discussing the merits of Boccherini's music;[294] this also reminds us that, given the flourishing market for published instrumental music, composers at this time undoubtedly knew more music than we might imagine they did. Many other recent writers have commented on the apparent gap between the theory and the predominant musical practice of the later eighteenth century; David Schroeder, for instance, sees an 'eerie cleft between theory and practice' and 'little connection between the music of the time and aesthetic opinion'.[295] But in naming Sulzer as a prime example of the seeming estrangement of the two domains, he shows how much our view has been skewed by the relative weight of German critical writings.

There might be a more positive interpretation to be put on this negative, though, at least in the cases of several famous figures. Caroline Pichler knew both Haydn and Mozart when she was a girl, and would later lead an eminent salon as she attained fame as a historical novelist. In her

---

[291] Burney, *General History of Music, Volume the Second*, 947: 'the great number of books of instruction and criticism on the subject of Music, which have been published during the present century chiefly in the German language'.

[292] Triest, 'Bemerkungen über die Ausbildung der Tonkunst', *Allgemeine musikalische Zeitung* 3 (25 March 1801), column 437; 'Remarks on the Development of the Art of Music, trans. Gillespie, 381.

[293] William Weber, 'The Contemporaneity of Eighteenth-Century Musical Taste', *The Musical Quarterly* 70/2 (1984), 186–187.

[294] Robert Stevenson, 'Los contactos de Haydn con el mundo ibérico', *Revista Musical Chilena* 36/157 (1982), 19–20.

[295] David Schroeder, 'Listening, Thinking and Writing', in *The Cambridge History of Eighteenth-Century Music*, ed. Simon P. Keefe (Cambridge: Cambridge University Press, 2009), 188.

reminiscences (*Denkwürdigkeiten aus meinem Leben*), published in Vienna in 1844, Pichler was considering the 'mysterious' nature of artistic creativity when she wrote:

> People to whom nature has given other capacities can have no idea of what goes on in the soul of a poet. . . . Perhaps one of the most remarkable puzzles involves the aptitude for music and composition. . . . There is something wonderful and mysterious in having a feeling for music [*Sinn für Harmonie*] and even more in the capacity to make up harmonies and melodies oneself. It is often found in people who aside from this heavenly gift have few mental capacities or even little education. They themselves have no clear idea of their capacities, and still less of the process that goes on inside them . . . Mozart and Haydn, whom I knew well, were people who in their personal dealings showed absolutely no outstanding mental capacities or education . . . An ordinary character, flat jokes, and with the former a thoughtless lifestyle were all that they showed in their relations, and yet what depths, what worlds of fantasy, harmony, melody and feeling lay hidden within these unprepossessing exteriors. What inner phenomena gave them the understanding of how to go about conveying such powerful effects and feelings?[296]

Whether Pichler truly thought like that when she encountered the composers, in the 1780s and 1790s, by the time she put her reminiscences together, well into the nineteenth century, her strains of expressing one's inner urges, of difficult creation that is inaccessible to the ordinary person, and above all of 'depth' obviously owe much to a later ideology of creativity. (Or at least it shows the triumph of the sort of outlook represented by Schubart.[297]) Assuming that her characterization of Haydn and Mozart's social behaviour contains some grain of truth, and assuming that we may make a connection between that behaviour and their musical practices, it suggests what one might call a sociable orientation: it shows the two not wishing to dominate, emphasizing humour, being perhaps studiedly unpretentious. Pichler's account does demonstrate that many others who frequented the salons were happier to 'show their depths'. Of course musicians were bound to be at some disadvantage in such situations, given that their professional skills would not necessarily demand high levels of verbal dexterity. Even James Webster makes a revealing comment in this regard when writing that Haydn 'circulated . . . with intellectuals

---

[296] Caroline Pichler, *Denkwürdigkeiten aus meinem Leben* (Vienna, 1844), ed. Emil Karl Blümml, two volumes (Munich: Georg Müller, 1914), volume 1, 293–294.

[297] In this connection one might recall Dahlhaus's aphorism that Romanticism was 'the *Empfindsamkeit* of the eighteenth century become the popular aesthetics of the nineteenth century'. Dahlhaus, *Die Music des 18. Jahrhunderts*, 68.

and freemasons, albeit without pretensions to being an intellectual himself';[298] yet who could have been more 'intellectual' in his chosen field than Haydn? Pichler's characterization might also inadvertently pinpoint an important element of creativity in later eighteenth-century music: that it was down to earth, more emerging from common properties than 'coming down from on high'. Trading on the everyday, which meant having a regard not just for familiarity but also for the variety that was out there in the musical world, was central. This also meant being set firmly against pretentiousness. As above, this might be a character trait as well as an artistic orientation. Haydn's biographer Dies combined the two when he remarked that Haydn 'never boasted of his accomplishments and entirely eschewed the wordy pomp of learned phrases. That may be the reason why in general he suffered Mozart's fate and, like him, was taken for an empiricist [ein Empyriker genannt ward].'[299] 'Empiricism', which clearly includes attributes such as a modest demeanour and receptiveness to a range of experiences, is a nice ingredient to add into the mix when we consider the nature of later eighteenth-century instrumental music.

[298] James Webster and Georg Feder, 'Haydn, (Franz) Joseph', in *Grove Music Online* www.oxfordmusiconline.com (30 October 2017).
[299] Dies, *Biographische Nachrichten von Joseph Haydn*, 23, cited in translation in Landon, *Haydn: Chronicle and Works*, volume 1: *Haydn: The Early Years, 1732–1765* (London: Thames and Hudson, 1980), 42.

3 | Formula

Convention

As we have already seen, the notion of a distinctive authorial voice emerged strongly in connection with our later eighteenth-century instrumental repertory. From the point of view of contemporary reception, this was one means of trying to control the understanding of a proliferating product. On the creative side, composers were leaving traces of their agency everywhere; the music they were providing was patently 'made', most obviously in cases of interference with a normal course of events, but also simply through variety of material. If this music was subject to more or less unpredictable change, both texturally and topically, who was pulling the strings except the composer? On the other hand, from the point of view of subsequent reception our era has an unparalleled reputation for conventionality – an era of quick, cheap, more or less anonymous mass production, with only a few individual brands having stayed the course through to posterity. And those brands have done so, so the story goes, by in various ways resisting the demands placed upon them by convention. 'Convention' here covers both the general expressive constriction that is often thought to characterize this music, as well as the specific units of sound that we recognize in their recurrence from piece to piece.

There is little doubt that, in the latter sense, some of this reputation is well merited. A relatively high level of syntactical-structural formality marks the style as a whole – hence the magnetic pull it has exerted on generations of theorists of form – and there is a sense of familiarity to many of its materials and typical concatenations of the same – hence the more recent appearances of topic and schema theories that attempt to classify those materials. More broadly, there is no real equivalent in other style periods of Western music for the sustained level of taxonomic activity that this repertory has inspired. On the other hand, from a historical point of view, this is not so much a formal as a distinctly informal style: its frequent juxtapositions and contrasts were perceived by many of the older school as a lack of 'good continuation', and its predilection for popular-sounding materials could be quite shameless. Then there are all the comic registers that might seem hardly compatible with the formal or the systematic, let alone with the image of an emotionally constricted conventionality. Further, we might recall the phenomenon of highly individualized motives discussed in the previous chapter, which give such a strong sense of particularity to the movements in which they are heard. That in spite of such features an undeniable sense of familiarity emerges from this repertory is a conundrum we have already considered. It is not as if familiar repeated features – conventions – are not found in baroque music, nor indeed in the music of the nineteenth century, even if few have cared to seek them out,[1] so why the lasting image? As I have suggested before, the difference seems to derive from the packaging, and this is above all a matter of large-scale rhythm, which we try to capture with reference to such terms as periodicity and reciprocity. This could be regarded as a triumph of accessibility, though the matter has rarely been conceived in such positive terms. Instead, the bogeyman of convention haunts the repertory.

Yet those who were inside the system – at least those who were positively disposed towards the modern musical style – do not seem to have seen things this way. In Chapter 1 we were able to cite pairings of composers with particular essential attributes ('Vanhall's liveliness', '[C. P. E.] Bach's seriousness', 'Kozeluch or Clementi's passion'), suggesting that the composers were readily distinguishable from one another. Certainly, the ability to deliver something fresh was often a matter of comment. The contemporary reception of the later Haydn in particular was for ever stressing the newness of his works, and in 1790 Ernst Ludwig Gerber praised his hero Boccherini with the exclamation 'notwithstanding the great quantity of his compositions, how ever new and almost inexhaustible!'.[2] Conversely, the inability to rise above the routine might not go down well. A reviewer in the *Musikalische Real-Zeitung* of sonatas by Johann Friedrich Schmoll (1739–1794) 'couldn't find a single thought that distinguished itself either through the allure of novelty *per se* or through a new presentation, like you find in

---

[1] For a recent serious attempt to grapple with specific conventions in the 'romantic' century see Michael Weiss, 'Theoretical and Analytical Reflections on the Role of Robert O. Gjerdingen's Galant Schemata in Nineteenth-Century Composition' (PhD dissertation, University of Auckland, 2018).

[2] Ernst Ludwig Gerber, 'Boccherini', in *Historische-Bibliographisches Lexikon der Tonkünstler*, two volumes, volume 1 (Leipzig: Breitkopf, 1790), column 174, cited in translation in Heartz, *Music in European Capitals*, 996.

the works of a Haydn or Kozeluch'.[3] The notion that novelty is not just an absolute quantity but also a relative one – that it could derive from making fresh what is familiar – was a fundamental aspect of the musical creativity of the time. Burney, though, seems to have understood the equation differently when he reported, 'it has already been remarked by critical observers, that [Pleyel's] fancy, though at first so fertile, is not so inexhaustible, but that he frequently repeats himself, and does not sufficiently disdain the mixture of common passages with his own elegant ideas'.[4] Here there is a more straightforward distinction between 'fertile' individual creativity and those 'common passages' that suggest a failure of creative imagination ('fancy'). But another part of the diagnosis involves the fact that Pleyel borrows, not so much from some sort of shared reserve of the commonplace, but directly from himself.

Both of these passages suggest that novelty could indeed be conceived in quite absolute terms. And some composers certainly claimed the same. In 1784 Mozart wrote to his father of his opera *L'oca del Cairo*: 'I guarantee that in all the operas which are to be performed until mine is finished, not a single idea will resemble one of mine.'[5] Significant here is that the composer focusses on 'novelty *per se*' rather than a 'new presentation' of existing ideas, in other words on the material itself rather than how it is manipulated. This corresponds to artistic originality in its 'strong' modern sense – creation out of nothing, as it were. Haydn, at least in later life, was also very keen to claim originality for his achievements, in a famous statement to Griesinger, which finishes with the phrase 'so mußte ich original werden' (and so I had to become original). This phrase itself could take several interpretations, as indeed could the larger passage from which it derives,[6] but it is sufficient to note here that the composer felt he was doing something different from his peers, something peculiar to himself that needed defending both from imitators and detractors (which was certainly one of the composer's motivations for the statement in the first place). Haydn was

---

[3] 'Zx', *Musikalische Real-Zeitung* 2/15 (15 April 1789), cited in Morrow, *German Music Criticism*, 25 (translation) and 168 (German original).

[4] Burney, *General History of Music, Volume the Second*, 952.

[5] Mozart, letter to Leopold Mozart, 10 February 1784; *Letters of Mozart*, ed. and trans. Anderson, 867.

[6] Detailed discussions of this famous passage include Bauman, 'Becoming Original: Haydn and the Cult of Genius'; Sisman, 'Haydn, Shakespeare, and the Rules of Originality'; and Ludwig Finscher, *Joseph Haydn und seine Zeit* (Laaber: Laaber, 2002), 82–83. Finscher finds Haydn's choice of words in this passage 'highly unusual, if not unique' for an eighteenth-century composer, given that his terminology suggests 'working in a scientific laboratory' ('das Arbeiten in einem naturwissenschaftlichen Laboratorium'): *Haydn und seine Zeit*, 83.

arguing for what we might call personal rather than collective intellectual property.⁷

Yet no amount of comment from the time culled from composers, critics and listeners seems likely to overturn the firm specific association between galant music and convention. Of course the distaste for what are perceived to be conventional artistic means is hardly confined to the music of our period. Richard Taruskin writes:

> Absolutely unchallenged 'normality' is perhaps the most boring mode of discourse. One rarely finds it in Haydn, or in any interesting or imaginative composer. Rather it is the existence of norms that allows departures to become meaningful – and thereby expressive. In that sense, rules are indeed made to be broken.⁸

While this is framed as a general proposition, it is no accident that these thoughts occur in an account of late eighteenth-century music. James Hepokoski and Warren Darcy say something similar, but with more particular reference to our repertory, and in defence of their core concept of 'deformation':

> on both the production and reception side of things, as part of the compositional 'game' it was *expected* ('normative') that, within the then-current boundaries of taste and decorum, a composer would apply conceptual force here and there to strain or alter what is otherwise a bland or neutral set of conventional options and procedures – mere starting-points for the mature and experienced artist. As has been observed over the decades by virtually all commentators on the sonata repertory, applying such forces and purposeful generic 'misshapings' is just what gives a composition personality, memorability, appeal, interest, expressive power.
>
> [If] transgressions of standardized shapes and procedures are not present at all, the work is more likely to be sidelined by historical consensus as unimaginative, composition-by-the numbers.⁹

There is a serious point of style history being made here – that deviations can also represent norms of a kind – but we should note once more the governing notion that conventions are more or less powerless to express

---

⁷ On the matter of 'authorial property', and its relation to the eighteenth-century concept of genius, see Melton, *Rise of the Public*, 140: 'The eighteenth-century concept of genius . . . shifted the locus of creative inspiration from outside to inside the author. If authors produced works of inspiration, they did so because of special gifts unique to their talent, not through some external agency.'

⁸ Taruskin, *The Oxford History of Western Music: Music in the Seventeenth and Eighteenth Centuries*, 533. Mark Evan Bonds also notes a general 'attitude of implicit disdain in musical scholarship toward the study of convention', but it is, once more, significant that this occurs in the service of a study of eighteenth-century music. Bonds, *Wordless Rhetoric*, 51.

⁹ Hepokoski and Darcy, *Elements of Sonata Theory*, 617.

anything in their own right. Their characterization as 'bland' and 'neutral' leaves little doubt about that.

Moving from the style-historical into the socio-political reading of convention, Susan McClary offered this comparative reading of Enlightenment musical style in 1985:

> The music with which today's dominant cultural group most strongly identifies is the music of the eighteenth-century Enlightenment: the music that is first articulated on the basis of the social values of the stabilizing middle class. This music appears (at least on some levels) to present itself as harmonious, perfect, organic, unified, formally balanced, capable of absorbing and resolving all tensions. In this way, it is very much unlike either the music produced in the seventeenth century (which celebrates in its fragmented structures and ornate, defiant arabesques the disruptive, violent struggles of the emerging bourgeoisie against the norms of the church and the aristocracy) or in the nineteenth century (which dramatizes the conflicts between the subjective self and the constraints of bourgeois society). In these musics, the ideology is far more evident, because their symbolic enactments of social antagonisms are to a large extent the message.[10]

It is clear enough that we are being asked to prefer struggle and conflict to the celebration of values that supposedly support the status quo, 'today's dominant cultural group', all the more insidious because of their covert nature. In this reading, convention, marked by its 'perfection' and 'balance', becomes cognate with consonance – albeit a false consonance because of what that perfect musical world suppresses. As Stephen Hinton has observed, attitudes to its opposite, dissonance, represent 'a consistent thread running through three [centuries] of music history': 'dissonance connotes subjective resistance to socially imposed order and constraint'.[11] McClary's musical seventeenth and nineteenth centuries are, by extension, periods that bring such dissonance to the creative foreground. This analogy, however, will not in fact take us very far given that precisely one of the features that most marked the galant style – that prompted its definition as new and modern – was its free treatment of dissonance, which could be encapsulated as a move away from the (prepared, 'correct') suspension in favour of the (unprepared, 'licentious') appoggiatura. And this was no 'merely technical'

---

[10] Susan McClary, cited in Joseph Horowitz, 'Musical Mavericks Fume and Blaspheme in Minnesota', *Opus* (October 1985), 17, cited in Richard Taruskin, 'Material Gains: Assessing Susan McClary' (review article), *Music & Letters* 90/3 (2009), 459.

[11] Stephen Hinton, 'The Emancipation of Dissonance: Schoenberg's Two Practices of Composition', *Music & Letters* 91/4 (2010), 570. Hinton is here characterizing Theodor Adorno's approach to the matter, but goes on to show how this attitude is much more widespread.

development; among the justifications given by the advocates for the new style was that it allowed greater freedom of expression.[12]

More fundamental, though, to the views given so far is that convention is a kind of empty shell: it 'says nothing' in its own right, at least nothing of artistic interest. Wye Allanbrook's account of Mozart reception has offered one of the strongest counterblasts both to this understanding of convention in general and to its particular application to our period. The 'pursuit of the Gloomy Mozart' has been underpinned by 'a presumption that these conventions [of the Classic style] have somehow been imposed from without, by the Enlightenment's musical thought police, and that it is intellectual progress to grow away from them'. Critics believe that 'they must distinguish between Mozart's true voice and his conventional mask, that the authentic Mozart is to be discovered buried under a mound of sedimented conventions'.[13] This approximates to the antagonistic conception of individual-social relations exemplified by McClary above. Allanbrook instead stresses the positive role played by some perceived larger-scale 'conventions', such as the preference for the major mode and for happy endings, and indeed the use of sonata-form structures: these and other conventions are for her not so much constraining as enabling. Another example on the larger scale would be the growing hold of periodic phrase construction, which I have argued has a symbiotic relationship with the growing taste for quick-fire contrasts of musical material.

Such an understanding has also in fact been backed up by Susan McClary. Between 1985, when her thoughts cited above were penned, and 2000, when the book *Conventional Wisdom: The Content of Musical Form* was published, McClary experienced something of a conversion not just on the role of convention in art but also on the moral integrity of eighteenth-century music. She noted that, since the nineteenth century, Western art has 'cultivated an aversion to conventions':

We interpret reliance on convention as betraying a lack of imagination or a blind acceptance of social formula. . . . [yet] a great deal of wisdom resides in conventions: nothing less than the premises of an age, the cultural arrangements that enable communication, co-existence, and self-awareness. . . . Consequently,

---

[12] The very nomenclatures 'strict style' and 'free style' as adopted by Koch, for instance, bear out this broad perception. That there was never in fact a clear separation between the two rhetorical opposites is entertainingly demonstrated in Keith Chapin, 'Strict and Free Reversed: The Law of Counterpoint in Koch's *Musikalisches Lexikon* and Mozart's *Zauberflöte*', Eighteenth-Century Music 3/1 (2006), 91–107.

[13] Allanbrook, 'Mozart's Tunes', 172.

conventions always operate as part of the signifying apparatus ... it is not the deviations alone that signify but the norms as well.[14]

In other words, McClary suggests we should think about how conventions themselves communicate. More commonly, as we have seen, formulaic gestures or expected events are thought of as being unmarked, even neutral, and disruptions to those events as bestowing meaning and expressive value on a discourse. Yet, in musical terms anyway, stylistic conventions tend to come and go – they have a shelf-life. They are not unchanging absolutes that we can take as read. For a convention to become a convention, it must serve some useful purpose at the time at which it operates.

As Allanbrook does, McClary devotes particular attention to conventions on the larger scale. For her this is, above all, tonality, in particular as it was practised in the eighteenth century – a quantity that we might struggle to understand as a convention at all, given its global reach into the present day (pedagogical as well as its manifestation in the various forms of popular music that McClary sees as the true descendants of the more communally oriented eighteenth-century musical art). Yet tonality too is an 'expressive apparatus' as well as a 'formal framework';[15] it was a 'device for prolonging a unified trajectory',[16] one of the 'premises of the musical language' that was 'sufficiently shared to permit genuine public exchange'.[17] This reminds us of the etymology of the very term convention: it denotes a 'meeting' or a 'coming together'.[18] Naomi Waltham-Smith has made this equation the basis for an encompassing affirmation of the 'ethical potential' of the style, one whose 'conventionality' creates a sense of shared ownership of musical materials.[19]

Many of the approaches to eighteenth-century musical convention, though, have had a more local focus, whether this involves topic, schema or form-functional analysis. Both William E. Caplin, with his work on formal function, and Robert O. Gjerdingen, with his work on schemata, stress the pleasure which listeners may experience when interacting with various kinds of convention. Gjerdingen's focus falls on the 'courtly'

---

[14] McClary, *Conventional Wisdom*, 3–6.   [15] McClary, *Conventional Wisdom*, 69.
[16] McClary, *Conventional Wisdom*, 73.   [17] McClary, *Conventional Wisdom*, 118.
[18] Compare Paul Alpers, *What Is Pastoral?* (Chicago: University of Chicago Press, 1996), 80: 'One source of our difficulty with the idea of convention that its root meaning, "coming together" (from Latin *convenire*)[,] has dropped out of sight when the word is used in literary contexts.'
[19] Waltham-Smith, *Music and Belonging*, 38 (where she affirms her aim to 'reclaim the Classical style ... by recuperating [its] ethical potential') and 17 (where 'conventionality' as an operating assumption is distinguished from 'convention', in its immediate sense of 'a set of shared figures and norms').

listeners of the time, who would have been primed to take an interest not just in the particular realization of an individual pattern or schema, but also in how one such instance was linked to another;[20] Caplin, on the other hand, considers the pleasure of contemporary listeners as it derives from 'the interaction of our (often unconscious) understanding of functional norms with their particular manifestations in a given work'.[21] Another larger-scale convention of a kind is, as previously discussed, the language model. Kofi Agawu notes that the concern to establish 'normative procedures' in the work of Charles Rosen, Leonard Ratner and others 'grows out of the feeling' that later eighteenth-century music 'approximates a *language* "spoken" by Haydn, Mozart, Beethoven, and their contemporaries'.[22] This language model – like tonality, hardly confined in its application to the music of this time, but most commonly invoked in connection with it – implies a collective agreement to operate on the basis of familiar material in order to communicate. It also suggests the sort of concern with the fine print of immediate continuity (word-by-word, sentence-by-sentence) that the more recent localized theoretical approaches also address.

A further writer who has mounted an explicit defence of eighteenth-century musical convention, in terms of the 'dialogue' that is one of the corollaries of a language model, is James R. Currie. Dialogue is taken as a metaphor for understanding the relationship between the language of late eighteenth-century instrumental music and 'the listening subject ... implied by that musical language'.[23] While this music 'depends upon the presence of recognizable musical conventions', often 'the conventional element occurs in a problematic or incorrect manner', meaning that pieces are then 'driven to solve such problems'. The disruption 'sets the discussion in motion, and the establishment of the accepted use of that convention is the goal'. And 'because the final resolution was earned through a process of discussion, it becomes imbued with a certain moral quality'; it manifests 'an ethics of convention'.[24] 'However, it is naïve not to recognize that conventions are also manifestations of socially objective forces that can determine us negatively', so that we are no longer conscious of the freedom that dialogue seems to offer us. Somehow this instrumental style manages

---

[20] Gjerdingen, *Music in Galant Style*, chapter 1, 'Introduction', 3–24, but the 'courtly' perspective is addressed at many other points, such as 45, 173 and 447–452. See my review of Gjerdingen's book in *Music & Letters* 90/3 (2009), 468–473, for some reservations about this audience model.
[21] Caplin, *Classical Form*, 3.   [22] Agawu, *Playing with Signs*, 6 (original italics).
[23] Currie, 'Waiting for the Viennese Classics', 138.
[24] Currie, 'Waiting for the Viennese Classics', 139.

to 'roam around restlessly ... between the determinate realm of conventions and the spontaneous realm of freedom, between givens and critique, law and dissent, stasis and movement, mimesis and metaphysics'.[25]

Unlike Hepokoski and Darcy, for whom transgression seems to be its own reward, Currie recognizes that transgression gives back to the convention, as part of an endless, 'restless' two-way dynamic. Disruptions or deviations may undermine, but they nevertheless also reaffirm the force of a convention; this is always the case perceptually anyway, since deviation is only perceived against a background of a norm, which therefore remains epistemologically in control. The true death of a convention, of an accepted way of doing things, musical or otherwise, is more likely to come about not through all-out 'attack', but less glamorously through gradual neglect – death through a thousand cuts, so to speak. Currie is certainly not the only writer to recognize the symbiotic relationship between deviation and norm, and the particular energy that it gives to the music of this time. Michael Spitzer aphoristically contends that 'convention is equally the vehicle for communication and its straitjacket'.[26] But we might note that the constraining side often only becomes evident when a particular convention has lost some of its force; when it still holds true, we might not even notice that we are under its thrall. On the larger scale, 'expression', understood in a particular way, is one such convention. Within that domain, something like the musical typology of the lament would serve as a good example, since it is likely to entail a whole host of devices that recur from work to work;[27] in spite of such replication, even sophisticated musicologists seem to have no problems believing in the personal 'authenticity' of every example of the genre that they hear. Every sigh figure represents direct, unmediated 'expression', every heavy chromatic step rings true. Another encompassing, living convention is, of course, the very attitude to convention that we have been considering, the widely held view it is intrinsically a bad thing – though just what the ideal conventionless music, of the eighteenth century, or any other time, might actually sound like, no one has yet been able to tell us.

---

[25] Currie, 'Waiting for the Viennese Classics', 142.
[26] Michael Spitzer, 'A Metaphoric Model of Sonata Form: Two Expositions by Mozart', in *Communication in Eighteenth-Century Music*, ed. Mirka and Agawu, 189.
[27] One of these devices is the stepwise descending bass, which forms the focus for William E. Caplin's study 'Topics and Formal Functions: The Case of the Lament', in *The Oxford Handbook of Topic Theory*, ed. Mirka, 415–452.

Renewal

Thus deviations from a norm may undermine, but they may also uphold. Norms may constrain, but they also enable utterance in the first place; they form a filter or starting-point for musical creativity. The out-and-out unconventional certainly features in our repertory, which of course is only perceived as such against the background of a more expected course of events, but more characteristic is to work with the conventional in various ways. This may indeed involve overt deviation, but such deviation operates on a sliding scale. The process of defamiliarization (*Verfremdung*) – making strange what is routine, making fresh what is familiar – can be quite low-key. The materials or processes that are subject to such treatment may appear almost normal, to the extent that many listeners may not even register that anything is amiss. And the freshening-up of familiar features can be accomplished simply through their particular arrangement, through the way in which these features are placed relative to others. No distortion or deviation need occur. In other words, timing and placement can count for a great deal. Dittersdorf relates how in his younger years he resolved to listen carefully to every passage that gave the impression of novelty in order to find out what made a beautiful thought sound beautiful. 'And how often I discovered that it was beautiful, simply because it was in the right place, so that, if it had occurred elsewhere, it would either not have been remarked at all, or have spoiled the whole work.'[28] Dittersdorf describes a musical equivalent of *le mot juste*: it's not what you say, it's how you say it – and when you say it. Timing and placement were bound to be important factors given the variety that was such a basic principle for the style, and variety itself was often regarded as insurance against deadening routine. This variety could be a topical one, meaning that familiar stylistic tokens could be made fresh simply through juxtaposition, but it could more fundamentally involve changes – often rapid ones – of texture, articulation or dynamic levels. The most conventional materials could come alive simply through artful arrangement.

This might seem to be drifting away from our earlier argument that conventions themselves communicate – that they are already 'alive', rather than being empty shells that require filling with deviant content. But from a perceptual point of view it is undeniable that while conventional materials do indeed do their own work and carry their own meanings, and while each individual usage acts to reinforce them, repeated exposure can nevertheless

---

[28] Dittersdorf, *Autobiography of Karl von Dittersdorf*, trans. Coleridge, 78.

make them worn around the edges. They become harder to perceive in their own right, and therefore are in danger of failing to make their mark. They may therefore require some explicit creative attention in order to restore them to mint condition, as it were. One should in any case bear in mind that for every convention being addressed in some such way, there are dozens of others simultaneously being upheld, on various levels, whether connected with the details of utterance or with larger-scale phenomena such as grouping, metre, phrase structure and harmonic grammar. What I am concerned with below are specific, smaller-scale events and materials rather than some of those broader conventions, including the ones outlined by Allanbrook and McClary. They may be described as formulas which are renewed through various forms of contextual manipulation.

Such renewal bespeaks a strong focus on the ordinary, the everyday, the unremarkable. The dialectics of convention outlined above can and do in fact apply well beyond the musical period with which we are concerned, yet this focus on the everyday is far more particular to the eighteenth century. And not just the musical one: favoured literary forms of the time such as novels, diaries and letters are much preoccupied with what Patricia Meyer Spacks calls 'the transformation of the trivial into the significant'.[29] Along similar lines, our instrumental repertory devotes enormous creative attention to the 'little things of life'. This is palpable not just in the high incidence of avowedly familiar materials but in the way in which those materials – cadences, repeated notes, melodic configurations and the like – are brought into the foreground of our consciousness through various forms of manipulation, of the sort that helped Haydn achieve his fame. This palpable creative focus is one further reason why the moniker 'conventional' might have attached itself with such tenacity to our period, since the music positively invites us to pay attention to apparently unremarkable things. As we saw earlier, one important aspect of 'originality' was precisely the ability to offer a fresh view of the familiar. Alexander Gerard, in his 1774 *Essay on Genius*, wrote that 'Invention is the capacity of producing new beauties in works of art, and new truths in matters of science; which can be accomplished only by assembling ideas in various positions and arrangements, that we may obtain uncommon views of them.'[30] This not only reinforces the premium Dittersdorf put on placement in order for

---

[29] Patricia Meyer Spacks, *Privacy: Concealing the Eighteenth-Century Self* (Chicago: University of Chicago Press, 2003), 14.

[30] Alexander Gerard, *An Essay on Genius* (London: W. Strahan and T. Cadell, 1774), 27, cited in Bauman, 'Becoming Original: Haydn and the Cult of Genius', 342.

'new beauties' to be perceived; it also suggests that the basic materials, the 'ideas', already exist, and it is the particular way in which they are presented that counts for most.

We may also understand this focus on the everyday in relation to a conversational ethos. By definition conversation is a brand of discourse that will often be preoccupied with unremarkable events. It will be rich in formulaic expressions, yet it also needs to sound and feel spontaneous. Similarly, it needs to be informal in character (in Chapter 2 we noted the increasing emphasis on conversational informality in the eighteenth century), yet without losing all structure; too loose an execution might well endanger the fundamental principle of reciprocity. Such tensions between formal and informal aspects are, as we have seen, shared by the instrumental music of our time. It offers relatively formal, clear-cut frameworks yet is also given to 'changing subjects' almost at will; there is both fixity and fluidity, giving rise to the 'restless' character identified by Currie. But more relevant in the present context is the shared concentration on small things. In his conduct manual Knigge noted that the 'spirit of conversation' means having 'a nice regard to trifles' ('Dieser Geist des Umgangs erfordert ... Achtsamkeit auf geringe Dinge, auf Kleinigkeiten').[31] These trifles, which will of course involve gesture as well as utterance, are to be taken seriously; if they are not, then such social interaction may well become a hollow exercise. No matter how stale they may seem, routine aspects – not just small talk in general, but also salutations, enquiries about state of mind and state of health, and so forth – need to be executed with conviction. They must sound as though they are meant, as though they are sincere. This social imperative, though, forms part of a broader concern. If communication becomes a virtual theme of the age – as reflected in the case of music in the rise of the language model, for instance – this is accompanied by an anxiety about whether the message will be received, about whether attention will be paid by the receiver, in sum, about whether communication will actually take place. There is a kind of scepticism at work that is also evident in the constant preoccupation with ideals of variety and accessibility,[32] as if these alone can help ensure that communication is

---

[31] Knigge, *Über den Umgang mit* Menschen, volume 2, 334; *Practical Philosophy of Social Life*, trans. Will, volume 2, 320.

[32] Inger S. B. Brodey writes of 'a growing distrust of the referential and communicative powers of language', for which the lachrymose sensibility is part of the remedy. Brodey, 'On Pre-Romanticism or Sensibility: Defining Ambivalences', in *A Companion to European Romanticism*, ed. Michael Ferber (Oxford: Blackwell, 2005), 13.

successful. Certainly when translated into artistic practice, these ideals may help to forestall incomprehension or a lack of engagement.

In the case of music, the focus on renewal of the smallest elements offers a means of combatting such doubts, as if re-examining a language from the ground up. One element that is subject to constant attention is cadence. Cadence, of course, hardly counts as small change – it is fundamental for the very existence of a musical language – yet it is certainly one of the most predictable, and potentially routine, of phenomena. And while its role as an organizing agent or a magnet for musical energy makes it a focal point across a wide range of Western musical styles, cadence somehow counts for even more than that in our style, as many writers have testified. Caplin, for example, states: 'In no other repertory does cadential articulation, and especially cadential play, assume such major significance for formal expression' as it does in later eighteenth-century music.[33] One element of that, as Allanbrook notes, is the greater scale of the operation, with cadence no longer being a 'perfunctory' matter but instead 'reach[ing] back to saturate the phrase. Areas of arrival were carefully planned and achieved serious proportions.'[34] This means, for instance, that the approach to a cadence is often signalled well in advance. Through various signalling techniques a cadence can be made a real event in its own right, one that is readily perceptible by a wide range of listeners – and the more important the cadence, the more likely it is to receive such extensive preparation. This already represents a form of renewal of the device, certainly on the global comparative level proposed by Allanbrook, but also effective on an intra-stylistic level.

The according of such prominence to cadential activity as well as to the point where the cadence is actually realized means that the common analogy made both then and now between cadence and punctuation is on shaky ground. Cadences are not like punctuation in that they still consist of sound, as did what came before them. Punctuation marks, of course, have some semantic content, but this is not exactly comparable to the nuanced richness of the words that they enclose. Cadences, on the other

---

[33] Caplin, 'Classical Cadence', 52. Just how one defines a cadence is hardly a matter of widespread agreement. Indeed, that was the very stimulus for Caplin's 'Classical Cadence' article. For another commentary on the situation see Markus Neuwirth and Pieter Bergé, 'Introduction: What Is a Cadence? Nine Perspectives', in *What Is a Cadence? Theoretical and Analytical Perspectives on Cadences in the Classical Repertoire*, ed. Neuwirth and Bergé (Leuven: Leuven University Press, 2015), 7–16. I follow Caplin's precepts in my understanding of cadence in this repertory.

[34] Allanbrook, *Secular Commedia*, 131.

hand, continue to convey meaning, form part of a continuous sonic process, and, as we have seen, 'reach back to saturate the phrase'.[35]

A key part of this process of cadential renewal is in fact to deny or delay the arrival of the cadence point itself. This is the 'cadential play' to which Caplin draws special attention above, and it typically involves evading or interrupting the cadence at the very point of arrival. But there are many degrees of denial, many shades of weakening of the cadence's effect. The deferral of listener satisfaction may be only short-lived, but it is often a longer wait. One characteristic location for such deferral is the second tonal area of a sonata-form structure.[36] In the first-movement exposition of Mozart's Quartet in D major K499 (1786) the plot seems to be to delay full cadential arrival on the dominant key for as long as possible. At the end of the transition the parts seem to be working smoothly towards a cadential confirmation of A major, but at the moment of seeming arrival, bar 57, this swerves into a harmony of F sharp minor – a classic interruption. The succeeding phrase makes its way back towards the harmonic goal, but a different submediant interruption now prevents completion, as the players slide into F major at bar 65. This phrase in turn makes its way back towards A major, and in fact uses the same material to do so as did the previous phrase (compare bars 61^4–65^1 with 69^4–73^1, which are identical apart from the initial replacement of C♯ in the former with C♮ in the latter). At the third time of asking, a close in the dominant key does take place, which features many of the ingredients necessary to be a strong point of arrival, including the presence of the local tonic A at the top of the texture. On the other hand, there is no clear-cut pre-dominant harmony to precede the V–I progression, a normal requirement for proper cadential articulation at the

---

[35] For a recent example of the equating of cadence with punctuation see Robert D. Levin, review of Karol Berger's *Bach's Cycle, Mozart's Arrow* in *Journal of the American Musicological Society* 63/3 (2010), 671: 'Cadences, which are indeed the equivalents of punctuation in language, are formulas; they set off the material that has come before, but they corroborate rather than define content.'

[36] Among others, Caplin notes that the evaded cadence 'is particularly well suited to subordinate themes, since dramatizing the subordinate key is a principal aesthetic objective of the classical style. ... But the need for dramatic articulation of the home key early in a movement is not pressing, and thus evaded cadences seldom appear in main themes': *Classical Form*, 107–109. Michael Spitzer states outright that the 'business' of S (the second thematic area) 'is not modulation but deferral of closure': 'Sonata Dialogues' (review of Hepokoski and Darcy, *Elements of Sonata Theory*), *Beethoven Forum* 14/2 (2007), 154. In his 'Sonata Form and the Problem of Second-Theme Beginnings', Mark Richards includes a close reading of the first movement of Beethoven's Sonata in D major Op. 10 No. 3, which offers an 'ST process which responds to, and indeed compensates for, the weakened signals in its non-normative beginning' in B minor' (17–18). Such signals 'may ... extend into one or more successive themes in the new key' and 'encourage us to hear [the] multiple themes as a broad unit' (21).

time.[37] Just as importantly, this 'cadence' lacks the time needed to make its effect. The strongest cadence points tend to be reinforced either by a following break in the texture or some form of postcadential affirmation of the arrival harmony. Here, though, the conclusion of the phrase barely has time to register before the entry of new material. The ensuing six-bar phrase does move through a pre-dominant harmony to conclude with a perfect authentic cadence, but once again the phrase is no sooner over than the music has moved on, this time via a varied repetition of the same.

As this varied version of the phrase reaches its end at the start of bar 83, there is even less time allowed for the cadence to have its effect: an overlap takes place, with second violin and viola immediately starting on new figuration, and, more subtly, the cello also beginning a new figure at this point. The phrase to which these materials contribute lasts for four bars, and now the pre-dominant harmony lasts for a full bar (85), followed by a full bar of dominant, which is then followed by the local tonic of A major. This could represent another firm point of arrival, but yet again it is allowed no time to resound as an immediate repetition of the phrase takes place from bar 87. This is a form of the 'one-more-time' reiteration that often characterizes closing material.[38] However, the repetition does not lead to the anticipated stronger close. Instead, bar 91 sees an interruption to the submediant chord of F sharp minor, as heard at the start of this whole section, only this time it is immediately corrected by a move to pre-dominant harmony, and this leads to a reiteration of the second two bars of the preceding phrase. This in turn is repeated, meaning that three consecutive two-bar units, bars 89–90, 91–92 and 93–94, have circled around the same material: will the teasing never end? But, finally, the third of these finishes on the tonic chord at the start of bar 95, and this produces an even smaller-scale form of reiteration as the material of bar 95 is repeated exactly in bar 96. Not only that, but the first violin's cadential formula, moving by step from the fifth scale degree up to the tonic, is a virtual replica of the formula used throughout this section: it has featured no fewer than six times, in bars 86, 90, 92, 94, 95 and 96.

---

[37] Caplin makes a persuasive case for this in 'Classical Cadence'; see in particular 70–72 (including note 63). One might argue that the F sharp minor and F major harmonies in these two phrases, whilst initially being heard as submediant interruptions, end up acting as pre-dominant harmonies that takes us on to the local dominants and so set up potential proper cadences. However, the proportions seem wrong for this to be a possibility. The two harmonies occupy the first six bars of their respective eight-bar phrases, and the subsequent moves back to dominant harmonies sound more like corrections back to the expected course rather than continuous logical harmonic progressions.

[38] This term originates in Janet Schmalfeldt, 'Cadential Processes: The Evaded Cadence and the "One More Time" Technique', *Journal of Musicological Research* 12/1–2 (1992), 1–52.

Thus what we have witnessed over the course of these forty-odd bars (57–96) is a seemingly endless deferral of firm closure in the new key. The sense of release that ensues from a strong cadential close is continually put off, even though, remarkably, every single phrase concludes with the local tonic in the uppermost voice and so reaches a point of melodic rest. What makes this deferral even more striking is the progressive shortening of phrase lengths over the course of the whole section. From bar 58 the pattern is 8 + 8 + 6 + 6 + 4 + 4 + 2 + 2 + 1 + 1, and one might argue that bar 97, which doubles the rate of alternation of V and I harmonies, increases that to 1/2 + 1/2. While the exact proportions are complicated by pervasive phrase overlaps, this is a near-symmetrical acceleration that increases anticipation – or frustration, given that each of these units closes with an expectant dominant and/or a complete cadential progression that could potentially lead to a firm demarcation point.[39] What this means cumulatively is that, when closure finally comes, it is far more marked an event than it would otherwise be, since so much effort has been expended, as it were, in the delivery. Yet by the time that finally happens, the dynamic level has dropped to *pianissimo*, a wry understatement after such a lengthy drive to the close.

The tenuous nature of any binary division into convention and transgression is evident in the use of such a technique. While it disrupts the most basic association of cadence – with closure – and so forces the listener to think twice, this technique is so commonly employed that it becomes more or less a convention in its own right. The same can apply to various devices that halt the cadential process at an earlier stage. The Indugio, for example, takes the typically third-to-last harmony of a cadential progression, a predominant chord of some kind, and dwells on it, throwing the expected progress of the music towards its cadential close into doubt.[40] The impression is of the music getting stuck, and the normal pattern is 'third time lucky', with the third repetition of the chord and its associated figuration leading on to the dominant. This schema is often allied with brilliant writing and a flourishing cadential conclusion, though that is not the case in the first movement of Haydn's Sonata in D major H33 (before 1778; Example 3.1). At bar 48 of the first section the cadential close on the dominant is undercut by a return to material heard earlier in the phrase; the

---

[39] Rosen, *The Classical Style*, 228–233, details a process of gradual acceleration in the first movement of Mozart's Piano Concerto in D minor, K466, though cast in terms of rhythmic values rather than the lengths of phrases or phrase units, and he describes the process as helping to create 'the "romantic" excitement generated by this concerto' (232).

[40] For a definition and discussion of the Indugio schema see Gjerdingen, *Music in the Galant Style*, chapter 20, 273–283.

Example 3.1 Haydn, Sonata in D major H33/i, bars 37–58

music loops back to bar 43 and proceeds to replay what we heard from that point. This has all the signs of being a 'one-more-time' repetition. But after three bars of the six-bar unit, instead of proceeding on to the cadence, the music stutters. The last five notes that we heard at bars 50^2–51^1 are isolated and repeated twice, the second version being followed by a pause over a quaver rest and the third marked 'adagio', with a lengthened final note likewise marked with a pause. There is no chordal reinforcement of the lone right-hand line, though the harmony may be understood as supertonic, and the impression is of energy draining away and momentum being lost – the opposite of the normal Indugio procedure. After the prolonged final note of the 'adagio' fragment, there is no resumption of the material heard in the first iteration of the whole phrase, in bars 46–48. Instead, Haydn brings in new material to achieve the cadential goal, more brilliant and in effect overwriting most of the previous 'failed' phrase. In the recapitulation, the effect is taken further. The one-more-time phrase, from bar 166, obstructs progress even more blatantly. Its first two bars form the basis for an eight-bar sequence based on the circle of fifths, a charming but irrelevant turn of events that sounds literally like playing for time. In bar 173 this lands us back on the phrase's starting material, which now unfolds as it did in the exposition, though the stuttering melodic figure is now played at a different octave on each of its three appearances, making the breakdown of the drive to the cadence even more overt. And thus the 'one more time' effectively expands into 'two more times', meaning that the cadence that first began to be signalled at bar 161 is not finally accomplished until bar 183.

There are many other ways of disrupting a cadential process and so renewing the perception not only of what is a grammatical essential, but also of the particular turns of phrase often associated with it.[41] Yet no overt manipulation need be present in order for a cadence to receive a new lease of life. The minuet from Haydn's Quartet in E flat major Op. 50 No. 3 (1787; Example 3.2a) is almost completely dominated by one of those highly individualized motives of the sort that we considered in Chapter 2, whereby the music seems to be a vehicle for the motive rather than the other way around. The motive consists of a three-crotchet rhythm beginning on the upbeat; it is also defined by pitch, with a note repeated over the bar line from anacrusis to downbeat, and by articulation, with staccato upbeat and first and second beats of the subsequent bar joined by a slur. The core of the motive, though, is the repeated note over the bar line, which is heard almost ad infinitum: it is present in most parts in most bars of the movement. The hard effect of all these repetitions is only softened towards cadence points. As we approach the cadence at the end of the first section, for example, bars 10–11 comprehensively break with all the motive's terms of reference: changes to grouping, articulation and pitch structure bring greater fluidity after the earlier insistence. But then, just as the cadential process is about to be completed, the motive obtrudes. We expect the root-position V chord heard from bar 11^1 to last the whole bar, and the tonic chord to follow at 12^1. But, courtesy of our motive, this tonic arrives a crotchet early, on the third beat of bar 11, and is then reiterated on the next downbeat. In effect, the motive interrupts 'the music', creating a very counterintuitive harmonic rhythm.

---

[41] A more overtly dramatic kind of disruption involves replacing the concluding tonic chord with a chromatic harmony followed by a gradual working-back towards resolution in the correct key. This is defined by Gabriel Fankhauser as 'cadential intervention' and is illustrated with an example from the minuet of Haydn's Quartet in C major Op. 74 No. 1, among other works, in his 'Cadential Intervention in Shostakovich's Piano Trio in E Minor, Op. 67', *Music Analysis* 32/2 (2013), 210–250.

Renewal 285

Example 3.2a Haydn, Quartet in E flat major Op. 50 No. 3/iii, bars 1–12[2]

Example 3.2b Haydn, Quartet in E flat major Op. 50 No. 3/iii, bars 43–57[2]

In the second half, there is a verbatim repetition of the first section until the very last moment. The cadence at bars 11–12 that was hijacked by our motive does not recur. Instead, in bar 47 the dominant harmony continues through to the third beat, as if to correct what had happened earlier (Example 3.2b). Then, as if to make sure, the harmony swerves away from a tonic conclusion, and in the next few bars pauses and nearly exclusive semitone movement in the parts suggest uncertainty. The motive then resumes in the first violin (from bar 51^3), and is answered by the cello, but overlapping with this answer are sustained notes in the three upper parts. These parts form the start of a falling cadential formula, the cello joining in once it has finished its imitation. The closing bars avoid any hint of the motive and give us a commonplace cadence point. The upper three parts present just about the first sustained diatonic stepwise motion heard in the movement, as smooth melodic conduct trumps motivic insistence. Thus, in this context, an entirely formulaic cadence acquires a much more pointed meaning than it otherwise would. It is an ironic turn to the familiar and the everyday, but at the same time this material can be understood actively to resist the motivic invasion, to counter the dominating idea of the movement with an agency of its own.

Such contextual renewal of the conventional can also take place on a purely metrical level: Danuta Mirka points out how 'contrast between the surrounding metric irregularity and the regularity of the cadential formula' may serve 'to dramatize the formal structure'.[42] One instance of this occurs in the finale of Haydn's Quartet in D major Op. 50 No. 6 (1787), in which 'metric relations are set right again only by the six-four chord' heard in bar 231 'that initiates the final cadence'. 'Most curiously', though, Mirka adds, 'this cadence is never carried through',[43] as the rest of the movement dissolves into a series of postcadential gestures. To fail to provide the expected continuation after a cadential 6/4 chord – a sonority that has the strongest possible implications for what is to happen next, a resolution to a plain root-position dominant chord, to be followed by the tonic – represents a radical act of defamiliarization. One should note that a series of embellished V–I progressions does follow this 6/4 chord, but they represent separate impulses; they do not form part of the larger phrase that has led to the cadence-preparing 6/4. Thus this most dependent of sonorities achieves perceptual independence; it becomes a thing in itself rather than simply a link in the chain. Haydn thereby refreshes not just the

---

[42] Mirka, *Metric Manipulations in Haydn and Mozart*, 251.
[43] Mirka, *Metric Manipulations in Haydn and Mozart*, 179.

conventional cadential 6/4, but the much larger-scale idea of proper grammatical closure. In this sense the movement fails to finish according to customary usage of the time, and so is a milder cousin of the famous ending of Op. 33 No. 2 that we considered in Chapter 1.

Another kind of cadential renewal depends less on any manipulation of proportions or progressions, and instead derives its effect from displacement. Haydn is renowned for this practice, which most commonly involves beginning with a closing cadence. However, no two cases are the same, as the composer applies almost infinite resource to this fundamental type of renewal. Sometimes what sounds like perfectly normal opening material recurs at the close and so is shown to be able to function in both positions; in the Minuet of the String Quartet in C major Op. 9 No. 1 (c1769) the opening four bars return at the end not as a final cadence, but as post-cadential reinforcement, something made possible by their being built on a tonic pedal. At the outset of Symphony No. 97 in C major (1792), though, we do indeed hear a closing cadence, and the effect is very strange (Example 3.3a). The tempo is Adagio, and first harmony we hear, after an initial bar of hovering on the tonic note, is a diminished seventh, which acts as an applied chord to the following V. This in turn cadences on the tonic in bar 4. The harmonic intensification represented by the diminished seventh, together with the contour of the first violins' lyrical line, suggest a valedictory quality, an eloquent conclusion to a larger stretch of music. But none of that larger stretch is heard; it is as though the listener has been dropped into proceedings not so much in the middle, but just at the point when a moving scene reaches its conclusion. To be instantly confronted with such a level of intensity is disconcerting.

It has been suggested that Haydn is quoting Mozart as a form of tribute soon after he learnt of that composer's death; what is being quoted is the oboe line from bars 97–101 of the duet 'Fra gli amplessi' in *Così fan tutte* (1789), that moment when Fiordiligi succumbs to Ferrando's seductive powers.[44] Whether or not this is what Haydn is doing, the comparison perfectly points to the sensation that attends his symphonic opening. In Mozart's duet the oboe line eloquently caps a Larghetto section of growing intensity, whereas Haydn's Adagio simply cuts to the climax. If this does represent a quotation, it takes the form of a romantic fragment, patently

---

[44] Heartz, *Mozart, Haydn and Early Beethoven*, 471 (though Heartz also notes that the passage is an instance of Haydn's 'putting the ending of a phrase before its beginning'), and Rice, *Music in the Eighteenth Century*, 244.

Example 3.3a Haydn, Symphony No. 97 in C major/i, bars 1–18

incomplete in effect. On the other hand, Haydn's fragment may be less a tribute to Mozart and more a way of renewing a shape that, if not exactly a familiar formula, represents a typology associated with pathos. Almost exactly the same melodic contour, beginning on the same sixth scale degree, features, for example, at the start of 'Nimm sie hin denn diese Lieder' from Beethoven's *An die ferne Geliebte* (1816). More directly comparable is the opening of Schubert's String Quintet in C major (1828), which opens with the same melodic line in the same key, harmonized with the same diminished seventh, though the first few notes are pitched a third higher. While Schubert's opening may in turn be a reference to Haydn's, more to the point is that all these extracts trade on the same contour that suggests expressive heightening.

Example 3.3a (continued)

That Haydn's opening is meant to disconcert is affirmed by what follows – a continuation in the same intense lyrical manner, followed, at bars 12–13, by an exact return of our earlier phrase to conclude the slow introduction. This first of all shows that bars 2–4^1 were indeed a closing cadential unit, which is now being restored to its proper place, and secondly that such a passage should follow directly from earlier material of comparable melodic and harmonic intensity, which it has now done. However, for all that the material is now more plausibly placed, it ends up not quite fulfilling its complete function, courtesy of an overlap, whereby the actual moment of cadential closure (bar 14^1) is absorbed into the loud C unison that opens the subsequent Vivace. In addition, slow introductions customarily finish on V, whereas the material we return to here is going to take us to a tonic close.[45] From that point of view, it has to be interrupted, or at least undermined – which is exactly what happens. Thus even the confirming, resolving return of

---

[45] Rice, *Music in the Eighteenth Century*, 244, also picks up on this unconventional end to a slow introduction.

Example 3.3a (continued)

the misplaced cadential phrase from the start – convention reaffirmed – is attended by problems and ambiguities of its own – meaning that this cadential close continues in one sense to go against the grain.

Haydn has not finished with his phrase, though. Just as we seem to be approaching the big moment of cadential confirmation of the dominant near the end of the Vivace's exposition, this opening material comes back, most unexpectedly, transposed into the dominant (Example 3.3b). It is preceded at bars 97–98 by repeated Es in the first violins, which are an equivalent for the Adagio's very opening bar of repeated Cs. Then the melodic line, together with the same succession of harmonies, diminished seventh leading to V6/4 then V5/3, is heard in plain crotchets, which means that in terms of duration it is heard at roughly the same speed as the Adagio phrase. Once again here it is preceded by plenty of prior material so that it does not enter out of the blue, as it did to start with, but in another sense the phrase does disconcert anew: its lyrical strains are not exactly compatible with what has largely been a robustious exposition in best C-major-

Example 3.3a (continued)

symphony style. The possibility that Schubert may indeed have been specifically referring to Haydn's opening is strengthened by the rhythmic conception here. Just as Haydn rewrites so that his phrase sounds at the same slow speed as at the start, so Schubert gives the opening phrase of his movement, an Allegro ma non troppo, in long note values so that it sounds much slower. In the recapitulation of his movement, Haydn once more reworks the Adagio's opening phrase into the temporal fabric of the Vivace, but now it is a closer match: it is transposed so as to yield the same pitch structure as heard in bars 2–4 of the Adagio. In addition, the material is greatly expanded: our closing cadential phrase acts as a portal into a world of sustained lyrical fantasy, extending from bar 240 to bar 267. Thus many times over what is in itself a humdrum musical event – a cadence – is made an object of attention. What is a collective musical

Example 3.3b Haydn, Symphony No. 97 in C major/i, bars 96–103[2]

property – not just the fact of cadence, but its particular turn of phrase – becomes an individual entity, with each subsequent appearance after the initial one in some way solving the problem but also adding something new. In this way the process of resourceful renewal seems exhilaratingly endless.

It is no surprise that this line of thinking, which we can quite firmly associate with Haydn, was taken up by other composers; it sets a challenge of communication, and of individual artistry, that must have seemed irresistible. In the first movement of his Quartet in E flat major Op. 1 No. 1, a set published in 1799 and dedicated to Haydn,[46] Andreas Romberg plainly takes up the challenge (Example 3.4). He opens in the first two bars with a closing cadential formation; the harmony is IV–V–I, and a typical

---

[46] Alongside the case of Hyacinthe Jadin noted in Chapter 2, Andreas Romberg was another of the sixteen composers to dedicate a set of string quartets to Haydn. See Walter, 'Haydn gewidmete Streichquartette'.

Example 3.4 Romberg, Quartet in E flat major Op. 1 No. 1/i, bars 1–18

closing melodic formula is heard on violin 1. To emphasize how out of place this opening is, Romberg continues with something apparently unrelated, three-part counterpoint based on a Romanesca schema that also features a *clausula vera*.[47] This is in fact a typical galant opening gambit, so it is as if the previous cadential gesture is simply being ignored. After a sequential repetition of this material in bars 5–6, the last three notes of the first violin's line, with its prominent rising semitone, are isolated and repeated over the following bars. By bars 10–11 this rising semitone, now

[47] Romberg's material closely resembles that used by Mozart in the opening of two of his works in the same key of E flat major, as schematically reduced by Robert O. Gjerdingen in his article 'Courtly Behaviors', 371–372.

B♮-C, has been further isolated, and is echoed by the second violin. The harmony being prolonged is the subdominant, which was the first chord we heard in the movement. In bar 13 this semitone melts into what is another standard pre-cadential melodic formula: a falling arpeggio each note of which is decorated by a lower neighbour note a semitone below. Thus the characteristic, the prominent rising-semitone figure, is transformed into the familiar; to state this in reverse, what would be a routine locution in another context is here reinvigorated as having a particular relevance to the argument at hand. The nicest touch of all is that the final neighbour-plus-main-note pair in bar 13, b♮^{1}-c^2, replicates the first two notes that were heard in the first violin in bar 1, and then as now they lead into a playing of the closing formation at 14–15. With this the initial syntactical impropriety is put right: the closing that was used as an opening now functions as a (local) close. That Romberg is not finished with his cadential formula is immediately apparent in what follows, as the cello takes up the opening/closing figure and uses it as a means of continuation.

What is renewed by this kind of cadential play is not just that fundamental operation, the cadence itself, but, more broadly, the whole notion of ending, and indeed, at least in retrospect, the other most fundamental part of a musical statement – its beginning. To begin with a stylistic impropriety, a functional dissonance, is to invite listener attention, and to recast it later on is to reward that attention. And we should bear in mind that cadences are among the most accessible of musical events; cognitive studies have found that cadences in tonal music can readily be perceived even by those with seemingly low levels of 'listening competence'.[48]

However, there are events in our repertory that send even more unmistakable signals. One is not so much cadential as postcadential in function; it consists of two or, more commonly, three repeated notes, which may be realized chordally or in unison, and which prolong the harmony that has just been affirmed by a cadence. The first note, which always occurs on the downbeat, generally has a double function: it both represents the point of cadential arrival but is also grouped with the note or notes that follow. This formula represents an extreme in the process known as liquidation: its very simplicity, and often brusqueness, 'kills off' the section of music that we have been hearing, tells us that no more of that material will be heard, and

---

[48] In 'The Perception of Cadential Closure', in *What Is a Cadence?*, ed. Neuwirth and Bergé, 253–286, David Sears combines theoretical-analytical and cognitive perspectives, and suggests that many cognitive studies may not be quite hitting the mark. While 'a vast number of [cognitive] studies employ cadences and other ending formulae as stimuli', in fact 'little experimental research explicitly investigates the perception of cadential closure' (255).

the silence that invariably follows enforces that understanding. Hepokoski and Darcy speak of 'several *forte* hammer-blows' and note there are generally three, though sometimes two, of them. They associate it in particular with the medial caesura of a sonata-form exposition, but recognize that it may also occur at the end of the whole section, or indeed at the very outset (in which case it has not a closing, but an enunciatory function).[49]

There is also a soft variant of the formula, more often found, naturally, in movements of a gentler character. One instance may be found at the end of the exposition of the first movement (Allegro maestoso) of Clementi's Piano Duet in E flat major Op. 3 No. 2 (1779). This three-part version, in bar 50, is played *pianissimo*, and instead of the customary full crotchet values we have quavers with quaver rests in between, together with staccato articulation. Commonly associated with this is a top part that goes $\hat{1}$–$\hat{3}$–$\hat{1}$ instead of the usual straight repetition of a note of the triad (normally $\hat{1}$). This variant is recognized by Gjerdingen, who groups it with a form that drops an octave or more between the final two notes. He dubs the pattern Final Fall, but excludes the downbeat from membership: for him it is a two-note phenomenon beginning on the second beat of the bar.[50]

There are in fact many further variants of pitch structure and timing. If the pattern is based on straight repeated notes, all three notes may be played at the same octave, in all parts, but the second note may also be either an octave lower or an octave higher, while the third note may retain the same pitch as the second, drop an octave lower, or even drop to an octave below either of its predecessors. And while in the three-note version the 'hammerblows' will always be equally spaced in time, the exact placement is variable. While the commonest realization would involve hearing notes or chords on the first three crotchet beats of a 4/4 metre, for example, those notes may be more widely spaced so as to occupy consecutive downbeats, or beats one, three and one of two consecutive bars, especially to give a more conclusive effect at the end of a movement. And while the formula may be adapted to the local expressive climate, this need not be the case. Boccherini, for example, has little compunction in using a brusque *subito forte* version even to end movements of distinctly gentle character. Of the thirteen diverse movements that make up Viotti's quartets Op. 1 (1783–1785), every single one ends with this formula. Yet most are significantly different in their exact realization, testifying to the versatility of the device as well as its undoubted utility.

---

[49] Hepokoski and Darcy, *Elements of Sonata Theory*, 34 (including note 12).
[50] Gjerdingen, *Music in the Galant Style*, 168.

Given what was said above about the dynamics of cadential play, it might seem inevitable that this postcadential formula was also going to prove an irresistible temptation for composers. Once again we must stress that a more or less unadorned realization will still have its effect, and is not in need of 'improvement'. We might infer this from the fact that this particular formula was employed just as enthusiastically by composers throughout the nineteenth century, as a final closing device, when it is especially likely to involve the variant of the second note or chord being heard at a higher octave, followed by a lower third note that is invariably played in unison. One way of playing with the formula is to create an overlap. On the downbeat of bar 116 of the Andantino grazioso from Brunetti's String Quartet in F major L186 (1785), it seems as though we have just heard the final full cadence of the movement, in B flat major. This is immediately followed on the second 2/4 beat by a further repeated B♭ in violin 1 that sounds like a typical confirmatory afterbeat gesture – it could be either the completion of a two-part version of our formula or else the middle of the three-part version. But instead of this leading to a punctual close, the movement's opening material returns from bar 117. This was initiated by the same solitary B♭ on an upbeat in the first violin, which means that the note acquires a double meaning: if it first sounds like part of a postcadential gesture, it now turns out to be a (return to the) beginning. Mozart does something very similar in the finale of his quintet K593 (1790): as we reach the end of a section in bar 54, a leap in the first violin from a first-beat e^3 down an octave to a second-beat e^2 sounds like a version of our reinforcing formula. As in the Brunetti movement, it could either be the completion of a two-note or the middle of a three-note realization. But from this point a quite different line unfolds, which turns out to be the subject of a short fugato section; and when the second violin enters with its dominant answer in bar 57, we realize that that e^2 heard in the first violin was an integral part of the subject. Thus that note fulfils a double role, and once more a formula is given a twist.

But it is the more decisive full three-part version of the formula that offers the greater opportunities. On the smaller scale, bars 98–99 of the finale of Haydn's Symphony No. 94 in G major ('Surprise'; 1791) signal the close of a section in D major by means of three loud repeated chords, but these hammerblows are instantly undermined at 100–101 by three *piano* unison C♮s in the strings alone, in a low tessitura. The three C♮s are then harmonized as V6/5 of G major to take us back to the theme in the tonic key. We scarcely have time to absorb the signals of strong closure in the dominant before, in a trice, the same figure is used to lead us back to the harmonic homeland.

A larger scale of operation is evident in the finale of Jadin's Quartet in B flat major Op. 1 No. 1 (1795). Three repeated chords are first heard affirming the dominant close at the end of the exposition, followed after the repeat by a long silence at the start of the second section, before there is a leap to the remote key of D flat major. The same formula is then heard at the end of the movement – at least so we think, as the three tonic chords are followed by a longer silence (four bars compared to two at the start of the development). But then the players suddenly start up again, using the same material that we heard after the shorter pause at the start of the development. This, though, turns out to be a relatively short detour, as the real end is eventually reached via the same formula of three repeated tonic chords. However, in terms of the listening experience, matters may not be as straightforward as this appears. Jadin marks a second-section repeat in addition to the more or less obligatory repeat of the exposition, so this means that by the actual end of the performance the listener will have encountered no fewer than six versions of this formula. Each of them is followed by a long notated silence, except for the very last. After the first playing of the ending, the performers return to the start of the second section, which begins with its own two bars of silence. After the second playing of the ending, no silence needs to be notated, since it will naturally occur. One could argue, though, that an exponentially increased equivalent of 'once bitten, twice shy' will be in operation – after so many false endings, the listener will surely no longer trust that the common turn of phrase actually means what it purports to mean. The silence at the end will be loaded; who will readily believe that the movement and work have truly finished? In this respect Jadin may have been taking his cue from the ending to Haydn's Op. 33 No. 2 – and since he dedicated his Op. 1 to Haydn, he no doubt wanted to show that composer that he understood the principle of using familiar means to achieve strange effects.

A virtuoso treatment of our closing formula, one that comes in all shapes and sizes, is found in the first movement of Gyrowetz's Quartet in B flat major Op. 44 No. 2 (1804). What would become the preferred nineteenth-century version forms the basic shape: the second part is higher and chordally fuller, and the third part is lower and in unison. It is first heard, in three-part form, in bars 20–21 to signal a firm arrival on V of V (Example 3.5a). Unusually, liquidation of more characteristic material is not total: interwoven with the formula is a quick rising scale in the second violin that continues an exchange of brilliant figuration between it and the

Example 3.5a Gyrowetz, Quartet in B flat major Op. 44 No. 2/i, bars 16–21[1]

Example 3.5b Gyrowetz, Quartet in B flat major Op. 44 No. 2/i, bars 42–46[3]

first violin. The second occurrence is heard shortly after the advent of the second subject, again on V of V, and is in fact very similar to what we hear in bars 20–21, minus the flourish from the second violin, which now joins with the others (Example 3.5b). By comparison with the first occurrence, this seems to be an 'incomplete' version, consisting only of the first two events – a cadential arrival at bar 44 followed by a more fully scored version of the same chord. This is followed by a figure in dotted rhythm heard in *piano* unison

Example 3.5c Gyrowetz, Quartet in B flat major Op. 44 No. 2/i, bars 83–86

Example 3.5d Gyrowetz, Quartet in B flat major Op. 44 No. 2/i, bars 262–266

which seems to interrupt completion of the full three-part form. But in fact this figure leads down in bar 46 to a unison C, which could in retrospect be heard to represent the third, low event. This third part has simply acquired a prefix, as it were. But if this is the case, the invariable timing of the schema – three equally spaced events – is being interfered with. On the other hand, the third appearance of the formula, at bar 85, which signals the end of the exposition, leaves no doubt: the third part has disappeared, being replaced by a silence of a whole bar that is also marked with a pause sign (Example 3.5c). This is unequivocally the two-part variant.

The ultimate manipulation, though, comes at the very end of the movement, from bar 264 – just where this kind of formula is most called for (Example 3.5d). Since bar 264 matches bar 85 at the end of the exposition, and a silent bar again follows, it seems we are to have a matching two-part version. But then after that empty bar all four instruments utter a low unison *piano* B♭. This is the most spectacular instance of playing with the timing of the formula that one could imagine – since the third component arrives fully a bar too late – and indeed also playing with the dynamic level, since a *forte* completion is essential for the gesture to work properly. If this sequence of events is disconcerting, then deliciously amusing, in its own right, it acquires even more force given the prominence of the pattern earlier on and the various ways it was inflected then. (Mixed in with these appearances of our hammerstroke formula are various other games with grand chordal closes that often fail to complete themselves or are oddly interwoven with other material.) Once more the listener learns that even the most routine of material cannot be taken for granted, can be made a 'subject of discourse'. The other aspect to the trick played by Gyrowetz is that the final, delayed part of the formula exactly matches the very first sound heard in the movement, which was also a soft low unison B♭, identically rendered in all four parts. Making this connection is quite plausible in the context of this movement given that unison playing has been an important textural-social subject throughout. So there is also a hint of circular return to the start, yielding yet another instance of the muddling of beginnings and endings.

A wider lesson to draw from such events is a preoccupation with formal edges – not just with what is heard at start and finish of a unit or a whole movement, but also with what happens in between, with how we get from one section to another. One manifestation of this is perhaps even more familiar than the various forms of (post)cadential play: the means by which previously heard material is reintroduced, in other words, a retransition. The classic case occurs in finales, particularly rondo or rondo-like finales, whereby an anacrusis that began the original theme is detached and repeated as a teaser, telling the listener that return to the familiar material is imminent. To play with the device, often by extending the reiterations beyond the point of expected return, is another one of those denials or deformations that is so common that it virtually constitutes a convention in its own right. And so to create a real stir with this brand of manipulation requires something out of the ordinary. The finale of Haydn's Symphony No. 93 in D major (1791) features an anacrusis of two repeated quavers followed by a leap up to a higher note on the downbeat. The anacrusis is detached and repeated on numerous occasions throughout, but the really remarkable one occurs in the middle of the movement. At bars 162–164 the orchestra settles on a repeated version of the anacrusis on C♯, which leaps up a full octave onto the following downbeat, marking the arrival on V of F sharp minor. After a general pause this C♯ anacrusis is reiterated twice, now with a gap in between, but this is accomplished by a solo cello, playing *piano* in its lowest register (bars 165–168). The sense of 'where to from here?' is dramatized by the shrinking of timbral weight to a lonely single string instrument. After a further pause, the answer comes: transpose the

Example 3.6 Haydn, Quartet in G major Op. 54 No. 1/iv, bars 185–193

anacrusis figure up a semitone to D, and we are home. But the scoring goes from one extreme to the other: the solitary soft cello is answered by the full orchestra (brass and timpani now joining in), declaiming the answer *fortissimo*. And this massed reply comes not twice, but once, an asymmetry which makes the contrast all the more shocking. The theme then returns promptly in the tonic, but after the massive sonic *Verfremdung* that has just been accomplished, it seems almost incidental. If reiteration of the lead-in figure is a standard retransitional device, often with the sort of irregular timing on display here, Haydn dramatizes the process so extravagantly that it arguably conveys greater 'content', a greater richness of information, than the reassembled theme of which it forms the first part.

Another way to put this is to say that such an anacrusis figure seems to become an agent in its own right rather than a means to an end – the same sort of conundrum that we noted in discussion of highly individualized motives in the previous chapter. This is apparent on the scale of a whole movement in the finale of Haydn's Quartet in G major Op. 54 No. 1 (1788). Its anacrusis figure is similar to that found in the finale of Symphony No. 93, consisting of two repeated quavers, though in this case the following downbeat stays on the same note rather than leaping upwards. It is played with, too, in a similar way to what we have observed of the symphony's retransition – by means of unexpected pitch, timing, dynamics and register – but in the quartet finale the play is more extended. The role of the anacrusis figure is for ever moving between beginning and middle, enunciation and transition. Each extended retransitional version, of course, promises to attach itself to a returning theme, thus changing function from transition to enunciation. At the end of the movement, though, the composer completes the set by turning the anacrusis into an ending gesture (Example 3.6). At bars 186–187 it is heard, for the first time, as a tonic chord. Played by all four parts in close position, *piano*, this new harmonic disposition immediately rules out the previous transitional function. Alternating with a low broken tonic triad played in *forte* unison, this tonic version of the anacrusis figure returns three times. While the cello remains stationed on a g^1, the other three parts move upward for the second and third versions, resulting in an almost freakishly high chordal tessitura third time around. After this, the *forte* broken triad fails to return, leaving an unexpected gap, after which the third version of the chord is repeated, but now *pianissimo*. And with that the movement is over. In the absence of any further sound we are forced to accept this gesture as signalling the end. A series of repeated tonic chords is no new way to finish a movement, though the manner in which it is accomplished here is something different. It is at once a brilliant piece of showmanship because of the extreme tessitura of the final chord, yet at the same time it is patently sketchy. While we are finishing with the most prominent material of the movement – and so from that point of view the ending makes sense – in other respects we are left more than literally up in the air. One reason for this is that one can sense behind this ending a ghost of our three-part postcadential formula, in the disposition used in Gyrowetz's movement, whereby the second part is high and chordal and the third part low and unison. In Haydn's ending the high tonic chords represent the middle term of the equation and the low unison arpeggios the final term, and so to finish in the middle of the formula, especially when it is repeated after the intervening silence, is both counter-intuitive and destabilizing.

More modest linking material may also be subject to the same sort of renewal. The Poco adagio from C. P. E. Bach's Symphony No. 2 in B flat major from the set written for Baron van Swieten (Wq182/2; 1773), to be played *senza Cembalo*, makes great play with a formulaic bass figure that drops an octave. It is the sort of figure whose role is normally confined to filling in the gaps that typically occur between the short phrase units of galant music, thus providing better continuity. It takes on such a role in this movement too, but so consistently as to defamiliarize the device. The bass line throughout the movement in fact consists of almost nothing but this figure, varied only through dynamics and sonority (pizzicato, arco, *piano, forte*), as well as placement within the bar. But this very variety, coupled with its insistent reappearances, gives the impression that the figure is an autonomous agent. It attains a perceptual prominence that goes well beyond the role of the discreet accompanist: the simple falling octave remains in focus when by definition it should, as it were, be seen but not heard. A more fluid version of the same kind of bass-line linking formula involves a rising rather than falling octave. Instead of leaping, it fills in the octave by means of a rising scale, only missing out scale degree 2, and it normally employs a sextuplet figure that leads to a longer final note. It often functions as a form of postcadential confirmation, which is what happens in the second movement of Brunetti's Symphony No. 36 in A major (no date), but with a difference: here it is heard at the very end of the movement, in lower strings and bassoons, and at a *forte* dynamic level, after the rest of the orchestra has seemingly played its final sound (bar 128). The figure thus disrupts a basic textural expectation, that all instruments will arrive at the end at the same time, and so what is usually a more or less discreet piece of textural glue draws attention to itself.

Another means of bringing such linking material alive is to integrate it into the phrase to which it leads. In the finale of Wanhal's Flute Quartet in C major Op. 7 No. 6 (1771) the first close on the tonic key is heard at the start of bar 13, and is followed by a typical bridging unit – repeated tonic notes followed by a falling tonic scale, played in unison. This leads to soft cantabile material that one would expect to continue in similar vein. The dashing unison figure is of the sort that normally occurs but once; it joins together two sections and then disappears, job done. But here it makes a second appearance, at bars 17–18, before a variant of the cantabile phrase unit then returns. Thus what seemed to be a purely functional element is made to come alive, integrated into a repeated gracious-riposte-like pattern. In the first movement of Hoffmeister's String Quartet in F major Op. 14 No. 1 (1791), immediately after a strong cadence in C major in bar 58, the viola plays a written-out turn figure in semiquavers on scale degree 5, which again would seem to have been played simply in order to bridge the gap until the next phrase begins. That function looks to have been fulfilled as the two violins then begin a new tune, but, as they continue, the cello answers the viola's figure, imitating it an octave below at the distance of a bar. The exchange between the two instruments is sustained as the phrase continues, and so once again the peripheral is made more central. While these are relatively localized events, such ambiguity of textural and functional roles can be maintained at greater length: the slow movement of Haydn's Symphony No. 52 in C minor (1772?) slyly manipulates both a melodic cadential formula and a bass linking figure to the point of confusion.[51]

Another kind of renewal may take place not so much at the formal edges, whether cadential or transitional, as within the phrase. Various kinds of

---

[51] A detailed account of this movement may be found in Sutcliffe, 'Expressive Ambivalence in Haydn's Symphonic Slow Movements', 98–110.

irregularity and extension may both complicate but also ultimately affirm the force of periodicity itself. And once more the irregularities may be quite indirect: a common procedure is have internal asymmetries of grouping that do not disturb the larger-scale arithmetic, whereby the complete phrase or theme still 'adds up' to a symmetrical four-or eight-bar duration. In the case of a C. P. E. Bach though, the disturbances are often more overt. In the Rondo in B flat major from the fourth *Kenner und Liebhaber* collection (Wq58/5; 1779), one return of the refrain (from bar 163) subjects the two initial one-bar cells to rhythmic augmentation, a stretching of the expected course of events. This stretched time is then filled with elaborate diminutions, which completely change the character of the refrain. What was chirpy and light-hearted is 'freed' into something far more lyrical. Although bar lines are retained through the expansion, the rhythms are so free that the two passages sound metrically unconfined. The impression is of a slow-motion exploration of 'voice', which suddenly, dramatically, has something quite different to tell us. After these extraordinary events, the rest of the rondo theme follows in its original symmetrical guise, as if nothing had happened – a patently ironic reversion to regularity and completion of the thought.

A more typical example of such internal expansion arises in the finale of the Sonata No. 1 in F major from Türk's *Sechs leichte Klaviersonaten* (1783). Its theme is a model of periodic construction, two eight-bar sentences making up a larger antecedent–consequent period. But when this theme is heard for the third time, in the movement's coda, from bar 70, its periodicity is disrupted. The continuation reaches the equivalent of bar 6^1 of the theme and then stops dead. The rest of the bar is silence, and then bars 5–6 of the theme are echoed at a higher register, *piano*, on a predominant harmony, before that too gives way to silence. The effect is of a musical question mark. After this further silence the original fifth bar is resumed at 78 and the theme carries on to a punctual close, thus matching Bach's basic shaping of disruption followed by restoration. Türk too reveals that while we might take periodic phrasing to be the natural order of things, it is in fact something that has to be constructed, a mechanism that can break down at any time. The final movement of the following work in the collection, Sonata No. 2 in A minor, applies such disruptions on a greater scale to an earlier part of its eight-bar phrase. Together these movements suggest that an artistic lesson – to startle in order to renew – is being 'taught' in works that are specifically being marketed at relatively unadvanced players.

Almost any musical element can be renewed through some sort of special treatment. Once more, though, this may happen without the element itself needing to sound anomalous. The keyboard works of Blasco de Nebra, for example, feature countless seemingly typical approaches to cadence points. These readily fit the template of what has become known as the *cadence galante*, involving a bass line that rises by step from $\hat{3}$ towards $\hat{5}$ before falling to $\hat{1}$, a melody that counteracts that by falling by step down to the tonic and a set harmonic progression of I^6–ii^6(or IV)–V6/4–5/3–I. Yet, especially in slower movements, the melodic lines are often realized with such idiosyncratic details (including lavish ornamentation and unusually timed and placed appoggiaturas) that the entire cadential exercise sounds anything but routine.[52] A more extensive example of the renewal of melodic formula comes in the Andantino. Arioso of Pleyel's Quartet Op. 1 No. 5 (1782–1783). For most of its duration this is an idyllic and lyrical movement, seemingly most remarkable for its key – it is set in B flat major in a G major work.[53] At several points, however, the first violin's eloquence fails, as it intones rather than sings long low notes while the other parts play in a rhythmically split unison. The first of these, from bar 25, is quite brief, but the second is more sustained (Example 3.7). The first violin's line from bar 104, to be played on the lowest string and marked *fortissimo*, has little of the normal periodic style of melodic construction about it. Rather, its long sustained notes, falling by step, suggest a kind of soliloquy.

However, the seemingly inexorable downward pull of the first violin's line does not lead it to the expected b♭ in bar 112. Instead, it cadences rather weakly on scale degree 3, then from 113 to 124 it plays a succession of commonplace cadential markers, suggesting a return to something more readily comprehensible, more socially attuned than the somewhat obscure passage of soliloquy. The unison of the other parts gives way around this point to full harmonization, so that the whole texture has once more taken on a more normal disposition. While the first violin's formulas take the plainest possible form, they come alive in this context. This is not just because of what has gone before, but also because of how they are realized, as a series of discrete attempts at closure above a bass loop. This represents an unusual level of paratactic organization, positively inviting us to hear a series of attempted farewells. Yet over the course of this passage, magically,

---

[52] For further discussion of this feature see Sutcliffe, 'Poet of the Galant', especially 310–311 and 316–317.

[53] The following account of Pleyel's movement is drawn largely from Sutcliffe, 'Simplifying Cadence', 178–181.

Example 3.7 Pleyel, Quartet in G major Op. 1 No. 5/ii, bars 102–126

renewal turns into estrangement. The normalizing, softening gesture ends up becoming too insistent through sheer repetition – there are at least six separate closing formulas played – and in fact ultimately fails. It has become the problem rather than the simplifying solution, and in bar 125

Example 3.8 Beethoven, Sonata in F minor Op. 2 No. 1/iii, bars 1–28²

the soliloquy material returns, *fortissimo* in all parts, together with a swerve into the relative minor, in which vein the movement comes to an end.

While all the formulas used in such a concatenation in Pleyel's movement sound familiar enough, sometimes the formula takes a very particular, more or less invariable form. One of those is the Cudworth Cadence, a variant of the *cadence galante*, which involves a particular rhythmic realization of the melodic descent.⁵⁴ Another is featured in the Menuetto third movement of Beethoven's Sonata in F minor Op. 2 No. 1 (1795; Example 3.8). Beethoven marks the end of the first section with a melodic line that follows a High 6 Drop (another Gjerdingen neologism⁵⁵) with the succession of scale degrees 1–3–2–1, which unit is then repeated with a decorated version of $\hat{6}$ (bars 10³–14¹). Not only the specific succession of scale degrees, but also the particular rhythmic-metrical organization, and, above that, the very decorated repetition of the unit, form part of this quite specific formula. The formula is used conventionally here, but then after the double bar, sooner than we would expect, it returns in iv. The first playing, at bars 19–20¹, has no High Drop from $\hat{6}$, though in the preceding bars the upper voice has been playing notes a fifth or sixth above the local tonic scale degree, and so the

---

⁵⁴ For definition and discussion see Gjerdingen, *Music in the Galant Style*, 146–149. In *Music in European Capitals* Heartz calls this simply a 'cadence galante', to which he adds a variant that he calls the 'wedge cadence' (23).

⁵⁵ For definition and discussion see Gjerdingen, *Music in the Galant Style*, 162–163.

basic shape of the formula is preserved. The complementary repetition, with a decorated High Drop inflected to become $\flat\hat{6}$–5, is *pianissimo*.

To this point, the use of the formula remains orthodox, though its placement after the double bar is mildly surprising: the formula would normally cap a complete melodic-thematic statement, rather than appearing five bars into a new section. But then the second part of the shape, involving the $\hat{3}$–$\hat{2}$–$\hat{1}$ close, is detached and repeated twice, still *pianissimo*. This is a more patent form of renewal, of a similar sort to that found in Pleyel's movement above. Once again there is an over-repetition that draws attention to the device, which normally has a set extent: two iterations only, the second lightly embellished. But the cognitive wake-up call becomes stronger when the three final melodic notes of the formula are repeated yet again from the upbeat to bar 25, and to quite different effect. They are now played *fortissimo* and in unison between the hands, and they have an initiating function, beginning a four-bar unit that moves us back to the dominant. This shows us in dramatic fashion that we cannot take the 'small things' for granted – the familiar turn of phrase is a live, rather than an automatic, part of the discussion, and it takes on sufficient agency to prompt a clear change of course in the music. Haydn disrupts this exact formula too in the minuet-finale of his Sonata H36 in C sharp minor (before 1780), whereby the second part swerves brutally back to the minor mode from an expected E major close. He achieves a different type of renewal of the formula in the tempo di menuetto finale of his Piano Trio H6 in F major (1784; see Example 5.6). As in Beethoven's movement, Haydn detaches the second, $\hat{3}$–$\hat{2}$–$\hat{1}$, half of the pattern and reiterates it, but this occurs across a formal divide. The formula is heard, without immediate repetition, at the end of the first section (bars 7–8), where it falls from a 'High 8'. Then straight after the double bar a fragmented version is heard, half-fulfilling the expectation of an immediate reiteration; this fragment then generates its own sequential continuation and leads to a quite unforeseen textural and dynamic climax. The effect of this enjambement is first disconcerting, then poetic.

However, smaller elements still can be given a new lease of life. The first movement of Boccherini's Quartet in E flat major Op. 32 No. 1/G201 (1780) fulfils the terms of its Allegretto lentarello e affettuoso indication through copious use of appoggiaturas (often restruck suspensions). These mark just about every beat of the opening theme, so that when another arrives at the end of the first two phrases (bars 4^1 and 8^1), it sounds both stylistically typical and also like part of the movement's profiled thematic material. But this double function takes on extra weight when another appoggiatura is used to mark the arrival on V of V at the end of a phrase in bar 16. Once again it sounds like a stylistically typical way of emphasizing the point of arrival, and one expects that the following phrase will move to something new. Instead, the suspension-cum-appoggiatura figure, with its crotchet-quaver rhythm, is used as a means of direct continuation. A rising sequence involving the figure is initiated by the first violin, so that once again a standard locution is shown to carry an unsuspected agency. What we would have heard as the ending of a phrase turns out to be the start of something else. The way in which this renewed figure carries us across a structural divide, as well as its treatment in rising sequence, are very similar to what Haydn achieves in the passage from his Piano Trio H6 discussed above.

If a phrase-ending appoggiatura is not an element one would expect to behave autonomously, as it were, the same might apply to another 'small' element, the trill. When sustained for any length of time, the trill most familiarly functions as a marker of impending cadence, and while the process to which the cadential trill contributes is frequently defamiliarized when the cadence is deflected or fails to arrive, it is rarer for the trill to form the focus in its own right. Beethoven, though, provides many instances of just this form of *Verfremdung*, perhaps most famously in the finale of his Sonata in C minor Op. 111 (1822). Another example would be the end of the development section in the opening Allegro of his Violin Sonata in F major, Op. 24 ('Spring'; 1801), where from bars 116 to 123 continuous trills at the extremes of the texture function as an arresting transition to the reprise. If in these instances the trill has become so disembodied that it has lost all of its familiar closing function, in his Quartet in B flat major L192 (1790; Example 3.9) Brunetti retains and renews that role. The first movement's exposition features a purple passage from bar 55 in which the harmony shifts to a remote D flat major and a turn figure, already an important thematic element, is isolated and reiterated in swift succession by the first violin. These reiterated turns grow by degrees into a very prolonged, and fully notated, cadential trill (bars 59–61), so that a routine gesture is made 'sincere' in context. Not only does it arise from the specific thematic circumstances of the piece, via the isolated turn figure, but it is made to sound like the natural climax to a process of gradual rhythmic diminution.

If trills and appoggiaturas would seem to represent just about the most untouchable of musical details, there are even more basic phenomena that can be held up for inspection. One would be simple repeated notes. Their main association, above all in galant music, is with an accompanimental

Example 3.9 Brunetti, Quartet in B flat major L192/i, bars 54–61

role. Yet as we saw in Chapter 2, repeated notes can interact with more obviously thematic material to create great fluidity of textural definition. If repeated notes are incorporated within say a melodic line, while also being present elsewhere in the texture, ambiguities about textural leadership can readily arise. The first movement of Haydn's Quartet in C major Op. 33 No. 3 (1781; Example 3.10), though, does something different with this conceit. In this case we begin with repeated-note quavers in second violin and viola, but there is no melody for them to support – they are an accompaniment to nothing. This immediately foregrounds the device, even though from bar 2 they take a back seat to the belated entry of a theme in the first violin. This theme, though, opens with a semibreve, followed by two grace-noted minims, all on the one note, and so it can be understood simply as a rhythmic augmentation of the repeated notes of the accompaniment. Not only does this blur the textural boundaries, but because the repeated notes occupy a full bar by themselves at the outset, they also gain an unusual perceptual prominence. And the fact that the first violin's line only achieves any strong rhythmic definition with the fourth bar of the movement increases that prominence still further. For such reasons, those repeated-note quavers are 'thematic' in that they form a memorable part of the whole shape that we retain and define in retrospect as a theme. But what is really different about this movement is what Haydn

Example 3.10 Haydn, Quartet in C major Op. 33 No. 3/i, bars 1–15

does *not* do after such an opening. He does not go on to exploit further the potential for textural integration by using repeated notes in conjunction with other material – which would mean that any other sequence of repeated notes could be referred back to their opening manifestation. Incredibly, the repeated-note quavers only appear in conjunction with the other materials presented in the opening phrases. They are used in no other context. In other words, this most standard of accompanimental devices has become so exclusively 'thematic' that it can never appear in its normal supporting role. Only the coda (see Example 3.25) provides a brief exception to this rule.

Even simpler than a repeated note is a single note – a drone. The finale of Haydn's Symphony No. 104 in D major (1795) opens with a soft low tonic drone on horns and cellos that is sustained for two bars before the entry of the rustic-sounding theme. But when its return in the recapitulation is approached by a lengthy pedal on C♯, it suddenly, as Simon McVeigh notes, 'achieves a dramatic compositional significance'.[56] A drone by definition does not move; it forms the ground for activities elsewhere in the texture. Yet the shift here from a sustained C♯ to a sustained D gives the lie to that; the device has changed from being static to being mobile, showing that even the simplest possible single-note phenomenon can be discursively and perceptually foregrounded.

One final example of renewal takes us back to accompanimental form and function. After a neat opening period to the first movement of Dussek's Sonata in D major Op. 31 No. 2 (1812), we start one of those 'melodic' transitions familiar from the work of Mozart (bars 16ff; see Example 3.11a). It remains firmly in D major, but the smaller-scale phrase syntax and the entry of an accompanying figure in constant semiquavers tell us that we are starting to 'travel' harmonically. After eight bars, though, this accompanimental figure, based on neighbour-note motion, abruptly takes over the whole texture at bar 24, suppressing the previous coherent melodic line. The dynamic swells to *fortissimo*, and the right hand joins the left in octaves, interspersing a simple alternating progression at the top of the texture.

This startling change of textural perspective is taken further in the recapitulation (Example 3.11b). For a start, the *fortissimo* version of the shape erupts after just four bars of the transition, instead of eight, at bar 119. The figuration is then subjected to a dramatic rising sequence (a Monte schema[57]), twice rising by a step at bars 123 and 127. When it reaches its plateau, on a tonicized F sharp minor chord, there is a textural change. We no longer hear the *fortissimo* presentation of the figure in octaves between the hands. Instead, it is played by the right hand alone, and it is now treated in a descending sequence, but with unpredictable harmonies and dynamics (which are different in each bar). What has happened here is that the material has, as it were, fulfilled its desire; it has become plainly melodic in character. It moves unpredictably, the very opposite of accompanimental behaviour, and it no longer supports but is supported, in this case by plainly subordinate repeated dyads in the left hand. The tables have been fully turned, and the former accompaniment is now the accompanied.

---

[56] McVeigh, *Concert Life in London*, 135.

[57] For definition and discussion of the Monte, a term derived from Riepel, see Gjerdingen, *Music in the Galant Style*, chapter 7, 89–106.

Example 3.11a Dussek, Sonata in D major Op. 31 No. 2/i, bars 8^2–31[1]

The Simplifying Cadence and the Soft Ending

In the foregoing discussion of renewal, the cadence formed a major point of focus; we saw how this most familiar and fundamental of devices could in various ways be made into an event rather than being a simple inevitability. A related phenomenon is what I call the simplifying cadence, in which cadence points act to calm the tone of the discourse.[58] In its succession of assertive and conciliatory gestures, it has much in common with the behavioural dynamic of the gracious riposte. But while the gracious riposte is most immediately recognizable when heard in an opening function and when composed of parts of equal length, even if neither aspect is binding, the simplifying cadence is different. As the name implies, it fulfills an ending function, and as a rule is used to inflect moments of strong formal closure. It also tends to take place on a larger canvas than the gracious riposte, and the two parts are not in proportion – typically a lengthy passage of animation, of some kind of heightened expression, is met by a concise and stylistically unremarkable cadential close.

---

[58] Much of the following section derives from Sutcliffe, 'Simplifying Cadence', 158–169 and 172–177.

Example 3.11b Dussek, Sonata in D major Op. 31 No. 2/i, bars 110–135

There is no question, to return to Caplin's thoughts, that cadential management is a particular focus of late eighteenth-century style. This includes, as we have seen, a tendency to stretch cadential progressions out and then delay the moment of their fulfillment, often leading the listener right to the point of arrival only to withhold its full articulation. The process becomes much more pronounced in the late 1700s than it had been in mid-century, and it means that the moment of relaxation – the moment when performers and listeners can breathe out – is postponed. Tension can therefore build up on quite a large scale, which is precisely what then makes the fact of closure so meaningful. Thus the formal process of a piece of music gains sharp edges, can offer expressive meaning in its own right; it is certainly no 'neutral' background for the 'real music'.[59]

[59] McClary, *Conventional Wisdom*, writes of the 'desire mechanism of the cadence' (16).

A concern with cadential process naturally forms a fundamental part of the theoretical revival that our repertory has recently been enjoying. Some of this literature in fact focusses specifically on the cadence, and while it aims to offer a comprehensive taxonomy of cadential types,[60] the social dimensions that are my concern are unlikely to be explicitly represented. To be fair, even the more humanizing topical analysis tends to run dry when trying to account for such points of the form. Allanbrook has noted that 'topical markedness often falls off when it comes time for closure despite the regular interplay between topic and syntax'.[61] Yet the less characteristic material that is used at such moments – more conventional, or simply plainer, beneath the level of recognizable formula – can be just as rich in social 'information'. This is a lesson we might draw from the various kinds of renewal covered in the previous section, though the simplifying cadence always involves conspicuously plain material, with few or no signs of 'added value' in the cadential formulation itself.

A laconic instance of such a simplification can be found in the first movement of Dittersdorf's Quartet in D major, K191 (1789; Example 3.12). The build-up to a decisive cadence in the dominant key begins in earnest from bar 37 with a series of roving chromatic harmonies in a slow harmonic rhythm of one chord per bar. The harmonic uncertainty is strengthened by the rhythmic agitation of the first violin's syncopated repeated notes, and a *crescendo* marking further dramatizes the process. With the arrival on V6/4 of the dominant in bar 41, we are back on track for a proper realization of the cadence. This is marked aurally by a quick rising scale, played in a higher register by the first violin alone. This is a common enough figure used to signal the approach to a cadence and would promise a strong point of arrival. But Dittersdorf ignores both the harmonic rhetoric and the soloistic rhetoric that have just been offered, and the cadence at 42–43 undercuts two types of more heated utterance, if in subtle fashion. There is no dynamic retrenchment – that is saved for the material that follows in the second half of bar 43 – but the first violin returns to a lower register and the four players act in complementary fashion to move the harmony on to V5/3 then I of A major. The rhythmic values used strike a mean between the longer and shorter notes that have featured in the

---

[60] See, for example, *What Is a Cadence?*, ed. Neuwirth and Bergé, and Pieter Bergé, Nathan John Martin, Markus Neuwirth, David Lodewyckx and Pieter Herregodts, *Concise Cadence Compendium: A Systematic Overview of Cadence Types and Terminology for 18th-Century Music* (Leuven: Leuven University Press, 2013).

[61] Wye J. Allanbrook, 'Mozart's K331, First Movement: Once More, with Feeling', in *Communication in Eighteenth-Century Music*, ed. Mirka and Agawu, 272.

Example 3.12 Dittersdorf, Quartet in D major, K191/i, bars 33–43

build-up, and the cadence arrives in an understated, matter-of-fact manner. The dramatic signals in the approach have simply been brushed aside.

Yet this is not the easiest of situations to read socially. Are we to hear a gentle irony in the abandonment of the higher-flown gestures that precede the cadence point, or is it a more straightforward return to normal collective behaviour? It is very characteristic of the ethos of this music that it is left up to the listener to judge, to try to read the tone, just as we would in a social situation that may contain conflicting signals. A passage in the first movement of Pleyel's Quartet in A major Op. 1 No. 3 (1782–1783) offers an instructive comparison (Example 3.13). Once again this involves arrival on the dominant in an exposition section. From bar 78 we can hear a standard full cadential approach, with the bass moving through scale degrees 1, 2, 3 and 4 of E major, then in bar 80 a sharpened 4 supporting a diminished-seventh chord. The ensuing V6/4 in bar 81 is expressed by violin 1 alone playing a rising arpeggio, suddenly marked *forte*. This is the right gesture for an expansive realization of a major cadence point, but it is odd that it fails to gain support from the other instruments. Instead, it is answered in bar 82 by a laconic single B in viola and cello, then the two violins alone add the tritone of the V7/3 harmony, suddenly marked *piano*. The arrival on I in bar 83 is accomplished solely by the cello, playing a low E *pianissimo* – even softer, in other words. The resolution of the tritone created by the D♯

Example 3.13 Pleyel, Quartet in A major Op. 1 No. 3/i, bars 75–83

and A in the two violins is withheld, and only happens indirectly, and crookedly, down an octave in the second half of the bar, in the two middle voices, by which time a new phrase has in fact begun. Thus we have witnessed the cadence unravelling in terms of texture, then dynamics, and finally voice leading.

If this represents a simplification, it does so radically, to the point of dysfunctionality. In this case one can hardly miss the sense of incongruity with the preceding material. The passage suggests that pretension has been cut down to size, that what could have been a brilliant and weighty close has been ironically undermined. There is a sort of moral wound up in such a sequence of events, that forceful expression should not be sustained, that it ought to give way at some point to a more modest demeanour. This is a lesson that one can glean from conduct books of the day, for instance in Knigge's *Über den Umgang mit Menschen*: 'The wiser a noble-minded man is, the more modest, diffident of his own knowledge, and the less intruding he will be'.[62] But it is also a 'lesson' that one can hear being taught in sound in Example 3.13.

---

[62] Knigge, *Über den Umgang mit* Menschen, volume 1, 4; *Practical Philosophy of Social Life*, trans. Will, volume 1, xviii. For further commentary on this aspect of the culture of the time, and its musical embodiments, see Sutcliffe, 'Before the Joke'.

Example 3.14a Kraus, Violin Sonata in C major VB160/ii, bars 57–60

Example 3.14b Kraus, Violin Sonata in C major VB160/ii, bars 1–2

A similar sequence of musical events can be found at the end of the slow movement of Kraus's Violin Sonata VB160 (1780–1782), a formally free and rhapsodic Adagio in F major. While we are securely in the tonic key as we approach its ending, in bars 57–58 (see Example 3.14a), the music feels unsettled: the dynamic markings seem to fight against the natural syntax of the music, with abrupt alternations of *forte* and *piano* disguising the simple repetition of a melodic figure. As if to move beyond such disruption, in bar 58 the violin alone plays something more fluent, a flourish that ends with a rising subdominant triad. What has been initiated with this material is the closing formula known as the Grand Cadence, which we encountered in Chapter 2. What one would expect to hear next according to that pattern is a low B♮ followed by C and then rapid rising figuration – a scale or an arpeggio – that would lead to a cadential trill. This would produce a brilliant, forceful finish. Example 3.15, from the finale of Haydn's Quartet in B flat major Op. 50 No. 1 (1787), shows a more or less orthodox realization of the pattern, heading likewise towards a close in F. But in the Kraus movement there is a lengthy silence, and then the two players outline a rising triad of F major, *pianissimo*. If this is disconcerting enough, since the expected style of continuation has simply been abandoned, it becomes even more so when we realize that this material recalls an early shape played by the piano alone in bars 1–2 (see Example 3.14b). Thus the

Example 3.15 Haydn, Quartet in B flat major Op. 50 No. 1/iv, bars 57–66

forward propulsion towards a firm finish to the movement is replaced by a reminiscence that suggests a more circular sense of time, and what had originally functioned as an opening gesture now has to be reheard as a closing one.

While this seems like a classic instance of an understated, simplifying close, in some ways what follows the violin's rising triad does fulfil expectations. While any linking B♮ is suppressed, we do then hear a low C, and this is followed by rising figuration. Thus both the basic pitch structure and the contour do accord with the model. A further part of the equation is harmonic ambiguity. The rising arpeggiation in bar 59 could readily be interpreted as a V6/4, the extended 6/4 which will lead to a firm dominant 5/3, as indeed sounds on the downbeat of bar 60; compare Haydn's version of the schema from bar 60 of his movement (Example 3.15), with its two full bars of V6/4. However, when we heard this figure in bar 1 of Kraus's movement (Example 3.14b), it clearly formed part of a simple prolongation of the tonic chord. Caught between these two possibilities, the listener may be unsure whether the harmonic function of bar 59 is to be understood as dominant or tonic.

Nevertheless, the Grand Cadence schema is undermined by being hollowed out in the middle. The incongruity between bars 58 and 59 suggests a gently comic effect, a wry withdrawal from the firmer closure that could have been. On the other hand, we might note that the violin's flourish in bar 58 leading to its subdominant triad is to be played *piano* rather than the much more likely *forte*. From this point of view, the entire schema is in fact understated, and the subsequent pause and softly stealing arpeggio are not so much incongruous as consistent with a larger-scale whole. This again renders the tone ambiguous; perhaps the whole passage can be understood as denoting an elevated, noble simplicity.

Example 3.16 Mozart, Sonata in F major K332/iii, bars 218–245

While all the examples we have encountered so far feature a single area of simplification, in the finale of Mozart's Sonata in F major K332 (1783) there are two stages to the process. This movement is predominantly in an animated, brilliant style, and from bar 222 a final close in this manner seems to be initiated (see Example 3.16). At the very point when we are about to complete a transposed equivalent of the end of the exposition, bar 227, the composer changes the expected root-position tonic chord. It has A in the bass instead of F, and is inflected by an E♭, thus becoming an applied dominant to the B flat major IV of the following bar. What Mozart has done here is to switch formulas: instead of a self-contained three-chord pattern that marks closure, the 'hammerblow' formula we considered in the previous section, we have a third component that points forwards. The formula that replaces this involves the same bass line we heard in our Pleyel movement (Example 3.13), using a chromatic rise in the bass from scale degrees 3 to 5, supported by a series of full loud chords. And to strengthen the sense of a grand peroration, it happens at a slower rate than the ending formula that has been overwritten. Instead of hearing a chord each dotted-crotchet beat, we hear just one chord per bar. This markedly slows the momentum, but once the whole pattern has concluded, we would expect a resumption of brilliance – the energy dammed up will then spill forth in an animated conclusion.

On two counts, though, this doesn't happen. The schema is realized in orthodox fashion harmonically, but not rhetorically. Thus the diminished-seventh harmony in bar 229 leads to a V6/4 then a V7/5/3, and each of these chords also lasts a bar. But in terms of right-hand register, dynamics and duration it is all change. We hear a soft close-position V6/4 chord held through the whole bar, and this is followed by a similarly sustained dominant seventh. The top voice, g^1, is decorated first by an a^1 appoggiatura and then by an anticipation of the f^1 note of cadential closure: this is a familiar cadential formula, similar to the one we saw being used in the minuet from Beethoven's sonata Op. 2 No. 1 (Example 3.8). The suddenly gentle, modest continuation of the schema takes the wind out of its rhetorical sails. This feels like a change from instrumental to vocal style, from brilliant instrumental declamation or display to simple song. It can also be heard to function ironically. The movement's brilliant, exuberant manner – previously self-evident, and especially when we are building up to the ending of a finale – is made to seem retrospectively overwrought. 'No need to shout', the player seems to suggest. Of course such a choking-back is considerably less likely to happen in an orchestral work, and this reminds us that the simplifying close will be most frequently found in chamber genres.[63]

Clearly after such a formula, no matter how unusually it is realized, something more needs to be added, but in this movement there is no further outbreak of brilliance. Instead the simplifying, withdrawing cadence colours what now follows from bar 232. This is in fact a verbatim restatement of a passage heard in the exposition but not then at the equivalent point in the recapitulation (compare bars 232–245 with bars 22–35). As the section now returns 'too late', as it were, it has a sort of retrospective quality that aids the sense of distancing accomplished by the

---

[63] Nevertheless, many examples will certainly be found in orchestral works. Some of the most striking seem to be found in slow movements, as in the Andantino e cantabile of Haydn's Symphony No. 42 (1771), bars 62–66, in which a prolonged pre-cadential *crescendo* to *fortissimo* in a full texture is undercut by a low *piano* understatement at the ensuing cadence point.

simplifying cadence. But it also encapsulates the pattern we have just heard of brilliance being met by a lyrical, stepwise rejoinder. The staccato figures heard here from bars 232 and 237 are hardly in full brilliant style, but they are *forte* and unison, and they move upwards. What answers them in each case is a single melodic line that moves mostly downwards. The second of these lines finishes at bars 241–242 with the exact cadential formula we heard earlier at 230–232, though played at twice the speed. The sonata then finishes as the original passage in the exposition did, with a *calando* and final dynamic of *pianissimo*. Soft confiding charm thus has the last word. At the same time we have clearly been manipulated, in that material originally having a relatively local ending function now fulfils a global one.[64] Both this rearrangement and the sudden reining-in, twice over, of any 'naturally' brilliant peroration testify to a discursively self-conscious style. Now the player seems to say 'Not only do I not need to shout, I don't need a flash new ending – there's one I used earlier that will work just fine.'

If the finale of K332 twice withdraws from an expected extroverted conclusion, in the first movement of Kozeluch's Quartet in E flat major Op. 32 No. 1 (1788) the simplifying cadence forms a persistent, and eventually dramatic, strain. There are two instances in the exposition, both in the name of establishing the dominant key (Example 3.17). After a heightening of rhythmic animation marked by a resumption of triplet values, bars 43–44 cap this by presenting an expansive V6/4 harmony, with the first violin peaking on a very high $b\flat^3$ on the downbeat of 45. Then, instead of running through to the cadence point with further brilliant material, the lower three instruments play *pianissimo* crotchets on a vii of V chord. V arrives in the next bar, complicated by a 4–3 suspension in the viola, and the first violin comes in on the second beat with a *pianissimo* falling-triplet figure that leads us quietly to the cadence, a definitive understatement. This spoiling tactic seems to demand another attempt to close firmly on the dominant key, since within a handful of bars another strong cadential approach is being created. If the previous one was redolent of the concerto, this one, from bar 52, suggests the overture: repeated crotchets in the cello, a gradual stepwise ascent in the violins and a continual *crescendo*. By bar 56 the players have cycled back to material heard during the previous cadential build-up (compare bars 56–58^1 with 39–41^1). But, as before, this is undercut, through exactly the same *pianissimo* phrase that creates the gentlest of closes.

---

[64] This ending perfectly exemplifies what Alfred Brendel calls Mozart's capacity to offer 'the surprise of the expected'. Brendel, 'A Mozart Player Gives Himself Advice', trans. Eugene Hartzell, *The New York Review of Books* (27 June 1985) www.nybooks.com/articles/1985/06/27/a-mozart-player-gives-himself-advice/ (30 June 2018).

Example 3.17 Kozeluch, Quartet in E flat major Op. 32 No. 1/i, bars 37–60

After a sustained passage of brilliant contrapuntal activity at the start of the development, our phrase returns, minus the first violin's falling-triplet figure. It is now marked to be played '[piano] e piu lento', which seems to stress its softening character. However, the material no longer has the function of quietly taking us to a cadence point. It is immediately repeated, in sequence, and is more dissonant, featuring full diminished sevenths, decorated by a painful dissonance in the first violin. This double version is repeated twice more as the harmony takes on an even more exploratory character, and the dynamic level switches to *forte*. All these factors mean that what was an understated, formulaic closing phrase has acquired a different, insistent character, and is now associated with harmonic instability – not resolution, as before. After further uncertain harmonic swerves, our original phrase returns, transposed into C minor, at bars 123^3–125^1.

Example 3.17 (continued)

Having become disruptive, harmonically and simply in the slowing of the tempo, it now resumes its role as the conciliating agent (and the *a tempo* presumably starts from this point).

In the recapitulation the softening phrase comes twice in similar circumstances to the exposition, though on both occasions the brilliant approach is extended by a bar or two, which makes the softly understated cadential completion all the more striking. Also striking is that the coda features a more or less complete reworking of what happened to this material in the development, complete with 'più lento' marking. This includes a final return to its conciliatory form, though now not marked *pianissimo*. Then, after a few bars of animation over a repeated tonic pedal, the first violin's falling-triplet figure returns by itself. It is now passed around in small-scale dialogue, and, on its final appearance, is coordinated with triple-stopped chords in the violins, *forte*. It seems as though our soft understated closing phrase, undertaken in the name of social equilibrium, in order to undercut the surrounding 'big talk', has itself become socially tedious, having been used so often. Therefore reworking it in this way at the end revives it. It still has an effective closing function, and achieves this in the more lively and assertive fashion that we would have originally expected to hear.

In all of our examples to this point, it seems to be the arrival on the cadential 6/4 that acts as a turning-point. This is not surprising, given that the 6/4 acts as a fulcrum for a cadence of any strength; as we saw earlier in the case of the finale of Haydn's quartet Op. 50 No. 6, an emphatic arrival on the 6/4 makes the cadential outcome seem inevitable. There, for once, it did not in fact happen, and we might also call to mind the concerto cadenza, which is all about delaying, more or less intricately, the subsequent arrival of a clear root-position dominant. Arrival on a 6/4 also leads to a simplifying cadence in the first movement of Dussek's Piano Trio in F major Op. 21 No. 3 (1793), but with a difference. After violin and piano have alternated playings of the second theme, the surface rhythm doubles, with brilliant continuous semiquavers in the piano right hand and the main motive from the first theme passed between cello and violin. The excitement level mounts as a series of quick repeated chords pushes us towards the dominant 6/4 at bar 92. This is then prolonged for several bars, the typical cue for arrival on the dominant 5/3, possibly to be marked by a cadential trill, and then the cadence. Dussek even begins, in bar 94, a rising arpeggio in the piano right hand, the sort of shape that would take us towards that 5/3, in Grand-Cadence fashion. But instead, from bar 96, we hear a lengthy further prolongation of the 6/4 via various chromatic sidesteps and an arching melodic line that replaces the expected brilliant figuration. And, notably, the dynamic level drops to *piano*. Eventually the harmony settles back on a straightforward 6/4 in bar 101 and there immediately follows the most understated, matter-of-fact slide to the 5/3, followed by the local tonic chord to create the cadence. Disproportionately short in time given the extended build-up, the cadence sounds like the last word in laconic utterance: once again a domineering brilliance has been thwarted. The difference in Dussek's movement is that the simplifying cadence does not represent an abrupt change of pose; there has been a long dissolve from the point of maximum animation.

While all the examples we have examined so far involve a denial or undercutting of brilliance, there are other characteristic contexts in which sudden simplification can take place. One of these comes especially in slow movements, and concerns passages that threaten to become too passionate or too heated – where it is not so much virtuosic or physical display that is ultimately tempered as emotional display. In the Adagio of Gyrowetz's Quartet Op. 44 No. 3 (1804) the passion that must be overcome is a collective affair. The elevated tone of this movement is already suggested by the remote relationship of its key, E major, to the tonic of the whole work, A flat. This is also the case with several contemporaneous slow movements that turn to E major from a flat-side overall tonic: the Adagio of Haydn's Sonata in E flat major H52 (1794) and the Largo of Beethoven's Piano Concerto No. 3 in C minor, Op. 37 (1800).[65] Not only do the three movements share a gravity of expression, but they also all make great play with the remoteness of their key from the work's tonic. In the case of Gyrowetz's movement this is plainest in the fact that much of the development section is set in that tonic of A flat major. This heightened harmonic awareness also helps to make sense of a feature we can see in Example 3.18, which shows the start of the recapitulation. The opening material returns from bar 44, but, as happened at the outset, the first phrase ends not in an expected dominant of B major but veers into C sharp minor; this can be seen in bars 46–47. The chord on which this phrase ends is G sharp major, the dominant of C sharp minor, but enharmonically this is nothing other than our overall tonic of A flat major. From a technical point of view, such an enharmonic pun is a witty procedure, yet the tone of the music does not betray this; it remains quite absorbed in itself. From 47 to 48 the G sharp major dominant resolves to the local C sharp minor tonic, which is prolonged through the next two bars, made more dramatic by the sudden repeated-note accompaniment in the lower strings and the first violin's more arioso style.

For a few bars we then move back into the orbit of E major, but a second intervention by C sharp minor soon arrives, in bar 54. This brings a sudden urgency of expression – those repeated notes return in the lower voices, now marked *forte*, and we hear a syncopated first-violin part. What helps to convey an abrupt heating of the temperature is the first violin's very lack of shapely melodic behaviour: instead of continuing in the same eloquent

---

[65] Slow movements in E major seem to have acquired a quite distinct identity altogether around this time, but they also form part of a wider pattern of moving to the extreme sharp side in works set in flat-side keys. See chapter 3 – '"High-Encrusted Jewels" and Their Puzzling Reflections: Large-Scale Sharpwards Movement and Multi-Movement Integration in Works by Haydn, Beethoven, Clementi, Hummel and Dussek' – in Rohan H. Stewart-MacDonald, *New Perspectives on the Keyboard Sonatas of Muzio Clementi* (Bologna: Ut Orpheus, 2006), 145–208.

Example 3.18 Gyrowetz, Quartet in A flat major Op. 44 No. 3/ii, bars 43–57

melodic vein, it becomes insistent, one could even say inarticulate. In bar 55 the phrase comes to rest on the dominant of C sharp minor, which is another enharmonic reference to A flat major. Then Gyrowetz magically juxtaposes his G sharp major chord with an E major 6/3 on the second beat

328   Formula

Example 3.18 (continued)

of the bar, with the common note G♯ highlighted in both cello and first violin. The dynamic abruptly drops from *forte* to *piano*, and the tonic 6/3 chord signals the start of the cadential approach proper.[66] After a poignant suspension in the first violin on the downbeat of bar 56, the violins suddenly play an entirely unremarkable cadential locution, one that we hear countless times in the works of Boccherini, for instance. The dotted rhythms and grace notes plus the descending stepwise contour all help to lighten the tone (a similar effect is achieved using very similar material in the Adagio of Latilla's Quartet Op. 1 No. 1 in C major (c1765), bars 20–22 and 24–26, in which duetting violins, using dotted rhythms and grace notes, also offer soft concessive replies to climactic material). This is a wonderful example of cadential simplification, where the use of formulaic material helps to unclot intensity, and enables us to return to a more generally intelligible brand of musical behaviour. At the same time, because of the context, the familiar is made to feel special, a response specific to the work at hand rather than a casual pleasantry. In the following bar 57, with its duet between viola and violin 1, there is a feeling that the movement has regained equilibrium of discourse, just as it has regained the tonic key.

While the move from something heated to something commonplace in this passage may suggest incongruity, it need not be taken in that way. Perhaps, as in Example 3.7 (Pleyel) or Example 3.14a (Kraus), we should hear not so much a lessening of intensity as simply a move towards a different style of utterance: an inspired simplicity. This might accord with the thesis of Carl Dahlhaus according to which both polite and courtly culture in the eighteenth century moved away from display and towards

---

[66] As noted earlier, William Caplin maintains that a tonic 6/3 chord (an 'initiating tonic') is the invariable starting-point for the approach to a true structural cadence in the music of this time: 'Classical Cadence', 83.

the ideal of 'noble simplicity', the very understatement guaranteeing the authenticity of feeling.[67] Indeed, for Dahlhaus and Ruth Katz, the equating of 'genuine' emotion with simple expression was the central thesis of the aesthetics of the Enlightenment, a subject to which Chapter 4 will return.[68]

While Gyrowetz's simplifying cadence dispels or diffuses one peak moment of intensity, the device is also subject to repeated appearances in other slow movements. In the Poco adagio of Kozeluch's Sonata in D minor Op. 20 No. 3 (1786) the same simplifying two-bar unit ends every phrase of the movement. This is always preceded by some clear signs of intensification, whether a quick rising chromatic flourish or a series of chromatic harmonies. The material that inevitably follows is coded 'plain', bringing us back down to earth with a simple tuneful closing line featuring dotted rhythms. The effect could be heard as one of noble simplicity or gentle irony, or indeed both. Near the end of the Andante from Mozart's Piano Concerto in B flat major K450 (1784), from bar 95, we hear a passage that consists of a chain of chromatic seventh chords built over a rising bass line, none of which resolves in orthodox fashion. The lack of resolution and a series of dynamic spasms – a repeated-note *forte-piano* figure that is played out of phase in the winds and piano – create an expressive knot that is suddenly untied by the simple cadential formula played by piano alone at bars 99–100. This gesture is in effect repeated for the rest of the movement, as the piano plays a series of elaborated closing formulas, initially punctuated by slightly menacing dynamic swells in the orchestra, continuing the process of 'purification'. The first two of these simplifying formulas in the piano use dotted rhythms for the same sort of lightening effect as found in the movements by Kozeluch, Latilla and Gyrowetz above.

The reduction of utterance evident in such contexts can be taken to quite extreme forms. In the slow movement of Haydn's Symphony No. 88 in G major (1787), which we glanced at in Chapter 2, the famously eloquent melody is at several points (bars 39–40 and 105–106) reduced to a skeleton form, all the more noticeable since these represent variants of what was originally a more melodically mobile phrase. The ultimate simplification, though, would be no melody at all. Near the end of the Andante from Mozart's Sonata for Two Pianos in D major, K448 (1781), an expected

---

[67] Dahlhaus, *Die Musik des 18. Jahrhunderts*, 2. Dahlhaus comments that this growing taste for noble simplicity was by no means confined to the bourgeoisie, but was also taken up by enlightened absolutism.

[68] 'The bourgeois conviction that a "genuine" emotion manifests itself simply, and that simplicity guarantees the "genuineness" of an emotion[,] was the central thesis of the aesthetics of the Enlightenment.' Katz and Dahlhaus, *Contemplating Music*, volume 2, 114.

strong cadence in the tonic is dramatically interrupted twice, first by a sequence of forceful chords that deflects us from the goal (a sort of misplaced Fonte schema[69]) at bars 106–107, and then at bar 109 by a *forte* diminished-seventh harmony that lasts a whole bar. This expansive diminished seventh, though, then takes its place as an applied chord back to a further dominant 6/4, and then the second piano alone proceeds to supply two full bars of simple repeated-quaver chords that at last allow the cadence in the tonic to arrive without any fuss at all. There is no melody to guide us home but, instead, something that sounds like a rudimentary realization of a figured bass. In both these works, such simplicity surely increases rather than reduces the eloquence of effect.[70]

Beethoven's 'crescendo to nothing' technique often allies itself with our phenomenon; this typically promises to deliver a strong cadence by means of loud dynamics, syncopated *sforzando* markings and the like, but then around the point when we expect the cadential arrival, there is a sudden withdrawal to *piano*. In the first movement of Sonata in E flat major Op. 31 No. 3 (1802; Example 3.19) this happens not at the end of a major section, as in most of our examples thus far, but right near the start. After the striking opening on a supertonic seventh chord, the phrase slows down and crescendos at the same time before arriving at a weighty pause on a 6/4 chord at bar 6. Instead of continuing in a similar vein through to the cadence, which would probably involve further warmly scored crotchet chords, we hear a reduction to *piano* and a common cadential formula in the melody. This formula is just another variant on the $\hat{3}$–$\hat{2}$–$\hat{1}$ pattern that has featured in a number of our simplifying cadences so far – in Mozart's K332 (Example 3.16), for instance. And so instead of a grand point of arrival we hear something that sounds modest, even coquettish.[71] The lightening of tone continues with the following staccato rising scale. In the counterstatement from bar 10, the registral unity of the first presentation is broken up. The same material is played at different registers that are in dialogue with each other. This variegation means that when we return to the little melodic formula in bar 16, with its middling tessitura, it

---

[69] On the Fonte, a term also derived from Riepel, see Gjerdingen, *Music in the Galant Style*, chapter 4, 61–71.

[70] Daniel Heartz comments how at this point the composer 'cut[s] back all figuration in the final pre-cadential area and let[s] a bare accompaniment speak by itself': *Mozart, Haydn and Early Beethoven*, 104.

[71] Charles Rosen, *Beethoven's Piano Sonatas*, 173, notes of this opening that 'The answer to the questioning pressure, when it comes in bars 7 and 8, is a shock after the unprecedented opening: it is simply a conventional cadence, sociable, courteous and deflating.' Roger Moseley, *Keys to Play*, 223, describes how at this point 'the right hand performs the cadential formalities with a flippant shimmy'.

Example 3.19 Beethoven, Sonata in E flat major Op. 31 No. 3/i, bars 1–25[1]

sounds even more like a wry understatement. From this point the lighter tone expressed by the formula takes over. From bar 17 Beethoven rewrites the opening material, adding a drum bass in repeated quavers and further grace notes, followed by the introduction of 'Scotch snap' rhythms and then trills, all of which increase the flirtatious tone of something that originally sounded introspective.

Beethoven's movement reminds us vividly of the type of renewal that is accomplished by the simplifying cadence: a hands-off treatment of the cadential formula itself, with the effect of *Verfremdung* achieved entirely through contextual manipulation. Any sense of estrangement, even shock, derives solely from the gap between preparation for and realization of the cadence. What is most unusual in Op. 31 No. 3 is how little preparation there is, given the appearance of the device so early in the movement – though one can argue that, with the Indugio-like repeated supertonic chords being the first thing we hear, Beethoven has in fact begun in the middle.

The opposite effect, but just about as disconcerting, occurs in the second and final movement of Haydn's Sonata in G minor, H44 (c1771–1773). Here the simplifying cadence occurs at the very end, and there is no direct approach to it; instead, it is preceded by silence. Prior to that, a passage of free figuration in bars 102–106 has dissolved the very consistent rhythmic basis for what is a virtually monothematic ABAB structure, in which tonic minor and tonic major alternate. This passage also clears away the heavy downbeat dissonances that have featured in almost every bar of the movement. Given these changes, the ensuing silence might be a particularly expectant one. Yet the simplifying cadence that follows, in G major, is not just a formula, but the most commonplace one of its time, the Cudworth Cadence. It concludes not just a movement, but a work that has been heavily melancholy throughout. While the Cudworth Cadence has already been heard some six or seven times in the movement, its final appearance here sounds less like a *lieto fine* than a wry anti-climax. It shares a certain sense of bathos with what Beethoven achieves at the other end of his sonata Op. 31 No. 3. In both cases, though, one result is to make us hear a common turn of phrase afresh, since through contextual manipulation it has been turned into an isolated, and questionable, entity.

One major difficulty with the category of simplifying cadence that I have proposed is that it could seem to be self-fulfilling. After all, isn't a certain simplification of material a precondition for a successful cadential close? We might recall Schoenberg's term 'liquidation', for instance, which captures the way in which characteristic thematic elements give way to conventional ones to enforce the closure of a tonal phrase.[72] However, given the typical syntax of later eighteenth-century style, with its emphasis on small-scale reciprocal activity, such a process is brought much more squarely to the listener's attention: the music is, once more, 'packaged' in such a way that we can hardly avoid noticing the concessive force of such a style of cadence. Further, from my perspective the process involves no lessening of character or interest, as the term 'liquidation' might imply. It may bring about the reinvigoration of formula, of everyday language, as we can hear in many of the cases treated above. The material that creates the simplified close may be entirely formulaic, but its placement in a particular context makes it surprising, invites us to hear it with fresh ears. On other occasions the result is even simpler, involving a reduction to material that is almost sub-formulaic – Example 3.13 by Pleyel was one instance of this,

---

[72] For a definition, according to which liquidation 'consists in gradually eliminating characteristic features', see Arnold Schoenberg, *Fundamentals of Musical Composition*, ed. Gerald Strang, with the collaboration of Leonard Stein (London: Faber, 1967), 58. William Caplin's version is also germane: 'the purpose of motivic liquidation is to strip the basic idea of its characteristic features, thus leaving the merely conventional ones for the cadence'. Caplin, *Classical Form*, 11. But it is, of course, in such 'merely conventional' elements that I have attempted to locate social meaning.

with its laconic B in viola and cello in bar 82 followed by the tritone of the dominant seventh in the two violins. What we hear sounds like a skeleton, a voice-leading reduction from a putatively more eloquent original. In this case too what is being foregrounded is something prized in sociable interchange, whereby even the simplest utterance, in the appropriate context, carries value, can function as *le mot juste*. What is being highlighted with the device of the simplifying close is a kind of musical behaviour that, as with the gracious riposte, negotiates between categorical and concessive tendencies. The process of reduction that underlies it is often realized so as to highlight incongruity, so that the act of softening is shot through with self-deprecating humour or even irony. This creates a double-edged quality appropriate to a sociable style that must inevitably mix calculation with consideration for others.

A related phenomenon is the soft ending to a movement. In several of our cases above the simplifying cadence also functioned as the ending altogether, but where this happens in a lyrical slow movement, such as the Andante of Mozart's K450, there can be no particular surprise: a gentle finish would be the rule rather than the exception. The soft ending becomes a marked event where it is generically less expected – this means in faster movements, and in particular in finales, where the expectation of a dynamically strong and expressively extroverted close is at its strongest. By definition the soft ending is a postcadential phenomenon, whereas the simplifying cadence generally occurs at a formal crux. And while the latter directly juxtaposes the expressively assertive with the expressively modest, in the soft conclusion the contrast may be more implicit and indirect.

A further distinction between the two events is that what the soft ending draws attention to, and thereby refreshes, is not so much the material itself, but the formal function of (final) closure. One might expect this, given that the primary role of postcadential material is to create an appropriate sense of an ending, to make the end of a movement 'feel right'. At the end of the first movement of Mozart's quartet K499 (Example 3.20) the material is in fact shaped in such a way as to make us expect a brilliant finish. From the upbeat to bar 254 the first violin plays the two-bar head motive of the movement – the soft fanfare that we studied earlier (Example 2.30) – starting on successively lower notes of a tonic triad, to the accompaniment of written-out trill figures. These help to create a sense of anticipation that is augmented from bar 259 when the first violin's material accelerates, turning the primary motive into the standard sort of flourish that would work up to a big cadence (a nice example of liquidation). The sense that a strong finish is imminent is encouraged by a *crescendo* to *forte* in all

Example 3.20 Mozart, Quartet in D major K499/i, bars 251–266

Example 3.21 Krommer, Oboe Quartet in F major, P IX:22/iii, bars 194–211

instruments in bars 259–260. At bar 261, however, the dynamic suddenly drops to *piano*. What ensues is a large-scale ascent by first violin up the tonic triad to balance the previous large-scale descent over bars 254–260. The very pronounced rise in register, evident in all parts, together with the active nature of the figuration, mean that this passage could easily provide the brilliant ending that might be anticipated from the rhythmic diminution heard in bars 259–260. One could readily imagine hearing bars 261–266 performed *forte* and thinking nothing was amiss; maybe only the cello's final four notes would be somewhat out of place, given their relatively high register. It is only the dynamic level – *piano* and then *pianissimo* from the penultimate bar – that undercuts the expected effect.

The material heard at the end of the rondo finale of Krommer's Oboe Quartet in F major, P IX:22 (date unknown; Example 3.21), is also not in itself out of the ordinary. The movement seems to have finished at bar 202, after an animated prolongation of the tonic, though our stylistic antennae may detect that another chord or two would be needed to secure complete closure (perhaps our three-chord formula). But then after nearly three bars of general pause, the theme returns, now introduced by a new anacrusis figure. The accompaniment is less active than at any previous point, with viola and cello playing a sustained chord. However, the fourth bar (209) does not give us the expected further reiteration of the motive that dominates the rondo theme – three repeated quavers. Instead, we hear a simple crotchet tonic chord, followed by a *pianissimo* V7–I close on the succeeding downbeats of bars 210 and 211. There is a clear functional reason for this change: the circularity of motivic construction within the rondo refrain (the repeated-note motive occurs in eleven of the theme's sixteen bars) means that some point of difference is needed from previous appearances of the theme if it is to function as a convincing close. Thus Krommer dissolves its most characteristic feature in bar 209, and this liquidation of the characteristic allows the ending promptly to take place. On the other hand, Krommer had already achieved ample liquidation via the repeated *forte* passagework that had all but secured a sense of proper closure by bar 202. The effect of wry understatement in what follows is enhanced by the suspicion that the whole closing phrase is more or less redundant.

Another kind of double-edged quality may obtain in the case of endings such as those provided by Mozart and Krommer. They are at once undemonstrative and conspicuous. To withdraw dynamically into an unexpectedly soft finish is, of course, to draw attention to the act of closure, to make us think about what makes for suitable closure – something that is considerably less likely to occur when the usual strong signals are sent out. In other words, understatement can be perceptually 'loud'. Considering the phenomenon in a study of Beethoven's sonatas, Rosen even says that such endings are 'not modest, but more pretentious than the standard closures. They prolong the atmosphere beyond the final chords.'[73] This reminds us of the double nature of such a compositional act from a behavioural point of view. While it would seem to count as a kind of deference, a token of good manners, a soft ending can readily take on a self-conscious aspect that potentially undercuts its 'modest charm'. The same was and is true of such human behaviour in general: deferential manners can walk a fine line between concern for others and a self-regarding display of one's superior sensibilities. From that point of view, highly cultivated, soft good manners

[73] Rosen, *Beethoven's Piano Sonatas*, 173.

can actually be a form of aggression. And such behavioural ambiguity is also apparent in the case of the simplifying cadence.

On many occasions, though, soft endings arise in association with a popular stylistic register that might make such suspicions seem out of place. This is particularly likely in finales, where 'downward' topical movement is, after all, very common; this is in itself a large-scale form of simplification. A number of Brunetti's most popular- and picturesque-sounding quartet finales, for instance, finish *piano* or *pianissimo*, and it is also striking that their soft postcadential extensions tend to be strictly regular in terms of phrase rhythm. Examples may be seen in the final movements of the Quartet in A major L191 (1792) and Quartet in E flat major L195 (1792–1793), where the four-square, no-nonsense nature of the endings invokes that apparent lack of artfulness that is intrinsic to the pastoral mode. In the finale of his Quartet in C major Op. 2 No. 2 (1784), which is framed by overtly rustic material, Pleyel allows the second violin to continue with its simple rocking accompaniment for two bars after the other three players have come to rest on pedal notes, and once that instrument joins them, the final chord – effectively a multi-part drone – is held for over two bars. The ending is marked 'Perden[dosi]', effecting a rare instance of a fade-out.[74]

The same idea is realized in less obviously pastoral fashion in the finale of William Shield's String Trio No. 8 in F major (1796). Marked 'Guioco Tempo Straniere', the movement is a series of variations on a theme in 5/4 time. (The dedication claimed that this and another movement from the published set bearing the same time signature had 'amused some of the most distinguished Professors both in England & Italy'.[75]) In its simplifying final section, the tune is reduced to a basic outline and features a Quiescenza. At the end the players hold an F major chord *diminuendo*, and then, in an unexpected picturesque touch, the viola plays a soft arpeggiated flourish while the other two players continue with their sustained triadic notes. A related conceit, whereby a finale features no sort of clearly punctuated ending-point, but simply stops, is found quite frequently in Kozeluch's sonatas. In the final movements of his Sonata in G minor Op. 15 No. 1 (1785) and Sonata in E flat major Op. 26 No. 3 (1788) the effect is achieved courtesy of busy repeated semiquaver figuration that

---

[74] My description of Pleyel's finale borrows from a slightly longer account of the movement in W. Dean Sutcliffe, 'Haydn, Mozart and Their Contemporaries', in *The Cambridge Companion to the String Quartet*, ed. Robin Stowell (Cambridge: Cambridge University Press, 2003), 196.

[75] Cited in Robert Hoskins, Foreword to William Shield, *String Trios* (the nine works are issued separately), ed. Hoskins (Wellington: Artaria, 2004), iv.

Example 3.22 Clementi, Violin Sonata in E flat major Op. 15 No. 1/iii, bars 187–199

comes to an abrupt halt. The harmonies alternate rapidly between tonic and dominant in typical postcadential fashion, but the continuity provided by moto-perpetuo-style figuration and the subdued dynamic levels that have been reached tend to override such markers of imminent closure. In both cases the effect partakes of the duality evoked above: self-evidently low-key ('I will stop now because I have nothing more to say') yet also something of a special effect, the modest conclusion immodestly drawing attention to itself.

The final movement of Clementi's Violin Sonata in E flat major Op. 15 No. 1 (1786; Example 3.22) subsides in just such a manner, but such effects are not confined to finales. The opening Allegro di molto of his Op. 15 No. 3 finishes with a particularly poetic take on the soft close. In the final three bars, as the dynamic level contracts to *pianissimo*, the piano reiterates a closing motive on tonic harmony while the violin plays falling dyads, in a realization of Gjerdingen's Final Fall formula. Coming almost immediately after two *fortissimo* reappearances of the opening theme, these final bars are quite disarming in the way that they continue a regular pulse until the very end.

Nor are such effects confined to the chamber, though they are certainly more readily achieved there. We have already encountered soft endings in the finales of orchestral works such as Mozart's concerto K415 and Haydn's 'Farewell' Symphony, the latter admittedly a very exceptional case. Rosetti showed a particular preference for subdued conclusions,[76] and had little compunction about using them in orchestral genres. The finale of his

---

[76] Sterling Murray writes that Rosetti was 'especially fond of the *perdendosi* conclusion and employed it throughout his career'. Murray, *Antonio Rosetti*, 195.

Symphony in B flat major Murray A45 (1777) features a conclusion not just to the whole movement, but to the exposition section as well, that is unexpectedly slow as well as unexpectedly soft, through the introduction of new Adagio material, on the latter occasion embellished with an oboe solo.[77] The last movement of Rosetti's Symphony in F major Murray A33 (1784–1785) seems set to finish emphatically via that typical device of dominant-tonic chordal alternation. But these strong closing signals are followed by a series of soft echoing fragments in individual parts. These do not coalesce into any sort of final corporate close; the texture is simply dispersed and the movement vanishes into thin air. We encountered a less extreme version of this effect in Chapter 2: the end of Brunetti's Symphony No. 9 in D major, which finishes with a *pianissimo assai* arpeggio for strings alone. What lends an extra frisson to all such gestures towards the expected close of a movement is that such material often functions as a tease, suggesting a drop in energy levels before the appropriate closing rhetoric eventually re-establishes itself. Wanhal plays with this expectation in the final movement of his Symphony in D major Bryan D17 (1781). At bar 237 a falling-step figure that derives from the first theme is changed into a falling third, which is passed antiphonally between pairs of instruments *pianissimo* to the accompaniment of a rocking-octave figure on first violins. The effect is the pastoral one of calls heard in the distance. These echoing calls also suggest a modest withdrawal after the typical brilliance and vigour of a symphonic finale, and hold up the prospect of a gentle ending. On this occasion, though, Wanhal follows through on an expectation that loud chords will eventually arrive to restore the proper closing rhetoric. Yet there is a sting in the tail. The previous textural dispersal is not entirely reversed, since while the strings play concluding *forte* I–V–I chords on successive downbeats, the winds and timpani play the equivalent chords on successive second beats of each bar. Thus some sense of loosening of a conventional finale ending remains. Through the dispersal of forces that should speak with one voice at such a point, Wanhal draws attention to the fact of closure, to the fact that there is nothing 'natural' about a musical ending: it is instead something that needs to be made.

Reduction

One way of framing the various kinds of operation evoked thus far in this chapter is to suggest that they all demonstrate a taste for reduction. Certainly

---

[77] See Murray, *Antonio Rosetti*, 200.

the simplifying cadence and the soft ending both manifest a desire to take away the thick, loud or heated and to reveal the virtues of the undemonstrative. This kind of stripping-back is also apparent in the way in which apparently simple phenomena such as trills or linking figures can be brought to the fore. From this perspective the emphasis falls not so much on 'renewal' as on simple creative curiosity, a wish to look intently at the small things that make the bigger things possible. This might be described as an intrinsically analytical orientation, with its traditional implications of picking an object apart to see how it works. But, as has always been the case with analytical operations, certainly when applied to music, they may alienate the receiver. They may, for instance, be perceived to interfere with one's untrammelled enjoyment of the whole; they may bring about a sense of disproportion through various kinds of over-emphasis and under-emphasis. They will almost certainly interfere with any smooth absorption of the discourse, and from that point of view are anti-rhetorical devices. We know that many auditors experienced discomfort with such procedures; accusations of 'comic fooling' were common, though by no means all of the operations described above need lend themselves to a comic interpretation.

An alternative way to describe this orientation would be via the interest in mechanism that has formed a significant part of recent eighteenth-century musical scholarship.[78] This also implies a preoccupation with understanding how structures are built up from simple discrete elements, and this may have been encouraged by the contemplation of periodicity as a sort of great machine, as suggested in Chapter 2. The music-theoretical literature of the period certainly displays an interest in mechanism thus defined, and we can see from his London diaries that Haydn, the most obvious musical engineer of his time, had a voracious appetite for all those small things that oiled the wheels of larger things, whether social, statistical or structural.[79]

At the same time, this taste for reduction has its behavioural and discursive implications, as explored earlier. 'To say more with less' might be a fitting maxim for this tendency, born of a distrust of a certain kind of eloquence. It is a kind of anti-sublime: instead of the listener's being overwhelmed with the unutterable or grand, the listener is instead offered a clear view of the underwhelming, as it were – ordinary, everyday musical

---

[78] See, for example, Annette Richards, 'Automatic Genius: Mozart and the Mechanical Sublime', *Music & Letters* 80/3 (1999), 366–389, and Emily I. Dolan, 'E. T. A. Hoffmann and the Ethereal Technologies of "Nature Music"', *Eighteenth-Century Music* 5/1 (2008), 7–26.

[79] For an encompassing interpretation of the composer's interest in such matters, and their musical consequences, see Nicholas Mathew, 'Interesting Haydn: On Attention's Materials', *Journal of the American Musicological Society* 71/3 (2018), 655–701.

objects. Of course, as we have seen, such objects may then be transformed to strange, not to say wondrous effect. Catherine Packham discusses the distrust of literary eloquence that was signalled by Hume's essay 'Of Eloquence' of 1742. As opposed to the easy, familiar fluency championed by the likes of Hume and Joseph Addison, there was the kind of eloquence that had more sublime aspirations; this brought problematic associations of 'authoritarianism, passivity, tyranny, passions, and excess'.[80] One musical reaction to such dangers was to cultivate the sort of understatement that issues from our simplifying, reductive manoeuvres. Nevertheless, we have seen that this socializing modesty can be loud and forceful in its way. In the case of Beethoven, this loudness is often literal. As Rosen writes, 'Beethoven knew how to strip naked the simplest elements of tonality in order to release their full power, to use the commonplace to reveal what made it so irresistible. . . . Beethoven's crudeness was provocative, never fortuitous or thoughtless . . . His art was never innocent, but it often deliberately skirts the edge of the artless.'[81] This is in fact a fine description of the reductive ethos that we are currently contemplating, even if the first Beethovenian examples that we are likely to call to mind hardly suggest modest understatement.

Nor might we think of Boccherini in connection with the matter, yet Rosen's description would also capture very nicely one of the composer's outstanding creative predilections. Boccherini's frequent loops – repetitions of short musical gestures that go beyond natural periodic bounds – also express this kind of reductive ethos.[82] In the minuet from his Quartet in E minor Op. 32 No. 2/G202 (1780), for example, bars 20–28 feature a loop in which the same two-bar module is repeated four times without alteration, each part reiterating its material verbatim.[83] The first violin's two-bar module is exactly palindromic, furthering the sense of repetitive overload. The effect is always disproportionate in context, in this case in the service of alternating 7/5/3 and 6/4 sonorities over a dominant pedal of E major. This too 'skirts the edge of the artless' – in this case sounding

---

[80] Catherine Packham, 'Cicero's Ears, or Eloquence in the Age of Politeness: Oratory, Moderation, and the Sublime in Enlightenment Scotland', *Eighteenth-Century Studies* 46/4 (2013), 504.

[81] Rosen, *Beethoven's Piano Sonatas*, 247.

[82] On this feature see Sutcliffe, 'Haydn, Mozart and Their Contemporaries', 193–194, and Elisabeth Le Guin, '"One Says that One Weeps, but One Does Not Weep": Sensible, Grotesque, and Mechanical Embodiments in Boccherini's Chamber Music', *Journal of the American Musicological Society* 55/2 (2002), 218–222.

[83] For further discussion of this movement see W. Dean Sutcliffe, 'Archaic Visitations in Boccherini's Op. 32', in *Boccherini Studies*, volume 1, ed. Christian Speck (Bologna: Ut Orpheus, 2007), 265.

distinctly rustic – yet is also insistent, not to say excessive. And as with Beethoven's insistence on the simple things, such passages can prompt quite opposed reactions. At one moment they may strike one as over the top, yet at another one's resistance can be broken down: as we are made to listen harder to the simplest sonic phenomena, a sense of fascination or wonder may take over. In the case of Boccherini's loops Elisabeth Le Guin has pinpointed the effect: during such repetitions what gradually reveals itself is 'the unsuspected richness of the everyday'.[84]

The same rubric may also profitably be applied to other simple elements that are reduced to a 'naked' state through a reductive process. Repeated notes are such an element. We have, for instance, encountered them in the service of textural ambiguity in works like Dittersdorf's Quartet K193 (Example 2.20a and b): as they hover between melodic and accompanying roles, they seem to consume the entire musical fabric. They also form an almost invariable part of those anacrusis figures that are so insisted upon in rondo forms. Even more pronounced in its reductive mania than those examples cited earlier would be something like the retransition section heard from bar 140 in the finale of Haydn's Symphony No. 88. Once more this is based on the common device of anticipating the return of the refrain via teasing repetitions of its anacrusis. Not only does this anacrusis also involve two repeated notes, but so does most of the theme that it initiates. This particular retransition features versions of the repeated-note cell beginning not only on the upbeat, but also on the downbeat, and the alternation of the two – one beginning-oriented, the other teasingly promising to lead to a thematic return that never seems to arrive – lasts for no fewer than nineteen bars. As before, this insistence on a small and seemingly simple bit of material may both repel and attract. In objectifying the element concerned, it may prompt irritation on the part of those who want the 'real music' to resume. On the other hand, given the sustained soft dynamic that occupies almost the entire retransition, the oscillations of the two forms of the cell might readily cast a hypnotic spell. Once again, even the smallest possible element of a musical discourse can be transformed into an object of attention.

As we saw above, the reductive process can go further, with the way in which the single-note drone was brought to consciousness in the finale of Haydn's Symphony No. 104. The raw power of a single note is also on display in the first movement of Rosetti's Symphony in D major Murray A20 (1786), which opens with a sort of minimalistic take on the Mannheim crescendo. It is built on a single note that begins as a repeated minim and

---

[84] Le Guin, 'One Says that One Weeps', 222. See also Le Guin, *Boccherini's Body*, 69.

accelerates successively through crotchets and quavers to a bar of repeated semiquavers, which effectively turns the note into a tremolo. This pattern is presented in canon by the strings, starting in violin 1 and imitated at a bar's distance by violin 2, then viola and cello, and finally by the bass. Symphony No. 1 in D major from C. P. E. Bach's set of *Orchester-Sinfonien mit zwölf obligaten Stimmen* (Wq183/1; 1775–1776) begins in similarly primal fashion, with a single note that is repeated in successive rhythmic diminutions. Many slow introductions of the time, too, begin in such a way – with a simple single impulse from which all else grows. Haydn's 'Representation of Chaos' from *The Creation* (1796) is the most celebrated of this class, and might indeed be regarded as the climax of our larger category altogether (as well as an influential model for countless nineteenth-century beginnings). In such a case, though, we can no longer properly speak of reduction, since that presupposes a fuller or more intricate fabric from which the simple element is subsequently extracted. What operates here and in the Bach and Rosetti openings is more like the opposite of this. Nevertheless, the same impulse to strip back, to dwell on individual elements, to contrast complete utterance with its constituent parts, is in operation; in the case of 'Chaos' Richard Kramer frames this as Haydn's 'quest to discover the beginnings of language'.[85]

A series of single notes grouped together into the most basic diatonic form constitutes a scale, which can also be presented in such reduced circumstances. The Trio from Haydn's String Quartet in E flat major Op. 76 No. 6 (1797) is built on alternating rising and falling scales of E flat major passed canonically between the four players, each time beginning with a monophonic presentation of the scale in iambic rhythm. This is a plan of seemingly nursery-rhyme simplicity, yet, as Georg Feder notes, it sounds 'as if one were consciously hearing a scale for the first time' ('Es ist, als ob man zum ersten Mal mit Bewußtsein ein Tonleiter hörte.').[86] This in itself, by drawing our attention to a feature that we would normally take for granted, creates a certain richness of perception – a 'thin' element becomes 'thickly' described by the composer. Furthering that sense of enrichment, on the basis of an initial unaccompanied tonic scale played by a single instrument, the texture is again and again built up from scratch into ever-new forms: we end up hearing a virtual compendium of harmonic and contrapuntal techniques.[87] Beethoven may well have been impressed by

---

[85] Kramer, *Unfinished Music*, 163.   [86] Feder, *Haydns Streichquartette*, 106.
[87] The last few sentences derive from W. Dean Sutcliffe, 'Musical Materials', in *The Cambridge Haydn Encyclopedia*, ed. Caryl Clark and Sarah Day-O'Connell (Cambridge: Cambridge University Press, 2019), 222.

Example 3.23 Mozart, Violin Sonata in E flat major K302/iii, bars 162–175

this particular instance of reduction: the finale of his Symphony No. 1 in C major (1800) begins with an Adagio in which, as noted in Chapter 2, the first violin hesitatingly works its way towards a complete rising scale of an octave, adding one further note on each attempt.

Even sound itself may be produced out of nothing, as it were. Near the start of the sixth and final movement of Haydn's Symphony No. 60 (1774) there occurs the famous passage where the violins interrupt the progress of the movement in order to retune their strings. What is at stake here is not a musical element as such, let alone an actual formula, but something much more basic – the very production of sound.[88] However, reduction need not take such radical forms as those detailed here. It is a more general taste, coming most obviously to the fore in the ways in which endings at various levels are effected. The very process of liquidation, observed and defined by Schoenberg primarily in relation to our repertory, clearly embodies a reductive ethos. The various features associated with liquidation are, of course, hardly confined to our repertory, but they are surely more conspicuous here. Mozart, for one, took great pains with such reductive manoeuvres. The last dozen bars of the finale of his Violin Sonata in E flat major K302 (1778; Example 3.23) offer a nice instance. The theme of this Rondeau movement returns for one last time at bar 164, but its

---

[88] That such attention to sonority is a new development of the time is the thesis of Dolan, *Orchestral Revolution*.

Romanesca-style falling bass line is replaced in the first two bars by a tonic arpeggio, followed by two bars of simple dominant. At the point when the dominant is reached, the piano departs from the expected continuation of the theme, replacing its stepwise movement with a decorated rising sixth that is then mirrored by a falling sixth in the following bar. The violin, meanwhile, plays simple semiquaver oscillations in a low register. These simplified first four bars are then repeated, so that the expected eight-bar unit does not eventuate. This is followed by further liquidation from bar 172: the melody just heard contracts into a simpler form, represented by its opening note and the falling sixth of its fourth bar, together with a dynamic reduction to *pianissimo*. This in turn contracts into reiteration of its opening note, E♭, alone, blending with a soft version of the three-part closing formula. This progressive shortening of the length of musical units matches what we noted earlier in the first movement of Mozart's K499, though to different effect: what we hear over the course of this final passage is a kind of purification, an emptying-out of more complex melodic and harmonic movement. We are left with something more elemental. This is all the more striking given that this passage has been preceded by a clearly climactic version of the theme's consequent phrase, from bar 153: *forte* after the previous *piano* dynamic, with a full and wide-ranging texture in the piano part, and with an effortful one-more-time repetition of the latter half. This creates a phrase of sustained intensity that lasts for eleven bars.

On occasion this kind of reductive process blends with the use of more popular-sounding material. In the case of Mozart this may even entail the arrival of a completely new tune, a process identified by Allanbrook, who describes the phenomenon as 'the tune that sprouts from the top'.[89] And it need not be confined to faster movements. The final bars of the slow movement of the Sonata in D major K311 (1777) feature what sounds like new melodic material from bar 90, though this is too short-lived to be called a tune. The left hand offers a new style of oom-cha-cha accompaniment that supports this topical swerve. Nothing that we have heard before in the movement has prepared us for such material, though it does not sound particularly incongruous. Rather, once again we witness a reduction to a simple core of utterance. This may indeed represent a kind of pastoral conceit, born of a shared conviction that simplifying processes 'take us further'.

---

[89] Allanbrook, 'Mozart's Tunes', 177.

Attention and Boredom

In the Preface to the first volume of his *General History of Music*, first published in 1776, Charles Burney sets out to define the approach he will take to his subject:

My subject has been so often deformed by unskilful writers, that many readers, even among those who love and understand music, are afraid of it. My wish, therefore, is not to be approached with awe and reverence for my depth and erudition, but to bring on a familiar acquaintance with them, by talking in common language of what has hitherto worn the face of gloom and mystery ... and though the mixing [of] biographical anecdotes, in order to engage attention, may by some be condemned, as below the dignity of science, yet I would rather be pronounced trivial than tiresome ...[90]

Burney's concern to avoid any sort of hermetic approach, trying to reach as wide a readership as possible, may have been understandable given the magnitude of his task, which was to write a large-scale history of Western music. It was a task that was by no means complete in 1776, as three further volumes would occupy him extensively until 1789, resulting in what is now seen as a milestone in music historiography. Clearly he did not wish his labours to be wasted upon the air, to be read only by a small learned circle. At the same time Burney's thoughts strike a strong chord with the music scholarship of our own era, and debates about the relevance and reach of such activity. His avowed desire to put a human face on the subject – which among other things involves avoiding excessive technical detail – and, indeed, the need to win a wider audience for this work can readily be related to recent disciplinary imperatives.

In another respect, though, Burney's preface seems to be more specifically characteristic of his time. His remark that he 'would rather be pronounced trivial than tiresome' encapsulates an important discursive ideal of later eighteenth-century culture, which demanded that one avoid giving the impression of high seriousness. In a world that continually declared itself to be a sociable one, a weighty, heavy, serious tone could suggest self-absorption, a relative lack of concern with whether other people shared one's views or indeed were even interested in knowing about them; recall William Weber's formulation concerning 'a sense of propriety that abhorred speaking in excessively serious terms'. Better too light than too heavy, Burney seems to say, but note how he precedes his

---

[90] Burney, Preface, *General History of Music, Volume the First*, 19.

alliterative pair of 'trivial' and 'tiresome': by the word 'pronounced'. What counts, in other words, is the perception of others. It is not a question of an intrinsic lack of serious intent, but rather the style in which one chooses to interact – in this case, the manner in which Burney downplays his natural position of authority as the writer in order to accommodate the reader, particularly those readers who might feel intimidated by the subject matter. Note that Burney does not in fact disavow 'depth and erudition', but would clearly regard it as a failure if his writing produced such an impression at the expense of promoting the understanding of the reader.

The style of address that Burney aimed to cultivate could also be seen to match his actual subject matter, at least in its most contemporary incarnation. The modern music for which Burney was such a strong advocate was also marked by a predominantly informal, friendly tone, which meant avoiding overt displays of learning (especially in the form of strict counterpoint): it seemed ever conscious of the need to engage its listeners. Indeed, one might argue that – most obviously in the hands of a composer such as Haydn – music had never before been so conscious of being listened to, had never before so actively engaged with its own immediate reception. The predilection for comedy and surprise are just the most obvious signs of this orientation. Lest this seem too anthropomorphic – music after all only arises through human agency – we might note how Burney himself framed the encounter with music, especially of the wordless instrumental kind. How to come to terms with such an art, when no text was present to channel one's reactions, was of course one of the most intensively debated problems of eighteenth-century music criticism. When Fontenelle posed his question 'Sonata, what do you want of me?', with 'sonata' standing in for all instrumental music in the modern style, Burney rose to the challenge with:

if a lover and judge of Music had asked the same question as Fontenelle; the Sonata should answer: 'I would have you listen with attention and delight to the ingenuity of the composition ... as well as to the charms of refined tones, lengthened and polished into passion.'[91]

What is most significant here is not what the sonata answers, but the fact that it answers at all. Such a personification suggests, as we saw in Chapter 1, that instrumental music could be understood to 'speak' to the listener, to engage in dialogue with the listener, as if it were its own agent. After all, the music can only answer back if it is granted a degree of autonomy, as though

---

[91] Burney, *General History of Music, Volume the Second*, 11.

it were a living, breathing life form of its own. And the tone of its reply is anything but heavy: this music suggests rather than decisively states a mode of listener understanding. It invites rather than determines a response.

One term of reference used by Burney not just in his mock-conversation between music lover and sonata, but also in the Preface to his *General History*, is 'attention'. This word, and its equivalents in other languages, lights up any number of later eighteenth-century writings on music. Its importance as a critical theme had been underappreciated until Matthew Riley signalled it in his study *Musical Listening in the German Enlightenment: Attention, Wonder and Astonishment*.[92] While Riley confines his treatment largely to north German writers, it seems that wherever one looks, 'attention' emerges as a watchword. The very debate on the nature of wordless instrumental music seems to have pivoted around the need to focus the interest of the listener. Noël-Antoine Pluche in 1746 stated that without accompanying words, it was difficult to engage attention: 'The most beautiful melody, when only instrumental, almost inevitably becomes cold, and then boring, because it expresses nothing. It is a fine suit of clothes separated from the body'.[93] This suggests that instrumental music is an inanimate object, certainly remote from Burney's personification of the sonata that talks back. And indeed one way of bringing this object to life was to imagine it in linguistic terms, as did Charles Avison in a preface to a set of accompanied sonatas published in 1760:

It is rather like a Conversation among Friends, where the Few are of one Mind, and propose their mutual Sentiments, only to give Variety, and enliven their select Company. . . . Thus Music may be said to discourse, and keep up our Attention like a methodical and intelligent Conversation.[94]

Thus music acquires its intelligibility through its language character. That music could be understood as a language became, as we have seen, one of the catch-cries of the eighteenth century, but it may not have been grasped in the literature that this metaphor seems to increase in direct proportion to the focus on listener attention. A favoured sub-category of language was, as Avison's preface shows us, conversation. The same rationale, of holding the attention, could be given for vaunting conversation itself. André Morellet in 1780 noted that 'Conversation gives us a lively and

---

[92] Riley, *Musical Listening in the German Enlightenment*.
[93] Pluche, *Le spectacle de la nature*, volume 7, 115, cited in translation in *Music and Culture*, ed. Fubini, 83.
[94] Avison, 'Advertisement' to Six Sonatas for the Harpsichord, with Accompaniments for Two Violins, and a Violoncello, Op. 7 (1760), cited in *Essay on Musical Expression*, ed. Dubois, 177.

alert attention that sometimes proves to be more useful than meditation itself. The latter is sometimes fatiguing ... conversation comes to the aid of the exhausted mind.'[95]

It is interaction that brings us most fully alive, ensuring that attention is held when we, as it were, lose interest in ourselves. Moving from conversation in the salon back to the musical world, and from the accompanied sonata to the genre of the concerto, we might note the concerns of Heinrich Christoph Koch that the listener should have a stake in the unfolding musical performance. He wrote that the listener is 'the third person, who can take part in the passionate performance of the concerto player and the accompanying orchestra'.[96] The idea of participation, of 'taking part', forms an important precondition for holding the attention of the listener. While the interaction between the various parties unfolds according to polite precepts in all these examples, it need not always be so. After all, even Edmund Burke's theory of the sublime, published in 1757, can be understood to proceed from the problem of maintaining human attention to our environment. In a less amiable vein than our previous writers, he posits the need for discomfort, even terror, to pull us out of a state of potential lethargy, an indifference to the ordinary experiences of our lives.[97]

Writers of musical treatises were also concerned with securing the concentration of the listener. While most authors stressed intelligibility of structure as a basic starting-point for attention, above all involving the use of regular periodic phrases, others looked elsewhere. In his *Essay on Musical Harmony* of 1796 Augustus Kollmann noted the absorbing effect of a digressive phrase – what he called the 'fancy period' – 'in which the composer seems to lose himself in the modulation, for the purpose of making the ear attentive to the resolution of the period'.[98] What Kollmann had in mind was what we would now call a development section or the sort of harmonic free fall found in some sections of a fantasia. And according to Türk in his keyboard treatise of 1789, listeners to concertos paid more

---

[95] Morellet, 'Réflexions', in *Mélanges de littérature et de philosophie du 18e siècle*, four volumes (Paris: Lepetit, 1818), volume 3, 21, cited in translation in Gordon, *Citizens without Sovereignty*, 204.
[96] Koch, *Versuch einer Anleitung zur Komposition*, volume 3, 332, cited in translation in Keefe, *Mozart's Piano Concertos*, 181.
[97] Edmund Burke, *A Philosophical Enquiry into the Origin of Our Ideas of the Sublime and Beautiful* (London: R. and J. Dodsley, 1757).
[98] Augustus Frederic Christopher Kollmann, *An Essay on Musical Harmony: According to the Nature of That Science and the Principles of the Greatest Musical Authors* (London: J. Dale, 1796), 84.

attention to their cadenzas than to anything else.⁹⁹ What Kollmann and Türk held to be the most ear-catching parts of a musical discourse were in fact also the freest, the least predictable, quite the opposite to the tight forms represented by periodic phrase syntax. In other accounts such passages would represent the most likely point at which a listener's mind would wander off. Thus both regularity and irregularity could be drafted in to serve the imperative of attention, so all-consuming had it become as a frame of reference.

Such differences of opinion certainly extended to the basic reception of modern instrumental style, yet, whether welcoming or hostile, everyone seemed to agree on the desirability of attention as such. But how surprising could this be? We could hardly imagine that previous generations of musicians didn't want and expect such concentration on their art. As William Hayes wrote in response to Avison's *Essay on Musical Expression* of 1752, 'he contenteth himself with telling us, it is only *keeping up our Attention from one Passage to another*; if that be all, his Discourses have no other Tendency than those of any other Author'.¹⁰⁰ Nevertheless, it is no accident that the concept of attention finds its way into so many intellectual frameworks of the time. The increasing frequency of reference bears witness to a shift from authority to taste as the basis for human judgment, not least in the realm of the arts. What this means in terms of music is a new emphasis on listener response. For a writer like Avison in his *Essay on Musical Expression*, this means a refusal to lay down rules about how music should be understood; instead, under the banner of 'expression', he refers listeners back to their own responses, appealing to sensuous individual experience. We can readily relate this to the pragmatism offered by Charles Burney, in which he refuses to stand above the reader and direct their thinking.

Such an orientation towards the listener has been fully acknowledged by more recent scholarship; in fact it forms an article of faith. However, this does not mean that the composer has to do all the work. As we saw in Chapter 1, in her study of metric manipulation in the string quartets of Haydn and Mozart, Danuta Mirka stresses the need for the listener to become 'an active partner of the eighteenth-century composer' in what she

---

⁹⁹ Türk, *Klavierschule*, 313, noted in Danuta Mirka, 'The Cadence of Mozart's Cadenzas', *The Journal of Musicology* 22/2 (2005), 292.

¹⁰⁰ William Hayes, *Remarks on Mr. Avison's Essay on Musical Expression* (London: J. Robinson, 1753), cited in Avison, *Essay on Musical Expression*, ed. Dubois, 116 (original italics). Note that Hayes believed that Geminiani was the real author of the treatise published under Avison's name.

calls 'a game played with the compositional rules of the time'.[101] Roger Mathew Grant also concentrates on the perception of rhythm and metre, but at a more fundamental level. He argues that changing metrical theories clearly embody a shift in how listening was conceptualized. The basic unit of cognition changes from that of the bar, within which accentuation was predetermined, to that of the beat – 'a stream of undifferentiated beats, which, upon hearing, the listener will divide into groups of two, three, or four to form measures'.[102] This equates to a move from metre as a given, a quantity that is beyond dispute, to something that requires the active participation of the listener to come into being. In a different field, Gjerdingen's schema theory argues for the immediate, small-scale nature of historical listening based on the identification of short stock patterns, or schemata. Given their familiarity, such patterns act as a 'medium of exchange' between composer and listener, and demand, he writes, a 'mode of listening that rewards experience, attention, and active engagement'.[103] Such patterns could only persist because of a mutually reinforcing relationship between listener and composer. Among other approaches, Annette Richards has shown how the critical category of the picturesque acts to 'excite attention', and we might note too the subtitle of Thomas Tolley's study *Painting the Cannon's Roar*: 'Music, the Visual Arts and the Rise of an Attentive Public in the Age of Haydn'.[104]

All such work testifies neatly enough to a general shift of emphasis in musicology from production to reception. But one might argue that this is nowhere more appropriate than for later eighteenth-century music, given the historical novelty that we can attach to its explicit courting of the listener. However, what recent scholarship has rarely considered directly is what lies in wait should our historical listeners not cooperate, should they fail to pay attention. They may get bored.

---

[101] Mirka, *Metric Manipulations in Haydn and Mozart*, xii. Floyd Grave, also dealing with metric manipulation in Haydn, suggests such manipulation means that we have to 'discard our attitude of unguarded absorption for one of alert detachment': 'Metrical Dissonance in Haydn', *The Journal of Musicology* 13/2 (1995), 202. Along similar lines, Ludwig Finscher writes in connection with the first movement of Haydn's Quartet in B flat major Op. 1 No. 1 (before 1762) that the composer 'demanded wide-awake listening from the listener, forced them to hear structures and processes' ('die Instrumentalmusik zu einer Komplexität geführt hatte, die den Hörer zum wachen Hören, zum Hören von Strukturen und Prozessen zwang'): *Joseph Haydn und seine Zeit*, 156–157.

[102] Roger Mathew Grant, 'Haydn, Meter, and Listening in Transition', *Studia musicologica* 51/1–2 (2010), 149. This is Grant's take on Kirnberger's 'description of metric hearing'.

[103] Gjerdingen, 'Courtly Behaviors', 367 and 381.

[104] Richards, *Free Fantasia and the Musical Picturesque*; Tolley, *Painting the Cannon's Roar*.

If this is a blind spot, though, it is one that has historical roots. In her 1995 study *Boredom: The Literary History of a State of Mind* Patricia Meyer Spacks argues that 'boredom' only comes into being from the middle of the eighteenth century.[105] This is no absolute matter, since the feeling of what we call boredom could hardly have been absent prior to this. What is new, though, is that boredom becomes a concept, a known quantity, to which one could refer when experiencing a lack of engagement with a particular stimulus. Spacks initially cites linguistic evidence for this argument, noting that the verb 'to bore' was first used in the mid-eighteenth century – and in fact the cognate term 'boredom' had to wait even longer, and dates from the nineteenth century.[106] This of course restricts us to an anglophone realm, but in a later study of the same subject, Elizabeth Goodstein notes that while the French 'ennui' and German 'Langeweile' were already well in existence, they were not used in the new sense until about this same time.[107]

This new sense can be understood to have arisen in tandem with an Enlightenment emphasis on individual experience and judgment. We have already traced this through the thoughts of figures like Burney and Avison. Validating personal reaction means that an individual's lack of engagement with a stimulus also becomes validated – it can be expressed under an emerging rubric of 'boredom'. Attending so intensively to the self might seem to sit uneasily with our rubric of sociability, but in fact the two can be understood to imply each other. A greater degree of individuation – believing in the intrinsic worth of one's own feelings and ideas – can feed a more overt concern with other people. This dialectic is apparent in another of the eighteenth century's favoured terms, sensibility. If sensibility implies a heightened sensitivity to one's own feelings, and indeed being prepared to express them openly, it should ideally also mean being alive to those of others, especially those who are suffering from misfortune. A similar feedback loop may be thought to operate for our term 'attention', even if its shadowy opposite is not often explicitly named. Even though he doesn't say it in so many words in his preface, Burney clearly does not want to 'bore' his readers.

But boredom, as a category of feeling, does not arise solely as part of some abstract history of Western subjectivity. In another symbiotic relationship, it seems to have been encouraged by the commercialization of

---

[105] Spacks, *Boredom*, 6.   [106] Spacks, *Boredom*, 9.
[107] Elizabeth Goodstein, *Experience without Qualities: Boredom and Modernity* (Stanford: Stanford University Press, 2005), 3.

leisure that took place over the eighteenth century, which includes the emergence of a concept of 'entertainment'. Cultural consumables proliferate, and imply a demand to be 'interested' at every turn.[108] This story has been told more frequently with regard to reading than to listening. As opposed to an older practice where precious books were read and reread, increased production of literature encouraged reading something once and then moving on to the next thing.[109] The market became crowded with items jostling for attention, which included not just books but weeklies of various kinds, offering short miscellaneous items that might attract the reader through sheer variety of topics covered. Naturally such developments were not always welcomed, for instance by the German publicist J. G. Pahl, who wrote in 1792, 'We ... have grown used to a hasty kind of reading. We rush fleetingly through an author, never penetrating below the surface ... ; we then begin to yawn and yet again reach for another book, for novelty amuses us.'[110] Pahl complains about the lack of attention that modern readers can sustain, and at same time, with his reference to 'yawning', boredom is the unspoken diagnosis.

The accusatory tone of Pahl's comment represents one of two basic reactions to these new market conditions. We might sum these up as 'blame the public' or 'blame the author'. No one was going to disagree that attention was desirable, and that by implication boredom was an experience to be avoided. But there was a view that to claim boredom was to indulge oneself, that it represented an ethical failure, as if simply failing to be grateful for the gift of life. In an issue of *The Rambler* from 1751, for instance, Dr Johnson opined that:

To be born in ignorance with a capacity of knowledge, and to be placed in the midst of a world filled with variety, perpetually pressing upon the senses and irritating curiosity, is surely a sufficient security against the languishment of inattention.[111]

In other words, an inability to remain mentally occupied represents a personal fault, when no special stimulus should be required. The problem

---

[108] Boredom may be said to be the evil twin of the more positively conceived 'interest', which was also acquiring a distinct identity around this time. For a recent exploration of 'interest' in relation to Haydn see Mathew, 'Interesting Haydn'.
[109] T. C. W. Blanning writes that 'Once there were thousands of titles available, ... new kinds of readers joined in, looking for topical information, practical advice, and recreation, reading books once and the discarding them. In short, they read extensively [rather than intensively].' Blanning, *Culture of Power*, 142.
[110] J. G. Pahl, 'Warum ist die deutsche Nation in unserm Zeitalter so reich an Schriftstellern und Büchern', *Der Weltbürger* 3 (1792), 621, cited in translation in Melton, *Rise of the Public*, 110.
[111] Samuel Johnson, *The Rambler* 124 (25 May 1751), cited in Spacks, *Boredom*, 45.

lies with the individual rather than with the phenomenon at hand. But since this is often represented as being a common malady of the times, as we can see from J. G. Pahl's comments, it also ends up being a collective failure: the great unwashed public is to blame. And the words of Dr Johnson clearly imply that what he calls 'inattention' is now a known quantity: Johnson is clearly writing against what he perceives as a failure to engage.[112] And being fashionably bored was already a known quantity. So much so, in fact, that in Frances Burney's *Camilla* (1796) the fop Sir Sedley Clarendel remarks during a ball in Tunbridge, 'I begin to tire of *ennui*. 'Tis grown so common. I saw my footman beginning it but last week.'[113]

The alternative view is that it is incumbent upon the author to capture attention. We can see this implied in some of the music-theoretical discourse of the time, with its pressing rubric of attention. The ability to engender interest becomes an essential ingredient of creativity. Skill is no longer enough; something more is needed, and a concept of 'originality' becomes one of the ways in which to capture this demand. The composer must adapt to the reality that audience attention is a finite resource; it must be stimulated on a regular basis. Once again a certain scepticism seems to underlie this, concerning whether (musical) language can capture attention in its 'natural' state.

These two different diagnoses of the problem of boredom can readily be mapped onto eighteenth-century patterns of reception of instrumental music – in particular, the ongoing debate between the ancients and the moderns. Neither party would have disputed that music had become more varied in its make-up. In comparison with the style of the early eighteenth century, within any individual movement textures had become more changeable, rhythmic values more mixed, and stylistic associations more unpredictable. It is just this plurality that has made the concept of a musical topic such a useful frame of reference for contemporary scholars: any movement may overturn stylistic hierarchies at any time, by juxtaposing

---

[112] A much later representative of this view is Johann Baptist Schaul, who in his 1809 *Briefe über den Geschmack in der Musik* (Karlsruhe: Macklots Hofbuchhandlung), 14, complained about 'bad listeners': 'it especially annoys me when I can see boredom painted on the faces of most of the listeners' ('wenn ich die Langeweile so recht nach dem Leben auf dem Angesichte der mehrsten zusammen berufenen Zuhörer abgemahlt sehe'). Clearly he regards experiencing such a state of mind as 'their fault', an ethical failure. Schaul's preferred style of music, with Boccherini at the head, is not described as combating boredom through variety; instead, listeners must 'sink into' it, become immersed.

[113] Frances Burney, *Camilla, or A Picture of Youth*, ed. Edward A. Bloom and Lillian D. Bloom (Oxford: Oxford University Press, 1972), 465.

types of material that would once have been heard in separate contexts. Thus a high dotted style might be succeeded by a rustic dance, a fanfare conjoined with a folksong.

Whether such stylistic attributes counted as 'pleasing variety' or maddening inconsistency depended very much on point of view. As we saw in the previous chapter, Burney had pointedly nailed his colours to the mast when writing that 'a liberal and enlightened musician, and hearer of music, receives pleasure from various styles and effects'. Variety was clearly something to be desired, and by dropping in the buzz-words 'liberal' and 'enlightened' he left no doubt that this was to be seen as the proper modern point of view. This variety could also be couched not so much as a totality that would hold the attention of any one listener at any one hearing, but as a sort of chocolate box from which individuals could pick out what appealed to their own taste. As we also saw in Chapter 2, in the Preface to his *Sechs leichte Klaviersonaten*, published in 1783, Türk hoped that the works would meet the expectations of most of the subscribers 'since, given how tastes vary, it is hardly possible to satisfy all'. The very notion that there exist different constituencies of listeners, who may be pleased with different musical materials, itself testifies to our cultural dynamic that gave greater emphasis to individual response. At the same time, given the placement of these sentiments in a preface, this is clearly a form of salesmanship, driven by the need to compete in a swollen musical market.

However, this is not to prop up the sort of binary opposition that has become so ingrained in our thinking about Western art music, whereby composers either write for themselves or sacrifice their art to commerce. Variety could, for example, be understood not just as a way of seeking out the attention of a maximum number of musical consumers but also as a way of improving human faculties. Pietro Verri, in his 1774 *Idee sull'indole del piacere* (Discourse on the Nature of Pleasure), noted that 'the same music will please different people at the same time, while the impressions it produces in them will be very different'.[114] As we saw in Chapter 1, Verri believed that such variety of reaction was less likely to occur in the reception of the visual and literary arts, whereas music left much more room for the imagination: 'With music, however, the listener has to go above himself', and is thus cognitively stimulated.[115] Along similar lines,

---

[114] Verri, *Idee sull'indole del piacere*, 64.

[115] Simon McVeigh shows how commercial and moralizing factors came together in the case of Haydn's symphonies in late eighteenth-century London. While commenting wryly that 'any notion of music as cultural responsibility rather than entertainment was still unformed', McVeigh states (as already seen in a note to Chapter 1) that the Haydn symphonies effected

Diderot had written in 1751, 'Painting shows the very object, poetry describes it, but music barely awakens a notion of it. ... How is it then that of the three arts that imitate nature, the one in which expression is the most arbitrary and the least precise speaks the most forcefully to the soul? Could it be that by revealing objects less it leaves freer rein to our imagination ... ?'.[116]

For all the sympathy shown in such accounts towards the modern, galant, style, there were many who heard instead a disorderly mixture. From our point of view, what is most notable is how often their complaints are framed precisely in terms of a market that aims for the lowest common denominator. These representatives of the 'ancient' school impute the faults of modern style to a need to entertain the listener, to keep them occupied, and to meet the demands of 'mere fashion'. Ascribing these faults to the Italians, whose composers and style were invading musical Europe, was a common critical gambit. For Johann Abraham Peter Schulz, as we have seen, the sonatas of present-day Italian composers were characterized by 'a great noise of notes following randomly one after another', and 'with no other purpose than to gratify the insensitive ears of the layman [das Ohr unempfindsamer Liebhaber zu vergnügen]'.[117] If many of the strongest criticisms came out of north Germany, they were certainly not confined to there. One of the many dialogues about music in Diderot's *Rameau's Nephew* refers to the *querelle des bouffons*, one of the most celebrated instances in the eighteenth century where an established musical order (in France) did battle with Italian modernity, this time on the field of operatic music. The character of the nephew states that the Italian *bouffons* 'have really given us a kick in the pants'. For defenders of the traditional French ways the *bouffons* can only offer what he describes as 'trashy fairground music',[118] cementing an association of Italian music with the currying of popular favour.

Burney's rival historian John Hawkins did not name the Italians in his account of the ills of modern music that was found in his *General History of the Science and Practice of Music* of 1776, but many of the same elements are in place. The contemporary symphony he characterized as a 'general uproar', made up of the 'interchange of little frittered passages and

---

a change in this regard: 'It was recognised at an early date that they required some application on the part of the listener ... This trend closely matched a current of improvement and instruction throughout the entertainment industry.' McVeigh, *Concert Life in London*, 64.

[116] Diderot, *Additions à la Lettre sur les sourds et les muets, a l'Usage de ceux qui entendent et qui parlent* (Paris, 1751), 109, cited in translation in *Music and Culture*, ed. Fubini, 104.

[117] [Schulz,] 'Sonate', 1095. [118] Diderot, *Rameau's Nephew*, trans. Mauldon, 65.

common-place phrases'.[119] In sum, for those who are hostile to it, the modern style is noisy, trivial and low. It is in thrall to the multitude, as Hawkins makes clear when he links the 'corrupt taste in music' to the manner in which it 'urges men to assume the character of judges of what they do not understand'.[120] This forms a pretty categorical refutation of any doctrine of listener authority, indeed of any notion of individual taste. Judgments of art should be left to the experts, he implies, to those who know their stuff, yet at the same time even the hostile Hawkins concedes that modern music can be heard to extend an invitation to the listener in the first place. Hawkins also brings to the surface an aspect of such criticisms that can remain as a subtext: the demonizing of 'public opinion'. One may even find this indirectly in the repeated descriptions of modern-day music as some form of 'meaningless noise', behind which seems to lurk the aural image of a crowd of people, an unruly public all clamouring to be entertained.

Whether welcomed or not, though, variety was an agreed attribute of the most modern musical style. Another aspect that certainly preoccupied theorists was more tightly technical: phrase syntax. As already mentioned, clarity of structure was widely agreed to be an essential basis for intelligibility, so that a listener would not simply get lost in the stream of sound. Only with the use of regular periodic phrases could attention be secured. From Johann Nikolaus Forkel, for example, we read:

The highest possible distinctness and clarity are necessary in the construction of periods, because without them the listener becomes either tired or distracted, and consequently is in no condition to follow the course of the whole and receive the pleasure expected from the piece. This general overview of the whole with all its individual parts must be eased as much as possible, insofar as music is a kind of language for which only very few listeners possess a complete dictionary.[121]

A different way of making the same point was to isolate the melodic component of a period, and Jacqueline Waeber has shown how this became an abiding concern of French writers on music under the banner of 'unité de mélodie', which she describes as 'a plea for ... attentive listening'.[122] On a larger scale, the very concentration on melody as a key

---

[119] John Hawkins, *General History of the Science and Practice of Music*, five volumes (London: T. Payne, 1776), volume 5, 430.
[120] Hawkins, *General History of the Science and Practice of Music*, volume 5, 432.
[121] Johann Nikolaus Forkel, *Allgemeine Geschichte der Musik*, two volumes, volume 1 (Leipzig: Schwickert, 1788), column 77, cited in translation in Riley, *Musical Listening in the German Enlightenment*, 17.
[122] Waeber, 'Rousseau's "Unité de Mélodie"', 118–119.

to securing attention was very characteristic of later eighteenth-century writings on music. Melody itself could even be understood as a peculiarly modern property, as we find in Vincenzo Manfredini's *Difesa della musica moderna e de' suoi celebri esecutori* (Defence of Modern Music), published in Bologna in 1788. Having just given a roll-call of recent masters – Corelli, Bononcini, Vinci, Pergolesi, the two Scarlattis (Alessandro and Domenico), Porpora, Marcello, Handel and Clari – Manfredini continues:

> Nevertheless, our good [modern] music excels that of these great maestros ... As I have already said, modern music is superior to ancient music in its most essential part, which is without the slightest doubt good melody ... If we examine the music by the aforementioned authors, with the exception of Pergolesi, we will find much counterpoint and much learning, but little melody, and consequently little naturalness [naturalezza] and variety. ... because they were lacking in invention, a few ideas or a few *cantilene* were enough for them to write a complete and lengthy composition. I leave it to those who have even a simple idea of what good taste is to imagine how monotonous and boring [monotona e nojosa] this type of music can be.[123]

In this case the emphasis falls not on the unity of melody but on what Manfredini takes to be its natural 'variety'. If it is not clear exactly how this variety comes about, maybe it lies in the fact that melodies, in order to function recognizably as such, have to mix up their rhythmic values. This allows them to project the individuality needed to act as the focus for listener perception. This is a connection that rarely seems to be made when we consider the importance of 'good melody' to the musical culture of this time. Because of this mixture of rhythmic values, melodies in and of themselves will naturally contain variety, even before one considers the matter of their periodic organization. Music of the earlier school concentrates on figure as the basic unit of syntax rather than the longer-breathed, and periodically organized, melody. This gives rise to the tighter continuity of baroque style, in which these figures are seamlessly knitted together. However, because Manfredini defines 'invention' primarily in melodic terms, this means that what was once an unmarked, default, compositional procedure is now understood as 'unnatural', and indeed so unlikely to engage a contemporary listener that it can be styled 'boring'. Boredom was all but invoked by Mozart when writing to his father in 1781 about the overture to *Die Entführung aus dem Serail*, but the means to combat it involved not melody as such but rapid changes of dynamics and harmony,

---

[123] Vincenzo Manfredini, *Difesa della musica moderna e de' suoi celebri esecutori* (Bologna: Carlo Trenti, 1788), 200, cited in translation in *Music and Culture*, ed. Fubini, 355–356.

and, not least, simple brevity: not only was the overture 'very short', and alternating continuously between 'fortes and pianos', but it 'modulates through different keys; and I doubt whether anyone, even if his previous night has been a sleepless one, could go to sleep over it'.[124]

The style strategies that we have reviewed, which were all blessed or cursed by contemporary writers under the rubric of attention, might not seem to be entirely compatible. An impression of variety surely depends on various kinds of irregularity or change, while periodic organization is premised on regularity, offering the listener the chance to grasp how the music is put together. More broadly, familiarity is needed to put listeners at their ease, to make them feel that they have a stake in the musical experience,[125] but on the other hand too much familiarity and regularity may breed contempt: music also needs to offer sharp edges and unexpected turns to lift the listener out of a potentially passive state. This is the conundrum we considered at the outset of this chapter, under the heading of convention. In more recent times it would seem to be the latter side that has captured more scholarly attention, according to which listeners are kept fully involved not just by means of continual variety of gesture but also, more overtly, by surprises, shocks, and what sounds like a whole repertoire of comic devices. This emphasis is doubly understandable. First, writers have had to fight against the image embodied by the style designation 'classical', which too readily connotes everything that is safe and sound. Beyond that, this emphasis responds appropriately to historical novelty: the later eighteenth century did after all bring the only style of Western art music in which comedy regularly plays a part. Comedy is a genre that not only rewards but in fact demands attention; it forces listeners to keep their wits about them if they are to follow a train of events.[126]

---

[124] Mozart, letter to Leopold Mozart, 26 September 1781; *Letters of Mozart*, ed. and trans. Anderson, 770.

[125] Elisabeth Le Guin has testified to her own positive musical experience of periodic organization itself in just the terms we are discussing, prompted by her listening engagement with Haydn's Sonata in G major H39: 'The periodic phrase structure and the building-up of phrases through identifiable, discrete sections ... also serve an important function in providing relief from this diaphragmatic intensity: frankly, they keep the listening experience from becoming too anaerobic. ... These moments, whether they are short cesura-silences, or clear-cut changes of texture, tune, or harmonic rhythm, serve to return me briefly "to myself", out of the piece altogether; and my attention is incrementally renewed thereafter.' Le Guin, *Boccherini's Body*, 266.

[126] Of Ferdinando Galiani's *Dialogues sur le commerce des bleds* (London, 1770), Dena Goodman writes 'Galiani demonstrated ... that gaiety was the rhetoric of Enlightenment because it forced readers to keep their wits about them, while it amused them and thus kept their interest.' Goodman, *Republic of Letters*, 195.

Thus comedy and more broadly variety can clearly be recruited as part of a campaign to secure the listener's attention – they enable composers to compose against boredom, as it were. But boredom need not just be implied in its absence, as it were, as the looming shadow of attention – the possibility of experiencing it can also be composed into the music. On the literary front, Darryl Domingo has linked the commercialization of leisure with 'the cultural moment at which writing began self-consciously to resist boredom and reading began to expect it to do so'.[127] Domingo notes that digression is the most pervasive technique, in which writers wander off topic and often comment on that fact. This of course brings the danger that reader-consumers will switch off, yet it is through just such interruptions, he believes, that 'readers are ingratiated and made to have a stake in the text'.[128]

Such digressive techniques are certainly also evident in the music of our time as producer-composers thematize the potential for boredom and distraction in the listening experience. This often involves playing with formal proportions. One instance of this, discussed earlier, is the handling of retransitions in rondo forms, whereby the use of part of the refrain material leads the listener to anticipate the return of the whole theme. Such material is often then extended beyond what would appear to be reasonable bounds, teasing the listener by creating a digression that seems to exist for its own sake; we noted one spectacular instance of this at bars 140–158 of the finale of Haydn's Symphony No. 88. Yet it would be easy to overplay the importance of digression as a means to hold the attention of an audience. Music, after all, also has the power to entrain its listeners simply through its patterns, whether these be metrical or phrase-structural: in other words, to return to the earlier point, regularity and familiarity may also play a full part in keeping an audience alert.

The particular phenomenon I would like to investigate under the current rubric would certainly seem to fall within a spectrum of normal, familiar musical behaviour – note repetition. Surely no musical gesture could be more basic, more routine than a simple repeated note – indeed, it was a prime exhibit in my earlier treatment of the aesthetic of reduction – yet in our historical context it was not as innocent as it might appear. In the music of this time, repeated notes could carry a charge of modernity about them. They were a common component of the simplified textures of a

---

[127] Darryl P. Domingo, 'Unbending the Mind: Or, Commercialized Leisure and the Rhetoric of Eighteenth-Century Diversion', *Eighteenth-Century Studies* 45/2 (2012), 208.
[128] Domingo, 'Unbending the Mind', 227.

galant style, whose 'natural' melodic lines demanded unobtrusive support. They could blend into the background, simply marking the pulse while the more rhythmically differentiated melody absorbed the listener's attention. That such an apparently simple technical means could be perceived as stylistically marked is apparent in the hostile testimony of William Hayes, in his response to Avison's *Essay on Musical Expression*. In this pamphlet of 1753 Hayes expressed his alarm at the weaknesses of the modern style:

> Shall no one endeavour to stem the Torrent? Surely, there never could be so much Occasion as at present: When the highest Pretensions to Harmony, amount to little more than the Bass continuing *tum, tum, tum* upon one Key for several Bars together, whilst two other Parts (at most) are moving in Thirds or Sixths incessantly.[129]

Hayes scornfully provides a textural recipe for the galant style, suggesting its musical impoverishment by implicit comparison with the older style that he upheld. This featured not idiot repetitions of a single note in the bass but rather fluid continuity, with its logical corollary of a more intricate harmonic language. In German-speaking realms, as we have seen, these note repetitions even acquired their own name of *Trommelbass* (drum bass). The term was used, for instance, by Christian Daniel Friedrich Schubart in his book on musical aesthetics completed in 1785, in which he praised the composer Graun for writing his basses 'with extreme contrapuntal correctness' and, 'contrary to Italian practice, he figured them all so conscientiously that each modulation was clear. In none of his pieces is the drum bass used'.[130] Once again the implication is that such note repetition is an index for sloppy modern ways. While Hayes and Schubart clearly found such a device altogether tiresome, my case studies hold it up for aural inspection, as if positively courting the dangers of dullness.

One composer who did just this was Haydn, who in the opening movement of his Quartet in B flat major Op. 50 No. 1 (1787) provocatively places a simple repeated note centre stage (Example 3.24). The movement starts with next to nothing, as what should be a purely subordinate part is all we are given to listen to. As if to illustrate Roger Grant's argument about changing conceptions of metre in the eighteenth century, we hear a series of undifferentiated pulses with as yet no clear hierarchy of strong and weak beats. Even a strong emphasis on first and third crotchets from the cellist will not entirely clarify the aural picture. A hierarchy of beats only emerges

---

[129] Hayes, *Remarks on Mr. Avison's Essay on Musical Expression*, 73.
[130] Schubart, *Ideen zu einer Ästhetik der Tonkunst*, 89 (my translation).

Example 3.24 Haydn, Quartet in B flat major Op. 50 No. 1/i, bars 1–6

once the three upper voices enter on a chord that contradicts the cello's B♭, embellished by a sort of turn figure in first violin and viola. The mystery is only solved towards the end of the movement, when it turns out that Haydn was invoking a typical postcadential formula in which the repeated-note bass acts to reinforce the tonic close, and to ground the movement through the process of liquidation.[131] As we have seen, this involves the removal of more characteristic features and their replacement by more conventional ones, creating the impression that the music has (nearly) finished what it has to say. At the same time, this would not do justice to the current movement, since those naked repeated notes from the start have been thoroughly integrated into the argument. Along with the turn figure, they have provided the primary thematic material. This means that the repeated notes have been at once conventional *and* characteristic features, both something a listener could take for granted and something that needs to be consciously attended to. Such a procedure, as we saw in Chapter 2, was commonly used to solve a compositional problem that arose in the simplified galant style: how to reconcile the need for textures that could readily be apprehended by the listener, which would be mainly homophonic, with the need for an interactive style in which all performers could play a part. By creating a textural ambiguity about the place of repeated notes in the scheme – are they

---

[131] For an excellent reading of this movement see Janet M. Levy, 'Gesture, Form, and Syntax in Haydn's Music', in *Haydn Studies: Proceedings of the International Haydn Conference, Washington, DC, 1975*, ed. Jens Peter Larsen, Howard Serwer and James Webster (New York: Norton, 1981), 355–362. Other readings of note include those by Rosen, *The Classical Style*, 120–125 (focusing on the structural implications of dissonance); Allanbrook, *Secular Commedia*, 121–124 (a topical reading); Naomi Waltham-Smith, 'Haydn's Impropriety', *Journal of Music Theory* 62/1 (2018), 137–139 (emphasizing the resourceful use of cadential convention); and Sutcliffe, *Haydn: String Quartets, Op. 50*, 66–73 (mainly following up on Levy's insights), the latter disputed in some of its details by Hepokoski and Darcy, *Elements of Sonata Theory*, 269–271.

Example 3.25 Haydn, Quartet in C major Op. 33 No. 3/i, bars 156–167

supportive, or are they primary? – Haydn is able to stimulate fresh appreciation of the musically routine. What could have been a by-word for the ordinary facts of modern musical life, basic note repetition, is manipulated so that it demands our attention.

The same also applies to the first movement of Haydn's Op. 33 No. 3, analysed above (Example 3.10), in which I argue that the repeated notes are never used in a normal accompanying role. The only exception comes in the coda (Example 3.25), when repeated notes enter in what is clearly a 'merely accompanimental' role. They support our Grand Cadence formula. The first violin performs it in full: descending steps from bar 156, followed by ascending leaps to a high point in bar 159, leading to a cadential trill. But at the very moment when the formula would be completed, the textural automatism is reversed. The first violin does move as expected to the tonic note in bar 161, but viola and cello play notes that deflect the harmonic resolution, demanding a continuation. Not only that, but the fact that the pair persist with their repeated quavers goes against the etiquette of the formula: once the Grand Cadence is completed, one expects textural and rhythmic change. Meanwhile, violin 2 starts to play the long-note motive that went with the repeated notes in the theme. This means that by association the lower two parts are now playing not any old repeated-note accompaniment, but the more thematically specialized repetitions

Example 3.26 Dittersdorf, Quartet in G major, K193/ii, bars 37–48

that we heard at the outset. Thus all three are failing to recognize the completion of the Grand Cadence; they are not cooperating with the leader. After two bars of this, the first violin, as if piqued, interrupts, not allowing its companion to complete the thought; from bar 163 it gives us a complete version of the theme, which now acts as a close. At the same point violin 2 resumes its original duties alongside the viola, and we can have no doubt that these repeated notes also refer back to the beginning, at the original pitches.

If Haydn's procedures in these two movements involve using repeated notes as opening gestures, before eventually recasting them in a closing function, in several of his quartet movements Dittersdorf does something like the opposite, as in the Alternativo from his Quartet in G major, K193 (1789; Example 3.26). The opening material is built on a version of the

Romanesca, in which above a circle-of-fifths motion in the bass the top line moves down by step from scale degree 3 (B♭) to scale degree 6 (D, reached on the last beat of bar 42 in the first violin). Each step of the progression is realized as repeated chords, either filling the whole bar together with a dotted first beat that gives a kink to the rhythm or else as two clearly separated quaver chords followed by a rest on the third beat of the bar. The fuller dotted version takes over in the second part of the eight-bar phrase before the two separate chords return in bar 44. After a repeat of the passage the second section opens with a near-exact repetition of that final bar, an aural double-take that can only confuse the listener. Have I misheard, the listener might ask himself, did I nod off for a moment? Or have the players become distracted and lost their place? Are they repeating the final bar of the section by accident? The confusion will be augmented by the fact that bar 45 not only matches bar 44, it also matches the earlier two-chord gestures of bars 38 and 40, and all of these have come at the ends of their respective units. Thus the two-chord figure has always functioned at some level as a close. And while bar 45 will initially sound like an echo of the previous bar, the way in which the phrase continues shows that its function has changed. In 44 it was an ending; now at 45 it is a beginning, as the sequential continuation of the rhythm makes clear. With this continuation of the rhythm into bar 46 and beyond, the two-crotchet figure now occupies the middle of a larger unit. Thus the figure suggests three formal functions in three bars: in bar 44 it closes a phrase, in bar 45 it opens a phrase, and then at 46 it acts as continuation. At the same time, its textural status changes. Having been the basis of the Alternativo's thematic material, the repeated chords are suddenly accompanying as the first violin breaks into a melodic flourish. This movement once more exemplifies how a style can trade in units of invention that may seem formulaic but which become individualized through contextual manipulation.

If we thought we were mishearing during this movement, a moment of inattention being punished by auditory confusion, the same applies even more strongly in another Dittersdorf Alternativo section, this one forming part of his Quartet No. 5 in E flat major, K195 (1789; Example 3.27). While the manner of this Alternativo may be simple, in line with the 'semplice' performance marking, in reality it is anything but. Each two-bar unit concludes with repeated-note crotchets on second and third beats of the bar, and these create a perceptual ambiguity: are these notes a parenthetical filler after an initial four-crotchet melodic unit, or do they form an integral part of a full two-bar shape? At the fourth time of asking, when these two crotchets are played by the cello rather than the first violin, this ambiguity

Example 3.27 Dittersdorf, Quartet in E flat major, K195/ii, bars 45–60

would seem to be eased. The interval outlined to reach the two notes in the cello in bar 52 is an octave, rather than the falling fifth that we heard three times from the first violin. The falling octave makes the shape sound like a typical postcadential filler, one that we have established as especially idiomatic to bass lines: the clearly sectioned phrase structures of galant style necessitate many such figures whose primary function seems to be to bridge the gap until the next clear periodic unit is ready to enter.

Immediately after the double bar, though, such an interpretation is thrown into doubt. What we heard in the final bar of the first section is immediately echoed, with the cello continuing its repeated crotchet Gs on second and third beats of the bar. This is patently similar to the equivalent section in Quartet No. 3 (Example 3.26), yet, if anything, the effect is even more disorientating on this occasion. This repeated-note figure leaves the strong beat of the bar empty, and is played by just one instrument. The cello continues on its lone path for three, almost four, bars with no intervention from the other voices. Has the cello become distracted, and have the other participants dropped off to sleep? While the repetitions may sound aimless, at the same time they move what should have been a peripheral figure into the foreground of our listening consciousness. This also, once more, means a potential change of formal function: the two repeated notes in bar 53 first of all sound like they form part of an ending (or, more accurately, a post-ending) and then seem to turn into a beginning; or should we hear simply a continuation and therefore an extended middle, rather like a series of musical ellipsis points?

The role of these notes must be reinterpreted anyway when in bar 56 the upper parts enter with a repeated figure occupying beats three and one, and the cello starts to provide an accompaniment to what sounds like a stylized rustic dance. Its repeated notes now oscillate between tonic and dominant, in true oom-pah-pah fashion. But we cannot ignore the agency of the cello in bringing about this unexpected change of tack. It is as though the other players have to listen for a while to pick up the topical cue, and yet all the cello provides is the simplest form of musical utterance, a series of bald repeated notes, something to which ordinarily no attention would need to be paid. At the same time there is an element of topical 'realism' to the procedure, in that bringing in an accompaniment first by itself, to set up the dance step, is a standard device of rustic representation. Certainly this moment, at which the music is suddenly transformed into something like a *Ländler*, represents the hard end of modern variety as a means of capturing or renewing listener attention. For proponents of modern instrumental style it could have been assimilated as a bracing contrast, and for its detractors viewed as an example of an unaccountable, not to say illogical, change. Schubart wrote that Dittersdorf 'has a completely individual manner which degenerates only too often' into 'burlesque and vulgar comedy',[132] while for Johann Triest, we might recall, the composer had '[written] too much' and 'succumbed too easily to the general tendency to write mixed compositions'.[133] In both cases, with the use of words like 'degenerates' and 'succumbs', we gain the sense of a sort of moral failure on the part of the

---

[132] Schubart, *Ideen zu einer Ästhetik der Tonkunst*, 239; DuBois, 'Schubart's *Ideen zu einer Ästhetik einer Tonkunst*: Annotated Translation', 288.

[133] Triest, 'Bemerkungen über die Ausbildung der Tonkunst', *Allgemeine musikalische Zeitung* 3 (25 February 1801), column 378; 'Remarks on the Development of the Art of Music, trans. Gillespie, 362.

composer. Yet the variety which Dittersdorf admits into these compositions is hardly as random as these critics believe it to be – it issues from careful attention to the smallest, simplest musical elements.

Repeated notes are thickened into repeated chords, in a comfortable iambic rhythm, at the outset of the Trio from Haydn's Symphony No. 101 ('The Clock'; 1794). Above these chords a flute enters with a line that is all pastoral charm. But when the flute reaches an e^3, demanding a change of harmony from the repeated pianissimo D major chords in the strings, no change eventuates: whether through absent-mindedness or through boredom, the strings stay exactly where they are, continuing in the same vein through the twelve bars of the flute's solo. When the flute tries again, the strings do notice what is going on, and oblige with a change of harmony (bar 102).

All our case studies so far may be said to embody 'constructedness', whereby the music foregrounds how it is put together and is premised on a listenership that is ready to understand its component parts. In one sense this is a global orientation, if an impetus behind galant style is to create a more intelligible, ear-catching brand of music for a more broadly conceived audience. And this was also encouraged by a marked increase in the rate of publication of instrumental music, creating a proliferation of items that needed to get noticed. In a more particular sense, 'constructedness' entailed an ironic glance at the very artificiality of the language, and this is a strain continued by Beethoven in a work like his Bagatelle in C major Op. 33 No. 2 (1803; Example 3.28a). The opening section embodies the most perfectly listener-friendly symmetrical syntax: a sixteen-bar sentence. This is initially split into two matching units that act as statement and response. The second unit is an exact transposition of the first up a major second, to the level of the supertonic – exactly the procedure we heard at the start of Haydn's Quartet Op. 33 No. 3 (Example 3.10, bar 7). What helps to create the sense of artificiality, of the music's having been as it were arbitrarily constructed, derives from a very compressed exchange of assertive and gracious gestures. The first bar has a *sforzando* on its second beat after an initial beat featuring a dotted rhythm played *piano*. There is then a loud low note on the third beat of the bar in the left hand, meaning that both second and third beats feature disruptions of the metrical sense. This is succeeded by material that is legato and *piano* and in which the hands now play together in a close middle register (whereas they only played separately and far apart in bar 1). Following that we hear a series of four repeated staccato chords in bars 3–4. Thus the odd, impetuous and aggressive gestures of the first bar are succeeded by material that sounds much smaller, even demure.

Example 3.28a Beethoven, Bagatelle in C major Op. 33 No. 2, bars 1–16

Example 3.28b Beethoven, Bagatelle in C major Op. 33 No. 2, bars 118–138

Especially after one has heard the parallel sequential phrase unit at bars 5–8, there is the impression that the repeated chords exist solely to fill in time until the unit can reach its allotted end according to the 'rules' of periodic discourse; they sound mechanical, relatively featureless.

This notion is strengthened once the next part of the musical sentence arrives from bar 9. We then hear just versions of the first two bars, transposed to the subdominant at 9–10 and then at 11–12 moving back to the tonic: the filling repeated chords have been removed. This yields a clear sense of acceleration, which is augmented from bar 13 when we hear only successive versions of the material of bar 1. These stake out a straightforward cadential progression in the tonic of ii6–V7–I. But this process finishes a bar too soon, in bar 15; it is to bar 16 that the material ought to extend in order to fulfil the symmetry, and so once more repeated notes are used to accomplish the task of filling out the phrase. But because the initial first-bar material is now in charge, the hands alternate rather than playing together.

The ending of this piece (see Example 3.28b) involves a prolonged alternation between the hands as we heard originally in bars 15–16, and eventually from bar 131 there is a kind of reductio ad absurdum of what is after all the simplest possible device – repeated notes and chords. First there is a plain hemiola as the hands alternate, creating a metrical disruption that contradicts the notion of stable closure. Then from 135, as the dynamic level decreases, the triple metre is restored, with a gap between the right-hand chord on the first beat and the low left-hand note on the third beat. But then bar 137 removes the metrically resolving rest as the left hand's note follows immediately on the second beat of the bar. This makes as if to generate another hemiola, but the music then trails off into soft silence, making for an ambiguous close. In this way the use of repeated tonic notes or chords to affirm closure is defamiliarized, as what is normally a standard device becomes marked for listener attention. The net effect is that the music finishes up in the air – quite the opposite to what the musical device of note repetition is meant to do in such a context.

Once more the net effect of this 'constructed' music is to elevate the routine, to suggest that even the simplest aspects of a musical movement – what John Hawkins disparaged as 'little frittered passages and commonplace phrases' – can in fact carry their own individual life. Boredom need never set in if nothing can be taken for granted, even when the musical phenomenon concerned is the most uneventful that one can conceive – note repetition. I am not of course claiming that repeated notes are intrinsically dull, but rather that they are unremarkable – and they do indeed express a certain literal kind of monotony. Maybe because music takes place in (measured) time, without specific semantic reference (more obviously so in the case of instrumental forms), it has the potential to mimic the experience of boredom and distraction more vividly than other media. At least, it can engage with it as a possibility and then set out to conquer it. The sort of versatile treatment of texture and formal function that we have observed in our examples implies a listener who can be persuaded to attend to the seemingly smallest, most 'trivial', details, who can exercise critical judgment on them and who can thus function as an active consumer of the musical discourse.

Versatility

The types of treatment accorded to repeated notes that we have reviewed above clearly show a taste for reduction, a desire to extract the maximum from the minimum. A related perspective would be to stress the versatility of thought that allows such simple (repeated) phenomena to carry so many different meanings. In fact, one might suggest that this is to look through the other end of the telescope: if reduction involves isolating the simple within the more complex, then versatility involves starting with the simple, or at least the single, and showing how variously it may be employed. And, in line with our main thesis, versatility – or flexibility – may be accounted a social as well as a musical virtue. It suggests the ability to see other points of view, the skill of making a lot out of what appears to be not very much at all. Much social interaction, we might remind ourselves, consists of outwardly unremarkable, often repeated words and actions, and successful interaction demands an alert, flexible response to them.

One of the most conspicuous kinds of versatility in our repertory is thematic-motivic: the redeployment of a prominent piece of material at various points within a movement. This has fascinated generations of writers, though it has often gone by the name of unity or economy – hallowed rubrics that offer a perspective that I find partial. However, this is not to reiterate the kneejerk reaction against a weighty thematicist tradition, understandable though that has been. If a fundamental aspect of later eighteenth-century musical style is its unprecedented pluralism, or variety of materials, it is only natural to seek some underlying thread. Unity, in other words, becomes a 'live' aesthetic issue precisely because it is no longer inbuilt through the concentration on a relatively narrow set of compatible materials.[134] Certainly complaints against the new varied manner often focussed on a perceived lack of unity or consistency, though this might be formulated in characteristic rather than thematic terms: in other words, the new music lacked stability or integrity of character. A more positive rationale, as we have seen, leant on periodicity – more broadly, rhythm – as the key unifying factor. This might then allow for contrasting materials to coexist within a periodic framework without fatal damage to musical-expressive logic. This could also, in fact, be framed in terms of melody rather than rhythm – recall our earlier discussions of 'unité de mélodie', which also pivoted on periodic organization. But if we broaden

---

[134] Compare the comments on this matter in my *Keyboard Sonatas of Domenico Scarlatti*, 322–323.

our definition of melody to encompass 'characteristic material', including the increased individualization of motive, it would be odd if unity had not been considered in those terms too.

That was indeed the case, but reception from the time suggests that our textbook 'thematic unity' was valued rather for its evidence of versatility: what counted was less the reuse of material per se and more the fact that it could be accommodated in different forms and different contexts. It was the differences rather than the similarities that impressed. This is most evident in the reception of the music of Haydn, who set the terms for this debate through an often conspicuous economy of materials. In Chapter 2 we cited a critic in the *Mercure de France* who described Haydn as 'this vast genius, who, in each of his pieces, knows so well how to draw such rich and varied developments from a single subject', and the critic continued by noting that this was 'so unlike those those sterile composers who continuously move from one idea to another for lack of knowing how to present one [idea] in varied forms'.[135] This bespeaks some ambivalence about the modern varied style, implying, in concert with many other northern critics, that one 'idea' should be the norm for any one movement (recall Judith Schwartz's formulation of the matter in Chapter 2).[136] More to the point here, though, is an emphasis on the richness and variety that results from Haydn's practice, rather than on 'unity'. Ultimately, of course, this is a symbiotic relationship: each term of reference sustains the other.

That this kind of economy need not lead to a straightforward 'unity', but might even result in contradiction, is apparent in Ignaz Arnold's account of the matter, whereby Haydn 'proceeds on the basis of a sentence that is universally recognized to be true, one with which everyone agrees, one that everyone must be able to understand; but he knows so cunningly just how to use this idea, that he can soon convince us of anything he wishes to, even if it is the very contrary of the original idea'.[137] This certainly counts as deriving the complex, or at least the multiple, from the simple – our working definition of versatility proposed above. A memorable formulation of this attribute comes from Johann Baptist Schaul in 1809, for whom Haydn's genius 'knows, like a chameleon, how to assume every possible form' ('wie ein anderes Cameleon alle möglichen Gestalten anzunehmen weiß'). In his quartets, 'once he has determined the motive of an Allegro, he delivers it in a hundred different ways, now giving it to the bass, now the

---

[135] Anonymous, 'Spectacles: Concert Spirituel', *Mercure de France* (12 April 1788), 77, cited in translation in Harrison, *Haydn: The 'Paris' Symphonies*, 22.
[136] See also the discussion in Bonds, *Wordless Rhetoric*, especially 98.
[137] Ignaz Arnold, *Gallerie der berühmtesten Tonkünstler des achtzehnten und neunzehnten Jahrhunderts* (Buren: Knuf, 1810), 110, cited in translation in Bonds, *Wordless Rhetoric*, 138.

viola, then to the second or the first violin, now transforming the whole in a trice, with a single brushstroke, and yet he always lets the theme shine through, so that one cannot help but be astounded'.[138] Schaul's image of a chameleon nicely captures the relationship between our unity and versatility: the chameleon is always one and the same thing, but what captivates us is the number of apparently different colours it can display, a supreme adaptability to circumstances.

Such an emphasis on changeability has marked some later reception of Haydn's thematic practice too. Bryan Proksch shows how Vincent D'Indy became greatly taken by the fact that 'a given thematic idea can express completely different things through a few small changes'.[139] In the opening movement of the Sonata in C sharp minor, H36 (before 1780), while the second theme seems to restate the opening idea in the mediant, a change of articulation from detached to legato and the addition of a new accompanimental figure create what D'Indy describes as 'something completely different from an expressive point of view'.[140] Later than this, some writers have chosen to do battle with the term that has so often been invoked to account for some elements of Haydn's economy, including the reuse of a theme as found in the Sonata in C sharp minor – monothematicism. While from our point of view this ought to imply the ability to see different angles to a 'subject', it has more often been flatly reported as a kind of careful husbandry of thematic resources. Jan LaRue objects to the word because it 'suggests limitation, the very opposite of the sense of boundless variety one experiences in the continual unfolding of Haydn's ideas. Haydn's sophisticated procedure evolves contrasting derivatives that give a polythematic effect ... even though genetically related'. LaRue offers the term 'multistage variance' to describe the way in which material could be developed in a chain of 'variants of variants of variants, and beyond'.[141] Pierpaolo Polzonetti proposes the term 'metathematicism', which applies 'when a theme tells us something more and different about itself'.[142] Taking the

---

[138] Schaul, *Briefe über den Geschmack in der Musik*, 10.
[139] Bryan Proksch, 'Vincent d'Indy as Harbinger of the Haydn Revival', *Journal of Musicological Research* 28/2–3 (2009), 173–174.
[140] Vincent d'Indy, *Cours de composition musicale*, three volumes, volume 2, part 1 (Paris: Durand, 1909), 209, cited in translation in Proksch, 'Vincent d'Indy as Harbinger of the Haydn Revival', 174.
[141] Jan LaRue, 'Multistage Variance: Haydn's Legacy to Beethoven', *The Journal of Musicology* 1/3 (1982), 265.
[142] Pierpaolo Polzonetti, 'Haydn and the *Metamorphoses* of Ovid', in *Engaging Haydn: Context, Culture, Criticism*, ed. Mary Hunter and Richard Will (Cambridge: Cambridge University Press, 2012), 229.

first movement of the String Quartet in F major Op. 74 No. 2 (1793) as his model, he notes how, through the sorts of apparently small changes also considered by D'Indy, a theme can be transformed into new shapes. And the conceit he uses to explain the process – the *Metamorphoses* of Ovid – makes a fitting companion to Schaul's evocation of the chameleon. Consistent with this comparison, the transformative capacity is described as inherent – 'the theme itself contains as its essential characteristic a readiness to change'[143] – as if it were beyond the direct control of the composer. This is like our earlier evocation of the individualized motive as seemingly autonomous, capable of making its own way through a musical universe. And the process of change also seems to be an infinite one. Floyd and Margaret Grave couple the 'relentless thematic process' that they associate with the string quartets in particular with Haydn's 'penchant for open-ended development in the unfolding of a musical idea' to argue for the 'impression of unlimited possibility' conveyed by such music.[144] This suggests a kind of liberation narrative realized in sound: the importance and significance of a thematic entity need not be fixed by the manner in which it first makes its way into the world. Recall David Lidov's formulation in which he asserted that to play with a theme is to 'set it partly free, free from one sound, one context, one definite arrangement'.[145] And, as already illustrated, musical material does not in fact have to merit the label 'thematic' in order to be accorded such treatment, since the apparently insignificant or routine may also appear and act in multifarious ways. And if brought to any sort of prominence, as we saw with our repeated notes above, or our simple cadential formulae earlier, then any distinction between characteristic/thematic and subordinate material falls right away. This is also the conclusion reached in a study of Haydn's 'improprieties' by Naomi Waltham-Smith: 'In its inexhaustible potential for other uses, material holds out against complete incorporation' into the supposedly stable categories of the conventional and the particular.[146]

This kind of versatility is evident in the first movement of Haydn's Symphony No. 96 (1791), in which, once more, simple note repetition is a feature. In this case repeated notes are both a focussed (thematic) proposition – they open the theme of the Allegro – and also part of the general flow. While the sheer frequency of the repeated-note motive could be accounted a demonstration of 'economy', Yoel Greenberg notes the

---

[143] Polzonetti, 'Haydn and the *Metamorphoses* of Ovid', 231.
[144] Floyd Grave and Margaret Grave, *The String Quartets of Joseph Haydn* (New York: Oxford University Press, 2006), 336.
[145] Lidov, *Is Language a Music?*, 57. [146] Waltham-Smith, 'Haydn's Impropriety', 132.

variety of treatment: the motive appears in forty-three of the exposition's sixty-five bars 'in a variety of guises, played by every instrument and in every possible metric position'.[147] The only caveat one might have with this account is that calling each and every manifestation of repeated notes the same 'motive' underplays the versatility of conception, when these repeated notes operate on a sort of sliding scale: at some moments they are plainly prominent, while at others they form a sort of vaguely familiar background. For instance, at bar 67 this motive becomes entirely accompanimental, part of a prolonged V6/4 harmony, while just before, from bar 57, only its rhythm is retained, as the original note repetition is replaced by stepwise chromatic movement. These particular transformations offer simple examples of LaRue's 'multistage variance': in the former instance, the originally anacrusic motive begins on the downbeat, while in the latter case the pitch structure is transformed. And, as D'Indy had remarked, such operations produce differences in character. In the current Allegro this is most striking towards the very end of the movement, from bar 191, when the repeated-note motive attains its most dramatic manifestation – with the help of a semiquaver flurry it becomes a repeated unison tattoo on A for almost the entire orchestra. So forceful is this transformation of the figure that it precipitates a shocking event: the repeated As pivot into D minor, *fortissimo*, instead of the overwhelmingly expected D major. This is a long way from the unassuming initial version of the repeated notes that opened the Allegro, and reminds us of our 'liberation narrative'; in this case, the modest has become grand.

Charles Rosen isolates this kind of affective reversal as a particular characteristic of Haydn's, though at the level of an entire theme rather than the smaller unit that operates in Symphony No. 96. With respect to the wildly differing presentations of the same theme in the first movement of the composer's Sonata in C major H50 (1794–1795) – which run from the dry, super-staccato presentation at the outset to the super-legato, 'Open Pedal' versions heard at bars 73–74 and 120–124 – he writes, 'It is clear that at this time any theme can be given whatever emotional significance the composer chooses'.[148] While this kind of larger-scale reversal may indeed be a particular Haydnesque specialty, and while the same may apply to the very intricacy of his thematic technique, the encompassing principle of versatility is by no means confined to Haydn; it may in fact have been the

---

[147] Yoel Greenberg, 'Minding a Gap: "Active Transitions" from the Slow Introduction to the Fast Section in Haydn's Symphonies', *The Journal of Musicology* 29/3 (2012), 307.

[148] Rosen, *Music and Sentiment*, 64.

most influential aspect of his art. Brunetti, for instance, is greatly given to making a little go a long way. This can involve changeability of function rather than of appearance, as it often also does in Haydn. In the third movement of his Quartet in F major L197 (1789–1793), for instance, one characteristic two-bar motive completely dominates first the minuet and then, reduced to a one-bar form, also the trio section; out of a total of fifty-six bars, there are just four where it is not in operation. The motive twists and turns into the shapes needed to fulfil all formal functions and harmonic requirements. Such writing plays with the stylistic expectation that contrasting or at least complementary material will arrive, yet it never does. The variety inheres solely in the varied applications of the same thing to different functional circumstances.

In the finale of Brunetti's Quartet in D major L199 (1791–1792), on the other hand, variety of appearance counts for much more. Much of the movement seems to arise from permutations of a basic shape of a simple rising third in minims, heard at the outset. From bar 41, for instance, the first violin reverses the direction of the cell and extends it so as to form a long chain of falling thirds, while the second violin simultaneously subjects it to rhythmic diminution, in two-quaver units. This contracted form is then presented in hectic dialogue between the three upper parts. From bar 89 the first violin returns to its extended and reversed version of the cell, but it is adjusted so as to fulfil a clear closing function; it now forms a falling arpeggio rather than the more open-ended chain of falling thirds that it did earlier, and this version is echoed in canon at the distance of a beat by the second violin. Then upon repetition the first violin's line is counterpointed by the contracted forms that we heard earlier, the second violin's falling quaver pairs being answered by rising versions in the viola. Throughout the section the various derived forms are so clearly laid out as virtually to enforce (and reward) analytical listening. We are aural witnesses to the seemingly spontaneous metamorphosis of a single simple musical idea.

In such instances my category of versatility is barely distinguishable from wit, which variously entails the ability to make unexpected connections, to show two sides to the same thing, or, conversely, to apply that same thing in apparently incompatible circumstances. Indeed, wit would be a conceptual means of encompassing many of the operations under review in this chapter – the reductive tendency, the renewal of perception that results – but it need not be aligned with a lighter or comic manner, as happens frequently in the critical literature. Wit – which of course demands nothing so much as versatility of thought – is more in the nature of a basic working method or mentality. While the aural outcome need not be amusing, the most recognizable instances certainly are, as is the case with both the Brunetti movements above.

Another aspect of this witty versatility is cleverness, deriving from the sense that not just the musical material, but also the listener, are subject to constant manipulation. We touched on this attribute in association with Clementi in Chapter 2, though it is hardly peculiar to his work. Mozart, for another, thrives in this climate, given his particular knack for permutation, whereby the versatility lies less in the changing forms of the materials themselves than in the surprisingly various ways in which they can be recombined. The impression of cleverness that ensues might, however, be equated with the not especially sociable trait of showing off, of lording it over the listener. This is certainly the conclusion that Germaine de Staël reached in her assessments of Haydn and Mozart, part of a broader critique that 'German composers' tend to 'think too much about what they are doing' ('ils réfléchissent trop à ce qu'ils font').[149] Her specific targets were in fact vocal works: Haydn's *Creation* was undermined by too much thought ('esprit', which also touches on what we would call 'wit'), while Mozart's *Requiem* was marred by an inappropriate cleverness ('l'ingénieux').[150] Clearly she disliked the self-consciousness that exuded from the sorts of operations we are describing in this chapter.

But even if one accepted such a critique, one should affirm that the musical results of such cleverness are often highly, not to say disarmingly, accessible. The technical means are generally far from hidden; the listener has a fair chance of picking up on the processes in play, is indeed invited to do so. In the first movement of Clementi's Sonata in G major Op. 40 No. 1 (1802), for instance, few can miss the permutations of the opening idea. After a decorated anacrusis on $\hat{5}$ this moves up by step from $\hat{1}$ to $\hat{5}$, supported by a thick texture of staccato chords (Example 3.29a). It then returns in the transition (from bar 26^4) in more cantabile guise, yet with most defining parameters reversed – falling instead of rising by step, legato instead of staccato, and minor instead of major (Example 3.29b). These reversals change the character of the shape so thoroughly that it might not be recognized, but the complementary two-bar phrase unit that follows from bar 28^4 gives the listener a chance to catch the connection: this unit restores the decorated version of the opening anacrusis that had been suppressed just before, and also initially follows the same rising contour as the original unit. The composer is always one step ahead, as it were, but then gives the listener the chance to catch up.

---

[149] de Staël, *De l'Allemagne*, 378.   [150] de Staël, *De l'Allemagne*, 380 and 381.

Example 3.29a Clementi, Sonata in G major Op. 40 No. 1/i, bars 1–8

Example 3.29b Clementi, Sonata in G major Op. 40 No. 1/i, bars 24–30²

Example 3.29c Clementi, Sonata in G major Op. 40 No. 1/i, bars 34–40

Similar help is offered shortly thereafter, at the arrival of the second theme from bar 36⁴ (Example 3.29c). The first two-bar unit has some features that might recall the opening idea – the use of the same decorated anacrusis, the same metrical layout – but sounds otherwise quite different, with its melodic falling thirds. The following two bars offer what sounds like an embellished complement to this unit, and hence a natural kind of continuation, but they are also in fact a direct transposition up a fifth of what we heard in bars 3 and 4: a gracious reply to the assertive upwards thrust of the opening idea. This then suggests, in an example of what Edward T. Cone calls 'reversed derivation',[151] that the two bars that open the second theme have amalgamated the paired two-bar units that opened the movement: rhythmically similar to bars 0^4–2^3, but with a pitch structure based on falling thirds that recalls bars 2^4–4^3 (note how bars 36^4–38^2 give us an augmentation of the falling thirds, moving from a^2 through $f\sharp^2$ and d^2 to b^1). It is the two-bar complement that follows, though, that makes this perception possible: bars 38^4–40^3 both act as continuation of two affectively opposed themes and also act as the broker to their differences.

A similar process is more vividly presented in the first movement of Gyrowetz's Op. 44 No. 2 (refer back to Example 3.5c). Near the end of the exposition, from bar 78, the opening motive, which had initially been presented in soft unison, returns *fortissimo* on first violin, urged on by energetic triplets in the lower voices – a pretty comprehensive instance of affective reversal. After a repetition of the two-bar unit, the final two notes of the motive, the minim appoggiatura d^3 that resolves to a c^3 crotchet, are subjected to two stages of rhythmic diminution. First, in bars 82–83, the d^3–c^3 pair contracts to half the previous duration, and then at 84 it contracts still further to a series of four dotted quaver-semiquaver units; cumulatively, bars 80–84 have the effect of a gradually accelerating final trill, but rendered in slow motion. This passage takes us directly to the 'incomplete' two-chords-only version of that closing formula that we considered earlier in the chapter. When the manipulation of the last two notes of the motive reaches its final stage, in bar 84, we may realize that this is something we have already encountered – the dotted-rhythmic figure that has been heard at various points during the second thematic group (see, for example, its appearance in the first half of bar 45 in Example 3.5b). Gyrowetz thus brings together – demonstrates before our ears – the underlying compatibility of two seemingly unrelated pieces of musical material. Once again, such a procedure could be understood in seemingly opposed ways. On the one hand there is the uncovering of surprising similarity amidst diversity – the composer as showman, pulling a rabbit from the hat – and on the other hand what is being highlighted is the variety that can

---

[151] Edward T. Cone, 'On Derivation: Syntax and Rhetoric', *Music Analysis* 6/3 (1987), 250: 'reversed derivation ... in which x precedes y yet x←y'.

issue from a single idea. The transformation involves not just a new context for the piece of material, but, more directly, a new character. As with the complete motive from which the last two notes are extracted, we hear the dotted rhythm change from being softly spoken, as it was at bar 45, to proclaiming itself in triumphal accents, in the present case. And once again the material being manipulated is in essence simple – in this case not the repetition of a single note, but the alternation between two notes.

A sort of negative image of the prized versatility of utterance is provided by the minuet from Haydn's Symphony No. 51 in B flat major (before 1774). The whole minuet is built on the exclusive basis of a four-note figure in the bass, played eight times at various transpositions. This makes possible a notational peculiarity in the original bass part: the four-note figure is written out just once, with various clefs attached, providing a visual puzzle for the players. As with many apparent examples of Haydnesque whimsy, the results turn out to be radical. The determined reiteration of this same bass figure, which consists of an octave leap up and then two steps down, means that no strong cadences will be possible at any point of the movement, since the only leap occurs at the start of the figure, and this is the harmonically insignificant octave. This bites particularly at the close of the two eight-bar sections, each of which ends with a I6–V4/3–I progression. The lack of a root-position dominant means that there can be no proper cadence at either point, which goes strongly against this most basic of grammatical essentials for a tonal piece.

But it is not just the bass line that seems to be stuck in a groove; the melodic line is not much less repetitive, effectively recycling the same two-bar module in tandem with the bass figure. However, it does offer more flexibility of pitch contour, and at the two main cadence points of 7–8 and 15–16 it relaxes into a typical formula, meaning that melodically at least a sense of cadence occurs. And the general tenor of the material is normal enough for a minuet in high style: a relatively regular marking of crotchet beats, the stepwise striding in the bass, the repeated-note melodic cell that sounds almost martial, the semiquaver flourish heard in the second bar of each unit that also has a ceremonial air.[152] But the failure of this material to do anything much more than repeat itself every two bars represents a reductio ad absurdum, a sort of caricatured rigidity, the humour at the expense of the mechanical in the music of this time that has been

---

[152] On such features as markers of a normal high minuet style see Melanie Lowe, 'Falling from Grace: Irony and Expressive Enrichment in Haydn's Symphonic Minuets', *The Journal of Musicology* 19/1 (2002), 172–178.

highlighted by Janet M. Levy.[153] On the other hand, the reiterated four-note bass figure does manage to appear in beginning, middle and end positions within each eight-bar section, which amounts to the kind of formal versatility that was noted above in the case of Brunetti's minuet and trio from the quartet L197. The difference here, though, is that the bass line remains utterly unchanged in form; it does not adapt to circumstances.

While the kinds of versatility we have considered can be accounted for under the rubrics of 'thematic' or 'motivic', on some occasions it is more concentrated than that: it is a single pitch, often initially dissonant, that forms the focus. In this case there can be little doubt that the 'economy' counts for little; the emphasis falls squarely on reinterpretation, on the way in which that note or pitch class can be placed in, or indeed generate, different harmonic contexts.[154] Often, though, it is the manipulation of rhythm rather than pitch that is most striking. This is worth noting as such given that this kind of manipulation has so often been missed amidst the popular prevailing image of symmetrical 'perfection'. In other words, the most striking flexibility is often evident simply in how that the given material interacts with supposedly set parameters such as metre or grouping. The finale of Haydn's Quartet in C major Op. 64 No. 1 (Example 2.17) offered a supreme instance of this: the main motive declared its independence above all through its refusal to align itself consistently with the metre or with one particular pattern of accentuation.

The versatility may in fact lie almost entirely in the rhythm, as it seems to in the finale of Haydn's Symphony No. 58 (c1767–1768; Example 3.30a), which plays endless games with downbeat versus offbeat placement of the main motive. At the start the two oboes play the first notes of the motive on the first beat of the 3/8 metre, which is then countered by the two violins entering with the same notes on the second beat, a hocket-like pattern that continues on odd-numbered bars. What makes this all the more teasing is that the continuation of the motive in the oboes in bar 2 occurs on the second beat, which then coincides with the violins' take on the matter, and this means an alternating pattern of rhythmic dislocation and rhythmic agreement. From a traditionally thematic point of view, 'nothing happens' to this oft-repeated motive, yet from the point of view of scansion, the motive never stands still. For instance, when the motive and its constituent

---

[153] Levy, 'Something Mechanical Encrusted on the Living'.
[154] This kind of procedure has been well covered in the literature; Rosen, in his chapter on Haydn's string quartets in *The Classical Style*, offers some especially memorable analyses, for example of the first movements of the quartets Op. 50 Nos 1, 5 and 6, Op. 55 No. 3 and Op. 64 No. 6 (120–134).

Example 3.30a Haydn, Symphony No. 58 in F major/iv, bars 1–12

Example 3.30b Haydn, Symphony No. 58 in F major/iv, bars 60–71

theme return to close the first half, from bar 61 (Example 3.30b), matters seem to be resolved in favour of off-beat execution by both oboes and violins; yet in the final three bars the oboes reassert the virtues of marking the downbeats. At the point of recapitulation (bar 107; Example 3.30c) the violins change their minds and start every second bar of the shape on the downbeat, while the oboes join the other instruments in playing a repeated-note figure that just happens to start on the second quaver of the bar, meaning that the tension between downbeat and off-beat execution is continued by different means. In fact, most of the material in the

Example 3.30c Haydn, Symphony No. 58 in F major/iv, bars 105–117

movement continues to enact this rhythmic battle in one way or another, and it is a battle that never resolves. At best we end with a stalemate, though that would hardly be the term with which to leave a movement that conveys such hyperactive ebullience. It creates an impression of near-endless resource, that there may be no end to the rhythmic possibilities, even while there is little thematic development in the customary sense of the term.

But accentual versatility need not reach the heights of nervous indecision that we hear in Haydn's finale. The Minuet of Krommer's Flute Quintet in C major, Op. 58 (published in 1807, but probably written much earlier), oscillates continually between the three possible metrical placements of a simple two-note slurred figure in triple time. The more common permutations occupy beats three to one and two to three, but eventually the downbeat-oriented placement on beats one and two also offers itself for consideration. Each stress pattern naturally suggests a quite different distribution of musical energy. The two-note motive that opens Beethoven's Sonata in E flat major Op. 7 (1796) seems unlikely to be in two minds: thickened chordally, and accompanied by a drum bass, the motive is plainly weighted towards the hypermetrically stronger first note, an emphasis that is in no doubt on its various reappearances through the movement. Yet near the very end, at bars 352–355, the accentual weight is reversed, together with its hypermetrical alignment, from being beginning-accented to being end-accented. In addition, the motive has also always been an initiating gesture (with the exception of the very end of the development), beginning a new section, and it almost always comes twice. These conditions apply from bar 352, but it is now also used with closing (postcadential) function, and is then subjected to rhythmic diminution, interlocking versions describing a rising arpeggiated contour. At the same time this is an instance of liquidation, whereby the thematic turns into the commonplace, giving a double perspective on the conventional affirmative triadic ending to the movement.

Formal Function

The versatility that is apparent near the end of Beethoven's Op. 7 movement involves not just rhythmic reinterpretation, but also a realignment of the motive within the larger structure. Such realignment may entail not so much a change in the actual form of the material as in our understanding of its place in the discourse – its formal function. There are but three such functions, beginning, middle and end, and material may typically be aligned with one of them, which the short phrase units of our musical style often make especially clear. Because of the strongly 'conventionalized' characteristics associated with each function, it is possible, as Caplin notes, to 'identify a given function without necessarily taking into account its position in a theme'. This means, for example, that 'model-sequence technique alone can signal the sense of continuation', and 'the presence of a cadential progression may in itself be sufficient to project a cadential function'.[155] Such separation of a piece of musical material from its functional associations, whether these arise through general custom or through the circumstances of a particular piece, is a signature technique of our period's instrumental music. We considered a classic instance of it with the finale of Haydn's quartet Op. 33 No. 2 (Example 1.1), where the very beginning has somehow to be re-heard and accepted as an ending to the whole movement. Caplin uses the term 'formal "dissonance"' to describe such a phenomenon,[156] and other writers have offered their own coinages – 'modular dislocation' from Hepokoski and Darcy, 'positional migration' as adapted from Leonard B. Meyer by Vasili Byros.[157] Agawu remarks that 'the constant rereading of [beginning-middle-end] signs' is 'one of the

---

[155] Caplin, *Classical Form*, 111.   [156] Caplin, *Classical Form*, 111.
[157] Hepokoski and Darcy, *Elements of Sonata Theory*, 66; Meyer, *Style and Music*, 124. Vasili Byros, in 'Towards an Archaeology of Hearing', 291–292, invokes Meyer's term, which refers primarily to a means of effecting 'style change', and adapts it to musical situations that fit with our current form-functional context.

sources of great excitement in listening to' our repertory.[158] Excitement might seem a strange sensation to claim for something that could readily appear to be a cerebral matter, principally of interest to critics and connoisseurs. But in fact it accords with the development of form – the big cousin of formal function, after all – into a 'live' parameter, something in which all can have a stake. If schema and topic theories envisage the existence of a listener who will recognize discrete units of invention, and then note how those units are arranged relative to each other, it should not be too big a jump to imagine that the same interest may be aroused when it comes to still larger concatenations of sound. In this particular context, that means the perception of one of three kinds of formal expression – being at the start, being in the middle, or being at or near the end. And 'expression' may be taken in its warm and fuzzy sense here as well. Far from occupying a neutral level, or representing an anachronistic academic layer, structural perception can contribute its own expressive force to a listening experience. From the point of view of formal function, for instance, different kinds of sensation are associated with each of the three basic categories; endings, for one, may prompt feelings of anticipation, resolution and satisfaction. For instance, Michael Talbot notes how the avoidance of strong cadences in the finale of Haydn's Sonata in C major H50, and in particular the avoidance of any full close in the tonic until almost the end of the movement, creates a 'restlessness' that is an 'important ingredient of the total effect'.[159]

But to go in this direction could be to miss part of the point of what we might call the formal energy of later eighteenth-century instrumental music. This is that the appeal to the listener – the way in which the listener is brought into the equation – need not be restricted to the customary critical category of emotional identification or empathy with the music. In the case of Haydn's Op. 33 No. 2 finale, we have already noted how any vaguely encultured listener will be turned into an analyst by the conclusion to the movement. Levy notes how we are 'forced to take part', made to 'attend to . . . the mechanism of structure'; Gretchen Wheelock writes of 'a strategy of inclusion, one that engages his listeners as highly self-conscious participants in a process of completing the jest'.[160] In fact Haydn's movement simply represents the extreme end of a development described by Laurenz Lütteken whereby 'music commands meaning via interplay with

---

[158] Agawu, *Playing with Signs*, 20.   [159] Talbot, *Finale in Western Instrumental Music*, 154.
[160] Levy, 'Something Mechanical Encrusted on the Living', 239 and 240; Wheelock, *Haydn's Ingenious Jesting with Art*, 13.

the structures of cognition', which he calls 'one of [the] most striking outcomes' of later eighteenth-century music.[161] In the case of Haydn this is apparent on many fronts besides his manipulation of formal functions. There is, for example, his habit of extensively recomposing recapitulations, as against the prevailing tendency to treat this section as a resolving rhyme. Materials may reappear well out of the expected sequence, or reiterated materials may go in unexpected directions. Haydn clearly thought deeply about this aspect of the musical experience: about what it means to sit and listen and how we experience, or can be made to experience, time. His constant playing with beginnings and endings can be thought to have the same conceptual basis: how we experience succession, temporal sequence, temporality altogether. From this perspective, Haydn might be dubbed a cognitivist composer. But this need not be as forbidding as it sounds: while such manipulation has its speculative, not to say forensic, side, betokening a spirit of constant, independent enquiry, it is also of course a means of engaging listener attention.

At the same time, when various kinds of 'formal dissonance' arise, those feelings of identification with, or absorption in, the musical process that are supposedly being encouraged can be put under strain. Listener incomprehension looms. And such manoeuvres might seem to cut against the trust inherent in a sociable communicative regime – how can we trust a composer who is, as it were, liable to tell such tall tales? Yet the irony is that deception is what seems to bring the communicative intent most vividly to life; we noted the same sort of conundrum with respect to convention itself, richly meaningful in its own right yet also regularly honoured in the breach. In other words, deception aids perception. By objectifying the musical materials, showing that they are not true for all times under all circumstances, Haydn encourages a critical spirit in his listeners, who must assess the fitness for purpose of what they are hearing. This in fact extends to a seeming opposite – silence. No prior music has such constant recourse to silence. This might be thought to grow naturally from the constant short breaks between phrases and phrase units that help to create an accessible formal transparency, but there can be a fine line between the helpful caesura and a less certain silence. One striking instance is heard at the start of the first movement of Haydn's Symphony No. 39 in G minor (1765?), in which segments of the theme are interspersed with lengthy breaks. What could have been brief caesuras are stretched so far that they

---

[161] Laurenz Lütteken, review of Lowe, *Pleasure and Meaning in the Classical Symphony*, *Eighteenth-Century Studies* 42/4 (2009), 629.

overplay their hand as punctuating devices. For Felix Diergarten, this movement embodies a shift from 'punctuation form' towards 'thematic form', since it is only the thematic connections across the 'spectacular grand pauses' that allow the discourse to achieve any coherence.[162]

Another case would be the slow movement of Haydn's Symphony No. 47 in G major (1772). The lengthy theme is based on two-part invertible counterpoint, laced with suspensions that help to impart a venerable character to proceedings. This is followed by a series of fairly literal variations on the theme, based on the principle of successively smaller rhythmic divisions: from the basic quaver rate at the start to semiquavers, sextuplets and demisemiquavers. These build up a sense of inevitable, inexorable movement, and even the theme itself was based on a steady flow of quavers that is never broken. From the upbeat to bar 121 we return to the original theme, which is now greatly enriched texturally compared with the original strict two-part basis. Just before this seemingly climactic version of the theme can complete itself, the whole ensemble pauses on and repeats a V6/5 chord, marked *crescendo* and leading to a suspenseful minim marked with a fermata (bars 150–151). This already breaks the steady flow of the movement. But what follows is electric – a silence and then a *piano* echo of these repeated chords in the strings, in a most unexpected tonic-minor harmony (bars 152–153). This is followed by another silence and a further set of soft repeated chords (bars 154–155). This use of silence, together with the irregular rhythm and fragmentation of material, would seem to be all but impossible stylistically, given the continuous contrapuntal basis of the movement to this point. Haydn has broken the topical code and exposed the contingency of musical time: the inevitable onward flow was not inevitable after all. Such silences as we find in these two symphonic movements not only testify to a discursive self-consciousness on the part of the composer, they also promote a perceptual self-consciousness on the part of the listener. The perceptually loud, infinitely extending silence at the end of the finale of Haydn's Op. 33 No. 2 is, once more, just a more extreme version of the same. Silence is no longer just an absence of sound; it is now music too.

The shared self-consciousness that seems to govern such operations need not be of the dramatic kind that is often embodied by outright silence. Many kinds of form-functional 'dissonance' may pass by unremarked; many have only been picked up for the first time by recent scholarship,

---

[162] Felix Diergarten, 'Time out of Joint – Time Set Right: Principles of Form in Haydn's Symphony No. 39', *Studia musicologica* 51/2 (2010), 109.

and the full extent of the practice remains far from common knowledge. For example, while it has often been noted that Haydn starts the Vivace assai of the first movement of his Symphony No. 94 in G major ('Surprise'; 1791) off-tonic, with a brief sequential pattern in A minor being repeated down a step in the tonic, schema theory enables us to be more specific. Haydn is using a particular two-voice nucleus known as the Fonte,[163] which is characteristic of middle or continuation function, often used immediately after the double bar of a minuet, for example. This pattern is therefore specifically out of place in its current formal position. That said, there is a twisted kind of logic at work: the Vivace assai is preceded by an Adagio, and does therefore represent a kind of continuation from the music already heard in the slow introduction. Nevertheless, there are multiple reworkings of this 'opening' unit through the rest of the movement, including some that incorporate it into a proper medial function within the larger phrase.

The first movement of Haydn's Symphony No. 90 in C major (1788) also plays on the functional ambiguity that was exploited in the first movement of Symphony No. 94: the double beginning first with slow and then with faster material. In this case the four-bar phrase that opens the Allegro assai has already been heard verbatim in the slow introduction. It occurs in bars 5–8 of the Adagio, forming the continuation of a larger phrase and then taking us to a cadence. When heard at this point, there is no cognitive dissonance – it fits perfectly. It is when this material begins the Allegro, at a faster speed, that it should strike the listener as at least a little odd. Harmonically, it represents a straight continuation from the end of the Adagio, which finished stranded on a diminished-seventh chord, but to reach a quite final-sounding cadence so quickly thereafter is hardly the done thing: in this case Haydn opens his fast section with a middle that leads to an ending.[164] This reverses what the composer does in his next (and last) C major symphony, No. 97, where, as we saw earlier, the closing phrase occurs in the wrong place in the slow introduction and is then properly situated in the subsequent Vivace (played in note values that will approximate the speed at which it was played in the slow introduction).

---

[163] This is also recognized by Byros in 'Towards an Archaeology of Hearing', 292.

[164] This movement is discussed by Yoel Greenberg in 'Minding the Gap', his study of 'active transitions' in Haydn symphonies: he notes how the composer presents three cycles of alternating material, of which the second encompasses the end of the introduction and the beginning of the Allegro. Greenberg does not mention, however, that our four-bar unit – which he describes as 'a sort of motto for the entire fast movement' (313) – represents a closing formula.

Inevitably, the first movement of No. 90 proceeds to rework its problem material in various ways, until its reaches its final destination in the coda. First the four-bar unit comes back verbatim in bars 218–221. Following this we hear three variously simplified versions of its last two bars: *piano* in the winds, *pianissimo* in the first violins with pizzicato accompaniment from the rest of the strings and then *forte* or *fortissimo* by the whole orchestra, which concludes the movement. These multiple references should confirm for even the most casual listener the form-functional conceit that has underpinned the movement. The material that had been a beginning to the Allegro now plainly acts as an ending. Yet it does not provide the formal close, which has already taken place prior to its re-entry. Instead, it functions more in postcadential manner, like a playfully ironic suffix.

While one is spoilt for choice in Haydn's output when it comes to the conflation of formal functions, it was not a one-man show, even though there were few areas in which Haydn more plainly set the terms of reference. Nor need the discursive affect always be the same each time, even if many of Haydn's infringements have a picaresque flavour about them. For example, the slow movement of Brunetti's Quartet in B flat major L185 (1785), Largo amoroso, starts in mid-phrase with a unit that lasts five bars. The bass line tells us this is a cadential approach – it starts on $\hat{3}$, supporting a tonic 6/3 harmony, and then moves chromatically up to $\hat{5}$. The dynamic level is initially *pianissimo*, followed by a continuous, carefully marked *crescendo* to a final *forte*. The sense of incongruity is strengthened through clear signs of intensification – chromatic passing notes in bars 1 and 2, imitation between the two violins over the first four bars, the fact that the final *forte* is marked by a unison texture, with the four parts playing a descending tonic arpeggio. All these factors suggest the closure of a large-scale section, with intensity having built up to the point at which we start; thus, as at the opening of Haydn's Symphony No. 97, there is the disconcerting sensation that we have walked in, as it were, in the middle of something. This five-bar opening is followed by a *piano* three-bar phrase that cadences again on the tonic, though in much more undemonstrative fashion. The eight-bar phrase that follows that uses the falling-arpeggio figure as the tune against a murmuring accompaniment. In its fifth bar, we hear once more the melodic line from bar 1, though it is now smoothly arrived at courtesy of a linking figure in the cello. It is not difficult to get the point – that what was improperly presented as an opening now takes its rightful place bang in the middle of a larger eight-bar unit. Nevertheless, while the continuation is momentarily the same, and the same basic linear rise to $\hat{5}$ in the bass takes place (from bar 13), what ensues is a plainer, less emotionally charged passage to the end of the phrase. While the thinking behind this may seem Haydnesque, the results sound different. The sense of discursive impropriety, of a kind of mock faux pas, that one might hear in Haydn is less pronounced; instead, one might hear the music simply emerging from silence, consistent with a slow-movement style that is gentle and 'amoroso'. These manoeuvres are witty in procedural but not in expressive terms.

Quite different from the Elysian fields occupied by such a movement is the Un poco andante from Kraus's Symphony in C major VB139 (1781), which also begins in mid-phrase, with what turns out in retrospect to be a tonicized supertonic chord of A minor. The phrase – ten bars long – eventually closes on the tonic G major, but only after considerable indirection (Example 3.31a). As the movement is a rondo, this theme comes back twice, both times recontextualized as to change our understanding of how it began. With the first return the material of original first bar is now heard in the middle of a phrase, as it should be, and its functional status as a predominant harmony is clarified (bars 36–44). The second return (Example 3.31b) is preceded by an extraordinary passage of harmonic mystification that closes in bars 68–69 in A minor. After a pause, the violins, *forte*, play a high falling scale that finishes on a D♯ – an ambiguous close to an alarming gesture that comes out of nowhere. This is followed in bar 72 by a *pianissimo* E7 chord in third inversion, which means that when the first bar of the theme returns at 73, it resolves that chord, which is now to be understood as V4/2 of ii. This time around, therefore, the tonicization of A minor has been prepared, and so the first bar of the refrain makes some logical harmonic sense. On the other hand, this material once more opens a phrase, and a section, that ought to be in G major. The effect of such dislocations, rather than the gentle ambiguity of Brunetti, is enigmatic, oblique and 'difficult'. In such circumstances one is reminded of Schwartz's equation that accompanying a shift from 'the older, single-theme notion of unity and the newer conception subsuming striking thematic contrast' is a shift in the sense of what a theme is and does: 'the idea of the theme as conveyer of expressive content, as a signal of the passion or affection intended to dominate the piece as its primary subject, gives way to the idea of the theme (with its associated affections) as object, to be manipulated into a larger pattern determined by the interplay of both musical and extra-musical elements, of which expression is only one'.[165] This is tantamount to the encouragement of analytical listening posited above, with the

---

[165] Schwartz, 'Conceptions of Musical Unity', 57 and 71.

Example 3.31a Kraus, Symphony in C major VB139/ii, bars 1–10

rider that such an experience cannot be excluded from the realm of 'expression', more broadly understood. In the case of Kraus's movement, the sense of estrangement from a fluid delivery of musical contents brings its own affective charge.

There are many other ways to deconstruct the formal function of beginning; it need not arise only through the purposeful muddling of material associations. False starts or ambiguous starts can do this just as

Example 3.31b Kraus, Symphony in C major VB139/ii, bars 64–82

well. Many of these occur at moments of reprise – in other words, not first beginnings but new beginnings. Leaving aside the matter of the so-called false reprise – the return of an opening in the apparently right place but in the wrong key – we encounter the reprise in the Trio section of the third movement of Haydn's Quartet in C major Op. 50 No. 2 (1787). This trio seems to parody the motivic concentration of the preceding minuet, transforming that section's head-motive into rustic guise. The reprise arrives quickly in the second half, but stops dead in its second bar (68), though the second violin continues with its quaver accompaniment for a beat longer than the others. After one of our 'loud' silences, another attempt at reprise is made, though the dynamic is now *piano* after an implied *forte*, suggesting uncertainty. In addition, the cello has dropped out. This attempt too falters, the first violin and viola stopping dead just as they had done before. But the second violin is even slower to cotton on this time and continues its accompanying quavers for the rest of the bar (71). After an even longer silence, viola and cello make a third attempt at reprise by themselves, and while the first violin subsequently enters with the correct thematic material, it is swept away in a rising sequence: the moment for a proper collective recapitulation has passed, one feels.[166] Through this sequence of events the musically 'natural', a return to earlier material, is made unnatural; through such manipulation it loses its innocence, and becomes a discursive subject. Best (or worst) of all, there is the delicious sense of embarrassment that arises when the second violin continues its actions in bar 71, seemingly oblivious to what is going on elsewhere – as when someone at a concert claps at the wrong place or continues to clap when others have stopped.

Another kind of conspicuous manipulation of function occurs through simple exaggeration, with no particular ambiguity involved. This can barely occur with opening function, but is very characteristic of middles, especially in the form of (re)transitions that last longer than they need to. Retransitions in particular characteristically involve an element of simplification which is straightforwardly listener-friendly: by reducing the cognitive load, they bespeak imminence, they tell us that something is on the way. But if this helpful formal sign lasts for too long, we gradually become aware of the redundancy, and hence what should be a means to an end emerges as an object in its own right. This may involve a disproportionately long standing on the dominant, as it does in the Minuet of Haydn's Symphony No. 66 in B flat major (before 1779), where an eight-bar retransition (bars 20–27) is nearly as long as the theme it purports to return us to, and the way in which it peters out rhythmically and dynamically makes it seem even longer. It can no longer be regarded as a lightening of the cognitive load.

This kind of functional exaggeration can also readily occur in the case of closure, as when too many ending signals are offered, often to comic ends. The finale of Pleyel's Symphony in C major Ben128 (1786) plays a series of tricks with a listener's perception of structure, based on a form that is one

---

[166] For a more detailed analysis of this movement, minuet included, see Sutcliffe, *Haydn: String Quartets, Op. 50*, 58–60.

of the easier ones to grasp and anticipate – the rondo. The opening theme is one of those that sounds like a typical rondo refrain and so promises the form even before anything else is heard. The first episode, in F major, begins at bar 49 and seems to finish at bar 94, but no immediate return to the rondo theme ensues, even though we have returned to the tonic key. From bar 102 the music delivers a clear form of closing rhetoric, as if it were a coda. However, in bar 120 it comes to rest decisively on the dominant. Then at last we hear something that is clearly (re)transitional in function: a repeated G pedal in the violas in quavers while the violins play anticipatory melodic fragments. This itself is quite prolonged, in line with the phenomenon of the exaggerated retransition that we have just considered, but eventually the music dies away into the silent bar 145. Then the rondo theme returns, some fifty bars after we might have expected it to do so. This section finishes at bar 169, from which point we would anticipate a simple cut to a further episode. Instead of that, we once more hear material that promises to wind the whole movement up, as the harmony sits firmly on the tonic. Perhaps we are now hearing the true coda, and the form is going to be, contrary to expectations, ternary plus coda. All the signs are there that the players are building up to the end. Then, in the midst of this process, the music stops in its tracks, and the first violins play a soft rising diminished-seventh arpeggio (bars 192–195). This moves into a completely syncopated line, against which the second violins plays staccato crotchets on the beat – *alla zoppa* figuration that sounds like a delaying tactic. Eventually, at bar 214, the diminished-seventh arpeggio returns and resolves to a V4/2 of C major. This takes us to a resumption of our noisy closing rhetoric, and the movement might have come to an end shortly thereafter, at bar 235. Indeed, for a second it seems to have done so. However, a new tune, based on a horn call, then 'sprouts from the top', the phrase Allanbrook has applied to those colloquial closing melodies that lead to a celebratory close.[167] This infectiously generates yet another new tune from bar 246 in the violins, one that has a real whiff of opera buffa about it, which is followed by a tutti answer. These three ingredients – the typical closing moves and the two new tunes – then rotate, which means that this coda is now becoming seriously prolonged, and Pleyel continues to add one closing gesture after another. This is clearly over the top. The proportions are wrong; the tail is wagging the dog.

Eventually it seems that the movement has ended at bar 339. The coda has lasted from bar 169 to bar 339: some 170 bars, which constitutes half

---

[167] Allanbrook, 'Mozart's Tunes', 177.

the movement. So was this a rondo interrupted by a coda? In fact, it transpires that the end has still not been reached, and we have been duped by another false ending: after a pause we hear the upper strings alone playing softly and Adagio. This turns out to be a reminiscence of the retransitional material that took us from the over-prolonged B section back to the rondo, and the scoring is identical. Then, after another silence, the rondo theme finally returns. So, after all that confusion, our formal expectation of a further refrain is finally being fulfilled. However, the proportions turn out to be quite wrong. We hear just the first six bars of the theme before it is liquidated into closing gestures that, this time, do deliver on their promise of a decisive tutti finish. In effect the rondo theme turns out to be the coda to the coda.

Quite apart from being an almost impossibly extended play on the formal function of closure, Pleyel's movement demonstrates a prime sociable attribute: it is aware of possible redundancy of utterance. It demonstrates this by 'getting it wrong', just as many of the most vivid moments of 'conversational' interplay in the repertory arise through various forms of misbehaviour, as we have noted in the case of Haydn. The movement has got stuck within its closing utterance, has gone on for too long, and the listener should gradually realize that a failure of discursive decorum is involved. The restoration of the refrain from bar 347 puts this right in a sense, though it is really far too late for such a rescue act: honour is not saved. Of course, this misrepresents the tone of the operation, which is in the nature of a hilarious shaggy-dog story. Rondo forms are perhaps particularly prone to such formal self-consciousness because, even when carried out in orthodox manner, they are 'about' alternations of the fresh and the familiar, an endless play on the basic facts of listening that involve departure ('something different') and return ('something the same'). That may help account for the enormous popularity of the form in later eighteenth-century musical culture: it was potentially a highly accessible listening experience, with a clear-cut design, but that very clarity could be utilized to complicate perception, to produce moments of shared self-consciousness.

If both endings and retransitions can be held up for inspection in this way, what about a transition, where we are headed, not back, but forwards? In the first movement of his Symphony in C major Murray A6 (published in 1782 by Sieber in Paris), Rosetti manages to undercut such a formal function. An extensive, predominantly loud and assertive tutti acts as a transition to the establishment of the new key – all very much as expected, certainly in a C major symphony. At bar 76 V of V is reached, which might

Example 3.32 Shield, String Trio No. 2 in D major/i, bars 10–19

be enough to bring about the medial caesura that will tell listeners that the section is over, but the harmony is prolonged by imitation involving a stretto of the opening subject, played in the lower strings and answered in inversion by violins. Oboes and horns, meanwhile, reiterate a grand dotted rhythm, and all parts are playing *fortissimo*. But instead of a final arresting gesture to cap this show of orchestral force, the transition dissolves. Harmonically it has already done its job, but rhetorically there is a kind of collapse. The violins are suddenly alone in bar 81, echoing a fragment of the opening subject, with an added grace note providing a comic touch. This fragment is repeated in a further dynamic reduction to *pianissimo* in the next bar, and a bar of silence marked by a pause follows. This means that we do now get our medial caesura, since the gap is followed by a new theme. However, the caesura is now marked for consciousness after the reduction in force and dynamic level, and the comical collapse of energy level; it is no longer simply a handy prop.

Middles and endings can also become beginnings via a common kind of linkage technique. We saw examples of this earlier in the chapter from C. P. E. Bach, Wanhal and others, there under the rubric of renewal of commonplace material. But what is also encouraged at such points is a renewed awareness of formal function. In the first movement of Shield's String Trio No. 2 in D major (1796) the close of the theme is marked by a rising scale in the violin at bars 11–12, and at the cadence point the cello plays a filling arpeggio figure (Example 3.32). As that finishes at the start of bar 13, the viola echoes the violin's rising scale, and then in bar 14 the violin echoes the cello's (mainly) falling arpeggio of bar 12. Thus we seem to have two bars of echoing repetition that confirm the cadential arrival. But on the last beat of bar 14, the viola goes its own way, and blossoms in bar 15 into something that is clearly melodic. When that reaches a point of rest, marked by a typical phrase-ending locution, in bar 16, we must adjust our perception, since the viola can now be understood to have initiated a four-bar melodic phrase at the start of bar 13 – and what we heard as postcadential, as having an ending function, turns out also to have been a beginning.

Another conspicuous type of form-functional play is to begin with an outright ending, which may be a cadential formula or even postcadential material. This category serves, as we saw earlier, as a form of cadential renewal. And the reverse is also common enough – to end with the beginning, either unexpectedly (as in our finale of Haydn's Op. 33 No. 2) or by reciprocal arrangement with the previous category (the finale of Haydn's Quartet in D major Op. 76 No. 5 (1797) begins with high-octane closing chords that then return in their natural position at the close). Thus the beginning = end equation may either surprise or satisfy. As such differing examples show, the play with formal functions cannot be neatly partitioned; interfering with middles, either by prolongation or by overlap, also of course interferes with an expected new beginning. One instance that seems to conflate all three possible functions is heard at the end of the opening ritornello of the first movement of Mozart's Piano Concerto in F major K413 (1782–1783). Following the decisive cadence in the tonic at bar 53, a gentle postcadential confirmation unfolds in the strings, based on the imitative treatment of a line that begins with simple repeated notes. The fourth imitative entry is provided by the soloist, and almost as soon as that has happened, the strings conclude their phrase at bar 57. But the piano has not finished; it is only just beginning, with the repeated notes forming the springboard for the soloist's opening theme. Thus while the phrase from bar 53 has an ending (postcadential) function, the soloist's entry in imitation with the strings represents continuation or middle function, and then the soloist proceeds unaccompanied, with the repeated-note figure opening its melodic line and constituting a fresh beginning. These rapid functional transformations are effected smoothly, and from a generic standpoint this is a modest way for the soloist to announce his presence. At the same time it is all rather conspicuous, with composerly technique plainly laid out for attention – the same duality we noted earlier with the gambit of the soft ending, which is both understated yet also draws attention to itself.

There are other, stranger ways to end at the beginning. Two works in C. P. E. Bach's fifth collection *für Kenner und Liebhaber*, the Sonata in E minor and Rondo in C minor, finish where they started; more precisely, they stop in the middle of doing so. Both were written in Hamburg in 1784, and it is difficult not to think that they show the composer trying his hand at something that Haydn had done so memorably at the end of his Op. 33 No. 2 of 1781. The Andantino finale of the sonata (Wq59/1) is in E major, and fluent and lyrical. It opens with a double period, an eight-bar unit that is followed by a varied version of the same. The reprise from bar 41 conflates the two – after a repetition of bars 1–2, we switch to a complete rendition of bars 9–16, creating a ten-bar stretch. However, the final bar of this unit begins a dramatic and brilliant extension of five bars, after which the theme starts again, in a gentle undercutting of this forceful display. The first four bars are heard verbatim (bars 55–58 = bars 1–4), but there is no continuation along the original lines. Instead of this, bars 59–60 replicate 55–56, though now *pianissimo* and one octave lower. Thus we seem to be starting again from the top. Except that we aren't. Instead the music simply ceases, and we are left with a similar puzzle to that which Haydn offered in Op. 33 No. 2: material that has been heard many times as a beginning now has to be accepted as an end. More exactly, we are two bars into a new beginning, and so we can also feel that the music ends in the middle of something we were expecting to last for longer. This ambiguity also precisely obtains in Haydn's finale, which likewise ceases to operate two bars into an apparently fresh start. Once again we see how manipulations of formal function, supposedly representing three distinct perceptual categories, readily run into each other. And Bach's final gambit leaves us with similar sensations. Syntactically the music is incomplete – we need a couple of extra bars at the very least for the music to come to a convincing point of rest – though in retrospect we realize the music is complete harmonically. Bach, like Haydn, does finish in the tonic key, if in weaker fashion: the final two bars offer inverted forms of dominant then tonic chords (V4/3 to I6).

In the skittish Rondo in C minor, Wq59/4, the listener has an even greater challenge (Example 3.33). Bar 108 presents a cadential formulation in the tonic that we have heard twice before, in bars 18 and 63. On both those occasions the material closed a section, and there is no reason to think it is acting differently in bar 108, at the same *forte* dynamic as before. Indeed, bar 108 seems to finish the movement. Immediately thereafter, though, Bach makes as if to start the rondo theme again, with its initial rising C minor arpeggio. However, this time it emerges from a lower register, two octaves down from all previous appearances, and is marked *piano*. It also stops dead after six notes, and the movement is over. In retrospect, this new beginning could be heard as a sort of throwaway

Example 3.33 C. P. E. Bach, Rondo in C minor, Wq59/4, bars 103–109

afterbeat, or a very eccentric kind of postcadential confirmation – it does after all consist of an arpeggiated tonic triad, the very stuff from which such confirmations are usually made. But whereas we may eventually make peace with other endings of this type, including that in Bach's sonata above, this one seems darker and physically more upsetting. If we have reached any degree of bodily entrainment with the music, the sensation at the end of this rondo is akin to stepping off a cliff.

Dittersdorf achieves a similarly haunting effect at the close of the first movement of his Quartet in G major, K193 (we have already studied the conflation of formal functions that he achieves in the second movement of the same work). This Moderato features a separate coda, to be played after a repetition of the second half of the movement. After an initial swerve to the flat submediant key (bar 179), the coda quickly returns to the material that finished the recapitulation. This means a return to a Grand Cadence schema, which is somewhat amplified, followed by material that has been used many times before in a postcadential capacity. Built on a repeated-note cell that featured in the movement's opening theme, this material consists of two complementary two-bar units which are then symmetrically repeated to yield an eight-bar whole. It signals the close of both the first and second groups in the exposition (bars 16–24 and 71–79 respectively), and then again of the second group in the recapitulation (170–178; shown as Example 3.34a). By the time the coda arrives, we are therefore more than familiar with this material and its functional role – if both repeats are taken we will have heard the whole thing six times. Its reappearance from bar 200 of the coda is both exactly the same as we have heard on those six previous occasions and radically different: it lasts for just four bars, without a complementary repetition, and with that the movement takes its leave (Example 3.34b). So accustomed are we to hearing the eight-

Example 3.34a Dittersdorf, Quartet in G major, K193/i, bars 167–178

Example 3.34b Dittersdorf, Quartet in G major, K193/i, bars 198–204

bar version of this postcadential gambit that it has come to seem like a single indivisible gestalt, and so only to hear half of that, followed by silence, is truly disconcerting. Once again, this will be a loaded silence, since cognition must continue. Yet this is different from our Bach and Haydn examples above. In no real sense can this ending be regarded as incomplete; we do not exactly finish in mid-stream, but rather with the firmest of postcadential confirmations. What Dittersdorf exposes is the arbitrary nature of our symmetrical syntactical expectations. It is only habituation to the particular form this material has always taken in the movement – two plus two times two – that could make us expect more. In itself the final four-bars-only version forms an entirely satisfactory pendant to the final structural cadence at bar 200. And we might even consider in retrospect that the more familiar eight-bar version was needlessly repetitive, that it contained a redundancy which the concluding four-bar version finally expunges.

Once more in this movement we have an effect that compels participation in the musical process – after the sound has stopped the listener must think about what has just happened, and in that sense it is the listener who completes 'the music'. Engaged, analytical listening is a premise for the effect to work. The same also applies if we zoom back to consider formal function on a larger scale, where big blocks of music can collide. In Chapter 2 we reviewed a series of movements by the likes of Andreas Romberg, Wranitzky, Pleyel, Mozart and Michael Haydn in which sudden changes of tempo and material could create large-scale formal ambiguity, and at the very least force listeners to think about musical succession. These cases all turned on the confrontation of different expressive typologies, typically one slow and lyrical and the other fast and more animated. While those ambiguities were found in slow movements and finales, the two typologies may also interact in first movements that feature a slow introduction. Kozeluch's Sonata in C minor Op. 2 No. 3 (1780) and Sonata in G minor Op. 15 No. 1 (1785) have similar structures: an initial slow movement (both Largo), harmonically incomplete and therefore functioning as a slow introduction, gives way to a quick movement in the same key, neither of which finishes, and instead the slow material returns to complete the movement with a finish in the tonic. Both works then proceed to a concluding movement in major. The respective first movements suggest functional versatility on a large scale, since what seem for a long time to be familiar successions of slow leading to fast could ultimately be understood as large-scale ternary designs. What seems to be the main (fast) material following the introduction turns out in the end to be a medial contrast – new beginning becomes middle – and there is also the ambiguity of when an initial slow movement is to be regarded as complete in itself. In both cases, the rhetoric is fantasia-like rather than clearly enunciatory, which tends to confirm the generic status of 'slow introduction'; on the other hand, both sections are very long for an introduction of this kind. The player-listener may well have to change her mind several times about the formal shaping of the whole. Such movements are prime examples of how a sociable aesthetic can operate within a cognitive, 'technical' domain: they actively engage the listener on the level of their large-scale form, yet the affects are far from 'sociable'. Instead the movements are heavily pathetic and agitated by turns, two of the expressive types that one expects to encounter in minor-mode works.

These two multi-part movements do not in fact unfold in quite so similar a fashion as I have implied. In Op. 2 No. 3 what returns is not the opening material of the Largo (very similar to the opening of Mozart's later Fantasia in C minor, K475 (1785), both being built on a falling chromatic tetrachord in the bass) but rather the material heard from the end of bar 8. In Op. 15 No. 1 it is the opening that returns, and in fact the preceding Allegro molto does plausibly finish, but then adds some further material that sounds coda-like before it is drawn to a prolonged dominant, out of which the opening Largo material re-emerges. Further, there are several later works by Kozeluch in which the same sort of structure emerges: the Sonata in C minor Op. 30 No. 3 (1789), for instance, where the opening of the Largo comes back, led into by an incomplete Allegro. It may be that this sort of unstable structure goes particularly well with minor-mode rhetoric. Beethoven's later Sonata in C minor Op. 13 ('Pathétique'; 1798), whose first movement also alternates between a weighty slow introduction and quicker material, suggests that this might be the case. The most intricate of such specimens, though, is neither a first movement nor in a minor key: the finale of Haydn's Quartet in C major Op. 54 No. 2 (1788) interweaves Adagio and Presto sections in such a way as to prompt what Cone called 'a series of mistaken interpretations, all encouraged by the composer and cleverly ordered in such a way that the subsequent correction of each merely exposes the listener to the next error'.[168] James Webster has subsequently detailed no fewer than nine stages to this evolving formal plot.[169]

Just a year before Haydn's Op. 54 appeared, Rosetti's Op. 6 string quartets were published in Vienna (1787). The third movement of No. 2 in E flat major is a Romance in Adagio tempo, in gavotte rhythm and with

---

[168] Edward T. Cone, 'The Uses of Convention: Stravinsky and His Models', *The Musical Quarterly* 48/3 (1962), 289.

[169] James Webster, *Haydn's 'Farewell' Symphony and the Idea of Classical Style* (Cambridge: Cambridge University Press, 1991), 300–308. Webster sums up the case by describing this finale as 'one of Haydn's most stunning examples of progressive form' (308).

serenade-style doublings of melodic lines at the octave and the tenth. The movement is quite short, and it is followed by an Allegro vivace in 6/8. This could and should be a finale, except for the disconcerting fact that it is in C minor. This too turns out to be rather brief, and after this closes on the dominant, we hear a verbatim repetition of the Adagio. And with that the quartet is over. Once again, large-scale functional reinterpretation seems to be called for. Is this a ternary-form finale, exceptionally involving a slow tempo at either end and a quick and not obviously related middle section? As one experiences the work, though, it seems like we have been listening to a fourth movement until the point when the Allegro fails to finish, or indeed to adjust itself to the key of the whole. One should also note that while the Allegro vivace turns to E flat major as expected after a C minor start, that very quickly gives way to the prolongation of its dominant, B flat major. This is what would expect from a finale in the tonic of the whole work, and maybe we should understand the opening in C minor as an initial deflection from that key.

In any case, this work, together with numerous others, suggests that these large-scale adventures of formal discovery were more widespread than is commonly thought. Another instance is the great Adagio of Kraus's Sonata in E major, VB196 (1787–1788), which seems to present the common pattern of an incomplete slow movement giving way to a quicker finale (an Allegretto at bar 44), but then the Adagio returns from bar 122, followed by a seemingly unrelated 'Arioso' section (bar 131) and then an 'a tempo' that takes us back to something like the original material. This is a particularly rich example of the interplay between formal and expressive typologies.[170] A finale proper then follows.

The ambiguity of such movement-complexes – challenging the listener to make sense of the relationship between different blocks of musical material – can in fact operate at the level of a complete work. This involves not any links of affect, texture, motive and so forth that may be discerned between seemingly separate movements, but rather verbatim repetition – what is often known as cyclic return. The consensus is that such outright sharing of material is rare. Peter A. Hoyt asks 'What aesthetic criteria made literal repetition between movements so rare in Haydn's and Mozart's instrumental music?',[171] suggesting it derives from an eighteenth-century

---

[170] I give a more detailed account of this movement in my review of *Joseph Martin Kraus: Keyboard Music*, two volumes, ed. Bertil van Boer (Wellington: Artaria, 2002), *Eighteenth-Century Music* 2/1 (2005), 164.

[171] Peter A. Hoyt, 'Haydn's New Incoherence' (review-essay of books by James Webster, Gretchen Wheelock, Elaine Sisman and Ethan Haimo), *Music Theory Spectrum* 19/2 (1997), 271.

belief in the 'inherent mobility of emotional states'. This means that any 'literal return of material from a previous movement entails an unnaturally static adhesion to a single passion'; it might even suggest '*monomanie*'.[172] Indeed, the premium placed on variety, as discussed in Chapter 2, might seem to rule out any regular use of large-scale thematic returns across separate movements. Well-known cases of the kind, such as the return of the first-movement opening at the end of Haydn's Symphony No. 31 in D major ('Hornsignal'; 1765) or the return of part of the minuet within the finale of Symphony No. 46 in B major (1772), might be exceptions that prove the rule.

Nevertheless, such remote repetitions are, once again, more often found than is commonly thought. We have already noted an instance in Dittersdorf's Quartet No. 4 in C major, in which the middle section of the minuet not only returns to act as the middle section of the trio, and then as a separate coda to the movement, but then reappears at the end of the finale, seemingly unrelated to the set of variations that has just been heard. To this we could add a work like Wanhal's Symphony in A major Bryan A9 (no date known), which is effectively a single-movement work. The initial Allegro moderato runs abruptly into an Andante molto in D major, which in turn runs into the final section, marked 'Tempo di primo' (though now written in cut time rather than 4/4). The reversion of a finale to the same basic pacing and metre as a first movement, even if the music is new, is in itself unusual. The listener might well think the movement has ended with bar 354, which follows a brilliant Grand Cadence formula plus several bars of confirming unison triadic figuration, finishing with our three-chord closing device. But then from bar 355 to the finish we hear a direct quotation of the first three bars of the first movement. They are played *piano* and lack the original driving quaver accompaniment, but are otherwise intact. This is like an echo of the start of the whole work, and perhaps also a kind of compensation for the fact that the first movement had failed to reach a close. After the three-bar quotation, the last two bars depart from the model and offer a very straightforward, unremarkable cadential close, one of those soft, low-key endings that is both amusingly self-deprecating and a kind of showing-off, in this case given extra point by the prior return to the work's very opening material.

---

[172] Hoyt, 'Haydn's New Incoherence', 272. Such a verdict is also backed up by Michael Talbot, who writes that the 'overt thematic links between the outer fast movements' found in works by composers such as Corelli and Castello 'become greatly attenuated in the course of the eighteenth century' before 'reasserting themselves once more in the nineteenth and twentieth centuries'. Talbot, *Finale in Western Instrumental Music*, 25–26.

Interestingly, two of the composers who cultivate 'cyclicity' quite consistently, C. P. E. Bach and Boccherini, seem relatively uninterested in the smaller-scale functional reinterpretations that we considered earlier. In Bach's case, though, we have only just dealt with two such instances, the movements in E major and C minor from the fifth collection of works *für Kenner und Liebhaber*. In fact, Bach is more likely to complicate the perception of closing function through outright denial, forming part of a general aversion that he displays towards strongly signalled endings. This often means that interior movements within a multi-movement instrumental work are run on: before a firm finish can be heard, we are transported to a different musical world. In some cases, this leads to outright return of previous material, as in several of the works published as *Sei concerti per il cembalo concertato* in 1772 (the composer played keyboard-only versions of these concertos to Burney when the latter visited Bach in that same year[173]). In Concerto No. 4 in C minor, Wq43/4, the initial Allegro assai gives way unexpectedly early to a modulating Poco adagio, which in turn leads without a break into a Tempo di minuetto in E flat major. Its phrase construction, its rounded-binary form and the fact that it is built on a recurring stepwise Romanesca bass line all provide an unprecedented stability to the musical discourse; in addition, this movement allies itself with the genre of the minuet-finale, and if it were not for the mediant tonality we might expect the work to come to a close with these strains. However, a second-time bar takes us back to the material of the Allegro assai, initially in F minor but then regaining the tonic. This return could hardly have been expected, though from the point of view of proportions it has its logic: the first movement seems to be only about half as long as we might have expected, and so this (second) finale simply provides what we were missing in the first place. Bach also acknowledges the cyclical design through a written-out piano cadenza that recalls the initial material of the two previous movements. Concerto No. 5 in G major, Wq43/5, is not much less remarkable, and again the movements are run on. A brief Adagio for the orchestra is quickly interrupted by the soloist introducing a Presto in 6/8. After this full-length movement the Adagio returns as slow movement proper, now including the soloist, before a concluding Allegro.[174]

---

[173] See Douglas A. Lee, Introduction to C. P. E. Bach, *Sei concerti per il cembalo concertato*, Carl Philip Emanuel Bach: The Complete Works, series 3, volume 8, ed. Lee (Los Altos: Packard Humanities Institute, 2005), xiii.

[174] This discussion of the two Bach concertos derives from my review of ten volumes of *Carl Philipp Emanuel Bach: The Complete Works* in *Notes: Quarterly Journal of the Music Library Association* 65/3 (2009), 845.

But it is Boccherini who, as Le Guin writes, cultivates cyclicity 'more consistently and inventively ... than any other composer of his generation'. She describes two of the cello sonatas, G17 and G569, as 'essays in the complex effects of memory and expectation upon the listener's perceptions'.[175] This is a nice way of capturing what is at stake with our category of large-scale functional reinterpretation. An extreme case is found in the Quintet in A major Op. 28 No. 2/G308 (1779), the finale of which is almost a mirror image of the first movement. More specifically, it presents the first four bars of the first movement followed by an exact repetition of its entire second half: thus what was a (big) beginning now acts as a (big) end. Spatial metaphors like 'mirror', of course, overlook the fact that musical form must be lived, or experienced, before it can be rationalized. 'Form' itself is just such a rationalization, and even to speak of 'return' overlooks the fact that identical material will mean something different when it is heard again, especially when we are dealing with such phenomena at the level of a whole work. As we saw earlier in 'Versatility', difference counts for more than similarity or sameness; it is how our perceptions can be dynamically changed rather than simply affirmed that counts for more.

We should also note that such sharing between movements need not involve outright thematic material. In the Quintet in G minor Op. 29 No. 6/G318 (1779), for example, the shared material is transitional.[176] The third movement, Preludio: Adagio, closes on the dominant with a repeated Phrygian cadence that recurs exactly in the rondo finale, as a retransition from its second episode back to the refrain (compare the respective bars 20–22 and 113–119). This may well play quite subtly on the ear, since such a formulation is less likely to be remembered with the same clarity that a theme or thematic section is; in other words, 'cyclic' returns may be perceived on a sliding scale. This is even more evident around this point in the finale, since the episode that this Phrygian progression succeeds is remarkably similar to the Trio to the second-movement Minuetto; it features the same Alberti-style figuration in the first cello, supporting the

---

[175] Le Guin, *Boccherini's Body*, 128.
[176] Le Guin also notes a 'category of recycling in Boccherini's music [that] involves the reiteration of material that, while striking, is not properly speaking thematic at all, but transitional': *Boccherini's Body*, 130. She goes on to suggest (131) that such recollections may owe something to the composer's 'hand memory'. While this is a very plausible and attractive line of enquiry, it could surely not be as specific to the composer as Le Guin seems to imply: Boccherini, after all, was hardly unique in being not just a composer but a high-quality performer, and the hand-memory perspective loses some force when the recycling occurs in works for multiple performers.

same sort of internally repetitive tune in octaves above (compare bars 50–56^1 and 103^2–109^1 of the rondo with the second movement's Trio). But it is no verbatim repetition.

The cyclical features found in these two works are combined in Boccherini's Quintet in C major Op. 25 No. 4/G298 (1778). Here the third-movement Trio, in C minor, opens with a slightly simplified version of what had opened the second movement, a Larghetto in the same C minor, and it follows that up with an oblique reference to an oscillating quasi-cadential formulation first heard during the Larghetto's first section (compare bars 49–57^1 of the Trio with bars 2–4^2 of the Larghetto, and in the slow movement this figuration returns in extended form at bars 16–20^2). The Trio does not finish; the point of expected recapitulation is replaced by a return to the start of the Minuetto (bar 73). The same in turn happens when the final version of the minuet's eight-bar unit is replaced by a return to the opening of the Trio (bar 105), creating an internally through-composed form in which the expected boundaries are broken. In fact it is only the first three and a bit bars of the Trio that are heard again; we then return to the cadential oscillations from the Larghetto. These steal in subtly, written in longer note values and suggestive of a tempo relationship between the two successive movements (the quavers of the Larghetto would equal the crotchets of the Minuetto and Trio). What Boccherini most explicitly returns to is not thematic as such, but rather a ritualistic cadential passage, which is thus defined less explicitly through its thematic identity than its most 'characteristic' syntax. Amidst all these interruptions and recollections, it appears that Minuetto, Trio and Larghetto have got in each other's way; a stalemate has apparently been reached. The over-repetition of the oscillating figuration (another Boccherinian 'loop') helps to make this point. A brief *a piacere* passage for first violin prolongs the suspense, and then something very unexpected occurs: a return to the material of the initial Allegro. This turns out to be a verbatim repetition of the recapitulation, in other words the most stable section of the opening movement. It is also a decisive return to the major mode, and given the rather grimly ritualistic minor-mode expression that has occupied much of the work, going back to something familiar may here be precisely the point.

Middle Function: What Are Development Sections Doing?

While sonata form has played a prominent role in the recent proliferation of new theoretical perspectives on eighteenth-century music, development sections have been considered rather briefly.[177] For instance, the chapter devoted specifically to the development occupies just thirty-five out of six-hundred-odd pages in Hepokoski and Darcy's *Elements of Sonata Theory*.[178] This makes sense given that a development constitutes, as Caplin puts it, 'the most loosely organized part of an entire sonata movement',[179] and one would naturally expect greater energies to be devoted to defining parts of the structure that are more formally obedient, as it were.[180] In any case, the typically loose-knit nature of development sections needs to be understood within a wider category – that of functional middles, which would also encompass such phenomena as transition sections and cadenzas, and can also include the central portion of a phrase or a theme group. These medial units share many of the properties that are widely agreed to characterize developments: harmonic and tonal instability, more variable organization of musical elements, fragmentation of previously heard material, use of sequence and the like. They are less likely to feature the sort of reciprocal binary organization that characterizes material with an opening or closing function. Spitzer describes this as a 'subversion of symmetry' that typically occurs 'within the second halves or middles of units at rising levels: consequent phrases, transitions, secondary groups, and development sections'.[181] Development sections proper, of course, are longer than any such related units and will contain at least several subsections, and they may present material not previously heard – all factors that lend them a relatively independent status, and make them a special type of musical middle. Further, a large-scale central development section was a new phenomenon, so on the grounds of historical novelty alone we are justified in treating it as something of a special case.

Yet just how new is it, in fact? Most of the individual developmental techniques noted above are also perfectly at home in earlier repertories. Rosen pointed out that 'the texture of the development section', for

---

[177] Much of this section is based on my chapter 'Laboring a Point: What Are Developments Doing?', in *SECM in Austin 2016: Topics in Eighteenth-Century Music II*, ed. Janet K. Page (Ann Arbor: Steglein, 2019), 89–113.

[178] Hepokoski and Darcy, *Elements of Sonata Theory*, chapter 10, 'The Development (Developmental Space)', 195–230.

[179] Caplin, *Classical Form*, 21.

[180] One exception to this is Christhard Zimpel's *Der kadenzielle Prozess in den Durchführungen: Untersuchung der Kopfsätze von Joseph Haydns Streichquartetten* (Hildesheim: Olms, 2010), in which the author argues that Haydn's string-quartet development sections are always organized on the basis of a central tonality that receives cadential confirmation. For a discussion of this thesis see the review by W. Dean Sutcliffe, *Music & Letters* 93/2 (2012), 238–241.

[181] Spitzer, *Metaphor and Musical Thought*, 116.

instance, 'generally resembles Baroque texture more than any other part of a sonata',[182] and even the notion of a distinct, relatively large-scale area featuring unstable behaviour had its precedents. One of the most interesting, and powerful, precedents may be found in the so-called 'vamp' sections in many of the keyboard sonatas of Domenico Scarlatti.[183] Perhaps the very word that we use to refer to this section obscures such similarities. The term development postdates the eighteenth century; it seems to have been first used to refer to our central section by Anton Reicha in 1814, and does not appear to have cemented itself until about a century later than that,[184] but now it is a fixed part of our intellectual apparatus. The problem is that the term tends to pre-judge the matter of what these sections are accomplishing musically. Hepokoski and Darcy soften it by referring to 'developmental space', noting that it need not entail fragmentation, motivic manipulation and so forth.[185] More significantly, with their theory of rotation these authors claim that the sequence of events in a development section may not be quite as random or 'free' as has been commonly thought. They describe rotation, whereby the development tends to use materials in the same order as the exposition, as a 'strong first-level default'.[186] This then means that sonata form as a whole can be conceived as a series of cycles through a similar sequence of events. Yet this need not contradict the traditional understanding that development sections take further some aspects of the given material, that they offer 'a space for reflection and commentary' on what we have already heard.[187]

However, if we consider such sections less from the point of view of 'formal logic' and focus instead on the sort of social behaviour they suggest, the role that they play seems less obvious. Why should such relatively freely

---

[182] Rosen, *Sonata Forms*, 275.
[183] They may be especially relevant given that such sections are often surrounded by a distinctly galant, periodic style of phrase syntax. For a discussion of the import of the 'vamp' see Sutcliffe, *Keyboard Sonatas of Domenico Scarlatti*, especially 196–216.
[184] See Hepokoski and Darcy, *Elements of Sonata Theory*, 195–196. The authors point out that Reicha's application of the term 'développement' does not completely correspond with our modern-day understanding, since it also included the subsequent recapitulation – in other words, it encompassed the entire second part of the form. Hepokoski and Darcy then report that in the germanophone realm it was only with the work of Hugo Leichtentritt (in his *Musikalische Formenlehre* of 1911 (Leipzig: Breitkopf & Härtel)) that the equivalent term, 'Durchführung', became standard.
[185] Hepokoski and Darcy, *Elements of Sonata Theory*, 196. 'Developmental space' is regarded as a more neutral way of referring to the central section of a sonata-form movement, pointing to its medial position but avoiding any automatic assumptions about the sorts of techniques that the composer will use.
[186] Hepokoski and Darcy, *Elements of Sonata Theory*, 206.
[187] Grave and Grave, *String Quartets of Joseph Haydn*, 60.

organized material – rotation or not – be required within a later eighteenth-century musical idiom that places such an unprecedented emphasis on periodic organization – on an arrangement of material that goes out of its way to ensure intelligibility for the listener? Often enough these middle sections seem to shed the 'discipline' of periodic construction, to lack the sort of reciprocal, varied presentation of material we expect to hear. Rather than pleasing through variety, they may suggest mechanical or obsessive behaviour, 'labouring' a particular musical point. These are not attributes that fit readily with a predominantly 'polite', sociable style.

Among the possible social-stylistic 'faults' that developments may demonstrate, obsessiveness must be one of the most glaring. In his conduct manual of 1788, Knigge counselled his readers to avoid any 'hobby-horse' in their interaction with others:

Some people are so weak as to abandon themselves entirely to a certain favourite *propensity*. People of this class speak of nothing with so much pleasure as of their favourite object; all their ideas revolve constantly round that point, and they miss no opportunity to introduce it on every occasion; their hobby-horse ... may consist in a predilection for hunting, horses and hounds, or for dancing and music, painting, prints or any other particular. They forget in that case that the person to whom they are speaking perhaps knows nothing at all of their favourite object, nor do they wish he should have much knowledge of it, if he but patiently listen to them, or admire their darling and seem to be delighted with it.[188]

Significantly, such offenders seem not to care whether their listeners can understand or follow their train of thought; any real social interaction is minimal. Not only could such behaviour prove tedious socially, it might actually be a sign of more serious maladjustment to the world: Knigge suggests that it is possible to cure mentally disturbed people 'if their mind can but be recalled from a single fixed idea'.[189] A related malady was 'enthusiasm', a term which at the time almost always carried negative connotations of unreasonable insistence on one's (often religious) point of view.[190] A musical equivalent of this state of mind is occasionally

---

[188] Knigge, *Über den Umgang mit Menschen*, volume 2, 254–255; *Practical Philosophy of Social Life*, trans. Will, volume 1, 137–138.

[189] Knigge, *Über den Umgang mit Menschen*, volume 2, 268; *Practical Philosophy of Social Life*, trans. Will, volume 1, 154. In fact my 'mentally disturbed' is a rather gentle way of describing those that Knigge characterized as 'schwermüthige, tolle, und rasende Menschen' (*Über den Umgang mit Menschen*, volume 2, 267), rendered in Will's translation as '*melancholy* people, *lunatics* and *madmen*' (volume 1, 153).

[190] Enthusiasm is invoked in a musical context by David P. Schroeder in the chapter 'Haydn and Shaftesbury: Music and Morality' of his book *Haydn and the Enlightenment*: 'In advocating religious as well as intellectual tolerance, [Shaftesbury's] thinking clearly runs counter to those

satirized in opera-buffa catalogue arias, in which, as Mary Hunter informs us, the construction of lists shows 'overinvolvement' on the part of the character with his subject matter. Such a list, she continues, 'often takes over the aria . . . stunning (or boring) its onstage listeners', which demonstrates 'the inability of the buffa aria singer to judge his audience'.[191] In fact, there is even an entire symphony of the time that demonstrates such a moral lesson: Brunetti's Symphony No. 33 in C minor, 'Il Maniatico', written in 1780. In the composer's words, his work represents

> the fixation of a delirious person on one subject, and this part is played by a violoncello solo, to which the other instruments join, as though friends obliged to free him from his delirium, offering him an infinite variety of ideas in a variety of motifs. The *Maniatico* remains for a long time fixed on the first subject until he meets a happy motif which persuades him to join with the others. After this, he falls anew (in his fixation), but at the end, transported by a feeling of common impulse, closes, happily united with the others.[192]

The particular obsession of the solo cellist takes the exclusive form of trills. Significantly, this is not material that makes any musical sense in its own right, as say a repeated motive could; it is meaningless in isolation from a larger context. Antisocial behaviour is embodied by a fixation not just on oneself – which involves not listening to others – but also on a single idea, and, as we saw with Knigge's 'hobby-horse', such obsessiveness is represented as an illness or mental disturbance. (Compare, too, Dittersdorf's symphonic minuet *Il Matto*, whose 'mad' concentration on limited material was noted in Chapter 2.) Variety, on the other hand, is construed as being inherently social; Brunetti's 'infinite variety of ideas' seems to arise naturally out of the plural social body that is the orchestra. Interaction with others, with their different musical perspectives and ideas, can provide a cure for the sufferer; it is a process that not only brings happiness but also lends coherence to the musical utterance.

If Brunetti's programmatic representation of the perils of obsession is exceptional, there is nevertheless no shortage of such over-repetition in

---

who hold to any form of "enthusiasm" or fanaticism' (19). That 'enthusiasm' did not invariably carry pejorative connotations is argued in Jan Goldstein, 'Enthusiasm or Imagination? Eighteenth-Century Smear Words in Comparative Context', *Huntington Library Quarterly* 60/1–2 (1997), 29–49.

[191] Mary Hunter, *The Culture of Opera Buffa in Mozart's Vienna: A Poetics of Entertainment* (Princeton: Princeton University Press, 1999), 124–125.

[192] Gaetano Brunetti, title-page to Symphony No. 33 in C minor, 'Il Maniatico', cited in translation in Newell Jenkins, Introduction to *Gaetano Brunetti, 1744–1798: Nine Symphonies*, ed. Jenkins (New York: Garland, 1979), xiv.

development sections of the time. For example, after a highly varied, not to say picaresque, exposition section in the first movement of Dittersdorf's Quartet in E flat major, K195 (1789), the development offers just one type of material – two-note sigh figures formed into chains that are exchanged unrelievedly for fifteen bars. These are underpinned by a chromatically rising bass line in the cello that begins on a C (bar 74) and works its way up to A♭ in bar 90; such stepwise bass movement is a common means of holding together 'free', aperiodic material. In the first-movement development section of William Shield's String Trio No. 3 in A major (1796), the first violin has just started to present the main theme in E minor when it seems to get stuck, resulting in some fifteen bars of obsessive repetition of a syncopated motive (bars 62–76). In the Adagio of Haydn's Symphony No. 43 in E flat major (*c*1771), during the first section, a Prinner schema is set up but then goes astray after an enharmonic reinterpretation of B♮ as C♭, resulting once more in a passage where the melodic line seems to get stuck (bars 27–31). The development returns to this passage and extends it vastly, with eighteen consecutive repetitions of the same melodic fragment in the first violin, complemented by eighteen consecutive repetitions of the same repeated-note accompaniment in the other strings (bars 63–80). While the harmonies shift constantly, and thus give a sense of open-ended progression, the repetitive 'monorhythmia', at an adagio tempo, sounds distinctly obsessive.

One common form that this over-repetition takes is a modulating sequence that features sequential repetition in all parts. To cite just a few examples from first-movement development sections: J. C. Bach's Symphony Op. 6 No. 6 in G minor (1770) features seven consecutive reiterations of a four-bar unit (bars 68–95); Haydn's Quartet in B flat major Op. 33 No. 4 (1781) repeats a one-bar unit eleven times (36–46); Wanhal's Symphony in C major Bryan C3 (1762?) likewise features eleven consecutive repetitions, though of a two-bar unit (61–82); while in Mozart's Violin Sonata in D major K306 (1778) the section is dominated by a huge sequence that features twelve repetitions of a two-bar unit derived from the start of the transition in the exposition (bars 12–15). For all that this is enmeshed in a process of dramatic harmonic free fall, it still makes twenty-four bars of the same thing many times over (83–106). This passage is preceded by a very differently scaled syntax, where melodic fragments in the piano are imitated at half a bar's distance by the violin (75–82). The obvious sense of give and take here makes the following block of sequence stand out all the more.

What are we to make of passages such as these? We could think of them in relation to the rubric of 'free fantasia' which has sometimes been applied to development sections. This captures some sense of improvisatory or 'free' action, illogical though that may seem in any genre apart from a solo piece.[193] On the other hand, there is also a sense of no freedom at all, of being locked obsessively inside one idea and unable to break out. From a purely style-historical point of view one can also arrive at contradictory conclusions. As Meyer reminds us, motivic constancy often acts as a stabilizing force when the harmony moves unpredictably,[194] and that is certainly the case with such passages. Nevertheless, the sheer amount of repetition in each constituent part of the texture and the sheer length of the whole are surely unstable in a stylistic sense, dissonant with the principles of periodic organization. Robert Hatten describes 'perpetual motion' as being a 'marked' attribute 'in opposition to the unmarked, stylistically established articulations of texture' that are characteristic of later eighteenth-century style;[195] in other words, while we may not actively notice all the typical breaks of phrase syntax and texture in this style, we certainly do notice when these breaks are overridden for any length of time. In this sense developments can present a discursive dark side, failing to mind their manners and being, as we have seen, potentially 'irrational' in their lack of self-control. On the other hand, such repetitions can undoubtedly convey excitement, and a particular kind of concentrated energy that arises from the symbiosis of fluid harmony and stubborn material. Certainly, in his *Versuch einer Einleitung zur Komposition* Koch invited the reader to admire the harmonic syntax of such passages – it 'requires much skill to lead the modulation into several keys in a good way' – and cites a development section by 'Pleyel' (in fact Rosetti) that has exactly the large-scale use of melodic sequence, together with consistent repeated-note accompanimental figuration, that has been discussed above.[196] In principle, the kinds of repetition we hear are not so different from the cyclic repetitions of

---

[193] Certainly such passages may seem to crop up especially frequently in pieces involving the keyboard in a solo capacity. The development section in the opening movement of J. C. Bach's Sonata in E flat major Op. 5 No. 4 (1766) immediately brings a long stretch of 'free' figuration that ranges widely over the keyboard, without clear relationship to exposition material. The first-movement development sections of C. P. E. Bach's keyboard concertos Wq11 in D major, Wq14 in E major and Wq25 in B flat major, which date from the 1740s, all contain central 'free fantasia' sections, consisting of sequential writing realized as propulsive figuration in the keyboard generally supported by longer notes in the string parts. Nevertheless, as should be clear, such 'improvisatory' writing is found in abundance in other instrumental genres too.

[194] Meyer remarks that 'harmonic instability tends, in Romantic as well as Classic music, to be complemented by motivic constancy': *Style and Music*, 316.

[195] Hatten, *Interpreting Musical Gestures*, 240.

[196] Koch, *Versuch einer Anleitung zur Komposition*, volume 3, 411; ed. and trans. Nancy Kovaleff Baker, *Introductory Essay on Composition: The Mechanical Rules of Melody, Sections 3 and 4* (New Haven: Yale University Press, 1983), 240.

mostly even-length phrases that act as the motor for periodic phrase organization; in both cases the large-scale rhythms are highly regular. But periodic syntax leavens its large-scale reiteration by complementary relationships, by reciprocal organization of varied elements, and this is just what is missing in the 'monomania' of large-scale sequential repetition.

We should note too that the repetition need not involve sequence. Especially towards the very end of the century, it is likely to be replaced by different kinds of insistence. The first-movement development section of Haydn's Quartet in C major Op. 76 No. 3 ('Emperor'; 1797), for example, finishes with a passage in flagrantly popular style, with the violins fiddling away in octaves above persistent open-fifth drones in viola and cello. This is not just 'over the top' stylistically, but also in terms of its duration; at ten bars in length (65–74), it clearly outstays its welcome, as it were, and is described by Rosen as 'relentless'.[197] Similarly too long for comfort is the final stretch of the first-movement development of Beethoven's Sonata in B flat major Op. 22 (1800). This does involve sequential repetition, of a four-bar version of material that has already dominated the whole section, here played softly throughout. But the final leg of this sequence prolongs itself well beyond a four-bar duration, lasting for some eleven bars as the right hand repeats the same broken-chord figure forty-four times over (from 113 to 123, changing one pitch after the fourteenth playing) and the left hand loops back to the same material again and again. With the very low tessitura of the left hand, the passage sounds menacing as well as obsessive.

A different negative spin on such developmental behaviour from a sociable point of view would see not so much irrationality as something that is pedantic. Allied with this is the galant behavioural ideal of naturalness and ease, according to which labouring a point is to be avoided. Johann Joachim Quantz, for instance, in counselling composers to avoid pedantry, stated that 'listeners should perceive no laborious industry, but nature alone shining forth everywhere'.[198] Earlier in the century, the Third Earl of Shaftesbury had characterized pedantry as an offence against manners: as Lawrence E. Klein has summed it up, 'What was inimical to politeness in learning was aspersed as "pedantry"'.[199] The dangers of the

---

[197] Rosen, *Sonata Forms*, 283.
[198] Quantz, *Versuch einer Anweisung die Flöte traversiere zu spielen*, 16; *On Playing the Flute*, trans. Reilly, 22.
[199] Lawrence E. Klein, *Shaftesbury and the Culture of Politeness: Moral Discourse and Cultural Politics in Early Eighteenth-Century England* (Cambridge: Cambridge University Press, 1994), 6. 'Politeness' here must be understood as much more than simply an adherence to rules of social conduct, as Klein's book explores throughout.

music seeming either 'unnatural' or 'impolite' were heightened in a development because of the likelihood, as Rosen had pointed out, that it will offer features reminiscent of the baroque past: textures may be polyphonic, material may be worked more intensively and at greater length, and extensive sequence may be used to bring this about.[200]

A wonderful example of such 'impoliteness' may be found in the first movement of Kraus's Quartet in B flat major, Op. 1 No. 2 (VB181; 1784). The movement as a whole is a model of the varied modern style. The opening seven bars offer no fewer than five separate types of material presented consecutively, and no material is reiterated until the ninth bar. Example 3.35a shows the five different gestures as (a) to (e), and suggests possible topical associations. The movement continues in similar vein, with many changes of tack. But in the central section, from bar 74, we hear a passage that really sticks out (Example 3.35b). The violins play a rising dotted figure in parallel thirds, which is imitated by viola and cello at the distance of a beat. From this a large-scale canon arises, organized into sequential groupings. This might suggest a learned style, though what we hear is far more convoluted than that, given the uneven grouping structures. While the basic figure lasts for three beats, it is sometimes followed by a one-beat rest, which means that the metre seems to alternate between 3/4 and 4/4. And the number of reiterated versions of the figure that we hear before it is transposed changes mid-way: initially it is two, but then expands to three (all these features are marked on Example 3.35b). If we then factor in the process of imitation, we will be completely thrown off the trail.

Also very strange is that this material, including the dotted rhythms, seems to come from nowhere. The only previous dotted rhythms we have heard arose in the brief suggestion of a march topic early on (this is (c) in Example 3.35a), but there is no compelling reason to link the two pieces of material. Further, the somewhat unpredictable dynamic markings don't do a lot to clarify perception. How might we read this passage? An important deciding factor is that the pitch structure follows a large-scale circle of fifths, with the pattern taking us from C in bar 74, through F in bar 76, followed by B♭ and finally to E♭: these notes are circled in Example 3.35b. The circle of fifths is of course a typical means of organizing sequential movement, and in the later eighteenth century often conveys Matthew Riley's 'untimely rhetoric',[201] an aural reminder of a past musical style. The

---

[200] Rosen discusses the sequential part of this equation in particular in *Sonata Forms*, 275.
[201] Riley, *Viennese Minor-Key Symphony*, 5.

Example 3.35a Kraus, Quartet in B flat major, Op. 1 No. 2/i, bars 1–13

use of this technique, together with the canonic imitation and sudden use of a dotted-rhythmic style, suggests that we might hear the whole passage as a parody. Kraus seems to be invoking a typical developmental gambit, but sabotages the expression of learning. This is reminiscent of the situation of those singers of catalogue arias whose self-importance ends up impressing nobody. Thus the passage could be understood as a parody of 'laborious industry'.

The point may be proven by what happens next, after this material finally runs dry at the end of bar 82. We hear perfect periodicity, a two-

Example 3.35b Kraus, Quartet in B flat major, Op. 1 No. 2/i, bars 72–87[1]

bar unit featuring an elegant first-violin line that is then repeated exactly. Sweet, lyrical, regular, it exemplifies the gracious riposte, tempering the previous assertive, and in this case decidedly strange, behaviour. What is particularly nice is the way this riposte begins – with a simple repeated note in the viola before the other parts enter. This gives the sense of a cautious, tentative continuation after something so bizarre has been heard, as if there has been an embarrassed silence during which no one is quite sure what to say next. We saw something similar in the long silence that followed the cello's histrionics in Boccherini's Op. 32 No. 4 (Example 2.7).

Example 3.36 Haydn, Symphony No. 93 in D major/i, bars 108–163

A similar story is told in a different way in the development section of the first movement of Haydn's Symphony No. 93 in D major (1791; see Example 3.36). Here a seemingly insignificant figure is taken from the tuneful second subject (at bars 76^3–77^2), augmented by an initial repeated crotchet and then reiterated insistently, turning it into a strongly rhythmic motto (marked *x* in Example 3.36). It is counterpointed by a running bass (marked *y*), itself an 'untimely' feature for the late eighteenth century. At bars 111–114 we hear a rising sequence in the violins which we might expect to be continued. Instead, those four bars are transposed up a fifth from bar 115, and this time a third version is heard to create the sequence of scale degrees 1–7–2–1–3–2 in B minor. This now fulfills a prototype of the 'ancient' style, a rising chain of suspensions à la Corelli. From 122 figure *x* is isolated, with no running bass, and is treated antiphonally and in inversion. Following this, in bar 128, the earlier passage is inverted, with the running bass now being heard in the top voice and figure *x* migrating to the bottom, demonstrating invertible counterpoint. From bar 137 our motto is then combined with the shape that preceded it in the second

Middle Function: What Are Development Sections Doing? 419

Example 3.36 (continued)

Example 3.36 (continued)

Middle Function: What Are Development Sections Doing? 421

Example 3.36 (continued)

subject, a falling arpeggio (marked *z*; compare bars 76 and 80 of the exposition). At this point, the running bass drops out, leaving *x* and *z* to contend in a dense, effortful imitative texture.

But all of a sudden, at bar 153, the music breaks off in the middle of another reiteration of the motto, followed by a pause. The last two-bar unit is then repeated *piano* by the two violins alone, followed by a further pause. After this the unit is reiterated by the two flutes, and its last two notes become part of a simple falling arpeggiated shape while first violins repeat a rising arpeggio in contrary motion. This utterly changes the flavour of the musical discourse. The speaker (as it were), having grown quite heated (and learned), suddenly breaks off – hesitates – repeats the last fragment, which sounds like a question mark – hesitates again – then hits upon a much gentler way of saying the same thing. A motto that formed the fulcrum of a learned contrapuntal furore is recast in a context of pastoral simplicity. The particular sting here is that the original second subject was very much in a tuneful pastoral style, and the modulation of social tone from heated to gentle is confirmed when from bar 161 part of the second subject now returns, in C major. There is humour in the incongruity of treatment of the motto material, as the learned or laboured gives way to the innocent and 'natural', but this swerve also undermines the authority of a 'speaker' who has just displayed considerable learning, and authority is one of the central expressive associations of a learned style.[202]

Naturally, development sections will consist of much more than lengthy sequences and learned working of material. Having concentrated on the social risks they may bring, I would now like to touch on more positive rationales for this type of musical behaviour, which, after all, composers consistently chose to feature in their larger-scale sonata structures, and elsewhere as well. For a start, it has been widely agreed that disrupting a normal flow of musical events and heightening harmonic tension make their eventual resolution – in the form of a reprise – more satisfying for the listener. This was recognized, as we saw earlier, by Augustus Kollmann in 1796; he used the term 'fancy period' for such a digression, 'in which the

---

[202] In her detailed account of this development section in *Pleasure and Meaning in the Classical Symphony* Melanie Lowe notes the prevailing learned style (and associated 'elevated stance' (141)) but also isolates a certain multivalence in the 'sigh motive' – what I have dubbed motive *x*. For her, this motive might be heard as opposed to the learned aspects of the section, or it might work 'in expressive tandem with the counterpoint it creates', such that the overall 'stormy effect' of the section could be 'heard as an expression of intense subjectivity' (142). Lowe's interpretation works in productive counterpoint with my own, though I would note that the 'sigh figure' is preceded in every case by two repeated notes, which somewhat distances it from the 'sentimental mode' that is claimed for it (142).

composer seems to lose himself in the modulation, for the purpose of making the ear attentive to the resolution of the period'.[203] In other words, instability heightens perception as listeners anticipate a return to more settled ways, and naturally the longer this is delayed, the more satisfying will be the sense of return.[204] But this could also apply from a purely social perspective. By being disruptive, unstable, effortful, possibly obsessional, developments make the subsequent restoration of more controlled communication all the more appreciated and meaningful. The pleasure of familiar ways – both thematically and behaviourally – is increased after it will in various respects have been denied.

To cite just one example, the first-movement development section of Pleyel's Quartet in C major Op. 1 No. 1 (1782–1783) quickly leaves the charm of the exposition behind, moving on to a large-scale three-part ascending sequence, various kinds of unison texture (heterophonic and staggered unisons as well as the literal kind) and prevalently loud dynamic levels. These all create an effortful impression, culminating from bar 114 in a *fortissimo* unison outburst (Example 3.37). The rhythms, which resemble nothing previously heard, have a French-overture flavour to them, with anacruses subdivided into quick note values. This outburst leads to huge 'tutti' chords with many multiple stops at bars 117–118. This passage 'misbehaves' in several ways: the material is not only new, but occurs at quite a late stage of the central section, when new material would be least expected; it sounds awkward, being not just a thematic but a gestural non sequitur; it is patently orchestral, a kind of generic dissonance in the context of a string quartet, and hence is out of scale with its surroundings; and, finally, the tutti chords affirm the tonic when the recapitulation has yet to start, creating an error of discourse. This material is answered by a gentle *piano* passage in which lower strings sustain long notes (so annulling the previous hectic activity) while violin 1 has a phrase whose pitch contour mirrors that of the previous unison. Based on the same D minor harmony, it rises from a D up to an A before falling by step down to a C (compare bars 115–116 with the first violin's 119–120). This C is then held for a whole bar while the lower parts move on to a dominant-seventh chord, creating a suspension; the dissonance sounds sweetly hesitant after the previous bullying gesture. The suspension resolves in the following bar (122), following which the first violin provides two bars of lead-in to the

---

[203] Kollmann, *Essay on Musical Harmony*, 84.
[204] William Caplin, for example, notes that 'As a formal function, a development generates the greatest degree of tonal and phrase-structural instability in the movement and thus motivates a restoration of stability (to be accomplished by the recapitulation).' Caplin, *Classical Form*, 139.

Example 3.37 Pleyel, Quartet in C major Op. 1 No. 1/i, bars 108–125

recapitulation (124). This clearly restores equilibrium, and gives us the pleasure of the familiar, which comes as a relief after the somewhat unaccountable, effortful material we have just heard. It is as if the development section exists to deny such simple pleasure.

But this raises the question of whether and what sort of pleasure is to be derived from such subversion of more normal manners in a development section. It is clearly unlikely that listeners obtained no pleasure – that a development is simply pain followed by recapitulatory gain. There is of course the immediate sense of excitement that developmental procedures may generate, the warmth and feeling of spontaneity that may arise. These attributes are important ones given the tension that surrounded the definition of sociable culture in the eighteenth century. As Klein has noted, there could be an uneasy relationship between politeness and sociability: politeness could degenerate into 'mere formality or ceremoniousness'.[205] Sociability may have had a strongly moral dimension – genuine goodwill towards other human beings, respect for their feelings and ideas – but its outward manifestation in good manners could also simply be a means of advancing socially, not animated by any concern for the welfare of others.[206] Translated into musical terms, this means that too much polish could be as bad as too little, and so the typically 'rougher', or more restless, expression heard in a development could be understood as a kind of behavioural corrective. The relative loss of traditional eloquence – and frequent suggestion of a greater directness of feeling – could suggest an all-too-human fallibility.

We could also consider development sections through the prism of another eighteenth-century touchstone, taste. Since there are no firm rules for the arrangement of the whole, a development will inevitably showcase taste, understood as the freedom to exercise individual judgment when choosing between alternatives. Taste is an opposite to pedantry, which insists on one proper way to do things.[207] Dittersdorf expressed a common creative view of his time when asserting in his autobiography that 'however profoundly versed a composer may be in the rules of musical science, he cannot dispense with the qualities of *taste* and *imagination*'.[208] Note how Dittersdorf allies taste with individual imagination and opposes these to both 'rules' and 'science,' which stand for knowledge vested in authority. For Roy Porter this was a central part of the ethos of the Enlightenment: what he calls a 'reliance upon first-hand experience rather than second-hand authority',[209] and indeed at their best development

---

[205] Klein, *Shaftesbury and the Culture of Politeness*, 4.

[206] This was a consistent source of anxiety to polite culture of the era. In *Privacy: Concealing the Eighteenth-Century Self* Patricia Meyer Spacks, for instance, describes how the conversational ideal of 'smoothness' could often mean 'superficiality' (119), and throughout her study she emphasizes concerns of the time about potentially hypocritical behaviour, 'the well-known eighteenth-century preoccupation with hypocrisy' (226). In his article 'The Figure of France: The Politics of Sociability in England, 1660–1715', *Yale French Studies* 92 (1997), Lawrence E. Klein notes how sociability could become a 'tool of domination or self-promotion: manners were not the expression of moral identity but techniques for advancement and conquest' (35). For further discussion of this see Chapter 4.

[207] George Dickie, *The Century of Taste: The Philosophical Odyssey of Taste in the Eighteenth Century* (New York: Oxford University Press, 1996), 3, notes how, at the start of the eighteenth century, 'the focus of theorizing' about what would come to be understood as aesthetic experiences 'shifted from objective notions of beauty to the subjective notion of taste'. To his 'objective' we might add 'authoritative'.

[208] Dittersdorf, *Autobiography of Karl von Dittersdorf*, trans. Coleridge, 78–79.

[209] Porter, *The Enlightenment*, 15.

sections offer the sensation of experience in the here and now, of sound unfolding unpredictably from moment to moment.

In more specific technical terms, while individual sections of a development may 'stick to the point' in baroque manner as they intensively work existing material, on a larger scale interest lies in the way in which the material as a whole may be rearranged. This may include the possibility that new material is introduced – the ultimate in spontaneity, one might say – or that material that had previously seemed incidental rises to prominence. We have seen an example of this in Haydn's Symphony No. 93, and another case would be the first movement of brother Michael Haydn's Symphony in E major ST151 (1771). Here the development is dominated by a two-bar fanfare motive that closed the exposition and whose role one would expect to have been confined to that, yet it in fact ends up assuming a pivotal role in shaping the argument of the whole movement.

It is a similar story in the finale of Mozart's Symphony in C major K425 ('Linz'; 1783), in which the development becomes entirely preoccupied with the jagged arpeggio shape that opened the transition section at bars 28–31. This soon turns into a canon between first violins and bass, before the shape is delivered successively in turn by first bassoon, first oboe, violas, second violins, first violins, and finally by the bass once more. And in the Presto finale of Clementi's Piano Duo Op. 12 in B flat major (1784), the development casts a shadow over the brilliant energy of the exposition. It is based on a brief moment of lyrical repose in that section, at bars 35–38, a phrase unit that had led unobtrusively to a cadence in the dominant. Immediately after the double bar similar material is heard over an F pedal, but turning to the minor. After a brief return to figuration, from bar 79 the same shape is greatly extended, on V of G minor, with a broad cantilena in the primo part, doubled in octaves, while the secondo plays a sustained accompaniment. In this case the most unassuming, seemingly incidental, of material from the exposition has not only risen to unexpected prominence, but has formed the basis for a marked expressive heightening. This once more suggests that from a sociable point of view the virtue of a development can be that it allows for maximum unpredictability and spontaneity.

When we ally such positive rationales with the social risks outlined before, we can see that developments have a paradoxical status. They may at many individual points be out of step with the behavioural and communicative ideals suggested by the surrounding sections, yet as complete entities they may offer variety and spontaneity, both desirable aspects of that behaviour. And then on a larger scale still, development sections will lend variety of gesture to a movement as a whole. Equally, while it may contradict the social conventions enacted elsewhere in the music, on a global scale a development is itself a convention, a consistently chosen mode of musical behaviour at the level of a whole musical repertory.

4 | Tone

Sociable Feeling

If we have in the last few chapters treated musical sociability primarily as a matter of discourse, as a style of utterance that involves various patterns and principles, we now direct our attention more fully towards its obvious emotional associations. This is the realm of what I have called affective sociability. It covers attributes such as the polite, pleasant, friendly, amusing and considerate, suggests an atmosphere of relatively undemonstrative comfort, implies a non-libidinal mode of behaviour. Yet, as we have already seen, it is precisely during the eighteenth century that music comes to be routinely understood as a language of feeling, that 'expression' becomes a dominant ontology for the art. So how might we attempt to square these two properties? If reference to 'feelings' suggests a directness of reaction or experience, sociability offers a more controlled, not to say guarded, image of human behaviour. Further, one seems personal in its import, the other more collective.

It would seem reasonable to propose that something has been lost in transmission – that the semantic goalposts have shifted between then and the present day. For instance, in some supplementary observations at the end of a 1789 Porro edition of Haydn songs, we find the comment that performers of the songs should possess 'une profonde connaissance de l'expression musicale' – a deep knowledge of musical expression.[1] This conveys the sense of something external to the performers that they need to cultivate; expression is not somehow intuited, it is instead 'known'. In other words, the language of feeling is something that must be learnt; it is an accomplishment that one must have in order to communicate properly with one's fellow human beings. Feelings are therefore shared phenomena; they represent codified signals within the regime of expression.

---

[1] Haydn, *Romances Et Chansons De Differens Caractères, avec Accompagnement de Clavecin ou Forté-Piano . . . Traduites ou imitées de l'Allemand en Français par une Société de Gens de Lettres, 2. recueil*, ed. Pierre Porro (Paris: Porro, 1789), 'Observation de L'Éditeur', 21.

The third edition of the *Encyclopedia Britannica* of 1797 said as much. Emotions were a 'universal language' that made interaction possible: 'Society among individuals is greatly promoted by that universal language.'² It is on such a basis that Wye J. Allanbrook defends the relevance of mimesis for the production and reception of art through to the end of the eighteenth century. Its 'central premise' is 'a world held in common among human beings. ... To find the form for his materials the artist looks outward to the originals in that world rather than inward, to the private chambers of the self'.³

However, for some those private chambers did appear to find outward expression. Leopold Mozart praised the violin playing of Regina Strinasacchi by exclaiming, 'She plays not a note without feeling, even in the orchestral ritornello she plays everything with expression, and the *Adagio* no one can play with more feeling or more touchingly than she. Her whole heart and soul are in the melody she is playing.'⁴ Within this sematic field, 'heart' was a common point of reference when assessing effective musical communication. We have seen it being invoked by figures from Koch to Haydn, with the ability to move the heart of the hearer being a touchstone of musical quality, an intrinsic part of the mission of music. But the particular relevance of 'heart and soul' in the current context is that it suggests an internal capacity, something not equally available to all. Rosetti thought the same, but on the collective scale of an orchestra. During his trip to Paris in 1781–1782 he found particular pleasure in the playing of the orchestra of the newly founded Société du concert de l'émulation, because 'only here do they strive for expressiveness; Haydn is their idol'.⁵ If Leopold Mozart does not exactly deny a shared understanding of feeling, his turn of phrase does suggest a sense of individual agency. It also seems to invert the direction proposed by Allanbrook: here expression, corresponding to its etymology, denotes something that moves from the inside ('heart and soul') to the outside. When Haydn was praising the music of Leopold's son, in a famous letter to the music patron Franz Rott in 1787, he referred to the composer's depth ('so tief') and great feeling

---

² *Encyclopedia Britannica*, third edition (Edinburgh: A. Bell and C. Macfarquhar, 1797), volume 14, 7, cited in Ute Frevert, 'Defining Emotions: Concepts and Debates over Three Centuries', in *Emotional Lexicons*, ed. Frevert, 25.
³ Allanbrook, *Secular Commedia*, 57–58.
⁴ Leopold Mozart, letter to Nannerl Mozart, 7–9 December 1784, cited in translation in Heartz, *Mozart, Haydn and Early Beethoven*, 56.
⁵ Rosetti, letter to Prince Kraft Ernst von Oettingen-Wallerstein, 25 January 1782, cited in translation in Murray, *Antonio Rosetti*, 123. Note how Haydn here acts, alongside 'expressive', as a touchstone of musical quality.

('mit einer so großen Empfindung'), and emphasized his own particular understanding of and feeling for those traits ('als ich sie begreife und empfinde').[6] Haydn was, in other words, personally affected in a way that not all others seemed to be (he wanted to impress Mozart's virtues 'on every music lover'), and it is also clear from his wording that those traits of Mozart's were understood to come from the 'inside', from the depths of his creative soul.

Such testimonies make for more comfortable reading for us today, since they seem to correspond to prevailing models of what 'expression' and 'feeling' should mean. They are not obviously compatible with the more socially situated perspectives on these categories. This is not just a historical problem, of course; understanding the nature of subjectivity and its conditioning through social organization is hardly a matter that has gone away. But in the Western music world there has long been an overwhelming rhetorical emphasis on inner responsiveness, and much less focus on how, and in what terms, that actually arises. If there is an imperative for students to learn to sing or play 'with expression', for example, that must in the first instance occur through emulation and imitation, yet the implication that it should 'all come from inside' remains secure.

In our eighteenth century there was certainly a tension, but not necessarily a gulf, between these conceptions of human consciousness and behaviour. Ideally, at least, sociability and individuality may be said to have enjoyed a symbiotic relationship. Much of what we call the Enlightenment involved a heightening of individual consciousness, including an acknowledgment of personal differences and an assertion of the need to judge for oneself rather than defer to authority. The primacy of 'feeling' – including but going well beyond its application to music – was an encapsulation of this. But the question then arose of what to do with this consciousness. To keep it to oneself was meaningless, and indeed unhealthy – this was a constant refrain of the time. The solitary life found relatively few advocates. For instance, when in Diderot's *Le neveu de Rameau* the theme of the dialogue turns to suspicions of society corrupting one's true nature, the alternative that is presented is to 'sequester

---

[6] Haydn, letter to Franz Rott, December 1787, cited in Franz Niemetschek, *Leben des k. k. Kapellmeisters Wolfgang Gottlieb Mozart* (Prague: Herrlische Buchhandlung, 1798), 66. Daniel Heartz remarks that while Haydn's letter now only exists as printed in Niemetschek's early biography, it is unlikely to be inauthentic: Niemetschek 'would not have dared invent such a document with Haydn still very much alive and flourishing in Vienna'. Heartz, *Mozart, Haydn and Early Beethoven*, 382. Making such a possibility even less likely is the fact that the author dedicated the book to Haydn himself ('Dem Vater der edlern Tonkunst, dem Lieblinge der Grazien Joseph Haydn').

yourself in a garret, live on dry bread and water, and attempt to know yourself.[7] This comes amusingly close to a later, and still entrenched, image of how a 'true artist' should subsist. Rather than follow this recipe, though, most deemed it more reasonable to share that individual consciousness – as expressed through opinions, preferences and the like. But an awareness of one's own individuality should give rise to the realization that others likewise bear a personal stamp – and so in order to interact productively with others some mediation will be required. An equally heightened emphasis on communication then arises as a means of avoiding the dangers of solipsism, of 'every man for himself'. After all, as members of the same animal species we are likely to have a remarkable amount in common. Self-awareness is thus fundamental to sociable exchange; it is not the tragic phenomenon that it can become in some treatments of art, and certainly of music. This is not to say that such interdependence of the social and the personal was accepted by all, or that it had to result in a pleasing equilibrium; unsurprisingly, it remained a source of anxiety that, as we shall see, is played out in our sociable style. We have already explored the ambiguous status of musical topics in this respect: by definition they should represent a common coinage readily understandable by all, but they can also be understood as incentives to the individual aural imagination. This was also the case when we considered that catch-all term, variety, in Chapter 2: at some points it suggests a benevolent world of fruitful interaction, yet it can also signify a sharp incompatibility between musical subjects.

It is also worth asserting the significance of the very term feeling – and its associates, sentiment and sensibility, in their various forms across various languages – since they historically marked a turn towards personal response. Georgia Cowart formulates this very handily for us:

Because the term 'aesthetics,' though coined in 1750, did not become current until the nineteenth century, the responsiveness to art – a topic of burning interest and wide discussion in the late eighteenth century – could only be described in terms of taste, sentiment, and *Empfindsamkeit*.

As these terms gained ascendancy, the older term *Leidenschaften* (passions) began to decline along with an older era of musical thought. The passions were inextricably tied to a rationalistic theory of music in their representation of objective emotional states dictated by a text. Their very objectivity and explicitness, however, made possible a pointedness of expression, an intensity and even sometimes violence of emotional statement. In contrast, sentiments, the heart's subjective responses to sensuous stimuli, were considered not only delicate and tender,

---

[7] Diderot, *Rameau's Nephew*, trans. Mauldon, 80.

but also – because wordless – necessarily vague. The rise of the aesthetic of *Empfindsamkeit* accompanied a turn towards the ideal of delicacy and subtlety in all the arts, and for the first time we encounter an aesthetic of musical expression capable of encompassing instrumental as well as vocal music.[8]

Cowart's historical formula, whereby passion gives way to sentiment, offers us a fresh spin on the mixed, changeable style of later eighteenth-century music and the sociable ethos that I believe contributes to it. While the mixture may in one sense reflect a greater worldliness – underpinned by ideals of accessibility that aim for a kind of music that can be open to all comers – it can also reflect a new focus on the sensory experiences of the individual, which were understood to be conflicting, uncertain, not susceptible of easy rationalization. Thus once again we can suggest that the sociable mixed style has roots in a turn towards introspection, the focus on the sensate individual; the mixed impressions left by the music might reflect the notion that feelings were not only 'vague', they were also fleeting. In that sense it is not so much feelings as the transitions between feelings that were the new element of the modern musical style, generated by the frequent, possibly unpredictable movements between different materials. We saw this thematized in the keyboard pantomime performed by the character of 'Him' in *Le neveu de Rameau*: 'His features revealed the play of successive emotions: tenderness, fury, pleasure, pain.'[9] Such successions, though, act as an inhibiting factor on the expression of any one particular sentiment, which helps to account for the 'inexpressive' image that clings to galant music as a whole. Embodiments of particular feelings, being often short-lived, may not therefore be able to build up a head of steam – this in contrast to the 'intensity' that Cowart notes can be achieved when determinate 'passions' are in play, and indeed also in contrast to our perceptions of the music of the following century. Even where one affect seems to dominate, the typical changeability of texture and highly articulated phrase syntax may tend to soften any form of categorical expression.

We should add to this a more pragmatic reason for the virtually programmatic emphasis on feeling and expression that arose specifically in relation to music: it was a way of trying to ground the critical uncertainties raised by the increasing prominence of purely instrumental genres, of the

---

[8] Cowart, 'Sense and Sensibility', 265.
[9] Diderot, *Rameau's Nephew*, trans. Mauldon, 22. For an account of shades of feeling fleetingly experienced within a real piece of music see Charles Rosen on the 'variety of affective nuances' contained in the opening of Mozart's Quartet in G major K387 in *Music as Sentiment*, 67.

sort explored in Chapter 2.[10] This could even amount to equating music with feeling pure and simple. For example, a critic in Flensburg wrote in 1792, 'Words affect reason, producing in it special ideas ... But music affects the feelings directly. As soon as it has aroused the sentiments, it has achieved its purpose.' If this sounds somewhat philistine, it is only a variant of a position that has survived healthily down to the present day: the special, seemingly indissoluble link between music and feeling (or emotion or expression). Significantly, this critic continued that while pure instrumental music could make 'a very lively impression', 'in this type of music always lies a great deal that is vague, ambiguous, uncertain – and you have to have a certain amount of musical training to get true pleasure from it'.[11] While this initially dovetails nicely with Cowart's characterization of the 'vagueness' of sentiment, the writer's subsequent comment that training is required returns us to the level whereby feeling must be learnt, within the bounds of a particular system, rather than intuited. More broadly, his comments remind us that instrumental music was able to flourish in tandem with an interest in – and from some quarters acceptance of – uncertain meaning and affect.[12]

If feelings could be fleeting and hard to define, this could encourage the ambivalence of tone that is one of the outstanding features of our instrumental repertory. Yet that has by no means always been grasped in later reception, nor indeed was it necessarily grasped at the time. One reason for this lies in the 'delicate and tender' ethos that Cowart rightly brings to the fore. The gentler aspects of diction and gesture can obscure any possible ambivalence, and it is these gentler aspects that we turn to at this point. Simplicity, naturalness, moderation and grace are among the key terms of reference. While subsequent reception has always acknowledged their relevance to the broader aesthetic, these expressive attributes have rarely been dwelt upon. This is understandable enough, since they tend not to

---

[10] See, for example, Christensen, Introduction, *Aesthetics and the Art of Musical Composition in the German Enlightenment*: 'The task of finding an aesthetic justification for instrumental music' found 'a solution ... in the psychological processes studied so intently by the empiricist philosophers. It was only by enfranchising the sentient responses of a listener that the strictures of traditional mimetic theory could be countered. If instrumental music was ever to attain a worth commensurate to vocal music, a strong aesthetic of sentiment needed to be formulated and defended.' (5)

[11] Anonymous, 'Ueber Musik, ihre Wirkung und Anwendung', *Flensburgsches Wochenblatt für Jedermann* 5/11 (12 September 1792) and 5/12 (19 September 1792), cited in Morrow, *German Music Criticism*, 12 (translation) and 162 (German original).

[12] Richard Will describes this as 'an interest in semantic indefiniteness sparked in no small part by the popularity of symphonies and other instrumental genres'. Will, *Characteristic Symphony*, 14.

excite the critical imagination; it is hard for them to compete with the more extreme states that are often taken to be badges of authentic emotional experience. Yet there is no doubt that 'moderate', or Cowart's 'delicate', affects are important at a global level of utterance in our repertory.

The most treasured category of expression was surely simplicity. It was a catch-cry of the time to which a positive evaluation was almost automatically attached. The simple formed the centre of a collocation of terms that also included the clear, pure and natural. The expression of similar ideals in other eighteenth-century art forms would eventually go by the name of neoclassicism, but that could not be the case for music, since there was no equivalent classical past to return to.[13] Instead, that label was reserved for a twentieth-century musical movement that took the eighteenth century as its glorious past. And that has created a problem of apprehension for us, since some elements of the neoclassicists' take on eighteenth-century music seem to have persisted. As translated into musical practice, that would include a discarding of emotional baggage from a previous 'romantic' relationship and a deliberate dryness of texture and rhetoric: in other words, using the eighteenth century as a stick with which to beat the nineteenth century. This means that neoclassical 'restraint' tends to carry a polemical edge, more or less advertising what is being withheld. While the musical eighteenth century's 'new simplicity' was certainly also marked by polemics, certainly also had its reactive element, its brand of restraint was more positively conceived. As I formulated it in Chapter 1, simplicity could be regarded as the highest form of eloquence. As Katz and Dahlhaus put it, 'that a "genuine" emotion manifests itself simply, and that simplicity guarantees the "genuineness" of an emotion[,] was the central thesis of the aesthetics of the Enlightenment'.[14] A writer in the *Morning Herald* of London remarked in 1791 that Pleyel 'is becoming even more popular than his master [Haydn]; as his works are characterized less by the intricacies of science than the charm of simplicity and feeling'.[15] Here we see precisely the conjunction of simplicity with 'genuine emotion'. Clearly anything 'difficult' could be thought antithetical to feeling, and we can certainly glimpse a polemical edge on this occasion – not of course against emotional excess, as with musical neoclassicism, but against an excess of 'science'.

---

[13] See Weber, 'Contemporaneity of Eighteenth-Century Musical Taste'.
[14] Katz and Dahlhaus, *Contemplating Music*, volume 2, 114.
[15] Anonymous, *Morning Herald* (22 November 1791), cited in Simon P. Keefe, Preface to *Ignaz Pleyel: Six String Quartets, Opus 1*, ed. Keefe (Ann Arbor: Steglein, 2005), vii.

Strictures against excessive learning were in fact a common part of the equation. For the dancing-master and choreographer Giovanni-Andrea Gallini, in his *Treatise on the Art of Dancing* of 1762, dancing the minuet ought to 'bring forth the natural graces, and not smother them with the appearance of study and art'. Simplicity was 'the great fountainhead of all the graces; from which they flow spontaneous, when unchecked by affectation, which at once poisons and dries them up'.[16] It is not so much learning, or 'study', that was wrong, but rather the appearance of it – carrying one's learning heavily and conspicuously, which was often associated with being insufficiently socialized. The prominence of a discourse that referred to relatively more and less learned types of listener, and player, was another way of making the point. C. P. E. Bach's keyboard collections *für Kenner und Liebhaber* put this discourse on the front page, as it were.[17] One hesitates to offer translations of the terms, since their precise import has been disputed – but certainly 'Liebhaber' validates the importance of a natural, spontaneous reception of music, not weighed down by learning or precedent.[18] Another kind of excess could also have a poisonous effect: virtuosity. This did not have to imply the full array of technical wizardry; it could denote something as specific as ornamentation practices. In his essay 'La Musica' of 1765 Pietro Verri, who affirmed that 'the simplest and most natural things in music make the best impression' ('le cose più semplici, le più naturali sono quelle appunto che fanno maggior impressione'), declared himself irritated by cadential trills, which were among the 'Gothic ornaments' that might prompt 'admiration' but not 'delight'.[19] He also distinguishes between 'professori' (by which he means performers) and composers on the one hand and music lovers on the other hand: the former don't actually love their medium, Verri believes,

---

[16] Giovanni-Andrea Gallini, *A Treatise on the Art of Dancing* (London: R. and J. Dodsley, 1762), 146 and 167, cited in Eric McKee, 'Mozart in the Ballroom: Minuet-Trio Contrast and the Aristocracy in Self-Portrait', *Music Analysis* 24/3 (2005), 389.

[17] Christopher Hogwood notes that 'the phrase [*Kenner und Liebhaber*] was new to printed music when C. P. E. Bach adopted it': Introduction to *'Kenner und Liebhaber' Collections I*, ed. Hogwood, xi.

[18] In '*Kenner und Liebhaber*: Yet Another Look' Jonatan Bar-Yoshafat offers six interpretations of the two terms. All are shown to be problematic except for the last, which suggests that the two are 'complementary characteristics' (46) and can be found in the same person – a complete 'man of music' who is familiar with the rules of art but is not constrained by them.

[19] Pietro Verri, 'La Musica', in *Il Caffè, o sia brevi e varj discorsi*, volume 2 (Venice: Pietro Pizzolato, 1766), 106 (the discussion of trills follows at 108-109). In *The Castrato: Reflections on Natures and Kinds* (Berkeley: University of California Press, 2015), 180, Martha Feldman notes that this essay was originally entitled 'L'evirazione' (Castration); this gives a little more point to Verri's strictures against ornamentation, and indeed his contrast between cold professionals and true music lovers.

and so here is another vote in favour of the natural and against forms of learning that leave the writer cold.[20] Of course Verri was far from alone in his strictures against ornament, which so readily prompted charges of being 'unnatural'.[21]

Naturally, an aesthetic equation of 'less is more' was not upheld by all at all times. It is quite consistently challenged by the music of C. P. E. Bach, for instance, for whom eloquence tends to be associated with a sense of effort rather arising from simplicity. Giorgio Pestelli describes this as an 'element of laboriousness', noting that Bach 'lacked the persuasive conversational style typical of even the least inspired moments of the Italian *galant* composers'.[22] Pestelli, nevertheless, sees this in a positive expressive light. Certainly understatement is not common in Bach's output; there is little of the subtle insinuating wrongness beneath a polished surface which is such a trademark of Haydn's, for instance. Instead, he likes to be demonstrative and *outré* from the outset. This is sensibility uncoupled from the delicacy that was often thought to accompany it, as instanced by Jérôme-Joseph de Momigny's verdict on Pleyel's quartets: 'full of a natural quality and grace, [they] appeal to the charm of sensitive and delicate souls'.[23] One index of Bach's aversion to a normal unfolding of contents is his practice of avoiding full closes within the parts of a multi-movement work, which would be the 'simplest and most natural' solution. For example, the four fast first movements of the *Orchester-Sinfonien mit zwölf obligaten Stimmen* (1775–1776), Wq183, are not allowed the release of a big celebratory close. In the first three works, just as the listener might be anticipating the end, rhythmic and melodic continuity is suddenly broken as pathos-ridden harmonies intrude; these can in the end be understood as transitions to the ensuing slow movements. What is suppressed by this run-on technique is applause, which would certainly have followed a completed first movement in accordance with the universal custom of that day. It is as if the moment of release and applause is replaced by a staging of the figure of the inspired composer, calling on the higher powers of sublime harmony.

---

[20] Verri, 'La Musica', 107.

[21] In *Sonata Forms* Charles Rosen writes of the development of a 'neoclassical aesthetic, which stressed simplicity and clarity of structure (and considered ornament as fundamentally unnatural and frivolous)' (11). Note in light of earlier discussions Rosen's adoption of the term 'neoclassical' to describe this tendency in eighteenth-century music.

[22] Giorgio Pestelli, *The Age of Mozart and Beethoven*, trans. Eric Cross (Cambridge: Cambridge University Press, 1984), 25.

[23] Jérôme-Joseph de Momigny, *Cours complet d'harmonie et de composition* (Paris: author, 1806), 693, cited in translation in Ratner, *Classic Music*, 128.

Critic and composer Carl Ludwig Junker (1748–1797) was also ready to question the simple life, but on a more purely affective plane; he criticized Rosetti, for example, for 'laps[ing] into an offensive French saccharine quality'.[24] Schubart, though, came to the composer's defence:

> Naiveté is his speciality. However simple his pieces may appear, they are nonetheless difficult to perform if one has no sentiment of his own. The mere musical acrobat, who seeks fame only in technical display, will fail if he tries to perform a piece by Rosetti. The grace and beauty are of such an infinitely delicate nature that the mere jerk of the hand destroys its fine contour and an image of Venus turns into a grimace.[25]

This is a nice summation of the many-sidedness of simplicity. Schubart makes clear that Rosetti's is an assumed simplicity, something he specifically cultivates ('his speciality'), rather than being a purely intrinsic quality: it is not a case of 'simple is as simple does'. On the other hand, simplicity is only available to those who have a 'natural' feeling for it; for those who lack the capacity for 'sentiment', the simple will prove difficult. It cannot readily be taught, and once more we find a withering glance at heavy-handed display, this time in the form of the virtuoso 'acrobat'. Simplicity is also demanding in the fine balance it requires between inconspicuous execution (both compositionally and performatively) and fine motor control, as it were (one misplaced gesture, a 'mere jerk of the hand', can ruin the impression of the whole). Above all, as evoked here by Schubart, simplicity is deeply felt; it is a source of rich expressive intensity, not simply a negative quality that arises from a kind of creative subtraction.

The mediated nature of this aesthetic can also be demonstrated on a more practical level. Daniel Heartz observes that many of the sketches that Mozart made – for numbers from *Le nozze di Figaro*, for example – show the pains the composer took in the name of 'further simplification'. He tells a similar tale of the Trio from Haydn's Symphony No. 86 (1786): 'Haydn jotted down a more complicated-sounding Trio that yielded almost nothing he finally accepted. What sounds so folklike and frolicsome in Haydn's music sometimes took him a struggle to achieve, which he did in this case by refining and simplifying. Seeming naiveté could be hard

---

[24] Carl Ludwig Junker, *Musikalischer Almanach auf das Jahr 1782* (Berlin: Alethinopel, 1782), 44, cited in translation in Murray, *Antonio Rosetti*, 385.

[25] Schubart, *Ideen zu einer Ästhetik der Tonkunst*, 174–175, cited in translation in Murray, *Antonio Rosetti*, 386. For further material on the reception of Rosetti see Lawrence F. Bernstein, 'Joseph Haydn's Influence on the Symphonies of Antonio Rosetti', in *Historical Musicology: Sources, Methods, Interpretations*, ed. Stephen A. Crist and Roberta Montemorra Marvin (Rochester, NY: University of Rochester Press, 2004), 143–187.

won.'[26] It is hard to top that final sentence as a summation of the case. It was an important communicative skill to be able to create clarity out of difficulty, whether that difficulty inhered in the thoughts themselves or simply in the creative process.[27]

To aim for naturalness whilst at the same time being aware that it could be the product of artifice, to allow for complexity as long as it was accessibly rendered: these are virtues of the middle way. The musical galant itself was often framed in such terms, for instance by Scheibe as a 'middle style'.[28] If it has often proved hard for us to enter imaginatively into the claims of simplicity, the same assuredly applies to moderation. Once again one might stress the social, communicative rationales for such a stylistic orientation, as Samuel Johnson did when praising the prose of Joseph Addison – 'familiar but not coarse, and elegant but not ostentatious'.[29] This was no tired old bromide of 'everything in moderation'; to aim to accommodate the widest possible audience (or readership) by avoiding extremes of style or affect was held to be something new. Hence the frequent jabs at a past style of address that was dismissed as heavy, excessive and the like. The attraction towards moderate states could also be justified from a phenomenonological point of view. They corresponded to a 'realistic' aspect of human consciousness, given the floating subjectivity associated with sentiment: one didn't, after all, actually go through life experiencing a series of definite, hard-edged feelings at every point. To do so could in fact be regarded as a failure of personal control, undesirable because of its effects on others in the social fabric, as well as on one's own well-being.

But moderation was not just a behavioural or a discursive principle; it could also amount to a virtual affect, allied to Cowart's 'delicacy and subtlety'. It connoted not expressive 'indifference', but rather gentleness, charm, sweetness and grace. It meant the moderating influence of what were perceived by the overwhelmingly male writers of the time as feminine virtues. According to this viewpoint, women represented a civilizing force, their 'natural' good taste and feeling saving men from their worst excesses.

---

[26] Heartz, *Mozart, Haydn and Early Beethoven*, 143 and 366.

[27] Compare the thoughts of Daniel Gordon on the importance of clarity to successful social interaction: 'Since obscurity was ugliness, the *honnête homme* was skillful in transforming the most difficult thoughts and subtle sentiments into clear expressions.' Gordon, *Citizens without Sovereignty*, 103.

[28] Scheibe, *Der critische Musikus*, 128 ('die mittlere Schreibart').

[29] Samuel Johnson, *Lives of the Poets*, two volumes (London: J. F. Dove, 1826), volume 1, 403, cited in Lawrence E. Klein, 'Addisonian Afterlives: Joseph Addison in Eighteenth-Century Culture', *Journal for Eighteenth-Century Studies* 35/1 (2012), 108.

They enjoyed the great advantage of not being weighed down with learning, which, as we have often seen already, could be social poison and could lead to 'unnatural' complexity and obscurity in art. Sociability itself could be understood as a feminine attribute. In society, as Hume expressed it, 'both sexes meet in an easy and sociable manner; and the tempers of men, as well as their behaviour, refine apace'.[30] Such mingling of the sexes was essential for a polite, civil society – just as sociable musical discourse clearly values mixed company, as it were. We have, to take one specific example, touched on the possible gendered implications of the gracious-riposte technique. The most overt contemporary applications to music of such terms of reference tend to be in the negative, equating the galant with the feminine (and, inevitably, the Italian). In 1751 William Hayes, then Professor of Music at Oxford, satirically (and just about pornographically) contrasted the 'manly Strokes' of 'the Man-Mountain, *Handel*' with the 'Ease and Negligence' and the 'pathetic Tenderness which breathes in every Strain of the modern *Italian Music*'.[31] 'Ease and Negligence' are not bad as a characterization of a style that aims to avoid the laborious, but we need to recall that the image of musical effeminacy had some geographical limits (it derived mainly from northern Europe). It may also have had some temporal limits: such aspersions were less commonly encountered in the last part of the century. Also worthy of note is that in the same pamphlet of 1751 Hayes equated modern music with 'polite Things', which is effectively a gloss on sociability, as well as the baleful feminine influence on it; for him, modern music has become a sort of fashionable accessory.

If one wants to find a ready musical reference-point for the virtues of moderation, it is hard to go past Boccherini. Moderate speeds are often involved too. To take a couple of examples at random, the initial Non tanto sostenuto of the Quintet Op. 10 No. 5 in E flat major (G269; 1771) and the Allegretto lentarello e affettuoso, in the same key, that opens the Quartet Op. 32 No. 1 (G201; 1780) do not so much proclaim what they are about as draw us in; they sound gentle, intimate and inviting, perfectly illustrating

---

[30] David Hume, 'Of Refinement in the Arts', in *Essays Moral, Political, and Literary*, ed. Eugene F. Miller, revised edition (Indianapolis: Liberty Classics, 1987), 164, cited in Head, *Sovereign Feminine*, 34. The essay, which was at other times called 'Of Luxury', originally appeared in *Essays, Moral and Political*, volume 2 (Edinburgh: A. Kincaid, 1742). Matthew Head's book offers a comprehensive guide to the eighteenth century's 'discourse of feminization', as E. J. Clery terms it in *The Feminization Debate in Eighteenth-Century England: Literature, Commerce and Luxury* (Basingstoke: Palgrave Macmillan, 2004), 6.

[31] William Hayes, *The Art of Composing Music By A Method entirely New, Suited To the meanest Capacity* (London: J. Lion, 1751), 8, cited in Todd Gilman, 'Arne, Handel, the Beautiful, and the Sublime', *Eighteenth-Century Studies* 42/4 (2009), 542.

Cowart's maxim of passion being replaced by delicate sentiment. Once again, we should not hear neutrality or negativity; this realm of 'moderate' affect has its own intensity, works its own spell, and any amount of contemporary testimony speaks to such movements being heard in these terms ('how often melting, how heartfelt is his melody!', exclaimed Gerber in 1790[32]). An important part of the affect involves dynamic levels: the movement from Op. 10 No. 5 has initial markings of *piano assai con espressione* and *sotto voce*. The composer's attention to various gradations of softness speaks of a concern for fine shades of feeling: Alessandro Dozio has counted eleven types of *piano* nuance in Boccherini's output.[33]

However, the primary technical focus for all these artistic aims lay elsewhere; to near-universal acclaim, it was found in melody, pure and simple. Melody provided a touchstone for the quality of eloquent simplicity that was sought. It was a capacious enough concept to be able to absorb just about any of the favoured epithets we have considered above – natural, graceful and, indeed, pure and simple. Such terms of reference arose in tandem with a certain kind of organization: periodic, which, as we saw with the Rousseauian 'unité de mélodie' described earlier, meant that the arrangement and proportions of the melodic materials counted for as much as the intrinsic contents, as it were. But textural and registral disposition was also important. Heartz has noted that the galant era 'was partial to high treble sounds' such as those made by violins, sopranos and castratos.[34] Melodies are, of course, most 'naturally' and accessibly situated at the top of the texture, and even an attraction to higher registers as such suggests a taste for the clear and bright.

The galant ideal of the pure singing voice is, naturally, most evident in slower movements, often in aria style. It could be more or less elaborately realized. We might compare, for example, the manner of many slow movements from Galuppi's keyboard sonatas with those by J. C. Bach. Galuppi's melodic lines unfold quite intricately, seemingly spontaneously, often over steady accompaniments in much slower rhythmic values,[35]

---

[32] Gerber, 'Boccherini', in *Historische-Bibliographisches Lexikon der Tonkünstler*, column 174, cited in translation in Heartz, *Music in European Capitals*, 996.

[33] Alessandro Dozio, 'Jubilus et suavitas: le malentendu de la légèreté dans la musique de Luigi Boccherini', *Boccherini Online* 3 (2010) www.boccherinionline.it (26 May 2014). For Elisabeth Le Guin, the composer's 'constant admonitions toward softness and sweetness' mean that 'one eventually develops an extremely sensitized, arguably *sensible* physical presence at the instrument'. Le Guin, 'One Says that One Weeps', 232.

[34] Heartz, *Music in European Capitals*, 208.

[35] For detailed commentary on mesmerizing examples of Galuppi's keyboard slow-movement art see Heartz, *Music in European Capitals*, 287-292, and Rohan Stewart-MacDonald, 'The

whereas in a movement like the Adagio from Bach's sonata Op. 5 No. 5 (1766) the accompaniment moves more quickly than the melody. We hear simple broken-chord accompanimental figuration in triplets, of the sort often used at slow tempos to signal an intense cantabile style. The melody that this figuration supports is plain by Galuppi's standards; the amount of ornamentation marked is minimal, and it would seem inappropriate to add much more. Here the expressive weight is felt between the notes, as it were; the outward demeanour is understated and 'moderate'. Many of these attributes feed into the 'sensitive style' that we visited in Chapter 2.

While Bach and Galuppi were writing their sonatas at more or less the same time,[36] it would appear as if the sort of relatively plainer melodic diction found in Bach's movement became more and more favoured as the century progressed. This often occurs in conjunction with the same sort of implied, but not overt, intensity that I argued for there. We noted at the outset that simplicity could be understood as the guarantee of 'genuine emotion', and this was far from being just a critical platitude. Listeners and players unquestionably had a voracious appetite for inspired simplicity; it was, for instance, an important factor in the widespread love for Pleyel's music. The Adagio of Pleyel's Symphony in C major Ben128 (1786) offers a nice example of what our critic from London's *Morning Herald* was attempting to capture. It presents a very pure cantabile, graceful and natural, and full of fine feeling – in other words, feeling that is sensed indirectly as much as stated outright. Plentiful appoggiaturas enhance this quality. The singing never lets up, even through transitions, and the development section moves into a kind of cavatina style. The use of horn-call material, with its 'natural' associations, from bar 20 strengthens the idyllic, Arcadian flavour. Further evidence of overwhelming *cantabilità* can be heard during the closing material of the first half. Beginning in bar 29, it could readily be over four bars later, but instead there is a lengthy parenthesis for the two violins alone. With the two parts always playing in parallel thirds, and very freely organized, this sounds like a vocal duet-cum-cadenza. Only at bar 39 do we reach a closing formula. (The functional version of the phrase can be reconstructed if we cut from halfway through bar 31 and go to about the middle of bar 38.) A slightly shorter parenthesis is heard at the equivalent point of the recapitulation, from bar 101. In keeping with the ethos of the 'cadenza', this one unfolds quite differently, though it once more consists solely of duetting parallel thirds. The urge to sing, as it were, bursts the bounds

---

Keyboard Sonatas of Baldassare Galuppi: Textures, Topics, and Structural Shapes', in *The Early Keyboard Sonata in Italy and Beyond*, ed. Stewart-MacDonald, 73–76.

[36] On the chronology of Galuppi's sonatas see Stewart-MacDonald, 'Keyboard Sonatas of Baldassare Galuppi', 70–72.

of what we are expecting to hear. Simple and modest though the movement may appear to be, it should also leave the listener feeling replete.

For all the galant emphasis on the purity and 'honesty' of the lone singing voice, it is rare to hear a literal monophonic texture. The keyboard works of C. P. E. Bach, though, offer some exceptions. One is the central movement of his Sonata in G major Wq55/6 (1765) from the first collection *für Kenner und Liebhaber*. This Andante in G minor starts with a long monody in continuous triplet semiquavers, unbarred and high in the keyboard, that gradually wends its way downward; it then slows down before reaching a purely melodic cadence point. A further melodic soliloquy then intrudes, most incongruously, into the exuberant Allegro di molto finale, this time in continuous quaver rhythm, and here minimally accompanied by single long bass notes. What is also missing from such moments of 'pure song' in C. P. E. Bach is the periodicity that elsewhere seems to be an intrinsic part of the expressive genre. For this composer, *cantabilità* comes in moments rather than movements; it seems to represent an unrepeatable passage of intensity. Instead of the differentiated rhythms and intervals that are normally required to constitute a melody as such, and the larger-scale reiterations that might turn it into a tune, Bach favours more or less uniform rhythms, stepwise intervals and a superlegato execution. These characteristically short-lived passages offer a different sense of repletion to that I have claimed for the Pleyel movement above; they give the impression of shutting out all the surrounding material and 'singing one's heart out'.

However it happens to be shaped by individual composers, the realm of pure song is, once again, something that may not speak very readily to us today. We may be a little impatient with something that seems obvious and not very interesting in its own right. Bernard Harrison considers this in the case of Haydn, who was one of so many who stressed the cardinal importance of clear melody, and comments that the 'seemingly inordinate emphasis placed on melody, by Haydn himself and other writers of the eighteenth century, is, in the first instance, of historical rather than stylistic significance'.[37] In other words, there seem to us to be many more remarkable things to Haydn's creative output than melodic clarity. Yet while the 'predominantly formalistic critique' of more recent times may find greater value elsewhere, 'we are ill advised to dismiss as irrelevant the apparent dogmatism of the eighteenth-century poetics of simplicity, nature and melody'. We should bear in mind, he continues wryly, 'that both eighteenth- and twentieth-century commentaries on Haydn's music are …

---

[37] Harrison, *Haydn: The 'Paris' Symphonies*, 42.

prisoners of contemporary thought'.[38] But we have seen that not every eighteenth-century writer or listener was enamoured of these poetics – just as we have seen that simplicity was no two-dimensional quality. The Scottish philosopher Adam Ferguson had clearly lost patience when he wrote: 'Of all the terms that we employ in treating of human affairs, those of *natural* and *unnatural* are the least determinate in their meaning. . . . the natural is an epithet of praise; but . . . all the actions of men are equally the result of their nature.'[39] If there is a way to make these qualities more palatable for modern critical sensibilities, it ought to be enough – in a time when we are told that classical music is losing its purchase on the public – to note the way in which they open up the field of art music to wider participation. Who cannot have a stake in melodious simplicity? As Matthew Head puts it, 'In sociological terms, the emphasis on music's capacity to move tended to valorize amateur and bourgeois musical practice, privilege performance and listening over composing, validate relatively untutored musical response over professional and technical appraisal, and lend music sensual, even erotic, power'.[40]

That last item on Head's list might bring us up short when our subject was supposed to be simple song, but in fact cantabile and eros may not have been such unlikely bedfellows. When Schubart was discussing the performances of the famous Plà brothers, oboe players from Catalonia, he marvelled that 'No one has better expressed the intimate connection of the tones, the swelling of *portamento* and the cantabile, which intimated, if I may say so, both the friendly and the amorous [das Verliebte und Freundliche]'.[41] The amorous, not to say the flirtatious, is of course implied in the very definition of galant – at least in that sense of the term that still survives today. The sort of 'smooth talking' of which the musical galant was capable is exemplified by the Boccherinian movement type considered above; some of these in fact carry the performance direction 'amoroso', alongside similar indications such as 'affettuoso'. Understated and 'moderate' such movements may be, but they can also sound seductive.

---

[38] Harrison, *Haydn: The 'Paris' Symphonies*, 43–44.
[39] Adam Ferguson, *An Essay on the History of Civil Society*, fourth edition (London: T. Caddel [sic], 1773), 15.
[40] Matthew Head, 'Fantasia and Sensibility', in *The Oxford Handbook of Topic Theory*, ed. Mirka, 267.
[41] Schubart, *Ideen zu einer Ästhetik der Tonkunst*, 160, cited in translation in Heartz, *Music in European Capitals*, 457. Schubart also described the joint performance of the Plà brothers as the 'mutual friendship of two closely united angels' ('wechselseitige Freundschaftserklärung . . . von zwei verschwisterten Engeln'; 160), cited in translation in Matthew Haakenson, 'Two Spanish Brothers Revisited: Recent Research surrounding the Life and Instrumental Music of Juan Bautista Pla and José Pla', *Early Music* 35/1 (2007), 87.

If we lower the emotional temperature somewhat, we arrive at the more disinterested side of that affect, Schubart's 'friendship'. The 'friendly' is another of the patent properties of our instrumental style that has not prompted much sustained contemplation. In this context we are considering not so much the listener-friendliness that arises out of all the discursive, syntactical aspects considered in previous chapters, but the naked affect: the undeniable sense, hiding in plain sight, that a high proportion of the instrumental music of the time has a gregarious orientation; it seems to welcome the listener with a smile. Historically, much of the scholarship on this repertory has emphasized the mechanics of the music. This is quite justified by the many new things the repertory has to offer, but it has also been a means of avoiding consideration of affect, especially those affects that have since been found less congenial. Not that there were no contemporary detractors, of course; Riepel, for instance, commented acidly that 'today most music lovers are no longer pleased to listen to sad things, except in church'.[42] On the other hand, we encountered earlier Charles Avison's view that 'it is the peculiar Quality of Music to raise the *Sociable and happy passions*, and to *subdue* the *contrary ones*': music, in other words, being 'naturally' melodious and harmonious, was intrinsically given to such an affect. That could then be contagious, since, as Adam Smith proposed, 'We have always ... the strongest disposition to sympathize with the benevolent affections.'[43] According to Smith, the very presence of these attributes predisposes us in favour of an individual or a type of behaviour; they prompt a more sympathetic, presumably more engaged, reaction from the onlooker. And the same might apply to a listener, who responds to an inviting, friendly tone by adopting a more 'sympathetic', interactive relationship with the music. When this is put in purely social, behavioural terms, few are likely to deny such a reciprocal equation – after all, as Kingsley Amis put it, nice things are nicer than nasty ones – but when applied to the matter of the receiver's response to art, we may not be so impressed. The same would apply to a related state, comfort, which Elisabeth Le Guin has investigated in the case of Boccherini; the composer shows a 'marked tendency to gravitate toward ease and comfort', with the author noting the problem that 'comfort as artistic currency is a notion that has gone somewhat out of style'.[44]

---

[42] Joseph Riepel, *Anfangsgründe zur musicalischen Setzkunst*, volume 4: *Erläuterung der betrüglichen Tonordnung* (Augsburg: Johann J. Lotter, 1765), 32, cited in translation in *The Musical Dilettante*, ed. and trans. Snook-Luther, 48n.

[43] Smith, *Theory of Moral Sentiments*, 39.   [44] Le Guin, *Boccherini's Body*, 26 and 9.

We need in any case to note that these are assumed rather than 'real' characteristics, whereby listener demands, preferred critical perspectives and compositional agency intersect to generate what we can describe as a predominant affective style. It is not that other moods or feelings do not find expression; it is rather a question of tone of address, or, as Le Guin has it, 'artistic currency'. Indeed, the complacent interpretation that is often put on such attributes might be nicely undercut with reference to a famous letter that Haydn wrote in 1802, to Jean Phillip Krüger as representative of the *Musikverein* in Bergen, on the German island of Rügen. Krüger had informed the composer of the great success of *The Creation* when performed in his town, and in reply the composer included this sentiment:

Often, when struggling against the obstacles of every sort that oppose my labours . . . a secret voice whispered to me: 'There are so few happy and contented people here below; grief and sorrow are always their lot; perhaps your labours will once be a source from which the careworn, or the man burdened with affairs, can derive a few moments of rest and refreshment.'[45]

This is, admittedly, darkened by Haydn's finding himself in a declining stage of life, to which he makes ample reference elsewhere in the letter (he describes his 'enfeebled health' and styles himself 'a gradually dying veteran'[46]). Nevertheless, it should be enough to confirm – if anyone ever doubted it – that the affective style that emanates from the music of Haydn and others is not born out of some sort of airhead optimism.

This tone of address – clear, simple, friendly, welcoming – may also be linked with another favoured term of reference from the time, pleasure. Like simplicity, it is a somewhat slippery concept, since it may mean less to us now than it did to the inhabitants of the eighteenth century. Certainly, evidence of its centrality to conceptions of music is easy to find. The theoretical writings of Koch refer frequently to the 'angenehm' or 'gefällig' (pleasant, agreeable);[47] Mozart wrote to his father that 'music,

---

[45] Haydn, letter to Jean Phillip Krüger, 22 September 1802, *Joseph Haydn: Gesammelte Briefe und Aufzeichnungen*, ed. Landon and Bartha, 410, cited in translation in H. C. Robbins Landon, *Haydn: Chronicle and Works*, volume 5: *Haydn: The Late Years, 1801–1809* (London: Thames and Hudson, 1977), 233, cited (with slight modifications) in David Wyn Jones, *The Life of Haydn* (Cambridge: Cambridge University Press, 2009), 211.

[46] Landon, *Haydn: The Late Years*, 233.

[47] For example, in the section of his *Versuch* on the trio Koch praises the flute trios of Graun on account of their 'gefälligste und schmeichelhafteste Melodie' (highly pleasing and 'flattering' melodies) and then recommends that budding composers 'können den Ausdruck der angenehmen Empfindungen, und zugleich die Kunst, mit der gefälligsten Melodie die größte Mannigfaltigkeit der Harmonie zu verbinden, nirgend besser studieren, als in diesen

even in the most horrifying situation, must never offend the ear, but must actually please'.[48] Avison not only associated music with the 'Sociable and happy passions', but also wrote that 'it is the natural Effect of Air and Harmony to throw the Mind into a pleasurable State'.[49] For Burney, 'Music may be defined [as] the art of pleasing by the succession and combination of agreeable sounds'.[50] Coming from such a central figure for our understanding of eighteenth-century music, such a definition is bound to disappoint many present-day readers; can Burney not offer a weightier evocation of the significance of the art of music? Part of the answer, it should be clear, lies in the fact that Burney's prose precisely embodies our affective style, which involves expressing oneself with a light touch, but his definition also suggests that we re-evaluate what 'pleasure' might have meant. One aspect of its significance we have already covered, in conjunction with 'friendliness' above. This is the pragmatic view that pleasure increases participation – the perfectly reasonable position that if something does not please us, we will not pay much attention to it. That early protagonist of the galant, Mattheson, had written in 1739 that 'We cannot have pleasure in a thing in which we do not participate'.[51] The desired consequence of that 'participation' is a heightened mental state, the improvement of the human faculties, so that pleasure may produce knowledge or understanding. This moves us from pragmatics to ethics. While offering itself up for pleasurable consumption, modern instrumental style – with its restless variety and predilection for setting various traps for the listener – could help to stimulate perception, demanding quick reactions that keep us alert and a relativistic, tolerant attitude to different

---

Graunschen Flötensonaten' (can study the expression of pleasant feelings and also the art of combining the greatest variety of harmony with the most pleasing melody nowhere better than in Graun's flute sonatas). Koch, *Versuch einer Anleitung zur Komposition*, volume 3, 325; *Introductory Essay on Composition*, trans. Baker, 206. David E. Sheldon singles out 'angenehm' for special mention in 'The Galant Style Revisited and Re-Evaluated', *Acta musicologica* 47/2 (1975), noting that 'it was Scheibe and later Quantz and his Berlin colleagues who gave to this word its highest aesthetic value in music' (259). However, the implication is that this is primarily a mid-century germanophone phenomenon, whereas I am suggesting that it remains fundamental for longer than that.

[48] Mozart, letter to Leopold Mozart, 26 September 1781, cited in translation in Heartz, *Mozart, Haydn and Early Beethoven*, 12. We should note that Mozart may well have been playing the part of the 'good son' when he wrote this letter to his father, but that would not necessarily invalidate the sentiment.

[49] Avison, *Essay on Musical Expression*, ed. Dubois, 7.

[50] Burney, *General History of Music, Volume the Second*, 7.

[51] Johann Mattheson, *Der vollkommene Capellmeister* (Hamburg: Christian Herold, 1739), 140; Ernest C. Harriss, *Johann Mattheson's 'Der vollkommene Capellmeister': A Revised Translation with Critical Commentary* (Ann Arbor: UMI, 1981), 311.

kinds of musical utterance. In other words, the alluringly 'easy' could blend into the more difficult without the listener necessarily being aware of it: the very cognitive stimulus provided by (modern) music had its moral dimension. This might not be so strange to a present-day mindset except for the fact that it is coupled with the notion of pleasure. For us, pleasure and instruction are somewhat different beasts. The same would go for the distinction between art on the one hand and pleasure/amusement/entertainment on the other. Yet, as William Weber writes, 'The mentality which blurred distinctions between art and amusement was general to eighteenth-century culture'; this differed greatly from the 'specialization [of amusement] in modern values'.[52] A specific instance of this would be the meaning of the generic term *divertimento* in the context of eighteenth-century Vienna; while it would later acquire connotations of stylistic lightness, 'music not to be taken too seriously', it originally carried no such baggage. It was instead a more matter-of-fact label for instrumental music that was to be played one to a part.[53] To be 'diverted', it would seem, was a value-neutral concept.

That the easy could blend into the difficult is evident in this account by Ignaz Arnold of what Haydn gets up to with his listeners:

Wahr ist es: seine Melodien scheinen im Anfange an etwas Bekanntes zu erinnern; aber schnell muß man den Gedanken verwerfen und bei sich selbst sagen: nein, ich irrte mich, ich habe doch nichts dem ähnliches gehört.... wir hören etwas Neues und staunen über den Meister, der so schlau Unerhörtes uns unter dem Anstrich des Allbekannten zu bieten wußte.... eine so unendliche Klarheit, allgemein Faßlichkeit und Verständlichkeit, daß wir mit Leichtigkeit das Schwerste vernehmen.[54]

It's true: his melodies seem at first to remind us of something familiar; but one must soon throw out such ideas, and say to oneself, 'No, I'm wrong, I've never heard anything like this.' ... We are hearing something quite new and marvel at the master, who so cunningly knows how to offer us something outrageous under the

---

[52] Weber, 'Contemporaneity of Eighteenth-Century Musical Taste', 191. For further consideration of the relationship between music and 'entertainment' in the later eighteenth century see Webster, 'Haydn's Symphonies: Art and Entertainment' and Hunter, *The Culture of Opera Buffa in Mozart's Vienna: A Poetics of Entertainment*, the very subtitle of which alerts us to the critical 'problem'.

[53] See James Webster, 'Towards a History of Viennese Chamber Music in the Early Classical Period', *Journal of the American Musicological Society* 27/2 (1974), 212–247.

[54] Arnold, *Joseph Haydn: Eine kurze Biographie*, 101–102. My translation that follows is unable to deal with Arnold's punning usages of 'Unerhörtes' and 'vernehmen', both of which refer to hearing as well as carrying broader meanings; these usages seem to correspond to the cognitive exhilaration that Arnold feels as one of Haydn's listeners.

banner of the everyday ... with such infinite clarity, lucidity and comprehensibility, that we can easily grasp the most difficult things.

In Arnold's account the composer shows the ability to extend the listener, to make that listener hear and think in different ways: the verb *staunen* ('to astonish', or in my translation 'to marvel') vividly suggests an expansion of mental horizons, even when the starting-point seems quite unremarkable. This returns us to the ethical, 'improving' side of such an art. One might even speak of a didactic aim, but a true galant artist would never, of course, put it in quite such forbidding terms.[55]

In one sense, to emphasize the refining, and possibly mind-altering, powers of this music is to have to try too hard, to concede too much to the furrowed-brow school of music scholarship. While the concept of pleasure has certain relatively specialized applications within our era – within the field of opera buffa, for instance, with Mary Hunter noting how comic operatic texts 'thematize pleasure in various ways'[56] – it is also just a fundamental starting-point for our engagement with all music, indeed art altogether. This is an inconvenient truth for that strong strain of reception that belittles the 'easy pleasures' of later eighteenth-century music. After all, pleasure need not derive only from the mixture of attributes we have been reviewing here, as constructed by eighteenth-century musical practitioners. It is evident, from its central place in the canon, that we thrill to the sounds of trouble and strife from the more 'committed' art music that was held to follow. What, after all, could be more deliciously pleasurable than having a good old cry?[57]

A further difficulty for us with pleasure: it now tends to denote individual gratification. That personal, libidinal perspective was, of course, also available to an eighteenth-century human being, but it is a fundamental part of a sociable view that the pleasure of the individual is connected with that of others. Thus self-centred desire might be modified by considering one's fellows, and one hopes that they will feel the same way in what is

---

[55] Allanbrook, though, is happy to affirm such an aim on behalf of the composers of the time: 'when thinking about eighteenth-century music one must take seriously the pervasive contemporaneous notion that music should and could instruct; it was not an antiquated piety'. Allanbrook, *Secular Commedia*, 78.

[56] Hunter, *Culture of Opera Buffa*, 19.

[57] Note the thoughts of Richard Taruskin in this respect: 'pleasure ... was certainly my own conduit into what has become my vocation. ... Isn't it everybody's? Can there be any other motivation for engagement with art? ... I must reject the claims of those who affect to pursue the arts for reasons other than pleasure or satisfaction.' Taruskin, 'The Musical Mystique' (review of books by Julian Johnson, Joshua Fineberg and Lawrence Kramer), *The New Republic* (22 October 2007) https://newrepublic.com (2 July 2014).

ideally a reciprocal operation. Shared pleasure has an ethical force because of its ability to bring people together. We touched earlier on the interdependence of the individual and the social, but not so directly on one of its behavioural consequences: politeness. Henry Fielding combined these strains in this passage:

Good Breeding ... is expressed in two different Ways, *viz.* in our Actions and our Words, and our Conduct in both may be reduced to that concise, comprehensive Rule in Scripture; '*Do unto all Men as you would they should do unto you*'. Indeed, concise as this Rule is, and plain as it appears, what are all Treatises on Ethics, but Comments upon it?[58]

Fielding prefaced this passage by making clear that 'good breeding' did not inhere in one's appearance or carriage ('Dress or Attitude of the Body'); it lay simply in 'the Art of pleasing, or contributing as much as possible to the Ease and Happiness of those with whom you converse'.[59] This was a markedly less elitist definition of politeness than had once obtained, with less emphasis on courtliness and more on simple warmth. Along similar lines, the 1771 edition of the *Dictionnaire de Trévoux* described the social virtues as entailing 'Sweetness of character, openness without rudeness, oblingingness without flattery, humanity [and] generosity'.[60] These do not match too badly with our catalogue of 'moderate' musical virtues, both as preached and as practised at the time, but the question does then arise: just what is 'polite', or well-bred, about later eighteenth-century instrumental music? One writer who has tried seriously to address this question is, as we saw in Chapter 2, Robert Hatten, who connects the two-note slur with 'gracious social gesturing'.[61] However, he notes that this figure can also represent a plaintive sigh. The finale of Beethoven's Sonata in E flat major Op. 7 opens with a gesture that Hatten describes as a combination of the two possibilities, through the addition of an anticipatory sigh before the sigh-figure proper: 'the two-note gesture combines galant graciousness with the sigh, troping the two gestural meanings to yield an effect that is neither superficial in its conventional graciousness nor tragic in its emotional context'.[62] This is nicely observed, though one detail of the wording is very revealing. 'Galant graciousness', and more broadly manners and

---

[58] Fielding, 'An Essay on Conversation', 125.
[59] Fielding, 'An Essay on Conversation', 124 and 125.
[60] *Dictionnaire universel françois et latin, vulgairement appelé Dictionnaire de Trévoux* (Paris: Compagnie des libraires associés, 1771), 'Social', cited in translation in Gordon, *Citizens without Sovereignty*, 53.
[61] Hatten, *Interpreting Musical Gestures*, 140.   [62] Hatten, *Interpreting Musical Gestures*, 142.

conventions, seem to run the risk of being 'superficial', while no such suspicions attach themselves to the plaintive, potentially 'tragic', sigh; this quality, it would seem, may automatically be taken on trust. Such priorities are widely shared: notions of politeness or restraint in relation to music are liable to send a chill of emotional 'inauthenticity'. Yet Hatten has at least tried to analyse just what can lead to that widespread impression of a style that conveys good manners.

I would suggest that musical politeness is more a technical than an affective matter; it arises from such features as the reciprocal arrangement of material (one piece of music 'defers' to another), length of individual utterance (closely monitored, as it were, so that no idea outstays its welcome) and the fine control of contours (as heard in the 'sensitive style'). We might also make the point that politeness, however defined, and whether in relation to music or applied more broadly, is not simply a restraining mechanism; it has its enabling side too. Through its disarming properties, it can enable one to say things that would otherwise not be sayable. It may be a means of avoiding conflict, but it can also, as André Morellet recognized, be a means of maintaining it, since the conflict is moderated by politeness.[63] We noted earlier his vaunting of the 'spirit of contradiction', and how that in sociable musical practice can mean that opposing materials 'agree to disagree'. And from the point of view of musical expression, a moderated, 'politely' expressed feeling need not be understood as a pale carbon-copy of the 'true' inner feeling – it is qualitatively different, and may be just as penetrating in its way as a less inhibited version.

Politeness by definition also means attending to 'the little things' of life. Small everyday deeds can bring pleasure and convey meaning; the precise way in which they are executed is a matter of interest. Such a mentality emerges vividly from Robert Gjerdingen's schema theory, which offers a picture in which the fine print of small-scale musical events counts for so much. In a different field, in his *Lectures of Rhetoric* from 1783, Hugh Blair noted the increasing importance of biographical detail for larger-scale historical understanding: 'it is from private life, from familiar, domestic and, seemingly trivial occurrences, that we often receive most light into the real character'.[64] In other words, small can be significant, as 'seemingly

---

[63] See the commentary by Gordon in *Citizens without Sovereignty*, 206.

[64] Hugh Blair, *Lectures on Rhetoric and Belles Lettres*, three volumes (Dublin: Whitestone, Colles, Burnet and others, 1783), volume 3, 75, cited in Annette Richards, 'Carl Philipp Emanuel Bach, Portraits, and the Physiognomy of Music History', *Journal of the American Musicological Society* 66/2 (2013), 370.

trivial' in particular conveys. It is what one does in ordinary circumstances that counts, as much as any publicly declaimed perspectives. This may be linked with my earlier assertion of the empirical nature of sociable instrumental music; it has a limited taste for the sweeping statement, for epic and heroic perspectives. These may too readily assume an authoritarian, 'tyrannical' tone of voice, may be associated with firm, inflexible 'passions' rather than the more uncertain world of 'sentiment'.[65] Instead, there is a preference for a relativistic type of discourse, one that grants different kinds of truth – and this may indeed include the grand as well as the modestly spoken. To return once more to the 'improving' side of the equation, this teaches the virtues of tolerance, and several studies have argued that this is just what Haydn is doing: Howard Irving, for instance, who takes as his point of departure the common contemporary connection drawn between Haydn and Laurence Sterne, and David Schroeder, who concentrates on the ways in which the London symphonies inculcate such a moral stance.[66]

The only problem with all this, from the point of view of later reception, is that Beethoven is waiting in the wings. Inevitably, this has meant that critics compare the moral compasses of Haydn and Beethoven. This is partly because, as explored in Chapter 1, Haydn is made to act as the representative of later eighteenth-century musical values, but it also owes much to some well-known circumstances, such as Haydn's having taught and advised the younger composer. But the comparisons also derive from evident musical similarities, whether technical or aesthetic-conceptual. Recall David Lidov's account of how Haydn bequeathed to Beethoven 'the method of giving a philosophical tone to music'.[67] And recent studies have offered persuasive accounts of the heroic and sublime aspects of Haydn's later output in particular.[68] Burnham, who has written sensitively about Haydn in his own right, feels that 'there is more at stake' when

---

[65] On this matter, and in particular the place of the sublime in a polite age, see Packham, 'Cicero's Ears, or Eloquence in the Age of Politeness'.

[66] Howard Irving, 'Haydn and Laurence Sterne: Similarities in Eighteenth-Century Literary and Musical Wit', *Current Musicology* 40 (1985), 34–49; Schroeder, *Haydn and the Enlightenment*.

[67] Lidov, *Is Language a Music?*, 56.

[68] See, for example, Hermann Danuser, 'Mishmash or Synthesis? On the Psychoagogic Form of *The Creation*', trans. Nicolas Betson, in *The Century of Bach and Mozart*, ed. Gallagher and Kelly, 41–78; Lawrence Kramer, 'Recalling the Sublime: The Logic of Creation in Haydn's *Creation*', *Eighteenth-Century Music* 6/1 (2009), 41–57; Nicholas Mathew, 'Heroic Haydn, the Occasional Work and "Modern" Political Music', *Eighteenth-Century Music* 4/1 (2007), 7–25; James Webster, 'Haydn's Sacred Vocal Music and the Aesthetics of Salvation', in *Haydn Studies*, ed. Sutcliffe, 35–69; James Webster, 'The *Creation*, Haydn's Late Vocal Music and the Musical Sublime', in *Haydn and His World*, ed. Sisman, 57–102; and James Webster, 'The Sublime and the Pastoral in *The Creation* and *The Seasons*', in *The Cambridge Companion to Haydn*, ed. Clark, 150–163.

Beethoven applies the techniques that he shared with Haydn. 'The precedence of some of the material features of Beethoven's heroic style in the works of Haydn permits us to give a more defined shape to what is truly unprecedented in Beethoven: the sense of an earnest and fundamental presence burdened with some great weight yet coursing forth ineluctably, moving the listener along as does the earth itself. . . . So compelling is the ethical thrust of the Beethovenian process that it carries the stamp and authority of necessity in mainstream musical thought.'[69]

While this appears to be caught somewhere between an account of reception and authorial value judgment, it sums up nicely some of the reasons why Haydn and sociable music in general find it hard to compete. The very way in which the comparison is framed shows the success of the Beethovenian paradigm. Why, after all, should 'weight' and 'authority' be absolute requirements of art music? And 'ethical thrust' virtually blackmails the reader into accepting the terms of reference; who, after all, is going to vote against musical ethics?[70] As I have aimed to suggest in this section, a sociable world-view has in fact a perfectly strong ethical dimension to it, but obviously less impressively so than clubbing the listener over the head with moral 'necessity'. As Nicholas Mathew has remarked of this strain of reception, 'It is as if Beethoven's interpreters need continually to refuel his masterpieces with the historical importance that their rhetoric calls for'. This might in turn seem unfair on the later composer, though it is a particular slice of the output that Mathew is considering, which involves 'that familiarly grand Beethovenian manner that proclaims its own importance'.[71] Of course, a great deal of Beethoven's music does not throw its weight about in this way; it offers many of the virtues that I have been describing under the banner of affective sociability, and it has already been suggested that certain musical elements that appear to contradict a sociable thesis are in fact perfectly compatible with it: the composer's habitual 'crescendo to nothing', for example. Of course when

---

[69] Scott Burnham, *Beethoven Hero* (Princeton: Princeton University Press, 1995), 64 and 65.

[70] See the comments on Burnham's argument by Marshall Brown in 'The Poetry of Haydn's Songs: Sexuality, Repetition, Whimsy', in *Haydn and the Performance of Rhetoric*, ed. Beghin and Goldberg. Brown does not dissent from Burnham's assertion of the 'lighter' weight of Haydn's music relative to that of Beethoven, but follows up by writing: 'Recent analysts properly remind us of the weight present even in Haydn, but his lightness represents a different cultural moment, with its own distinctive insights and pleasures. If we deny or depreciate them, we sacrifice both a part of our culture and a part of ourselves.' (248). The idea that Haydn's lightness, as defined in Brown's article, has obscured his weight is an attractive one.

[71] Mathew, *Political Beethoven*, 196. Along similar lines, Rosen writes of 'a sententious moral earnestness that many people have found repellent', though there is little evidence of such repulsion in the literature. Rosen, *The Classical Style*, 385.

one writes about reception at this level, musical caricature becomes inevitable – we have the familiar figures of a friendly Haydn and a turbulent Beethoven – but one premise of this study is that such images count for a great deal, since they help to determine how – and what – we hear. David Wyn Jones remarks, 'It suited the nineteenth century to exaggerate [the] incompatibility [of Haydn and Beethoven] in order to stress the questing individuality of Beethoven', and it has often suited later times well enough too. It also seems at times to have suited Beethoven, and he may be regarded as an 'early adopter' of the narrative, setting the terms of reference for later interpretation: as Jones subsequently notes, 'even a casual reading of Beethoven's correspondence and other documents relating to his life shows that Haydn and his status were constant preoccupations; Mozart's name, in contrast, never features in this way'.[72]

Sociable Surface

To this point I have stressed the brighter side of affective sociability, attempting to show how a series of interconnected qualities – the simple, natural, moderate, friendly, pleasant and polite – may bear an ethical weight that is rarely contemplated, at least in relation to art music. But also noted was that such values, and the general good intentions they convey, can mask the ambivalence of tone that is just as fundamental to the instrumental music of the time. In order to get at this quality, we now move to the shadier side of sociable theory and practice. If our era showed a constant concern with the interrelationship between individual and social, this cannot have always been a productive one. The very frequency of warnings against the solitary life suggest that many individuals did indeed wish to forgo the pleasures of social intercourse. To Diderot's facetious alternative – 'sequester yourself in a garret, live on dry bread and water, and attempt to know yourself' – we might add the words of Moses Mendelssohn: 'Man is by nature social and will not achieve success without help from others of his kind; if he remains alone, his mental faculties and attributes will not pass from potentiality to actuality, and he will resemble the animals, and will perhaps not even achieve their merits.'[73]

---

[72] David Wyn Jones, 'First among Equals: Haydn and His Fellow Composers', in *The Cambridge Companion to Haydn*, ed. Clark, 55.

[73] Moses Mendelssohn, commentary to Genesis 2:18, cited in translation in Matt Erlin, 'Reluctant Modernism: Moses Mendelssohn's Philosophy of History', *Journal of the History of Ideas* 63/1 (2002), 90.

For another writer, the solitary life 'approaches too near the Life of a *Vegetable*, and has nothing to stir the Passions, or keep them awake'.[74] But whether it reduced its sufferer to an animal or a vegetable state, solitariness was definitely a male malady. Adam Smith confirms this, but then casts the problem in an interesting light: 'Men of retirement and speculation, who are apt to sit brooding at home over either grief or resentment, though they may often have more humanity, more generosity, and a nicer sense of honour, yet seldom possess that equality of temper which is so common among men of the world.'[75]

Smith's image of men 'brooding at home' is a variant on Diderot's 'sequester yourself in a garret'; the sense of confinement is not only physical, but, by implication, mental and emotional. Giving vent to one's feelings in isolation may suggest a kind of liberation, but it can also represent a kind of enslavement, whereby the individual is 'locked in' to particular affects or patterns of thought. For all that, though, Smith suggests that such individuals may have finer moral qualities than 'men of the world'. Being better socialized may well help to polish off some rough edges, but that might occur at some expense to those finer sensitivities. On the other hand, we should not assume that Smith's 'equality of temper' is meant to be as bloodless as it might sound to us. After all, individual 'integrity' can readily turn into intolerance. As Alain Viala writes, 'when it is radical, sincerity is above all else a relationship of self to self more than an attention to others; it shatters social commerce by turning into intolerance'.[76] We have seen such 'sincerity', translated into over-insistence, thematized musically on many occasions in this study.

Another association of solitude is with a state of sadness, as expressed in Smith's 'grief or resentment' above. More broadly, we might link this with the basic dualism whereby authentic individual expression is linked with melancholy, while the collective or social are more likely to be associated with uplift. As already explored at some length, it is very difficult to escape from these terms of reference. Even someone like William Weber, in an attempt to defend the culture of eighteenth-century musical life, ends up having recourse to such terms: 'for all the importance of sociability within

---

[74] David Fordyce, *Dialogues concerning Education* (London, 1745), 169, cited in Spacks, *Boredom*, 35.
[75] Smith, *Theory of Moral Sentiments*, 23.
[76] Alain Viala, '*Les Signes Galants*: A Historical Reevaluation of *Galanterie*', trans. Daryl Lee, *Yale French Studies* 92 (1997), 19. See also Daniel Gordon, 'The City and the Plague in the Age of Enlightenment', *Yale French Studies* 92 (1997), including an account of the changing views of La Rochefoucauld on the matter: 'the cult of integrity engenders persons who lack integrity, because they pretend to know something in themselves that is not in fact knowable' (73).

18th-century musical values, we can discern a certain internality in the dark affects that pieces set in slow tempos and in the minor mode often contained'.[77] Weber's equating of slow and minor with the deep, dark and personal is part of an attempt to show that 'introspective' listening did indeed exist, in spite of the general image held of distracted frivolous audience behaviour at public musical events. It has to be said, though, that there is a logic to these associations: positive feelings are more likely to be shared with one's peers, and negative ones less so, precisely because of social constraints, and so these are more likely to remain 'locked inside'. A similar logic could also operate at that time. Germaine de Staël wrote that 'The wish to appear amiable tells us to adopt an expression of gaiety, whatever the interior disposition of the soul', the implication being that the soul is often not in the mood to rejoice. Yet, she continued, 'the physiognomy gradually influences what one feels, and what one does to please others soon dulls what one is feeling inside'.[78] This puts a more optimistic spin on any contrast between inner and outer dispositions – 'put on a happy face' would seem to be the advice. According to this way of thinking, and because feelings are after all malleable rather than for ever fixed, acting sociably can in fact come to the aid of the inner life.

If inner feelings can be socially influenced in this way, another perspective would be to say that they are socially produced. To broaden that, we might consider the extent to which individuality and identity are also socially produced. In other words, it is not so much a matter of how individual and social claims are balanced as recognizing that selfhood represents a social construction through and through. We can only know ourselves through interaction and comparison with others, and how others react to us determines who we are. We are no 'autonomous substance, but rather ... a relational entity that comes into being only in its encounter with society'.[79] Hence the aspersions cast on the status of him who seeks solitude; in the absence of interaction with one's fellows, one simply has no meaningful identity at all[80] – hence the comparisons with animal and

---

[77] Weber, 'Did People Listen?', 684. The danger of conflating dark affect with true emotional expression is also apparent, for example, in Clive McClelland, *Ombra: Supernatural Music in the Eighteenth Century* (Lanham: Lexington, 2012). Given the premise of his study in topic theory, McClelland might have noted that 'ombra' is a set of characteristics intended to convey affect, no more 'genuine' than any other expressive typology.

[78] de Staël, *De l'Allemagne*, 56–57.

[79] Elena Russo thus characterizes the views of David Hume and Pierre de Marivaux in 'The Self, Real and Imaginary', 136–137.

[80] A contemporary expression of this view, in relation ultimately to music, comes from Christopher Small: 'No one has an identity except in relation to others, and an entirely solitary person, a person with no relationships whatever ... can have no identity.' Small, *Musicking*, 60.

vegetable life-forms. Not only is individual identity, according to this point of view, socially constructed, but subjectivity itself is similarly derived. We glanced at this in Chapter 1: the notion not only that an individual's feelings are 'learnt', but also that the core of 'character' to which they contribute is a culturally specific assumption. Indeed, the wider composite of those states of feeling is not so much a unified whole as a series of separate sensations of the soul – what David Hume, on a more purely cognitive level, styled 'a bundle or collection of different perceptions'. Hume went on to describe the mind as 'a kind of theatre',[81] and this is a useful metaphor for the way in which individuality is created within a social network. Identity becomes a question not of essence, but of performance: as Gillian Russell and Clara Tuite put it, the individual is 'not ... an isolate, but ... a socially recognized entity who is required to *perform* his or her individuality within a repertoire of codes and modes of affect'.[82]

To a significant degree the century's many disputes over modern musical style may be framed in terms of this line of thought: galant 'variety' may be conceived as embodying such a relativistic, constructed sense of identity, and this was vehemently opposed by those who advocated an 'authentic', stable self, based on a belief in the natural consistency of human character and feeling. Recall Pluche's criticism of modern instrumental music in just these terms: 'we never think well of a mind that passes from sadness to great bursts of laughter, and from banter to seriousness, to tenderness, to anger, and to rage without having any cause to laugh or to become angry'. This issue, one might argue, was more vividly experienced in relation to music than in other domains, not just because of the widely held view that music was a 'language of feeling', but because of the very nature of the art, its encompassing blend of physical, aural, mental and emotional entrainments. Thus any revelation that no core of identity or feeling was being offered by this wordless music would be particularly crushing to the more conservative school of thought.

But the texted, vocal genre of opera buffa also routinely suggests such a perspective. Allanbrook and Hunter are at pains to explicate this aspect in order to forestall objections to the impersonal, even mechanistic take on

[81] David Hume, *A Treatise of Human Nature* (London: J. Noon, 1739), ed. L. H. Selby-Bigge, second edition, revised by P. H. Nidditch (Oxford: Clarendon, 1978), 252.
[82] Gillian Russell and Clara Tuite, 'Introducing Romantic Sociability', in *Romantic Sociability: Social Networks and Literary Culture in Britain, 1770–1840*, ed. Russell and Tuite (Cambridge: Cambridge University Press, 2006), 9. The authors are discussing Niklas Luhmann's study of 'affect-management'.

human identity and behaviour that the genre may seem to present. For Allanbrook, characters reveal themselves through action, through *interac*tion with others, since the genre 'focus[es] on its characters' social rather than interior natures'; this represents a collective rather than an introspective poetics. Along similar lines, Hunter remarks that most larger ensemble numbers 'define individuality as the result of social processes rather than as something stemming from a unique and fully expressed selfhood'.[83] Hunter then considers the matter with respect to solo numbers:

> Individuality in the opera buffa aria ... is normally constructed not in opposition to the conventions of the genre, but rather by means of the manipulation of a dizzying array of conventional possibilities ... Conventions work in at least two ways to develop a character's individuality: on the one hand the use of one archetype rather than another may assert his or her distinctness from other characters in the same opera, and on the other, a particular combination and layering of conventional associations can contribute to a sense of a character's depth and psychological plausibility.[84]

This is perfectly defensible in its own terms; it fits with the idea that character may derive from a 'bundling' of learnt behaviours and responses, none of which is unique to that person. From that point of view, what opera buffa offers is not comic artifice but comic realism based on a particular view of human nature. And a little reflection might persuade us that even our modern individuality is unlikely to be made up of traits not also found in others. Perhaps what is most significant is that Allanbrook and Hunter need to define and defend such a perspective at all. That they need to do so shows the extent to which they are having to argue against the grain, against the absolute value with which we prefer to invest individual feeling and identity. However, if this perspective might fit uncomfortably with later views of the mission of music, it could also, as we have seen, prove traumatic to inhabitants of the eighteenth century. Le Guin describes 'the ultimate elusiveness of a centered subjectivity' as felt in the eighteenth century as 'one of European culture's rawest moments of alienation'.[85]

Among the countercurrents to such a 'relational' perspective on human identity – whereby individuality was socially manufactured rather than intrinsic – was what is generally known as sensibility. Sensibility was a badge of the individual capacity for feeling, both as found within oneself and as applied to others. Thus it could connote both a personal quality, involving an inner sensitivity to outer stimuli, including the musical, as well

---

[83] Allanbrook, *Secular Commedia*, 16; Hunter, *Culture of Opera Buffa*, 23.
[84] Hunter, *Culture of Opera Buffa*, 100.   [85] Le Guin, 'One Says that One Weeps', 207.

as the way in which that sensitivity was extended outwards beyond the personal domain. The latter would result in sympathy for other people, especially those in some form of distress.[86] Tears were the accepted major currency.[87] While such tears found their clearest musical depiction within vocal genres, music in general was in a good position to ride the wave of the 'cult of feeling' because of its very association with the idea. Music was an eminently suitable medium through which to build the capacity for feeling.[88] It was morally improving both in the way it could increase sensitivity, both sensory and emotional, and because such sensitive reactions might be shared; this could create sympathy between human beings who react in the same way to a particular 'moving' phenomenon, whether that was virtue in distress or simply a beautiful tune. And music was also often, of course, taken as the very model of sympathetic harmony both in its constitution and as manifested in the cooperative sensitivity needed for its performance.

Where the difficulty arises, though, is in the expectation that such sensibility will manifest itself openly; otherwise, how are others to know how we feel, and how could they sympathize in turn? Because of the need to 'express', indeed to 'perform', such finer feelings, the danger is that it is nothing but performance, a show that needs an audience, rather than being a genuine, inbuilt quality. There is no true sensitivity, no true empathy, merely self-dramatization and self-gratification. If a social 'spectator' entertains such a suspicion, then sympathy and fellow-feeling will quickly be replaced by their opposites, distance and alienation.[89] What should be an innate capacity is revealed as something that has been 'learnt',[90] and, worse still, learnt because it is a fashionable accomplishment. Thus sensibility could readily lose its authentic associations and become yet further evidence of the 'relational' aspects of human nature.[91] From this perspective, the common

---

[86] James Webster usefully distinguishes between 'inner' and 'outer' forms of sensibility in 'Haydn's Sensibility', 14.

[87] This will no doubt make readers think of their manifestation in such genres as novels and sentimental opera. For something closer to home, see the autobiography of Dittersdorf, where tears are shed copiously throughout (*Autobiography of Karl von Dittersdorf*, trans. Coleridge).

[88] See Dahlhaus, *Die Musik des 18. Jahrhunderts*, 9, for discussion of the 'gefühlsbildend' capacities of music within a broader culture of feeling ('Gefühlskultur').

[89] David Marshall characterizes the conundrum thus: 'The dream of sympathy, the fiction of sympathy, is that an interplay and interchange of places, positions, persons, sentiments, and points of view could cancel out the theatricality of the most theatrical of situations.' Marshall, *The Figure of Theater: Shaftesbury, Defoe, Adam Smith, and George Eliot* (New York: Columbia University Press, 1986), 192.

[90] For a somewhat different slant on the question of whether sensibility was innate or acquired see Frevert, 'Defining Emotions', 12–13.

[91] To this one might add the anxiety that sensibility was simply mechanically produced. This is literally so in the case of the female piano-playing automata investigated in Adelheid Voskuhl,

vaunting of musical simplicity acquires a further dimension: if feelings are expressed simply and moderately rather than histrionically and heavily, one might be more likely to trust that they are genuine.

In this light we might consider Hunter's reading of the aria 'Porgi amor', sung by the figure of the Countess as she makes her first appearance at the start of Act 2 of *Le nozze di Figaro*. As Hunter notes, this carries all the signs of later eighteenth-century 'sentimental' style. But we would be wrong to assume that we are somehow eavesdropping on this expression of fine feeling as the Countess bemoans her loveless fate. Instead it would be better to think of it as a performance that assumes an audience, born out of the 'theatricality' inherent in contemporary notions of sympathy: 'sympathy involves imagining oneself in the position of the one-to-be-sympathized-with, and consequently requires on the part of the sympathizer a "dramatization" of the plight of the "sympathizee". To perform a plea for sympathy is thus merely a realization of the idea of dramatization inherent in the notion of sympathy itself.' This is especially clear given the Countess is alone on stage, and so her plea can only be meant for an audience.[92] While Hunter confirms the fundamentally performative nature of sensibility/sympathy, there is no suggestion here that we should doubt the genuineness of the character's feeling. Certainly, the nature of the aria itself helps in this regard: it is not only simply rather than histrionically expressed, but it is also relatively short and so does not try too hard to engage our sympathies.

To turn from a consideration of sensibility to the field of manners might appear to be engaging behavioural opposites, to be moving from the spontaneous individual feeling of one to the collective formality of the other. Certainly within music criticism, sensibility – often denoted by its rough German equivalent, *Empfindsamkeit* – has often been treated as a kind of saving grace of the times, a precious trace of human warmth within a convention-bound, relatively inexpressive 'classicism'. But the reference above to the performative nature of sensibility immediately starts

---

Androids in the Enlightenment: Mechanics, Artisans, and Cultures of the Self (Chicago: University of Chicago Press, 2013).

[92] Mary Hunter, 'Rousseau, the Countess, and the Female Domain', in *Mozart Studies 2*, ed. Eisen, 16. For a nice epistolary equivalent of this, consider Rebecca Green's interpretation of a well-known letter that Haydn wrote to Maria Anna von Genzinger in 1790: 'Though [the letter] appears to record the spontaneous expression of his deepest feelings (to represent his self), it is highly rhetorical, beginning with the operatic cadences of a sentimental heroine: "Well, here I sit in my wilderness – forsaken – like a poor waif...".' Green, 'A Letter from the Wilderness: Revisiting Haydn's Esterházy Environments', in *The Cambridge Companion to Haydn*, ed. Clark, 28. Haydn, in other words, is 'performing' sensibility too.

to close any perceived gap, since manners too patently need to be demonstrated. And further, since sensibility involves being sensitive to the feelings of others, that should ideally result in treating those others with consideration. Even making a distinction between the two on the basis of levels of formality is dubious, given the increasing stress that was laid on informality of manners; one's social behaviour was meant to be relatively free, easy and relaxed, and in Chapter 2 we saw how this principle applied to the practice of conversation.[93]

More fundamentally, though, manners could be subject to the same sceptical reading as sensibility: as a performance from outside oneself, as Rousseau would have had it, rather than an illumination of true good intentions and real fellow feeling. Antoine Lilti describes this as a tension 'between a pessimistic and an optimistic anthropology' of sociability,[94] which we might translate into a series of paired terms. Were one's good manners natural or calculated, real or feigned? Was one's behaviour motivated by moral or instrumental considerations? The latter would imply that manners were being adopted simply as a means of social advancement, of earning the good opinions of one's fellows, and thus were purely selfish in origin. Politeness could in fact turn into its colder cousin, mere civility.[95] Then there is the larger contradiction, which comes to the fore when one reads through manuals on behaviour and conversation: they advocate an easy, natural, spontaneous manner, then proceed to instruct the reader on how this is to be achieved. Naturalness, in other words, involves study and artifice. The same is apparent in all those treatises on ornamentation, feeding a general sense of insecurity about exactly how one should demonstrate natural good taste (in this case, performers are being put on the spot).

However, this encompassing anxiety of the time, the inability to know the true intentions behind the behaviour of others, also had its positive side. As Lawrence Klein has it in his account of Shaftesbury, the

---

[93] Because of this informality, I cannot quite agree with Suzanne Aspden's thesis that 'As these learned [courtly] behaviours became commodified as a means of facilitating social movement within burgeoning cities, suspicion of their superficial nature prompted the search for new authenticities – a search resulting in the mid-century vogue for *sensibilité*.' However, Aspden's remarks pertain to a specifically (north) German context and focus on an earlier part of the eighteenth century than I am principally concerned with. Aspden, 'Bach and the Feminised Galant', *Understanding Bach* 5 (2010), 13.

[94] Lilti, *World of the Salons*, 125.

[95] For discussion of this dominant theme of the age see, for example, Susan Dalton, 'Searching for Virtue: Physiognomy, Sociability, and Taste in Isabella Teotochi Albrizzi's *Ritratti*', *Eighteenth-Century Studies* 40/1 (2006), 85–108; Goodman, *Republic of Letters*; and Klein, *Shaftesbury and the Culture of Politeness*.

'opaqueness of the inner self served to protect it from the pity or ridicule of others'; it 'was also a form of courtesy to others, an acceptable "Dissimulation" that "hides what passes within"'.[96] From the point of view of the individual, protection also meant privacy. If by avoiding the fullest declaration of one's personal feelings or circumstances one could avoid embarrassing others – because one might go beyond their capacity to sympathize – one could also maintain what we would now call 'personal space'. From this point of view, sociability, ironically, could facilitate privacy.[97]

But even if one accepted the pessimistic view of this 'opaqueness' of individual motivation, one could adopt a 'soft' instrumentalist perspective: that while genuineness of feeling was an important principle, it need not matter too much if the effect of kind manners was the same. As John Constable expressed it in a conversation manual of 1738:

as Vanity and Self-love are apt to fix our Minds upon ourselves, and diminish our Esteem and Love for others, it frequently happens, that Civilities are feigned Expressions of Good-will and Esteem. Yet even when we are persuaded, or at least suspect they are not very sincere, still they generally please. Partly because they keep People at a Distance from offensive Rudeness; and partly because we think, a good Share, at least, of the Respect or Affection implied in Civilities, is too unquestionably our Due, to be totally feigned.[98]

In other words, self-interest and the interests of others can coincide; 'everyone wins'. This is a governing irony of so many conduct and conversation manuals of the century, that they are written in wide-eyed awareness of the potential unsociality of individuals, of their likely 'Vanity and Self-love'. All the more reason, then, to aim to rise above it. And such considerations are hardly confined to the eighteenth century. One might cite the world of the academic conference and current etiquette when it comes to question time. Since this raises the possibility of confrontation or disagreement, and in a public space to boot, a certain social awkwardness is in prospect. This is commonly overcome by the questioner's beginning with a congratulatory 'Thank you for your wonderful paper'. Whether such a statement is meant or whether it is purely phatic – and it may of course be a bit of both, for all we know – seems not to matter that much, as honour is satisfied all round.

---

[96] Klein, *Shaftesbury and the Culture of Politeness*, 92.
[97] This is a central theme that emerges from Patricia Meyer Spacks's very entertaining book *Privacy: Concealing the Eighteenth-Century Self*.
[98] John Constable, *The Conversation of Gentlemen Considered, in most of the Ways, that make their mutual Company Agreeable, or Disagreeable: In Six Dialogues* (London: J. Hoyles, 1738), 187–188.

This homely anecdote brings us to a point that should already be clear enough from my treatment of the subject of manners, and more broadly the affective principles that help to make up what we call sociability. I am applying what Leonard B. Meyer calls the 'axiom of constancy', without which 'the past would be irrelevant, and the future ... inconceivable'.[99] This means I believe that it is not so difficult for us to get inside the mentality of the time concerning inter-human behaviour. Most of us, after all, dislike politeness without warmth and informality without respect – and we like our interlocutors to be friendly but not needy. We are certainly less formal now than then, but the principles by which we relate to one another are surely not so different – even if technology may currently be shifting the sense of what represents normal and acceptable human interaction. What is much harder for us to believe is that such precepts could form a major source for a style of musical art; this is the real sticking-point. Even those aspects that might seem so remote to us now may not truly be so. Sensibility, for example, which conjures up an age of swooning sensitivities, surely seems like a lost world. Yet one might argue that we are living through our own age of sensibility, with its own lachrymose imperatives and ritualized performances of sympathy. After all, only the most tearful interviewees make it into the news cycle, and public (and also frequently tearful) demonstrations of fellow feeling are a matter of course (candlelit vigils, leaving bouquets *in memoriam* and the like). And the same uncomfortable questions might be asked about the (self-)dramatization of feeling.

How might all these complexities of definition and orientation with regard to human nature and human behaviour play out musically? Most evidently, they do so when a text is there to lead us on. The pervasive metatheatrical aspects of comic opera spell out the uncertain boundaries between what is real and what is simply performance. These are most obvious with the device of the (sung) play within the play, or may involve more specific phenomena such as the 'singing lesson' as part of the plot, as in Haydn's *La canterina* (1766).[100] But it is a constant theme, as in the string of arias at the start of Act 2 of Haydn's *L'infedeltà delusa* (1773) that offer an extended play on the theme of appearance versus reality – a world of hypocrisy, disguises and trickery. For example, in her attempt to win back her lover Nencio, Vespina adopts a series of disguises that are musical

---

[99] Meyer, *Style and Music*, 89.
[100] On 'meta-opera' more broadly see Alice Bellini, 'Music and "Music" in Eighteenth-Century Meta-Operatic Scores', *Eighteenth-Century Music* 6/2 (2009), 183–207.

as well as sartorial. Thus in 'Ho un tumore in un ginocchio,' dressed up as an old woman, she presents a catalogue of devices signalling pathos: two-note sigh figures to denote weeping (bars 25–28), further two-note figures to denote being out of breath (bars 34–38), supported by diminished-seventh harmonies and stabbing off-beat accents. In another context such devices would tug at our heart-strings, but here the very same devices signal only deceit. In addition, a syncopated *alla zoppa* rhythm is literally used to illustrate lameness (bars 18–22). That this is all a show is proved by some very healthy vocal lines sung in between the pantomime, which would be unlikely to issue from the mouth of an old woman.[101]

If we zoom back to encompass the art of music as a whole, the plot thickens. In Chapter 1 I suggested that music, because of its association with 'pure feeling', could represent a sort of ideal sphere of sociability; it could rise above the suspicions that might attend real-life social conduct. This is most obviously the case with straight instrumental music, when there is no text to mediate the 'purity' of expression. And part of that ideal state involved the fact that performers must cooperate with, and listen to, each other in order for that music to come about. But that very fact can be twisted around to offer another parallel with our central problem. And this is simply that music is literally performed. At least when reading from a score, musicians are not offering any pure, spontaneous bursts of feeling; these feelings are instead rehearsed, not just in the context of one particular piece but also because performers will have encountered similar means of creating affect in other music. This was a moral dilemma that exercised the mind of Quantz, in his flute treatise of 1752. In musical performance,

Simulation [Verstellungskunst] is not only permitted, it is even of the utmost necessity, and it does not violate ethical behavior. If one attempts, as much as possible, to be the master of one's passions in daily life, it will not be difficult at any time during a performance to place oneself into the affect the piece demands. Then one will perform really well and, so to speak, always from the soul [gleichsam allezeit aus der Seele spielen].... Although, unfortunately, many dissimulate very often in their daily lives, in music they rarely practise the desirable art of simulation.[102]

Quantz makes quite clear that music demands simulation just as social interaction does – that there can be no question of music's entailing raw,

---

[101] Most of the last few sentences derive from my entry 'Musical Materials' in *The Cambridge Haydn Encyclopedia*, 228.

[102] Quantz, *Versuch einer Anweisung die Flöte traversiere zu spielen*, 248–249, translation adapted from *Music and Culture*, ed. Fubini, 307.

natural 'expression'. It might at first seem odd that he connects the everyday control of one's 'passions' – which one needs in order to survive as a social animal – with readily slotting into the affect (single affect, it would appear) of a particular movement, but the connection must lie in control and mastery of 'performance', whether musical or social. The phrase 'always from the soul' surely needs to be read ironically, since that impression can only be given to a witness or listener – it is patently not true of the 'performer', and Quantz's use of 'gleichsam' here ('so to speak') seems to bear this out. On the other hand, Quantz distinguishes between unethical social simulation and an ethically neutral musical simulation. He further suggests that not enough performers are able to do this, that they should take a leaf out of the book of everyday 'dissimulators', able to assume a role at will. Does this mean that performers need to be soulful hypocrites? That they should feel less in order to move more? This would seem to be the conclusion in a study of another performing art, acting: Diderot's *Paradoxe sur le comédien* (1773).[103] On the other hand, the advice that Quantz's Berlin colleague C. P. E. Bach gives to performers approximates rather to 'method acting', demanding utter uncompromising immersion,[104] but even this can be understood as part of the wider anxiety about how to convince a listener or witness of the sincerity of one's intentions. The idea of impersonation or simulation is not only given concrete form in those moments when singers step out of character, as it were; instrumentalists may do the same. In the finale of Haydn's Symphony No. 60 (1774), 'Il Distratto', the violins stop proceedings a few bars in, in order to retune their strings. In the final Adagio of Haydn's Symphony No. 45 in F sharp minor (1772), the 'Farewell', the orchestra knows itself to be an orchestra: individual members and sections gradually withdraw their services, leaving the stage as the music ebbs into silence.[105] Similar questions about

---

[103] On this see Daniel Larlham, 'The Felt Truth of Mimetic Experience: Motions of the Soul and the Kinetics of Passion in the Eighteenth-Century Theatre', *The Eighteenth Century: Theory and Interpretation* 53/4 (2012), 432–454: Diderot argues that sensibility 'incapacitates the actor, robbing him of his ability to deliver a controlled and composed performance. Diderot's consummate performer is an unmoved mover' (447).

[104] See Bach, *Versuch über die wahre Art das Klavier zu spielen*, part 1, 122; *Essay on the True Art of Playing Keyboard Instruments*, trans. Mitchell, 152, where players are counselled to 'assume ... the emotion which the composer intended'. Earlier comes Bach's famous advice 'Aus der Seele muß man spielen, und nicht wie ein abgerichteter Vogel.' ('Play from the soul, not like a trained bird!'): *Versuch*, part 1, 119; *Essay*, 150.

[105] For a different take on the implications of this famous ending see Kevin Korsyn, 'Reception History and the Trauma of Real History: Decoding the Pantomime in Haydn's "Farewell" Symphony', *Musikološki Zbornik/Musicological Annual* 45/2 (2009), 143–158. Describing the work as being 'as radical a violation of generic expectations as Beethoven's introduction of

impersonation are raised by the indication 'smorfioso', or 'con smorfia', that Boccherini writes into some of his scores (see, for example, the first movement of the quartet Op. 8 No. 1/G165 of 1769). Since the indication seems to have some visual basis, asking the performer to play 'with a grimace',[106] Le Guin believes that it 'emphasizes the disjuncture between visual and aural modes of communication, encouraging the player to telegraph visually a distance from the sounds he is making'.[107] In the current context, though, one might tie this up with worries about sincerity as a result of a 'performative' culture of feeling and fellow-feeling: what is staged and what is real?[108]

One of the most vivid embodiments of the anxiety about musical performance takes place soundlessly, within the pages of Diderot's *Le neveu de Rameau*. We have already witnessed the scene where the character of 'Him' mimes the playing of Alberti or Galuppi sonatas on a harpsichord, his face conveying the emotions that cannot be realized in actual sound. Further elements of 'realism' are gestural: 'You could tell when he was playing *piano*, when *forte*'; 'the curious thing was that at times he'd stumble in his playing, then correct himself as if he'd played a wrong note'.[109] In a subsequent, famous passage, 'Him' mixes and muddles 'some thirty airs of every style'. For the character 'Me', the performance was 'taking possession of our souls and keeping them suspended in the most extraordinary state of being I have ever known'; yet 'a tinge of ridicule' is mixed with feelings of admiration and pity.[110] 'Him' then imitates all the various instruments. He completely loses touch with reality, becoming 'utterly spent' by his expressive efforts[111] – which reminds one of another famous description, Burney's account of the playing of a perspiring C. P. E. Bach. Again we encounter themes of performance and sincerity, with the performance being at once of overpowering immediacy and capable of 'transporting' the

---

a chorus in the Ninth Symphony' (143), Korsyn evaluates the sexual and political implications of Haydn's close, which he describes as a form of 'performance art *avant la lettre*' (156).

[106] For an interesting discussion on the meaning and implications of this term see the Colloquy contained in the *Journal of the American Musicological Society* 59/2 (2006), 459–472, featuring contributions by Beverly Jerold, Marco Mangani and Elisabeth Le Guin.

[107] Le Guin, 'One Says that One Weeps', 234.

[108] Not that such notions of one particular culture being 'performatively' inclined should be taken too far; Peter Burke discusses the scholarly context for the recent widespread 'performative turn' within the humanities in 'Performing History: The Importance of Occasions', *Rethinking History* 9/1 (2005), 35–52. And he notes that 'Emotions too are viewed increasingly as being performed.' (40)

[109] Diderot, *Rameau's Nephew*, trans. Mauldon, 22 and 23.

[110] Diderot, *Rameau's Nephew*, trans. Mauldon, 68.

[111] Diderot, *Rameau's Nephew*, trans. Mauldon, 69.

performer and listener, but also suspect because of its being divorced from what may really be felt. And because the whole thing is a dumb show in the service of a sounding art, it is also plainly ridiculous. Beyond the matter of literal performance (or, in the current case, non-literal performance), one might suggest that music altogether proved a peculiarly suitable medium through which to consider such questions about social behaviour. Most obviously with instrumental music – because it is 'abstract', about 'feelings', since in the absence of words those feelings may be sensed but are not directly knowable – the medium vividly embodies questions about the reality of a particular affect or series of affects. To ascribe some agency to this question, this means we should consider the 'performance' of a role or an emotion by the actual composer. If one can doubt the intentions of a performer, one can also doubt the intentions of a composer.

To take this further, we might consider one of the particular behavioural values associated with the eighteenth century's 'polite' culture: equanimity. Adam Smith, as we saw earlier, referred to an 'equality of temper which is so common among men of the world'. This need not imply an absence of strong feelings, but it does involve regulating their open expression, as part of an agreed social contract.[112] Baron Freiherr von Knigge defined it as *esprit de conduite*, which included 'the ability to fall in unaffectedly with the tone of every company without losing one's originality of character or demeaning oneself to low flattery' ('sich ungezwungen in den Ton jeder Gesellschaft stimmen zu können, ohne weder Eigentümlichkeit des Charakters zu verlieren, noch sich zu niedriger Schmeichelei herabzulassen').[113] This meant one should be sympathetic but also hold something of oneself in reserve; diplomacy takes the place of honesty, as it were. Such a value has certainly proved problematic when considered in relation to our repertory. It has contributed to the common image of an expressively circumscribed style, from which only a few exceptional composers managed to escape – hence the emphasis on apparently more direct, personal creative expression in the reception histories of Mozart or C. P. E. Bach, for example. Marshall Brown, on the other hand, states plainly that 'concealment rather than passionate

---

[112] Michael Spitzer aptly describes this as 'a general principle of self-command which resonates ... with our sensibility to the feelings of others', discussed in an investigation of the 'display rules' involved in the expression of angry affect in Mozart. What Spitzer hears in the Minuet from the Symphony in G minor K550 is not just 'anger' but 'the control of anger ... too'. Spitzer, 'The Topic of Emotion', in *Music Semiotics: A Network of Significations*, ed. Esti Sheinberg (Farnham: Ashgate, 2012), 222.

[113] Knigge, *Über den Umgang mit Menschen*, volume 1, 8; *Philosophy of Social Life*, trans. Will, volume 1, xxi.

utterance is a core value of Enlightened manners',[114] and asks us to evaluate such an attribute more positively. While he concentrates on Haydn's songs and the lyric poems that they set, his study also aims more widely. One way to build on his lead is to consider the ambivalent tone of much musical utterance of the time: the uncertainty about whether a particular passage or gesture is to be taken at face value. To use the words of Diderot's 'Me', this amounts to the question 'Are you being ironic, or sincere?'.[115] Thus politeness, which I earlier suggested was more obviously a technical than an affective property of this repertory, now takes on a more global discursive import.

That Diderot's question must be asked constantly of later eighteenth-century instrumental music has not always been evident to all. This may be partly because we tend to 'trust' music as the great 'expressive' art, and need very clear evidence to the contrary before we disengage from that trust. Overt comedy provides a clear first step away from expressive sincerity, but even that may lie in the ear of the listener: Ratner writes of how much instrumental music of the time is 'saturated with comic rhetoric which may be vaguely sensed but is not often fully savored'.[116] When we move further away into the realms of wit and irony, there is a greater chance that they will not be recognized.[117] Recognition will depend on stylistic competence and individual mentality, and there may be regional-cultural differences as well (Goethe, when discussing the reception of his *Die Leiden des jungen Werthers*, commented that 'the humorous irony of the British was not given to us'[118]). And these differentiating factors have not changed overmuch through time: while we would like to imagine that the 'authentic' listeners of the time were more attuned to various forms of linguistic play, or alert for a possible double meaning, this was certainly not always the case. In terms of later reception, while 'classical' music may have become renowned for its comic properties, it is also often thought highly direct and transparent in its style of utterance. Such an impression is by no means wrong, but tells only half the story. In fact, ambiguities of tone – by which we mean the music's 'tone of voice' – may be most potent in places where we would least expect them: not in the rough-and-tumble of a fast outer

---

[114] Brown, 'Poetry of Haydn's Songs', 238.
[115] Diderot, *Rameau's Nephew*, trans. Mauldon, 44.   [116] Ratner, *Classic Music*, 387.
[117] For a discussion of the recognition or otherwise of irony and parody in relation to the learned style see Tamara Balter, 'Canon-Fodders: Parody of Learned Style in Beethoven', *Journal of Musicological Research* 32/2-3 (2013), 199–224.
[118] Cited in Daniel Heartz and Bruce Alan Brown, 'Empfindsamkeit', in *Grove Music Online* www.oxfordmusiconline.com (10 August 2018).

movement, for instance, but in moments of seeming innocence or lyricism. Indeed, humour, especially in the form of 'jokes', may put us off the trail by encouraging the sense of a localized phenomenon after which the music reverts to its default 'serious' mode. Humour is treated as a delimited technique brought to bear by the composer rather than forming part of a more fundamental orientation or mentality.[119] In her account of the first movement of Beethoven's Sonata in G major Op. 31 No. 1 (1802) Claudia Maurer Zenck, for example, seems much concerned to separate the 'serious' from the 'jocular'. While she presents this primarily as a problem of reception, as something that listeners and performers had and have to wrestle with, the possibility that the music could be both things at the same time is not entertained.[120] The same applies to Melanie Wald's study of the reception of the finale of Haydn's 'Farewell' Symphony; it has at various times been found both amusing and melancholy, and Wald believes that the latter is historically the proper affect.[121] In this case too, though, we need to consider whether 'both/and' might be a more appropriate reading than 'either/or', both now and then.

One manifestation of duality of discourse arises in the shape of so-called romantic irony. Contrary to the associations that the label brings, this is by no means confined to music that we like to label romantic. Through shifts of material, topic and stylistic level, through interference with the expected course of musical events – and above all through any technique that conveys the sense that the music has been made rather than simply arising 'naturally' – the composer forces the listener to distrust him, to doubt that what has been heard is to be taken for real. And this means that everything is thrown into doubt – not just the moments of comic 'interference', for instance, but also passages that seem to bespeak sincerity and 'seriousness' of feeling. We have positive evidence from the time that this was

---

[119] When, for example, David Schroeder makes an unfortunate comparison between Haydn's preference for 'rustic quips' and Mozart's 'more sophisticated' humour in their respective quartet outputs, it suggests that he can hear only localized joking, but not Haydn's consistent contingency of tone. Schroeder, *Experiencing Mozart: A Listener's Companion* (Lanham: Scarecrow, 2013), 45.

[120] Claudia Maurer Zenck, '"Mannichfaltige Abweichungen von der gewöhnlichen Sonaten-Form": Beethoven's "Piano Solo" Op. 31 No. 1 and the Challenge of Communication', in *Communication in Eighteenth-Century Music*, ed. Mirka and Agawu, 73. She subsequently asks, 'How can later generations ... identify the transgression of norms ... with certainty as intentionally humorous and not, for example, as daring ideas of a genius or, on the other hand, as sheer mistakes of a composer possibly not of the first rank?' (74).

[121] Melanie Wald, '"Ein curios melancholisches Stückchen": Die düstere Seite von Haydns fis-moll Sinfonie Hob. I:45 und einige Gedanken zur Pantomime in der Instrumentalmusik', *Studia musicologica* 51/1–2 (2010), 79–90.

understood in the case of Haydn, given the comparisons that were made between his oeuvre and the novels of Laurence Sterne.[122] There was also, of course, plenty of negative evidence, for example in the writings of Koch. We noted earlier his criticism of what may be Haydn's Symphony No. 60: 'Instead of using art to work on the heart, one tries to occupy the minds of the listeners with wit'. To say that feeling has been undermined by mental activity, by the distancing effects of wit, is to recognize the effects of irony and to dislike them. Haydn has formed a natural focus for discussions of ironic musical discourse, since this was one area in which he plainly set the tone. Michaelis acknowledged this when he wrote in his 1807 essay 'Über das Humoristische oder Launige in der musikalischen Komposition' that 'our most recent music is largely humorous, especially since Haydn, as the greatest master in this vein, ... set the tone. ... Haydn was the first to do this ... and awakened a great number of the most celebrated composers of most recent times to write in this manner' ('Hingegen ist unsere neueste Musik grossentheils humoristisch, besonders seitdem Joseph Haydn, als der grösste Meister in dieser Gattung ... den Ton dazu angab. ... Haydn that es zuerst ... und weckte eine Menge berühmter Tonkünstler der neuesten Zeit, in diesem Charakter zu schreiben').[123]

While giving primacy to Haydn, Michaelis also makes clear that 'this manner' had become a foundational attribute of the times. This is worth noting given that the attribute has often been associated almost exclusively with Haydn – and, indeed, within that, it has often been only the more obvious and gentler 'humour' that has registered rather than the more encompassing irony. This has been a convenience to help keep the composer in his place within the classical chain of command,[124] but it also reflects what I take to be a lack of understanding of the tone of address offered not just by Haydn but by many of his contemporaries. With the kind of irony reviewed above the breaks of style or discourse are relatively conspicuous, but this can grade into a softer style of irony that has received

---

[122] For an anglophone context for this see, for example, McVeigh, *Concert Life in London*, 160. See also Bonds, 'Haydn, Laurence Sterne, and the Origins of Musical Irony'.

[123] Christian Friedrich Michaelis, 'Über das Humoristische oder Launige in der musikalischen Komposition', *Allgemeine musikalische Zeitung* 46 (12 August 1807), column 729.

[124] For example, in his *Interpreting Musical Gestures* Robert Hatten prefers to take romantic irony more literally, discussing it with reference to later Beethoven and Schubert, where the 'shifts in level of discourse' (47) are more obviously signalled than they may be in Haydn. Curiously, in his 'Irony and Incomprehensibility: Beethoven's "Serioso" String Quartet in F Minor, Op. 95, and the Path to the Late Style', *Journal of the American Musicological Society* 70/2 (2017), 285–356, Mark Evan Bonds all but ignores Haydn's prior claims in the matter of musical irony. Yet his earlier article 'Haydn, Laurence Sterne, and the Origins of Musical Irony' offers perhaps the definitive account of how Haydn's ironic discourse can operate.

far less written recognition. In this case the tone is relatively more even, in line with Smith's 'equality of temper', and the gestural sense more akin to a raised eyebrow than anything more overt. This kind of approach understands the potential irony of speaking a gracious galant language when underlying feelings may not be so altruistic, and it manifests itself most strongly with gentler styles of musical utterance.

It is in the literature on Mozart's operas that this has found most consistent recognition. Stefano Castelvecchi considers the mixture of direct sentimental writing and the 'explicit parody' of the same in *Le nozze di Figaro* and concludes that 'it is impossible to settle on either side'; Burnham writes of the quality of 'distance without disdain, involvement without credulity' found in *Così fan tutte*; and Hunter of the 'eternally ambiguous relation between sympathy and ridicule that is one of [*Così*'s] principal topics'.[125] Hunter in fact notes that this ambiguity is found most clearly in the numbers with 'beautiful music',[126] which accords with my suggestion that this type of tone attached itself most strongly to gentler expression. In these operatic cases the ambiguity often arises out of music that has strong pastoral attributes, and this goes beyond any particular topical affiliation to encompass the pastoral as a cultural mode. At this level the pastoral typically evokes idyllic scenes but is always on the outside looking in, resulting in a characteristic combination of direct simplicity and elaborate irony. Outside of the realm of Mozartean opera, this kind of tone has been identified and memorably described by Charles Rosen with particular relation to the 'heroic pastoral' style of Haydn's late symphonies:

> The pretension of Haydn's symphonies to a simplicity that appears to come from Nature itself is no mask but the true claim of a style whose command over the whole range of technique is so great that it can ingenuously afford to disdain the outward appearance of high art. Pastoral is generally ironic, with the irony of one who aspires to less than he deserves, hoping he will be granted more. But Haydn's pastoral style is more generous, with all its irony: it is the true heroic pastoral that cheerfully lays claim to the sublime, without yielding any of the innocence and simplicity won by art.[127]

---

[125] Stefano Castelvecchi, 'Sentimental and Anti-Sentimental in "Le nozze di Figaro"', *Journal of the American Musicological Society* 53/1 (2000), 21; Burnham, 'Mozart's *felix culpa: Così fan tutte* and the Irony of Beauty', *The Musical Quarterly* 78/1 (1994), 92; and Hunter, *Culture of Opera Buffa*, 287.

[126] Hunter, *Culture of Opera Buffa*, 286 (the phrase is found here, but commentary on its conjunction with an ambiguity of tone is given on the following page).

[127] Rosen, *The Classical Style*, 163.

The point of this style of utterance, in other words, is not simply to 'get the irony'; it is also to understand that there is (or may be) no irony at all. The precise point of view adopted by the composer is undecidable, and we will also therefore be hard put to arrive at a 'finalizing judgment', as George Edwards writes of Haydn's Op. 76 string quartets, with their 'constant shift[s] of points of view'.[128] This relates to what I have called a stance of relativism about the materials of the musical world; this is born out of their pluralistic employment in ever-different combinations whereby no one type of material carries absolute authority. And it also follows that different listener reactions to a piece's tone of voice are allowable – indeed, to be expected – under these terms of reference. This could mean coming down firmly on the side of ironic interpretation or else hearing pure 'innocence and simplicity', as well as finding some sort of admixture of the two. My only problem with this lies in the sheer imbalance of opinion that has prevailed. Taking the music at face value, taking the music on trust, has been the rule. Recognition of irony has been in short supply.

This applies even more to the recognition of 'soft irony'. For example, Burnham notes of the theme that opens the finale of Haydn's Symphony No. 98 in B flat major (1792) that its 'terse, choppy patter seems to parody the Classical-style penchant for appositely paired phrases: the often decorous reliability of such pairings is here downgraded to a clownish predictability'.[129] This is a good way of trying to capture a quality that one hears in so many of Haydn's finale themes in particular, but it is surely missing a point not to note that the theme is outwardly unimpeachable. It is a question of 'tone': the theme is as much innocent as parodistic, as breezily popular as flippant. On the other hand, in his reading of the cancrizans minuet and trio in Haydn's Symphony No. 47 (1772), Balázs Mikusi notes how 'the conspicuous dynamic contrasts and the differentiated orchestration ... suggest that Haydn intended to render the underlying structural trick of the piece perceptible to all attentive listeners'. At the same time Mikusi wonders whether the composer is not making sport of the technique: the abrupt dynamic alternations that do so much to aid perception sound odd whether played in their original sequence or played backwards, in retrograde inversion, resulting in 'an estranged character'.[130] This yields the sort of 'generosity' of perspective that Rosen defines above: two quite different interpretations of communicative intent, one direct, the other more indirect, are held in uncertain balance.

---

[128] Edwards, 'Nonsense of an Ending', 248. [129] Burnham, 'Haydn and Humor', 63.
[130] Mikusi, 'More than a Copy', 14 and 18.

However, on most occasions any ambiguity of tone does not involve complicated compositional callisthenics. It derives instead from a much simpler surface. One central category is the theme that has an air of innocence about it. The slow movement of Haydn's Symphony No. 96 in D major (1791) opens with such a theme, simple and songful. When this theme is repeated from bar 5, solo woodwind instruments take turns to imitate its anacrusis, a simple rising arpeggio, creating antiphony between the woodwind lines themselves and between them and the tune of the first violins. This confirms the Arcadian leanings of the material, evoking an idealized rural landscape across which shepherds are calling to each other. At the same time, it is hard not to smile when one hears this anacrusis figure being echoed around the orchestra. While these woodwind additions straightforwardly amplify the effect, they might also sound too cute by half. The addition of horn calls and a bassoon duet in thirds upon repetition of the theme from bar 22 adds to this conundrum – the effect is both charming and too obviously picturesque. Michaelis clearly recognized such an effect when he wrote that with the category of naive humour 'the composer with his simple notes ends up saying more than he seemed to want to say' ('wenn der Komponist mit seinen simpeln Noten am Ende mehr sagt, als er zu wollen schien').[131] Of similar movements in the London symphonies, from Nos 94 ('Surprise') and 101 ('Clock'), Simon McVeigh comments that 'the *innocente* Andante is taken to an absurd naivety', as a form of 'self-parody'.[132] It is difficult to dissent from this view, though we do then lose the sense that these movements also offer something that is disarmingly, self-sufficiently 'natural' and attractive.

On most occasions, this expressive ambivalence is not entirely intrinsic, but rather emerges by comparison with other kinds of material. This may mean that surrounding movements throw the innocence of a particular movement into doubt. The Adagio cantabile of Boccherini's String Quintet in F minor Op. 42 No. 1/G348 (1789), as we saw in Chapter 2, features a seemingly inexplicable disruption to its course after the double bar, with a sequence of loud diminished-seventh chords that leads to an eerie close on the dominant of F minor. The ensuing finale, a Rondeau Allegro giusto in the tonic major, features a very catchy refrain. This spends its first eight bars hovering *pianissimo* on a dominant seventh, with all parts being static. The first violin's 'tune' consists simply of eight bars of the seventh b♭^{1},

---

[131] Michaelis, 'Über das Humoristische oder Launige in der musikalischen Komposition', column 727.
[132] McVeigh, *Concert Life in London*, 136 and 135.

decorated minimally by upper and lower neighbour notes. This is followed by eight bars of tonic that reiterate the same melodic module four times. This sequence of events returns verbatim on three further occasions in the movement. We can account for the static quality by categorizing this material as one of Boccherini's characteristic 'loops', but the particular impression given here is of rustic vamping, as if the band is warming up before beginning in earnest. This suggests that a kind of pastoral simplicity overcomes the tragic accents delivered towards the end of the slow movement, a straightforward change of manner, but one might also hear bathos in the comparison. Are we hearing self-sufficiently 'natural' music or something that is clearly too simple to be taken seriously? Even the *pp* dynamic allocated to the refrain could be a positive special effect – the rustic band heard from afar? – or part of the joke, since this is hardly much of a theme, especially for a rondo, and such rustically 'limited' music is incompatible with the 'preciousness' and control implied by the very soft collective dynamic.

The innocence that is in play need not have any strong pastoral associations, though it generally has at least some sort of popular, tuneful flavour. The slow movement of Hoffmeister's String Quartet in D minor Op. 14 No. 3 (1791) offers a typical example. While it is marked Adagio cantabile, the movement embodies an expressive typology that one more readily associates with Andante tempo – not just tuneful, but also smooth and flirtatious. But are we getting true charm and modesty of gesture, or is it all laid on a bit thick? The sense of a mask being in place may be strengthened by passages within the subsequent variations in which the *dolce* quality is abruptly undermined by strident dotted-style passages; deriving from a surprisingly aggressive central portion of the original theme (bars 13–19), these passages act as a foil to open up a possible ironic perspective on the manner of the original theme. Yet we must bear in mind that later eighteenth-century instrumental style is 'naturally' variable in its moods and type of delivery. As explored in Chapter 2, we might therefore hear such contrasts as self-evident rather than loaded.

The finale of Haydn's Sonata H34 in E minor (1784), Vivace molto, raises the stakes somewhat by adding the marking 'innocentemente' at the outset. This surely guarantees that we can't hear the movement as innocent. Why would the composer add such a marking if it were all above board? This Vivace presents a pure, uninterrupted stream of melody, which is 'natural', but on the other hand it is in minor, and stays there till the end. This is certainly as undisruptive, even-tempered a minor-mode movement as one could hear; the nearest we get to a dramatic moment is the very final cadence, but even that is firm rather than especially assertive.[133] If the 'innocentemente' does indeed mean more than it says, it might derive from the contrast between the naturally flowing melody and an undercurrent of agitation that derives, strangely enough, from the very ubiquitousness of the Alberti-bass accompaniment. This would normally be unmarked, and indeed no accompanying figuration more directs us towards the primacy of a singing melodic line. But there is an awful lot of it. The only time it is absent is in the first episode in E major, but when that returns in decorated form, the Alberti bass persists from the preceding E minor section. The accompaniment hurries the melody along, as it were, not allowing it any opportunity to expand. The resulting impression is of a mood that cannot quite declare itself: there is more to say, but it cannot be said. This suggests a quite different kind of double meaning compared to our previous case studies. The middle movement of Haydn's Piano Trio in E flat major H29 (1797) also moves in this direction with its Andantino ed innocentemente marking. The fact that it is set in the flat submediant key of B major may already represent an unlikely setting for true innocence, idyllic though the material may be, but that quality is then more vividly undercut when the opening figure is subjected to a rather tortured form of imitation in rising sequence first at bars 21–23 than at bars 37–39.

The most common staging of innocence occurs in recursive forms, above all in rondos with strongly contrasting episodes. Richard Will comments on the effects that such contrasts can have on our perception of an innocent theme in Haydn's rondo finales: 'The incongruity of dance tunes generating fugues or chromatic modulation is pronounced, so much so that the eventual reprise of the theme in something like its original guise stretches credibility; the naïveté thus restored has come to seem impossibly distant.'[134] On the other hand, the boot may be on the other foot when a 'naïve' refrain returns in this way, often in identical form, as if nothing had happened. Such material exemplifies what William Empson called 'comic primness'. As glossed by Paul Alpers in a discussion of 'the power

---

[133] Floyd Grave's category of 'galant minor', which implies that the choice of mode is relatively unmarked, might seem to fit this movement very well, and he does in fact cite this finale as an exemplar, though it would rather weaken the argument I am making here about a play between surface innocence and a different underlying affect. Grave, 'Galant Style, Enlightenment, and the Paths from Minor to Major in Later Instrumental Works by Haydn', *Ad Parnassum* 7/13 (2009), 11–12.

[134] Richard Will, 'Eighteenth-Century Symphonies: An Unfinished Dialogue', in *The Cambridge History of Eighteenth-Century Music*, ed. Keefe, 642.

of pastoral simplicity', this is 'a form of irony which works by having a character say something in (apparently) perfect innocence which at the same time is felt to open up a range of critical attitudes and ironic perspectives'.[135] And such perspectives may be applied just as readily to the more complicated musical machinery that has grown out of the innocent theme as to the theme itself.

Both possibilities are alive in the keyboard rondos of C. P. E. Bach, which differ from the late eighteenth-century norm in that the refrain is normally quite short, and it returns more often and in different keys. It is also mixed with contrasting material on a smaller scale than in the more customary clearer-cut sectional forms such as ABACA. The Rondo in E major (Wq57/1; 1779) and Rondo in G major (Wq 57/3; 1780) published in the third collection *für Kenner und Liebhaber* offer instructive examples. The master narrative for these works seems to be that of the innocent abroad. There is a kind of Panglossian optimism in the air as the theme undergoes all sorts of adventures, being translated into very remote keys and being subjected to various unexpected developments, and it is often interrupted by various passages whose brilliance or intensity is at odds with the more temperate charm of the refrain. Yet this refrain keeps on popping up unperturbed, bright and fresh.[136] Are we to infer irony from these returns, as the expansive gestures give way to the controlled repetitions of the refrain? In other words, are we encouraged to be slightly sniffy about the returns of the material, so often and so literally and so doggedly, as if it were a straitjacket; is the refrain material now to be heard as too simple to satisfy, an ironic restoration of a contemporary norm? Or is it in fact a more self-evident reappearance, highlighting the virtues of material that gives pleasure through its melodic integrity and structural transparency? After all, the refrain is complete in itself, and able to make the sort of lucid statement which all the huffing and puffing heard in the interim could not accomplish. The final four bars of the Rondo in E major sum up the two possible perspectives (Example 4.1, and compare Example 2.9, which shows the first eight bars of the movement). Preceded by a final blaze of soloistic rhetoric, the refrain returns for a final time at a very gentle *pianissimo* dynamic. This is sustained until the consequent phrase

---

[135] Alpers, *What Is Pastoral?*, 40.
[136] L. Poundie Burstein notes that 'Major-key rondos are particularly suited for comedic expression, since they often involve a jovial-sounding theme which remains basically unchanged in face of its increasingly turbulent surroundings.' Burstein, 'The Off-Tonic Return in Beethoven's Piano Concerto No. 4 in G Major, Op. 58, and Other Works', *Music Analysis* 24/3 (2005), 336.

Example 4.1 C. P. E. Bach, Rondo in E major Wq 57/1, bars 89–94

suddenly swells to *forte* on its second beat, and this coincides with a rewriting of the basic material. Instead of circling around a fixed point, it is transformed into a series of falling parallel 6-3 chords, suggesting that a grander, more expansive finish to the phrase, and the piece, is in prospect. But then the dynamic is cut to *piano* in the following (and final) bar, and each beat of the cadential descent is softened by an appoggiatura, creating a gentle, sweet, charming ending. This also counts as a form of simplifying cadence, ironically modest when we were led to expect something else.

This kind of punctual close, leaving the listener expecting more, is a fairly sure sign of innocence abroad. We hear it also in the final movement of Kraus's Quartet in B flat major, Op. 1 No. 2 (1784), a more traditional five-part rondo in which the relaxed popular-sounding tune returns twice amidst a welter of contrasting, not to say incongruous material. Neither return is properly prepared harmonically, which furthers the sense of the refrain's being a thing apart; this is especially marked given the generic code for rondos, in which retransitions often feature prominently. And on each occasion the rondo theme is repeated exactly, as if entirely unaffected by its surroundings, which are so changeable and relatively dramatic. After the final return of the refrain in bars 71–78 there is a full bar of silence. Then the very last part of the refrain is repeated *smorzando*. And with that the music is over. This makes not only for an unexpectedly abrupt ending in its own right, but if the movement is really to finish at this point, it simply sounds too short relative to the previous two movements.[137] As with Bach's Rondo in E major, we can account for this as a simplifying close, yielding a wry, apologetic tone. But if it is concessive in one sense – a gentle withdrawal of utterance – it is also challenging and socially cheeky in its very unexpectedness and the sense of disproportion it leads to the movement and the whole work. The modest, innocent refrain is insistent about its self-sufficiency.

If ambiguities of tone often arise in the case of innocent or naive material, they can also arise where more elevated feelings seem to be in play. Such instances can be even more destructive of the trust that the listener wants to repose in the composer and performers. After all, naive material often carries an air of comedy, or at least lightness, about it, but that is less likely to be the case with a more earnest lyricism. Not that there need be a clear dividing-line between the two. The slow movement of Haydn's Symphony No. 57 in D major (1774) is dominated by its opening figure, a simple three-chord sequence, I–V–I, played pizzicato by the strings.[138] The composer plays his customary structural riddles with it, as at various points in this variation movement it acts as opening, continuation and close. It can readily be heard as a humorous device, particularly given the relative unpredictability of its appearances. Peter Brown describes the movement that results as 'quirky',[139] and one could readily imagine that for Haydn's north German critics it would have been accounted yet another instance of 'comic fooling' by means of an intrusive gimmick. On the other hand, for Daniel Heartz this Adagio is 'a vision of serene beauty ... at once simple and profound'. Regarding the returning pizzicato material, he writes, 'There is something deeply expressive about this return to the simplest kind of beginning, reenacted over and over, leading us to ponder the identity of beginnings and endings in a broader sense.'[140] Heartz offers a useful intervention by suggesting that the structural self-consciousness imparted to the listener by this movement need not destroy a sense of beauty; this Adagio can move as well as amuse.[141] We

---

[137] Presumably because of this problem of proportions, the Lysell Quartet, in their recording of this movement, offer a repeat of bars 1–27 in order to pad things out a bit: *Joseph Martin Kraus, Stråkkvartette* (Musica Sveciae MSCD 414, 1990).

[138] The characteristic 3–2–1 shape of the top line seems to reverse the 1–2–3 motto that Haydn used to similar ends in the finale of his Symphony No. 35 in B flat major (1767).

[139] A. Peter Brown, 'Symphony: 5. Esterházy Symphonies from *c.* 1772 to *c.* 1781', in *Oxford Composer Companions: Haydn*, ed. David Wyn Jones (Oxford: Oxford University Press, 2002), 393.

[140] Daniel Heartz, *Haydn, Mozart and the Viennese School, 1740–1780* (New York: Norton, 1995), 371.

[141] For a study of the uncertain affects that mark out many of the slow movements of Haydn's 'middle period' in particular see Sutcliffe, 'Expressive Ambivalence'.

saw Tom Service suggest something similar in the case of the finale of the composer's Op. 33 No. 2. Once more, 'both/and' rather than 'either/or' may be an appropriate reaction. Rosen offers a further possible example in his account of the opening of Haydn's 'Lark' Quartet, Op. 64 No. 5 (1791). As we saw in Chapter 2, the opening eight bars present what seems to be a staccato main theme that the following eight bars reveal to be an accompaniment to the famously soaring tune in the first violin. For Rosen this realizes 'a double sentiment of scherzando and passionate lyricism that is both serious and not without humour. The effect is as thrilling as it amuses.'[142] However, such even-handedness of reaction may not always be possible. Eric F. Clarke suggests that the slow movement of Haydn's quartet Op. 54 No. 2 (1788) – a short but startlingly intense Adagio in C minor with extravagant melodic arabesques in the first violin, often taken to represent gypsy fiddle playing – 'hovers between "heartfelt authenticity" and parody'.[143] Can anyone honestly feel such a movement in both ways at once?

Certainly the more intense the sentiment appears to be, the harder it is for us to take if there is any suggestion of distancing parody. The Adagio grazioso of Beethoven's Sonata in G major Op. 31 No. 1 (1802) is a similar case to Haydn's Op. 54 quartet movement, with its lavish ornamentation – this time operatically inspired, it would appear – suggesting flights of daring inspiration. And there are many signs of heightened sentiment, such as the lengthy chromatic transition heard at bars 53–64. Yet, as the movement draws to a close after a full ten minutes or so, one might struggle to suppress a feeling that it has been inflated in length as well as in expressive pretensions: the ornamentation could be heard less as eloquent and more as parodistically over the top.[144] Another intriguing case is provided by the slow movement of Rosetti's Symphony in D major Murray A12 (1782). This Andantino is a theme and variations, and after the final one, in bar 64, there is an unexpected arrival of brilliance after a 'sentimental' set. This quickly turns into the sort of figuration that typically prepares a cadenza. A V6/4 harmony then does arrive in bar 68 to confirm this, but the dynamic is immediately hushed to *pianissimo*, and instead of brilliance we have display of another sort. This is the sentimental close that

---

[142] Rosen, *Music and Sentiment*, 71.   [143] Clarke, *Ways of Listening*, 121.
[144] Charles Rosen hears some ambivalence here, describing the movement as 'a delightful imitation, only partly humorous but mostly affectionate, of the traditional but already outdated style of operatic singing of long decorative passages'. Rosen, *Beethoven's Piano Sonatas*, 38. Maurer Zenck points out that the very tempo indication contains an internal contradiction: 'grazioso' is 'an expression always used in conjunction with lively movement (e. g. *allegretto grazioso*)': 'Mannichfaltige Abweichungen von der gewöhnlichen Sonaten-Form', 73.

features heightened pathetic chromaticism, based on falling lines in all parts and a series of sighs. Then the theme starts again, remarkably marked *ppp*, but is quickly abandoned for a simplified close, a basic chordal IV–V7–I in strings alone, with the final two chords played pizzicato. These recall the device used in Haydn's Symphony No. 57. As in that case, the pizzicato does not necessarily have to indicate any change of tone. The final simplicity can be entirely touching, but there is also surely a possible irony in the abandonment of the previous heightened utterance in favour of such a naked close.

This kind of gentle, but ambivalent conclusion is found in two of the slow movements from Gyrowetz's Op. 44 string quartets (1804). In the coda of the Adagio of Op. 44 No. 3 (which we considered earlier in discussion of the simplifying cadence; see Example 3.18), the cello intones the movement's opening motive in bar 76, which viola and first violin answer by playing a rising scalic figure in parallel sixths (Example 4.2). The cello's repetition of its motive from bar 78 prompts a reversal of motion in the upper three voices; they now descend to create a larger-scale symmetry of gesture. At the end of a movement that is full of heightened lyrical expression, and immediately preceded by a broad cadential confirmation of the tonic, this passage could be heard as a simple form of liquidation, perfectly in keeping with the tone of what has gone before. On the other hand, there is a nursery-rhyme simplicity to these scales – all the way up and then all the way back down again – that might be heard as incongruously playful, if undemonstratively so. Perhaps they represent not so much a break in tone as an appropriate means of withdrawing from the earlier intensity.

At the equivalent point of the Adagio non tanto of Op. 44 No. 2, following the final structural cadence in the tonic in bar 96, there is a more conspicuous lightening of mood, after a movement that has been solemn and dramatic throughout (Example 4.3). Gyrowetz uses a short chain of dotted rhythms to effect this, presented by the upper then the lower pair of instruments. Those dotted rhythms are continued in the cello as the music continues to fragment. We expect the final tonic harmony to arrive at bar 101, after the pre-dominant chord at 99 and dominant that follows in bar 100. What happens instead is that all players take up the cello's dotted-rhythmic figure from the previous bar, alternating between C and B♮, but this figure now continues through the whole bar rather than simply happening on the first beat. It is also expanded texturally, being spread out over three octaves, while the dynamic level lowers to *pianissimo*. Harmonically, this material has to be heard as a continuation of the dominant reached in bar 100. In bar 102 the continuous dotted motion is arrested, and all players have a minim C. On the third beat this moves to a unison A,

Example 4.2 Gyrowetz, Quartet in A flat major Op. 44 No. 3/ii, bars 74–82

Example 4.3 Gyrowetz, Quartet in B flat major Op. 44 No. 2/ii, bars 95–103

and then in bar 103 to a unison F, after which the movement is finished. These final notes prompt a retrospective reinterpretation of the harmonic sense of the last three bars: instead of representing a dominant sonority, and so being tense and forward-leading, they may now be heard as a prolonged resolving tonic, but unfolded with extreme deliberation. These oddities of timing and gesture, together with the fact that the material of the coda bears little relation to what has gone before in the movement, suggest that we might hear a hint of facetiousness to this conclusion. On the other hand, the passage could readily be heard as a continuation of the elevated style that has gone before, the final stretched-out harmony simply being a rather eccentric form of noble simplicity. As in all our previous examples of ambivalence of tone, the policy seems to be 'neither confirm nor deny'; it is up to us as listeners to read the signs and judge for ourselves.

The same would apply to the Rondo in F major, VB191, by Kraus (1778–1782). It carries what for the genre is an unusual tempo designation of Larghetto.[145] Yet this suits the character of the theme, which exemplifies the galant ideal of simple but affecting melodic eloquence (Example 4.4a). It is high in register, markedly symmetrical in phrase syntax and exquisitely polished, yet 'natural'. The remarkable feature of the piece as a whole is the contrast between the expansiveness of the retransitions that follow each episode and the miniaturism of the returning theme's syntax. Each retransition is made up of a rhythmic module that seems to repeat itself endlessly, building up a momentum that makes the return of the theme sound somewhat incongruous: there is an abrupt gear-change back to the courtesies of periodic syntax.

The first retransition (bars 38–52; Example 4.4b) is extravagantly long. There was an increasing predilection for such effects, of course – we associate them above all with Haydn – but this one is different. It features the increasing fragmentation of a repeated melodic unit, fading away dynamically, but at an exceptionally high tessitura, and the left hand's $b\flat^2$ runs into the right hand's $b\natural^2$ at 44–47 to complicate the aural picture. Further, just when the passage has reached its most fragmented it starts to build up again, first rhythmically and then dynamically. The norm is for such liquidation of material to continue to vanishing point. In addition, the beginning of the build-up (bars 48–49) uses the device of anticipating an element of the rondo theme, but Kraus again deforms the implied model – what is anticipated here is not the initial element of the rondo theme so much as the dotted-rhythmic repeated note found in bar 3. Altogether the tone is ambiguous here:

---

[145] Some of the ensuing material derives from my review of *Joseph Martin Kraus: Keyboard Music*, ed. van Boer, 162.

Example 4.4a Kraus, Rondo in F major, VB191, bars 1–20

Example 4.4b Kraus, Rondo in F major, VB191, bars 37–54

the passage could be heard as humorously disproportionate, but this is not signalled, and it could readily be played as inspired, 'improvisatory' and entirely 'serious'.

The second retransition (bars 117–126; Example 4.4c) features a large-scale rising sequence built on a stepwise ascent in the bass. Even more here, the

Example 4.4c Kraus, Rondo in F major, VB191, bars 118–128

Example 4.4d Kraus, Rondo in F major, VB191, bars 173–191

surging momentum of the section collides awkwardly with the returning theme, though the theme then alternates louder and softer phrase units, and straight and more expansive versions of the earlier material, as if now less sure of its role. The dynamics oscillate from *mf* to *p* to *f* to *p* over the course of bars 127–133. The third retransition (bars 173–187; Example 4.4d) rhythmically augments material that had been heard in the middle of the previous episode (at bars 158–164), creating in the comparison a magical slow-motion effect. As if recognizing the difficulty of wedding this to the returning theme, Kraus lets the figuration slow down and disappear into silence, and then introduces entirely new material, a quickly repeated note followed by a rising chromatic scale in the right hand (182–183); this is then doubled upon repetition in the left hand, as the dynamics rise from *pianissimo* to *forte*. Sounding nothing so much as Lisztian, these figures seem quite out of place, as if the performer-composer is at a loss as to how to return to the theme. A longer silence then ensues. All this means that when the theme does then re-enter, in bar 188, it sounds more incongruous than ever. Thus while the retransitions contain their own oddities, the primary wrench comes when these sections abut upon the rondo refrain. Yet nothing is 'said' about this fundamental incongruity; the theme simply returns and goes about its business in seeming ignorance of the intervening material. 'Don't ask, don't tell' would seem to be the operative phrase. Is the theme to be heard as limited in its range (expressive as well as textural) next to the expansive retransitions, or are the retransitions pretentiously over-composed compared to the simple beauty of the theme? Neither need be the case. Once more, it is left to the listener to judge. This is Rosen's 'generosity' of perspective, and it should have become clear by now that it is by no means confined to music by Haydn.

If we can absorb this lesson, it helps to explain the decidedly anti-scholastic, anti-authoritarian orientation of our instrumental style. At the end of Chapter 2 we found Haydn's biographer Dies noting that his subject, like Mozart before him, had been 'taken to be an empiricist'. Dies is evidently uneasy with the description, but it fits very well in the current context. The implicit exhortation that arises from our case studies above, when the musical tone of voice remains uncertain, is something like 'Listen and decide for yourselves'. This anti-scholastic bent was a matter of compositional word as well as deed. Haydn made a point in London of saying that had managed to please all constituencies of listener 'apart from the professors'.[146] He might have been referring not just to his critics of old, but indeed to the 'ancients' who were quite a force in the land he was visiting. Burney no doubt had them in mind when he penned his ode to welcome Haydn to London: 'No treatise, code, or theory of sound, / Whose narrow limits, fixt by pedants

---

[146] Haydn, letter to Maria von Genzinger, 17 October 1791; *The Collected Correspondence and London Notebooks of Joseph Haydn*, ed. and trans. H. C. Robbins Landon (London: Barrie and Rockliff, 1959), 120, cited in translation in Schroeder, *Enlightenment*, 93. Schroeder notes, though, that 'professors' may denote not so much the grizzled academics that we might call to mind, but more broadly those who were involved in London's Professional Concerts.

vain, / Thy bold creative genius can restrain'.[147] Around the same time, in 1791, Pierre-Louis Ginguené was referring to the 'infinite art' of Tartini, 'without the air of slavery and pedanticism that even Corelli, more occupied with counterpoint than with melody, did not always avoid'.[148] When Türk included a cancrizans minuet (*minuetto riverso*) in the *Klavierschule* that he published in 1789, he felt that he had to excuse himself for his learning, writing 'Nowadays one wastes less time and effort on such tricks than formerly …, and I think rightly so; since they are for the most part more for the eye than for the feelings'.[149]

'More for the eye' reminds us that learning and pedantry were often associated with the practice of strict counterpoint. At its most severe, this meant the *stile antico* that, as William Weber has established, was the nearest thing the music profession had to a venerable, institutionalized kind of learning, 'intended to create a learned musical elite'.[150] To its proponents, its 'timelessness' was precisely one of its greatest merits. As Friedrich Wilhelm Marpurg wrote in his *Abhandlung der Fuge* of 1753–1754, 'An advantage of counterpoint is that it is not based on the changeable style of the day and its wretched traits, which creates a dubious taste … all nations agree that counterpoint is truth in music.'[151] Counterpoint could stand above mere fashion, absolving composers of the need to cater slavishly to their audiences. However, what represented dignity and independence of spirit to Marpurg was 'slavery' in turn to Ginguené, and a cluster of similar terms was used to dismiss the various forms of strict counterpoint and thereby emphasize the modern credentials of the writer. For Burney, 'Canon and Fugue' were by-words for 'restraint and labour',[152] and he praised Vinci for disentangling the voice part from 'fugue, complication, and laboured contrivance'.[153]

However, it was by no means simply learning or counterpoint as such against which so many writers routinely fulminated – it was the perceived wider attitude of laying down the law, of not listening to listeners, as it were. Johann Adolph Scheibe, that famous critic of J. S. Bach, transferred this to an

---

[147] [Charles Burney,] 'Verses on the Arrival of Haydn in England', cited in Mathew, *Political Beethoven*, 54.

[148] Pierre-Louis Ginguené, *Encyclopédie méthodique*, two volumes, volume 1 (Paris, 1791), 'Concerto', 300, cited in translation in Heartz, *Music in European Capitals*, 230.

[149] Türk, *Klavierschule*, 408, cited in translation in Mikusi, 'More than a Copy', 22.

[150] Weber, 'Contemporaneity of Eighteenth-Century Musical Taste', 189.

[151] Friedrich Wilhelm Marpurg, *Abhandlung der Fuge*, two volumes (Berlin: A. Haude and J. C. Spener, 1753–1754), volume 2, 30–31, cited in translation in David Yearsley, *Bach and the Meanings of Counterpoint* (Cambridge: Cambridge University Press, 2002), 228.

[152] Burney, *General History of Music, Volume the Second*, 96.

[153] Burney, *General History of Music, Volume the Second*, 917.

imagined social situation when he wrote that 'a composer usually sinks into the bombastic manner when he gives all parts the same amount to do and when they constantly squabble with one another'. This is a doubly unattractive image: the parts 'squabble' amongst themselves and so fail to observe any social niceties, while the composer who sets up this drawing-room nightmare is himself 'bombastic', and so, as noted in Chapter 1, only interested in listening to the sound of his own voice(s).[154] This widens the sphere of censure to include anything that can be said to be heavy-handed or self-absorbed, as in the case of the London critic who found the music of the 'Prussian school' excessive in its 'gravity, self-importance [and] pedantry'.[155] In Vienna, the Empress Maria Theresa wrote that Hasse 'was the first one who made music more delightful and less heavy', a neat encapsulation of a galant ethos.[156] At the outset of this study we cited Matthew Riley on the vein of 'polite criticism' that characterized eighteenth-century letters. As he subsequently explains, 'Critics tried to meet their readers on common ground and scrupulously avoided the technical jargon and formal manner of "the schools", along with all forms of "pedantry" and any hint of "magisterial" tone.'[157] Talking down to the reader was impolite, and we need to bear in mind that this is more than a matter of etiquette; it encompasses a whole attitude to one's fellow creatures. And anti-academicism was more than a mantra; it had some practical consequences. The authority and prestige of universities suffered an eclipse during the eighteenth century,[158] and even

---

[154] Scheibe, *Der critische Musikus*, 132, cited in translation in Kirkendale, *Fugue and Fugato*, 23. Elisabeth Le Guin captures something of this in the simulated conversation that makes up her chapter 'A Visit to the Salon de Parnasse' in *Haydn and the Performance of Rhetoric*, ed. Beghin and Goldberg. Channelling the *salonnière* Suzanne Necker, she writes 'in the salon . . . we are more likely to feel indifference toward a very ingenious work; our taste will be for a simple but useful reading. . . . In the one, the author speaks to me of myself, and in the other he speaks to me only of himself' (18). Keith Chapin outlines the aesthetic lineage of Scheibe's perspective in 'Scheibe's Mistake: Sublime Simplicity and the Criteria of Classicism', *Eighteenth-Century Music* 5/2 (2008), 165–177, noting how Scheibe departs from his French models and how he misapplies strictures against complexity ('Scheibe's mistake').

[155] Anonymous, *The European Magazine* 9 (1786), 321, cited in McVeigh, *Concert Life in London*, 127. McVeigh tells us that this critic approved only of the music of Graun.

[156] Maria Theresa, letter to Maria Beatrice d'Este, 17 August 1771, in *Briefe der Kaiserin Maria Theresia an ihre Kinder und Freunde*, ed. Alfred Arneth, four volumes (Vienna, 1881), volume 3, 119, cited in translation in Heartz, *Haydn, Mozart and the Viennese School*, 135–136.

[157] Riley, 'Sonata Principles', 596.

[158] This was brought home to me during my time at St Catharine's College Cambridge. As was intoned on 25 November of every year, the day on which the college holds its Commemoration of the Founder and Benefactors, 'During the eighteenth century there was little regard for the universities, and so benefactions largely ceased.' Lawrence Klein, *Shaftesbury and the Culture of Politeness*, writes of 'the decline in prestige of the English universities in this period and their abandonment by the English elite' (10). T. C. W. Blanning, *Culture of Power*, writes, 'In the

where one would most expect a laying-down of the law, in the church, the 'magisterial' could be muted. In the case of Catholic church music in Austria, for instance, Jen-yen Chen notes that 'spiritual mystery and clerical authority' were replaced late in the century by 'a pragmatic morality directed towards the public good'.[159] And of course the church was home base for the *stile antico*, yet this did not preclude the adoption of 'more delightful and less heavy' accents, with some well-known consequences for reception in the case of say Haydn's masses. Chen writes of how a judgmental attitude to the 'graceful expression of popular religious sentiment' has 'plagued' this area.[160]

If it was not so much learning as such that was the object of this sustained attack, as the way in which it was expressed, the sources of that knowledge were also critical. Hume in 1742 divided the world into 'learned' and 'conversible', writing that in the previous generation philosophy had been cultivated by 'Men without any Taste of Life or Manners', which once more evokes the image of the man locked away in his cell or ivory tower. The 'conversible' orientation could lead to a better understanding of mankind, since it was based on 'common Life and Conversation'.[161] Adam Ferguson echoed this when writing that 'learning may arise from the bustle of an active life. Society itself is the school, and its lessons are delivered in the practice of real affairs.'[162] This approximates to what we would now call the university of life. Germaine de Staël turned the terms of reference around when she described the French as paradoxically possessing 'une ... grande pédanterie de frivolité'.[163] In other words, to express oneself in an acceptably light manner was a weighty matter. It required study, but the hard work had to be invisible.

German-speaking lands in the eighteenth century, there was a significant move from using the words *die Gelehrten* (the learned) to *die Gebildeten* (the educated or cultivated). ... a move from regarding professional academics ... as the epitome of intellectual achievement to preferring the autodidact' (207) – in other words, a preference for informal self-education over formal institutionalized education. Compare, however, the view of David Blackbourn that the German Enlightenment 'developed within established institutions – universities, academies of science, churches', whereas 'The French Enlightenment owed nothing to the University of Paris' and 'the English Enlightenment (if there was one) certainly owed nothing to Oxford'. Blackbourn, 'The German Eighteenth Century: Marking Time', in *The Century of Bach and Mozart*, ed. Gallagher and Kelly, 11–12.

[159] Jen-yen Chen, 'Catholic Sacred Music in Austria', in *The Cambridge History of Eighteenth-Century Music*, ed. Keefe, 106.
[160] Chen, 'Catholic Sacred Music in Austria', 87–88.
[161] David Hume, 'Of Essay-Writing', in *Essays Moral, Political, and Literary*, ed. Miller, 289, cited in Elena Russo, 'Editor's Preface' to 'Exploring the Conversible World: Text and Sociability from the Classical Age to the Enlightenment', *Yale French Studies* 92 (1997), 1. The essay originally appeared in Hume, *Essays, Moral and Political*, volume 2 (Edinburgh: A. Kincaid, 1742).
[162] Ferguson, *Essay on the History of Civil Society*, 295.   [163] de Staël, *De l'Allemagne*, 59.

This empirical orientation meant that systems of any kind were objects of suspicion. It was virtually implicit that heavy-handed learning entailed being locked into a particular viewpoint and therefore unable to respond to the human realities of an everyday environment. Knigge, who warned against the effects of 'stiff seriousness' and a 'shew of stateliness',[164] made the point by means of another kind of reversal. 'Tradesmen', he wrote, 'may be less given to prejudices than those of superior rank who have perverted their sound reason by study and a slavish devotion to systems' ('die durch Studieren und Systemgeist ihre gesunde Vernunft verschroben haben').[165] It was, in other words, easier to trust the judgment of the relatively uneducated than of those who, once more, were in a state of 'slavery' to their views. Calls on the basis of this rhetoric to trust the evidence of one's ears were therefore a matter of routine, and not just in the musical world. In his *Course of Lectures on Elocution* (1762) Thomas Sheridan asserted that where accentuation within a word is uncertain, 'the ear beyond all doubt ought to be consulted, as to that which forms the most agreeable sound, rather than an absurd, pedantic rule, attempted to be laid down'.[166] Haydn for one had made similar pronouncements in response to complaints about the correctness of his writing;[167] apart from anything else, these terms of engagement offered him a ready means to escape censure.

A flexible pragmatism was often evident in music-theoretical works too. The very title of Joseph Riepel's treatise of 1752–1768, *Anfangsgründe zur musicalischen Setzkunst: nicht zwar nach alt-mathematischer Einbildungs-Art der Zirkel-Harmonisten, sondern durchgehends mit sichtbaren Exempeln abgefasset*, explicitly dismisses mathematical speculation in favour of the hands-on and practical.[168] His is a theory that will always attend to the particular context rather than grand abstractions and rules. The very fact that the treatise is

---

[164] Knigge, *Über den Umgang mit Menschen; Philosophy of Social Life*, trans. Will, volume 2, 140.

[165] Knigge, *Über den Umgang mit Menschen*, volume 2, 138; *Philosophy of Social Life*, trans. Will, volume 2, 236.

[166] Thomas Sheridan, *A Course of Lectures on Elocution* (London: A. Millar and others, 1762), 56, cited in Amit Yahav, 'The Sense of Rhythm: Nationalism, Sympathy, and the English Elocutionists', *The Eighteenth Century* 52/2 (2011), 179.

[167] For example, in conversation with biographer Griesinger, Haydn stated that 'an anxious compliance with the rules often produces works that are the most lacking in taste and feeling ... and that in music the only thing absolutely forbidden is what offends a delicate ear'. Griesinger, *Biographische Notizen*, 16, cited in translation in Sisman, 'Haydn, Shakespeare, and the Rules of Originality', 7.

[168] See Stefan Eckert, '*Einschnitt, Absatz,* and *Cadenz* – The Description of Galant Syntax in Joseph Riepel's *Anfangsgründe zur musicalischen Setzkunst*', *Theoria* 14 (2007), 116: Riepel 'rejects any speculative mathematics in the form of ratios and proportions since they prove useless for composition'.

couched in dialogue form, especially of the relatively informal kind that Riepel employs, is also significant in this regard. The magical word that arose out of such a pragmatic orientation was, as we have seen, taste. Avison was another theoretician who disavowed heavy theory when he asserted that 'Example is of much greater Force than any Rule or Precept whatever'. He continued by suggesting that 'the Energy and Grace of *Musical Expression* is of too delicate a Nature to be fixed by Words: it is a Matter of Taste, rather than of Reasoning'.[169] Once again music functions as a kind of ideal proving-ground for one of the bywords of the era. Given its lack of concrete reference relative to most other arts, music – in particular instrumental music – could provide a perfect embodiment of sensuous experience untarnished by 'systematic' thought. It demanded in the first instance an unmediated reaction, and an attention to particularities. That it could not readily be 'fixed by Words' was all to the good. Further, the very notion of taste implies an awareness of difference, of alternatives, and it implies that negotiation and discussion will be involved – which might take place within the individual as well as interpersonally. And so the exercise of taste might seem particularly called for in the case of a style that is full of quick contrasts, as if presenting constant challenges to the listener's powers of discernment and judgment. And even then, that taste might be pragmatically variable. Quantz, for instance, offers highly relativistic views on the question of how one judges a piece of music; for him it depends on the time of day at which one plays or listens, differences in temperament, changes in one's mood from day to day, the venue, the quality of performance and so forth.[170] There are no absolutes any more – taste and circumstance determine everything.

We have already encountered works that address the matter of 'devotion to systems' in its specific musical sense, strict counterpoint. That generally means that the textural 'heaviness' will, sooner or later, be conspicuously undercut. There was the laboured canon in the first movement of Kraus's Quartet in B flat major, Op. 1 No. 2, which seems to embody Quantz's dismissal of 'laborious industry', or the contrapuntal furore in the development of the first movement of Haydn's Symphony No. 93, stirring enough in its own right but then suddenly dissolving into more colloquial accents. To these we might add the first movement of Krommer's Flute Quintet in C major, Op. 58 (1807),[171] which begins with a fugal exposition for the four stringed instruments (violin, two violas and cello). But almost as soon as the flute in turn enters with the

---

[169] Avison, *Essay on Musical Expression*, ed. Dubois, 32.
[170] See Quantz, *Versuch einer Anweisung die Flöte traversiere zu spielen*, 279–280; *On Playing the Flute*, trans. Reilly, 298.
[171] This was republished as an oboe quintet in 1812.

subject, the topic changes to something stylistically much lighter. There is a sudden profusion of repeated turn figures that sound almost like 'laughing music'. Thus are the 'learned' and 'conversible' brought into contact – and that is not the end of the stricter idiom, which returns several times later in the movement.

Naturally, composers were hardly going to do without such a significant textural resource as strict counterpoint, even in secular instrumental music, and we need to remember that it did not have to be learning as such that occasioned disapproval; it was how that learning was expressed that mattered most. If strict counterpoint wore its learning lightly and took care to attend to 'feelings', as Türk required, then honour could be satisfied. In practical terms, this meant that strict style was generally episodic rather than constituting a complete movement. The widespread genre of the canonic minuet would be one of several obvious exceptions, but use of the minuet form meant that any such movements would automatically have a relatively restricted length. And these movements tended to express a very clear character rather than being merely 'music for the eye', whereby the counterpoint is sufficient in itself, as it were. Well-known examples would include the canonic minuets of Haydn's Symphony No. 44 in E minor (c1771), Mozart's Serenade in C minor, K388 (1782), and Haydn's Quartet in D minor Op. 76 No. 2 (1797), the last of these with pronounced gothic accents that have earnt it the name of 'Witches' Minuet'. While all of these are in minor keys, Mozart's movement switches to major for further contrapuntal display, a 'Trio in canone al roverscio'. On the other hand, the third movement of Clementi's Sonata in G major Op. 40 No. 1 (1802) features a jaunty canon in major followed by a minor-mode canon 'per moto contrario' for the trio, marked 'dolce' on five separate occasions within its fifty-odd bars. This suggests some anxiety on the part of the composer – who was greatly given to the device of canon[172] – that the strict procedure be rendered 'expressively'.

There are also larger-scale instrumental movements that are more or less strictly contrapuntal throughout, almost always finales.[173] Celebrated examples

---

[172] For a sensitive account of this Clementian trait see Rohan Stewart-MacDonald, 'Canonic Passages in the Later Piano Sonatas of Muzio Clementi: Their Structural and Expressive Roles', *Ad Parnassum* 1/1 (2003), 51–107.

[173] To start with a fugue is almost unknown before the famous example of Beethoven's Quartet in C sharp minor, Op. 131 (1826). One precursor, though, is the first movement of Kraus's String Quartet in G minor, Op. 1 No. 3, of 1784. A double fugue unfolds from bar 5, which eventually devolves into freer counterpoint. The strict style seems to exhaust itself and the players come to rest on a pause at bar 43. After a silence, a *fortissimo* unison D♭ creates an electrifying effect. It is followed by *pianissimo* sigh figures, before a *stringendo il tempo* marking leads to a resumption of the double fugue.

include the three fugal finales that feature in Haydn's Op. 20 quartets (1772), but these are all marked to be performed 'sempre sotto voce', which not only lends a special character to the multi-subject textural intricacies of each movement, but also patently avoids any suspicion of what Scheibe called 'bombast'. Less well known are the many fugal finales that brother Michael Haydn wrote to his symphonies. The final movement of his Symphony in D major ST287 (before 1781), marked Fugato. Presto ma non troppo, is one such instance. Very long and brilliant, it mixes its fugal writing with a modern, comic, homophonic style in a way that Mozart is celebrated for having done in the finale of his quartet K387 (1782). Indeed, the similarities go further than that. The movement is built on a traditional long-note subject similar to that used by Mozart in his quartet. Near the end, after a dramatic pause that ensues following a V7 harmony, the long-note subject is presented harmonized and *pianissimo*, which is just what Mozart does right near the end of his finale. On both occasions this procedure has a wry effect: what had generated so much contrapuntal animation is 'cut down to size', via a simple, understated presentation in chorale style.

Such a mixture of strict and free elements characterizes many finales in particular, though the textural balance tips away from lengthy passages in strict style. An unusual instance is the finale of Hummel's Quartet in G major, Op. 30 No. 2 (1804), which twice quotes material from No. 10, 'Fugetta', from J. S. Bach's *Goldberg Variations*.[174] But these are incorporated in such a way that they barely intrude upon the humorous exuberance of the whole. As we saw in Chapter 2, counterpoint and comedy become constant companions in the later eighteenth century, which more or less guarantees that charges of pedantry cannot be laid. The polyphonic texture can range from a proper fugato (in the finale of Beethoven's Piano Concerto No. 3 in C minor of 1800) to something more allusive: the finale of Mozart's Piano Concerto in E flat major K449 (1784) plays with a series of contrapuntist's tricks and 'untimely' devices without ever being too open about its stylistic sources. The preference for comic counterpoint was noted by Koch, who observed, not without regret, that 'the strict fugue is too austere nourishment for the fashionable taste of our time, which likes fugal composition and double counterpoint in an instrumental work only when it is combined with comic ornaments in one and the same movement to provoke laughter'.[175]

---

[174] For commentary on this and other Hummel borrowings see Rohan Stewart-MacDonald, 'The Undiscovered Flight Paths of the "Musical Bee": New Light on Hummel's Musical Quotations', *Eighteenth-Century Music* 3/1 (2006), 7–34.

[175] Koch, *Versuch einer Anleitung zur Komposition*, volume 3, 301; *Introductory Essay on Composition*, trans. Baker, 197.

The ways in which instrumental music of the time engages with heaviness and authority in a wider behavioural sense, rather than in the narrower textural sense discussed above, barely need to be addressed again here. Devices that I have identified and named such as the gracious riposte and simplifying cadence are built on a spirit of concession, deflating or toning down any statement or affect that could be perceived as too absolute in its claims. Those two devices may be aligned with the broader functional categories of beginning and ending, which are both naturally sensitive locations from a sociable point of view. Allanbrook notes how one of Haydn's most assertive opening gestures, the thick loud chords that open his Sonata H52 in E flat major (1794), is immediately toned down: a 'prim echo' of the opening gesture in bar 3 is followed by an 'echo of the cadence of the echo', which is immediately repeated, a 'quiet repetition [that] obliterates one's memory of previous splendor'.[176] Grandeur is similarly undercut in the first movement of Haydn's Symphony No. 92 ('Oxford'; 1789): Riley notes how it 'continually sets up grand entrances' that stand 'in ironic contrast to the relative insignificance of what actually "enters"'.[177] William Caplin meanwhile discerns a more widespread ambivalence about the ways in which sonata-form movements make their first moves: 'Many main themes exhibit a certain hesitancy or uncertainty . . ., often bringing sudden, striking changes in texture and marked discontinuities in rhythmic momentum. In fact, it often is not until the beginning of the transition that the movement seems finally to "get under way".'[178]

It might seem harder to hesitate when it comes to the opposite formal juncture, since endings do need do carry a certain authority if they are to do their job at all. Yet we have seen how widespread equivocations are, to the point of some endings more or less failing in their rhetorical duty. More common, though, is for the grand affirmative close to be undermined just enough to remind the listener of the constructed, contingent nature of even the most basic discursive habits, before that close is then realized. A simple example occurs near the end of the finale of Haydn's Symphony No. 94 ('Surprise'; 1791). With the wind-up to the finish all but completed, and rapturous applause surely only seconds away, the wind band alone performs a V–I progression, a puny sound after the sustained noise we have been hearing from the full orchestra. That timbrally undernourished V–I progression is immediately corrected by a tutti version of the same, and the work is over.

---

[176] Allanbrook, 'Theorizing the Comic Surface', 205.
[177] Matthew Riley, 'Hermeneutics and the New *Formenlehre*: An Interpretation of Haydn's "Oxford" Symphony, First Movement', *Eighteenth-Century* Music 7/2 (2010), 203.
[178] Caplin, *Classical Form*, 197.

In considering certain strands of affective sociability above, I have touched on forms of what we might call the comic mode, which encompasses phenomena variously styled as humour, comedy, wit and irony (whether hard or soft). In varying degrees of directness, these phenomena interfere with any literal, straightforward reception of a musical discourse. To this point, though, they have not played a particularly prominent role; I have preferred to concentrate on those aspects that have been less well acknowledged and less widely understood. The comic mode, on the other hand, has been frequently addressed in the literature, even if its more ambivalent, indirect aspects have largely drawn a critical blank. But it is worth dwelling on the comic mode at this point, as a counterweight to the roles played by inhibition and qualification in the discursive patterns of sociable music. However, this will be no simple celebration of the 'liberating' qualities of comedy, overturning the stuffed-shirt formalities of polite society behaviour. Not only does politeness, as explored earlier, liberate as much as it constrains, but the comic mode itself arises out of constraint. Inhibition creates the conditions for comedy. The inhibiting forces of custom and habit, the gap between how one feels and how one acts – in musical terms, anything that represents an 'accepted way to do things' – set themselves up for comic deconstruction. That said, we must remember that music cannot conduct a real conversation, is not a straightforward equivalent of real-life social behaviour; it plays by different rules. We noted in Chapter 2 how music in many respects parts company with the behavioural ideals suggested by the conduct manuals of the time, with their prohibitions against puns, interruptions and excessive cleverness.[179] We find many forms of musical 'rudeness' that only make the sense of social interaction more vivid; cleverness, often taken to extremes, is a basic attribute of our instrumental style; and double meanings are found everywhere, often at the expense of immediate clarity. (Of course these could be taken to be 'realistic' traits of real-life social behaviour too, against which the treatises compose their lists of proprieties.) And indeed, the physical immediacy of music gives its 'body language' an altogether different dimension to that which one would encounter in the drawing-room. When we combine this immediacy with various forms of the comic mode, we often find an exuberant – not to say irreverent and indecorous – side that does take us some way distant from the gentler aspects of musical sociability.

---

[179] Morellet, 'De la conversation', writes disapprovingly of puns and general word-play – '*pointes et calembourgs*' (200) – describing them as a pest – 'une peste de la conversation' (202).

There is a larger-scale reason why the comic mode should be dwelt on. One can hardly overemphasize the historical uniqueness of a strongly humour-based instrumental style; its prominence in our repertory represents an aberration in the history of Western music, just the most obvious reason why the law-giving implications of the term 'classical' are so inappropriate. Prominence may be too weak a word, though, given that comedy is more akin to a dominating mentality, an encompassing orientation. It is spurred on not just by various kinds of 'inhibition' but also by the variety that was such a desideratum for musical communication. Variety opens up the possibility of incongruous combination; it is, as Allanbrook notes, intrinsic to a comic orientation, as opposed to the unity associated with the tragic mode.[180] If musical variety is underpinned by an acknowledgment of difference, this was also implicit in the dynamic relation between the individual and the collective that we considered earlier, for instance when it comes to the concept of taste. W. H. Auden connected these two poles when he wrote that 'A sense of wit and humor develops in a society to the degree that its members are simultaneously conscious of being each a unique individual and of being all in common subjection to unalterable laws.'[181]

As we saw before, Michaelis granted Haydn the leading role in the development of a comic mode while also acknowledging how widespread the orientation was: 'our most recent music is largely humorous'. While it is important to note its collective aspects, this hardly means that there was some kind of identikit humour shared by all. That is not only implausible from the point of view of reception, given all the differences in cognitive capacities and stylistic expertise that existed, to say nothing of the workings of irony and tone detailed above; it is also not likely at the production end either. Kozeluch, for example, tends to offer pleasant humour and playfulness, but seems little interested in emphasizing incongruity. Kraus, on the other hand, relishes sharp juxtaposition, though the expressive register often remain oblique. Haydn's various manipulations of expected events often have an edgy, nervous quality that is rarely found in Mozart, who seems to prefer a more controlled style of delivery. The difficulties that one runs into when attempting such thumbnail descriptions reflect a wider truth. There aren't many memorable evocations of say Haydn's humour or

---

[180] Allanbrook, 'Mozart's Tunes', 176, notes the 'new emphasis on the variety of the comic surface', and cites Charles Rosen's affirmation that 'unity is a quality characteristic of the tragic'. Rosen, *The Classical Style*, 235, writes in a discussion of Mozart's Piano Concerto in D minor, K466, of 'the sustaining of a unified tone demanded by the tragic style'.

[181] W. H. Auden, 'Notes on the Comic', *Thought: Fordham University Quarterly* 27/1 (1952), 57.

wit, simply because it's harder to evoke with stirring prose, of the sort that flows so easily when the writer has the good fortune to be dealing with music of tragedy and misery. Stirring prose, in fact, would precisely miss the point, which is a core of self-deprecation or detachment, incompatible with a messianic style of delivery.

If comedy can be described as a dominating mentality or a governing orientation, this does not, of course, mean that everything we will hear is funny. As noted earlier, many writers seem to see humour as a localized phenomenon – a garment that the composer whips on and off – after which the music resumes its default mode of sincere intent. But humour (and its cognates irony, parody and the like) insinuates itself anywhere and everywhere; once its presence has been felt, nothing may be quite the same again. The development section of the first movement of Haydn's Symphony No. 96 in D major (1791) is something of a virtuoso exercise in using the same material to create different affects, as the manner swings from learned to pathetic to grand to popular; it is back in grand, not to say threatening, mode as the full orchestra settles on V of B minor from bar 123, with the brass belting out repeated-note tattoos and the flute holding a high, piercing pedal note. This could well signal the end of the middle section: V of vi was a common nodal point from which to return to the tonic for a recapitulation. After a long silence, the popular-sounding opening theme does return, but it is in the subdominant, G major – the wrong key.[182] Even if it were in the correct key of D major, the effect would not be so different, which is that, after a dramatic halt to proceedings, the 'big' is undercut by the 'small'. Such an effect is related to the gracious riposte, but here the appearance of the more modest material sounds humorously incongruous. There is nothing especially humorous in the material that returns – it is amiable and relatively light-hearted, but the incongruous continuation after the stormy preceding passage and the dramatic silence is enough to create the effect. The tragic or grand cannot endure such contrast and remain rhetorically in control, whereas humour can. It naturally thrives on contrast and pluralism, is at home with not being overtly in control at every moment, since once the seeds of doubt are sown, it has 'won'.[183]

---

[182] While controversy remains about the so-called false reprise, as noted in Chapter 2, that primarily concerns an 'early' return in the tonic key; in the current case there seems little doubt that this thematic return is supposed to sound less than definitive.

[183] Compare Allanbrook's remarks to this effect: 'The mixed mode of comedy undermines the elevated style, making it difficult to take the serious seriously.' (*Secular Commedia*, 19–22) and 'it is one thing for wit to remind the serious of its tendentiousness, another for seriousness to

Along similar lines, the development of the finale of Haydn's Symphony No. 98 in B flat major (1792) alternates insouciant passages for a solo violin, furnished with an oom-pah-pah accompaniment, with tempestuous tuttis. On one level this exemplifies the tolerance or relativism that underpins the mixed style; both types of expression have their place in the musical world, and listeners may witness the passing parade without needing to take sides. On the other hand, the lighter, indeed outrageously popular, material seems to be immune from the effects of the turbulence. It always pops up again fresh as a daisy, immediately rendering the tutti material heavy-handed by comparison; that material stands revealed as just so much bluster, not to be taken as seriously as it would like to be. The reappearance of an 'innocent' tune apparently unaffected by its surroundings recalls our earlier cases of ambivalence, where it seemed impossible to say whether a particular piece of material was to be taken 'seriously' or not. The current Haydn movements would be susceptible of similar interpretation, yet their sharper incongruities suggest a less uncertain outcome. The lighter side does seem to prevail, in an instance of what Jean Paul called Haydn's 'annihilating' humour. Comedy becomes a force for misrule – it pulls things apart, undoes 'systems' and tidy equations.

It is perhaps because of this spoiling tendency that so many writers, from that time to the present, have fenced off the comic mode, in all its shapes and sizes, from 'proper' discourse. It is not allowed the status of 'serious' art. Serious it indeed is not in tone of voice, but, as we saw in Chapter 1, that description all too readily elides with a judgment about artistic intent.[184] Even Burney, that great defender of Haydn, once wrote as much. Having noted that 'the first exclamation of an embarrassed performer and a bewildered hearer is, that the Music is very *odd*, or very *comical*', he then reassured readers that while Haydn has 'movements that are sportive, *folatres*, and even grotesque ... they are only the *entre-mets*, or rather *intermezzi*, between the serious business of his other movements'.[185] The operatic metaphor – a byword for the short, light and comic – suggests that we are to hear such music as light relief. But Burney, writing before the

---

reconstitute itself after it has been undermined by wit. It may be that the transaction is not reversible.' ('Two Threads through the Labyrinth', 144–145)

[184] From personal experience, I can vouch for the continuing force of the 'serious' when the two connotations collide, for example in James MacKay's (mild) attack on me and Paul Griffiths for suggesting that the finale of Haydn's quartet Op. 50 No. 6 is comic and therefore 'not serious'; MacKay believes that to say something is comic is to be negative about a piece or a composer's intentions. MacKay, '*Bariolage* and Formal Design: Haydn's "The Frog", Opus 50, No. 6, Finale', *Haydn-Studien* 10/1 (2010), 105.

[185] Burney, *General History of Music, Volume the Second*, 959–960.

composer's first visit to London, clearly felt he needed to stress Haydn's prevalent 'seriousness' to counter all the negative criticism about his composing hero.[186] It is for similar reasons that James Webster has made the point that 'humour' can be too easy (and indeed often too friendly) a category within which to place all that is unaccountable and odd in Haydn,[187] and the start of the Burney quotation above makes clear that oddity, eccentricity, even grotesquerie might have been the impressions of many early listeners.

Another problem in the reception of the comic mode is that its various named properties (humour, wit, irony), and the responses they evoke (including smiles and laughter), are often ring-fenced not just from 'proper' art, but also from 'proper' emotion. Mere comedy was routinely opposed to true feeling by those who were uneasy with the modern instrumental style. Koch, we have seen, wrote of the composers of such music that 'instead of using art to work on the heart, they try to occupy the minds of the listeners with wit'.[188] He was certainly right that wit makes one think. Much earlier, in 1726, Rameau had written à propos of the new Italian style that 'the comic genre almost never deals with the expression of feeling [le sentiment]'.[189] And precisely because of the all-encompassing capacity of comedy, its ability to undermine and relativize everything around it, opponents could feel that the whole musical world had gone comic, that 'nothing was sacred any more'. This could be coupled, as we saw in Chapter 3, with the image of a rapacious musical marketplace that would inevitably cater for the lowest common denominator, creating what John Hawkins lamented as a 'a corrupt taste in music'. Hawkins also opined: 'That music was intended merely to excite ... mirth, is a notion most illiberal, and worthy only of those vulgar hearers who adopt it.'[190] The

---

[186] For some background to this – a 'publicity war waged between [Haydn's] supporters and detractors' – see Alan Davison, 'The Face of a Musical Genius: Thomas Hardy's Portrait of Joseph Haydn', *Eighteenth-Century Music* 6/2 (2009), 209–227.

[187] This passage derives from my review of *Haydn & das Streichquartett*, ed. Feder and Reicher, in *Music & Letters* 86/3 (2005), 482, and is a paraphrase of a James Webster statement in the section 'Abschlußdiskussion', 190–191.

[188] Koch, *Versuch einer Anleitung zur Komposition*, volume 2, 40. For a further relevant account of this issue see Tilden A. Russell, '"Über das Komische in der Musik": The Schütze-Stein Controversy', *The Journal of Musicology* 4/1 (1985–1986), 70–90. Russell examines the debate of the 1820s and 1830s between Stephan Schütze, for whom music was all about feelings and did not allow for humour, and Gustav Adolph Keferstein, who believed instrumental music could be funny in its own right.

[189] Rameau, *Observations sur notre instinct pour la musique, et sur son principe* (Paris: Prault, Lambert and Duchesne, 1754), viii.

[190] Hawkins, *General History of the Science and Practice of Music*, volume 5, 432 and 431.

negative reception of comedy has often run along such lines, and not just in the field of music. There is also a long history of humour, and the laughter it may provoke, being seen not as a species of feeling but rather as something that stands outside any system of emotions or affects. There is in fact some justification for this. After all, in order for amusement to be felt or expressed, some sort of objectification is normally required on the part of the receiver, some recognition of an incongruity that draws one back from taking events literally. And as soon as one stands outside the system or discourse in this way, then the immediacy associated with 'feeling' or 'emotion' can be lost.

On the other hand, the comic mode, and the smiles and laughter that it often prompts, can generate a sense of happiness and well-being, not to say exhilaration, that are among the sensations that our repertory most regularly transmits. These surely count as feelings too, even if they do not always appear to be so highly prized within the fields of art criticism. An overt reaction like laughter need not be involved, especially in the case of the more indirect forms of wit and irony, but an inner smile is at least to be expected. In order to cover this eventuality, Wallace Chafe, in his study *The Importance of Not Being Earnest: The Feeling behind Laughter and Humor*, uses the term 'nonseriousness', which also has the utility that it gets us around all the various labels for humour that tend to collide so awkwardly in any analysis.[191] I have not adopted it above simply because it remains too loaded a term, certainly in the case of music criticism. Nevertheless, when one is in company, the understanding of just about any form of humour is likely to be signalled by demonstrative behaviour such as a laugh. Indeed, laughter surely represents the ultimate shared, social experience; it is not as a rule a solitary activity. One could argue that human communication is at its most direct and immediate in the case of humour – it can be a meeting of minds, a peak form of empathy, with any barriers of difference (temporarily) forgotten. And barriers of language will also matter for little in the case of instrumental genres. For Knigge laughter presupposes a certain openness of temper that was a key social attribute: 'Malice and cunning render us serious, pensive and close; but a man who can laugh heartily is not dangerous' ('Tücke und Bosheit machen zerstreuet, ernsthaft, nachdenkend, verschlossen, mais un homme, qui rit, ne sera jamais dangereux').[192] For Hugh Blair a happy tone was a sign of

---

[191] Wallace Chafe, *The Importance of Not Being Earnest: The Feeling behind Laughter and Humor* (Amsterdam and Philadelphia: John Benjamins, 2007), 8–9.
[192] Knigge, *Über den Umgang mit Menschen*, volume 2, 256; *Philosophy of Social Life*, trans. Will, volume 1, 138.

civilization: 'chearfulness is one of the many blessings which we owe to formed society. The solitary wild state is always a serious one.'[193]

However, this is the sunnier side of the equation. As we have seen, various forms of humour exist on a sliding scale, from outright jokes all the way up (or down) to 'soft irony', and individual reactions can also vary strongly: what one person finds hilarious is a non-event for another. Thus humour can be a strongly differentiating property: from a social perspective, it can exclude as well as include, it may pit individuals and groups against each other as well as bring them together. There is also the question of whether humour always involves a spirit of openness, or whether some of Knigge's 'malice' may not sometimes be mixed in as well – in other words, a less charitable 'laughing at' rather than 'laughing with' someone. Satirical, parodistic, sardonic and irreverent elements in fact exist aplenty within the repertoire of later eighteenth-century instrumental humour.[194] The subtly rude aspects of Haydn's comic mode were, I have already proposed, an important ingredient in his contemporary success, just as much as the more abrupt discourtesies. Howard Irving, exploring the common comparisons that were made at the time between Haydn and Sterne, compares the shocking drumstroke that intrudes on the pastoral calm of the slow movement of Symphony No. 94 (hence its nickname of 'Surprise') with the equally famous event in *Tristram Shandy* in which the eponymous character is accidentally circumcised by a falling window sash as he tries to urinate out of the bedroom window. For Irving, both passages are 'original, eccentric, irreverent' and, of particular relevance here, 'indelicate'.[195] Such indiscretions are common in Haydn, even if their critical fate has largely been to be domesticated into the harmlessly

---

[193] Hugh Blair, *A Critical Dissertation on the Poems of Ossian, the Son of Fingal* (London: T. Becket, 1763), 22.

[194] Richard Taruskin thinks he has spotted such an instance in the Trio of Haydn's quartet Op. 33 No. 2, whereby the composer is encouraging his upmarket devotees to laugh at the musical portrayal of rustic simpletons. See *The Oxford History of Western Music: Music in the Seventeenth and Eighteenth Centuries*, 550, wherein we are told that the composer's 'frequent evocations of peasant music were no class solidarity, ... but a bit of humorous rustic exoticism'. This is hardly convincing, in the first instance because the main analytical point used to support the argument – that the close of the first section of the Scherzo shows a rustic incapacity to modulate ('The tonal trajectory is askew. The first strain never leaves the tonic.' (548)) – is spurious. To close the (generally quite short) first section of a rounded-binary form of this kind in the tonic key is very common. The Trio is then said to reproduce this 'impoverished sequence of events' (548), which involves the same close of the first strain in the tonic and an exact return of this strain in the second half, both perfectly normal events. The author's point speaks more to a lingering element of Haydn reception than anything else, though there is little doubt that this movement is meant to amuse.

[195] Irving, 'Haydn and Laurence Sterne', 35.

humorous. One means of coping with any incomprehension or discomfort at the time – the sort of 'bewildered' reaction that Burney describes above – was to ascribe it to the personality of the composer, to the 'personal and original manner of Herr Hayden'.[196]

Another aspect that is often highlighted by the comic mode is sheer compositional cleverness. As with risk-taking indelicacy above, this might not seem especially compatible with the image of a warm-hearted humour. We considered such cleverness in association with the first movement of Clementi's Sonata in G major Op. 37 No. 2 of 1798, suggesting that the composer may come across as a master manipulator or raconteur. The finale of that same work exemplifies a similar heightening of creative agency, the sort of staging of authorship that led listeners to interpret musical events as a reflection of compositional personality. At the outset a series of six repeated notes alternates irregularly with the melodic parts in a kind of comic hocket. The repeated notes act as a sort of tic, and after a while their nervous energy is translated into a more intricate form, with the first and last pairs of repeated notes being decorated with lower neighbour notes, creating a palindrome (first heard at bars 149–151). This decorated form of what remains ostensibly an accompanimental figure then just about takes over the movement, becoming the sustained focus of various episodes and being worked intensively into thematic returns. As it juggles this figure with other shapes, the movement demonstrates a comic versatility of discourse in which textural and other hierarchies are constantly being upset, generating a sense of spontaneity, of brilliant thoughts being incorporated on the wing, realized in the real time of music. This kind of cleverness may alienate, just as various forms of humour will not appeal to all, but it may also entertain; such speed of thought can, after all, be a very desirable social attribute. With his bent for permutation of all kinds, Mozart, we have noted, is also greatly given to such brilliance. In a sort of double-counterpoint mentality writ large, he loves nothing more than to show how a set sequence of materials may be reallocated and work just as well in their new configuration. It is a form of showing-off, and this kind of exhibitionism is by no means confined to Mozart and Clementi.

[196] Anonymous, review of Haydn symphonies, in *Wöchentliche Nachrichten und Anmerkungen die Musik betreffend*, ed. Johann Adam Hiller, volume 4: *Musikalische Nachrichten und Anmerkungen auf das Jahr 1770* (Leipzig: Verlag der Zeitungs-Expedition, 1770), 37, cited in Wheelock, *Ingenious Jesting*, 40–41. Wheelock also comments how Haydn's 'personality became a matter of interest to those seeking to explain the humorous, playful, "teasing strain" in his music. The retrospective view offered by Georg August Griesinger in his *Biographische Notizen* (1810) indicates an easy reconciliation of the humor of the man with that of his music. In such a portrait one wonders if the style has become the man' (31).

A main reason why such showing-off is rarely noted as such is that it tends to go with a kind of physical exhilaration, a sense of sheer fun that is another important aspect of our comic instrumental mode. The oft-remarked playfulness of this music is not just a cognitive matter; it manifests itself physically. And as with humour in general, it can take many different inflections. Of Haydn's often nervous, hyperactive manner Giorgio Pestelli writes that it 'produce[d] for the first time a type of music that made one feel like moving and fidgeting'.[197] The sense of bodily exuberance, often comic, meant that listeners of the time could be inclined to understand instrumental music theatrically, as if what they were hearing was populated with moving figures.[198] But an impression of comic theatricality will also depend on how a composer times musical events, and Triest had something like this in mind when he stated that 'The quintessence of [Haydn's greatness] seems to me to lie in the exceptionally light treatment of rhythm, in which no one can compete with him'.[199] The way in which Haydn handles the conclusion of the minuet in his Quartet in B flat major Op. 55 No. 3 (1788) offers a neat example. The return of the opening twelve-bar section proceeds unremarkably until the very last minute, when a flattened submediant harmony at bars 32–34 helps turn what should have been the conclusion into a climax (see Example 4.5). An emphatically repeated dominant-seventh chord leads to a suspenseful silence. What we then hear invokes the opening motive, a bold rising arpeggio in dotted rhythm, but it is expressed with increasing hesitation, as the motive gradually loses its swagger. There are all told no fewer than five collective silences either side of and within the ensuing phrase,[200] and the original arpeggiated shape is gradually liquidated until by bar 40 the first violin is playing purely in stepwise intervals. There is a vivid sense of social discomfort as the structure of the music seems to be falling apart. Yet at the end of the phrase, a perfect cadence is reached, and there has been a full I6–ii6–V6/4–V5/3 preparation for it. But while everything has

---

[197] Pestelli, *Age of Mozart and Beethoven*, 122.

[198] See, for example, Sisman, 'Haydn, Shakespeare, and the Rules of Originality', who notes that Ferdinand Hiller's (negative) reaction to comic elements suggests that these inspire 'a mode of "theatrical listening" in which musical segments become agents of the drama by causing interruptions in tone' (22), and Le Guin, *Boccherini's Body*: 'Numerous eighteenth-century accounts of listening to instrumental music show us that the Perfect Listener's visualistic responses will tend to refer to the stage' (263).

[199] Triest, 'Bemerkungen über die Ausbildung der Tonkunst in Deutschland im achtzehnten Jahrhundert, *Allgemeine musikalische Zeitung* 3 (11 March 1801), column 407; 'Remarks on the Development of the Art of Music, trans. Gillespie, 373.

[200] For an analysis of the metrical and accentual play here see Mirka, *Metric Manipulations in Haydn and Mozart*, 109–110.

Example 4.5 Haydn, Quartet in B flat major Op. 55 No. 3/iii, bars 32^3–42^2

worked out well harmonically, from the point of view of rhythmic gesture matters are far from settled. The awkwardness is seemingly dissolved through the entry, in the final bar of the movement, of brand-new material that uses a triplet rhythm heard nowhere before. Together with an accompanying *forte* dynamic and firm chordal support, this gesture makes for a strong ending in its own right, but in the context of what has gone before it sounds like a rather desperate remedy. The following Trio then does little but reiterate this very triplet figure, as if to smooth over the sudden swerve in the discourse; or it may act more like a teasing reminder of the previous antics.

A much larger-scale manipulation of events is evident in Boccherini's String Quintet in E flat major Op. 10 No. 2/G266 (1771), which is remarkable for being played entirely with mutes until the finale. After an Amoroso first movement, an Allegro non tanto that might almost be a normal specimen of its type except for the continuation of the muted string timbre and a rather indolent minuet, marked to be played 'espressivo vibrato', the

Presto finale offers timbral relief when the mutes are finally removed. The more open timbre, which will sound particularly brilliant after what has gone before, is combined with high-octane physical comedy to create an upbeat resolution. The Presto seems to make light of or even dismiss the much more introverted manner that has prevailed up to that point. High spirits run riot.

The Minor Mode

Lurking in the shadows to this point is what might be perceived as the polar opposite to the high comedy found in Boccherini's finale – music in the minor mode. The various negative aspects to the reception of later eighteenth-century instrumental music are crystallized in the near-uniformly positive attitudes displayed towards works and movements in the minor. The particular praise that generally comes the way of such works is directed against the 'inexpressive' properties of the repertory as a whole. The minor mode is a refuge from convention, from a marketplace that demanded a creative chorus of 'accentuate the positive, eliminate the negative'. It enabled composers to give vent to personal feelings, to demonstrate their humanity. These views are encapsulated in the reception history of the 'Gloomy Mozart', as related in Chapter 1.

There certainly is something special about the use of the minor mode across the eighteenth century – it becomes increasingly rare. This applies less to the use of minor-mode material per se than to the setting of works as a whole in the minor. But even this is a very striking development: the change from relative statistical parity between minor and major at the beginning of the eighteenth century to the strong predominance of major towards its end. Ludwig Finscher describes the initial state of affairs as one of relative neutrality[201] – in other words, using a minor key was, so to speak, a matter of routine – whereas later on, minor becomes 'marked'. This much is implicit in Hatten's describing the major mode as 'typically unmarked in the Classical style',[202] meaning that the other term in the binary equation, minor mode, will have more perceptual salience. It is defined in part by being 'not major', whereas the major mode in itself has no such dependency relationship. If the major mode does become the

---

[201] Finscher, *Joseph Haydn und seine Zeit*, 189–190 ('die Entwicklung … vom gleichsam neutralen Moll der barocken Tradition').
[202] Hatten, *Interpreting Musical Gestures*, 25.

default expectation, we should not lose sight of the bigger stylistic picture – that, as Allanbrook remarks, the prevalence of major keys represents a 'striking new trope'[203] in comparison with baroque practice. However, baroque must not be taken to mean 'until the death of Bach', as is often enough maintained; Michael Talbot dates the 'change in the status of the minor mode' to Neapolitan innovations of the 1720s and their subsequent influence on much of musical Europe.[204] Certainly by 1776 the relative avoidance of minor could form part of Hawkins's attack on modern music: shortly before the withering glance at the predominance of 'mirth' cited above, Hawkins noted that composers 'uniformly' avoided 'the use of all the keys with the minor third, upon a pretence that they tend to excite melancholy ideas'.[205] For him, hilarity and the major mode were allies in the campaign to take over the musical world.

'Melancholy' takes us back to our familiar particularized definition of 'expression', in which sadness plays a major part. And thus in the subsequent reception of our style the minor mode – incontestably (though not exclusively) associated with such a state – becomes viewed as an outlet for the individual expression denied by the crushing conformity of major-mode optimism. (For Hawkins, though, 'melancholy' was probably more nearly connected to the gravity that he missed in contemporary instrumental music rather than to any imperative of self-expression.) To use the minor meant a kind of liberation, both stylistic and personal. The problem with these entrenched assumptions, though, is that they are simply not borne out in musical reality. Because it was 'marked' in opposition to the dominant major mode, the ways in which the minor mode was typically employed in fact involved a narrowing of options, quite the opposite of any liberation narrative. In terms of actual compositional practice – the sorts of figures and devices that were employed, the sorts of affects that were projected – minor was more, not less, convention-bound than major. Since composers were more likely to adopt similar approaches when writing in minor, it was arguably less revealing of individual creative agency.

Among the few writers that acknowledge this state of affairs are Hatten, for whom the 'unmarked' status of the major mode meant that it could encompass 'a much broader realm of meaning' than the minor,[206] and Floyd Grave, who notes the logical converse, a 'tendency to channel minor

---

[203] Allanbrook, 'Mozart's Tunes', 175. [204] Talbot, *Finale in Western Instrumental Music*, 73.
[205] Hawkins, *General History of the Science and Practice of Music*, volume 5, 430.
[206] Hatten, *Interpreting Musical Gestures*, 25.

discourse into increasingly narrow spaces'. Grave correlates this with contemporary views on the acoustical instability of minor harmony;[207] for example, the theorist Bernard Germain Lacépède, in his *La poétique de la musique* of 1785, found in the minor mode only a 'somewhat impaired consonance [un accord un peu altéré]' that would leave a listener dissatisfied.[208] In many respects Matthew Riley's study of the Viennese minor-key symphony of the 1760s to 1780s, which he proposes as a specific subgenre peculiar to that environment, also fits the bill. Riley is explicit about the many conventions that recur in the individual works written within this loose tradition – and in fact many of these are also found more widely in minor-mode works of that time. Yet he also plainly believes that these symphonies are more 'expressive' than their major-mode counterparts, and indeed that they are taking a stand against the diminished aesthetic circumstances of their era: the subgenre was 'a mode of resistance to the contemporary practices of compositional overproduction and distracted listening, in short, a decline in the quality of musical experience'.[209] Hawkins would certainly have approved of such sentiments.

Riley amplifies such commentary when writing subsequently that 'the celebration of the entertainment character of music and the aristocratic values that supported it tends to reduce late eighteenth-century music and theater to the image that the *ancien régime* itself wanted to promote: an unchanging world in which each social class had its place and shared conventions were manipulated and combined but not transformed or replaced'.[210] That this is being written against Allanbrookian views becomes clear when we then read that the 'confidence in the social equilibrium' supposedly expressed by this music is a mirage given the 'turbulent change' and 'clashing views' that characterized the era. But music did not have to fall into line; it 'could engage with reality, express the thoughts and feelings of the individual, and propose alternatives to the present settlement'.[211] By extension, this reaffirms the association of the major mode with complacency; writing in minor, on the

---

[207] Grave, 'Galant Style, Enlightenment, and the Paths from Minor to Major', 20–21. Grave also lists typical associations and affects of the minor mode at this time (9–10), some of which overlap with those I am proposing in the current section.

[208] Bernard Germain Lacépède, *La poétique de la musique*, two volumes (Paris: L'Imprimerie de Monsieur, 1785), volume 1, 189, cited in translation in Floyd Grave, 'Recuperation, Transformation and the Transcendence of Major over Minor in the Finale of Haydn's String Quartet Op. 76 No. 1', *Eighteenth-Century Music* 5/1 (2008), 27.

[209] Riley, *Viennese Minor-Key Symphony*, 31–32.

[210] Riley, *Viennese Minor-Key Symphony*, 35.

[211] Riley, *Viennese Minor-Key Symphony*, 35–36. Riley makes sure to hold Mozart above the fray, in time-honoured fashion, by stressing the 'difficulty' of his music: 'Mozart is notable for his frequent failure to communicate effectively with his audiences.' (35)

other hand, is not just a personal and stylistic outlet for 'real' expression, it is also a political act. All this offers a useful recent confirmation of views that are widely held but not often so plainly stated, and against which I have written the current study.

Among the characteristic expressive associations – conventions – of the minor mode as employed in the later eighteenth century is what Riley himself has so usefully dubbed the 'untimely'. This can range from recollections of baroque practice to the downright archaic. For example, Kozeluch's Piano Trio Op. 28 No. 3 in E minor (*c*1786; Example 4.6) starts with a motto-type theme played in octaves (though *piano*) that includes a 'pathotype' falling diminished seventh (from the C of bar 3 to the D♯ of bar 4) and a falling chromatic tetrachord (moving from the E of bar 3 to the B of bar 5).[212] The consequent phrase from bar 9, played *forte*, is counterpointed by a line in continuous quavers that sounds like a baroque walking bass. The phrase does not cadence in the tonic but veers off to the mediant, G major; however, this tonal twist only brings a transposed version of the same material (bar 14). This soon leads to rapid figuration in normal contemporary style, but within a few bars the walking-bass subject enters once more (bar 23), together with a falling suspension chain entwined with another chromatic falling tetrachord. Thus the initial older-style material refuses to give way entirely to a more modern manner.[213] Hoffmeister's Trio Op. 31 No. 6 in E minor for Two Flutes and Cello (no date), another 'modest' genre, features a first movement in which the transition to the second group begins with a canon, and this returns in the recapitulation, expanded to include chains of suspensions. We should also recall the predominance of the minor mode in the canonic minuets discussed above.

The untimely gestures could take very particular forms, as in the second movement of Pleyel's Quartet in A major Op. 1 No. 3 (1782–1783). This is a set of variations, with Variation 4 being the customary Minore. Both halves of the variation conclude with a more or less archaic cadential progression that had been common in the earlier eighteenth century: this proceeds from a flattened Neapolitan second directly to the leading note, so producing an awkward melodic interval of a diminished third (see bars 71 and 79). Such a feature reflects the acoustical 'difficulty' of the minor mode, the 'impaired consonance' that it represented. This results in a generally more complex sound image to works in minor, including the emphasis on

---

[212] The 'pathotype' formula was so dubbed by Warren Kirkendale in *Fugue and Fugato*, 91–92, and always involves 'awkward' intervals like the falling diminished seventh.

[213] Discussion of this Kozeluch movement derives from Sutcliffe, 'Topics in Chamber Music', 133.

Example 4.6 Kozeluch, Piano Trio in E minor Op. 28 No. 3/i, bars 1–28 (piano part only)

dissonant melodic intervals that Pleyel's progression represents as well as a particular emphasis on dissonant, chromatic harmony. Such a sonority is by no means confined to the later eighteenth century, but it is striking how saturated minor-mode works of the time often are by diminished-seventh, augmented-sixth and Neapolitan chords.

Perhaps partly to compensate for such greater aural difficulty, the older musical manners that we find in so many minor-mode works and movements of the time tend to feature a relatively lean helping of musical material. But this also derives from an older, more economical style of thematic invention. A sense of rigour and sparseness can obtain even when the primary material is not especially untimely, as in the first movement of Mozart's Violin Sonata in E minor, K304, though this does include a canonic treatment of the theme in the recapitulation. The final work of J. C. Bach's Op. 5 sonatas (1766), No. 6 in C minor, presents an enormous contrast to the galant ways of the previous five works. Instead of that familiar combination of pleasing modern variety and syntactical clarity, all three movements are highly continuous and concentrated. The initial Grave, which has echoes of a sarabande, features much heavier textures than anything so far encountered in the opus, and it goes out of its way to avoid pronounced periodic construction and gaps between phrases. This is followed, without a break ('Siegue subito') by a lengthy fugue, which by definition is not going to stray thematically, and then a gavotte-like Allegretto, stately and self-contained.

More pointedly older in pedigree is the Andante di molto introduction to Kraus's Symphony in C sharp minor (VB140; 1782), full of suspensions in the pathetic style, and finishing with a signature technique of the baroque slow movement: a Phrygian progression in which the bass proceeds down the scale degrees 8-7-6-5. One might argue that later eighteenth-century musical style was not readily suited to the evocation of solemn or weighty moods, not just because of a distaste for categorical expression, but also because the articulate phrase syntax tends to break up the necessary sense of concentration. In order to convey such attributes it was necessary to draw on an idiom – a set of topical traces – that connoted such authority, and that was especially likely when minor keys were in operation. Indeed, one could further suggest that the minor mode over this period never fully developed a new manner akin to what happened with major keys, which were a 'natural' home for variety and plurality. One can also feel the force of this equation in the case of many of C. P. E. Bach's slower movements. While often praised for their 'personal' intensity, they tend in fact to represent variations on a single expressive typology, that of the baroque lament. This means frequent recourse to an idiom laced with suspensions, appoggiaturas and various chromatic chords, often counterpointed against the steady movement of the bass, promoting an atmosphere of consistently heavy pathos.[214] Not that there is anything wrong with such an idiom, or indeed with its conventionality: conventions only become conventions because they communicate, because they (continue to) work in the ears of a listener. And the same applies to the various untimely means that we have considered above.

[214] For example, Richard Kramer writes of the slow movement of the Sonata in F major Wq55/5, from the first collection *für Kenner und Liebhaber* (1779), that 'Everywhere, the intensity of gesture is felt. ... No phrase can be attributed to the demands of an imposed convention.' Kramer, *Unfinished Music*, 81–83. There is no doubt about the intensity, but also surely little doubt that the outer parts of the movement in particular derive from the expressive convention of the baroque lament, imposed or otherwise.

But while minor-mode means were often of long stylistic acquaintance, the ends to which they were put could indeed be novel. One behavioural trait common to much later-century minor-mode music is an obsessiveness that does not fit especially well with notions of weighty venerability. This represents the harder end of the economy or rigour to which minor-mode works were commonly given. The obsessiveness will often involve the reiteration of a single motive or motto. This sometimes overlaps with what one finds in structural middles – transitions and development sections – where such reiteration is more of a stylistic norm. In Chapter 3 we noted a number of development sections that feature such over-insistence on one piece of material, repeated almost ad infinitum, and to these we could add the development sections of the outer movements of Dittersdorf's Symphony in G minor Grave g1 (c1768), which feature long modulatory passages expressed in exact sequence in all parts. But more distinctive is an obsessive treatment that is more widely spread over a complete movement. The D minor theme from the second movement of Mozart's Violin Sonata in F major K377 (1781) offers an example. It consists of almost nothing but repeated cells of a rising third or octave decorated by a turn, accompanied by an implacable bass line that moves almost entirely in even crotchets. Such steady bass rhythms, in their recollection of genres like the passacaglia, are clearly marked as older style in such a context. They also arguably embody a circular temporal dynamic, suggesting movement around a fixed point rather than movement forward. The finale of Mozart's Sonata in C minor, K457 (1784), features long chains of a syncopated sighing figure,[215] while the first movement and following minuet of Rosetti's Symphony in G minor, Murray A42 (1787), are dominated by obsessive references to a single motto figure, with consistently crowded orchestration, so that there is little fresh air either thematically or texturally.

In all such cases what I have styled as obsessive might also be thought of as getting stuck – inside a labyrinth of thought and feeling, in which alternatives to the present state of affairs do not readily come to mind.[216] This brings us close to the figure of the solitary individual and to the world

---

[215] Hatten writes that the 'fourth-species-derived sequential treatment of the conventional sigh figure' in the finale of Mozart's K457 'is expressively marked as obsessive': *Interpreting Musical Gestures*, 152.

[216] On the image of the labyrinth in association with melancholy see Elaine Sisman, 'Music and the Labyrinth of Melancholy: Traditions and Paradoxes in C. P. E. Bach and Beethoven', in *The Oxford Handbook of Music and Disability Studies*, ed. Blake Howe, Stephanie Jensen-Moulton, Neil Lerner and Joseph Straus (New York: Oxford University Press, 2015), 601–602.

of the 'passions', both of which we have considered earlier and both of which from a contemporary perspective could be thought to represent a lack of flexibility. Translated into musical terms, this means a lack of the ability to consider alternatives, a lack of reciprocal thinking. None of this should suggest that listeners of the time would have been expected to tut-tut their way through the aural embodiment of such obsession; the sense of urgency offered by such insistent reiteration could surely generate visceral excitement. At the same time a certain discomfort might have been felt, given that such insistence was not a natural outcome of a periodic style of musical syntax; we have seen in Chapter 1 how Adam Smith felt that periodic organization tended to constrain the more antisocial types of utterance.

In any case, 'obsession' may be too strong a term for the kind of monothematic impulse often expressed within the minor mode. This is particularly the case when the minor-key material occupies an internal section of a movement. Typical places would be a Minore within a theme-and-variations movement or a Trio within a minuet movement. Here the minor-mode manner may act as a straightforward contrast to the major-mode material that surrounds it. On such occasions we often hear a kind of mechanically propulsive, relatively undifferentiated kind of musical motion, as in the second and third movements of Haydn's Piano Trio in E major H34 (c1760). The first of these uses the *alla zoppa* technique characteristic of earlier Haydn in which one line drags 'lamely' behind the other, off the beat, but both lines are quite inflexible in their own right. A much later example would be the G minor Trio in Beethoven's Sonata in B flat major Op. 22 (1800), which gives us a continuous stream of semiquavers punctuated by off-beat chords, all the greatest possible contrast to the largely gracious Minuetto. In such instances it can seem as though the employment of minor in conjunction with this kind of monothematic writing only makes the eventual return to major all the more pleasurable. Lacépède wrote of such returns to major from minor in general that if the soul 'does take great pleasure in [the] contrived consonances' of the minor mode, 'this is only because it feels it will soon get back to pure, perfect and natural consonances, that the cause of its anxiety will soon be removed, that it has only been deprived of the things it loves in order to lay hold of them soon again, that in doing so it will find them more beautiful and touching still'.[217] This is more than theoretical wishful thinking; it

---

[217] Lacépède, *La poétique de la musique*, volume 1, 189, cited in translation in Grave, 'Recuperation, Transformation and the Transcendence of Major over Minor', 27–28.

describes quite nicely the sensation we might feel when such Minore sections are succeeded by the 'natural simplicity' of the major mode.

If obsession is one term under which we can file much that feels new about the use of the minor mode in later eighteenth-century instrumental music, a related behavioural trait is one of effort. This becomes most apparent when contrasts of mode come into play, and these are perhaps most striking in continuous forms rather than the sectional forms just considered. The effort and 'tightness' of the minor mode gives way to greater ease and variety in major. One might argue that such a contrast is just about built in, given the fact that the mediant major becomes more or less the default secondary key after a movement has started in minor. Historically, though, this is telling in its own right, given that the dominant minor was once the more common tonal destination. A characteristic example is the F minor slow movement of Pleyel's Quartet in C major Op. 1 No. 1 (1782–1783). The Adagio molto opens with a series of short-lived, pathos-ridden gestures, and the first real melodic fluency arrives only once A flat major has been secured, from bar 13: the first violin's cantilena is supported by the sort of regular accompaniment that creates a sense of natural flow to proceedings. It is as if we have moved from recitativo accompagnato to aria mode. The recapitulation of the opening material, from bar 26, quickly fragments into even shorter units, together with greater dynamic instability. The first violin's cantilena re-enters sooner than expected (bar 35), but almost immediately runs aground; it seems that the minor-mode environment in which it now finds itself hinders its eloquence. A second attempt from bar 45 is no more successful. Rather than progressing forward, the melody turns in on itself, so to speak. This blockage culminates in a sort of cadenza for the first violin from 50, though this is no melodic flight of fancy; instead we hear a laboured cross-string passage that lasts for two and a half bars at Adagio tempo before the first violin's companions come in to help create a dissonant dominant-minor-ninth chord. Ultimately, the expressive effect of this movement comes from the sense it conveys of a thwarted lyricism, from its sheer effortfulness. The fluency that seems 'natural' to the major mode becomes a sort of subject of compositional enquiry in the minor mode.

A telling change of detail in the first movement of Kozeluch's Sonata in D minor Op. 20 No. 3 (1786) would be susceptible of a similar interpretation. The close of the second group in the exposition, which had in fact opened in the mediant minor, is signalled by a filled-in High 6 Drop, confirming that the mediant major is the point of arrival (bars 49–50). This is the same formula that Beethoven plays with in the Minuet of his sonata Op. 2 No. 1, shown in Example 3.8. At the equivalent point in Kozeluch's recapitulation, where we are bearing down on a close in D minor, this familiar formula is set aside. Instead, we hear something that is less obviously a shared device, mixing sigh figures into a line that keeps the earnest lyricism going (bars 137–139). What was an 'easy' compositional solution in the more affirmative major mode is replaced by something less clear-cut.

On many occasions, of course, the minor mode does not survive through to the end of a movement but gives way to major. Such a course of events has caused much anguish amongst commentators, especially on Mozart, and especially when the close in major does not seem to have been achieved after great effort; it survives as a perceived compositional-aesthetic problem through to the apparently trivial conclusion to Beethoven's 'Serioso' Quartet in F minor, Op. 95.[218] The slow movement of Krommer's Oboe Concerto No. 2, Op. 52 (1805), moves from C minor to C major at its end, but has an immaculate model for doing so. It bears many traces of a composer who has heard Haydn's 'Representation of Chaos', one of Western music's most definitive progressions from minor to major. Not only does Krommer use the same key, but the soloist's opening melody, together with its harmonic support, recalls the oboe and clarinet lines that are heard shortly before the entry of the voices in Haydn's movement (see bars 51–54). Krommer's Adagio is just as oblique harmonically: after the oboe's initial lament we move to E flat major, thence to E flat minor and B flat minor. This takes us to the remote region of G flat major, which winds its way back to C minor, but no sort of thematic return eventuates, and thus the sense of obscurity remains. When a proper cadence on C finally arrives, the mode changes to major, and a new openness of sonority is heard, with the 'clear pure air' of horns being prominent. This exemplifies another conceptual pair that may be associated with major and minor modes respectively – open versus closed.

One can also understand such conceptual oppositions in topical terms. The second movement of Boccherini's Quintet in A major Op. 10 No. 1/G265 (1771), an A minor Largo in 6/8, begins with the common minor-mode topic of siciliano. A falling chromatic tetrachord in the bass and fragmentary melodic writing both give this siciliano the flavour of a lament. But when the music moves to major in bar 9, there is a topical modulation to musette, with a long octave pedal held by the second cello and a greater degree of melodic continuity. A further change is that melodic lines, previously carried by a single

---

[218] For a recent discussion of this movement in these terms see Bonds, 'Irony and Incomprehensibility'.

instrument, are now carried by two instruments at a time in parallel intervals; together with the pedal note this forms the standard textural signifier of the pastoral. To put the change in extra-topical terms, we might say that the major mode replaces tightness with lyrical plenitude, and solitariness with companionship. In the recapitulation, which stays in minor, this pastoral section is simply omitted. Here the two modes inspire not just different topics but also different types of phrase syntax and texture.

Boccherini in fact is particularly given to projecting such distinctions onto the canvas of a complete work. For example, the Quintet in G minor Op. 29 No. 6/G318 (1779) and the Quartet in E minor Op. 32 No. 2/G202 (1780) operate to a similar large-scale plan: first and third movements in an untimely, not to say archaic, minor mode (the third movement of the quintet carries the overtly old-fashioned title Preludio), a vigorous minuet in the major, and a rondo finale that is not just major but modern in its variety. Both finales in fact open with the two violins playing the theme in octaves, a decidedly popular texture that immediately opens up a stylistic chasm from the previous well-wrought writing in the minor mode. After the tension and 'labour' of first and third movements, this sounds almost aggressively relaxed. However, the key point of difference in both finales is the sheer variety of materials they contain. As opposed to the more 'mono' manner of earlier movements in the minor, these finales can incorporate 'minor-mode style' as part of their varied modern palette; the major mode represents a sort of universal set that can encompass all brands of expression. In the case of the quintet movement, this includes a C section that, as we saw in Chapter 3, opens with material that strongly recalls the Trio and closes with exactly the same Phrygian progression we had heard at the end of the Preludio.

It is, of course, hardly the case that all minor-mode movements written at this time can be understood under any of the expressive or behavioural rubrics proposed above – and indeed even those movements that might fit quite comfortably will still offer a relative variety and flexibility of delivery. The first movement of Haydn's Sonata in E minor, analysed in Chapter 2 (Example 2.26), could certainly count as rigorous and obsessive in its conduct, but that does not stop it being highly interactive in its fundamental make-up. Grave has proposed a category of minor-key works that is relatively unmarked against the major-mode norm: 'galant minor', which presents a 'relatively subdued, well domesticated manner'.[219] He offers the finale of the same Haydn Sonata in E minor as an example – the movement I considered earlier in connection with its 'innocentemente' marking. In

---

[219] Grave, 'Galant Style, Enlightenment, and the Paths from Minor to Major', 11–12.

addition, we might note how in a number of finales the retention of the minor mode seems calculated to increase the sense of comic energy. A nice example is found in the final movement of Boccherini's Quintet in G minor Op. 42 No. 4/G351 (1789), which is just about a moto perpetuo, to which the minor mode adds an edgy, dark flavour; there is, unusually for Boccherini, a *pianissimo* conclusion. While in this case the minor is retained through to the very end, it is more common in such instances for the movement to turn to major at this point, as we find in three Beethoven finales to works in C minor: the sonata Op. 10 No. 1 (1798), the quartet Op. 18 No. 4 (1800) and the piano concerto Op. 37 (1800). In all three cases tempestuous gestures mix with comic elements, meaning, as we have seen before, that the comic atmosphere prevails. The finale of Michael Haydn's Symphony in D minor, ST393 (1784), is based on a catchy, somewhat exotic-sounding refrain that embodies a similar kind of comic energy. This movement turns to major well before the end, and includes one of Allanbrook's celebratory 'tune[s] that sprout ... from the top'.[220] After we seem to have reached a forceful ending, the minor-mode refrain then briefly reappears. Abruptly placed after all the celebratory moves of a symphonic *tierce de Picardie*, this sounds most disconcerting. In the end, though, it only strengthens the rhetorical force of the major mode when it returns to close out the work.

Similar complicated modal manoeuvres in a final movement arise in the quartets Op. 76 Nos 1 and 3 (1797) by brother Joseph. These offer an innovative twist – finales that start in the tonic minor in works that are set in major. In these movements there is no initial impression of lightness; a rather more threatening tone is struck. Yet in the case of Op. 76 No. 1 the ending is nothing if not comic, suggesting that the 'serious' material that had gone before might have been just so much bluster; alternatively, we can contemplate the hard incompatibility of gesture and affect evoked in Chapter 2. Parody of the minor mode's *agitato* manner became a real possibility, as we find in the first movement of Haydn's Symphony No. 80 in D minor (1784), though once more this is because the turbulent material seems to be undermined by comedy: both here and in the finale of Op. 76 No. 1 the agent of this undermining is a trivial-sounding tune, all 'innocence'. We need not hear anything intrinsically 'wrong' with the minor-mode writing; instead, once more, we are faced with the ambiguities of tone that count for so much in later eighteenth-century instrumental style.

[220] Allanbrook, 'Mozart's Tunes', 177.

5 | Final Focus

The Pastoral

One term of reference that has played around the edges of our central theme of sociability is the pastoral. While the pastoral is commonly thought of as a musical topic, as one possible element within the constellation of stylistic references in the instrumental music of this time, it can also be understood as something much more encompassing. It intersects, for example, with the taste for reduction that I discussed in Chapter 3, evident in a phenomenon like the simplifying cadence, in which the simple and understated abruptly replace more forceful accents. I also invoked the pastoral as a 'cultural mode' in connection with the exploration of affective sociability in Chapter 4. There again the power of simplicity, in both its critical and its musical embodiments, came to the fore, together with cognate terms such as naturalness and moderation. This did not, however, exclude the playfulness and irony that are likely to attend the pastoral mode. One way to take the sociable-pastoral equation further would be to consider the reception of Boccherini, so strongly associated with some of the above attributes. In his *Briefe über den Geschmack in der Musik* of 1809, Johann Baptist Schaul wrote of Boccherini, and by implication of his string chamber music:

> And what melody cannot be found in the simplest accompanying parts! Everything sings. There is not one note that does not speak, that is not in harmonious conversation with the main part. It requires no great investigation or tiresome study to divine the sense of this. Every part represents, so to speak, a person in a family, the members of which mutually impart their secrets and their sorrows, with such affection, compassion and warmth, that every listener will believe himself returned to the times of innocence and honesty.[1]

---

[1] Schaul, *Briefe über den Geschmack in der Musik*, 12, trans. Elisabeth Le Guin on website *Boccherini's Body* epub.library.ucla.edu/leguin/boccherini/ (2 March 2007).

While some aspects of this panegyric sound very familiar notes in the music criticism of this time – in particular the understanding of music as a language and of the interaction of several players in an instrumental work as a form of conversation – less usual is that Schaul does not ally utterance with melody and confine subordinate parts to the role of listeners, as so many did and have done since. Here, even the 'simplest accompanying parts' also 'speak', indeed 'sing', as part of the 'harmonious' whole. More unusual still is that Schaul extends the metaphor of conversation to encompass the vision of a family; not, in other words, the polite company or 'society' that is more commonly thought to be embodied. This suggests a greater degree of intimacy between participants, whereby many matters may be understood rather than directly addressed, where there is no need for outer show or display; witness the emphasis on 'warmth' rather than wit, for instance. Of course such ideals of empathy were hardly foreign to the ethos of the polite conversation as it was theorized in the eighteenth century. Naturalness and a genuine fellow feeling were always ideals, but these were attended with the contradictions we have already considered. First of all they had to be practised, and the publication of conversation manuals, for instance, attests to the need to rehearse one's verbal behaviour and sympathetic demeanour. Then there was the difficulty of distinguishing between feigned and genuine conduct in such a context. Cultivating one's speech and behaviour was both a desirable part of the social contract yet also potentially a barrier to authenticity in self-expression and in interaction. From such standpoints Schaul seems to be implicitly contrasting society conversation with what happens within the four walls of the family home, in effect to be positing the latter as an ideal type. Boccherini's music becomes a form of utterance in which no suspicion attends efforts at communication with others.

Schaul was certainly not the only figure of his time to write in such terms of Boccherini. For Pierre-Marie Baillot in 1804, this music would 'transport us into a better world, and allow us to taste the pleasures of the golden age';[2] the poet Chênedollé, writing in 1808, heard 'something of Heaven' in it;[3] and the *Dictionnaire historique des musiciens* of 1810 by Alexandre Choron and François Fayolle compared the composer's Adagios to 'the music of angels'.[4] While Schaul's imagery is decidedly more domestic in scale, it is

---

[2] Pierre-Marie Baillot, Jean-Henri Levasseur, Charles-Simon Catel and Charles Baudiot, *Méthode de Violoncelle et de Basse d'Accompagnement* (Paris: Janet & Cotelle, 1804), 3.

[3] Charles-Julien Lioult de Chênedollé, journal entry for 4 February 1808, cited and trans. Elisabeth Le Guin, *Boccherini's* Body epub.library.ucla.edu/leguin/boccherini/ (2 March 2007).

[4] Alexandre Choron and François Fayolle, *Dictionnaire historique des musicians artistes et amateurs, morts ou vivants* (Paris: Valade, 1810), 86, trans. Elisabeth Le Guin, *Boccherini's* Body epub.library.ucla.edu/leguin/boccherini/ (2 March 2007).

born from a similar perspective. Such superlative rhetoric may have been a defence against the perception that Boccherinian poetics were passing out of fashion, just around the time of his death in 1805, from which period all these testimonials derive. However, we should not be too keen to specify the historical moment of this phase of Boccherini reception, since in many respects this image of the composer is still powerfully felt. In 1993 Francesco Degrada, for instance, initially querying whether 'a musician so rich in humours, so varied and contradictory, ... can be enclosed within the limits of an Arcadian taste', then suggests that 'what Boccherini really transmits to us is the dream-like idea of an ideal world in which we can rediscover the lost synthesis between man and nature'.[5] At least as common, though, has been the attitude encapsulated by Charles Rosen, for whom the bulk of the composer's works are 'bland' and 'anodyne'.[6] Such an attitude – in all its shades from indifference through to something approaching contempt – may apply not so much to Boccherini in particular as to the gentler aspects of later eighteenth-century musical utterance altogether, which we considered in Chapter 4.

One means of dealing with such strands of thinking, both in their more recent manifestations and in the earlier context of Schaul's remarks, is to consider the case for Boccherini as pastoral composer. Such an alignment has already been more or less explicit in the reception we have traced, from Baillot's evocation of a golden age to the more recent reference by Degrada to an Arcadian taste. On a different scale, in his recent study of the topic, Raymond Monelle asserts that the pastoral as a complete cultural discourse operated as 'an allegory of music; ... music was for Europeans simply the pastoral without its shepherds'.[7] In other words, this is the old topos of a music that disarms the listener through its sheer freedom of signification and its consequent power to suspend us in a different realm of experience, one that frees us from the identities we assume in our ordinary lives. However, such a possible function would have been sharpened by the concentrated attention that the eighteenth century devoted to matters of language, communication and sociability, in other words everything that pertains to how we get along with others. Music could be seen as an ideal medium in which to convey unsullied sentiment and through which to construct models of an ideal type of human interaction – most powerfully so, in the latter part of the century, in textless, instrumental music.

---

[5] Francesco Degrada, 'Luigi Boccherini e la musica strumentale dei maestri italiani in Europa fra Sette e Ottocento', *Chigiana* 43 (1993), 369.
[6] Rosen, *The Classical Style*, 48.   [7] Monelle, *Musical Topic*, 185.

But this concerns more than reception; one way of accounting for the momentous changes in European musical style during the eighteenth century is to think in terms of a pastoralization of art music, the movement away from the higher-flown diction of the late Baroque towards something that was, or at least announced itself to be, simpler and more unassuming.[8] Monelle links the musical pastoral in the early eighteenth century more or less specifically with the genre of the siciliano,[9] and while I think this is too rigid an equation, the siciliano can usefully symbolize a particular relationship of high art to modest subject matter – one that is formalized and self-contained. The later eighteenth century sheds much of the high pastoral manner represented by the siciliano, and instead the pastoral spreads itself much more generously. A tone of popular simplicity becomes fundamental to art music; it is no longer an occasional discourse. This can be seen even on a more technical level – the parataxis characteristic of the pastoral mode, the tendency towards short, seemingly self-contained statements,[10] comes to dominate compositional practice. Accompanying this is the move towards what Quantz called the 'mixed style', the free play of musical topics within a single formal frame, which will of course include the pastoral. Thus the generic purity of the older pastoral is compromised; the contrast between low and high styles which animated it, but was not spelt out, may now be directly addressed through juxtaposition. Further, the pastoral I have in mind need not carry its traditional musical signifiers of compound time signature, drone bass and melodic lines moving in parallel intervals.[11] These are still heard often enough, but such features become just one option in wider compositional practices that are informed by a new consciousness of social relationships, whether between composer and player, composer and listener, player and listener, or of course between the players themselves. Accompanying this development is a stronger emphasis on pleasure and play, tied up with a clear acknowledgment of the power of conventions to bring the various parties together. These features too may be regarded as the spirit of pastoral writ large.

---

[8] Much of this paragraph derives from Sutcliffe, 'Topics in Chamber Music', 135–136.

[9] See Monelle, *Musical Topic*, 215–220.

[10] Writing of the earliest pastoral poets, Thomas G. Rosenmeyer describes an 'emphasis on brief, disconnected sentences; the stress on things rather than the relations between them . . . ; and the perception of a world that is not continuous, but a series of discrete units'. Thomas G. Rosenmeyer, *The Green Cabinet: Theocritus and the European Pastoral Lyric* (Berkeley: University of California Press, 1969), 46.

[11] Michael Beckerman identifies these elements, bar the compound time signature, as part of what he calls the 'pastoral set': 'Mozart's Pastoral', *Mozart-Jahrbuch* (1991), 94.

However, this pastoral does not necessarily carry that sense of nostalgia and loss which so clearly weighs down the encomiums of Schaul, Baillot and their contemporaries. This of course was and still is a fundamental part of the pastoral mode in itself, the illusion of a golden age that occasions melancholy reflection on the part of the writer or listener, and it helps to explain the apparent contradiction that Schaul's family have any 'sorrows' to share in their idyllic existence. The later eighteenth-century musical pastoral, though, tends to offer a more optimistic vision – a democratic and worldly rather than courtly pastoral – with rustic effects, for example, becoming less stylized and more vigorous.

This move towards greater informality of style, certainly when it comes to instrumental genres, tends to be underplayed in many accounts of our repertory, and also seems to figure weakly in the popular imagination. It has to compete with other associations, above all the formal control that arises from the *Formenlehre* tradition and from generations of pedagogical practice. This is reflected, for instance, in the characterization of sonata form by James Hepokoski and Warren Darcy as 'an abstract metaphor for disciplined, balanced action in the world' and 'a feat of engineering'.[12] Such imagery takes us far away from any 'pastoralization of art music', though it can hardly be said to be entirely anachronistic. As we saw in Chapter 2, the perception of formal machinery, generally at a lower structural level than what we now call sonata form, induced the likes of Adam Smith to speak admiringly of a 'great system' in modern music. But alongside such careful communicative mechanisms we have to budget for the more informal aspects of later eighteenth-century diction, whether that means a mixed, heterogeneous subject matter or, in the current case, the increasing strength of popular musical accents.

How might Boccherini fit here? The reception we have traced would seem to suggest that he retains something of the older brand of pastoral. The recurring emphasis on melancholy expression and the focus on sheer sonority that many have remarked upon,[13] together with the pronounced, often musing repetitiveness that invades many Boccherinian scores,

---

[12] Hepokoski and Darcy, *Elements of Sonata Theory*, 15.

[13] Such a perception forms a basic starting-point for Le Guin, 'One Says that One Weeps' and *Boccherini's Body*; a more negative, traditional view is represented by Donald Francis Tovey, for instance in his entry 'Luigi Boccherini (1743–1805)' for the *Encyclopedia Britannica* of 1929. The 'surprising beauty of colour' in a work like the composer's Quintet in E major Op. 11 No. 5 is ultimately judged as 'purely decorative' next to the 'dramatic' variety and contrasts that Haydn was simultaneously working to develop. In Donald Francis Tovey, *The Classics of Music: Talks, Essays, and Other Writings Previously Uncollected*, ed. Michael Tilmouth, edition completed by David Kimbell and Roger Savage (Oxford: Oxford University Press, 2001), 343.

suggest a taste for the static and contemplative that might fit more naturally within the pastoral constellation as traditionally understood. Such features suggest a relatively low level of social tension, a sort of music of retreat – which Schaul seems to affirm by setting his Boccherinian conversations within a domestic rather than a worldly environment. The modern sociable sphere surely demands a more dynamic, changeable manner, in which dwelling for too long on one subject would represent a lapse in decorum. Yet Boccherini certainly also qualifies as a practitioner of the mixed style, with many very sharp contrasts of material, and certainly also is a master of the racier 'new pastoral' manner. The quintet Op. 30 No. 6/G324 (1780), *Musica notturna delle strade di Madrid* (Night Music on the Streets of Madrid), is just one particularly celebrated example of this strain, and it reminds us that the new pastoral does not confine itself to traditionally bucolic imagery – it also draws its vigorous popular idioms from urban environments.

In trying to negotiate our way through these various perspectives on the pastoral, it rather depends where we choose to look. Clearly what stayed in the memory of many of Boccherini's contemporaries was a particular kind of slower movement, of the sort that caused Choron and Fayolle in their *Dictionnaire historique des musiciens* to pronounce that it was 'The adagios of Boccherini', 'the admiration of connoisseurs and the despair of artists', that gave 'the idea of the music of angels.'[14] This certainly suggests the perception of an idiom representing what W. H. Auden called the 'dreamer Arcadian' side of the pastoral tradition,[15] which would seem to be embodied in those many movements marked by an intense *dolcezza* of manner. The tender addresses of this style often occasioned the sort of melancholy reflection that we earlier associated with the pastoral tradition; it is evident, for instance, in the letters exchanged between Burney and Thomas Twining about the respective merits of Haydn and Boccherini, who for Twining conveyed 'a force of *serious* expression, a pathos, that is not so much Haydn's fort, I think'.[16] This pathos does not have to be linked to use of the minor mode; one example is the Grave from Boccherini's Quintet in C major Op. 28 No. 4/G310 (1779), which achieves a similar fusion of the idyllic and the melancholy in spite of its being set in G major. It includes

---

[14] Choron and Fayolle, *Dictionnaire historique des musicians*, 86, trans. Elisabeth Le Guin, *Boccherini's Body* epub.library.ucla.edu/leguin/boccherini/ (2 March 2007).

[15] W. H. Auden, 'Dingley Dell and the Fleet', in *The Dyer's Hand and Other Essays* (London: Faber, 1963), 410.

[16] Thomas Twining, letter to Charles Burney, 5–6 July 1783; *The Letters of Dr Charles Burney, Volume 1: 1751–1784*, ed. Alvaro Ribeiro (Oxford: Clarendon, 1991), 376n.

many duets that involve elaborate melodic diminutions, sometimes moving in parallel intervals, yet these need not be traced to operatic precedent; rather, one might hear the kind of intimate communal introspection envisaged by Schaul.

Brunetti, another Italian transplanted to Spain, also left many memorable examples of this idiom, again primarily found in slow movements. As with Boccherini, the expressive typology often suggests a kind of sublimated serenade, though in Brunetti's case this is achieved less through the duetting melodic behaviour of Boccherini's players than through various kinds of rhythmic ostinato. Some kind of accompanimental motive typically courses through the texture to hypnotic effect. The slow movement of the Quartet in E flat major L195 (1792–1793) – an Andantino in the traditional siciliano metre of 6/8, played *con sordino*[17] – contains its fair share of eloquent melodic lines, but the most striking feature is arguably the simple repeated-note chords that in several places carry the discourse by themselves. The way in which they build up texturally from a single repeated-note line, leading to some unexpected harmonic twists, makes one wonder whether Haydn's Op. 54 string quartets of 1788 had reached the Madrid court by the time of composition. The second movement of Op. 54 No. 1 in G major, also moving at a quickish 6/8 gait (here Allegretto) is similarly constituted, though in this case the repeated-note 'accompaniment' carries even more affective weight. Both movements convey that blend of overtly artless material with various complexities of treatment – a sort of virtuosity with simplicity – that we have encountered so often in this study.

To bring this movement by Haydn into play reminds us that in fact the dreamy-idyllic-poignant pastoral mode continued to flourish widely in the latter half of the century, in the slower movement type where it was already established, even if the intense *dolcezza* and *tenerezza* of Boccherini and Brunetti are not often matched. This may take the more historically embedded form of a movement in compound time (normally 6/8) with siciliano rhythms – aside from the Allegretto of Op. 54 No. 1 noted above, one might cite the slow movements of Haydn's Quartet in F minor Op. 20

[17] Miguel Ángel Marín notes the use of mutes in three slow movements from earlier Brunetti quartets, one each from the Op. 3, Op. 4 and Op. 5 sets, written in the mid-1770s. These movements open their respective works, which Marín suggests means that the works and players are 'calling for silence and for listeners to pay attention in a particularly subtle manner'. The current instance from the quartet L195 is therefore, as Marín remarks, different in occupying an intermediate position. Marín, 'Haydn, Boccherini and the Rise of the String Quartet in Late Eighteenth-Century Madrid', in *The String Quartet in Spain*, ed. Christiane Heine and Juan Miguel González Martínez (Bern: Peter Lang, 2016), 102.

No. 5 (1772) or of Mozart's Piano Concerto in A major K488 (1786) – but there are many other ways in which this mode may be maintained. In the broadest terms, countless slow movements ally themselves with its gentle, contemplative side; various forms of unbroken rhythmic motion over which lyrical melodic lines are projected help induce a sense of reverie. And the virtues of simplicity and naturalness that we studied in Chapter 4 will come to the fore, a conviction that 'less is more', whether that involves textural or harmonic or melodic simplicity. This is the reductive aesthetic that I have already described as a pastoral conceit. While the prevalent reception of such simplicity has emphasized the 'less', I have argued for the 'more', in the current case that the kind of idyllic writing we are considering carries its own kind of intensity, as I have suggested above in the case of Brunetti and Boccherini.[18] For Schaul this was felt as a kind of family warmth.

If it may be argued that I am simply trying to rebrand some basic attributes of modern-galant eighteenth-century style as pastoral, that is exactly the point. The two quantities are not easily extricated from each other. Matthew Gelbart is a rare writer who has explicitly equated the two, writing, 'In music, the *galant* style in general shared many of the stylistic markers associated with pastoral, as well as a similar attitude toward nature as simple, universal moral balance. (Indeed, the pastoral and *galant* style sometimes appear almost coextensive in the eighteenth century.)'[19] In either case, the idyllic aspects of our current type of slower pastoral movement might seem to sit uneasily with the sharper sense of social action that I am arguing for in the case of this repertory as a whole. But while some feeling of retreat is undeniable, a sense that such movements encourage unselfconscious absorption, this can only be relatively true. As already explored in the previous chapter, both pastoral and sociable are marked by a tension between the artificial and the natural. The pastoral is premised on a gap between its simplicity of appearance and its very existence in a high-art context, but that does not mean we should mistrust its intentions, as it were. We have also already signalled the similar tensions involved in sociable culture, given the way, for instance, in which interlocutors were encouraged to cultivate their spontaneous speech and behaviour in advance.

---

[18] For such a reason I cannot altogether agree with Robert Hatten's formulation that a 'fundamental principle of pastoral expression in music' is 'mollified tension and intensity'. Hatten, *Interpreting Musical Gestures*, 56 (italics removed).

[19] Matthew Gelbart, *The Invention of 'Folk Music' and 'Art Music'* (Cambridge: Cambridge University Press, 2007), 43.

The inbuilt tension between nature and artifice becomes overt when more or less explicitly pastoral material is mediated by contrast within the same movement – in other words, when this material, which in its native habitat ought to be uninterruptible, is indeed interrupted, and becomes merely one element of a more mixed style. Such interruptions are often abrupt, if not brutal. The celebrated *fortissimo* chord that appears out of nowhere to sabotage the opening tune in the Andante of Haydn's Symphony No. 94 in G major ('Surprise'; 1791) is a particularly concise example of this. According to a review in the *Oracle*, 'The surprise might not be unaptly likened to the situation of a beautiful Shepherdess who, lulled to slumber by the murmur of a distant Waterfall, starts alarmed by the unexpected firing of a fowling-piece.'[20] What this suggests is that an ostentatiously simple theme in the context of a slow movement, even if it carried none of the traditional markers of the idiom, could readily prompt the most literal of pastoral associations. On most occasions, though, the contrast is more sustained, and often takes the form of a central section that puts the idyll into perspective, such as in the Andante of Rosetti's Symphony in E flat major Murray A28 (1786), which in the middle reaches a blazing *fortissimo* climax on V of vi.

The sense of outside forces threatening Arcadia may even take the explicitly programmatic form of the storm in the countryside, as realized, for example, by the young Arriaga in the 'Pastorale' slow movement of his String Quartet No. 3 in E flat major (1824). Here the singing of the birds and the shepherds, and the murmuring of a brook, translated into the traditional texture of a drone that supports a melody doubled in thirds, are twice interrupted by a thunderstorm. And our category of interrupted slow movement, as explored in Chapter 2, seems to partake of a comparable plot archetype. In that case, though, the interrupting material does not so much darken as lighten the mood, by moving to a swifter tempo and, in most cases, the accents of a comic finale. And, as with the movements we have just cited, what had seemed 'natural' is now revealed to be just one possible mode of utterance, a stylistic pose – in other words, the ironic gap that is at the heart of the pastoral mode is made explicit. This is, of course, how the mixed style works in general, but pastoral – rather like that umbrella topic at the other end of the spectrum, the learned style – brings stronger inbuilt expectations of absolute, uninterrupted, continuity.

If there is ample historical precedent for this type of slower lyrical pastoral, the same cannot readily be claimed of the more vigorous, racier

---

[20] Anonymous, *The Oracle* (24 March 1792), cited in Finscher, *Joseph Haydn und seine Zeit*, 367.

and generally faster brand that I have noted above. Compared to the former type, it offers what sounds like a bracing 'realism'. Leonard B. Meyer recognized this development when writing of how 'the conventions of the mythic, arcadian pastoralism of the ancien régime were gradually replaced by the egalitarian folk-pastoralism of Romanticism'.[21] But this is surely to underestimate how quickly such a development took place. The sonatas of Domenico Scarlatti, all written by the 1750s at the latest, already offer startling proof of that. And the three-movement Pastorelas of Manuel Blasco de Nebra (no later than 1784) explicitly thematize the growth of a demotic idiom. As already mentioned, their central movements, also called 'Pastorela', offer a rhythmically exuberant, 'undisciplined' style which is in each case countered by a brief minuet finale that returns, even if equivocally, to a higher style of diction. But the first movements quite clearly present a more traditional idyllic vision. Marked Adagio, they all suggest the endless lyrical present of Arcadian myth through a patent simplicity of melodic material and various kinds of hovering, oscillating figuration.[22] These movements are then succeeded by that much rougher, ruder, physically bracing brand of pastoralism. When it comes to such qualities in the more familiar repertory of the time, Haydn is the name that will spring to mind, with that tearing vitality that courses through so many of his faster movements. But this may be yet another area where the composer in fact represents an extreme that has retrospectively been turned into a kind of harmless norm. Simon McVeigh, noting the 'strongly pastoral folk-imagery' that is particularly striking in later Haydn, asserts that 'the exaggeratedly popular style in which these [pastoral] ideas masqueraded was an outrageous departure'.[23]

However, this brand of 'new pastoral' did not have to invoke lower stylistic registers. It could often take a gentler form, offering a broadly popular and accessible manner where, once more, it is hard to distinguish between the pastoral and a normal modern-galant tone of voice: it is as if the later galant in particular aspires to the condition of folk music. Every listener will be familiar with the kind of thematic material from this time, catchy and immediately memorable, that sounds like a popular tune, yet is no such thing: the theme of the finale of Mozart's Clarinet Quintet in A major, K581 (1789), would be just one of innumerable examples. And there are composers of the time who primarily cultivate this gentler type of

---

[21] Meyer, *Style and Music*, 175.
[22] See Sutcliffe, 'Poet of the Galant', 313–324 (some of the wording I use here derives from page 318).
[23] McVeigh, *Concert Life in London*, 135.

pastoral idiom – Mozart himself is one, and Krommer and Kozeluch are others who spring to mind. But Haydn also often employs this idiom, and it is really better to think of popular accents and materials existing along a spectrum, at the harder end of which Haydn typically goes further than his contemporaries. A movement like the finale 'in the German Style' from his Piano Trio in E flat major H29 (1797), rushing along at a Presto assai tempo, is rowdy and dishevelled, anything but a picture of idyllic perfection, and while a finale is the most common position for such 'low' pastoral representation, this need not be so. A work such as the 'Surprise' Symphony features strong rustic elements throughout, including an especially earthy 'minuet'. The first movement of Clementi's Piano Trio in F major Op. 27 No. 1 (1791) creates a riotous impression through its constant manipulation of a quick triplet figure that appears in a multitude of cross-rhythmic guises. This is all the more pointed through its being preceded by an Adagio slow introduction and followed by a 'Siciliano. Andante' movement, to which, significantly, the instruction 'innocente' is added. Along similar lines, the finale of Haydn's Trio H29 is preceded by the Andantino ed innocentemente movement that was briefly discussed in the previous chapter, which is also in 6/8 time. It seems that both composers, like Blasco de Nebra, wanted to juxtapose the more established and newer types of pastoral imagery.

One attribute that both these types share, by definition, is a surface innocence, part of the imperative of (overt) simplicity that ties the pastoral to the modern-galant. This is given a programmatic role in the opening movement of Dittersdorf's symphony *The Four Ages of the World*, which depicts the Golden Age. This prelapsarian musical paradise expresses its harmonious nature, as we saw in Chapter 2, through perfectly balanced periodic constructions, a 'natural' symmetry that is the very embodiment of galant phrase syntax and shows the roots of the modern galant in the idyllic and pastoral.[24] But innocence can also mean ignorance, and this offers composers the chance to write outright unorthodox music – another established ingredient of the pastoral tradition. This can take the form of bum notes, as it does in the increasingly strange last section of Domenico Zipoli's Pastorale for organ (1716), which the indication 'piva' tells us has been inspired by the sound of bagpipes. In the first movement of Boccherini's Quintet in D major Op. 10 No. 6/G270 (1771), a Pastorale

---

[24] Richard Will hears a gavotte rhythm underpinning this movement, which would further cement the notion of a marriage between (civilized) galant and (innocent) pastoral. Will, *Characteristic Symphony*, 34.

in 6/8 time, the idyll is marked by a use of increasingly strong dissonance, culminating in bars 37 and 39 in a bitter clash between an a^1 and a $b\flat^1$. This owes something to the tradition we see realized in Zipoli's work, though it is also surely a sign that this music inhabits a world after the fall; the painful dissonances suggest a loss of earlier innocence.

The lack of orthodoxy may also involve unlikely harmonic progressions: both outer movements of Clementi's Op. 27 No. 1 piano trio, for example, feature progressions that are not so much 'incorrect' as subtly strange, such as the rather modal-sounding succession of G minor and C major chords heard at bars 120–124 of the finale. On other occasions, it is not so much that the harmony is faulty, but that it is limited; there may, for example, be a distinct lack of the pre-dominant harmonies that are normally required to manoeuvre the music towards a firm cadence. This is the case in the 'Allemande' finale of Dussek's Piano Trio in B flat major Op. 31 No. 1 (1795), for example, which is built on a musette-like pedal point. In the output of Brunetti, though, such harmonic behaviour leaves a major imprint, along with a distinct tendency for the music to hover around pedal points and to reach for the flat side at every opportunity (notably through use of the Quiescenza schema that begins by flattening the leading note of the key).[25] This applies not just to his typically idyllic slow movements, but equally to his finales, which often have a picturesque flavour to them. This trait creates a low centre of harmonic gravity.

A further possibility is the use of untutored phrase syntax. Here the seemingly natural compatibility of pastoral and galant that we saw thematized in Dittersdorf's 'Golden Age' is subject to strain; nature remains unimproved, as it were. This may mean a relative lack of flexibility with regard to phrase extension, where sections and whole movements finish without ceremony, of the kind that we noted in respect of Pleyel's 'Rondo Ecossois' in Chapter 2. Conversely, it can also mean a kind of wandering looseness of construction. This is the case in the third movement of Haydn's Symphony No. 50 in C major (1773). After a robust minuet dominated by its opening fanfare-like idea, the trio (Example 5.1) begins as though it were yet another repetition of the minuet's opening, if for strings only, but there is a sudden swerve via a sustained dotted-minim B♭ towards F major and the start of the 'real' trio. But even this is ambiguous: if it sounds like the section properly begins with the oboe solo at bar 63, this

---

[25] For further comment on this harmonic tendency see my review of *Gaetano Brunetti: Cuartetos de Cuerda L184–L199*, ed. Miguel Ángel Marín and Jorge Fonseca, *Eighteenth-Century Music* 11/1 (2014), 129–131.

Example 5.1 Haydn, Symphony No. 50 in C major/iii, bars 56^3–102

would leave at least two bars unaccounted for: the strings' bars 61–62, once F major seems to emerge as the true key of the section. One might feel that the trio has in fact no definite starting-point; rather, we simply slide into it. This turns out to be consistent with how the trio is shaped as a whole: it is effectively through-composed, with no repeat marks, and has no more of a proper ending than it had a proper beginning. There is no final cadence on the putative tonic of F, and instead we finish on a prolonged E major, from bars 94 to 102. This is probably to be understood as the dominant of A minor (V of vi relative to the C major of the minuet), though even this isn't entirely clear, since there is a careful avoidance of a C in the diminished chords (built on a D♯) that alternate with the E major chords above the sustained E in the bass, at 95–100. Thus we could be hearing a prolongation of E major in its own right rather than a standing on the dominant of A minor.

Example 5.1 (continued)

Such informal behaviour really dramatizes the difference between the two sections of the movement, which is based on the very common plan of a stately or grand minuet followed by a more modest, rustic trio. The minuet is lengthy, formally controlled and punctual, whereas the trio 'innocently' knows nothing of such imperatives. Haydn even expresses this notationally, since bars 63–74 of the trio are written out again as

75–86 even though they are identical and could thus be represented by repeat marks. This innocence is personified by the solo oboe. Its phrases are six bars long, not necessarily irregular in itself, but the phrases sound irregular because of a certain imbalance of rhythmic values and melodic contour: there is little trace of the sorts of internal organization that one expects under a regime of periodicity. In addition, the oboe's first phrase finishes in odd manner, perched on a V4/2 chord at bars 67–68 and with the melody falling triadically to $\hat{5}$. As with the Clementi trio above, the result sounds subtly strange rather than plainly wrong. After an answering phrase, and the written-out reiteration of the complete oboe tune, we hear from bar 86^3 a rising sequence featuring suspensions in the top two parts, with an extension on the third limb that takes us seemingly to V of A minor. The music then settles mysteriously there, with two forms of pedal (drone in the violas, repeated notes in the bass) and oscillations in the violin parts, suggesting musette style, while the oboe repeats in isolation its initial falling-arpeggio motive (compare bars 96–97 with 63–64), but transposed downwards. This produces an uncomfortable clash between the oboe's e^1 and the first violin's $d\sharp^1$, a bittersweet dissonance that we might compare with those highlighted above in the first movement of Boccherini's Op. 10 No. 6. Then the strings fall silent and the oboe, all by itself, repeats its falling E major arpeggio in consecutive bars, *pianissimo*. This is not only a strikingly poetic effect in its own right, but makes for a huge contrast with the returning minuet, loud and collectively performed. These final bars of the trio evoke the most central of Arcadian images – the solitary shepherd playing on his pipe.

It is another brand of wind-playing, though, that develops into one of the most striking tokens of the newer pastoral manner – the horn call. It becomes a virtual signature sonority of the time, cutting across all movement types. According to most topical taxonomies, the horn call and the pastoral are different beasts, and for ostensibly good reasons. As Raymond Monelle comments in his study of these topics, 'no shepherd is ever portrayed playing a brass horn. The horn is normally a huntsman's instrument.'[26] Yet most of the horn calls that haunt our instrumental repertory do not seem to evoke the world of the hunt, which does, after all, carry quite different associations from that of the modest pastoral. Where the two clearly overlap is in suggesting the great outdoors – though,

---

[26] Monelle, *Musical Topic*, 101. Monelle goes on to note how 'the connection of the horn with the pastoral spirit becomes standard' (102), though he cites only post-eighteenth-century examples in support.

as noted earlier, many of the racy 'pastoral' evocations that we hear may just as well imply an urban outdoors, music heard on the streets rather than in the fields. On many occasions horn-call material, rather than projecting itself strongly as a distinct 'topic', seems to connote something that is simple and open in sonority, readily comprehensible, a 'natural' part of the sonic environment. This then returns us to the overlap between a pastoral mode and a galant aesthetic.

Another aspect of topical definition is salience: characteristic materials may be more or less overtly presented, and so not every incidence of a 'topic' carries the same perceptual weight. On the one hand we have the horn call that opens the finale of Haydn's Symphony No. 103 in E flat major ('Drumroll'; 1795), which is quite unambiguous – the classic two-voice pattern involving intervals of a sixth leading to a fifth leading to a third, which is then reversed, and it is played by two horns. On the other hand, in the Adagio of the composer's Sonata in E flat major H52 (1794), famously set in the remote key of E major, a horn call is fleetingly heard in bar 4 as part of a linking passage between antecedent and consequent phrases (G♯-E to F♯-B on the last two triplet semiquavers leading to E-G♯ on the downbeat of bar 5). This does not return at the corresponding point of the recapitulation, bar 36, since the horn fifth is avoided, and only at one other point in the movement do we hear any real suggestion of the same horn-call sonority (bar 25, in the contrasting middle section). It is hard to hear these brief occurrences as carrying the same straightforward 'pastoral' connotations as in the finale of Symphony No. 103. Instead, they seem to form part of a different affective register, an elevated mood that links many of the slower movements that make use of horn-call material. We can hear this more plainly, for example, at the outset of the slow movement of Brunetti's Symphony No. 36 in A major (no date). This Andantino sostenuto, in E major, opens with the two violins playing a horn-call figure *pianissimo assai* in dotted rhythms, as if heard from the distance. Even more evocative is the return of this material in the minor mode from bar 28, a Schubertian effect.

On the other hand, horn-call material often appears to be a more integrated part of our galant-pastoral panorama, as is the case in Kozeluch's three piano trios Op. 28 (*c*1786). In this set such material occupies a range of positions and is variously prominent. A horn call opens the first movement of Trio No. 1 in E flat major; in the finale of No. 2 in D major horn calls from bar 117 effect a retransition back to the main theme; in Trio No. 3 in E minor a horn-call sonority appears within the opening theme of the Adagio (bar 2), more or less in passing; while in the finale of the same work, which retains the minor mode, an episode in E major from bar 151 is built on horn calls in the piano part, offering a warmth of sonority that contrasts with the sparer textures elsewhere. The context in which this last horn call occurs reminds us of another link between such material and the broader galant within which it is embedded: the horn call is an intrinsically major-mode phenomenon. Kozeluch's piano trios Op. 41 (c1800) also make frequent reference to horn sonority, and once again they may simply sound like a 'natural' part of a wider discourse or bear a more specific affective weight. This set also demonstrates the extent to which the pastoral altogether forms a more or less intrinsic part of a wider modern-galant orientation. The Andantino con Variazioni of Op. 41 No. 1, for example, proceeds from a simple tune that sounds like a folk melody together with a simple harmonic style, with pervasive doublings in thirds and sixths.[27] The coda section (see Example 5.2) returns to the tune and sets it almost entirely over a tonic pedal, expressed as minims in the lowest part in the keyboard's left hand and as repeated semiquavers an octave above, thus adding the missing ingredient to create the standard pastoral texture. After the tune ends there are several bars of fade-out (marked *mancando* in the cello), featuring pure tonic triadic degrees and marked *aperto* (open) in the keyboard part. While picturesque enough, and easy to hear as an evocation of pastoral simplicity, there is really nothing especially marked about such musical imagery – rather, the 'open', (mock-)innocent, fresh quality is one towards which the composers of our time more generally aspired.

The Tempo di Menuetto Finale

If the pastoral has been widely recognized as a distinct quantity in the make-up of our instrumental style – even if I have just argued that we may not collectively have the measure of its extent, and that it is more than a topic or even a genre – the tempo di menuetto[28] finale has barely been recognized as a category in its own right. Yet, like pastoral, if within narrower confines, it helps us to unlock some key aspects of musical sociability. While anything making reference to the minuet might seem to promise a formality that takes us far from pastoral imagery, the two have some common properties.

The tempo di menuetto finale represents a real blind spot in the reception of our instrumental style. It seems to have been assumed that tempo di menuetto

---

[27] Much of the rest of this paragraph derives from Sutcliffe, 'Topics in Chamber Music', 134–135.
[28] I am using the spelling favoured by Haydn and some other composers, as opposed to the linguistically purer 'tempo di minuetto'. Other polylinguistic designations sometimes found include 'tempo di minuet' and 'tempo di menué'.

Example 5.2 Kozeluch, Piano Trio in B flat major Op. 41 No. 1/ii, bars 124–141

is simply a minuet placed last in the cycle and hence demands no separate consideration, but this is the case neither formally – since a straightforward ternary construction involving a designated trio is rare – nor expressively. It is the emerging difference in expressive typology that most interests me here, linked with the claim that the tempo di menuetto finale comes to constitute a distinct musical genre.[29]

If we reflect on its generally moderate speed, it is clear that the tempo di menuetto finale doesn't really have that dynamic character with which we

---

[29] A good recent index for the neglect of the genre is Michael Talbot's study *The Finale in Western Instrumental Music*, in which over several hundred pages the tempo di menuetto finale makes it to a single footnote.

want to associate a movement in such a position. Historically it has been overwhelmed by a faster type of close, often indeed involving those 'new pastoral' elements considered earlier. It presents a gentler way of closing that hangs on in smaller chamber genres – principally sonatas for one to three players – before disappearing. This may in turn promote the feeling that it lacks sufficient musical substance to justify its position. A representative verdict – where the subject even comes up for discussion – comes from Giorgio Pestelli, who writes, 'The minuet as a finale for the whole composition was bound to die out; it was jeopardized by the weight of the first movement and was obliged to give up its position to a closing Allegro which strengthened a structure that would otherwise have leaned towards the opening.'[30] In fact, chances are that tempo di menuetto will not even form part of most listeners' conscious experience of later eighteenth-century music. We might note its near-complete absence from what have become most intensively studied and performed instrumental genres of that time, the symphony and string quartet, as practised by the famous figures of late eighteenth-century Vienna, which of course tends to govern our perception of the wider state of affairs.[31] Logically, minuet finales are not going to occur in the four-movement versions of those genres that are most familiar to us today, since a minuet will already have featured as an inner movement.

If Pestelli suggests that such movements are retrogressive, this is not just on the basis of musical style, but also because of all the nasty political connotations of the ancien régime that attach to the minuet. This much is apparent in Hepokoski and Darcy's assessment that when a three-movement instrumental cycle closes with a minuet or other dance movement as finale, 'now the whole piece stages its progress from a dynamic sonata-form world into one of stylized, *ancien-régime* grace and short-winded *galant* symmetries. In this case the pathway brings us to affirmation

---

[30] Pestelli, *Age of Mozart and Beethoven*, 110–111.

[31] However, tempo di menuetto finales are not completely absent from string quartets of the later eighteenth century. The final movement of Kraus's String Quartet in G minor, Op. 1 No. 3 (1783), besides being a cancrizans in its outer sections, is also marked Tempo di Minuetto, and Pleyel employs the indication not just for the occasional quartet finale, but also in string quintets. Tempo di menuetto movements conclude, for example, the String Quintet in A minor, Op. 9/Ben276 (1786), and the Quartet in F minor Op. 22 No. 6/Ben358 (1791), both carrying the additional marking *dolce*. Marín notes the rarity of minuet finales in quartets within this area of Europe; on the other hand, 'this trait, Italian in origin but regularly used by French composers', is commonly found in Boccherini and works by his compatriots. Note, though, that Marín does not distinguish between minuet-as-finale and the tempo di menuetto finale: 'Haydn, Boccherini and the Rise of the String Quartet', 81.

of high-prestige (if slightly empty) aristocratic stabilities.'[32] Leaving aside the question of why sonata forms should be held to be intrinsically more 'dynamic' in their constitution than other formal types, this offers a further reminder of the bad press that quantities like grace and (small-scale) symmetry can continue to attract: they remain expressively 'empty'.[33]

However, a distinction needs to be drawn between a concluding minuet – what I call minuet-as-finale – and our tempo di menuetto finale. For much of the eighteenth century such a concluding minuet was a standard option – a self-evident, and therefore an 'unmarked', placement within the cycle. While tempo di menuetto must partly have evaded definition since it arose out of the minuet-as-finale, its very development as a designation, as opposed to the simple 'Minuet', suggests a consciousness that a straightforwardly presented dance movement doesn't go as a finale. It more or less openly proclaims its relatively extreme distance from functional versions of the dance. One way in which this independence is commonly expressed, as touched on earlier, is through design. The common ternary form of the minuet (and also the minuet-as-finale) reflects functional origins in that multiple minuets, together with repetitions of their constituent sections, were normally needed to generate the hundred or so bars required for the actual dancing of a minuet. The tempo di menuetto tends by comparison not only to be longer, but it has no fixed design: the nearest to a formal precept is simply the common avoidance of a simple succession of minuet followed by a named trio (or indeed second minuet) followed by the minuet da capo.

To return to its placement as a finale, we might assume, along with the writers cited above, that composers and their audiences came to find a concluding minuet incompatible with the 'modern manner' (although this was of course hardly a uniform process, either with respect to various instrumental genres or with respect to different musical centres). Perhaps, though, there is a point where some composers positively exploited the difference in affective weight and character of the minuet finale from a normally more rapid rondo or sonata-form finale. But this applies only to the tempo di menuetto. The minuet-as-finale virtually dies out relatively early in this process – Haydn, for example, had more or less abandoned it by the end of the 1760s – and the tempo di menuetto starts to acquire

---

[32] Hepokoski and Darcy, *Elements of Sonata Theory*, 336.
[33] Indeed, Hepokoski and Darcy show themselves wary of most of the 'moderate' virtues of later eighteenth-century style that were our particular subject in Chapter 4. While they do occasionally invoke a term like grace in positive contexts, in general it is obscured by a vaunting of heavy expressive intensity, 'big' emotions like despair and activities like striving.

a separate identity as the parent structure falls from use. Then, as the fast finale becomes the most likely option, the tempo di menuetto develops more conspicuous generic characteristics, playing against the expected brilliance and animation. It may therefore be conceived as a countergenre, inviting listeners to understand it in pointed contrast to others. But for this to carry any force we need to consider just what sort of expressive attributes it could convey. As a countergeneric construct, the tempo di menuetto finale is marked above all by its tone, by typically modelling an intimate sensibility, full of feeling but disciplined by a minuet gait that promotes continuity of motion. It becomes a 'characteristic' manner in the same way that rondo style, for instance, did – and it perfectly illustrates the intensity that is possible within a prevailing affect of 'moderation', as argued in Chapter 4.

The tempo di menuetto finale of Haydn's Piano Trio in F major H17 (1790; Example 5.3a), offers us something like this flavour. Here a relatively plain melodic style is the base from which great lyrical intensity is achieved. Indeed, what we hear is really a continuous lyrical stream. Normal minuet syntax moves essentially in two-bar units, to accommodate or reflect the six-beat duration of the minuet dance step. What we find here is not only much more broadly conceived than that, it has a slightly meandering, informal quality. Most notable perhaps is the passage heard from bar 37 (Example 5.3b). In functional terms it can be heard as the typical 'closing figuration' of a sonata-form exposition, yet the combination of a long-breathed cello pedal with the gentle fall and rise in piano right hand and violin creates a sort of poetry out of plainness. What this movement offers that is typical of many tempo di menuetto finales is a relaxed, even homely, warmth, at the slower end of possible minuet tempos. Such finales are much more likely than the minuet to suggest such qualities as the idyllic, nostalgic or ruminative. They seem to luxuriate in the feeling of time to spare, as one might judge from the notably slow harmonic rhythm of this example, which hardly ever moves above one chord per bar. At the same time, for all this warmth, the tempo di menuetto preserves a certain grace and reserve through the discipline of its minuet gait. This can lend a certain ambivalence of tone that is one of the most tantalizing attributes of the whole genre. How, we might ask, were listeners to react to this enactment of minuet style? What sort of behaviour or deportment was read into such a piece?

Given this ambivalent tone, we must once again avoid suggesting too firm a distinction from the minuet. It would in any case be hard to be too categorical: of all eighteenth-century types and forms, the minuet in

Example 5.3a Haydn, Piano Trio in F major H17/ii, bars 1–11

particular is so pervasive that one can barely fix the limits of its influence and definition. Charles Pauli, writing in Leipzig in 1756, defined it as 'the universal dance that all nations prefer to their own national dances'.[34] Minuet style can after all, as Ratner reminds us, be used in all movement positions – in first movements, slow movements and finales, quite apart from its specific presentation as a dance movement.[35] And this omnipresence has encouraged a practice of permissive labelling of almost any

---

[34] Charles Pauli, *Elemens de la danse* (Leipzig: U. C. Saalbach, 1756), 64, cited in translation in Arnfried Edler, *Gattungen der Musik für Tasteninstrumente. Teil 2: Von 1750 bis 1830* (Laaber: Laaber, 2003), 338.
[35] Ratner, *Classic Music*, 11.

Example 5.3b Haydn, Piano Trio in F major H17/ii, bars 33–43

quickish movement in 3/4 time as embodying minuet style – often rather unconvincingly, as with the common assertion that the last movement of Haydn's Sonata in C minor (H20; 1771?) at least begins as a minuet.[36] Wye Allanbrook has described the minuet as 'the ultimate survivor',[37] given that it was the one French courtly dance that remained fully alive in both musical and dance practice from its origins in the mid-seventeenth century through to the end of the eighteenth, and it did so on a truly European scale. In order to last like this, it had to be very versatile,[38] and this applied to its choreography, its tempo and its social function. As a dance form, there was such variety of practice and indeed speed that it is somewhat misleading to talk about *the* minuet at all, although certain precepts seem

---

[36] For example, in *The Keyboard Sonatas of Joseph Haydn: Instruments and Performance Practice, Genres and Styles*, trans. author in collaboration with Charlotte Greenspan (Chicago: University of Chicago Press, 1995), László Somfai describes this movement, along with the finale of the Sonata in E flat major H45 (1766), as representing an 'accelerated minuet type' (299), and later describes the two finales as being 'in faster tempos, but with first themes in minuet character' (317).

[37] Allanbrook, *Rhythmic Gesture in Mozart*, 48.

[38] Jennifer Thorp, for example, writes that the minuet 'displayed a huge capacity for adaptation and change during its long life from the 1660s until the early years of the 19th century': 'In Defence of Danced Minuets', *Early Music* 31/3 (2003), 101–102.

to have remained constant, such as the beginning of the minuet step on the upbeat. And the common image of the minuet as a prime representational tool of the aristocracy, as we saw being affirmed a few pages back, is also misleading; it was eventually far more widely danced than that.[39] Even in purely musical terms, while there was a broadly understood courtly style – involving such features as dotted rhythms, a fairly constant crotchet bass and rising scales and arpeggios, especially at phrase openings – this is no global attribute of minuets of the time. And even in that case, it did not imply a character of stiff dignity. Naturalness and precisely a lack of affectation were the desirable attributes stressed in endless treatises, both dance and musical: recall the injunction of dancing master Gallini in Chapter 4 to dance the minuet without the poisonous presence of 'study and art'. Even regularity of rhythm and phrase structure was not essential: conflict between dance and music was inevitable since the initiation of the minuet step on the upbeat would always lead to cross-rhythms against the music and continuity of motion across phrase boundaries.[40] So we should not hold the image of minuets being danced by aristocratic automatons, and not every minuet or tempo di menuetto with irregular features need be understood as socially subversive.

On the other hand, the regularity of rhythm and phrase syntax in the overwhelming majority of at least later eighteenth-century minuets is remarkable, even for an age that valued the 'naturalness' of binary symmetrical constructions so highly. Perhaps it was the very fact that listeners would feel the performance of a minuet through their bodies, ghosting out step sequences that often cut against the rhythmic grain of the music, that allowed most composers most of the time to produce such unswerving regularity. The very regularity must have been enticing enough in its own way.

So we need to exercise care before we play the tempo di menuetto finale off against the minuet in terms of its syntactical character. Indeed, the tempo di menuetto is considerably less likely than the minuet to feature possibly disruptive phrase rhythms or angular contours. And we must be wary of thinking that the tempo di menuetto in some way 'improves on' the

---

[39] Among many testimonies to this see, for example, David Charlton, '"Minuet-Scenes" in Early Opéra-Comique', in *French Opera 1730–1830: Meaning and Media* (Aldershot: Ashgate, 2000). Reporting on the 'fashion craze' for the minuet that 'united the poorest classes with theatre professionals', Charlton notes that 'through such mixing of different people in semi-public dances and balls ... there arose a specific belief that social dance brought moral danger' (269–270).

[40] See, for example, Wye J. Allanbrook and Wendy Hilton, 'Dance Rhythms in Mozart's Arias', *Early Music* 20/1 (1992), 145.

minuet. One of the minuet's greatest virtues was simply its widespread currency as a lingua franca, both musically and choreographically (for all the local variety of practice). Its very intelligibility was itself desirable from an Enlightenment point of view. And its very pervasiveness meant that it could bear a great expressive range. Perhaps the minuet proper was such a fundamental category of musical production that, when presented in its 'applied' form within an instrumental cycle, it could almost act as a blank canvas. Counterbalancing such a possibility is the fact that any minuet movement or derivative carries that specific physical and gestural weight through its avowed linkage with a widely practised dance form.

Such considerations only re-emphasize the tempo di menuetto's inherent ambiguity, its relative instability as a category. And this was reflected as much in contemporary writings as it has been in those that have followed. More recent commentators have tended to see tempo di menuetto as distinct from the minuet only in its form; in other words, they have defined it as a formal rather than an affective type. David Wyn Jones, for example, writes that 'Such movements have the gait of a minuet but the customary compact structure of minuet and trio is replaced with other approaches'.[41] That this implies stylistic equivalence between the two is apparent in Howard Irving's summation with respect to Haydn: 'Although the minuet disappears from the finales of Haydn's keyboard works as a titled dance movement in rounded binary form early in his career, the style of the minuet is retained ... in numerous movements in *Tempo di menuetto*.'[42] Even in William S. Newman's huge survey *The Sonata in the Classic Era* no distinction is suggested.[43] Sandra Rosenblum, on the other hand, sees tempo as the definitive parameter. She notes the existence of two types of minuets in the eighteenth century: the 'more usual' piece, which, 'although often headed Allegretto, moves with one pulse per measure'; and the 'more moderate' type, 'frequently headed Menuetto, Moderato or Tempo di menuetto', which moves with three beats per bar and may contain subdivisions of the beat into quaver triplets and semiquavers. She suggests this division may derive from original differences between the generally fast Italian minuet, often written in 3/8 or 6/8, and the stately French minuet in

---

[41] David Wyn Jones, 'Minuet', in *Oxford Composer Companions: Haydn*, ed. Jones, 235.
[42] Howard Irving, 'Haydn's *Deutscher Tanz* Finales: Style versus Form in Eighteenth-Century Music', *Studies in Music* 20 (1986), 15–16.
[43] For example, William S. Newman's discussion of the finale of Haydn's Sonata in E flat major H25 (c1773), a self-contained Tempo di Menuet without any contrasting section, shows that he makes no distinction between the minuet-as-finale and the tempo di menuetto. Newman, *The Sonata in the Classic Era* (Chapel Hill: University of North Carolina Press, 1963), 162.

3/4.⁴⁴ Certainly a consensus has arisen that tempo di menuetto is slow or relatively slow within the possible range of minuet speeds. Frederick Neumann, for instance, takes tempo di menuetto to connote 'relaxed ease', 'anything but fast'.⁴⁵ But then he suggests an equivalent tempo marking for this of Allegretto, which for Rosenblum belongs to the faster type. To add to the uncertainty, we might recollect the finale of Rosetti's oboe concerto Murray C33 from Chapter 2, which features the unaccountable appearance of a tempo di menuetto section that is also marked 'Adagio'.

Defining the tempo di menuetto in terms of its relative speed seems to have been the commonest gambit in the work of eighteenth-century theorists. Heinrich Christoph Koch and Johann Gottfried Walther did so, but simply equated this with the speed of the minuet proper.⁴⁶ Türk, in his *Clavierschule* of 1789, seems to follow suit in writing 'there are some pieces which should be performed in the tempos of various dances. They are entitled: . . . tempo di minuetto, gavotta, sarabande, etc., [meaning] in the tempo of a minuetto, gavotte, sarabande, etc.'⁴⁷ If we read this carefully, though, it also emphasizes the relative abstraction from functional origins that I suggested earlier. Türk describes a piece that is written in the tempo of the dance, conceptually distinct from a piece that simply carries the name of the dance itself and hence more closely approximates the functional dance form. But the ambiguity of defining a piece as being 'in the tempo of a minuetto', whether as a compositional act or as a theoretical interpretation, is apparent when Türk later states: 'The *minuet* . . ., a well-known dance of noble and charming character in 3/4 measure . . ., is played moderately fast and agreeable, but executed without embellishments[.] (In some regions, the minuet is played much too fast when it is not used for the dance.)'⁴⁸ This not only reveals that there was disagreement about and variability of minuet tempos in performance, it renders problematic the earlier assertion that tempo di menuetto should go at the speed of a minuet. A different sort of definition comes from Riepel, in his *Anfangsgründe der*

---

⁴⁴ Sandra P. Rosenblum, *Performance Practices in Classic Piano Music* (Bloomington: Indiana University Press, 1988), 338.

⁴⁵ Frederick Neumann, 'How Fast Should Classical Minuets Be Played?', *Historical Performance* 4 (1991), 7, cited in William Malloch, 'The Minuets of Haydn and Mozart: Goblins or Elephants?', *Early Music* 21/3 (1993), 437, who describes this as an oversimplification.

⁴⁶ Cited and discussed by Jürgen Brauner in his *Studien zu den Klaviertrios von Joseph Haydn* (Tutzing: Schneider, 1995), 385–392.

⁴⁷ Türk, *Klavierschule*, 110; *School of Clavier Playing*, trans. with Introduction and notes by Raymond S. Haggh (Lincoln: University of Nebraska Press, 1982), 106.

⁴⁸ Türk, *Klavierschule*, 401; *School of Clavier Playing*, trans. Haggh, 395.

musicalischen Setzkunst. He denies the validity of recent minuets containing periods with uneven numbers of bars: 'I . . . believe that a minuet must remain a proper minuet, if it is to be pleasing to the listener . . . as such. Anything else is a *tempo di menuetto*.'[49] But, as always with such attempted codification, one must consider whether the author was as much writing against as describing contemporary practices, and Riepel's admonition implies a situation where minuets often did contain uneven numbers of bars and where terminology was not as purely or consistently applied as the theorist would wish.

Rather more encouraging for our purposes is a passage found elsewhere in Riepel's treatise, written in dialogue form. In the second chapter the student asks, 'The final Allegro of a symphony and so forth can sometimes be in 2/4, or even in *alla breve* tempo. Or perhaps instead of that one could have a singing *Tempo moderato* or *Tempo di minué*?', to which the teacher replies 'That is indeed possible.'[50] This ventriloquized exchange shows an explicit recognition of a slower finale type, in which cantabile style predominates, and tempo di menuetto is allied with this. It also suggests that, even by mid-century, a fast finale ('final Allegro') could be perceived as the default option for an instrumental cycle ('a symphony and so forth').

It is significant that a cantabile quality was already associated by Riepel in 1752 with the tempo di menuetto finale, since it is not always easy to hear this in retrospect in movements of this time. Of course such a movement may feature a more explicit singing style than an average allegro conclusion, but it is hard to hear this as exceptional against our other point of reference, the minuet proper. This continues to be the case in orchestral music, especially in the concerto, where the tempo di menuetto finale remained common for some time. Among instances in Mozart one could cite the finales of the Concerto for Two Violins in C major, K190 (1774), the Bassoon Concerto in B flat major, K191 (1774), the Flute Concerto in G major, K313 (1778), and the Piano Concerto in F major K413 (1782–1783). In these and in less well-known concerto finales their labelling as tempo di menuetto may represent a relatively 'unmarked' compositional decision. For example, in the final movement of Leopold Hofmann's Flute Concerto in D major, Badley D3 (no later than 1767), a constant crotchet pulse together with a predominance of dotted rhythms tend to suggest a high minuet style, but there is no grandeur here. The tone is friendly, and a similar amiable flavour, more a middle than a high style, marks the

---

[49] Riepel, *Anfangsgründe zur musicalischen Setzkunst*, volume 1, 10.
[50] Riepel, *Anfangsgründe zur musicalischen Setzkunst*, volume 2, 82.

'Tempo di Menuet' finale of Abel's Keyboard Concerto in E flat major, Op. 11 No. 3 (1774), though this features a notably plaintive central section where the soloist takes off lyrically.

There is a relative intimacy to both these finales, but this seems a self-evident one. These movements exemplify the tradition of the easily paced finale, a wider phenomenon of which tempo di menuetto forms just a part. It may be most familiar to us as found in such movements as the finales of Beethoven's sonatas Opp. 7, 22 or 90. Many of these movements share a 2/4 time signature and the heading Allegretto, and are in fact comparable to tempo di menuetto as a distinct complex of gesture and affect: both show that tempo types, in association with specific metres, not only carry particular characteristics, but can do so to the extent that they form subgenres. That neither has been widely discussed as such only shows how thoroughly ingrained certain tempo types have become as the 'natural' options not just through the weight of practice in the later eighteenth century, but also in subsequent centuries. Indeed, we are not very good in general at dealing with moderately paced movements that do not offer pronounced Allegro/Presto or Adagio/Andante characteristics. Movements of such 'uncertain' tempo character, often suggesting a delicacy that is not among our favoured affects, can in fact occur in all positions in the cycle – not just the moderate finale, but also the moderate first movement, and perhaps in particular the not-very-slow movement.

I now turn to some cases that might cast a more positive light on the specific typology of the tempo di menuetto finale. The tempo di menuetto finale of Johann Schobert's Sonata Op. 6 No. 1 forms part of a group of three works for keyboard with violin and bass accompaniments ad libitum, published in Paris between 1761 and 1767 (Example 5.4). It is a quite definitive example of how tempo di menuetto can differ from the minuet-as-finale, for which we have a convenient point of comparison, since the final movements of the two subsequent sonatas are minuets. (And both are ternary movements with a designated trio as opposed to the rounded-binary structure of No. 1.) Our tempo di menuetto movement operates mostly in four-bar units, a level of regularity, but on both smaller and larger scales it is irregular. On the smaller scale, there is very little sense of movement by two-bar units that was the norm for the minuet, a norm that is consistently upheld by the relevant movements of Sonatas 2 and 3. On the larger scale, any sense of antecedent–consequent or similar parallel relationship between the four-bar phrases is weak – in fact, radically so. In terms of material, syntax and affect this movement seems to go out of its way not to resemble a minuet.

Example 5.4 Schobert, Sonata in E flat major Op. 6 No. 1/iii, bars 1–29

The very first four bars proclaim a distance from the minuet model – although not with too much of a flourish, since tempo di menuettos do tend to be gentle creatures. The sustained tonic pedal clearly removes much sense of danceability, especially striking at the very start, when momentum and carriage must be defined. The continuous triplets represent another level of softening from any tight metrical-gestural outline, and, within that, we might note the change from downbeat to upbeat beginnings of the units within the phrase. The second and third units, at bars 2^3–3^2 and 3^3–4^2, build sequentially on bars 1^3–2^2, which does suggest impetus and direction, but the realization of each quasi-suspension on the first beat is different – another level of informality. The second phrase offers relatively more normal diction in itself, but it fails to match the first unit; it therefore forms part of a contrasting, rather than parallel, period. It does complement the antecedent in certain ways, by introducing a more normal harmonic rhythm, by pivoting around V (when the first phrase was based on I) and by having a more functional melodic character (bars 7–8 present a converging cadence[51]). On the other hand, bars 5 and 6 both introduce a new rhythmic base value, first semiquavers at 5 then quavers in 6. The strongest connection to bars 1–4 is the cadential figure at 7^3–8^2, which matches the form it took at bar 4. The bass figure in bar 8, while complementing the right hand's semiquaver figure from bar 5, provides an impulsive link to something distinctly odd: three bars of undifferentiated quavers in repeated-note close-position chords. This will surely inspire few thoughts of the dance. In principle the static repetition – with the pedal note now effectively in the top voice's F – suggests a return to the world of 1–4. Once more the only real continuity comes at the end of the phrase, which closes in bar 12 with the same figure we heard at the end of the two previous units.

Further continuity comes with the lengthy semiquaver anacrusis figure in bar 12, similar to what we heard in the left hand in bar 8. But once more this leads to something completely different, with repeated Alberti triplets in the left hand, the first time triplets have been sustained through a whole phrase. The bass line of b♭ (13)–b♭ (14)–a (15)–b♭ (16) in fact repeats that which underpinned the previous four bars, but above this we find something that once more seems to have very little to do with what went before: lyrically expansive as opposed to the lack of melodic activity in 9–12. Schobert does refer to earlier shapes – bar 15 is very close to bar 5 and bar 16 clearly refers to the initial triplet contour of bar 1^{1-2}, yet the impression of a highly informal discourse persists. The following unit from bar 17 provides a continuation, not yet another new start, suggesting that a sentence structure is unfolding, with bars 13–14 and 15–16 functioning as statement and restatement respectively, and these bars have a clear pre-cadential function. This is then fulfilled when bar 19 leads us towards the movement's first authentic cadence.

---

[51] The converging cadence is defined and illustrated in Gjerdingen, *Music in the Galant Style*, 159–163.

The formula heard in bar 19 – the Cudworth – does indeed produce a kind of cadence, but its effect is greatly reduced by the overlapping of the fourth bar with the first bar of the next unit – bar 20 acts as the last bar of one phrase as well as the first bar of the next. Thus the most unexceptionable writing heard so far, from bar 17 on, is undermined at the point of completion. This is even more noticeable because scale degree 2 does not fall as expected to 1 at the start of bar 20 – which the Cudworth formula ought to make inevitable – but rises to scale degree 5, the F. And the overlap sounds even more like a straight interruption when we consider the nature of the material. The sustained local tonic pedal for four bars from this point reminds us of the opening unit. And the melodic style has the sort of freedom we found in the first four bars, but even more so, as it expansively and ravishingly fills the four bars with continuous quavers in a falling arc.

A rude interruption follows from bar 24, which gives us yet another new rhythmic type – continuous demisemiquavers – in the right hand. This, in conjunction with the familiar semiquaver scale in the left hand, clearly evokes orchestral writing, another sort of disjunction. The pre-cadential bar 26 again looks likely to deliver us a proper cadence, but once more this is effectively evaded. The right hand's b♭^{2} at 27 is an octave too high, which creates another clear point of discontinuity. In the following unit, bar 28 reactivates the pre-cadential bar 26, and at bar 29 this leads at last to melodic resolution – and, indeed, to the first satisfactorily articulated (perfect authentic) cadence of the movement. But the end has been reached too early, and this is an absolutely bare three-bar phrase. The provocative melange of material suggests a composer testing the bounds of his generic contract with the player and listener,[52] and it is surely the conception of the movement within the frame of a tempo di menuetto that helps to make this possible. The net effect is a victory for an oblique, even inefficient, approach to the topic of the minuet.

At the same time, on a broader scale, this music represents the sharp end of the 'mixed style', with its constant changes of gesture and, above all, its radical admixture of rhythmic values. One can readily understand that common critical perspective of the time that saw an unprincipled lack of unity in the modern style. Yet this piece also shows how periodic regularity could cover all sins: the cornucopia of ideas is held together by the medium-scale regularity of four-bar phrases, which is only compromised towards the end of the section we have been studying.

---

[52] The phrase 'generic contract' derives from the well-known article by Jeffrey Kallberg, 'The Rhetoric of Genre: Chopin's Nocturne in G Minor', *19th-Century Music* 11/3 (1988), 238–261.

However, the radical distinction drawn between tempo di menuetto finale and minuet-as-finale in Schobert's Op. 6 is less apparent in other parts of his output. Complicating the picture is a comparison with movements such as the Menuetto. Grazioso from his Violin Sonata in C minor, Op. 14 No. 3, and the Tempo di Minuetto finale from a Quartet for Two Violins, Bass and Keyboard in G major, Op. 7 No. 3 (both 1761–1767). Both works feature a designated trio, and it is difficult to say why the tempo di menuetto finale is called such in distinction to the minuet finale of the violin sonata. It is unlikely that a tempo difference could account for the different titles: both movements would seem to demand a moderate execution. However, there are some possible distinctions of rhythmic organization. The tempo di menuetto movement operates more clearly in groups of four, whereas the minuet movement works in two-bar modules, meaning that the tempo di menuetto suggests greater sweep and continuity. Secondly, the rhythmic values in the quartet movement are much more varied, impulsive, if one will, so that this tempo di menuetto once again suggests a relatively greater informality of rhythm and rhetoric.

In other cases, though, it seems that composers used minuet and tempo di menuetto interchangeably, either because they meant much the same thing or because the composers were indifferent to any distinction. One might expect this as we move further back into the eighteenth century: for instance, Wagenseil's six sonatas Op. 1 (1753) contain two tempo di menuetto finales and four minuet movements, two of these placed centrally and two placed in final position. All six movements have named trios. It is hard to distinguish the tempo di menuetto movements from the others, although there may be a case for their looser or more varied rhythmic organization. Or we could compare two sonatas for flute and continuo by C. P. E. Bach. The Sonata in G major Wq123 (1735) has a tempo di menuetto finale with two variations on a sixteen-bar theme; the Sonata in E minor, Wq124 (1737), features a finale that is identical in its layout but is called 'Minuetto'. This suggests that the names are alternatives, at least at this time and in this place. Of course we are all enjoined nowadays to attend carefully to the contingencies of local circumstance, but we must be careful not to overestimate the autonomy of various European centres in the eighteenth century, above all when we are dealing with an avowed international success story like the minuet. Thus if one remarks that Boccherini seems to stand quite outside all the developments suggested, since for him minuet and tempo di menuetto seem to be fully interchangeable right through to the century's end, we should not assume it was because he was cut off in Spain. Apart from anything else, he was having works published in all the major centres and undoubtedly had a good sense of his market. By my reckoning Boccherini wrote over fifty tempo di menuetto movements in his instrumental cycles, but there are only isolated suggestions of a distinction in usage. It seems that almost regardless of designation, a trio is included, and all his minuets move in two-bar units. Yet one could hardly claim that Boccherini was indifferent to the finer points of minuet style. The very frequency of designations like 'Minuetto con moto', 'Minuetto non presto' and 'Minuetto tempo giusto' suggests he understood the minuet within a highly differentiated spectrum of possible tempo and affective characters. He also, in common with some others, uses tempo di menuetto to designate an internal movement, what we might imagine ought more properly to be called minuet alone – a further complication in our composite picture.

At the other end of things, Clementi wrote remarkably few tempo di menuetto movements, but they all seem conceptually distinct from a minuet. The finale of the duet sonata Op. 3 No. 2 (1779) offers an instance (Example 5.5). The most remarkable aspect of this movement is hard to articulate: it is almost an indeterminacy of expression. We can't exactly say it goes against an idealized 'spirit of the minuet', as there is clearly elegance and control of deportment here, and the tone seems perfectly 'natural'. Of course such qualities could also follow from wider generic factors – this is after all domestic music, whose rhetoric does not demand projection of affect. Perhaps the dual personality of the tempo di menuetto, issuing both from the minuet and from the finale as a type, aids the cultivation of such indeterminacy. If the tempo di menuetto seems to come into its own as it loses ground in favour of the racy, popular finale, above all the rondo, this seems to encourage a focus on its potential ambivalence of tempo character: it is neither slow nor fast music. Yet this vagueness of definition may have been not so much a hindrance as an opportunity. In offering a tempo di menuetto movement composers could exploit the sense that they were working with a not altogether distinctive set of generic parameters. The relatively weak expectations that arise as a consequence might help explain why comedy seems so rare in this genre. I have yet to discover a single tempo di menuetto movement with overt humorous elements, a remarkable circumstance given the comic preoccupations of this time. Again, the supposedly more restricted minuet does much better here, and witty effects abound.

Various features seem to embody indeterminacy in this particular case. Clementi's very first bar is ambiguous. Given the entry of the bass and the

Example 5.5 Clementi, Sonata for Piano Duet in E flat major Op. 3 No. 2/ii, bars 1–30

Example 5.5 (continued)

beginning of melodic motion in the second bar, we are forced to understand the whole of bar 1 as a bar-long anacrusis. Yet the unit to which this upbeat leads lasts just three bars, so perhaps bar 1 is to be understood as integral to the phrase after all. A further part of the ambiguity is that bar 3 could be heard as hypermetrically stronger than bar 2, in other words that its first beat carries a relatively stronger accent: the implication of a Heartz schema in this first phrase, with its typical proportions of 2:1:1 accompanying the I5/3–6/4–5/3 motion, supports this.[53] The contrary-motion scales that follow in bars 5–6 also have an ambivalent character. They ought to represent a brilliant gesture but in context feel more like part of a tenderly lyrical stream. In this respect they are reminiscent of the closing figuration found in our Example 5.3, the finale of Haydn's piano trio H17.

A further feature is the use of alternating octave figuration, the so-called murky bass, in the first few bars of the secondo part. This suggests a musette topic, more broadly the world of the pastoral, but no more than that. The parallel melodic thirds heard above this, in conjunction with just such a static bass, are a familiar textural embodiment of the pastoral, but they also feature refined chromatic contours that blur any pastoral flavour. We also heard a bass pedal at the start of our Schobert sonata (Example 5.4), indeed the very same low E♭ octave. In fact, the sustained pedal note or drone is a common presence in the tempo di menuetto finales I have examined, and most of them seem to be as topically reserved about this stylistic signal as are the Schobert and Clementi examples. An outright low style is rarely found. One might think that such reserved deportment issues from the minuet itself, but then, as I have suggested, the minuet itself often seems to be both more varied and less

---

[53] The Heartz schema was identified and named by John A. Rice in his article 'The Heartz: A Galant Schema from Corelli to Mozart', *Music Theory Spectrum* 36/2 (2014), 315–332.

inhibited. It almost seems as if this tempo di menuetto manner represents a distillation of the essence of minuet as writers of the time liked to define it, enacting the virtues of noble simplicity and a lack of ostentation. Also relevant here is that the two episodes in the ABACA rondo form of Clementi's movement are clearly nothing like trios – they are unimaginable as such. Rather, they amplify the mood and indeed material of the A section, showing different facets of what feels like an expressive whole. This minimizing of potential contrast and relative unity of tone is very characteristic of tempo di menuetto finales, contributing to their poetics of 'moderate' interiority. It is quite unlike the typical trio section of the ternary-form minuet, which normally formed a sharp internal contrast, often, of course, precisely in the direction of the pastoral. We find this also in the tempo di menuetto finale of the Violin Sonata in B flat major (Š88; 1780s?) by Joseph Anton Steffan (1726–1797). It occupies a leisurely 248 bars, taking its time over a remarkably small amount of material. While it is in a sectional ternary form, its (unlabelled) middle section never strays very far thematically.

We should also note that Clementi's finale carries a tempo marking, Andante, in addition to its tempo di menuetto designation. Such additional markings are common enough in the genre – for instance, the opening movement of a Sonata in B flat major S1 (1774) by Frantisek Xaver Dusek (1731–1799) marked 'Tempo di minuetto più tosto allegro'; the finale of a Concertino in A major, Badley A2, by Hofmann for Flute, Violin, Cello, Keyboard and Bass (1769) marked 'Tempo di Minuetto poco vivace'; the finale of Mozart's Violin Sonata in F major K377 (1781) marked 'Tempo di Menuetto. Un poco allegretto'; or the middle movement from Beethoven's Violin Sonata in G major Op. 30 No. 3 (1802) marked 'Tempo di Minuetto ma molto moderato e grazioso'. Such indications would seem to help our quest to determine the understood tempo character of the tempo di menuetto. However, all these could bear two meanings: confirmatory (making explicit the assumption of a more or less standard tempo di menuetto speed) or exceptional (instructing performers that the particular movement should be performed outside the normal range). For instance, Clementi's 'Andante' could be counselling a somewhat slower than normal tempo di menuetto speed, just as Hofmann's 'poco vivace' would seem to suggest a somewhat quicker one.

In the case of Haydn, there is first of all a formal rationale for the tempo di menuetto designation. Haydn uses it to indicate a minuet movement that does not take the form minuet-trio-minuet da capo, so that any other treatment of the topic, normally more extended, qualifies as tempo di menuetto.⁵⁴ It is also clear that tempo di menuetto becomes a full replacement for the minuet-as-finale after the 1760s. Before that point, the evidence for a clear distinction between the two types is partial. The tempo di menuetto finales of the early string trios are full of quirks, especially rhythmic and syntactic, that embody a milder form of what we saw in the Schobert sonata. Of course Haydn's rhythmic wit, which is in place from the start, also leaves its mark on ordinary minuet movements, as in the early string quartets, but the sheer extent of the oddities in the string trios surely relates to the use of tempo di menuetto and its potentially looser relationship with the functional parent dance. The Trio in E major H1, for instance, is determinedly irregular, with many three-bar phrases and a general avoidance of the normal concatenations of minuet language. On the other hand, the six sonatas for violin and viola (before 1769?) all have minuet finales with variations, all marked tempo di menuetto except for one, called 'Minuet', which is indistinguishable from the others.

From the 1770s, however, the expressive typology of the tempo di menuetto finale becomes quite distinct in Haydn's hands, in his piano sonatas and trios. Example 5.6a shows the start of the second and final movement of the Piano Trio in F major H6 (1784). The descending steps heard after the initial anacrusis suggest a certain gravity of expression, while a series of ornaments gestures towards a courtly minuet style. But the presence of yet another initial sustained bass pedal helps to suppress this flavour, although it may not do enough to create a pastoral tone as such. Outweighing its claims is the violin's inner part, almost duetting with the piano's tune in a series of wave motions, almost sounding in fact like a Schumannesque 'inner voice'. And the syntax is very continuous, moving decidedly in four- rather than two-bar units. The net impression is of a certain heaviness of sensibility kept in order by the minuet.

From bar 4^3 there is no parallel consequent phrase, though thematically it starts like one. Bar 5^3, with its trill, matches what we heard at the equivalent point of the previous phrase (bar 1^3), but when it leaps up to the start of bar 6, this leap then followed by descending steps, we are also hearing a version of the first four beats of the melody. Bar 5^3 thus has

---

[54] One seeming exception is the third movement of Haydn's Quartet in F major Op. 50 No. 5 (1787), which is marked Tempo di Menuet. However, this is not quite the standard ternary form. Rather like the third movement of Symphony No. 50 that we considered earlier in this chapter, the 'trio' (Haydn does not name the central sections in his Op. 50 set) begins with a further version of the movement's opening gambit, if now rendered by all four players in unison, before sliding into its new tonality. For further discussion see Sutcliffe, *Haydn: String Quartets, Op. 50*, 42–46, 55–56 and 98–99.

Example 5.6a Haydn, Piano Trio in F major H6/ii, bars 1-32[2]

a double role: it forms part of a symmetrical match for the opening of the previous phrase, while at the same time representing the start of a heightened form of that shape. The net result is that bar 6 witnesses further stepwise falling motion instead of the compensating stepwise ascent that we heard in bars 2–3. Then on the second beat of that bar the trill comes a beat too early – it should be on the third beat of the bar if the unit is to continue matching the model (compare bar 1^3). The third beat of bar 6 then rises by a fourth, from E to A, as did the initial anacrusis to the first bar. This means we have a sort of stretto effect thematically, and also in terms of ornaments – with a turn following on the a^2 of bar 7^1, we are now hearing an ornamental flourish every two beats. With the bass pedal having

Example 5.6a (continued)

disappeared and the melody continuing to rise in register, the consequent represents a much heightened form of the antecedent of bars 1–4.

After the double bar Haydn detaches the cadential formula we have just heard and repeats it by itself – a reflexive treatment of the familiar that we investigated in Chapter 3 (which included a glance at this particular passage). In fact, this is just the formula that was given special treatment, via the device of the simplifying cadence, in the finale of Mozart's sonata K332 (Example 3.16). But here the bottom falls out of the texture and the formula is exposed. Without its customary root-position-dominant foundation, it sounds naked and vulnerable – an extraordinary effect in these circumstances. Obviously this functions as an echo of the previous close melodically; at the same time this is the start of a new section, clarified by the sequential continuation – so there is a double function. The cadential formula, the musical equivalent of a common courtesy, an automatic utterance, comes into quite a different perspective through this repetition and even more through the continuation by sequence up a fourth. Originally the cadence point, through its easy familiarity, lightened the tone after the heavy intensity of earlier material. But now it partakes of just this same heaviness. If Haydn has already lifted the cadential figure out of the ordinary and made it strange, at the third time of asking it is hugely dramatized. The third limb of the sequence brings something like a primal cry, a convulsion. Instead of the repeated note over the barline the melody at 10–11 rises by a fourth, from C to F, as at the opening. Suddenly the texture has depth again, and indeed far more so than at the opening – the piano plays its highest available note, f^3, while the cello re-enters on a sustained low G. To come down from this high, the piano uses the first grouping of continuous semiquavers we have heard, finishing on the first two beats of bar 12 with the falling-step figure that featured prominently in the first section.

This leads, from bar 12, to a texture encountered at the opening, with a drone in the cello and a sinuous stepwise inner voice in the violin, while the piano carries a continuous lyrical line. But this is affectively heightened, as one might expect after such a momentous irruption. The melodic wave motions from the first section return with rising and falling steps in the piano, but these now sound freer and more urgent. The ornaments seem to take their place in this free cantilena rather than having the more formal, even French, flavour of the earlier ones. At 16 the ecstatic long line continues, but is broken up into three two-note pairs, as if to reflect the two-note pairs heard immediately after the double bar (also three in number). This leads to a longer two-note appoggiatura figure in bar 17, the music almost draining away at this point. Bars 18–19 seem to be a standard filler, another formulaic approach to a cadence point. But they are also a diminution of the previous two bars, more exactly of the melody beginning on the third quaver of 16 – we hear the same pitch succession of G–F (paired) to E–D (paired) followed by a longer C (minim)–B♮. This must also refer to the pairs after the double bar, especially since the piano is once more unaccompanied. But here we seem to have a reversal of the earlier process, a completion of the circle, as what was passionate becomes more dispassionate, what was expressively unexpected is transformed into the formulaically expected.

The opening phrase returns intact, but from the end of bar 24 we have what seems to be a better, or at least more likely, continuation of the thought. From 24^3 to 25^1 the opening unit is simply transposed up an octave, but then it stops after the downbeat, so there is no ensuing heavy descent. Then bar 25^3 continues the upbeat turn figure, but this is joined to a recollection of the melody from bars $13–14^1$ and $15–16^1$, the rising sixth filled in by step followed by a leap down. And here again what was heightened melts into formula. The legato is replaced by a lighter staccato, and the texture is again bare: note how key moments in the dialectic of formula and sensibility are highlighted by this piano-only texture. This rising staccato scale then leads to the return to the cadential formula that was heard at the end of the first section and then so dramatically reworked immediately after the double bar. In fact the cadential formula that Haydn is preoccupied with is slightly larger than we have yet acknowledged. It also includes a High Drop, in this case down a fourth from the b♭^{1} of bar 26^3 to the f^1 on the following downbeat (compare the version of the formula used in the minuet of Beethoven's sonata Op. 2 No. 1 seen in Example 3.8, and which led to the brief discussion of Haydn's movement at that point). This has a corrective function: we in fact heard a High Drop in the original version of the formula in bars 7–8, but there the formula was unnaturally compressed as a result of the stretto-like accumulation of melodic intensity. The initial high portion, which customarily sounds on an upbeat, followed by the intervallic drop and the arrival of a V6/4 harmony, was instead heard on the downbeat of bar 7.

After the phrase is completed with this metrical realignment of the cadential formula, Haydn backs up and starts to repeat this new consequent phrase. Its first two bars (24^3–26^1) are repeated up an octave, *forte*, at 28^3–30^1, but the ensuing rising staccato scale does not return. Instead the phrase merges into a transposition of material that ended the first part, but, crucially, our cadential formula is once more presented in its metrically corrected guise: compare bars 7–8^1 with bars 30^3–32^1. The last part of this section altogether represents the purest minuet style we have encountered, with no 'inner voice' and plenty of air in the texture. Note too how the earlier climactic f^3 from bar 11 is recaptured and made less exceptional – it occurs twice in the final phrase unit, so being absorbed into the voice-leading continuity. This whole section of the movement plays with the gestures and particulars of minuet style as it investigates levels of formality and interiority.

The middle section in F minor from bar 33 (not, of course, given the name of trio) clarifies this interiority, with the clear thematic relationship of the incipits being part of this process. Here we find a far higher proportion of intervallic leaps: the violin's melody, inhabiting a higher register, soars much more easily, not needing to feel its way step by step. The texture is homophonic as opposed to the more linear writing of the A section, which means it is now consistently aerated. The real rhetorical difference, though, is found in the broadly unfolding melody, natural and artless – unlike the (productive) inhibitions of the first section. Haydn has in fact reversed the normal rhetorical distinction between the modes – here the major is full of inflections while the minor is broader and more settled.

The short coda from bar 142 (Example 5.6b) recalls the passage from bar 8^3 onwards and indeed the whole process of manipulation of the cadential formula. Its echoing repetitions after a firm cadence point to the earlier passage, but this is a foil for the more important differences. Here the figure

Example 5.6b Haydn, Piano Trio in F major H6/ii, bars 135³–148

has been absorbed to become an entirely normal part of melodic diction and of phrase syntax – the familiar postcadential gambit of repeating a formula to strengthen the rhetoric of closure. So the figure reverts to a more purely formal role, but this is also an expressive simplification, one might even say a catharsis. And note how it is surrounded by a halo of horn calls in the piano, creating an idyllic finish after the eventful interiority of the movement. A return to a more normal linguistic register is suggested by the familiar formulation and its familiar treatment, but the convention is deepened – made more sincere, if one will – by what has gone before.

For my own idyllic finish, this is how I would formulate the elements and tendencies of the tempo di menuetto finale that help to define it as a more or less independent genre. It is for small forces, normally one to three players; the tempo is relatively slow; its design is variable, but when in ternary form, a 'trio' designation is rare; the alternating parts (or, if in sonata form, second-subject materials) often show minimal contrast from the initial section, creating relative unity of tone; phrase syntax is broader and more continuous than in the minuet; linear writing and smooth intervals are characteristic; the declamatory monophony of unisons and octaves is rare; sustained pedals are often found, as indeed are horn calls, but neither ever leads to a pronounced rustic flavour; tessitura tends to be on the low side; mellow flat-side keys are more likely; and overt humour is rare. And then there are the more intangible elements that model a behaviour that, while full of inner warmth, is reserved, undemonstrative and frequently ambivalent. Such an intimate, confidential tone must have been flattering to the player or listener, absorbing them in a concentrated expression of the minuet's official virtues, its moderate manner and relaxed grace. It codified, and perhaps also helped to preserve, a kind of sociability that demanded composure and polite shaping of discourse, but also allowed for the feelings that are connoted by that familiar term, sensibility.

For all such notional independence, the genre dies out sooner than the minuet itself. Yet while tempo di menuetto disappeared as a finale, it remained as a distinct expressive quantity, normally migrating to other movement positions. There are instances in the piano sonatas and other chamber forms of Dussek (for example in his sonatas Op. 70 (1807) and Op. 77 (1812)) and Beethoven (as in the violin sonata Op. 30 No. 3, mentioned earlier, or the first movement of the Sonata in F major Op. 54 of 1804), not forgetting the last section of the Diabelli Variations (1819–1823), which takes the form of a wryly mannered, yet also moving tempo di menuetto. Czerny's verdict of 1846 on one such example – 'simple grace and gentle feeling'[55] – shows that that flavour was still understood, and in

---

[55] Czerny was writing of the tempo-di-menuetto middle movement of Beethoven's violin sonata Op. 30 No. 3. Carl Czerny, *Über den richtigen Vortrag der sämtlichen Beethoven'sche Klavierwerke*, ed. Paul Badura-Skoda (Vienna: Universal, 1963), facsimile edition of chapters 2 and 3 of *Die Kunst des Vortrags der älteren und neueren Klavierkompositionen* (Vienna: Diabelli, 1846), cited in Rosenblum, *Performance Practices in Classic Piano Music*, 346.

fact many later so-called minuets adopted tempo di menuetto traits. So its interiority became absorbed into the expressive code of a minuet form that was increasingly bathed in a retrospective glow.

The tempo di menuetto offers a nice final point of focus for some of the attributes that have been sidelined in the reception of later eighteenth-century instrumental music. Just as my project has not attempted an encompassing view of all the musical-cultural currents that might be traced in later eighteenth-century instrumental works, so the tempo di menuetto finale is no complete incarnation of what the period had to offer. But, with its undemonstrative depth, it provides some clue as to what has been missing or misunderstood in the reception of musical sociability.

References

Agawu, Kofi. *Playing with Signs: A Semiotic Interpretation of Classic Music*. Princeton: Princeton University Press, 1991.

Allanbrook, Wye J. [Jamison] 'Mozart's K331, First Movement: Once More, with Feeling', in *Communication in Eighteenth-Century Music*, ed. Danuta Mirka and Kofi Agawu, 254–282. Cambridge: Cambridge University Press, 2008.

'Mozart's Tunes and the Comedy of Closure', in *On Mozart*, ed. James M. Morris, 169–186. Cambridge: Cambridge University Press, in association with the Woodrow Wilson Center Press, 1994.

Rhythmic Gesture in Mozart: 'Le nozze di Figaro' and 'Don Giovanni'. Chicago: University of Chicago Press, 1983.

'Theorizing the Comic Surface', in *Music in the Mirror: Reflections on the History of Music Theory and Literature for the Twenty-First Century*, ed. Andreas Giger and Thomas Mathiesen, 195–216. Lincoln: University of Nebraska Press, 2002.

The Secular Commedia: Comic Mimesis in Late Eighteenth-Century Instrumental Music, ed. Mary Ann Smart and Richard Taruskin. Berkeley: University of California Press, 2014.

'Two Threads through the Labyrinth: Topic and Process in the First Movements of K. 332 and K. 333', in *Convention in Eighteenth- and Nineteenth-Century Music: Essays in Honor of Leonard G. Ratner*, ed. Wye J. Allanbrook, Janet M. Levy and William P. Mahrt, 125–171. Stuyvesant: Pendragon, 1992.

Allanbrook, Wye J. and Wendy Hilton. 'Dance Rhythms in Mozart's Arias', *Early Music* 20/1 (1992), 142–149.

Almén, Byron. *A Theory of Musical Narrative*. Bloomington: Indiana University Press, 2008.

Alpers, Paul. *What Is Pastoral?* Chicago: University of Chicago Press, 1996.

Anderson, Emily, ed. and trans. *The Letters of Mozart and His Family*, third edition, revised by Stanley Sadie and Fiona Smart. London: Palgrave Macmillan, 1985.

Applegate, Celia. 'Introduction: Music among the Historians', *German History* 30/3 (2012), 329–349.

Arnold, Ignaz. *Gallerie der berühmtesten Tonkünstler des achtzehnten und neunzehnten Jahrhunderts*. Buren: Knuf, 1810.

Joseph Haydn: Eine kurze Biographie und ästhetische Darstellung seiner Werke. Erfurt: Müller, 1810.

Aspden, Suzanne. 'Bach and the Feminised *Galant*', *Understanding Bach* 5 (2010), 9–22.

Auden, W. H. 'Notes on the Comic', *Thought: Fordham University Quarterly* 27/1 (1952), 57–71.

The Dyer's Hand and Other Essays. London: Faber, 1963.

Bach, Carl Philip Emanuel. Autobiography, in *Carl Burney's der Musik Doktors Tagebuch seiner musikalischen Reisen*, volume 3: *Durch Böhmen, Sachsen, Brandenburg, Hamburg und Holland*. Hamburg: Bode, 1773.

Versuch über die wahre Art das Klavier zu spielen. Part One, Berlin: Christian Friedrich Henning, 1753. Part Two, Berlin: Georg Ludewig Winter, 1762.

Badley, Allan. Notes to *Dittersdorf: Sinfonias*, Failoni Orchestra, conducted by Uwe Grodd. Naxos 8.553975, 1998.

Baillot, Pierre-Marie, Jean-Henri Levasseur, Charles-Simon Catel and Charles Baudiot. *Méthode de Violoncelle et de Basse d'Accompagnement*. Paris: Janet & Cotelle, 1804.

Baker, Keith Michael. 'Enlightenment and the Institution of Society: Notes for a Conceptual History', in *Main Trends in Cultural History: Ten Essays*, ed. Willem Melching and Wyger Velema, 95–120. Amsterdam: Rodopi, 1994.

Baker, Nancy Kovaleff and Thomas Christensen, ed. and trans. *Aesthetics and the Art of Musical Composition in the German Enlightenment: Selected Writings of Johann Georg Sulzer and Heinrich Christoph Koch*. Cambridge: Cambridge University Press, 1995.

Balter, Tamara. 'Canon-Fodders: Parody of Learned Style in Beethoven', *Journal of Musicological Research* 32/2–3 (2013), 199–224.

Bandur, Markus. 'Plot und Rekurs – "eine gantz neue besondere Art"?', in *Haydns Streichquartette: Eine moderne Gattung*, Musik-Konzepte 116, ed. Heinz-Klaus Metzger and Rainer Riehn, 62–84. Munich: edition text + kritik, 2002.

Bar-Yoshafat, Jonatan. '*Kenner und Liebhaber*: Yet Another Look', *International Review of the Aesthetics and Sociology of Music* 44/1 (2013), 19–47.

Barnett, Gregory. 'The Early Italian Keyboard Sonata: Origins, Influences, and Disseminations', in *The Early Keyboard Sonata in Italy and Beyond*, ed. Rohan Stewart-MacDonald, 3–58. Turnhout: Brepols, 2016.

Bartha, Denes. 'On Beethoven's Thematic Structure', *The Musical Quarterly* 56/4 (1970), 759–778.

Bauman, Thomas. 'Becoming Original: Haydn and the Cult of Genius', *The Musical Quarterly* 87/2 (2004), 333–357.

Beckerman, Michael. 'Mozart's Pastoral', *Mozart-Jahrbuch* (1991), 93–100.

Beghin, Tom. *The Virtual Haydn: Paradox of a Twenty-First-Century Keyboardist*. Chicago: University of Chicago Press, 2015.

Beghin, Tom and Sander M. Goldberg. 'Coda', in *Haydn and the Performance of Rhetoric*, ed. Tom Beghin and Sander M. Goldberg, 327–331. Chicago: University of Chicago Press, 2007.

Bellini, Alice. 'Music and "Music" in Eighteenth-Century Meta-Operatic Scores', *Eighteenth-Century Music* 6/2 (2009), 183–207.

Benton, Rita. 'Form in the Sonatas of Domenico Scarlatti', *The Music Review* 13/4 (1952), 264–273.

Bergé, Pieter, Nathan John Martin, Markus Neuwirth, David Lodewyckx and Pieter Herregodts. *Concise Cadence Compendium: A Systematic Overview of Cadence Types and Terminology for 18th-Century Music*. Leuven: Leuven University Press, 2013.

Berger, Karol. *Bach's Cycle, Mozart's Arrow: An Essay on the Origins of Musical Modernity*. Berkeley: University of California Press, 2007.

Bernstein, Lawrence F. 'Joseph Haydn's Influence on the Symphonies of Antonio Rosetti', in *Historical Musicology: Sources, Methods, Interpretations*, ed. Stephen A. Crist and Roberta Montemorra Marvin, 143–187. Rochester, NY: University of Rochester Press, 2004.

Blackbourn, David. 'The German Eighteenth Century: Marking Time', in *The Century of Bach and Mozart: Perspectives on Historiography, Composition, Theory, and Performance*, ed. Sean Gallagher and Thomas Forrest Kelly, 3–15. Cambridge, MA: Harvard University Press, 2008.

Blainville, Charles Henri. *Histoire générale, critique et philologique de la musique*. Paris: Pissot, 1767.

Blair, Hugh. *A Critical Dissertation on the Poems of Ossian, the Son of Fingal*. London: T. Becket, 1763.

Lectures on Rhetoric and Belles Lettres, three volumes. Dublin: Whitestone, Colles, Burnet and others, 1783.

Blanning, T. C. W. [Tim] *The Culture of Power and the Power of Culture: Old Regime Europe 1660–1789*. Oxford: Oxford University Press, 2002.

The Triumph of Music: The Rise of Composers, Musicians and Their Art. Cambridge, MA: Belknap Press of Harvard University Press, 2012.

Blom, Eric. *Mozart* (The Master Musicians). London: Dent, 1962.

Blume, Friedrich, trans. M. D. Herder Norton. *Classic and Romantic Music: A Comprehensive Survey*. New York: Norton, 1970.

Bonds, Mark Evan. 'Haydn, Laurence Sterne, and the Origins of Musical Irony', *Journal of the American Musicological Society* 44/1 (1991), 57–91.

'Irony and Incomprehensibility: Beethoven's "Serioso" String Quartet in F Minor, Op. 95, and the Path to the Late Style', *Journal of the American Musicological Society* 70/2 (2017), 285–356.

'Replacing Haydn: Mozart's "Pleyel" Quartets', *Music & Letters* 88/2 (2007), 201–225.

Wordless Rhetoric: Musical Form and the Metaphor of the Oration. Cambridge, MA: Harvard University Press, 1991.

Botstein, Leon. 'The Consequences of Presumed Innocence: The Nineteenth-Century Reception of Joseph Haydn', in *Haydn Studies*, ed. W. Dean Sutcliffe, 1–34. Cambridge: Cambridge University Press, 1998.

Bracht, Hans-Joachim. 'Überlegungen zum Quartett-"Gespräch"', *Archiv für Musikwissenschaft* 51/3 (1994), 169–189.

Brauner, Jürgen. *Studien zu den Klaviertrios von Joseph Haydn*. Tutzing: Schneider, 1995.

Brendel, Alfred, trans. Eugene Hartzell. 'A Mozart Player Gives Himself Advice', *The New York Review of Books* (27 June 1985) www.nybooks.com/articles/1985/06/27/a-mozart-player-gives-himself-advice/.

'Must Classical Music Be Entirely Serious?: 1 The Sublime in Reverse', in *Alfred Brendel on Music: Collected Essays*, 90–112. London: Robson, 2001.

Brodey, Inger S. B. 'On Pre-Romanticism or Sensibility: Defining Ambivalences', in *A Companion to European Romanticism*, ed. Michael Ferber, 10–28. Oxford: Blackwell, 2005.

Brown, A. Peter. 'Symphony', in *Oxford Composer Companions: Haydn*, ed. David Wyn Jones, 381–398. Oxford: Oxford University Press, 2002.

The Symphonic Repertoire, volume 2: *The First Golden Age of the Viennese Symphony: Haydn, Mozart, Beethoven, and Schubert*. Bloomington: Indiana University Press, 2002.

Brown, John. *A Dissertation on the Rise, Union, and Power, the Progressions, Separations, and Corruptions, of Poetry and Music*. London: L. Davis and C. Reymers, 1763.

Brown, Marshall. 'Editorial', *Eighteenth-Century Music* 5/1 (2008), 3–6.

'The Poetry of Haydn's Songs: Sexuality, Repetition, Whimsy', in *Haydn and the Performance of Rhetoric*, ed. Beghin and Goldberg, 229–250.

Burke, Edmund. *A Philosophical Enquiry into the Origin of Our Ideas of the Sublime and Beautiful*. London: R. and J. Dodsley, 1757.

Burke, Peter. 'Performing History: The Importance of Occasions', *Rethinking History* 9/1 (2005), 35–52.

The Art of Conversation. Ithaca: Cornell University Press, 1993.

Burney, Charles. *A General History of Music from the Earliest Ages to the Present Period*, three volumes, first edition. London: author, 1776–1789; *Volume the First* and *Volume the Second*, with critical and historical notes by Frank Mercer. New York: Dover, 1957.

Review of William Jackson, *Observations on the Present State of Music, in London*, *Monthly Review* (October 1791), 196–202.

The Present State of Music in Germany, the Netherlands, and United Provinces, two volumes. London: T. Becket, J. Robson and G. Robinson, 1773.

Burney, Frances. *Camilla, or A Picture of Youth*, ed. Edward A. Bloom and Lillian D. Bloom. Oxford: Oxford University Press, 1972.

Burnham, Scott. 'Haydn and Humor', in *The Cambridge Companion to Haydn*, ed. Caryl Clark, 61–76. Cambridge: Cambridge University Press, 2005.

'Mozart's *felix culpa*: *Così fan tutte* and the Irony of Beauty', *The Musical Quarterly* 78/1 (1994), 77–98.

Mozart's Grace. Princeton: Princeton University Press, 2013.

'The Criticism of Analysis and the Analysis of Criticism', *19th-Century Music* 16/1 (1992), 70–76.

Burstein, L. Poundie. 'The Off-Tonic Return in Beethoven's Piano Concerto No. 4 in G Major, Op. 58, and Other Works', *Music Analysis* 24/3 (2005), 305–347.

Byros, Vasili. 'Meyer's Anvil: Revisiting the Schema Concept', *Music Analysis* 31/3 (2012), 273–346.

'Towards an "Archaeology" of Hearing: Schemata and Eighteenth-Century Consciousness', *Musica Humana* 1/2 (2009), 235–306.

Campbell, Archibald. *An Enquiry into the Original of Moral Virtue*. Edinburgh, 1733.

Caplin, William E. *Classical Form: A Theory of Formal Functions for the Instrumental Music of Haydn, Mozart, and Beethoven*. New York: Oxford University Press, 1998.

'The Classical Cadence: Conceptions and Misconceptions', *Journal of the American Musicological Society* 57/1 (2004), 51–117.

'Topics and Formal Functions: The Case of the Lament', in *The Oxford Handbook of Topic Theory*, ed. Danuta Mirka, 415–452. New York: Oxford University Press, 2014.

Cascudo, Teresa. 'Iberian Symphonism, 1779–1809: Some Observations', in *Music in Spain during the Eighteenth Century*, ed. Malcolm Boyd and Juan José Carreras, 144–156. Cambridge: Cambridge University Press, 1998.

Castelvecchi, Stefano. 'Sentimental and Anti-Sentimental in "Le nozze di Figaro"', *Journal of the American Musicological Society* 53/1 (2000), 1–24.

Chafe, Wallace. *The Importance of Not Being Earnest: The Feeling behind Laughter and Humor*. Amsterdam and Philadelphia: John Benjamins, 2007.

Chapin, Keith. 'Learned Style and Learned Styles', in *The Oxford Handbook of Topic Theory*, ed. Mirka, 301–329.

'Scheibe's Mistake: Sublime Simplicity and the Criteria of Classicism', *Eighteenth-Century Music* 5/2 (2008), 165–177.

'Strict and Free Reversed: The Law of Counterpoint in Koch's *Musikalisches Lexikon* and Mozart's *Zauberflöte*', *Eighteenth-Century Music* 3/1 (2006), 91–107.

Charlton, David. *French Opera 1730–1830: Meaning and Media*. Aldershot: Ashgate, 2000.

Chastellux, François-Jean de. *Essai sur l'union de la poésie et de la musique*. Paris: Merlin, 1765.

Chen, Jen-yen. 'Catholic Sacred Music in Austria', in *The Cambridge History of Eighteenth-Century Music*, ed. Simon P. Keefe, 59–112. Cambridge: Cambridge University Press, 2009.

Choron, Alexandre and François Fayolle. *Dictionnaire historique des musiciens artistes et amateurs, morts ou vivants*. Paris: Valade, 1810.

Churgin, Bathia. 'Francesco Galeazzi's Description (1796) of Sonata Form', *Journal of the American Musicological Society* 21/2 (1968), 181–199.

Clark, Stephen L., ed. and trans. *The Letters of C. P. E. Bach*. Oxford: Clarendon, 1997.

Clarke, Eric F. 'Subject-Position and the Specification of Invariants in Music by Frank Zappa and P. J. Harvey', *Music Analysis* 18/3 (1999), 347–374.

Ways of Listening: An Ecological Approach to the Perception of Musical Meaning. New York: Oxford University Press, 2005.

Clery, E. J. *The Feminization Debate in Eighteenth-Century England: Literature, Commerce and Luxury*. Basingstoke: Palgrave Macmillan, 2004.

Cobley, Paul. 'Communication and Verisimilitude in the Eighteenth Century', in *Communication in Eighteenth-Century Music*, ed. Mirka and Agawu, 13–33.

Comen, Craig. 'Hoffmann's Musical Modernity and the Pursuit of Sentimental Unity', *Eighteenth-Century Music* 15/1 (2018), 9–28.

Cone, Edward T. 'On Derivation: Syntax and Rhetoric', *Music Analysis* 6/3 (1987), 237–255.

The Composer's Voice. Berkeley: University of California Press, 1974.

'The Uses of Convention: Stravinsky and His Models', *The Musical Quarterly* 48/3 (1962), 287–299.

Constable, John. *The Conversation of Gentlemen Considered, in most of the Ways, that make their mutual Company Agreeable, or Disagreeable: In Six Dialogues*. London: J. Hoyles, 1738.

Cowart, Georgia. 'Sense and Sensibility in Eighteenth-Century Musical Thought', *Acta musicologica* 56/2 (1984), 251–266.

Cross, Ian. 'Music, Speech and Meaning in Interaction', in *Music, Analysis, Experience: New Perspectives in Musical Semiotics*, ed. Costantino Maeder and Mark Reybrouck, 19–30. Leuven: Leuven University Press, 2015.

Currie, James R. *Music and the Politics of Negation*. Bloomington: Indiana University Press, 2012.

'Waiting for the Viennese Classics', *The Musical Quarterly* 90/1 (2007), 123–166.

Czerny, Carl. *Über den richtigen Vortrag der sämtlichen Beethoven'sche Klavierwerke*, ed. Paul Badura-Skoda. Vienna: Universal, 1963.

D'Indy, Vincent. *Cours de composition musicale*, three volumes. Paris: Durand, 1903–1950.

Dahlhaus, Carl. *Geschichte der Musik*, seven volumes, *volume 5: Die Musik des 18. Jahrhunderts*. Laaber: Laaber, 2010. (Reprint of *Neues Handbuch der Musikwissenschaft*, ed. Carl Dahlhaus and Hermann Danuser, thirteen volumes, volume 5. Laaber: Laaber, 1985.)

Dalton, Susan. 'Searching for Virtue: Physiognomy, Sociability, and Taste in Isabella Teotochi Albrizzi's *Ritratti*', *Eighteenth-Century Studies* 40/1 (2006), 85–108.

Danuser, Hermann, trans. Nicolas Betson. 'Mishmash or Synthesis? On the Psychoagogic Form of *The Creation*', in *The Century of Bach and Mozart*, ed. Gallagher and Kelly, 41–78.

Daube, Johann Friedrich. *Der musikalische Dilettant*. Vienna: Johann Thomas edlen von Trattnern, 1773.

Davison, Alan. 'The Face of a Musical Genius: Thomas Hardy's Portrait of Joseph Haydn', *Eighteenth-Century Music* 6/2 (2009), 209–227.

Degrada, Francesco. 'Luigi Boccherini e la musica strumentale dei maestri italiani in Europa fra Sette e Ottocento', *Chigiana* 43 (1993), 363–375.

DeNora, Tia. *Music in Everyday Life*. Cambridge: Cambridge University Press, 2000.

Dickie, George. *The Century of Taste: The Philosophical Odyssey of Taste in the Eighteenth Century*. New York: Oxford University Press, 1996.

Diderot, Denis. *Additions à la Lettre sur les sourds et les muets, a l'Usage de ceux qui entendent et qui parlent*. Paris, 1751.

Diderot, Denis, trans. Margaret Mauldon, with Introduction and notes by Nicholas Cronk. *Rameau's Nephew and First Satire*. Oxford: Oxford University Press, 2006.

Diergarten, Felix. '"Auch Homere schlafen bisweilen": Heinrich Christoph Kochs Polemik gegen Joseph Haydn', *Haydn-Studien* 10/1 (2010), 78–92; trans. Michael Schubert, '"At Times Even Homer Nods Off": Heinrich Christoph Koch's Polemic against Joseph Haydn', *Music Theory Online* 14/1 (2008) www.mtosmt.org.

 'Time out of Joint – Time Set Right: Principles of Form in Haydn's Symphony No. 39', *Studia musicologica* 51/2 (2010), 109–126.

Dies, Albert Christoph. *Biographische Nachrichten von Joseph Haydn*. Vienna: Camesinaische Buchhandlung, 1810.

Dittersdorf, Carl, trans. A. D. Coleridge. *The Autobiography of Karl von Dittersdorf, Dictated to His Son*. London: Richard Bentley and Son, 1896.

Doe, Julia. 'Two Hunters, a Milkmaid and the French "Revolutionary" Canon', *Eighteenth-Century Music* 15/2 (2018), 177–205.

Dolan, Emily I. 'E. T. A. Hoffmann and the Ethereal Technologies of "Nature Music"', *Eighteenth-Century Music* 5/1 (2008), 7–26.

 The Orchestral Revolution: Haydn and the Technologies of Timbre. Cambridge: Cambridge University Press, 2013.

Domingo, Darryl P. 'Unbending the Mind: Or, Commercialized Leisure and the Rhetoric of Eighteenth-Century Diversion', *Eighteenth-Century Studies* 45/2 (2012), 207–236.

Dozio, Alessandro. 'Jubilus et suavitas: le malentendu de la légèreté dans la musique de Luigi Boccherini', *Boccherini Online* 3 (2010) www.boccherinionline.it.

Dubois, Pierre, ed. *Charles Avison's 'Essay on Musical Expression', with Related Writings by William Hayes and Charles Avison*. Aldershot: Ashgate, 2004.

DuBois, Ted Alan. 'Christian Friedrich Daniel Schubart's *Ideen zu einer Ästhetik der Tonkunst*: An Annotated Translation'. PhD dissertation, University of Southern California, 1983.

Dürr, Walther. 'Music as an Analogue of Speech: Musical Syntax in the Writings of Heinrich Christoph Koch and in the Works of Schubert', in *Eighteenth-Century Music in Theory and Practice: Essays in Honor of Alfred Mann*, ed. Mary Ann Parker, 227–240. Stuyvesant: Pendragon, 1994.

Eagleton, Terry. *The Illusions of Postmodernism*. Oxford: Blackwell, 1996.

Eckert, Stefan. '*Einschnitt, Absatz,* and *Cadenz* – The Description of Galant Syntax in Joseph Riepel's *Anfangsgründe zur musicalischen Setzkunst*', *Theoria* 14 (2007), 93–124.

'"[...] wherein good Taste, Order and Thoroughness rule": Hearing Riepel's Op. 1 Violin Concertos through Riepel's Theories', *Ad Parnassum* 3/5 (2005), 23–44.

Edler, Arnfried. *Gattungen der Musik für Tasteninstrumente. Teil 2: Von 1750 bis 1830*. Laaber: Laaber, 2003.

Edwards, George. 'The Nonsense of an Ending: Closure in Haydn's String Quartets', *The Musical Quarterly* 75/3 (1991), 227–254.

Erlin, Matt. 'Reluctant Modernism: Moses Mendelssohn's Philosophy of History', *Journal of the History of Ideas* 63/1 (2002), 83–104.

Fankhauser, Gabriel. 'Cadential Intervention in Shostakovich's Piano Trio in E Minor, Op. 67', *Music Analysis* 32/2 (2013), 210–250.

Feder, Georg. *Haydns Streichquartette: Ein musikalischer Werkführer*. Munich: Beck, 1998.

Feldman, Martha. *The Castrato: Reflections on Natures and Kinds*. Berkeley: University of California Press, 2015.

Ferguson, Adam. *An Essay on the History of Civil Society*, fourth edition. London: T. Caddel [sic], 1773.

Ferraguto, Mark. 'Haydn as "Minimalist": Rethinking Exoticism in the Trios of the 1760s and 1770s', *Studia musicologica* 51/1–2 (2010), 61–77.

Fielding, Henry. 'An Essay on Conversation', in *Miscellanies*, volume 1, 115–178. London: A. Millar, 1743.

Finscher, Ludwig. *Joseph Haydn und seine Zeit*. Laaber: Laaber, 2002.

Studien zur Geschichte des Streichquartetts. Die Entstehung des klassischen Streichquartetts: Von den Vorformen zur Grundlegung durch Joseph Haydn. Kassel: Bärenreiter, 1974.

Fisher, Stephen Carey. 'Haydn's Overtures and Their Adaptations as Concert Orchestral Works'. PhD dissertation, University of Pennsylvania, 1985.

Fordyce, David. *Dialogues concerning Education*. London, 1745.

Forkel, Johann Nikolaus. *Allgemeine Geschichte der Musik*, two volumes. Leipzig: Schwickert, 1788–1801.

Frevert, Ute. 'Defining Emotions: Concepts and Debates over Three Centuries', in *Emotional Lexicons: Continuity and Change in the Vocabulary of Feeling, 1700–2000*, ed. Ute Frevert and others, 1–31. Oxford: Oxford University Press, 2014.

Fubini, Enrico, ed., Wolfgang Freis, Lisa Gasbarrone and Michael Louis Leone, trans., Bonnie J. Blackburn, trans. ed. *Music and Culture in Eighteenth-Century Europe: A Source Book*. Chicago: University of Chicago Press, 1994.

Fuller, David. 'The "Dotted Style" in Bach, Handel, and Scarlatti', in *Bach, Handel, Scarlatti: Tercentenary Essays*, ed. Peter Williams, 99–117. Cambridge: Cambridge University Press, 1985.

Galand, Joel. 'Form, Genre, and Style in the Eighteenth-Century Rondo', *Music Theory Spectrum* 17/1 (1995), 27–52.

Galeazzi, Francesco. *Elementi teorico-pratici di musica*, two volumes, volume 2. Rome: Puccinelli, 1796.

Gallini, Giovanni-Andrea. *A Treatise on the Art of Dancing*. London: R. and J. Dodsley, 1762.

Garratt, James. 'Haydn and Posterity: The Long Nineteenth Century', in *The Cambridge Companion to Haydn*, ed. Clark, 226–238.

Geiringer, Karl. 'Joseph Haydn, Protagonist of the Enlightenment', in *Joseph Haydn and the Eighteenth Century: Collected Essays of Karl Geiringer*, ed. Robert N. Freeman, 55–64. Warren, MI: Harmonie Park Press, 2002.

Gelbart, Matthew. *The Invention of 'Folk Music' and 'Art Music'*. Cambridge: Cambridge University Press, 2007.

Gerard, Alexander. *An Essay on Genius*. London: W. Strahan and T. Cadell, 1774.

Gerber, Ernst Ludwig. *Historische-Bibliographisches Lexikon der Tonkünstler*, two volumes. Leipzig: Breitkopf, 1790–1792.

Gerhard, Anselm. *London und der Klassizismus in der Musik: Die Idee der 'absoluten Musik' und Muzio Clementis Klavierwerke*. Stuttgart: Metzler, 2002.

Gilman, Todd. 'Arne, Handel, the Beautiful, and the Sublime', *Eighteenth-Century Studies* 42/4 (2009), 529–555.

Ginguené, Pierre-Louis. *Encyclopédie méthodique*, two volumes. Paris, 1791.

Gjerdingen, Robert O. *A Classic Turn of Phrase: Music and the Psychology of Convention*. Philadelphia: University of Pennsylvania Press, 1988.

  'Courtly Behaviors', *Music Perception: An Interdisciplinary Journal* 13/3 (1996), 365–382.

  Music in the Galant Style. New York: Oxford University Press, 2007.

Gmeiner, Josef. *Menuett und Scherzo: Ein Beitrag zur Entwicklungsgeschichte und Soziologie des Tanzsatzes in der Wiener Klassik*. Tutzing: Schneider, 1979.

Goldstein, Jan. 'Enthusiasm or Imagination? Eighteenth-Century Smear Words in Comparative Context,' *Huntington Library Quarterly* 60/1–2 (1997), 29–49.

Goodman, Dena. *The Republic of Letters: A Cultural History of the French Enlightenment*. Ithaca: Cornell University Press, 1994.

Goodstein, Elizabeth. *Experience without Qualities: Boredom and Modernity*. Stanford: Stanford University Press, 2005.

Gordon, Daniel. *Citizens without Sovereignty: Equality and Sociability in French Thought, 1670–1789*. Princeton: Princeton University Press, 1994.

  'The City and the Plague in the Age of Enlightenment', *Yale French Studies* 92 (1997), 67–87.

Gottsched, Johann Christoph. *Auszug aus des Herrn Batteux schönen Künsten aus dem einzigen Grundsätze der Nachahmung hergeleitet*. Leipzig: Breitkopf, 1754.

Gotwals, Vernon, ed. and trans. *Haydn: Two Contemporary Portraits*. Madison: University of Wisconsin Press, 1968.

Granot, Roni Y. and Nori Jacoby. 'Musically Puzzling II: Sensitivity to Overall Structure in a Haydn E-Minor Sonata', *Musicae Scientiae* 16/1 (2011), 67–80.

Grant, Roger Mathew. 'Haydn, Meter, and Listening in Transition', *Studia musicologica* 51/1–2 (2010), 141–152.

Grave, Floyd. 'Freakish Variations on a "Grand Cadence" Prototype in Haydn's String Quartets', *Journal of Musicological Research* 28/2–3 (2009), 119–145.

'Galant Style, Enlightenment, and the Paths from Minor to Major in Later Instrumental Works by Haydn', *Ad Parnassum* 7/13 (2009), 9–41.

'Metrical Dissonance in Haydn', *The Journal of Musicology* 13/2 (1995), 168–202.

'Recuperation, Transformation and the Transcendence of Major over Minor in the Finale of Haydn's String Quartet Op. 76 No. 1', *Eighteenth-Century Music* 5/1 (2008), 27–50.

Grave, Floyd and Margaret Grave. *The String Quartets of Joseph Haydn*. New York: Oxford University Press, 2006.

Green, Rebecca. 'A Letter from the Wilderness: Revisiting Haydn's Esterházy Environments', in *The Cambridge Companion to Haydn*, ed. Clark, 17–29.

Greenberg, Yoel. 'Minding a Gap: "Active Transitions" from the Slow Introduction to the Fast Section in Haydn's Symphonies', *The Journal of Musicology* 29/3 (2012), 292–322.

Griesinger, Georg August. *Biographische Notizen über Joseph Haydn*. Leipzig: Breitkopf & Härtel, 1810.

Griffiths, Paul. *The String Quartet: A History*. London: Thames and Hudson, 1983.

Haakenson, Matthew. 'Two Spanish Brothers Revisited: Recent Research surrounding the Life and Instrumental Music of Juan Bautista Pla and José Pla', *Early Music* 35/1 (2007), 83–94.

Hanning, Barbara. 'Conversation and Musical Style in the Late Eighteenth-Century Parisian Salon', *Eighteenth-Century Studies* 22/4 (1989), 512–528.

Harrison, Bernard. *Haydn: The 'Paris' Symphonies*. Cambridge: Cambridge University Press, 1998.

Harriss, Ernest C. *Johann Mattheson's 'Der vollkommene Capellmeister': A Revised Translation with Critical Commentary*. Ann Arbor: UMI, 1981.

Hatten, Robert S. *Interpreting Musical Gestures, Topics, and Tropes: Mozart, Beethoven, Schubert*. Bloomington: Indiana University Press, 2004.

'The Troping of Topics in Mozart's Instrumental Works', in *The Oxford Handbook of Topic Theory*, ed. Mirka, 514–536.

Hawkins, John. *General History of the Science and Practice of Music*, five volumes. London: T. Payne, 1776.

Hayes, William. *Remarks on Mr. Avison's Essay on Musical Expression*. London: J. Robinson, 1753.

The Art of Composing Music By A Method entirely New, Suited To the meanest Capacity. London: J. Lion, 1751.

Head, Matthew. 'Fantasia and Sensibility', in *The Oxford Handbook of Topic Theory*, ed. Mirka, 259–278.

'"Like Beauty Spots on the Face of a Man": Gender in 18th-Century North-German Discourse on Genre', *The Journal of Musicology* 13/2 (1995), 143–167.

Sovereign Feminine: Music and Gender in Eighteenth-Century Germany. Berkeley: University of California Press, 2013.

Heartz, Daniel. *Haydn, Mozart and the Viennese School, 1740–1780*. New York: Norton, 1995.

Mozart, Haydn and Early Beethoven, 1781–1802. New York: Norton, 2009.

Music in European Capitals: The Galant Style, 1720–1780. New York: Norton, 2003.

Heartz, Daniel and Bruce Alan Brown. 'Empfindsamkeit', in *Grove Music Online* www.oxfordmusiconline.com.

Hennebelle, David. 'Nobles, musique et musiciens à Paris à la fin de l'Ancien Régime: les transformations d'un patronage séculaire (1760–1780)', *Revue de musicologie* 87/2 (2001), 395–418.

Hepokoski, James and Warren Darcy. *Elements of Sonata Theory: Norms, Types, and Deformations in the Late-Eighteenth-Century Sonata*. New York: Oxford University Press, 2006.

Hinton, Stephen. 'The Emancipation of Dissonance: Schoenberg's Two Practices of Composition', *Music & Letters* 91/4 (2010), 568–579.

Hirschmann, Wolfgang. 'Editorial', *Eighteenth-Century Music* 11/2 (2014), 167–172.

Hogwood, Christopher, ed. Introduction to *'Kenner und Liebhaber' Collections I*, Carl Philip Emanuel Bach: The Complete Works, series 1, volume 4.1, xi–xxi. Los Altos: Packard Humanities Institute, 2009.

'The Keyboard Sonatas of Leopold Kozeluch', *Early Music* 40/4 (2012), 621–637.

Hoskins, Robert, ed. Foreword to William Shield, *String Trios*. Wellington: Artaria, 2004.

Hosler, Bellamy. *Changing Aesthetic Views of Instrumental Music in 18th-Century Germany*. Ann Arbor: UMI, 1981.

Hoyt, Peter A. 'Haydn's New Incoherence' (review-essay of books by James Webster, Gretchen Wheelock, Elaine Sisman and Ethan Haimo), *Music Theory Spectrum* 19/2 (1997), 264–284.

'The "False Recapitulation" and the Conventions of Sonata Form'. PhD dissertation, University of Pennsylvania, 1999.

Huehls, Mitchum. 'Structures of Feeling: Or, How to Do Things (or Not) with Books', *Contemporary Literature* 51/2 (2010), 419–428.

Hume, David. *A Treatise of Human Nature*, ed. L. H. Selby-Bigge, second edition, revised by P. H. Nidditch. Oxford: Clarendon, 1978.

Dialogues concerning Natural Religion, second edition. London, 1779.

'Of Essay-Writing', in *Essays Moral, Political, and Literary*, ed. Eugene F. Miller, revised edition, 289–291. Indianapolis: Liberty Classics, 1987.

'Of Refinement in the Arts', in *Essays Moral, Political, and Literary*, ed. Miller, 163–169.

Hunter, Mary. 'Rousseau, the Countess, and the Female Domain', in *Mozart Studies 2*, ed. Cliff Eisen, 1–26. Oxford: Clarendon, 1997.

The Culture of Opera Buffa in Mozart's Vienna: A Poetics of Entertainment. Princeton: Princeton University Press, 1999.

'Topics and Opera Buffa', in *The Oxford Handbook of Topic Theory*, ed. Mirka, 61–89.

'Unisons in Haydn's String Quartets', *HAYDN* 4/1 (2014) www.rit.edu/haydn.

Hyer, Brian. Review of Rose Rosengard Subotnik, *Deconstructive Variations: Music and Reason in Western Society* and Lawrence Kramer, *Classical Music and Postmodern Knowledge*, *Journal of the American Musicological Society* 51/2 (1998), 409–424.

Irvine, Thomas. '"Das Launigste Thema": On the Politics of Editing and Performing the Finale of K. 593', *Mozart-Jahrbuch* (2003–2004), 3–23.

Irving, Howard. 'Haydn and Laurence Sterne: Similarities in Eighteenth-Century Literary and Musical Wit', *Current Musicology* 40 (1985), 34–49.

'Haydn's *Deutscher Tanz* Finales: Style versus Form in Eighteenth-Century Music', *Studies in Music* 20 (1986), 12–21.

Ivanovitch, Roman. 'Mozart's Art of Retransition', *Music Analysis* 30/1 (2011), 1–36.

Jan, Steven. 'The Evolution of a "Memeplex" in Late Mozart: Replicated Structures in Pamina's "Ach, ich fühl's"', *Journal of the Royal Musical Association* 128/1 (2003), 30–70.

Jander, Owen. 'Beethoven's "Orpheus in Hades": The *Andante con moto* of the Fourth Piano Concerto', *19th-Century Music* 8/3 (1985), 195–212.

Jenkins, Newell, ed. Introduction to *Gaetano Brunetti, 1744–1798: Nine Symphonies*. New York: Garland, 1979.

Jerold, Beverly. 'Fontenelle's Famous Question and Performance Standards of the Day', *College Music Symposium* 43 (2003), 150–160.

'The Bach-Scheibe Controversy: New Documentation', *Bach: Journal of the Riemenschneider Bach Institute* 42/1 (2011), 1–45.

Jerold, Beverly, Marco Mangani and Elisabeth Le Guin. 'Colloquy' (on Boccherini's indications 'smorfioso' and 'con smorfia'), *Journal of the American Musicological Society* 59/2 (2006), 459–472.

Jones, David Wyn. 'First among Equals: Haydn and His Fellow Composers', in *The Cambridge Companion to Haydn*, ed. Clark, 45–57.

'Minuet', in *Oxford Composer Companions: Haydn*, ed. Jones, 234–236.

The Life of Haydn. Cambridge: Cambridge University Press, 2009.

Jones, William. *A Treatise on the Art of Music; in which the Elements of Harmony and Air are practically considered, and illustrated by an hundred and fifty examples in notes[,] Many of them taken from the best Authors: The whole being intended as a Course of Lectures, preparatory to the practice of Thorough-Bass and Musical Composition*. Colchester: W. Keymer, 1784.

Junker, Carl Ludwig. *Musikalischer Almanach auf das Jahr 1782*. Berlin: Alethinopel, 1782.

Kallberg, Jeffrey. 'On the *Scherzando* Nocturne', in *Variations on the Canon: Essays on Music from Bach to Boulez in Honor of Charles Rosen on His Eightieth Birthday*, ed. Robert Curry, David Gable and Robert L. Marshall, 172–184. Rochester, NY: University of Rochester Press, 2008.

'The Rhetoric of Genre: Chopin's Nocturne in G Minor', *19th-Century Music* 11/3 (1988), 238–261.

Karl, Gregory. 'Structuralism and Musical Plot', *Music Theory Spectrum* 19/1 (1997), 13–34.

Katz, Ruth. *A Language of Its Own: Sense and Meaning in the Making of Western Art Music*. Chicago: University of Chicago Press, 2009.

Katz, Ruth and Carl Dahlhaus. *Contemplating Music: Source Readings in the Aesthetics of Music*, volume 2: *Import*. Stuyvesant: Pendragon, 1989.

Keefe, Simon P. '"An Entirely Special Manner": Mozart's Piano Concerto No. 14 in E Flat, K. 449, and the Stylistic Implications of Confrontation', *Music & Letters* 82/4 (2001), 559–581.

Mozart's Piano Concertos: Dramatic Dialogue in the Age of Enlightenment. Woodbridge: Boydell, 2001.

ed. Preface to *Ignaz Pleyel: Six String Quartets, Opus 1*, vii–x. Ann Arbor: Steglein, 2005.

'The Concertos in Aesthetic and Stylistic Context', in *The Cambridge Companion to Mozart*, ed. Simon P. Keefe, 78–91. Cambridge: Cambridge University Press, 2003.

Keller, Hans. *The Great Haydn Quartets: Their Interpretation*. London: Dent, 1986.

Kerman, Joseph. 'Mozart's Concertos and Their Audience', in *On Mozart*, ed. Morris, 151–168.

Kirkendale, Warren, trans. Margaret Bent and Warren Kirkendale. *Fugue and Fugato in Rococo and Classical Chamber Music*, revised and expanded second edition. Durham, NC: Duke University Press, 1979.

Klein, Lawrence E. 'Addisonian Afterlives: Joseph Addison in Eighteenth-Century Culture', *Journal for Eighteenth-Century Studies* 35/1 (2012), 101–118.

Shaftesbury and the Culture of Politeness: Moral Discourse and Cultural Politics in Early Eighteenth-Century England. Cambridge: Cambridge University Press, 1994.

'The Figure of France: The Politics of Sociability in England, 1660–1715,' *Yale French Studies* 92 (1997), 30–45.

Klorman, Edward. *Mozart's Music of Friends: Social Interplay in the Chamber Works*. Cambridge: Cambridge University Press, 2016.

Knigge, Adolph Freiherr von. *Über den Umgang mit Menschen*, two volumes, first edition. Hanover: Schmidt, 1788; trans. P. Will as *Practical Philosophy of Social Life, or The Art of Conversing with Men*, two volumes. London: T. Cadell junior and W. Davies, 1799.

Koch, Heinrich Christoph. *Musikalisches Lexikon*. Frankfurt am Main: August Hermann der Jüngere, 1802.

Versuch einer Anleitung zur Komposition, three volumes. Rudolstadt: Adam Friedrich Boehme, 1782; Leipzig: Adam Friedrich Boehme, 1787 and 1793.

Koch, Heinrich Christoph, ed. and trans. Nancy Kovaleff Baker. *Introductory Essay on Composition: The Mechanical Rules of Melody, Sections 3 and 4*. New Haven: Yale University Press, 1983.

Kollmann, Augustus Frederic Christopher. *An Essay on Musical Harmony: According to the Nature of That Science and the Principles of the Greatest Musical Authors*. London: J. Dale, 1796.

Korsyn, Kevin. 'Reception History and the Trauma of Real History: Decoding the Pantomime in Haydn's "Farewell" Symphony', *Musikološki Zbornik/Musicological Annual* 45/2 (2009), 143–158.

Kramer, Lawrence. *Classical Music and Postmodern Knowledge*. Berkeley: University of California Press, 1995.

  'Recalling the Sublime: The Logic of Creation in Haydn's *Creation*', *Eighteenth-Century Music* 6/1 (2009), 41–57.

  'The Devoted Ear: Music as Contemplation', in *Musical Meaning and Human Values*, ed. Keith Chapin and Lawrence Kramer. New York: Fordham University Press, 2009.

  'The Mysteries of Animation: History, Analysis and Musical Subjectivity', *Music Analysis* 20/2 (2001), 153–178.

Kramer, Richard. *Unfinished Music*. New York: Oxford University Press, 2008.

Krumhansl, Carol L. 'A Perceptual Analysis of Mozart's Piano Sonata K. 282: Segmentation, Tension, and Musical Ideas', *Music Perception* 13/3 (1996), 401–432.

  'Topic in Music: An Empirical Study of Memorability, Openness, and Emotion in Mozart's String Quintet in C Major and Beethoven's String Quartet in A Minor', *Music Perception* 16/1 (1998), 119–134.

Lacépède, Bernard Germain. *La poétique de la musique*, two volumes. Paris: L'Imprimerie de Monsieur, 1785.

Landon, H. C. Robbins. *Haydn: Chronicle and Works*, five volumes. Volume 1: *Haydn: The Early Years, 1732–1765*. London: Thames and Hudson, 1980. Volume 2: *Haydn at Eszterháza, 1766–1790*. London: Thames and Hudson, 1978. Volume 3: *Haydn in England, 1791–1795*. London: Thames and Hudson, 1976. Volume 5: *Haydn: The Late Years, 1801–1809*. London: Thames and Hudson, 1977.

  ed. and trans. *The Collected Correspondence and London Notebooks of Joseph Haydn*. London: Barrie and Rockliff, 1959.

Landon, H. C. Robbins and David Wyn Jones. *Haydn: His Life and Music*. London: Thames and Hudson, 1988.

Landon, H. C. Robbins and Dénes Bartha, eds. *Joseph Haydn: Gesammelte Briefe und Aufzeichnungen*. Budapest: Corvina, 1965.

Langlois, Mathieu. 'Haydn's "Irregularities": Ambiguous Openings in the B-Minor String Quartets, Op. 33/1 and Op. 64/2', in *Topics in Eighteenth-Century Music*

I: Selected Papers from the Fourth Biennial Conference of the Society for Eighteenth-Century Music at St. Francis College in Brooklyn, NY, 8–11 April 2010, ed. Margaret R. Butler and Janet K. Page, 103–130. Ann Arbor: Steglein, 2014.

Larlham, Daniel. 'The Felt Truth of Mimetic Experience: Motions of the Soul and the Kinetics of Passion in the Eighteenth-Century Theatre', *The Eighteenth Century: Theory and Interpretation* 53/4 (2012), 432–454.

Larson, Steve. *Musical Forces: Motion, Metaphor, and Meaning in Music*. Bloomington: Indiana University Press, 2012.

LaRue, Jan. 'Multistage Variance: Haydn's Legacy to Beethoven', *The Journal of Musicology* 1/3 (1982), 265–274.

Le Guin, Elisabeth. 'A Visit to the Salon de Parnasse', in *Haydn and the Performance of Rhetoric*, ed. Beghin and Goldberg, 14–35.

Boccherini's Body: An Essay in Carnal Musicology. Berkeley: University of California Press, 2006. Website *Boccherini's Body* epub.library.ucla.edu/leguin/boccherini/.

'"One Says that One Weeps, but One Does Not Weep": *Sensible*, Grotesque, and Mechanical Embodiments in Boccherini's Chamber Music', *Journal of the American Musicological Society* 55/2 (2002), 207–254.

Lee, Benjamin. *Talking Heads: Language, Metalanguage, and the Semiotics of Subjectivity*. Durham, NC: Duke University Press, 1997.

Lee, Douglas A., ed. Introduction to C. P. E. Bach, *Sei concerti per il cembalo concertato*, Carl Philip Emanuel Bach: The Complete Works, series 3, volume 8, xi–xvi. Los Altos: Packard Humanities Institute, 2005.

Leichtentritt, Hugo. *Musikalische Formenlehre*. Leipzig: Breitkopf & Härtel, 1911.

Levin, Robert D. 'Performance Practice in the Music of Mozart', in *The Cambridge Companion to Mozart*, ed. Keefe, 227–245.

Review of Karol Berger, *Bach's Cycle, Mozart's Arrow*, *Journal of the American Musicological Society* 63/3 (2010), 658–684.

Levinson, Jerrold. *Music in the Moment*. Ithaca: Cornell University Press, 1997.

Levy, Janet M. 'Gesture, Form, and Syntax in Haydn's Music', in *Haydn Studies: Proceedings of the International Haydn Conference, Washington, DC, 1975*, ed. Jens Peter Larsen, Howard Serwer and James Webster, 355–362. New York: Norton, 1981.

'"Something Mechanical Encrusted on the Living": A Source of Musical Wit and Humor', in *Convention in Eighteenth- and Nineteenth-Century Music*, ed. Allanbrook, Levy and Mahrt, 225–256.

'Texture as a Sign in Classic and Early Romantic Music', *Journal of the American Musicological Society* 35/3 (1982), 482–531.

Lidov, David. *Is Language a Music? Writings on Musical Form and Signification*. Bloomington: Indiana University Press, 2005.

Lilti, Antoine, trans. Lydia G. Cochrane. *The World of the Salons: Sociability and Worldliness in Eighteenth-Century Paris*. New York: Oxford University Press, 2015.

London, Justin. 'Musical and Linguistic Speech Acts', *The Journal of Aesthetics and Art Criticism* 54/1 (1996), 49–64.

Lowe, Melanie. 'Amateur Topical Competencies', in *The Oxford Handbook of Topic Theory*, ed. Mirka, 601–628.

'Falling from Grace: Irony and Expressive Enrichment in Haydn's Symphonic Minuets', *The Journal of Musicology* 19/1 (2002), 171–221.

Pleasure and Meaning in the Classical Symphony. Bloomington: Indiana University Press, 2007.

Lütteken, Laurenz. Review of Melanie Lowe, *Pleasure and Meaning in the Classical Symphony*, *Eighteenth-Century Studies* 42/4 (2009), 628–630.

MacKay, James. '*Bariolage* and Formal Design: Haydn's "The Frog", Opus 50, No. 6, Finale', *Haydn-Studien* 10/1 (2010), 93–110.

MacKay, Nicholas. 'On Topics Today', *Zeitschrift der Gesellschaft für Musiktheorie* 4/1–2 (2007), 159–183.

Malloch, William. 'The Minuets of Haydn and Mozart: Goblins or Elephants?', *Early Music* 21/3 (1993), 437–444.

Manfredini, Vincenzo. *Difesa della musica moderna e de' suoi celebri esecutori*. Bologna: Carlo Trenti, 1788.

Regole armoniche, o sieno precetti ragionati per apprender la musica, second edition. Venice: Adolfo Cesare, 1797.

Margulis, Elizabeth Hellmuth. *On Repeat: How Music Plays the Mind*. New York: Oxford University Press, 2014.

Marín, Miguel Ángel. 'Haydn, Boccherini and the Rise of the String Quartet in Late Eighteenth-Century Madrid', in *The String Quartet in Spain*, ed. Christiane Heine and Juan Miguel González Martínez, 53–119. Bern: Peter Lang, 2016.

Marmontel, Jean-François. *Essai sur les révolutions de la musique en France*. Liège: Bassompierre, 1777.

Marpurg, Friedrich Wilhelm. *Abhandlung der Fuge*, two volumes. Berlin: A. Haude and J. C. Spener, 1753–1754.

Marshall, David. *The Figure of Theater: Shaftesbury, Defoe, Adam Smith, and George Eliot*. New York: Columbia University Press, 1986.

Martin, Robert L. 'Musical "Topics" and Expression in Music', *The Journal of Aesthetics and Art Criticism* 53/4 (1995), 417–424.

Mathew, Nicholas. 'Heroic Haydn, the Occasional Work and "Modern" Political Music', *Eighteenth-Century Music* 4/1 (2007), 7–25.

'Interesting Haydn: On Attention's Materials', *Journal of the American Musicological Society* 71/3 (2018), 655–701.

Political Beethoven. Cambridge: Cambridge University Press, 2013.

Mattheson, Johann. *Der vollkommene Capellmeister*. Hamburg: Christian Herold, 1739.

Maurer Zenck, Claudia. '"Mannichfaltige Abweichungen von der gewöhnlichen Sonaten-Form": Beethoven's "Piano Solo" Op. 31 No. 1 and the Challenge of

Communication', in *Communication in Eighteenth-Century Music*, ed. Mirka and Agawu, 53–79.

Maus, Fred Everett. 'Music as Drama', *Music Theory Spectrum* 10/1 (1988), 56–73.

Mayes, Catherine. 'Turkish and Hungarian-Gypsy Styles', in *The Oxford Handbook of Topic Theory*, ed. Mirka, 214–237.

McClary, Susan. 'A Musical Dialectic from the Enlightenment: Mozart Piano Concerto in G Major, K. 453, Movement 2', *Cultural Critique* 4 (1986), 129–169.

  Conventional Wisdom: The Content of Musical Form. Berkeley: University of California Press, 2000.

  Desire and Pleasure in Seventeenth-Century Music. Berkeley: University of California Press, 2012.

  'Editorial', *Eighteenth-Century Music* 6/1 (2009), 3–5.

McClelland, Clive. *Ombra: Supernatural Music in the Eighteenth Century*. Lanham: Lexington, 2012.

McKee, Eric. 'Mozart in the Ballroom: Minuet-Trio Contrast and the Aristocracy in Self-Portrait', *Music Analysis* 24/3 (2005), 383–434.

McMurran, Mary Helen. 'The New Cosmopolitanism and the Eighteenth Century', *Eighteenth-Century Studies* 47/1 (2013), 19–38.

McVeigh, Simon. *Concert Life in London from Mozart to Haydn*. Cambridge: Cambridge University Press, 1993.

Mellers, Wilfred. *The Masks of Orpheus*. Manchester: Manchester University Press, 1987.

Melton, James van Horn. 'School, Stage, Salon: Musical Cultures in Haydn's Vienna', in *Haydn and the Performance of Rhetoric*, ed. Beghin and Goldberg, 80–108.

  The Rise of the Public in Enlightenment Europe. Cambridge: Cambridge University Press, 2001.

Meyer, Leonard B. 'Exploiting Limits: Creation, Archetypes, and Style Change', *Daedalus* 109/2 (1980), 177–205.

  'Nature, Nurture, and Convention: The Cadential Six-Four Progression', in *Convention in Eighteenth- and Nineteenth-Century Music*, ed. Allanbrook, Levy and Mahrt, 473–516.

  Style and Music: Theory, History, and Ideology. Chicago: University of Chicago Press, 1989.

Michaelis, Christian Friedrich. 'Über das Humoristische oder Launige in der musikalischen Komposition', *Allgemeine musikalische Zeitung* 46 (12 August 1807), columns 725–729.

Mikusi, Balázs. 'More than a Copy: Joseph Haydn's *Menuet al roverso* in Context', *HAYDN* 3/2 (2013) www.rit.edu/haydn.

Mirka, Danuta. *Metric Manipulations in Haydn and Mozart: Chamber Music for Strings, 1787–1791*. New York: Oxford University Press, 2009.

'Punctuation and Sense in Late-Eighteenth-Century Music', *Journal of Music Theory* 54/2 (2010), 235–282.

'The Cadence of Mozart's Cadenzas', *The Journal of Musicology* 22/2 (2005), 292–325.

Mitchell, William J., ed. and trans. *C. P. E. Bach, Essay on the True Art of Playing Keyboard Instruments*. New York: Norton, 1949.

Momigny, Jérôme-Joseph de. *Cours complet d'harmonie et de composition*. Paris: author, 1806.

Monahan, Seth. 'Action and Agency Revisited', *Journal of Music Theory* 57/2 (2013), 321–371.

Monelle, Raymond. *The Musical Topic: Hunt, Military and Pastoral*. Bloomington: Indiana University Press, 2006.

Morellet, André. 'De la conversation', in *Éloges de Mme Geoffrin, contemporaine de Madame du Deffand, par MM. Morellet, Thomas et D'Alembert*, ed. André Morellet, 155–226. Paris: Nicolle, 1812.

'De l'esprit de contradiction', in *Éloges de Mme Geoffrin*, ed. Morellet, 229–270.

Mélanges de littérature et de philosophie du 18e siècle, four volumes. Paris: Lepetit, 1818.

Morgan, Robert P. 'The Concept of Unity and Musical Analysis', *Music Analysis* 22/1–2 (2003), 7–50.

Morrow, Mary Sue. *German Music Criticism in the Late Eighteenth Century: Aesthetic Issues in Instrumental Music*. Cambridge: Cambridge University Press, 1997.

Moseley, Roger. *Keys to Play: Music as a Ludic Medium from Apollo to Nintendo*. Oakland: University of California Press, 2016.

Murray, Sterling E. *The Career of an Eighteenth-Century Kapellmeister: The Life and Music of Antonio Rosetti*. Rochester, NY: University of Rochester Press, 2014.

Neuwirth, Markus and Pieter Bergé. 'Introduction: What Is a Cadence? Nine Perspectives', in *What Is a Cadence? Theoretical and Analytical Perspectives on Cadences in the Classical Repertoire*, ed. Markus Neuwirth and Pieter Bergé, 7–16. Leuven: Leuven University Press, 2015.

Newman, William S. *The Sonata in the Classic Era*. Chapel Hill: University of North Carolina Press, 1963.

Ngai, Sianne. *Ugly Feelings*. Cambridge, MA: Harvard University Press, 2005.

Niemetschek, Franz. *Leben des k. k. Kapellmeisters Wolfgang Gottlieb Mozart*. Prague: Herrlische Buchhandlung, 1798.

November, Nancy, ed. Introduction to *Paul Wranitzky, Six Sextets for Flute, Oboe, Violin, Two Violas, and Cello*, vii–xi. Middleton, WI: A–R Editions, 2012.

'Theatre Piece and *Cabinetstück*: Nineteenth-Century Visual Ideologies of the String Quartet', *Music in Art* 29/1–2 (2004), 135–150.

Packham, Catherine. 'Cicero's Ears, or Eloquence in the Age of Politeness: Oratory, Moderation, and the Sublime in Enlightenment Scotland', *Eighteenth-Century Studies* 46/4 (2013), 499–512.

Pauli, Charles. *Elemens de la danse*. Leipzig: U. C. Saalbach, 1756.

Pestelli, Giorgio, trans. Eric Cross. *The Age of Mozart and Beethoven*. Cambridge: Cambridge University Press, 1984.

Pichler, Caroline. *Denkwürdigkeiten aus meinem Leben*, two volumes, ed. Emil Karl Blümml. Munich: Georg Müller, 1914.

Prosaische Aufsätze, two volumes. Vienna: Anton Pichler, 1822.

Pluche, Noël-Antoine. *Le spectacle de la nature*, seven volumes, volume 7. Paris: chez la veuve Estienne, 1746.

Polzonetti, Pierpaolo. 'Haydn and the *Metamorphoses* of Ovid', in *Engaging Haydn: Context, Culture, Criticism*, ed. Mary Hunter and Richard Will, 211–239. Cambridge: Cambridge University Press, 2012.

'Tartini and the Tongue of Saint Anthony', *Journal of the American Musicological Society* 67/2 (2014), 429–486.

Porter, Roy. *The Enlightenment*, second edition. Basingstoke: Palgrave, 2001.

Pritchard, Matthew. '"The Moral Background of the Work of Art": "Character" in German Musical Aesthetics, 1780–1850', *Eighteenth-Century Music* 9/1 (2012), 63–80.

Proksch, Bryan. *Reviving Haydn: New Appreciations in the Twentieth Century*. Rochester, NY: University of Rochester Press, 2015.

'Vincent d'Indy as Harbinger of the Haydn Revival', *Journal of Musicological Research* 28/2–3 (2009), 162–188.

Quantz, Johann Joachim. *Versuch einer Anweisung die Flöte traversiere zu spielen*. Berlin: Johann Friedrich Voß, 1752; *On Playing the Flute: A Complete Translation with an Introduction and Notes by Edward R. Reilly*. London: Faber, 1966.

Raab, Armin. 'Ein Porträt des Künstlers als alter Mann: Joseph Haydn und seine Biographen', *Haydn-Studien* 10/3–4 (2013), 369–380.

Rasch, Rudolf. 'Luigi Boccherini and the Music Publishing Trade', in *Boccherini Studies 1*, ed. Christian Speck, 63–142. Bologna: Ut Orpheus, 2007.

Ratner, Leonard. *Classic Music: Expression, Form, and Style*. New York: Schirmer, 1980.

'Topical Content in Mozart's Keyboard Sonatas', *Early Music* 19/4 (1991), 615–619.

Reicha, Anton. *Art du compositeur dramatique, ou cours complet de composition vocale*. Paris: Richault, 1833.

Traité de mélodie. Paris: J. L. Scherff, 1814.

Ribeiro, Alvaro, ed. *The Letters of Dr Charles Burney, Volume 1: 1751–1784*. Oxford: Clarendon, 1991.

Rice, John. *Music in the Eighteenth Century*. New York: Norton, 2013.

'New Light on Dittersdorf's Ovid Symphonies', *Studi musicali* 29/2 (2000), 453–498.

'The Heartz: A Galant Schema from Corelli to Mozart', *Music Theory Spectrum* 36/2 (2014), 315–332.

Richards, Annette. 'Automatic Genius: Mozart and the Mechanical Sublime', *Music & Letters* 80/3 (1999), 366–389.
   'Carl Philipp Emanuel Bach, Portraits, and the Physiognomy of Music History', *Journal of the American Musicological Society* 66/2 (2013), 337–396.
   'Haydn's *London* Trios and the Rhetoric of the Grotesque', in *Haydn and the Performance of Rhetoric,* ed. Beghin and Goldberg, 251–280.
   The Free Fantasia and the Musical Picturesque. Cambridge: Cambridge University Press, 2001.
Richards, Mark. 'Sonata Form and the Problem of Second-Theme Beginnings', *Music Analysis* 32/1 (2013), 3–45.
Ridgewell, Rupert. 'Biographical Myth and the Publication of Mozart's Piano Quartets', *Journal of the Royal Musical Association* 135/1 (2010), 41–114.
Riepel, Joseph. *Anfangsgründe zur musikalischen Setzkunst,* five volumes. Volume 1: *De Rhythmopoeïa, oder von der Tactordnung.* Regensburg and Vienna: Emerich Felix Bader, 1752. Volume 2: *Grundregeln der Tonordnung.* Frankfurt and Leipzig: Christian Ulrich Wagner, 1755. Volume 4: *Erläuterung der betrüglichen Tonordnung.* Augsburg: Johann J. Lotter, 1765.
Riley, Matthew. 'Hermeneutics and the New *Formenlehre*: An Interpretation of Haydn's "Oxford" Symphony, First Movement', *Eighteenth-Century Music* 7/2 (2010), 199–219.
   Musical Listening in the German Enlightenment: Attention, Wonder and Astonishment. Aldershot: Ashgate, 2004.
   'Sonata Principles' (review article), *Music & Letters* 89/4 (2008), 590–598.
   The Viennese Minor-Key Symphony in the Age of Haydn and Mozart. New York: Oxford University Press, 2014.
Robinson, Jenefer and Robert S. Hatten. 'Emotions in Music', *Music Theory Spectrum* 34/2 (2012), 71–106.
Rosen, Charles. *Beethoven's Piano Sonatas: A Short Companion.* New Haven: Yale University Press, 2002.
   Music and Sentiment. New Haven: Yale University Press, 2010.
   Sonata Forms, revised edition. New York: Norton, 1988.
   The Classical Style: Haydn, Mozart, Beethoven. London: Faber, 1971.
Rosenblum, Sandra P. *Performance Practices in Classic Piano Music.* Bloomington: Indiana University Press, 1988.
Rosenmeyer, Thomas G. *The Green Cabinet: Theocritus and the European Pastoral Lyric.* Berkeley: University of California Press, 1969.
Rothstein, William. *Phrase Rhythm in Tonal Music.* New York: Schirmer, 1989.
Rousseau, Jean-Jacques. *Discours sur l'origine et les fondemens de l'inégalité parmi les hommes.* Amsterdam: Marc-Michel Rey, 1755.
Rumph, Stephen. *Mozart and Enlightenment Semiotics.* Berkeley: University of California Press, 2012.
   'Topical Figurae: The Double Articulation of Topics', in *The Oxford Handbook of Topic Theory,* ed. Mirka, 493–513.

Rushton, Julian. *Classical Music: A Concise History from Gluck to Beethoven.* London: Thames and Hudson, 1986.

Russell, Gillian and Clara Tuite. 'Introducing Romantic Sociability', in *Romantic Sociability: Social Networks and Literary Culture in Britain, 1770-1840*, ed. Russell and Tuite, 1-23. Cambridge: Cambridge University Press, 2006.

Russell, Tilden A. '"Über das Komische in der Musik": The Schütze-Stein Controversy', *The Journal of Musicology* 4/1 (1985-1986), 70-90.

Russo, Elena. 'Editor's Preface' to 'Exploring the Conversible World: Text and Sociability from the Classical Age to the Enlightenment', *Yale French Studies* 92 (1997), 1-7.

'The Self, Real and Imaginary: Social Sentiment in Marivaux and Hume', *Yale French Studies*, 92 (1997), 126-148.

Schaul, Johann Baptist. *Briefe über den Geschmack in der Musik.* Karlsruhe: Macklots Hofbuchhandlung, 1809.

Scheibe, Johann Adolph. *Der critische Musikus.* Leipzig: Breitkopf, 1745.

Schiff, Andras. 'Did You Hear the One about ... ', *The Guardian* (29 May 2009) www.theguardian.com.

Schmalfeldt, Janet. 'Cadential Processes: The Evaded Cadence and the "One More Time" Technique', *Journal of Musicological Research* 12/1-2 (1992), 1-52.

Schmalzriedt, Siegfried. 'Charakter und Drama: Zur historischen Analyse von Haydnschen und Beethovenschen Sonatensätzen', *Archiv für Musikwissenschaft* 42/1 (1985), 37-66.

Schroeder, David [P.]. *Experiencing Mozart: A Listener's Companion.* Lanham: Scarecrow, 2013.

Haydn and the Enlightenment: The Late Symphonies and Their Audience. Oxford: Clarendon, 1990.

'Listening, Thinking and Writing', in *The Cambridge History of Eighteenth-Century Music*, ed. Keefe, 183-200.

Schubart, Christian Friedrich Daniel. *Ideen zu einer Ästhetik der Tonkunst*, ed. Ludwig Schubart. Stuttgart: J. Scheible, 1839.

Preface ('Klavierrezepte') to *Musicalische Rhapsodien*, volume 3. Stuttgart: Buchdrukerei der Herzoglichen Hohen Carlsschule, 1786.

[Schulz, Johann Abraham Peter.] 'Sonate', in Johann Georg Sulzer, *Allgemeine Theorie der Schönen Künste*, volume 2, 1094-1095. Leipzig: M. G. Weidmann und Reich, 1774.

Schwartz, Judith L. 'Conceptions of Musical Unity in the 18th Century', *The Journal of Musicology* 18/1 (2001), 56-75.

Schwindt-Gross, Nicole. *Drama und Diskurs: Zur Beziehung zwischen Satztechnik und motivischem Prozeß am Beispiel der durchbrochenen Arbeit in den Streichquartetten Mozarts und Haydns.* Laaber: Laaber, 1989.

Sears, David. 'The Perception of Cadential Closure', in *What Is a Cadence?*, ed. Neuwirth and Bergé, 253-286.

Seidel, Wilhelm. 'Haydns Streichquartett in B-Dur Op. 71 Nr. 1 (Hob. III: 69): Analytische Bemerkungen aus der Sicht Heinrich Christoph Kochs', in *Joseph Haydn: Tradition und Rezeption. Bericht über die Jahrestagung der Gesellschaft für Musikforschung, Köln 1982*, ed. Georg Feder, Heinrich Hüschen and Ulrich Tank, 3–13. Regensburg: Bosse, 1985.

Service, Tom. 'Haydn Composed Existential Comedy', *The Guardian* (29 May 2009) www.theguardian.com.

Shadko, Jacqueline A., ed. Introduction to *The Symphony in Madrid: Seven Symphonies*, xi–xix. New York: Garland, 1981.

Shaftesbury, Anthony Ashley Cooper, Third Earl of. *Characteristicks of Men, Manners, Opinions, Times*, three volumes. London: John Darby, 1714.

Sheldon, David E. 'The Galant Style Revisited and Re-Evaluated', *Acta musicologica* 47/2 (1975), 240–270.

Sheridan, Thomas. *A Course of Lectures on Elocution*. London: A. Millar and others, 1762.

Sisman, Elaine. 'Genre, Gesture, and Meaning in Mozart's "Prague" Symphony', in *Mozart Studies 2*, ed. Eisen, 27–84.

'Haydn's Career and the Idea of the Multiple Audience', in *The Cambridge Companion to Haydn*, ed. Clark, 3–16.

'Haydn, Shakespeare, and the Rules of Originality', in *Haydn and His World*, ed. Elaine Sisman, 3–56. Princeton: Princeton University Press, 1997.

'Music and the Labyrinth of Melancholy: Traditions and Paradoxes in C. P. E. Bach and Beethoven', in *The Oxford Handbook of Music and Disability Studies*, ed. Blake Howe, Stephanie Jensen-Moulton, Neil Lerner and Joseph Straus, 590–617. New York: Oxford University Press, 2015.

'Six of One: The Opus Concept in the Eighteenth Century', in *The Century of Bach and Mozart*, ed. Gallagher and Kelly, 79–107.

Small, Christopher. *Musicking: The Meanings of Performing and Listening*. Hanover, NH: Wesleyan University Press, 1998.

Smith, Adam. *Essays on Philosophical Subjects*. London: T. Cadell junior and W. Davies, 1795.

The Theory of Moral Sentiments, ed. D. D. Raphael and A. L. Macfie. Oxford: Clarendon, 1976.

Snook-Luther, Susan, ed. and trans. *The Musical Dilettante: A Treatise on Composition by J. F. Daube*. Cambridge: Cambridge University Press, 1992.

Somfai, László, trans. author in collaboration with Charlotte Greenspan. *The Keyboard Sonatas of Joseph Haydn: Instruments and Performance Practice, Genres and Styles*. Chicago: University of Chicago Press, 1995.

Spacks, Patricia Meyer. *Boredom: The Literary History of a State of Mind*. Chicago: University of Chicago Press, 1995.

Privacy: Concealing the Eighteenth-Century Self. Chicago: University of Chicago Press, 2003.

Spitzer, Michael. 'Haydn's *Creation* as Late Style: Parataxis, Pastoral, and the Retreat from Humanism', *Journal of Musicological Research* 28/2-3 (2009), 223–248.

'Haydn's Reversals: Style Change, Gesture and the Implication-Realization Model', in *Haydn Studies*, ed. Sutcliffe, 177–217.

Metaphor and Musical Thought. Chicago: University of Chicago Press, 2004.

Review of Anselm Gerhard, *London und der Klassizismus in der Musik: Die Idee der 'absoluten Musik' und Muzio Clementis Klavierwerke*, *Eighteenth-Century Music* 3/2 (2006), 330–336.

Review of Charles Rosen, *Music and Sentiment*, *Music & Letters* 93/2 (2012), 222–223.

'Sonata Dialogues' (review of Hepokoski and Darcy, *Elements of Sonata Theory*), *Beethoven Forum* 14/2 (2007), 150–178.

ed. Special Issue on Music and Emotion, *Music Analysis* 29/1-2-3 (2010) (including 'Guest Editorial', 1–7).

'The Topic of Emotion', in *Music Semiotics: A Network of Significations*, ed. Esti Sheinberg, 211–223. Farnham: Ashgate, 2012.

Staël, Madame de. *De l'Allemagne*. Paris: Didot, 1868.

Stafford, William. 'The Evolution of Mozartian Biography', in *The Cambridge Companion to Mozart*, ed. Keefe, 200–211.

Stevens, Jane. 'Georg Joseph Vogler and the "Second Theme" in Sonata Form: Some 18th-Century Perceptions of Musical Contrast', *The Journal of Musicology* 2/3 (1983), 278–304.

Stevenson, Robert. 'Los contactos de Haydn con el mundo ibérico', *Revista Musical Chilena* 36/157 (1982), 3–39.

Stewart-MacDonald, Rohan [H.]. 'Canonic Passages in the Later Piano Sonatas of Muzio Clementi: Their Structural and Expressive Roles', *Ad Parnassum* 1/1 (2003), 51–107.

New Perspectives on the Keyboard Sonatas of Muzio Clementi. Bologna: Ut Orpheus, 2006.

'The Keyboard Sonatas of Baldassare Galuppi: Textures, Topics, and Structural Shapes', in *The Early Keyboard Sonata in Italy and Beyond*, ed. Stewart-MacDonald, 69–108.

'The Undiscovered Flight Paths of the "Musical Bee": New Light on Hummel's Musical Quotations', *Eighteenth-Century Music* 3/1 (2006), 7–34.

Stockigt, Janice B. and Michael Talbot. 'Two More New Vivaldi Finds in Dresden', *Eighteenth-Century Music* 3/1 (2006), 35–61.

Sulzer, Johann Georg. *Allgemeine Theorie der Schönen Künste*, four volumes. Leipzig: M. G. Weidmann und Reich, 1771–1774.

Sutcliffe, W. Dean. 'Archaic Visitations in Boccherini's Op. 32', in *Boccherini Studies*, volume 1, ed. Speck, 245–276.

'Before the Joke: Texture and Sociability in the Largo of Haydn's Op. 33 No. 2', *Journal of Musicological Research* 28/2-3 (2009), 92–118.

'Expressive Ambivalence in Haydn's Symphonic Slow Movements of the 1770s', *The Journal of Musicology* 27/1 (2010), 84–133.

'Haydn, Mozart and Their Contemporaries', in *The Cambridge Companion to the String Quartet*, ed. Robin Stowell, 185–209. Cambridge: Cambridge University Press, 2003.

Haydn: String Quartets, Op. 50. Cambridge: Cambridge University Press, 1992.

'Laboring a Point: What Are Developments Doing?', in *SECM in Austin 2016: Topics in Eighteenth-Century Music II*, ed. Janet K. Page, 89–113. Ann Arbor: Steglein, 2019.

'Musical Materials', in *The Cambridge Haydn Encyclopedia*, ed. Caryl Clark and Sarah Day-O'Connell, 218–229. Cambridge: Cambridge University Press, 2019.

'Poet of the Galant: The Keyboard Works of Manuel Blasco de Nebra', in *Instrumental Music in Late Eighteenth-Century Spain*, ed. Miguel Ángel Marín and Màrius Bernardó, 303–343. Kassel: Reichenberger, 2014.

Review of *Gaetano Brunetti: Cuartetos de Cuerda L184-L199*, ed. Miguel Ángel Marín and Jorge Fonseca, *Eighteenth-Century Music* 11/1 (2014), 127–132.

Review of *Haydn & das Streichquartett*, ed. Georg Feder and Walter Reicher (Tutzing: Schneider, 2003), *Music & Letters* 86/3 (2005), 478–482.

Review of *Joseph Martin Kraus: Keyboard Music*, two volumes, ed. Bertil van Boer, *Eighteenth-Century Music* 2/1 (2005), 160–164.

Review of Melanie Lowe, *Pleasure and Meaning in the Classical Symphony*, *Music & Letters* 89/4 (2008), 628–633.

Review of recording *Ignaz Pleyel: Piano Trios*, played by Trio 1790, *Eighteenth-Century Music* 9/2 (2012), 284–286.

Review of ten volumes of *Carl Philipp Emanuel Bach: The Complete Works*, *Notes: Quarterly Journal of the Music Library Association* 65/3 (2009), 840–850.

'Temporality in Domenico Scarlatti', in *Domenico Scarlatti Adventures: Essays to Commemorate the 250th Anniversary of His Death*, ed. Massimiliano Sala and W. Dean Sutcliffe, 369–399. Bologna: Ut Orpheus, 2008.

The Keyboard Sonatas of Domenico Scarlatti and Eighteenth-Century Musical Style. Cambridge: Cambridge University Press, 2003.

'The Shapes of Sociability in the Instrumental Music of the Later Eighteenth Century', *Journal of the Royal Musical Association* 138/1 (2013), 1–45.

'The Simplifying Cadence: Concession and Deflation in Later Eighteenth-Century Musical Style', in *Haydn and His Contemporaries II: Selected Papers from the Fifth Biennial Conference of the Society for Eighteenth-Century Music at the College of Charleston in Charleston, SC, 13–15 April 2012*, ed. Kathryn Libin, 155–177. Ann Arbor: Steglein, 2015.

'Topics in Chamber Music', in *The Oxford Handbook of Topic Theory*, ed. Mirka, 118–140.

Talbot, Michael. *The Finale in Western Instrumental Music.* Oxford: Oxford University Press, 2001.

Taruskin, Richard. 'Material Gains: Assessing Susan McClary' (review article), *Music & Letters* 90/3 (2009), 453–467.

'The Musical Mystique' (review of books by Julian Johnson, Joshua Fineberg and Lawrence Kramer), *The New Republic* (22 October 2007) https://newrepublic.com/.

The Oxford History of Western Music, volume 2: Music in the Seventeenth and Eighteenth Centuries. New York: Oxford University Press, 2005.

Thomas, Antoine-Léonard. 'À la mémoire de Madame Geoffrin', in *Éloges de Mme Geoffrin*, ed. Morellet, 77–100.

Thormählen, Wiebke. 'Playing with Art: Musical Arrangements as Educational Tools in van Swieten's Vienna', *The Journal of Musicology* 27/3 (2010), 342–376.

Thorp, Jennifer. 'In Defence of Danced Minuets', *Early Music* 31/3 (2003), 100–108.

Tolley, Thomas. *Painting the Cannon's Roar: Music, the Visual Arts and the Rise of an Attentive Public in the Age of Haydn, c.1750 to c.1810*. Aldershot: Ashgate, 2001.

Tovey, Donald Francis. *A Companion to Beethoven's Pianoforte Sonatas (Bar-to-Bar Analysis)*. London: Associated Board of the Royal Schools of Music, 1931.

The Classics of Music: Talks, Essays, and Other Writings Previously Uncollected, ed. Michael Tilmouth, edition completed by David Kimbell and Roger Savage. Oxford: Oxford University Press, 2001.

Treitler, Leo. 'The Historiography of Music: Issues of Past and Present', in *Rethinking Music*, ed. Nicholas Cook and Mark Everist, 356–377. Oxford: Oxford University Press, 1999.

Triest, Johann Karl Friedrich. 'Bemerkungen über die Ausbildung der Tonkunst in Deutschland im achtzehnten Jahrhundert', *Allgemeine musikalische Zeitung* 3 (1801); trans. Susan Gillespie, 'Remarks on the Development of the Art of Music in Germany in the Eighteenth Century', in *Haydn and His World*, ed. Sisman, 321–394.

Türk, Daniel Gottlob. *Klavierschule, oder Anweisung zum Klavierspielen für Lehrer und Lernende*. Leipzig: Schwickert and Halle: Hemmerde und Schwetschke, 1789; trans. with introduction and notes by Raymond S. Haggh as *School of Clavier Playing*. Lincoln: University of Nebraska Press, 1982.

Preface to *Sechs leichte Klaviersonaten, Erster Teil*. Leipzig and Halle: Breitkopf, 1783.

Tyre, Jess. 'Reviving the Classic, Inventing Memory: Haydn's Reception in Fin-de-Siècle France, *HAYDN* 2/1 (2012) www.rit.edu/haydn.

Unverricht, Hubert. 'Carl Ditters von Dittersdorf als Quartettkomponist: Ein Konkurrent Haydns, Mozarts und Pleyels?', *Haydn-Studien* 7/3-4 (1998), 315–327.

van Boer, Bertil H. *The Musical Life of Joseph Martin Kraus: Letters of an Eighteenth-Century Swedish Composer*. Bloomington: Indiana University Press, 2014.

Verri, Pietro. 'La Musica', in *Il Caffè, o sia brevi e varj discorsi*, volume 2, 101–109. Venice: Pietro Pizzolato, 1766.
　Idee sull'indole del piacere. Milan: Giuseppe Galeazzi, 1774.
Vial, Stephanie D. *The Art of Musical Phrasing in the Eighteenth Century: Punctuating the Classical 'Period'*. Rochester, NY: University of Rochester Press, 2008.
Viala, Alain, trans. Daryl Lee. '*Les Signes Galants*: A Historical Reevaluation of Galanterie', *Yale French Studies* 92 (1997), 11–29.
Voskuhl, Adelheid. *Androids in the Enlightenment: Mechanics, Artisans, and Cultures of the Self*. Chicago: University of Chicago Press, 2013.
Waeber, Jacqueline. 'Jean-Jacques Rousseau's "Unité de Mélodie"', *Journal of the American Musicological Society* 62/1 (2009), 79–143.
Wald, Melanie. '"Ein curios melancholisches Stückchen": Die düstere Seite von Haydns fis-moll Sinfonie Hob. I:45 und einige Gedanken zur Pantomime in der Instrumentalmusik', *Studia musicologica* 51/1–2 (2010), 79–90.
Walter, Horst. 'Haydn gewidmete Streichquartette', in *Joseph Haydn: Tradition und Rezeption*, ed. Feder, Hüschen and Tank, 17–53.
　'Zum Wiener Streichquartett der Jahre 1780 bis 1800', *Haydn-Studien* 7/3–4 (1998), 289–314.
Waltham-Smith, Naomi. 'Haydn's Impropriety', *Journal of Music Theory* 62/1 (2018), 119–144.
　Music and Belonging between Revolution and Restoration. New York: Oxford University Press, 2017.
Watkins, Holly. 'From the Mine to the Shrine: The Critical Origins of Musical Depth', *19th-Century Music* 27/3 (2004), 179–207.
Weber, William. 'Did People Listen in the 18th Century?', *Early Music* 25/4 (1997), 678–691.
　'The Contemporaneity of Eighteenth-Century Musical Taste', *The Musical Quarterly* 70/2 (1984), 175–194.
　'The Myth of Mozart, the Revolutionary', *The Musical Quarterly* 78/1 (1994), 34–47.
Webster, James. *Haydn's 'Farewell' Symphony and the Idea of Classical Style*. Cambridge: Cambridge University Press, 1991.
　'Haydn's Sacred Vocal Music and the Aesthetics of Salvation', in *Haydn Studies*, ed. Sutcliffe, 35–69.
　'Haydn's Sensibility', *Studia musicologica* 51/1–2 (2010), 13–27.
　'Haydn's Symphonies between *Sturm und Drang* and "Classical Style": Art and Entertainment', in *Haydn Studies*, ed. Sutcliffe, 218–245.
　'The Century of Handel and Haydn', in *The Century of Bach and Mozart*, ed. Gallagher and Kelly, 297–315.
　'The *Creation*, Haydn's Late Vocal Music and the Musical Sublime', in *Haydn and His World*, ed. Sisman, 57–102.

'The Sublime and the Pastoral in *The Creation* and *The Seasons*', in *The Cambridge Companion to Haydn*, ed. Clark, 150–163.

'The Triumph of Variability: Haydn's Articulation Markings in the Autograph of Sonata No. 49 in E Flat', in *Haydn, Mozart, & Beethoven: Studies in the Music of the Classical Period. Essays in Honour of Alan Tyson*, ed. Sieghard Brandenburg, 33–64. Oxford: Clarendon, 1998.

'Towards a History of Viennese Chamber Music in the Early Classical Period', *Journal of the American Musicological Society* 27/2 (1974), 212–247.

Webster, James and Georg Feder. 'Haydn, (Franz) Joseph', in *Grove Music Online* www.oxfordmusiconline.com.

Weiss, Michael. 'Theoretical and Analytical Reflections on the Role of Robert O. Gjerdingen's Galant Schemata in Nineteenth-Century Composition'. PhD dissertation, University of Auckland, 2018.

Wheelock, Gretchen A. *Haydn's Ingenious Jesting with Art: Contexts of Musical Wit and Humor*. New York: Schirmer, 1992.

'The "Rhetorical Pause" and Metaphors of Conversation in Haydn's Quartets', in *Haydn & das Streichquartett*, ed. Feder and Reicher, 67–88.

Will, Richard. 'Eighteenth-Century Symphonies: An Unfinished Dialogue', in *The Cambridge History of Eighteenth-Century Music*, ed. Keefe, 613–647.

'Pergolesi's *Stabat Mater* and the Politics of Feminine Virtue', *The Musical Quarterly* 87/3 (2004), 570–614.

The Characteristic Symphony in the Age of Haydn and Beethoven. Cambridge: Cambridge University Press, 2002.

'When God Met the Sinner, and Other Dramatic Confrontations in Eighteenth-Century Instrumental Music', *Music & Letters* 78/2 (1997), 175–209.

Williams, Raymond. *Marxism and Literature*. Oxford: Oxford University Press, 1977.

Woodfield, Ian. 'Haydn Symphonies in Calcutta' (Correspondence), *Music & Letters* 75/1 (1994), 141–143.

Yahav, Amit. 'The Sense of Rhythm: Nationalism, Sympathy, and the English Elocutionists', *The Eighteenth Century* 52/2 (2011), 173–192.

Yearsley, David. *Bach and the Meanings of Counterpoint*. Cambridge: Cambridge University Press, 2002.

Zimpel, Christhard. *Der kadenzielle Prozess in den Durchführungen: Untersuchung der Kopfsätze von Joseph Haydns Streichquartetten*. Hildesheim: Olms, 2010.

Index

Note: Pages on which music examples are found or begin are indicated in **bold**.

Abel, Carl Friedrich, 68, 86
  Concertos
    Op. 11 No. 2, **64**, 64
    Op. 11 No. 3, 541–542
Accessibility, 11, 12–13, 14, 44–45, 47, 48, 52–53, 148, 150, 159, 182–183, 214, 220, 236, 268, 278–279, 377, 386, 432, 524
Addison, Joseph, 4, 47, 341, 438
Adorno, Theodor, 271
Agawu, Kofi, 11, 274, 384–385
Agency, 17, 120–140, 143–144, 187, 190–191, 199, 237, 253–254, 267, 301, 302, 308, 309, 347–348, 367, 466, 500, 504
Alberti, Domenico, 253, 465
Alla zoppa, 204, 394, 463, 510
Allanbrook, Wye Jamison, 2, 8, 9, 26–27, 32, 33, 35, 36, 68, 100, 150, 164, 194, 219, 225, 233–234, 272, 273, 277, 279, 315, 345, 362, 394, 429, 448, 456–457, 492, 494, 495–496, 503–504, 505, 514, 537
Allanbrook, Wye Jamison and Wendy Hilton, 538
Almén, Byron, 30–31
Alpers, Paul, 273, 474–475
Amis, Kingsley, 444
Anti-learned orientation, 45, 263, 265–266, 346–347, 358, 414–422, 434–436, 439, 484–491
Applegate, Celia, 6, 14
Appoggiaturas, 58, 68, 83, 244, 271–272, 305, 308–309, 441, 476
Aprile, Giovanni, 64
Arnold, Ignaz, 53, 372, 447–448
Arriaga, Juan Crisóstomo de
  Quartet No. 3, 523
Aspden, Suzanne, 460
Attention, 25, 48, 49–50, 86, 87, 108, 278, 294, 332, 336, 342, 346–370, 386, 521
Auden, W. H., 494, 520
Austin, J. L., 8

Avison, Charles, 18, 147, 148, 234, 263, 348, 350, 352, 361, 444, 446, 489

Bach, C. P. E., 17, 18, 24, 35, 46, 54, 117–120, 122, 232, 248, 249, 255, 260, 261, 262, 263, 268, 396, 405, 435, 436, 442, 464, 465, 466, 508
  Concertos
    Wq11, 413
    Wq14, 413
    Wq25, 413
    Wq43/4, 405
    Wq43/5, 405
  Flute Sonatas
    Wq123, 546
    Wq124, 546
  Rondos, 475
    Wq57/1, 83, **86**, 475–476, **476**, 477
    Wq57/3, 475
    Wq58/5, 304
    Wq59/4, 397–399, **399**, 401, 405
    Wq61/1, 177–183, **178**, 185, 186, 191
  Sonatas
    Wq55/4, 183
    Wq55/5, 508
    Wq55/6, 442
    Wq56/4, 118, 119
    Wq58/2, 119–120
    Wq59/1, 397–398, 401, 405
    Wq61/5, 118
  Symphonies
    Wq182/2, 302
    Wq183, 436
    Wq183/1, 343
  Trio Sonata Wq161/1, 164
Bach, J. C., 63, 66–67, 86, 261, 440–441
  Catone in Utica, 259
  Sonatas
    Op. 5 No. 2, 72
    Op. 5 No. 3, **86**, 86–87
    Op. 5 No. 4, 413

Op. 5 No. 5, 441
Op. 5 No. 6, 507–508
Symphonies
  Op. 6 No. 6, 91–94, **93**, 412–414
  Op. 9 No. 2, 202, 203
Bach, J. S., 7, 260, 485, 491, 504
Badiou, Alain, 33
Badley, Allan, 76, 249
Baillot, Pierre-Marie, 516, 517, 519
Balter, Tamara, 467
Bandur, Markus, 152
Barnett, Gregory, 250
Baroque, 1, 25, 35, 67, 89, 92, 94, 110, 122, 126, 210, 222, 238, 241, 268, 358, 409, 415, 426, 504, 506, 508, 518
Bartha, Denes, 144
Bar-Yoshafat, Jonatan, 435
Bauman, Thomas, 258, 269
Beaumarchais, Pierre-Agostin Caron de, 38
Beckerman, Michael, 518
Beethoven, Ludwig van, 31, 88–89, 125, 168, 216, 232, 274, 330, 336, 341, 342, 451–453, 469
  An die ferne Geliebte, 288
  Bagatelles
    Op. 33 No. 2, 368–370, **369**
    Op. 119 No. 1, 205
  Cello Sonata Op. 5 No. 2, 205
  Concertos
    Op. 37, 326, 491, 514
    Op. 58, 77–78
  Diabelli Variations, 557
  Quartets
    Op. 18 No. 4, 514
    Op. 59, 230
    Op. 95, 512
    Op. 131, 490
  Sonatas
    Op. 2 No. 1, 74, 82, **307**, 307–308, 321, 511–512, 555
    Op. 7, 383–384, 449, 542
    Op. 10 No. 1, **61**, 61, 514
    Op. 10 No. 2, 239
    Op. 10 No. 3, 89, 131, 280
    Op. 13, 402
    Op. 14 No. 2, 203, 205
    Op. 22, 414, 510, 542
    Op. 28, 89
    Op. 31 No. 1, 468, 478
    Op. 31 No. 3, 330–331, **331**, 332
    Op. 54, 557
    Op. 90, 542
    Op. 111, 309

Symphony No. 1, 132, 343–344
Violin Sonatas
  Op. 24, 309
  Op. 30 No. 3, 550, 557
Beghin, Tom, 248
Beghin, Tom and Sander M. Goldberg, 142
Behaviour, 7–8, 9–10, 123, 140, 167, 193, 336–337, 340–341, 409–411, 414–415, 422–427, 493, 535, 557
Bellini, Alice, 462
Benton, Rita, 124
Bergé, Pieter, 315
Berger, Karol, 37, 89
Bernstein, Lawrence F., 437
Binary relationships. *See* Reciprocity
Blackbourn, David, 487
Blainville, Charles Henri, 108
Blair, Hugh, 450, 498–499
Blanning, T. C. W., 3, 4, 34, 353, 486–487
Blasco de Nebra, Manuel, 305, 525
  Pastorelas, 115–116, 524
Blom, Eric, 37
Blume, Friedrich, 47–48, 102–103
Boccherini, Luigi, 17, 24, 124, 157, 215, 254, 264, 268, 295, 328, 341–342, 354, 405, 406, 439–440, 443, 444, 473, 513, 515–517, 519–521, 522, 533, 546–547
  Cello Sonatas
    E flat major, fuori catalogo, 69
    G17, 406
    G569, 406
  Con smorfia, smorfioso, 464–465
  Piano Quintet Op. 57 No. 6/G418, 246
  Quartets
    Op. 8 No. 1/G165, 465
    Op. 32 No. 1/G201, 308–309, 439–440
    Op. 32 No. 2/G202, 341–342, 513
    Op. 32 No. 3/G203, **160**, 160
    Op. 32 No. 4/G204, 79–80, **80**, 81, 82, 149–150, 417
  Quintets
    Op. 10 No. 1/G265, 512–513
    Op. 10 No. 2/G266, 502–503
    Op. 10 No. 4/G268, 95
    Op. 10 No. 5/G269, 439–440
    Op. 10 No. 6/G270, 203–204, 525–526, 529
    Op. 11 No. 5/G275, 519
    Op. 25 No. 1/G295, 161
    Op. 25 No. 4/G298, 407
    Op. 28 No. 1/G307, 159
    Op. 28 No. 2/G308, 406
    Op. 28 No. 4/G310, 520–521
    Op. 29 No. 6/G318, 406–407, 513

Boccherini, Luigi (cont.)
    Op. 30 No. 6/G324, 520
    Op. 42 No. 1/G348, 222, 472–473
    Op. 42 No. 4/G351, 514
    String Trios Op. 7/G125-130, 145
Bonds, Mark Evan, 32, 39, 124, 372, 469, 512
Bononcini, Giovanni, 358
Boredom, 11, 351–370
Botstein, Leon, 125, 194
Bracht, Hans-Joachim, 150–151
Brahms, Johannes, 7, 168
Brauner, Jürgen, 540
Brendel, Alfred, 28, 322
Brodey, Inger S. B., 278
Brown, A. Peter, 202, 205, 207, 245, 477
Brown, John, 10
Brown, Marshall, 54, 452, 466–467
Brunetti, Gaetano, 376, 390, 521, 522, 526
    Quartets, 337
        L160, 521
        L163, 521
        L172, 521
        L185, 389–390
        L186, 296
        L191, 71, 337
        L192, 309, **310**
        L195, 521
        L197, 376–377, 381
        L199, 376–377
    Symphonies, 245
        No. 9, 192–193, 194, 339
        No. 33, 411
        No. 36, 302–303, 530
Burke, Edmund, 349
Burke, Peter, 146, 465
Burney, Charles, 17, 21, 46, 49–50, 56, 66–67, 94, 248, 255, 262–264, 269, 346–348, 350, 352, 355, 405, 446, 465, 484–485, 496–497, 500, 520
Burney, Frances, 354
Burnham, Scott, 31, 36, 90, 451–452, 470, 471
Burstein, L. Poundie, 475
Byros, Vasili, 51, 384, 388

Cadence, 11, 68, 117–118, 277, 279–294, 305–308, 309, 374, 380, 397
    Cadence galante, 305, 307
    Simplifying, 313–333, 336–337, 339–340, 476, 477, 479, 492, 515, 553
Campra, André, 109
Caplin, William E., 2, 86–87, 107, 113, 208, 218, 273–274, 275, 279, 280, 281, 314, 328, 332, 384, 408, 423, 492

Cascudo, Teresa, 164
Castello, Dario, 404
Castelvecchi, Stefano, 470
Chafe, Wallace, 498
Chapin, Keith, 239, 272, 486
Character, 65, 76–78, 91, 95, 163–164, 177, 190–191, 192, 195, 203, 205, 231, 237, 245–246, 254, 371, 456, 457
Charlton, David, 538
Chastellux, François-Jean de, 108, 109
Chen, Jen-yen, 487
Chênedollé, Charles-Julien Lioult de, 516
Chopin, Frédéric François, 34
Choron, Alexandre and François Fayolle, 516, 520
Christensen, Thomas, 66, 433
Churgin, Bathia, 72
Clari, Giovanni Carlo Maria, 358
Clarke, Eric F., 47, 62, 120–121, 478
Classical, Classicism, xii, 11, 16, 25, 26, 28, 39, 55, 56, 69, 101, 229, 231, 359, 459, 467, 494
Clementi, Muzio, 24, 53, 101, 216, 263, 268, 377, 500, 547
    Capriccio in F major Op. 34, 117
    Piano Duets
        Op. 3 No. 2, 295, 547–550, **548**
        Op. 6, 101
        Op. 12, 101
    Piano Duo Op. 12, 195–196, 197–198, 426–426
    Piano Trio Op. 27 No. 1, 525, 526, 529
    Sonatas
        Op. 37 No. 2, 117, 183–188, **184**, 191, 500
        Op. 40 No. 1, 377–379, **378**, 490
    Violin Sonatas
        Op. 15 No. 1, 72–74, **73**, 82, **338**
        Op. 15 No. 3, 338
Clery, E. J., 439
Cleverness, 187, 377, 493, 500–501
Cobley, Paul, 14
Comedy. *See* Humour
Comen, Craig, 254
Cone, Edward T., 15, 121, 379, 402
Constable, John, 461
Convention, 5, 7, 24–25, 99, 204, 267–277, 332, 359, 386, 427, 449–450, 503, 504, 505, 506, 508, 518, 557
Conversation, 19–20, 45, 49, 133, 144–162, 163, 164, 167, 188, 238, 249, 252, 278, 348–349, 395, 460, 493, 516
Corelli, Arcangelo, 92, 194, 240, 241, 256, 358, 404, 418, 485
Cosmopolitanism, 251–252, 256–257, 262

Cowart, Georgia, 8, 254, 431–432, 433, 434, 438, 440
Cramer, Carl Friedrich, 249
Cross, Ian, 143
Currie, James R., 2, 48, 239, 274–275, 278
Cyclic return, 403–407
Czerny, Carl, 557

D'Indy, Vincent, 373, 374, 375
Dahlhaus, Carl, 20, 44, 63, 82, 262, 263, 265, 328–329, 434, 458
Dalton, Susan, 460
Danuser, Hermann, 451
Daube, Johann Friedrich, 110–111, 114, 142, 240, 254–255
Davison, Alan, 497
Defamiliarization. See Renewal
Degrada, Francesco, 517
DeNora, Tia, 9
Development sections, 113, 349, 407–427, 509
Dialogue, 91–94, 99, 144–145, 146, 150, 163, 226, 238, 274–275, 347, 489
Dickie, George, 425–425
Diderot, Denis, 356, 464
    Le neveu de Rameau, 109, 110, 253–254, 257, 356, 430–431, 432, 453, 454, 465–466, 467
Diergarten, Felix, 18, 256, 387
Dies, Albert Christoph, 14, 24, 266, 484
Digression, 360
Discourse, 8, 9, 59, 122, 123, 140, 233, 322, 340–341, 342, 346–347, 395, 428, 450–451, 493, 496
Dittersdorf, Carl Ditters von, 77, 213, 215, 234–235, 259–260, 261, 276, 277, 425–425, 458
    Quartets, 215
        K191, 315–316, **316**
        K193, 152–154, **153**, 342, **364**, 364, 366, 399–401, **400**
        K194, 207–215, **209**, 240, 404
        K195, 80–81, 82, 365–367, **366**, 412
        K196, 240
    Symphonies
        Grave g1, 509
        Il combattimento delle passioni umani, 76, 113–114, 160, 250, 411
        Les Quatre Ages du Monde, 112–113, 241, 525, 526
        Sinfonia nazionale nel gusto di cinque nazioni, 248–250, 259, 263
Divertimento, 447
Doe, Julia, 22
Dolan, Emily I., 192, 201, 340, 344

Domingo, Darryl, 360
Dozio, Alessandro, 440
Drum bass, 78, 183–187, 331, 361, 383
Dubos, Jean-Baptiste, 47
Duni, Egidio, 22, 109
Dürr, Walther, 91
Dusek, Frantisek Xaver
    Sonata S1, 550
Dussek, Jan Ladislav
    Piano Trios
        Op. 21 No. 3, 325
        Op. 31, 114
        Op. 31 No. 1, 526
        Op. 31 No. 3, 114–115
    Sonatas
        Op. 31 No. 2, 312, **313**
        Op. 70, 557
        Op. 77, 557

Eagleton, Terry, 251–252
Eckert, Stefan, 44, 488
Edwards, George, 201, 471
Effort, 45, 78–79, 263, 282, 345, 410, 414, 422, 422, 423–424, 436, 485, 489, 511–512, 513
Empson, William, 474
Esterházy, Nikolaus II, 34
Everyday, the. See Familiarity
Expression, xi, 5–8, 9, 25, 27, 53, 90–91, 102, 122, 123, 275, 350, 385, 390–391, 428–434, 463–464, 466, 467, 497–498, 503, 504, 505–506, 534

Familiarity, 2–3, 13, 47, 52, 54, 61–62, 143, 183, 266, 267, 268, 269, 277–278, 286, 294, 297, 342, 359, 360, 423
Fankhauser, Gabriel, 284
Fantasia, 117–118, 349, 401, 412–413
Feder, Georg, 110, 343
Feeling. See Expression
Feldman, Martha, 435
Femininity, 68–69, 261, 438–439
Ferguson, Adam, 443, 487
Ferraguto, Mark, 205–206
Fielding, Henry, 4, 19, 147, 449
Finscher, Ludwig, 33, 145, 269, 351, 503
Fischer, Ferdinand, 258
Fisher, Stephen, 228
Flexibility. See Versatility
Fontenelle, Bernard le Bovier de, 49, 347
Forkel, Johann Nikolaus, 249, 357
Form, 2–3, 11, 13, 25, 26, 38, 40, 43, 102, 163, 193, 267, 272, 314, 385, 406, 519

Formal function, 11, 47, 106, 124, 135–140, 153, 186, 187, 214, 224, 273–274, 287–294, 296–297, 300–303, 322, 333, 365, 367, 376, 381, 383–408, 492, 509, 553
Formula, 2, 9, 11, 109, 132, 277, 286, 292–308, 318–322, 328–333, 553–557
Fortspinnung, 110–111, 124
Fowke, Joseph, 257
French overture. *See Topics: Dotted style*
Frevert, Ute, 6, 458
Friedrich Wilhelm II, King of Prussia, 41
Friendliness, 1–2, 22–23, 444, 446, 453
Fuller, David, 238

Galand, Joel, 249
Galeazzi, Francesco, 71, 108
Galiani, Ferdinando, 359
Gallini, Giovanni-Andrea, 435, 538
Galuppi, Baldassarre, 248, 253, 440–441, 465
Garratt, James, 41
Gay, Peter, 24
Geiringer, Karl, 33
Gelbart, Matthew, 522
Geminiani, Francesco, 350
Genzinger, Maria Anna von, 459
Geoffrin, Marie Thérèse Rodet, 252
Gerard, Alexander, 277
Gerber, Ernst Ludwig, 268, 440
Gerhard, Anselm, 16, 18
Ginguené, Pierre-Louis, 485
Giustini, Lodovico, 250
Gjerdingen, Robert O., 2, 12, 13, 25, 51, 56, 63–64, 81, 87, 102, 108, 118, 176, 204, 224, 273–274, 282, 293, 295, 307, 312, 330, 351, 450, 544
Gluck, Christoph Willibald
  Orfeo ed Euridice, 77
Goethe, Johann Wolfgang von, 467
Goldstein, Jan, 411
Goodman, Dena, 145, 359, 460
Goodstein, Elizabeth, 352
Gordon, Daniel, 3, 4, 10, 438, 450, 454
Gottsched, Johann Christoph, 257–258
Gracious riposte, 57–89, 90–91, 94, 97, 99–100, 103, 113, 126, 135, 154, 162, 164, 165, 179, 180, 198–199, 207, 242, 303, 313, 333, 368, 379, 416–417, 492, 495
Granot, Roni Y. and Nori Jacoby, 165
Grant, Roger Mathew, 351, 361
Graun, Carl Heinrich, 361, 445–446, 486
Grave, Floyd, 224, 351, 474, 504–505, 513
Grave, Floyd and Margaret Grave, 374, 409

Green, Rebecca, 459
Greenberg, Yoel, 374–375, 388
Griesinger, Georg August, 258, 269, 488, 500
Griffiths, Paul, 43, 496
Grillparzer, Franz, 215
Gyrowetz, Adalbert
  Notturno Op. 31, 217
  Quartets
    Op. 29 No. 2, 111
    Op. 44 No. 2, 159, 246, 297–300, **298**, 302, 379–380, 479–481, **480**
    Op. 44 No. 3, 326–329, **327**, 479, **480**

Handel, George Frideric, 17, 124, 215, 256, 358
Hanning, Barbara, 147–148, 149
Hänsel, Peter, 76
  Quartet Op. 5 No. 3, 74
Harrison, Bernard, 442–443
Hasse, Johann Adolph, 486
Hatten, Robert S., 7, 62, 68, 242, 244, 413, 449–450, 469, 503, 504, 509, 522
Hawkins, John, 356–357, 370, 497, 504, 505
Haydn, Joseph, 4, 7, 14, 15, 17, 18, 22–24, 32–34, 37, 38, 39–42, 53, 54, 62, 103, 124, 125, 133, 143, 149, 161, 216, 257, 258–259, 263, 264–266, 268–270, 274, 277, 287, 297, 340, 350, 372–374, 377, 386, 389, 390, 395, 429–430, 434, 436, 442, 445, 451–453, 459, 468–469, 474, 481, 484–485, 488, 494–495, 496–497, 499–500, 501, 519, 520, 524, 525, 534, 550–551
  Creation, The, 40, 113, 343, 377, 512
  Flute Trio H15, 132
  La canterina, 462
  L'infedeltà delusa, 462–463
  Masses, 487
  Piano Trios
    H6, 308, 309, 551–557, **552**
    H17, 535, **536**, 549
    H18, 103
    H27, 206
    H28, 116–117, 240
    H29, 474, 525
    H34, 204, 510
  Quartets, 156–157, 263, 372–373, 374, 408, 551
    Op. 1 No. 1, 351
    Op. 9 No. 1, 287
    Op. 20, 491
    Op. 20 No. 3, 205
    Op. 20 No. 5, 522
    Op. 33, 43

Op. 33 No. 1, 150–152, **151**, 154, 167
Op. 33 No. 2, 28–32, **29**, 37, 43, 47, 48, 52, 143, 287, 297, 384, 385, 387, 397, 398, 401, 478, 499
Op. 33 No. 3, 310–311, **311**, **363**, 363–364, 368
Op. 33 No. 4, 412–414
Op. 50, 41
Op. 50 No. 1, 41, 318–319, **319**, 361–363, **362**, 364, 381
Op. 50 No. 2, 392–393
Op. 50 No. 3, 284–286, **285**
Op. 50 No. 4, 101–102
Op. 50 No. 5, 149, 381, 551
Op. 50 No. 6, 133, 286–287, 325, 381, 496
Op. 54, 521
Op. 54 No. 1, **301**, 301–302, 521
Op. 54 No. 2, 224–225, 402, 478
Op. 54 No. 3, 149, 206
Op. 55 No. 3, 70, 159, 381, 501–502, **502**
Op. 64, 50
Op. 64 No. 1, 125–133, **127**, 135, 140, 146, 381
Op. 64 No. 5, 159, 478
Op. 64 No. 6, 381
Op. 71 No. 1, 201
Op. 74 No. 1, 284
Op. 74 No. 2, 374
Op. 76, 471
Op. 76 No. 1, 514
Op. 76 No. 2, 490
Op. 76 No. 3, 414, 514
Op. 76 No. 4, 201, 202
Op. 76 No. 5, 229–230, 397
Op. 76 No. 6, 343
Op. 77 No. 2, 163
Salve regina in G minor, 205
Seven Last Words, The, 113
Sonatas
 H12, 204
 H20, 536–537
 H25, 539
 H31, 116–117
 H33, 282–284, **283**
 H34, 74–76, **75**, 164–177, **169**, 179, 181, 185, 186, 188, 191, 473–474, 513
 H36, 248, 308, 373
 H39, 248, 359
 H44, 331–332
 H45, 537
 H50, 375, 385
 H52, 326, 492, 530
Sonatas for Violin and Viola, 551
Songs, 428, 467
String Trios, 551
 H1, 551
Symphonies, 33–34, 40, 355–356, 470
 No. 31, 197, 404
 No. 35, 477
 No. 39, 386–387
 No. 42, 321
 No. 43, 188–189, 191, 192, 201, 412
 No. 44, 490
 No. 45, 226, 338, 464–465, 468
 No. 46, 404
 No. 47, 111, 387, 471
 No. 50, 189–191, 192, 526–529, **527**, 551
 No. 51, 380–381
 No. 52, 303
 No. 57, 477, 479
 No. 58, 204–206, 381–383, **382**
 No. 60, 219, 237–238, 256, 344, 464, 469
 No. 66, 239, 393
 No. 67, 95–97, **96**, 227–229
 No. 71, 62, 71
 No. 79, 220–222
 No. 80, 28, 514
 Nos 82–87, 41
 No. 82, 71
 No. 86, 437–438
 No. 88, 201–202, 206, 329–330, 342, 360
 No. 90, 388–389
 No. 92, 492
 Nos 93–104, 192
 No. 93, 207, 300–301, 418–422, **418**, 426, 489
 No. 94, 296–297, 388, 472, 492, 499, 523, 525
 No. 96, 245, 374–375, 472, 495
 No. 97, 287–292, **288**, **292**, 388, 389
 No. 98, 471, 496
 No. 101, 368, 472
 No. 103, 530
 No. 104, 311–312, 342
Haydn, Michael
 Symphonies
  ST62, 219, 401
  ST151, 426
  ST287, 196–198, 491
  ST393, 514
Hayes, William, 350, 361, 439
Head, Matthew, 68–69, 261, 439, 443
Heartz, Daniel, 62, 251, 287, 307, 330, 430, 437–438, 440, 477
Hennebelle, David, 251

Hepokoski, James and Warren Darcy, 2, 63, 70, 72, 95, 126–130, 187, 227, 270–271, 275, 295, 362, 384, 408, 409, 519, 533–534
Herregodts, Pieter, 315
Hiller, Ferdinand, 501
Hinton, Stephen, 271
Hirschmann, Wolfgang, 36
Hoffmeister, Franz Anton, 38, 158, 161
  Quartets
    Op. 14 No. 1, 154–155, **155**, 303
    Op. 14 No. 2, 155–157, **156**
    Op. 14 No. 3, **157**, 157–158, 473
  Trio Op. 31 No. 6, 506
Hofmann, Leopold
  Concertino Badley A2, 550
  Flute Concerto Badley D3, 541–542
Hogwood, Christopher, 435
Homophonic polyphony, 156–157
Hoyt, Peter A., 189, 403–404
Huehls, Mitchum, 21
Hume, David, 200, 341, 439, 455, 456, 487
Hummel, Johann Nepomuk
  Quartet Op. 30 No. 2, 491
Humour, 25, 28–30, 32–33, 42, 48, 54, 79, 112, 203, 216, 219–220, 223–224, 250, 260, 261, 268, 319, 340, 347, 359–360, 376–377, 380–381, 393, 395, 422, 467–468, 491, 493–503, 514, 547, 557
Hunter, Mary, 159, 231, 411, 447, 448, 456–457, 459, 470
Hyer, Brian, 142, 143

Incongruity, 25, 199–230, 333, 450, 494, 496, 514
Individual, Individuality, 5, 6, 18, 123, 147, 237, 251, 253–254, 350, 352, 355, 357, 429–432, 448–449, 453–461, 494
Innocence, 191, 227, 341, 422, 467–468, 471–477, 496, 514, 525–526, 528–529, 531
Interest, xi–xii, 11, 353
Irony, 23, 78–79, 113, 224, 321, 329, 467, 468–479, 494, 515, 523
Irvine, Thomas, 36
Irving, Howard, 451, 499, 539
Italian style, 17, 85, 232, 251, 252, 256–258, 259–263, 356, 361, 436, 439, 497
Ivanovitch, Roman, 36

Jadin, Hyacinthe, 292
  Quartets
    Op. 1 No. 1, 297
    Op. 1 No. 3, 161–162, **162**, 240

Jan, Steven, 132
Jander, Owen, 77
Jerold, Beverly, 45, 49, 465
Johnson, Samuel, 353–354, 438
Jones, David Wyn, 177, 453, 539
Jones, William, 16–17, 18, 123
Joseph II, Emperor, 259
Junker, Carl Ludwig, 437

Kallberg, Jeffrey, 15, 545
Kant, Immanuel, 254
Karl, Gregory, 65
Katz, Ruth, 44, 48, 329, 434
Keefe, Simon P., 46, 77, 91, 146, 148
Keferstein, Gustav Adolph, 497
Keller, Hans, 156
Kerman, Joseph, 36
Kirkendale, Warren, 240, 506
Kirnberger, Johann Philipp, 18, 66, 351
Klein, Lawrence E., 414, 424, 460–461, 486
Klorman, Edward, 148
Knigge, Adolph Freiherr von, 19, 145, 252, 278, 317, 410, 411, 466, 488, 498, 499
Koch, Heinrich Christoph, 17–18, 51, 68, 91, 110, 235–236, 237, 239, 256, 258, 272, 349, 413, 429, 445–446, 469, 491, 497, 540
Kollmann, Augustus, 349–350, 422
Körner, Christian Gottfried, 254
Korsyn, Kevin, 464–465
Kozeluch, Leopold, 46, 53, 220, 268, 269, 494, 525
  Piano Trios
    Op. 28 No. 1, 530
    Op. 28 No. 2, 530
    Op. 28 No. 3, 506, **507**, 530–531
    Op. 41, 531
    Op. 41 No. 1, 531, **532**
  Quartets
    Op. 32 No. 1, 322–325, **323**
    Op. 32 No. 3, 159
  Sonatas, 337
    Op. 2 No. 3, 401–402
    Op. 15 No. 1, 337–338, 401–402
    Op. 20 No. 3, 329, 511–512
    Op. 26 No. 3, 337–338
    Op. 30 No, 402
Kramer, Lawrence, 40, 47, 229–230, 451
Kramer, Richard, 119, 343, 508
Kraus, Joseph Martin, 23, 494
  Quartets
    Op. 1 No. 2/VB181, 415–417, **416**, 476–477, 489
    Op. 1 No. 3/VB183, 111, 490, 533

Rondo VB191, 481–484, **482**
Sonata VB196, 403
Symphonies
    VB128, 198–199
    VB139, 390–391, **391**
    VB140, 111, 508
Violin Sonata VB160, **318**, 318–319, 328
Krommer, Franz, 525
    Flute Quintet Op. 58, 383, 489–490
    Oboe Concerto Op. 52, 512
    Oboe Quartet P IX 22, **335**, 335–336
Krüger, Jean Phillip, 445
Krumhansl, Carol L., 143, 235
Kühnau, Johann Christoph, 35

La Rochefoucauld, François de, 454
Labour. *See Effort*
Lacépède, Bernard Germain, 505, 510
Landon, H. C. Robbins, 205
Langlois, Mathieu, 193
Language model, 9, 14, 20, 43–44, 45, 50, 122, 123, 140–144, 246, 250, 274, 278, 348, 357, 516
Larlham, Daniel, 464
Larson, Steve, 107
LaRue, Jan, 227, 373, 375
Latilla, Gaetano
    Quartets
        Op. 1 No. 1, 328, 329
        Op. 1 No. 3, 95
Le Guin, Elisabeth, 69, 80, 341, 342, 359, 406, 440, 444, 445, 457, 465, 486, 501, 519
Leichtentritt, Hugo, 409
Lessing, Gotthold Ephraim, 49
Levin, Robert D., 247, 280
Levinson, Jerrold, 13
Levy, Janet M., 153, 159, 163, 362, 380–381, 385
Lidov, David, 90, 125, 374, 451
Lilti, Antoine, 16, 255, 460
Liquidation, 203, 294, 332, 333, 336, 344, 362, 384, 479, 481, 501
Listener, Listening, 2, 8–9, 12–13, 24, 28–30, 31–32, 42–54, 108, 110, 124–125, 133, 214–215, 223, 228, 233, 234–237, 241, 254, 263, 273–274, 279, 294, 297, 300, 314, 319, 340–341, 347–351, 355–365, 368, 370, 376, 377, 385–386, 387, 390, 393, 401–402, 403, 406, 423, 444, 471, 481, 484, 485, 489, 496–497, 501, 505, 508, 518, 535, 557
Lodewyckx, David, 315
Löhlein, Georg Simon, 68

London, Justin, 143
Louis Duc de Noailles, 251
Lowe, Melanie, 39, 40, 380, 422
Luhmann, Niklas, 456
Lully, Jean-Baptiste, 109
Lütteken, Laurenz, 385–386
Lyrical breakthrough, 172, 175, 177, 304
Lysell Quartet, 477

MacKay, James, 496
MacKay, Nicholas, 234
Mackenzie, Henry, 4
Malloch, William, 540
Manfredini, Vincenzo, 142, 358
Mangani, Marco, 465
Manners, 9–10, 149, 224, 336–337, 425, 450, 459–462, 467
Mannheim crescendo, 342
Marcello, Benedetto, 358
Margulis, Elizabeth Hellmuth, xi, 15
Maria Theresa, Empress, 486
Marín, Miguel Ángel, 521, 533
Marivaux, Pierre de, 455
Market conditions. *See Public taste*
Marmontel, Jean-François, 108
Marpurg, Friedrich Wilhelm, 485
Marsh, John
    'Conversation Sinfonie', 145
Marshall, David, 458
Martin, Nathan John, 315
Martin, Robert L., 237
Mathew, Nicholas, 31, 340, 353, 451, 452
Mattheson, Johann, 446
Maurer Zenck, Claudia, 468, 478
Maus, Fred Everett, 122
Mayes, Catherine, 114
McClary, Susan, 6, 12, 36, 54, 194, 271, 272–273, 277, 314
McClelland, Clive, 455
McMurran, Mary Helen, 252
McVeigh, Simon, 50–51, 312, 355–356, 469, 472, 486, 524
Medial caesura, 94, 295, 395–396
Mellers, Wilfred, 201
Melody, 45, 108–109, 158, 357–358, 371–372, 440–443, 481
Melton, James van Horn, 3, 47, 145, 252, 270
Mendelssohn, Moses, 18, 453
Meyer, Leonard B., 12, 25, 51, 107, 218, 384, 413, 462, 524
Michaelis, Christian Friedrich, 469, 472, 494
Mikusi, Balázs, 111, 471

Minor mode, 35, 38, 55, 91–92, 250, 402, 407, 455, 503–514, 555
Miranda, Francisco de, 264
Mirka, Danuta, 51, 124, 286, 350–351, 501
Mixed style, 123, 231, 239, 252–253, 432, 496, 518, 520, 523, 545
Moderation, 5, 433–434, 438–440, 449, 459, 515, 534, 535, 542, 550, 557
Molina y Saldívar, Gaspar de, 5
Möllering, Monika, 177
Momigny, Jérôme-Joseph de, 436
Monahan, Seth, 121–122, 124
Monelle, Raymond, 231, 517, 518, 529
Morellet, André, 149, 200, 348–349, 450, 493
Moreno, Francisco Javier
   Sinfonia 'Superbia ed Umiltà', 76–78, 164
Morgan, Robert P., 235–236
Morley, Thomas, 213
Moseley, Roger, 16, 330
Motive, 37, 121, 124–140, 162–163, 191, 268, 284–286, 301–302, 372, 374, 381, 411
Mozart, Leopold, 429
Mozart, Wolfgang Amadeus, 14, 18, 24, 26–27, 33, 34–39, 40, 41, 42, 46, 53, 54, 62–63, 67, 86, 100, 103, 122, 231–232, 259, 263, 264–266, 269, 272, 274, 293, 312, 345, 350, 377, 429–430, 445–446, 453, 466, 468, 470, 484, 490, 494, 500, 503, 505, 512, 524, 525
  Concertos, 36
    K190, 541
    K191, 541
    K271, 226
    K313, 541
    K413, 46, 50, 397, 541
    K414, 46, 50
    K415, 46, 50, 225, 228, 338, 401
    K449, 77, 491
    K450, 70, 329, 333
    K466, 282, 494
    K482, 226
    K488, 522
    K491, 160
  Così fan tutte, 287–288, 470
  Die Entführung aus dem Serail, 227, 228, 358–359
  Fantasia K475, 35, 402
  L'oca del Cairo, 269
  Le nozze di Figaro, 437, 459, 470
  Piano Quartet K478, 38
  Quartets
    K387, 432, 491
    K428, 70, 159
    K499, 242–244, **243**, 280–282, 333–335, **334**, 336, 345
    K575, 41
    K589, 41
    K590, 41
  Quintet for Piano and Winds K452, 62
  Quintets
    K515, 62
    K593, 36, 62, 87–88, **88**, 244–245, 296
  Requiem, 377
  Serenade K375, 78–79, 82
  Sonata for Two Pianos K448, 329–330
  Sonatas
    K283, 135
    K311, 345
    K332, 232, **320**, 320–322, 330, 553
    K457, 35, 62, 509
  Symphonies
    K297, 41
    K425, 62, 70–71, 76, 77, 94–95, 246–247, 426
    K504, 233
    K550, 466
    K551, 62–63
  Variations for Piano Duet, K501, 103–106, **104**
  Violin Sonatas
    K301, 133–140, **134**, 144
    K302, **344**, 344–345
    K304, 161, 507
    K306, 35, 226–227, 412–414
    K376, 97, 99
    K377, 509, 550
    K380, 35
    K454, 62, 100–101, **101**
    K526, 35, 116–117
    K547, 35
Murky bass, 549
Murray, Sterling E., 225–226, 228, 338

Naturalness, 11, 20, 44, 109–110, 254–255, 393, 414, 433–434, 435–439, 442–443, 460, 515, 516, 522, 523, 530, 538
Necker, Suzanne, 486
Neoclassicism, 434, 436
Neumann, Frederick, 540
Neuwirth, Markus, 315
Neuwirth, Markus and Pieter Bergé, 279
Newman, William S., 539
Ngai, Sianne, 6
Niemetschek, Franz Xaver, 430
Nineteenth century. *See Romanticism*
Nissen, Georg Nikolaus von, 38

Norm. *See* Convention
November, Nancy, 145–146, 216

Obsessiveness, 410–414, 509–511, 513
Opera buffa, 231, 394, 411, 416, 448, 456–457, 462
Overture idiom, 61, 215, 232, 322
Ovid, 112, 374

Packham, Catherine, 341, 451
Pahl, J. G., 353, 354
Passions, 8, 68, 254, 390, 431, 432, 440, 451, 510
Pastoral, 115, 204, 205, 231, 245, 337, 339, 345, 422, 470, 473, 475, 512–513, 515–531, 533, 549, 550, 551
Pattern, 12, 13–14, 20, 43, 90, 351, 360, 428
Pauli, Charles, 536
Pedagogy, 16, 25, 55–56, 273, 519
Pedantry. *See Anti-learned orientation*
Performance, Performativity, 8, 456, 458–466
Pergolesi, Giovanni Battista, 21, 22, 219, 358
Periodicity, 19, 55–57, 84–85, 91, 107–113, 124, 142, 144, 161–162, 175, 181–182, 190, 208, 233, 246, 247–248, 256, 268, 272, 303–304, 305, 340, 349, 350, 357, 359, 369, 371, 409–410, 413–414, 440, 442, 481, 508, 510, 525, 529, 538, 545
Pestelli, Giorgio, 436, 501, 533
Piccinni, Niccolò, 22
Pichler, Caroline, 4, 264–266
Plà, Juan Bautista and José, 443
Pleasure, 20, 51, 69, 110, 111, 255, 273–274, 355, 423–424, 445–449, 510, 518
Pleyel, Ignaz, 39, 269, 413, 434, 441, 533
　Piano Trio Op. 42 No. 3/Ben448, 115, 526
　Quartets, 436
　　Op. 1 No. 1/Ben301, 78, 423–424, **424**, 511
　　Op. 1 No. 2/Ben302, 57–59, **58**, 223–224, 401
　　Op. 1 No. 3/Ben303, 316–317, **317**, 320–321, 332–333, 506–507
　　Op. 1 No. 5/Ben305, 159, 305–307, **306**, 308, 328
　　Op. 2 No. 2/Ben308, 337
　　Op. 22 No. 6/Ben358, 533
　Quintet Op. 9/Ben276, 533
　Symphony Ben128, 393–395, 441–442
Pluche, Noël-Antoine, 253–254, 255, 257, 348, 456
Politeness, 149–150, 414–415, 424, 449–450, 460, 466, 467, 486, 493, 557
Polzonetti, Pierpaolo, 14, 373–374

Popular style, 30, 31, 44, 115, 144, 190, 214, 218, 225, 268, 337, 345, 414, 471, 473, 476, 495, 496, 513, 518, 519, 524, 547
Porpora, Nicola, 358
Porter, Roy, 251, 425
Pritchard, Matthew, 164, 254
Proksch, Bryan, 41, 373
Public taste, 35, 38, 39, 260–261, 353, 356–357, 497, 503
Punctuation. *See Periodicity*

Quantz, Johann Joachim, 44, 45, 46, 72, 414, 446, 463–464, 489, 518

Raab, Armin, 14
Rameau, Jean-Philippe, 109, 497
Rasch, Rudolf, 21
Ratner, Leonard, 25, 62, 67–68, 109, 230–232, 233–234, 236, 241, 274, 467, 536
Reciprocity, 11, 55–107, 113–114, 116, 117, 120, 199, 256, 268, 332, 408, 410, 450, 510
Reconciliation, 176–177, 188, 192–199, 214, 225–226, 244–245, 249
Reduction, 329, 332–333, 339–345, 360, 370, 371, 376, 515, 522
Regnard, Jean-François, 219
Reicha, Anton, 91, 148, 409
Reichardt, Johann Friedrich, 249
Renewal, 276–312, 315, 331, 340, 376, 553
Repeated notes, 150–155, 277, 309–311, 342, 360–370, 374–375
Repeated-note close, 78, 222, 294–300, 302, 320, 336, 345, 370, 379, 404
Resolution. *See Reconciliation*
Retransitional material. *See Formal function*
Rhetoric, 16, 37–38, 123, 144, 147, 229, 340
Rice, John, 22, 241, 287, 289, 549
Richards, Annette, 16, 118, 340, 351
Richards, Mark, 72, 280
Richter, Jean Paul, 32, 496
Ridgewell, Rupert, 38–39
Riepel, Joseph, 26, 51, 64, 110, 116, 145, 247, 312, 330, 444, 488–489, 540–541
Riley, Matthew, 2, 92, 204, 209, 240, 348, 415, 486, 492, 505–506
Robinson, Jenefer, 7
Romanticism, 1, 7, 25, 27, 38, 48, 54, 57, 122–123, 146, 163, 168, 198, 207, 215, 261–262, 265, 268, 271, 296, 343, 432, 434, 448, 468, 524, 529
Romberg, Andreas
　Quartet Op. 1 No. 1, 218–219, 221, 292–294, **293**, 401

Rondo, 30, 132, 204, 207, 223, 249, 300, 342, 360, 393–394, 395, 474–477, 534, 535
Rosen, Charles, 33, 62–63, 70, 103–104, 116, 126, 150, 151–152, 154, 167, 183, 188, 203, 206, 227, 274, 282, 330, 336, 341, 362, 375, 381, 414, 415, 432, 436, 452, 470, 471, 478, 484, 494, 517
Rosenblum, Sandra, 539–540
Rosenmeyer, Thomas G., 518
Rosetti, Antonio, 338, 413, 429, 437
   Concertos
      Flute, Murray C21, 225–226, 228
      Oboe, Murray C33, 226, 540
   Quartet Op. 6 No. 2, 402–403
   Symphonies
      Murray A6, 395–396
      Murray A12, 478–479
      Murray A20, 342–343
      Murray A28, 194–195, 197–198, 523
      Murray A33, 339
      Murray A42, 509
      Murray A45, 338–339
Rothstein, William, 57
Rott, Franz, 429
Rousseau, Jean-Jacques, 20, 108, 440, 460
Rumph, Stephen, 37–38, 40, 69–70, 90, 123, 124, 144, 194, 239, 242
Rushton, Julian, 14, 41, 56
Russell, Gillian and Clara Tuite, 456
Russell, Tilden A., 497
Russo, Elena, 455

Sala, Nicola, 176
Salomon, Johann Peter, 23, 24
Salzer, Felix, 56
Sammartini, Giovanni Battista, 263
Saussure, Ferdinand de, 90
Scarlatti, Alessandro, 6, 358
Scarlatti, Domenico, 37, 125, 172, 200–201, 358, 409, 524
   Sonatas
      K202, 200
      K236, 200
Schaul, Johann Baptist, 354, 372–373, 374, 515–517, 519, 520, 521, 522
Scheibe, Johann Adolph, 45, 69, 438, 446, 485–486, 491
Schemata, 2, 25–26, 42–43, 47, 51–52, 81–82, 132, 267, 273–274, 351, 385, 450
   Cadenza lunga, 176, 226
   Clausula vera, 293
   Converging Cadence, 544
   Cudworth Cadence, 118, 307, 332, 545
   Final Fall, 295, 338
   Fonte, 388
   Grand Cadence, 224, 318–319, 325, 363–364, 399, 404
   Heartz, 549
   High 6 Drop, 307–308, 511, 555
   Indugio, 75, 282–284, 331
   Monte, 247, 312
   Prinner, 64, 67, 412
   Quiescenza, 87, 136, 337, 526
   Romanesca, 152, 160, 203, 293, 345, 365, 405
Schenker, Heinrich, 107
Schiff, Andras, 28
Schiller, Friedrich, 254
Schmalfeldt, Janet, 281
Schmalzriedt, Siegfried, 71
Schmoll, Johann Friedrich, 268
Schobert, Johann, 260–261
   Quartet Op. 7 No. 3, 546
   Sonatas
      Op. 6, 542
      Op. 6 No. 1, 542–546, **543**, 549, 551
   Violin Sonata Op. 14 No. 3, 546
Schoenberg, Arnold, 332, 344
Schroeder, David P., 264, 410–411, 451, 468, 484
Schubart, Christian Friedrich Daniel, 53, 112, 260–262, 265, 361, 367, 437, 443, 444
Schubert, Franz, 34, 469, 530
   Quintet D956, 288, 291
Schulz, Johann Abraham Peter, 18, 66, 258, 356
Schumann, Robert, 551
Schütze, Stephan, 497
Schwartz, Judith L., 256, 262, 372, 390
Schwindt-Gross, Nicole, 37
Sears, David, 294
Seidel, Wilhelm, 201
Sensibility, 352, 431, 436, 457–460, 462, 535, 554, 557
Sensitive style, 100, 102, 119, 246, 441, 450
Sentiment, 254, 431–433, 437, 438, 440, 451, 517
Serenade, 202, 403, 521
Seriousness, 22–23, 26–28, 31–33, 35, 39, 48, 112, 219–220, 239, 240, 261, 346–347, 468, 496–497
Service, Tom, 32, 33, 477–478
Shaftesbury, Third Earl of, 4, 414, 460
Sheldon, David E., 446
Sheridan, Thomas, 488
Shield, William
   String Trios
      No. 2, **396**, 396–397

No. 3, 412
No. 8, 337
Simplicity, 44, 48, 319, 328–329, 333, 433–438, 441–443, 445, 458–459, 481, 511, 515, 521, 522, 524, 525, 550
Simplifying cadence. *See Cadence*
Sincerity, 20–21, 44, 278, 309, 424, 454, 464–468, 557
Sisman, Elaine, 39, 65, 229, 233, 269, 501, 509
Small, Christopher, 15, 40–41, 120, 455
Smith, Adam, 18–19, 111–112, 146, 444, 454, 466, 470, 510, 519
Sociability, affective, 5, 11, 12, 66, 69, 265–266, 347, 428, 445, 452, 453, 493, 515
Sociability, technical, 11, 12, 55, 65, 66, 69, 90, 402, 450
Soft ending, 333–340, 397, 404
Solitude, 147, 430–431, 453–454, 455–456, 487, 499, 509, 513
Somfai, László, 168–, 537
Sonata form, 26, 40, 163, 407–408, 492, 519, 533–534, 535, 557
Spacks, Patricia Meyer, 15, 277, 352, 425, 461
Spitzer, Michael, 6, 18, 34, 51–52, 63, 89, 122–123, 275, 280, 408, 466
Staël, Germaine de, 19–20, 133, 146, 188, 377, 455, 487
Stafford, William, 38
Stamitz, Johann, 84–86, 87
   Symphonies
      Op. 4 No. 1, 87
      Op. 4 No. 6, 82–83, **83**
Steffan, Joseph Anton
   Violin Sonata Š88, 550
Sterkel, Johann Franz Xaver, 23
Sterne, Laurence, 451, 469, 499
Stevens, Jane, 65–66
Stewart-MacDonald, Rohan, 326, 440, 441, 490, 491
Stockigt, Janice B., 62
Strinasacchi, Regina, 429
Sublime, the, 340–341, 349
Sulzer, Johann Georg, 7, 66, 123, 255–256, 260, 264
Sutcliffe, W. Dean, 37, 125, 149, 172, 200, 215, 274, 303, 341, 362, 393, 403, 408, 409, 474, 477, 551
Swieten, Baron Gottfried van, 52, 302
Symmetry. *See Periodicity*

Talbot, Michael, 62, 238, 385, 404, 504, 532
Tartini, Giuseppe, 62, 248, 485
Taruskin, Richard, 40, 78, 270, 448, 499

Taste, 1–2, 7, 38, 46–47, 236, 251–252, 350, 425–426, 489, 494
Tempo di menuetto (finale), 226, 227, 405, 531–558
Theatricality, 149, 164, 219, 231, 232, 233, 245, 501
Thematic interaction, 11, 69, 95, 162–200, 230, 235
Thompson, George, 115
Thormählen, Wiebke, 52
Thorp, Jennifer, 537
Tolerance, 200, 215, 230, 231, 241, 249, 251, 447, 451, 496
Tolley, Thomas, 7, 351
Tone, 48, 316, 433, 453, 467–484, 494, 514, 535
Topics, 2, 16, 25–26, 42–43, 47, 90, 123, 158, 162, 203, 230–246, 253, 267, 273, 276, 315, 337, 354–355, 367, 385, 387, 415, 431, 508, 512–513, 515, 518, 530
   Alla turca, 114
   Archaic, 205, 208–213, 234
   Chorale, 203
   Dance, 230, 238
   Dotted style, 76, 77, 117, 204, 237–238, 241, 242, 355, 423, 473
   Fanfare, 192–193, 219, 230, 237, 242–244, 355, 526
   Horn call, 207–213, 230, 234, 244, 394, 441, 529–531, 557
   Learned style, 239–240, 415, 422–, 523
   March, 203, 244, 246, 415
   Military, 207, 231, 242
   Musette, 512, 526, 529, 549
   Siciliano, 512, 518, 521
   Singing style, 188
Tovey, Donald Francis, 203, 519
Treitler, Leo, 14
Triest, Johann Karl Friedrich, 259, 264, 367, 501
Trills, 309
Trommelbass. See Drum bass
Türk, Daniel Gottlob, 65, 66, 68, 111, 236, 349–350, 355, 485, 490, 540
   Sechs leichte Klaviersonaten
      No. 1, 304
      No. 2, 304
      No. 4, 59–61, **60**
Twining, Thomas, 10, 520
Tyre, Jess, 41

Unison texture, 57, 70, 76, 77, 82–83, 97–98, 114, 115, 134–140, 159–162, 191, 240, 241, 242, 244, 300, 302, 303, 423, 557

Unity, 66, 108, 131, 255–257, 371–373, 390, 494, 545
Untimely rhetoric, 204, 209, 240–242, 245, 415, 418, 506–508, 513

Variety, 46, 49, 114, 144, 197, 199–200, 214–215, 226, 228–229, 236, 245–262, 266, 267, 276, 278–279, 354–360, 367–368, 371, 404, 410, 411, 426, 431, 456, 473, 494, 508, 511, 513
Verri, Pietro, 50, 355, 435–436
Versatility, 94, 125, 130–131, 140, 164, 182–183, 186–187, 371–384, 406, 500
Vial, Stephanie, 108
Viala, Alain, 454
Vinci, Leonardo, 108, 358, 485
Viotti, Giovanni Battista
    Quartets Op. 1, 295
Vivaldi, Antonio, 62, 238
Vogler, Georg Joseph, 65–66
Voskuhl, Adelheid, 458

Waeber, Jacqueline, 108, 357
Wagenseil, Georg Christoph
    Sonatas Op. 1, 546
Wald, Melanie, 468
Walter, Horst, 161, 292
Waltham-Smith, Naomi, 33, 273, 362, 374

Walther, Johann Gottfried, 540
Wanhal, Johann Baptist, 53, 268, 396
    Flute Quartet Op. 7 No. 6, 97–99, **98**, 303
    Symphonies
        Bryan A9, 404
        Bryan C3, 412–414
        Bryan D17, 339
Watkins, Holly, 262
Weber, William, 24, 27, 38, 264, 346, 447, 454–455, 485
Webster, James, 34, 36, 62, 247, 265–266, 402, 447, 451, 458, 497
Weiss, Michael, 268
Wheelock, Gretchen, 49, 132, 133, 144, 149, 385, 500
Will, Richard, 48, 71, 76, 112, 146, 164, 241, 433, 474, 525
Williams, Raymond, 21
Willing, Johann Ludwig, 53, 67
Wit, 198, 326, 376–377, 390, 467, 469, 497
Wranitzky, Paul
    Quartet Op. 23 No. 2, 217
    Sextet No. 4, 216–217, 401

Zimpel, Christhard, 408
Zipoli, Domenico, 525
    Pastorale, 525–526